T0190331

Communications
in Computer and Information Science
2012

Rationale

The CCIS series is devoted to the publication of proceedings of computer science conferences. Its aim is to efficiently disseminate original research results in informatics in printed and electronic form. While the focus is on publication of peer-reviewed full papers presenting mature work, inclusion of reviewed short papers reporting on work in progress is welcome, too. Besides globally relevant meetings with internationally representative program committees guaranteeing a strict peer-reviewing and paper selection process, conferences run by societies or of high regional or national relevance are also considered for publication.

Topics

The topical scope of CCIS spans the entire spectrum of informatics ranging from foundational topics in the theory of computing to information and communications science and technology and a broad variety of interdisciplinary application fields.

Information for Volume Editors and Authors

Publication in CCIS is free of charge. No royalties are paid, however, we offer registered conference participants temporary free access to the online version of the conference proceedings on SpringerLink (http://link.springer.com) by means of an http referrer from the conference website and/or a number of complimentary printed copies, as specified in the official acceptance email of the event.

CCIS proceedings can be published in time for distribution at conferences or as postproceedings, and delivered in the form of printed books and/or electronically as USBs and/or e-content licenses for accessing proceedings at SpringerLink. Furthermore, CCIS proceedings are included in the CCIS electronic book series hosted in the SpringerLink digital library at http://link.springer.com/bookseries/7899. Conferences publishing in CCIS are allowed to use Online Conference Service (OCS) for managing the whole proceedings lifecycle (from submission and reviewing to preparing for publication) free of charge.

Publication process

The language of publication is exclusively English. Authors publishing in CCIS have to sign the Springer CCIS copyright transfer form, however, they are free to use their material published in CCIS for substantially changed, more elaborate subsequent publications elsewhere. For the preparation of the camera-ready papers/files, authors have to strictly adhere to the Springer CCIS Authors' Instructions and are strongly encouraged to use the CCIS LaTeX style files or templates.

Abstracting/Indexing

CCIS is abstracted/indexed in DBLP, Google Scholar, EI-Compendex, Mathematical Reviews, SCImago, Scopus. CCIS volumes are also submitted for the inclusion in ISI Proceedings.

How to start

To start the evaluation of your proposal for inclusion in the CCIS series, please send an e-mail to ccis@springer.com.

Yuqing Sun · Tun Lu · Tong Wang · Hongfei Fan ·
Dongning Liu · Bowen Du
Editors

Computer Supported Cooperative Work and Social Computing

18th CCF Conference, ChineseCSCW 2023
Harbin, China, August 18–20, 2023
Revised Selected Papers, Part I

Springer

Editors
Yuqing Sun
Shandong University
Jinan, China

Tong Wang
Harbin Engineering University
Harbin, China

Dongning Liu
Guangdong University of Technology
Guangzhou, China

Tun Lu
Fudan University
Shanghai, China

Hongfei Fan
Tongji University
Shanghai, China

Bowen Du
Tongji University
Shanghai, China

ISSN 1865-0929   ISSN 1865-0937 (electronic)
Communications in Computer and Information Science
ISBN 978-981-99-9636-0   ISBN 978-981-99-9637-7 (eBook)
https://doi.org/10.1007/978-981-99-9637-7

This Springer imprint is published by the registered company Springer Nature Singapore Pte Ltd.
The registered company address is: 152 Beach Road, #21-01/04 Gateway East, Singapore 189721, Singapore

Paper in this product is recyclable.

Preface

Welcome to ChineseCSCW 2023, the 18th CCF Conference on Computer Supported Cooperative Work and Social Computing.

ChineseCSCW 2023 was organized by the China Computer Federation (CCF), and co-hosted by the CCF Technical Committee on Cooperative Computing (CCF TCCC) and the Harbin Engineering University, in Harbin, Heilongjiang, China, during 18–20 August 2023. The conference was also supported by HLJ E-LINK Network Co., Ltd., Guangdong Xuanyuan Network Technology Co., Ltd. and SCHOLAT. The theme of the conference was *Human-Centered Collaborative Intelligence*, which reflects the emerging trend of the combination of artificial intelligence, human-system collaboration, and AI-empowered applications.

ChineseCSCW (initially recognized as CCSCW) is a highly reputable conference series on computer supported cooperative work (CSCW) and social computing in China with a long history. It aims at bridging Chinese and overseas CSCW researchers, practitioners and educators, with a particular focus on innovative models, theories, techniques, algorithms and methods, as well as domain-specific applications and systems, from both technical and social aspects in CSCW and social computing. The conference was initially held biennially since 1998, and has been held annually since 2014.

This year, the conference received 221 submissions, and after a rigorous double-blind peer review process, only 54 of them were eventually accepted as full papers to be orally presented, resulting in an acceptance rate of 24%. The program also included 28 short papers, which were presented as posters. In addition, the conference featured 6 keynote speeches, 5 high-level technical seminars, the ChineseCSCW Cup 2023 Collaborative Intelligence Big Data Challenge (Final Round), the Forum for Outstanding Young Scholars, the Forum for Presentations of Top-Venue Papers, and an awards ceremony. We are grateful to the distinguished keynote speakers, *Weimin Zheng* (CAE Member) from *Tsinghua University*, *Yanning Zhang* from *Northwestern Polytechnical University*, *Junzhou Luo* from *Southeast University*, *Nong Xiao* from *Sun Yat-sen University*, *Chunming Hu* from *Beihang University*, and *Zili Zhang* from *Southwest University*.

We hope that you enjoyed ChineseCSCW 2023.

November 2023

Yong Tang
Zhiwen Yu

Organization

Steering Committee

Yong Tang	South China Normal University, China
Weiqing Tang	China Computer Federation, China
Ning Gu	Fudan University, China
Shaozi Li	Xiamen University, China
Bin Hu	Beijing Institute of Technology, China
Yuqing Sun	Shandong University, China
Xiaoping Liu	Hefei University of Technology, China
Zhiwen Yu	Harbin Engineering University, China
Xiangwei Zheng	Shandong Normal University, China
Tun Lu	Fudan University, China

General Chairs

Yong Tang	South China Normal University, China
Zhiwen Yu	Harbin Engineering University, China

Vice Chair

Zheng Dou	Harbin Engineering University, China

Program Committee Chairs

Yuqing Sun	Shandong University, China
Tun Lu	Fudan University, China
Dongning Liu	Guangdong University of Technology, China
Tong Wang	Harbin Engineering University, China

Organization Committee Chairs

Xiaoping Liu	Hefei University of Technology, China
Chunhui Zhao	Harbin Engineering University, China

Publication Chairs

Bin Hu   Beijing Institute of Technology, China
Hailong Sun   Beihang University, China

Proceedings Editors

Yuqing Sun   Shandong University, China
Tun Lu   Fudan University, China
Tong Wang   Harbin Engineering University, China
Hongfei Fan   Tongji University, China
Dongning Liu   Guangdong University of Technology, China
Bowen Du   Tongji University, China

CSCW Cup Competition Chairs

Chaobo He   South China Normal University, China
Lu Wang   Harbin Engineering University, China
Ronghua Lin   South China Normal University, China

Paper Award Chairs

Shaozi Li   Xiamen University, China
Yichuan Jiang   Southeast University, China

Paper Recommendation Chairs

Honghao Gao   Shanghai University, China
Yiming Tang   Hefei University of Technology, China

Publicity Chairs

Xiangwei Zheng   Shandong Normal University, China
Jianguo Li   South China Normal University, China
Zhongjie Wang   Harbin Engineering University, China
Guangsheng Feng   Harbin Engineering University, China

Finance Chairs

Shan Gao   Harbin Engineering University, China
Min Ouyang   Harbin Engineering University, China

Website Chairs

Jianguo Li   South China Normal University, China
Chengzhe Yuan   Guangdong Polytechnic Normal University, China

Program Committee

Tie Bao   Jilin University, China
Zhan Bu   Nanjing University of Finance and Economics,
                              China
Hongming Cai   Shanghai Jiao Tong University, China
Xinye Cai   Nanjing University of Aeronautics and
                              Astronautics, China
Yongming Cai   Guangdong Pharmaceutical University, China
Yuanzheng Cai   Minjiang University, China
Zhicheng Cai   Nanjing University of Science and Technology,
                              China
Buqing Cao   Hunan University of Science and Technology,
                              China
Donglin Cao   Xiamen University, China
Jian Cao   Shanghai Jiao Tong University, China
Jingjing Cao   Wuhan University of Technology, China
Chao Chen   Chongqing University, China
Jianhui Chen   Beijing University of Technology, China
Liangyin Chen   Sichuan University, China
Long Chen   Southeast University, China
Longbiao Chen   Xiamen University, China
Ningjiang Chen   Guangxi University, China
Qingkui Chen   University of Shanghai for Science and
                              Technology, China
Wang Chen   China North Vehicle Research Institute, China
Weineng Chen   South China University of Technology, China
Xin Chen   Taiyuan University of Science and Technology,
                              China
Yang Chen   Fudan University, China

Zhen Chen	Yanshan University, China
Zonggan Chen	South China Normal University, China
Shiwei Cheng	Zhejiang University of Technology, China
Xiaohui Cheng	Guilin University of Technology, China
Yuan Cheng	Wuhan University, China
Lizhen Cui	Shandong University, China
Weihui Dai	Fudan University, China
Wei Dao	Tisson Regaltec Communications Tech. Co., Ltd., China
Xianghua Ding	University of Glasgow, UK
Wanchun Dou	Nanjing University, China
Bowen Du	Tongji University, China
Guodong Du	Yanshan University, China
Hongfei Fan	Tongji University, China
Yili Fang	Zhejiang Gongshang University, China
Lunke Fei	Guangdong University of Technology, China
Liang Feng	Chongqing University, China
Shanshan Feng	Shandong Normal University, China
Honghao Gao	Shanghai University, China
Jing Gao	Guangdong Hengdian Information Technology Co., Ltd., China
Liping Gao	University of Shanghai for Science and Technology, China
Ying Gao	South China University of Technology, China
Yunjun Gao	Zhejiang University, China
Ning Gu	Fudan University, China
Bin Guo	Northwestern Polytechnical University, China
Kun Guo	Fuzhou University, China
Wei Guo	Shandong University, China
Yinzhang Guo	Taiyuan University of Science and Technology, China
Tao Han	Zhejiang Gongshang University, China
Fei Hao	Shaanxi Normal University, China
Fazhi He	Wuhan University, China
Chaobo He	Zhongkai University of Agriculture and Engineering, China
Haiwu He	Chinese Academy of Sciences, China
Bin Hu	Beijing Institute of Technology, China
Daning Hu	Southern University of Science and Technology, China
Wenting Hu	Jiangsu Open University, China
Yanmei Hu	Chengdu University of Technology, China

Changqin Huang	South China Normal University, China
Faliang Huang	Nanning Normal University, China
Yongjian Huang	Guangdong Xuanyuan Network Technology Co., Ltd., China
Lu Jia	China Agricultural University, China
Tao Jia	Southwest University, China
Min Jiang	Xiamen University, China
Bo Jiang	Zhejiang Gongshang University, China
Wenchao Jiang	Guangdong University of Technology, China
Bin Jiang	Hunan University, China
Jiuchuan Jiang	Nanjing University of Finance and Economics, China
Weijin Jiang	Xiangtan University, China
Yichuan Jiang	Southeast University, China
Miaotianzi Jin	Shenzhen Artificial Intelligence and Data Science Institute (Longhua), China
Lanju Kong	Shandong University, China
Yi Lai	Xi'an University of Posts and Telecommunications, China
Chunying Li	Guangdong Polytechnic Normal University, China
Dongsheng Li	Microsoft Research Asia, China
Guoliang Li	Tsinghua University, China
Hengjie Li	Lanzhou University of Arts and Science, China
Jianguo Li	South China Normal University, China
Jingjing Li	South China Normal University, China
Junli Li	Jinzhong University, China
Li Li	Southwest University, China
Pu Li	Zhengzhou University of Light Industry, China
Renfa Li	Hunan University, China
Shaozi Li	Xiamen University, China
Taoshen Li	Guangxi University, China
Weimin Li	Shanghai University, China
Xiaoping Li	Southeast University, China
Yong Li	Tsinghua University, China
Lu Liang	Guangdong University of Technology, China
Hao Liao	Shenzhen University, China
Bing Lin	Fujian Normal University, China
Dazhen Lin	Xiamen University, China
Cong Liu	Shandong University of Technology, China
Dongning Liu	Guangdong University of Technology, China
Hong Liu	Shandong Normal University, China

Jing Liu	Guangzhou Institute of Technology, Xidian University, China
Li Liu	Chongqing University, China
Shijun Liu	Shandong University, China
Shufen Liu	Jilin University, China
Xiaoping Liu	Hefei University of Technology, China
Yupeng Liu	Harbin University of Science and Technology, China
Yuechang Liu	Jiaying University, China
Zhihan Liu	Central South University, China
Tun Lu	Fudan University, China
Dianjie Lu	Shandong Normal University, China
Hong Lu	Shanghai Polytechnic University, China
Huijuan Lu	China Jiliang University, China
Qiang Lu	Hefei University of Technology, China
Haoyu Luo	South China Normal University, China
Zhiming Luo	Xiamen University, China
Chen Lv	Shandong Normal University, China
Jun Lv	Yantai University, China
Mingjie Lv	Zhejiang Lab, China
Peng Lv	Central South University, China
Pin Lv	Guangxi University, China
Xiao Lv	Naval University of Engineering, China
Chaoqing Ma	Yantai University, China
Hui Ma	University of Electronic Science and Technology of China and Zhongshan Institute, China
Keji Mao	Zhejiang University of Technology, China
Chao Min	Nanjing University, China
Li Ni	Anhui University, China
Haiwei Pan	Harbin Engineering University, China
Li Pan	Shandong University, China
Yinghui Pan	Shenzhen University, China
Yijie Peng	Peking University, China
Lianyong Qi	Qufu Normal University, China
Sihang Qiu	National University of Defense Technology, China
Jiaxing Shang	Chongqing University, China
Limin Shen	Yanshan University, China
Yanjun Shi	Dalian University of Science and Technology, China
Yuliang Shi	Shanda Dareway Company Limited, China
Xiaoxia Song	Datong University, China

Kehua Su	Wuhan University, China
Songzhi Su	Xiamen University, China
Hailong Sun	Beihang University, China
Ruizhi Sun	China Agricultural University, China
Yuqing Sun	Shandong University, China
Yuling Sun	East China Normal University, China
Lina Tan	Hunan University of Technology and Business, China
Wen'an Tan	Nanjing University of Aeronautics and Astronautics, China
Yong Tang	South China Normal University, China
Shan Tang	Shanghai Polytechnic University, China
Weiqing Tang	China Computer Federation, China
Xiaoyong Tang	Changsha University of Science and Technology, China
Yan Tang	Hohai University, China
Yiming Tang	Hefei University of Technology, China
Yizheng Tao	China Academy of Engineering Physics, China
Shaohua Teng	Guangdong University of Technology, China
Fengshi Tian	China People's Police University, China
Zhuo Tian	Institute of Software, Chinese Academy of Sciences, China
Jingbin Wang	Fuzhou University, China
Tao Wang	Minjiang University, China
Binhui Wang	Nankai University, China
Dakuo Wang	Northeastern University, USA
Hongbin Wang	Kunming University of Science and Technology, China
Hongjun Wang	Southwest Jiaotong University, China
Hongbo Wang	University of Science and Technology Beijing, China
Lei Wang	Alibaba Group, China
Lei Wang	Dalian University of Technology, China
Tianbo Wang	Beihang University, China
Tong Wang	Harbin Engineering University, China
Wanyuan Wang	Southeast University, China
Xiaogang Wang	Shanghai Dianji University, China
Yijie Wang	National University of Defense Technology, China
Yingjie Wang	Yantai University, China
Zhenxing Wang	Shanghai Polytechnic University, China
Zhiwen Wang	Guangxi University of Science and Technology, China

Zijia Wang	Guangzhou University, China
Yiping Wen	Hunan University of Science and Technology, China
Ling Wu	Fuzhou University, China
Quanwang Wu	Chongqing University, China
Wen Wu	East China Normal University, China
Xiaokun Wu	South China University of Technology, China
Zhengyang Wu	South China Normal University, China
Chunhe Xia	Beihang University, China
Fangxiong Xiao	Jinling Institute of Technology, China
Jing Xiao	South China Normal University, China
Zheng Xiao	Hunan University, China
Xiaolan Xie	Guilin University of Technology, China
Zhiqiang Xie	Harbin University of Science and Technology, China
Yu Xin	Harbin University of Science and Technology, China
Huanliang Xiong	Jiangxi Agricultural University, China
Jianbo Xu	Hunan University of Science and Technology, China
Jiuyun Xu	China University of Petroleum, China
Meng Xu	Shandong Technology and Business University, China
Heyang Xu	Henan University of Technology, China
Yonghui Xu	Shandong University, China
Xiao Xue	Tianjin University, China
Yaling Xun	Taiyuan University of Science and Technology, China
Jiaqi Yan	Nanjing University, China
Xiaohu Yan	Shenzhen Polytechnic, China
Bo Yang	University of Electronic Science and Technology of China, China
Chao Yang	Hunan University, China
Dingyu Yang	Shanghai Dianji University, China
Gang Yang	Northwestern Polytechnical University, China
Jing Yang	Harbin Engineering University, China
Lin Yang	Shanghai Computer Software Technology Development Center, China
Tianruo Yang	Hainan University, China
Xiaochun Yang	Northeastern University, China
Yan Yao	Qilu University of Technology, China
Shanping Yu	Beijing Institute of Technology, China

Xu Yu	Qingdao University of Science and Technology, China
Jianyong Yu	Hunan University of Science and Technology, China
Yang Yu	Zhongshan University, China
Zhengtao Yu	Kunming University of Science and Technology, China
Zhiwen Yu	Northwestern Polytechnical University, China
Zhiyong Yu	Fuzhou University, China
Chengzhe Yuan	Guangdong Engineering and Technology Research Center for Service Computing, China
Junying Yuan	Nanfang College Guangzhou, China
An Zeng	Guangdong Polytechnical University, China
Dajun Zeng	Institute of Automation, Chinese Academy of Sciences, China
Zhihui Zhan	South China University of Technology, China
Changyou Zhang	Chinese Academy of Sciences, China
Chaowei Zhang	Yangzhou University, China
Jia Zhang	Jinan University, China
Jifu Zhang	Taiyuan University of Science and Technology, China
Jing Zhang	Nanjing University of Science and Technology, China
Liang Zhang	Fudan University, China
Libo Zhang	Southwest University, China
Miaohui Zhang	Energy Research Institute of Jiangxi Academy of Sciences, China
Peng Zhang	Fudan University, China
Senyue Zhang	Shenyang Aerospace University, China
Shaohua Zhang	Shanghai Software Technology Development Center, China
Wei Zhang	Guangdong University of Technology, China
Xin Zhang	Jiangnan University, China
Ying Zhang	Northwestern Polytechnical University, China
Zhiqiang Zhang	Harbin Engineering University, China
Zili Zhang	Southwest University, China
Hong Zhao	Xidian University, China
Tianfang Zhao	Jinan University, China
Jiaoling Zheng	Chengdu University of Information Technology, China
Xiangwei Zheng	Shandong Normal University, China
Jinghui Zhong	South China University of Technology, China
Ning Zhong	Beijing University of Technology, China

Yifeng Zhou	Southeast University, China
Huiling Zhu	Jinan University, China
Jia Zhu	South China Normal University, China
Jianhua Zhu	City University of Hong Kong, China
Jie Zhu	Nanjing University of Posts and Telecommunications, China
Nengjun Zhu	Shanghai University, China
Tingshao Zhu	Chinese Academy of Science, China
Xia Zhu	Southeast University, China
Xianjun Zhu	Jinling University of Science and Technology, China
Yanhua Zhu	First Affiliated Hospital of Guangdong Pharmaceutical University, China
Qiaohong Zu	Wuhan University of Technology, China

Contents – Part I

Social Media and Online Communities

Collaborative Mechanisms, Models, Approaches, Algorithms and Systems

Contents – Part II

Cooperative Evolutionary Computation and Human-Like Intelligent Collaboration

Domain-Specific Collaborative Applications

Social Media and Online Communities

HGNN-T5 PEGASUS: A Hybrid Approach for Chinese Long Text Summarization

Xuhui Luo, Jianguo Li[✉], and Zhanxuan Chen

School of Computer Science, South China Normal University, Guangzhou 510631, China
{lxhui,lijianguo,czxuan}@m.scnu.edu.cn

Abstract. Currently, the performance of abstractive summarization is generally superior to extractive summarization, but it is inhibited for the long text by the complexity. Extractive summarization, though high speed, is redundancy and lack of sentences coherence. Based on the above, for Chinese long text summarization, we propose a hybrid model HGNN-T5 PEGASUS which includes two stages. In the first stage, we use a heterogeneous graph-based extractive model to obtain a shorter extractive summarization than the original text. The heterogeneous graph-based neural network (HGNN) incorporates sentence-level and word-level semantic nodes, which can enrich the relationship between sentences. In the second stage, we choose the T5 PEGASUS as our base model and add a category prediction mechanism to alleviate the Out-Of-Vocabulary problem and improve fidelity. Moreover, a more simplified sparse softmax is introduced to T5 PEGASUS to avoid overfitting. To demonstrate the effectiveness of our model, we constructed the SCHOLAT text summarization dataset. The results of our experiments show that the proposed model outperforms other baseline models on both the NLPCC 2018 and SCHOLAT datasets.

Keywords: Text Summarization · HGNN · T5 PEGASUS · Category Prediction · SCHOLAT Dataset

1 Introduction

With the continuous development of social networks, we have entered the digital age, and social networks have become an essential aspect of our everyday existence. As an academic social networks platform, SCHOLAT has accumulated massive amounts of text data. As a result, managers of SCHOLAT need to spend a lot of time checking each text's content for misinformation or bad information, and users of SCHOLAT will also spend more time reading these long texts to get the content they need. A good automatic text summarization (ATS) technology will help them get the main content of the text faster.

ATS aims to convert the long text into a concise and smooth summary that contains the important information. ATS is categorized as extractive or abstractive summarization, depending on how the summary is generated. Extractive

Y. Sun et al. (Eds.): ChineseCSCW 2023, CCIS 2012, pp. 3–16, 2024.
https://doi.org/10.1007/978-981-99-9637-7_1

summarization scores the original text sentences and extracts the ones with higher scores to obtain a summary. Its advantage lies in the ability to obtain complete semantics and syntax. However, extractive summarization is too redundant and incoherent, resulting in poor readability.

Another method of abstractive summarization is more similar to the way humans think. First, it needs to understand the original text and analyze the semantics of each sentence, and then it generates a more coherent and smoother summary. Hence, abstract summarization can generate a higher quality summary, but sometimes with lower fidelity. Rush et al. [1] and Nallapati et al. [2] applied the RNN in the field of abstractive summarization. However, these models face some shortcomings, including RP (Repeating Phase) and OOV (Out-Of-Vocabulary) problems, resulting in poor generation effect. Over the past few years, as pre-trained models have advanced, the performance of transformer-based pre-trained models in abstractive summarization has improved significantly. The integration of a self-attention mechanism into pre-trained models has mitigated the issue of RP to a certain degree. They are more suitable for short texts, but their processing ability for long texts is very limited because of the high computational overhead. In practice, the meaning of summarizing short texts is limited, and we pay more attention to the ability of long text summarization. Based on the long text summarization problems, we present a model named HGNN-T5 PEGASUS.

The key contributions we have made are as follows:

- For the Chinese long text summarization, we design a hybrid model HGNN-T5 PEGASUS combining extractive and abstractive summarization.
- We propose a heterogeneous graph neural network (HGNN) based extractive model, which contains sentence and word nodes at different granularity levels. The model updates the node representation based on the relationships and importance between nodes using a multi-headed Graph Attention Network.
- We use the Chinese pre-trained model T5 PEGASUS [3] for our abstractive model and add a category prediction mechanism to avoid the OOV problem and enhance fidelity, and introduce the sparse softmax to avoid overfitting.
- The SCHOLAT text summarization dataset is constructed to evaluate our model. And the text summarization model will be deployed to the backend text review and search system of SCHOLAT.

2   Related Work

2.1   Extractive Summarization

Early extractive summarization work is mainly based on statistics and linguistic features, specifically relying mostly on frequency, probability, and centrality models. In 2004, Mihalcea et al. [4] proposed constructing a graph with sentences as vertices and sentence similarity as edges, and applying the PageRank graph algorithm to obtain the summary. Since most algorithms for extractive summarization use sentence scores calculated heuristically, there is no explicit probabilistic interpretation of sentence scores. Kupiec et al. [5] have started to study the application of probabilistic models to text summarization. With the development of deep learning, Nallapati et al. [6] proposed SummaRuNNer, which used the GRU-RNN structure to capture inter-sentence relations and sentence-document relations. Xu et al. [7] and Wang et al. [8] started using graph neural networks for extractive summarization. Liu et al. [9] was the first to utilize BERT in the field of text summarization with their proposed BERTSUM model. On the basis of BERTSUM, Bdel-Salam et al. [10] reduced about half of the parameters using the method of knowledge distillation and compression, but the performance was full with only a 2% decrease. Gu et al. [11] introduced reinforcement learning to extractive text summarization and proposed the SUMmarizer extractive model.

2.2 Abstractive Summarization

Considerable advancements have recently been made in abstractive summarization. Since 2014, when Sutskever et al. [12] proposed the seq2seq model, abstract summarization has gradually become the focus of current research in text summarization. The Seq2Seq model was first utilized in the task of summarization along with the introduction of the attention mechanism by Rush et al. [1] in 2016. Subsequently, Nallapati et al. [2] improved their work by fusing multifeatures with word embedding at the encoding layer. Gulcehre et al. [13] and See et al. [14] incorporated a pointer generator network into the above abstractive model, while Gu et al. [15] incorporated a copy mechanism. Furthermore, See et al. [14] proposed a coverage mechanism to solve the problem of generating repeat summaries. In 2019, Li et al. [16] proposed the UniLM extractive model, which differed from BERT only by the self-attention mask. As pre-trained models continue to evolve, performance on Natural Language Generation (NLG) tasks continues to improve. Zhu et al. [17] integrated the factual relationships in the text into the transformer models for summarization through neural graph computation to improve the factual consistency. Xu et al. [18] further enhanced factual consistency through contrastive learning.

2.3 Hybrid Summarization

Unfortunately, the complexity of the transformer-based pre-trained model is O (tokens^2), resulting in much worse results for long texts than for short texts. Recently, some have conducted hybrid summarization studies of long texts, which include two stages: extractive and abstractive. Gidiotis et al. [19] utilized a divide-and-conquer strategy for long document summarization. Bae et al. [20] adapted BERT to get contextualized representations to complete the extraction and used the seq2seq model to generate the final summary. Li et al. [21] proposed an end-to-end two-stage summarization model based on the idea of minimizing redundant information during processing while retaining sufficient information.

3   Our Model: HGNN-T5 PEGASUS

In this section, we present the proposed HGNN-T5 PEGASUS model in detail. The process of our hybrid model shown in Fig. 1 divides the process of generating a summary into two stages. The extractive stage is a process rather than a result. It generates shorter transitional summaries that contain as much information as possible. And the abstractive stage uses the transitional summaries to produce a concise and informative final summary.

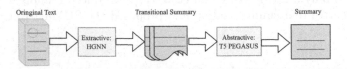

Fig. 1. The process of our hybrid model.

3.1   Extractive Model: HGNN

The extractive summarization divides each sentence in the original text into two categories: significant and nonsignificant. Some researchers [7] have suggested text summarization methods using graph neural networks. Yet these methods only capture the mutual interaction between sentences. Inspired by Cui et al. [22] and Wang et al. [8], we propose a heterogeneous graph neural network based for extractive summarization as shown in Fig. 2, which incorporates word nodes at different granularity levels in addition to sentence nodes. These additional word nodes serve as intermediaries connected to the sentence nodes, enriching the relationships between sentences. In fact, using higher-level features such as entities or topics can further improve the semantic representation of sentences. Considering that the extractive model in this paper is a process rather than a result, higher-level features are not used in this study.

Graph Initializes. A graph can be represented as $G = \{V, E\}$, where V represents the set of nodes and E represents the set of edges. In this paper, the undirected heterogeneous graph for the original text is defined as follows: $V = V_S \cup V_W$, where $V_S = \{s_1, \ldots, s_m\}$ denotes m sentences from the original text and $V_W = \{w_1, \ldots, w_n\}$ denotes n different words of the original text; $E = \{e_{11}, \ldots, e_{mn}\}$, where $e_{ij} \neq 0$ indicates the concatenation of the i-th sentence with the j-th word. To initialize the sentence vectors, we use Sentence-BERT [23], a model based on sentence-level semantic representation learning. However, it only learns intra-sentence features but not inter-sentence relations. So, we introduce multi-layer dilated convolutions to enable sentence vectors generated by Sentence-BERT that can learn the inter-sentence relationships. The GloVe model is used to initialize the word vectors. Wang et al. [8] used the TF-IDF technique to construct edge weights to further include the links between phrases and words in the graph.

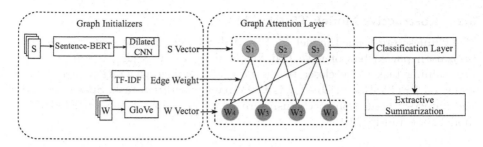

Fig. 2. The overview of the HGNN model.

Graph Attention Layer. After constructing the heterogeneous graph and initializing the node vectors, Graph Attention Network with multiple heads of attention is used to revise the nodes representation. The update process is formulated as:

$$z_{ij} = \text{LeakyReLU}\left(W_a\left[W_q h_i \| W_k h_j \| \tilde{e}_{ij}\right]\right), \tag{1}$$

$$\alpha_{i,j} = \frac{\exp\left(z_{i,j}\right)}{\sum_{l \in \mathcal{N}_i} \exp\left(z_{i,l}\right)}, \tag{2}$$

where W_a, W_q, and W_k are trainable weights, h_i represents the i-th node vector, $\tilde{e}_{ij}$ symbolizes edge weight of the i-th node and j-th node, and α_{ij} is attention weight between h_i and h_j. The multi-dimensional space vector $\tilde{e}_{ij}$ is obtained by discretizing the TF-IDF values into integer values and then using the embedding matrix. The representation of node i updated by multi-head attention is represented as follows:

$$h_i' = \|_{m=1}^M \sigma\left(\sum_{j \in N_i} \alpha_{ij}^M W_v^M h_j\right), \tag{3}$$

where σ denotes the tanh activation function, and M is the number of heads using attention. To alleviate gradient vanishing and enhance information flow, we introduce residual structures represented as: $\tilde{h}_i = h_i + h'_i$. Similar to Transformer, we incorporate an FFN layer after each Graph Attention Layer to improve the capabilities of the model. We use an iterative update strategy, where in each update step, the sentence nodes are first updated using the word nodes, and then the word nodes are updated using the updated sentence nodes.

Classification Layer. Finally, we plug all sentence nodes into a Classification Layer to get the important sentences as extractive summarization.

3.2   Abstractive Model: T5 PEGASUS

The Chinese pre-trained model T5 PEGASUS [3] adopts the structure and initialization parameters of mT5 [24]. Inspired by Pegasus [25], it improves the pre-training task to be closer to the natural language generation task. These make T5 PEGASUS suitable for the summary generation task. Sparse softmax and category prediction mechanism are added to improve the T5 PEGASUS model shown in Fig. 3.

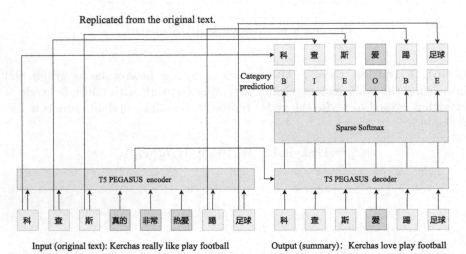

Fig. 3. The T5 PEGASUS model with sparse softmax and category prediction mechanism.

Sparse Softmax. The idea of sparse softmax is derived from Article [26,27], which can effectively avoid the problem of over-fitting. A more simplified sparse softmax [28] is proposed, which is depicted as follows:

$$P_i = \begin{cases} \frac{e^{S_i}}{\sum_{j \in Top_k} e^{S_j}}, i \in Top_k \\ 0, i \notin Top_k \end{cases}, \tag{4}$$

where Top_k is the first k elements of the Set S sorted from largest to smallest. It means that sparse softmax uses the activation function softmax to calculate possibilities only for the top k elements and $P_i = 0$ (i $\notin Top_k$). And the cross-entropy loss function is changed to that shown in the following equation:

$$\mathcal{L} = \log \left(\sum_{i \in Top_k} e^{S_i} \right) - S_t, \tag{5}$$

where S_t denotes the score of the target category. Sparse softmax is generally suitable for pre-trained scenarios to avoid overfitting because the pre-trained model has been trained sufficiently.

Category Prediction. Most existing solutions to the OOV problem only consider single word copying from the original text. These solutions may result in the loss of necessary tokens when long continuous sequences need to be copied. Therefore, we introduce the category prediction mechanism into the T5 model to better solution the OOV problem. The prediction categories include "S, B, I, E, and O", which originate from the field of named entity identification [29]. Figure 3 illustrates the category prediction mechanism, which is actually an additional sequence prediction task in the T5 PEGASUS decoder. The original decoder only predicted the probability of each token, which is defined as:

$$p\left(b_t \mid b_{<t}, a\right),\tag{6}$$

where $b_{<t}$ is the output of the previous t-1 series token prediction and a is the input at time t. And now we add an additional category prediction:

$$p\left(c_t, b_t \mid b_{<t}, a\right) = p\left(c_t \mid b_{<t}, a\right) p\left(b_t \mid b_{<t}, a\right),\tag{7}$$

where $c_t \in \{\mathbf{S}, \mathbf{B}, \mathbf{I}, \mathbf{E}, \mathbf{O}\}$. Category **S** (Single) denotes that the present token is replicated, and the continuous sequence only includes 1-gram. Category **B** (Begin) denotes that the present token is replicated, and the continuous sequence includes more than 1-gram. Category **I** (Inside) denotes that the present token is replicated from the original text and the previous token is B or I. Category **E** (End) denotes that the present token is replicated, and the end of the continuous sequence. Category **O** (Outside) denotes that the present token is not replicated, but generated from the model vocabulary list.

The category prediction label construction rules for the training model are as follows: Initially, we extract the longest common subsequence between the original text and the summary. Next, set the extracted tokens to S, B, I, or E according to the previous rules. Other tokens are set to O. Figure 3 shows an example of category construction. In the inference phase, we first predict the current token category and then mask all the tokens that are not in the category. The category prediction can alleviate the OOV problem and copy essential continuous sequences from the original text to improve fidelity.

4 Experiments

We will introduce two datasets used in our experiments, evaluation metrics, and model implementation details in this section.

4.1 Datasets

NLPCC. The dataset[1] is from the NLPCC 2018 Single Document Summarization competition track and contains mainly 50,000 article-summary pairs on Toutiao.com.

---

[1] http://tcci.ccf.org.cn/conference/2018/taskdata.php.

SCHOLAT. Since there are few high-quality Chinese long text summarization datasets, we constructed the SCHOLAT text summarization dataset. The dataset mainly includes team dynamics, personal dynamics, and institution number dynamics, which are written mainly by university professors, and contains 18709 article-summary pairs. The detailed construction process is shown in Fig. 4.

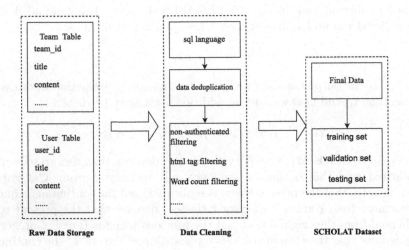

Fig. 4. The building process of the SCHOLAT dataset.

The statistics of the NLPCC and SCHOLAT datasets are shown in Table 1.

4.2   Evaluation Metrics

Evaluating summary quality automatically mainly includes internal and external methods. The external evaluation method is in view of the summary results of effectiveness evaluations of other application tasks. An internal method named ROUGE metrics [30] are widely used to evaluate text summarization, which

Table 1. The statistics of the NLPCC and the SCHOLAT datasets. (N means NLPCC, S means SCHOLAT.)

Datasets	max article length	average article length	max summary length	average summary length
N train	12007	945	128	48
N test	8120	940	66	39
S train	38411	946	165	50
S test	7858	974	94	39
S dev	9300	935	129	48

include R^2-{N, L, W, S}. We choose R-{1, 2} to assess informativeness, and R-L to assess sentence fluency.

4.3   Implementation Details

In the extractive stage, we limit the number of word nodes to 50,000 and remove some high-frequency words that have no real meaning. Initialized sentence nodes dimension size is 128. We use two GAT layers, and the number of multi-headed attentions per GAT layer is 6. We apply the Adam optimizer with a learning rate of 5e–4. In the inference phase, the length of extractive summarization is approximately α which is a hyperparameter. According to the experimental results of the paper [31], we use the sentence-level alignment method to construct the extractive reference summary and adopt R-{1, 2, L} as the evaluation criterion. In the abstractive stage, we initialize the model using the T5 PEGASUS base version weights.

5   Results and Analysis

5.1   Comparison Experiments

We choose some extractive and abstractive baseline models as a comparison. The results of the experiments on the NLPCC and the SCHOLAT datasets are shown in Table 2.

- TextRank [4]: The model splits the original text into sentences, constructs a sentence graph, and extracts the n sentences with the highest importance as extractive summarization.
- BERTSUM [9]: This model first uses BERT in extractive summarization.
- Pointer-Generator [14]: This model adds a pointer network to the Seq2Seq+ Attention model to avoid the OOV problem.
- UniLM [16]: This model is based on the BERT model using three special masks, which allows the model to be used for abstractive summarization (NLU task).
- BART [32]: A pre-trained model that we fine-tune for the task of generating abstractive summarization.

It can be deduced from Table 2 that the simple extractive model of TextRank has good results, but models based on pre-training will give better results. By comparing with the traditional seq2seq model, it is noted that the transformer-based pre-training model with the self-attention mechanism can better obtain dependencies between words. Crucially, our model is superior to other models in terms of R-{1, 2, L} on both datasets. Our models R-{1, 2, L} are higher than the same full-structure transformer-based pre-training model BART 4.27, 5.27, and 4.62 on the NLPCC dataset and 7.46, 9.40, and 6.99 on the SCHOLAT dataset, respectively. Illustrated by the data in Table 2, the proposed approach provides stable performance irrespective of the dataset.

---

[2] R-ROUGE.

Table 2. Comparison with different models on the NLPCC dataset and the SCHOLAT dataset.

Model	Type	NLPCC			SCHOLAT		
		R-1	R-2	R-L	R-1	R-2	R-L
TextRank	Ext	35.90	24.87	31.01	42.64	33.03	39.99
BERTSUM	Ext	38.62	27.81	33.48	52.56	43.78	51.05
Pointer-G	Abs	36.78	26.42	30.98	50.29	40.45	43.96
UniLM	Abs	57.78	40.06	52.09	62.33	51.28	60.15
BART	Abs	64.64	50.52	59.93	69.31	60.06	68.29
Our model	Hyb	**68.91**	**55.79**	**64.55**	**76.77**	**69.46**	**75.28**

5.2   Ablation Experiments

In this set of experiments, we conduct ablation studies to elucidate the impact of each part of the proposed method on the final performance. The results of the ablation experiments are shown in Table 3. By comparing the experimental results of T5 PEGASUS and HGNN-T5 PEGASUS, we are able to demonstrate that the hybrid model has better efficiency. We can also prove that our sparse softmax and category prediction mechanism are effective and can avoid overfitting and OOV problems. Our models R-1, R-2, and R-L are higher than the base model T5 PEGASUS 2.96, 3.47, and 3.53 on the NLPCC dataset and 2.56, 2.35, and 2.55 on the SCHOLAT dataset, respectively.

5.3   Sparse Softmax Top_k Experiments

In order to determine the value of k for which the sparse softmax effect is better, we conduct experiments without adding the category prediction mechanism. Considering the training time, we only set k $\in$ {10, 20, 100, 200, 300, 1000} for evaluation in both datasets separately. As shown in Fig. 5, the results are better when k is equal to 200.

5.4   Qualitative Analysis

To better illustrate the effect of our model, we show the summary generated from the NLPCC dataset and the SCHOLAT dataset in Table 6. The red-underlined part of the Table represents the important information in the reference summary that our model can generate but the BART model cannot. These two examples demonstrate the ability of our model to generate high-quality summaries.

Table 3. Ablation experiments on each part of the proposed method on two datasets. (TP means T5 PEGASUS, H means HGNN, SS means Sparse Softmax, CP means Category Prediction.)

Model	NLPCC			SCHOLAT		
	R-1	R-2	R-L	R-1	R-2	R-L
TP	65.95	52.32	61.02	74.21	67.11	72.73
H-TP	67.79	54.90	63.61	74.63	67.23	73.21
H-TP-SS	68.51	55.69	64.23	76.16	68.64	74.92
H-TP-CP	68.02	55.18	63.79	75.13	68.01	74.31
H-TP-SS-CP	**68.91**	**55.79**	**64.55**	**76.77**	**69.46**	**75.28**

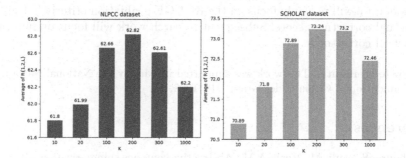

Fig. 5. The average of R-{1, 2, L} of the D-TP-SS model when k ∈ {10, 20, 100, 200, 300, 1000}.

NLPCC original text:湖人已经打算留住尼克杨。北京时间7月15日，据《湖人国度》报道，此前洛杉矶湖人队一直都在兜售他们的板凳得分手尼克-杨，但是由于没能找到愿意接手的下家，湖人队已经打算留下杨。为了腾出薪金空间来引进新球员，有消息称湖人管理层曾试图兜售尼克-杨、萨尼雷以及莱恩-凯利。但是据《橘县纪事报》记者比尔-奥拉姆得到的最新的消息，由于无法找到下家，湖人队目前并不打算交易尼克-杨。"今天听说湖人队已经没有交易尼克-杨的打算。他们曾给其他球队打电话并寻找下家，并希望能迅速腾出薪金空间。但是(这个想法)并没有实现。"奥拉姆在推特上写道。上赛季，尼克-杨在湖人队表现得十分挣扎。他理应成为这支球队的主要得分点，但是由于伤病和表现不稳定，杨一共只打了42场比赛，场均得到13.4分，投篮命中率仅为36.6\%，创下生涯新低。...... (省略)
Reference summary:美媒体称因没有球队接手，湖人队打算留下尼克扬，上赛季杨场均13.4分命中率仅36\%。
BART summary:湖人打算留下尼克-杨，他场均13.4分，投篮命中率仅36.6。
Our model generated summary:《湖人国度》报：湖人队已考虑留尼克-杨，去年夏天双方续约了4年2150万美元的合同，上赛季杨打42场场均13.4分，投篮命中率仅为36.6%。

SCHOLAT original text:2019年12月21-22日，广东省计算机学会CCF广州分部年会暨学术会议在江门市顺利召开。华南师范大学数据智能团队部分老师和研究生参加了学术活动。汤庸教授主持了陈国良院士、於志文教授和郝志峰校长的学术报告，朱佳教授获优秀学术论文二等奖，李建国副教授获优秀秘书长表彰。本届年会包括学术报告、年度表彰和专业委员会分论坛等环节。大会报告阶段邀请了省学会名誉理事长陈国良院士、佛山科学技术学院校长郝志峰教授、国家杰青、长江学者特聘教授、西北工业大学计算机学院院长於志文教授、国家优青、中山大学郑子彬副教授以及浪潮集团、广东轩辕公司、广东君略公司等企业做大会报告。......（省略）
Reference summary:华南师范大学大数据智能团队组织参加2019年广东省计算机学会&CCF广州分部年会暨学术会议。
BAET summary:广东省计算机学会在江门召开学术年会，陈国良院士等出席会议。
Our model generated summary:华南师范大学大数据智能团队参加2019年广东省计算机学会ccf广州分部年会暨学术会议并喜获学术论文奖

Fig. 6. Examples

6   Conclusion and Future Work

In this paper, we have designed a HGNN-T5 PEGASUS model for long text summarization. The key to success comes from designing a hybrid model to capture the more critical information in the long text. First, we used the extractive model HGNN to get the transitional summary. And then, we used the transitional summary as input to the abstractive model T5 PEGASUS. For improved effects, we added the sparse softmax and the category prediction mechanism to the T5 PEGASUS model. The experiments were conducted on two datasets, which demonstrated the appealing performance of the proposed model.

Subsequently, we will deploy this model to SCHOLAT as soon as possible to help administrators review SCHOLAT articles faster. We will also apply it to the search engine of SCHOLAT, providing a summary for each search result. For our model, we will not only focus on the ROUGE evaluation criteria but also on the factual correctness score. Subsequent research work will focus on improving the factual correctness.

Acknowledgements. This work was supported in part by the National Natural Science Foundation of China under Grant U1811263.

References

1. Chopra, S., Auli, M., Rush, A.M.: Abstractive sentence summarization with attentive recurrent neural networks. In: Proceedings of the 2016 Conference of the North American Chapter of the Association for Computational Linguistics: Human Language Technologies, pp. 93–98 (2016)
2. Nallapati, R., Zhai, F., Zhou, B.: Summarunner: a recurrent neural network based sequence model for extractive summarization of documents. In: Thirty-first AAAI Conference on Artificial Intelligence (2017)
3. Su, J.: T5 PEGASUS - ZhuiyiAI. Technical Report (2021)
4. Mihalcea, R., Tarau, P.: Textrank: bringing order into text. In: Proceedings of the 2004 Conference on Empirical Methods in Natural Language Processing, pp. 404–411 (2004)
5. Kupiec, J., Pedersen, J., Chen, F.: A trainable document summarizer. In: Proceedings of the 18th Annual International ACM SIGIR Conference on Research and Development in Information Retrieval, pp. 68–73 (1995)
6. Nallapati, R., Zhou, B., Gulcehre, C., Xiang, B., et al.: Abstractive text summarization using sequence-to-sequence RNNs and beyond. arXiv preprint arXiv:1602.06023 (2016)
7. Xu, J., Gan, Z., Cheng, Y., Liu, J.: Discourse-aware neural extractive text summarization. arXiv preprint arXiv:1910.14142 (2019)
8. Wang, D., Liu, P., Zheng, Y., Qiu, X., Huang, X.: Heterogeneous graph neural networks for extractive document summarization. arXiv preprint arXiv:2004.12393 (2020)
9. Liu, Y.: Fine-tune bert for extractive summarization. arXiv preprint arXiv:1903.10318 (2019)
10. Abdel-Salam, S., Rafea, A.: Performance study on extractive text summarization using bert models. Information **13**(2), 67 (2022)

11. Gu, N., Ash, E., Hahnloser, R.H.: Memsum: extractive summarization of long documents using multi-step episodic markov decision processes. arXiv preprint arXiv:2107.08929 (2021)
12. Sutskever, I., Vinyals, O., Le, Q.V.: Sequence to sequence learning with neural networks. In: Advances in Neural Information Processing Systems, vol. 27 (2014)
13. Gulcehre, C., Ahn, S., Nallapati, R., Zhou, B., Bengio, Y.: Pointing the unknown words. arXiv preprint arXiv:1603.08148 (2016)
14. See, A., Liu, P.J., Manning, C.D.: Get to the point: summarization with pointer-generator networks. arXiv preprint arXiv:1704.04368 (2017)
15. Gu, J., Lu, Z., Li, H., Li, V.O.: Incorporating copying mechanism in sequence-to-sequence learning. arXiv preprint arXiv:1603.06393 (2016)
16. Dong, L., et al.: Unified language model pre-training for natural language understanding and generation. In: Advances in Neural Information Processing Systems, vol. 32 (2019)
17. Zhu, C., et al.: Enhancing factual consistency of abstractive summarization. arXiv preprint arXiv:2003.08612 (2020)
18. Xu, S., Zhang, X., Wu, Y., Wei, F.: Sequence level contrastive learning for text summarization. In: Proceedings of the AAAI Conference on Artificial Intelligence, vol. 36, pp. 11556–11565 (2022)
19. Gidiotis, A., Tsoumakas, G.: A divide-and-conquer approach to the summarization of long documents. IEEE/ACM Trans. Audio Speech Lang. Process. **28**, 3029–3040 (2020)
20. Bae, S., Kim, T., Kim, J., Lee, S.G.: Summary level training of sentence rewriting for abstractive summarization. arXiv preprint arXiv:1909.08752 (2019)
21. Li, H., et al.: Ease: extractive-abstractive summarization end-to-end using the information bottleneck principle. In: Proceedings of the Third Workshop on New Frontiers in Summarization, pp. 85–95 (2021)
22. Cui, P., Hu, L., Liu, Y.: Enhancing extractive text summarization with topic-aware graph neural networks. arXiv preprint arXiv:2010.06253 (2020)
23. Reimers, N., Gurevych, I.: Sentence-bert: Sentence embeddings using siamese bert-networks. arXiv preprint arXiv:1908.10084 (2019)
24. Xue, L., et al.: mt5: a massively multilingual pre-trained text-to-text transformer. arXiv preprint arXiv:2010.11934 (2020)
25. Zhang, J., Zhao, Y., Saleh, M., Liu, P.: Pegasus: pre-training with extracted gap-sentences for abstractive summarization. In: International Conference on Machine Learning, pp. 11328–11339. PMLR (2020)
26. Martins, A., Astudillo, R.: From softmax to sparsemax: a sparse model of attention and multi-label classification. In: International Conference on Machine Learning, pp. 1614–1623. PMLR (2016)
27. Peters, B., Niculae, V., Martins, A.F.: Sparse sequence-to-sequence models. arXiv preprint arXiv:1905.05702 (2019)
28. Sun, S., et al.: Sparse-softmax: a simpler and faster alternative softmax transformation. arXiv preprint arXiv:2112.12433 (2022)
29. Dai, Z., Wang, X., Ni, P., Li, Y., Li, G., Bai, X.: Named entity recognition using BERT BiLSTM CRF for Chinese electronic health records. In: 2019 12th International Congress on Image and Signal Processing, Biomedical Engineering and Informatics (CISP-BMEI), pp. 1–5. IEEE (2019)
30. Lin, C.Y.: Rouge: a package for automatic evaluation of summaries. In: Text Summarization Branches Out, pp. 74–81 (2004)

31. Ladhak, F., Li, B., Al-Onaizan, Y., McKeown, K.: Exploring content selection in summarization of novel chapters. arXiv preprint arXiv:2005.01840 (2020)
32. Lewis, M., et al.: Bart: denoising sequence-to-sequence pre-training for natural language generation, translation, and comprehension. arXiv preprint arXiv:1910.13461 (2019)

Prompt-Based and Two-Stage Training for Few-Shot Text Classification

Zexin Yan$^{(\boxtimes)}$, Yan Tang, and Xin Liu

College of Computer and Information, Hohai University, Nanjing, China
{zexinyan,tangyan,201807010003}@hhu.edu.cn

Abstract. Text classification is a crucial task in the field of Natural Language Processing (NLP), which aims at predicting the category where a text belongs. Recently, prompt-based learning has emerged as a powerful approach to handling a wide variety of tasks in NLP. It effectively bridges the gap between pre-trained language models (PLMs) and downstream tasks. Verbalizers are key components in prompt-based tuning. Existing manual prompts heavily rely on domain knowledge, while automatically generated verbalizers, whether on discrete or continuous space, have been suboptimal. In this work, we propose a two-stage training strategy for few-shot text classification, combining prompt-based learning and contrastive learning to learn appropriate verbalizers. In the first stage, we construct positive and negative samples for each input text and obtain soft verbalizers by integrating prompt-based learning and contrastive learning. In the second stage, we leverage the verbalizer learned in the first stage, along with prompt tuning, to train the entire model. Through experiments on some text classification datasets, our method outperforms other existing mainstream methods, which demonstrates its significance.

Keywords: Text classification · Prompt-based learning · Two-stage training · Contrastive learning

1 Introduction

Text classification is a significant task within the field of NLP [1]. Its objective is to categorize text documents into predefined classes or categories. This task plays a vital role in automating the analysis of extensive amounts of text data, facilitating efficient information retrieval, content organization, and decision-making across various industries and applications [2].

Although pre-trained language models (PLMs) combined with fine-tuning have become a prevailing paradigm in recent years, they still possess certain limitations. To bridge the gap between PLMs and downstream tasks, such as text classification, drawing inspiration from the concept of "in-context learning" in GPT-3 [3], a new approach called prompt-based learning has emerged. Prompt-based learning revolves around reformulating the original downstream

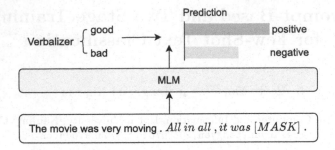

Fig. 1. An example of classical prompt-based learning, where MLM denotes Masked Language Model, which is a kind of PLMs.

task into a closely-related task using a prompt template [4]. For instance, consider the sentence: "The movie was very moving." It can be wrapped with a manual template, resulting in the following input: "The movie was very moving. *All in all, it was [MASK]*." The process of prompt-based learning is illustrated in Fig. 1. Template engineering and answer (verbalizer) engineering are two crucial aspects of prompt-based learning. Apart from employing manual templates for prompt tuning, researchers have also dedicated their efforts to exploring alternative methods to enhance the adaptability of PLMs to downstream tasks.

Regarding verbalizers, two primary approaches have been employed thus far. The first approach treats verbalizers as vectors in a discrete space. Schick et al. [5] designed manual verbalizers, which achieved significant success by incorporating rich domain knowledge. However, this approach is limited when domain knowledge is unavailable. In contrast, [6–8] utilized various algorithms to automatically generate verbalizers. Nevertheless, this automatic approach was found to be suboptimal compared to manual verbalizers that leverage extensive domain knowledge. The second approach treats verbalizers as vectors in a continuous space. Hambardzumyan et al. [9] introduced soft verbalizers, initializing them and optimizing them with the model together. However, even in the few-shot scenario, this approach was found to be suboptimal compared to the use of manual verbalizers.

To address these concerns, we propose a prompt-based and two-stage training strategy for few-shot text classification. Our approach utilizes a model backbone consisting of a masked language model (MLM) followed by a projection head. In the first stage, drawing inspiration from the concept of MoCo [10], we combine contrastive learning and prompt-based learning to train the model. We construct positive and negative samples for each input text and adopt the InfoNCE contrastive loss function [11] to minimize the distance between the target sample and positive examples, while simultaneously maximizing the distance between the target sample and negative examples. Subsequently, we freeze the model parameters from the first training stage and input texts from the training set to obtain the optimal verbalizer. In the second stage, our focus is primarily on prompt tuning using the trained verbalizer to enhance prediction accuracy.

To validate the effectiveness of our method, we conducted a series of experiments on text classification datasets. The experimental results demonstrate that our model significantly enhances classification performance in few-shot scenarios compared to other existing mainstream methods. Our contributions can be summarized as follows:

1. We propose a prompt-based and two-stage training strategy for few-shot text classification, aiming to bridge the gap between pre-trained language models (PLMs) and downstream tasks in the few-shot scenario.
2. We construct positive and negative samples and combine contrastive learning and prompt-based learning to obtain soft verbalizers. This approach addresses scenarios where there is insufficient domain knowledge to manually construct verbalizers.
3. Experimental results show that our model improves the classification performance in the few-shot scenario compared with other existing mainstream methods.

2   Related Work

2.1   Prompt-Based Learning

The success of GPT-3 [3] has made NLP tasks more dependent on PLMs. Inspired by the idea of "in-context learning" in GPT-3, researchers have recently focused on the prompt-based learning paradigm using medium-scale models such as BERT and RoBERTa [12,13]. Typically, two important aspects remain to be addressed in prompt-based learning: template construction and verbalizer construction [4]. Regarding template construction, Schick et al. [5] designed manual prompts based on domain knowledge, resulting in significant improvements in downstream task performance. Gao et al. [6] adopted T5 [14] to automatically generate prompt templates mapped into discrete spaces, achieving promising results. Other researchers have focused on constructing continuous prompt templates as an alternative to traditional discrete prompt templates [15–17]. In this work, our main focus is on the construction of verbalizers. For simplicity, we utilize manual prompt templates instead of automatically generating them.

2.2   Verbalizer Construction

Verbalizer construction is an important part of prompt-based learning. The quality of verbalizers can affect the performance of the model directly. Schick et al. [5] designed manual verbalizers with domain knowledge. However, the main disadvantage of manual verbalizers is that the cost of designing high-quality verbalizers is huge in the lack of domain knowledge. In order to avoid this situation, Gao et al. and Wang et al. [6,7] utilized the PLMs to generate verbalizers automatically. Shin et al. [19] utilized the language model and gradient-guided search to generate additional verbalizers. Hu et al. [8] utilized knowledge graphs and pre-trained embeddings to enrich the prompt verbalizer with relevant information and improve its ability to generate effective prompts. However, some researchers focused on learning soft verbalizers, a kind of verbalizer on continuous space. Hambardzumyan et al. [9] viewed verbalizers as embeddings on continuous space and optimize with the model together. Cui et al. [18] combined prototype learning with prompt-based learning to learn appropriate prototype vectors as soft verbalizers. In this work, we also focus on soft verbalizers as these kinds of verbalizers have more potential for optimization.

2.3   Contrastive Learning

Contrastive learning has gained significant attention in recent years as a crucial research topic in computer vision. The purpose is to learn useful representations of data by contrasting positive samples against negative samples. Chen et al. [20] proposed a framework for learning visual representations called SimCLR using contrastive learning. He et al. [10] proposed a novel approach to unsupervised visual representation learning called Momentum Contrast. After that, they further improved the methodology by integrating the strengths of SimCLR [21]. The application of contrastive learning is not limited to computer vision alone; it has also found practical utility in the field of NLP. SimCSE [22] provided a simple and effective approach to learning sentence embeddings using contrastive learning, which achieved better performance and was computationally efficient. DeCLUTR [23] trained a model to contrast positive and negative pairs of text sequences and the model was also computationally efficient.

3   Method

3.1   Task Formulation

Overall, there are two stages of the training process in our method. In the first stage, our primary objective is to generate the best verbalizer, which will play a crucial role in the subsequent stage. Given a batch of texts from the training dataset wrapped with the manual prompt. Our goal is to train the best verbalizer via contrastive learning. In the second stage, we focus on tuning the model through prompt-based techniques by incorporating the verbalizer acquired from the first stage. The objective of this stage is to further enhance the model's predictive capabilities.

3.2   Auxiliary Few-Shot Training Dataset

An auxiliary few-shot training dataset $\mathcal{D}_{aux}$ is transformed from the original training dataset which will be used in the first stage of training. Texts with the same label are gathered in one batch. So, the number of batches equals the number of classes in each dataset, and batch size is the number of samples K in few-shot learning.

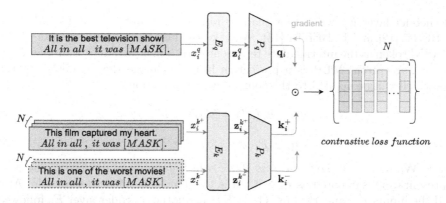

Fig. 2. An overview of our model's framework. Raw texts from the training dataset combined with the prompt will be fed into the backbone. In the first training stage, the contrastive loss function will be used to learn the best verbalizer. In the second training stage, we will reuse the backbone E_q and P_q to optimize the model.

3.3   Positive and Negative Samples

Given a batch of texts from few-shot training dataset $\mathcal{D}$ sampled from the original training set. Wrap each text $s_i \in \mathcal{B}$ with prompt:

$$x_i^q = prompt(s_i), \ s_i \in \mathcal{D}, \tag{1}$$

where the sentence wrapped with a prompt is denoted as x_i^q, which will be viewed as a query. For each input x_i^q in a batch, select K samples whose labels are the same as x_i^q from auxiliary training dataset $\mathcal{D}_{aux}$ mentioned above:

$$x_i^{k^+} = prompt(s_i), \ s_i \in \mathcal{D}_{aux}, \ y_{s_i} = y_{x_i^q}, \ i \in \{1, ..., K\}, \tag{2}$$

where y_{s_i} is denoted as label, and k^+ means positive keys. In the meanwhile, select N samples whose labels differ from x_i^q from auxiliary training dataset $\mathcal{D}_{aux}$:

$$x_i^{k^-} = prompt(s_i), \ s_i \in \mathcal{D}_{aux}, \ y_{s_i} \neq y_{x_i^q}, \ i \in \{1, ..., K\}, \tag{3}$$

where k^- means negative keys.

3.4   First Stage of Training

The entire process of the first stage of training is to learn the best verbalizer for the following prediction. The first step is to train the whole model via the contrastive loss function. An overview of the training model is illustrated in Fig. 2. Then, fix the parameters of the model which are trained well to get the appropriate verbalizer, the detail is illustrated in Fig. 3 (a).

Given a batch of texts wrapped with the prompt, each input x_i^q in this batch is combined with K positive samples $\{x_1^{k^+}, ..., x_K^{k^+}\}$ and K negative samples $\{x_1^{k^-}, ..., x_K^{k^-}\}$ which have been mentioned above. Feed the input x_i^q into an encoder layer E_q, which is actually a Masked Language Model (MLM) such as BERT [12] and RoBERTa [13]. We take the last layer's hidden state of the [MASK] token as the intermediate representation. Then, we adopt a simple (Multilayer Perceptron) MLP as a projection head to change the dimension to the one which will be applied to the contrastive loss function:

$$\mathbf{z}_i^q = E_q(x_i^q) = \mathbf{MLM}_q(x_i^q) \tag{4}$$

$$\mathbf{q}_i = P_q(\mathbf{z}_i^q) = \sigma(\mathbf{W}_q \mathbf{z}_i^q), \tag{5}$$

where $\mathbf{W}_q$ denotes weight and σ is ReLU which denotes nonlinearity. The final representation is denoted as $\mathbf{q}_i \in \mathbb{R}^d$, d is the dimension of representation. Also feed the inputs $x_{ij}^{k^+}$ and $x_{ij}^{k^-}$ ($j \in \{1, ..., K\}$) to another encoder layer E_k followed by a simple MLP to generate positive and negative sample representations:

$$\mathbf{z}_{ij}^{k^+} = E_k(x_{ij}^{k^+}) = \mathbf{MLM}_k(x_{ij}^{k^+}) \tag{6}$$

$$\mathbf{z}_{ij}^{k^-} = E_k(x_{ij}^{k^-}) = \mathbf{MLM}_k(x_{ij}^{k^-}) \tag{7}$$

$$\mathbf{k}_{ij}^+ = P_k(\mathbf{z}_{ij}^{k^+}) = \sigma(\mathbf{W}_k \mathbf{z}_{ij}^{k^+}) \tag{8}$$

$$\mathbf{k}_{ij}^- = P_k(\mathbf{z}_{ij}^{k^-}) = \sigma(\mathbf{W}_k \mathbf{z}_{ij}^{k^-}) \tag{9}$$

Inspired by DeCLUTR [23]. For each query, we take the mean of K positive embeddings as its positive counterpart:

$$\mathbf{k}_i^+ = \frac{1}{K} \sum_{j=1}^{K} \mathbf{k}_{ij}^+ \tag{10}$$

Contrastive Loss Function. Given an encoded and projected query $\mathbf{q}_i$, its correspond positive embedding $\mathbf{k}_i^+$ and K negative embeddings $\{\mathbf{k}_{i1}^-, \mathbf{k}_{i2}^-, ..., \mathbf{k}_{iK}^-\}$. We adopt InfoNCE loss [11], a contrastive loss that maximizes the similarity between the query and positive embedding and minimizes the similarity between the query and negative embeddings, where similarity is measured by the dot product. The loss function is defined as:

$$\mathcal{L}_{contrastive} = -\sum_{i=1}^{n} \log \frac{\exp(\mathbf{q}_i \cdot \mathbf{k}_i^+ / \tau)}{\sum_{j=1}^{K} \exp(\mathbf{q}_i \cdot \mathbf{k}_{ij}^- / \tau)}, \tag{11}$$

where $\mathcal{L}_{contrastive}$ denotes the contrastive loss function in the first training stage, n is the batch size and τ is a temperature hyperparameter that affects the degrees of penalties on hard negative samples.

Parameters Updating. The parameters of this model are combined with two parts:

$$\theta = \theta_E + \theta_P, \tag{12}$$

where θ_E denotes parameters of an encoder and θ_P denotes parameters of the projection head mentioned above. We follow the method of parameters updating proposed in MoCo [10], which can be defined as:

$$\theta_k \leftarrow m\theta_k + (1-m)\theta_q, \tag{13}$$

where θ_q denotes parameters of the query, θ_k denotes parameters of the keys and $m \in [0,1)$ is a momentum coefficient. In detail, only update the parameters θ_q through back-propagation, while employing a momentum coefficient to update θ_k with greater smoothness compared to θ_q. Empirically, m is commonly set to 0.999, and we will demonstrate the impact of this hyperparameter in the subsequent experiments.

Verbalizer Generation. After training our model with the contrastive loss function, the corresponding parameters are fixed. Then, the texts from the training dataset are passed through E_q followed by P_q to obtain the verbalizer representation in the continuous space:

$$\mathbf{v}_k = \frac{1}{K} \sum_{i=1}^{K} P_q(E_q(x_i^q)), k \in \{1, ..., N\}, \tag{14}$$

where N represents the number of classes in each dataset. The process is illustrated in Fig. 3 (a).

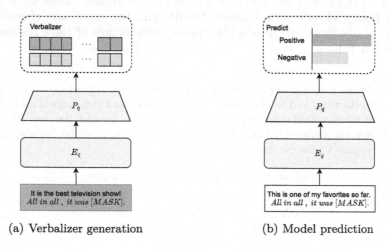

(a) Verbalizer generation   (b) Model prediction

Fig. 3. An illustration of using our model to learn verbalizer and make a prediction.

3.5   Second Stage of Training

The second stage of the training process mainly focuses on employing prompt-based learning to fine-tune the model. During this stage, we take E_q and P_q as the backbone. Rather than starting from scratch, the parameters of E_q and P_q are inherited from the first training stage. The whole input is fed into the backbone to generate $\mathbf{q}_i$ (mentioned in Eq. 5). We adopt cross-entropy loss, combining with $\mathbf{q}_i$ and verbalizer $\mathbf{v}_k$ learned in the first stage to optimize the model, which is defined as:

$$\mathcal{L}_{prompt} = -\frac{1}{N} \sum_i \sum_{k=1}^{N} \mathbf{q}_i \log(\mathbf{v}_k), \tag{15}$$

where $\mathcal{L}_{prompt}$ denotes cross-entropy loss in the second training stage.

3.6   Prediction

The process of prediction is illustrated in Fig. 3 (b). After getting representations of inputs, calculate their similarity with the verbalizer by dot product. Subsequently, the probability of predicting the class is determined:

$$p(y_k|x) = \frac{\exp(\mathbf{q} \cdot \mathbf{v}_k)}{\sum_{k'} \exp(\mathbf{q} \cdot \mathbf{v}_{k'})} \tag{16}$$

4   Experiments

4.1   Datasets

In order to verify the effectiveness of our model, we conduct these experiments on one binary classification dataset: IMDB, and two multiclass classification datasets: AG's News and Yahoo [24]. The specific details of these datasets are provided in Table 1.

Table 1. Datasets used in our experiments, the second column illustrates the categories of each task, the third and fourth columns show the train and test items of each dataset, and the last column illustrates the samples of few-shot K for each dataset, which were sampled from the training dataset. It is important to note that the few-shot samples for the train and validation sets are the same.

Dataset	Class	Train	Test	Samples
IMDB	2	25,000	25,000	16
AG's	4	120,000	7,600	16
Yahoo	10	140,000	60,000	16

4.2   Experimental Settings

All experiments are performed on one NVIDIA RTX 3090 GPU. To ensure consistent and fair comparisons, we set the configuration as N-way 16 shots (K=16). Accuracy was chosen as the primary evaluation metric to assess the performance of our model in relation to other baselines. Specifically, we employed the best-performing model from the validation dataset for evaluating the test dataset. As the primary objective of this study is to construct verbalizers in the context of few-shot prompt learning, we utilized fixed manual templates for prompting.

4.3   Implementation Details

Our model is implemented with Pytorch framework basically. Besides, we adopt RoBERTa-large model from Huggingface[1] as our basic PLM [13]. In order to integrate raw data with manual templates for training, verifying, and testing our model, we leverage Openprompt[2] toolkit developed by NLP researchers at Tsinghua University. The experimentation process consists of two crucial training stages: training the best verbalizers and training the complete model to achieve enhanced performance. In the first stage, we introduce the InfoNCE loss [11] to facilitate training the best verbalizers. Our model optimization is carried out using the AdamW [26] optimizer. In the second stage, we focus on training the complete model, utilizing cross-entropy loss as the loss function. Throughout our experiments, the batch size is 4 and we train the model in the second stage for 50 epochs. However, it is important to note that hyperparameter settings differ between the two groups of datasets, which are detailed in Table 2.

Table 2. The differences between the two groups of datasets on both two training stages. *dims* denotes verbalizer vector dimensions, which are trained in the first stage. lr_{first} denotes learning rate and $epoch_{first}$ denotes training epochs in the first stage. lr_{second} denotes the learning rate in the second stage.

	First training stage	Second training stage
IMDB, AG's	$lr_{first} = 1\mathrm{e}{-2}$ $epoch_{first} = 10$ $dims = 128$ $dropout =$ False	$lr_{second} = 5\mathrm{e}{-3}$
Yahoo	$lr_{first} = 1\mathrm{e}{-4}$ $epoch_{first} = 1$ $dims = 512$ $dropout =$ True	$lr_{second} = 3\mathrm{e}{-4}$

---

[1] https://huggingface.co.
[2] https://github.com/thunlp/OpenPrompt.

4.4 Baselines

To compare our approach with other existing mainstream methods of few-shot text classification based on prompt learning, we consider the following methods as baselines:

Manual Verb [5]. This baseline utilizes prompt patterns designed by humans. Due to the requirement for extensive domain knowledge, we adopt the manual verbalizers provided by Openprompt.

PETAL [27]. Appropriate verbalizers are determined by searching the entire vocabulary. The token with the highest score from the probability distribution is selected.

WARP [9]. This method treats verbalizers as token embeddings in a continuous space. The token embeddings are learned and updated during fine-tuning. These verbalizers are referred to as soft verbalizers.

ProtoVerb [18]. This model learns the prototype vectors as soft verbalizer representations through contrastive learning. There are two versions of this baseline. The first version utilizes single verbalizers and does not incorporate the knowledge of manual verbalizers. The second version, which we consider, merges the knowledge of manual verbalizers.

ProtoVerb+ [18]. This version incorporates the knowledge of manual verbalizers, but the PLMs are unturned.

Table 3. Results of our model compared to other baselines. We use $K = 16$ (per class) for few-shot experiments and take mean accuracy(%) over 3 random seeds.

	IMDB	AG's	Yahoo
Manual Verb	89.43	84.74	58.77
PETAL	-	83.40	59.66
WARP	91.85	80.57	58.20
ProtoVerb	88.20	84.48	**64.35**
ProtoVerb+	89.79	84.78	60.89
Ours	**93.14**	**85.69**	62.77

4.5 Main Results

The experimental results of our model and the baselines are presented in Table 3. Based on the results, we can draw the following conclusions: (1) Our model demonstrates a significant performance improvement compared to manual verbalizers, particularly on the IMDB and Yahoo datasets. This suggests that our method can train models with superior verbalizers compared to those designed by humans with domain knowledge. (2) For the IMDB and AG's News datasets, our model outperforms the best baseline model by 1.29% and 0.91%, respectively. This indicates the effectiveness of our model, especially on the IMDB dataset. (3) However, our model's performance is lower than ProtoVerb on the Yahoo dataset. We speculate that the high number of categories in Yahoo leads to increased dataset complexity [25]. The model may encounter difficulties in handling such a large number of categories and a highly complex dataset. Despite not achieving the top performance, our model still outperforms other baselines by over 2%.

Table 4. The impact of templates used in our experiments, where s denotes a raw sentence in a dataset.

Datasets	Templates	Accuracy
AG's	A [MASK] news : s	82.54
	s This topic is about [MASK]	85.28
	[Category : [MASK]] s	**85.69**
	[Topic : [MASK]] s	85.42
IMDB	It was [MASK] . s	88.72
	s Just [MASK] !	82.98
	s All in all , it was [MASK]	**93.14**
	s In summary , the film was [MASK]	92.22
Yahoo	A [MASK] question : s	49.88
	s This topic is about [MASK]	61.94
	[Category : [MASK]] s	**62.77**
	[Topic : [MASK]] s	61.62

4.6 Influence of Manual Templates

As mentioned by Gao et al. [6], the choice of templates can significantly impact the performance of prompt learning. To investigate this, we conducted a series of studies on the IMDB, AG's News, and Yahoo datasets. Table 4 reveals that different manual templates have varying effects on the accuracy of our model. For example, when using the manual template "*A [MASK] news : s*" for AG's News, we observed that it leads to the lowest accuracy compared to the other three templates, which exhibited relatively consistent accuracy. This indicates that the manual template "*A [MASK] news : s*" may not be suitable for our model. Similarly, for the IMDB and Yahoo datasets, there was one template that resulted in significantly lower accuracy compared to the other three templates, with a difference of approximately 10% for each dataset. In conclusion, our findings align with the notion that different templates can impact the performance of prompt learning models.

4.7   Parameter Analysis

There are two important hyperparameters in our model that significantly impact its performance. The first one is the momentum coefficient, denoted as $m \in [0, 1)$, illustrated in Fig. 4 (a). This coefficient controls the update of θ_k and plays a crucial role in the stability of our model. Through experimentation, we found that the optimal value for m is 0.999 on the AG's News dataset and 0.99999 on the IMDB dataset. This indicates that incorporating the historical gradient in the query part of our model improves its stability. However, on the Yahoo dataset, the impact of this hyperparameter on the model's performance is minimal, and the optimal value is found to be 0.9. We speculate that the dropout function we specifically implemented for this dataset contributes more to the prevention of overfitting. The second hyperparameter is the temperature coefficient, denoted as τ, illustrated in Fig. 4 (b). It influences the strength of penalties on hard negative samples [28]. A smaller τ value focuses more on hard negative samples. Through our experiments, we determined the optimal value for τ to be 0.20 on both AG's News and IMDB datasets. This suggests that the model achieves a good balance in penalizing hard negative samples at this temperature coefficient. However, on the Yahoo dataset, the optimal value for τ is 0.07. In summary, a smaller τ enables our model to better classify positive samples and hard negative samples.

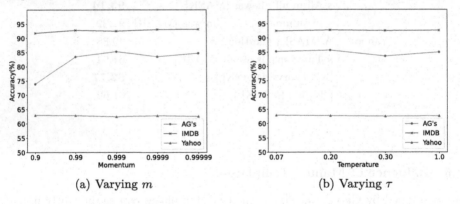

(a) Varying m (b) Varying τ

Fig. 4. Hyperparameter analysis over three datasets.

5   Conclusion

In this paper, we present a novel training strategy for few-shot text classification. It is based on prompt learning and is divided into two stages. In the first stage, we construct positive samples and negative samples for each input text in the dataset, combing contrastive learning and prompt-based learning to train the best verbalizer. In the second stage, we mainly focus on prompt tuning to enhance the model's performance. Through a series of experiments, we validate the effectiveness of our proposed method. Furthermore, various analyses support the significance of our approach.

References

1. Sun, X.J.: Paradigm shift in natural language processing. Mach. Intell. Res. **19**(3), 169–183 (2022). https://doi.org/10.1007/s11633-022-1331-6
2. Minaee, S., Kalchbrenner, N., Cambria, E., Nikzad, N., Chenaghlu, M., Gao, J.: Deep learning-based text classification: a comprehensive review. ACM Comput. Surv. **54**(3) (2021). https://doi.org/10.1145/3439726
3. Brown, T., et al.: Language models are few-shot learners. In: Advances in Neural Information Processing Systems, pp. 1877–1901. Curran Associates Inc (2020)
4. Liu, P., Yuan, W., Fu, J., Jiang, Z., Hayashi, H., Neubig, G.: Pre-train, prompt, and predict: a systematic survey of prompting methods in natural language processing. ACM Comput. Surv. **55**(9) (2023). https://doi.org/10.1145/3560815
5. Schick, T., Schutze, H.: Exploiting cloze-questions for few-shot text classification and natural language inference. In: Proceedings of the 16th Conference of the European Chapter of the Association for Computational Linguistics: Main Volume, pp. 255–269. Association for Computational Linguistics (2021). https://doi.org/10.18653/v1/2021.eacl-main.20
6. Gao, T., Fisch, A., Chen, D.: Making pre-trained language models better few-shot learners. In: Proceedings of the 59th Annual Meeting of the Association for Computational Linguistics and the 11th International Joint Conference on Natural Language Processing, ACL/IJCNLP 2021, (Volume 1: Long Papers), Virtual Event, 1–6 August 2021, pp. 3816–3830. Association for Computational Linguistics (2021). https://doi.org/10.18653/v1/2021.acl-long.295
7. Wang, H., Xu, C., McAuley, J.: Automatic multi-label prompting: simple and interpretable few-shot classification. In: Proceedings of the 2022 Conference of the North American Chapter of the Association for Computational Linguistics: Human Language Technologies, pp. 5483–5492. Association for Computational Linguistics (2022). https://doi.org/10.18653/v1/2022.naacl-main.401
8. Hu, S., et al.: Knowledgeable prompt-tuning: incorporating knowledge into prompt verbalizer for text classification. In: Proceedings of the 60th Annual Meeting of the Association for Computational Linguistics (Volume 1: Long Papers), ACL 2022, Dublin, Ireland, 22–27 May 2022, pp. 2225–2240. Association for Computational Linguistics (2022). https://doi.org/10.18653/v1/2022.acl-long.158
9. Hambardzumyan, K., Khachatrian, H., May, J.: WARP: word-level adversarial ReProgramming. In: Proceedings of the 59th Annual Meeting of the Association for Computational Linguistics and the 11th International Joint Conference on Natural Language Processing, ACL/IJCNLP 2021, (Volume 1: Long Papers), Virtual Event, 1–6 August 2021, pp. 4921–4933. Association for Computational Linguistics (2021). https://doi.org/10.18653/v1/2021.acl-long.381
10. He, K., Fan, H., Wu, Y., Xie, S., Girshick, R.: Momentum contrast for unsupervised visual representation learning. In: 2020 IEEE/CVF Conference on Computer Vision and Pattern Recognition, CVPR 2020, Seattle, WA, USA, 13–19 June 2020, pp. 9726–9735. Computer Vision Foundation/IEEE (2020). https://doi.org/10.1109/CVPR42600.2020.00975
11. Oord, A.V.D., Li, Y., Vinyals, O.: Representation Learning with Contrastive Predictive Coding. CoRR, abs/1807.03748 (2018)
12. Devlin, J., Chang, M.W., Lee, K., Toutanova, K.: BERT: pre-training of deep bidirectional transformers for language understanding. In: Proceedings of the 2019 Conference of the North American Chapter of the Association for Computational Linguistics: Human Language Technologies, Volume 1 (Long and Short Papers),

pp. 4171–4186. Association for Computational Linguistics (2019). https://doi.org/10.18653/v1/N19-1423

13. Liu, Y., et al.: RoBERTa: a robustly optimized BERT pretraining approach. CoRR, abs/1907.11692 (2019)

14. Raffel, C., et al.: Exploring the limits of transfer learning with a unified text-to-text transformer. J. Mach. Learn. Res. **21**, 140:1–140:67 (2020)

15. Liu, X., et al.: GPT understands, Too. CoRR, abs/2103.10385 (2021)

16. Lester, B., Al-Rfou, R., Constant, N.: The power of scale for parameter-efficient prompt tuning. In: Proceedings of the 2021 Conference on Empirical Methods in Natural Language Processing, EMNLP 2021, Virtual Event/Punta Cana, Dominican Republic, 7–11 November, 2021, pp. 3045–3059. Association for Computational Linguistics (2021). https://doi.org/10.18653/v1/2021.emnlp-main.243

17. Li, X.L., Liang, P.: Prefix-tuning: optimizing continuous prompts for generation. In: Proceedings of the 59th Annual Meeting of the Association for Computational Linguistics and the 11th International Joint Conference on Natural Language Processing, ACL/IJCNLP 2021, (Volume 1: Long Papers), Virtual Event, 1–6 August 2021, pp. 4582–4597. Association for Computational Linguistics (2021). https://doi.org/10.18653/v1/2021.acl-long.353

18. Cui, G., Hu, S., Ding, N., Huang, L., Liu, Z.: Prototypical verbalizer for prompt-based few-shot tuning. In: Proceedings of the 60th Annual Meeting of the Association for Computational Linguistics (Volume 1: Long Papers), ACL 2022, Dublin, Ireland, 22–27 May 2022, pp. 7014–7024. Association for Computational Linguistics (2022). https://doi.org/10.18653/v1/2022.acl-long.483

19. Shin, T., Razeghi, Y., Logan IV, R.L., Wallace, E., Singh, S.: AutoPrompt: eliciting knowledge from language models with automatically generated prompts. In: Proceedings of the 2020 Conference on Empirical Methods in Natural Language Processing, EMNLP 2020, 16–20 November 2020, pp. 4222–4235. Association for Computational Linguistics (2020). https://doi.org/10.18653/v1/2020.emnlp-main.346

20. Chen, T., Kornblith, S., Norouzi, M., Hinton, G.: A simple framework for contrastive learning of visual representations. In: Proceedings of the 37th International Conference on Machine Learning, ICML 2020, 13–18 July 2020, Virtual Event, pp. 1597–1607. PMLR (2020)

21. Chen, X., Fan, H., Girshick, R., He, K.: Improved Baselines with Momentum Contrastive Learning. CoRR, abs/2003.04297 (2020)

22. Gao, T., Yao, X., Chen, D.: SimCSE: simple contrastive learning of sentence embeddings. In: Proceedings of the 2021 Conference on Empirical Methods in Natural Language Processing, EMNLP 2021, Virtual Event / Punta Cana, Dominican Republic, 7–11 November, 2021, pp. 6894–6910. Association for Computational Linguistics (2021). https://doi.org/10.18653/v1/2021.emnlp-main.552

23. Giorgi, J., Nitski, O., Wang, B., Bader, G.: DeCLUTR: deep contrastive learning for unsupervised textual representations. In: Proceedings of the 59th Annual Meeting of the Association for Computational Linguistics and the 11th International Joint Conference on Natural Language Processing, ACL/IJCNLP 2021, (Volume 1: Long Papers), Virtual Event, 1–6 August 2021, pp. 879–895. Association for Computational Linguistics (2021). https://doi.org/10.18653/v1/2021.acl-long.72

24. Zhang, X., Zhao, J., LeCun, Y.: Character-level convolutional networks for text classification. In: Advances in Neural Information Processing Systems 28: Annual Conference on Neural Information Processing Systems 2015, December 7–12, 2015, Montreal, Quebec, Canada, pp. 649–657 (2015)

25. Collins, E., Rozanov, N., Zhang, B.: Evolutionary data measures: understanding the difficulty of text classification tasks. In: Proceedings of the 22nd Conference on Computational Natural Language Learning, CoNLL 2018, Brussels, Belgium, October 31–November 1, 2018, pp. 380–391. Association for Computational Linguistics (2018). https://doi.org/10.18653/v1/k18-1037
26. Loshchilov, I., Hutter, F.: Decoupled weight decay regularization. In: 7th International Conference on Learning Representations, ICLR 2019, New Orleans, LA, USA, 6–9 May 2019. OpenReview.net (2019)
27. Schick, T., Schmid, H., Schütze, H.: Automatically identifying words that can serve as labels for few-shot text classification. In: Proceedings of the 28th International Conference on Computational Linguistics, COLING 2020, Barcelona, Spain, 8–13 December 2020, pp. 5569–5578. International Committee on Computational Linguistics (2020). https://doi.org/10.18653/v1/2020.coling-main.488
28. Wang, F., Liu, H.: Understanding the behaviour of contrastive loss. In: IEEE Conference on Computer Vision and Pattern Recognition, CVPR 2021, virtual, 19–25 June 2021, pp. 2495–2504. Computer Vision Foundation/IEEE (2021). https://doi.org/10.1109/CVPR46437.2021.00252

A Fine-Grained Image Description Generation Method Based on Joint Objectives

Yifan Zhang[1], Chunzhen Lin[1], Donglin Cao[1,2]([✉]), and Dazhen Lin[1]

[1] Artificial Intelligence Department, Xiamen University, Xiamen 361005, China
`another@xmu.edu.cn`
[2] The Key Laboratory of Cognitive Computing and Intelligent Information Processing of Fujian Education Institutions, Wuyi University, Wuyishan 354300, China

Abstract. The goal of fine-grained image description generation techniques is to learn detailed information from images and simulate human-like descriptions that provide coherent and comprehensive textual details about the image content. Currently, most of these methods face two main challenges: description repetition and omission. Moreover, the existing evaluation metrics cannot clearly reflect the performance of models on these two issues. To address these challenges, we propose an innovative Fine-grained Image Description Generation model based on Joint Objectives. Furthermore, we introduce new object-based evaluation metrics to more intuitively assess the model's performance in handling description repetition and omission. This novel approach combines visual features at both the image level and object level to maximize their advantages and incorporates an object penalty mechanism to reduce description repetition. Experimental results demonstrate that our proposed method significantly improves the CIDEr evaluation metric, indicating its excellent performance in addressing description repetition and omission issues.

Keywords: Image description generation · Fine grained · Joint objectives

1 Introduction

Image description generation aims to depict visual content in natural language accurately. Presently, research in image description generation focuses on two levels: coarse-grained and fine-grained. Coarse-grained image description generation primarily addresses the image's main elements, summarizing the image content. Conversely, fine-grained image description generation aims to generate a more detailed text, delving into the image's subject, intricate details, and environmental context. Fine-grained image description generation demands a model capable of handling complex visual object relationships and generating fluent, coherent descriptions. Studying fine-grained image description generation assists in a more comprehensive understanding of image information, significantly propelling the development of image understanding and processing technology. Hence it bears significant research value.

However, due to the complex relationships between objects within images and semantic disparities between images and texts, current fine-grained image description generation methods face two main issues: (1) Repetition: Existing methods often over-emphasize the image's primary objects, resulting in repetitive and incoherent descriptions; (2) Omission: These approaches typically focus only on a few or significant objects, overlooking other objects within the image, leading to a failure to describe the image comprehensively.

Existing Methods in fine-grained image description generation [2,11,15,17, 26] often applies a sequence-to-sequence construction approach, combined with hierarchical design principles. However, without hierarchical constraints, such strategies may overemphasize significant portions of the image, neglecting less obvious objects and other information, thereby failing to ensure the completeness and uniqueness of the descriptions. To address these challenges, we propose a Fine-grained Image Description Generation method based on Joint Objectives (FIDG-JO). This method establishes connections between sentences and their corresponding objects, extracts multi-object features, filters out interference from other information, and retains spatial relationship information among objects. In addition, we introduce an objective penalty mechanism, effectively mitigating issues of repetition and omission in descriptions.

Our main contributions can be summarized as follow:

- We propose a novel fine-grained image description generation method based on joint objectives that establish correspondences between sentences and their respective objects. This approach extracts multi-object features corresponding to each sentence, thereby maintaining inter-object spatial relations while minimizing the interference of other information while generating descriptions. Additionally, the proposed method integrates an object penalty mechanism to reduce repetition in the descriptions.
- We introduce new object-based evaluation metrics that intuitively reflect the severity of repetition and omission in image description generation. By gathering statistics on the frequency of object occurrences and the total and proportional numbers of objects described, we can more accurately assess a method's performance in addressing repetition and omission issues in image description generation.
- Comprehensive experimental results indicate that our method significantly improves the CIDEr score, demonstrating its effectiveness in addressing description repetition and omission to a considerable extent.

2   Related Work

2.1   Visual Language Models

Current research in visual language models can be divided into two categories: understanding-based models [3,13] and models based on both understanding and generation [21]. While capable of handling a relatively limited set of tasks, the former falls short in addressing open-ended queries such as image description generation and open-ended visual question-answering tasks. The latter garners more attention owing to its broader task coverage and enhanced generalizability. Models such as SIMVLM [25], Oscar [14], OFA [24], and VinVL [29] belong to the category of understanding and generation-based models.

Pre-training visual-language models require an object detection dataset and a paired image-text dataset. The pre-training process is complex and highly demands datasets, while data annotation is costly. Thus, to lower these dataset requirements and training costs, Wang et al. [25] proposed a Simplified Visual Language Model (SimVLM), which employs a prefix language model for end-to-end pre-training. SimVLM does not require pre-training for object detection or auxiliary losses, instead leveraging large-scale weak supervision to reduce training complexity. Without the need for additional data or task-specific customizations, SimVLM's pre-training approach significantly outperforms previous methods.

Traditional visual-language model training paradigms primarily adopt a pre-training finetuning approach. However, Yang et al. [28] have integrated a new finetuning paradigm - prompt tuning [1] into multimodal pre-training, significantly enhancing the model's robustness.

The research on visual-language models is evolving continuously. Despite the enduring challenges, we can anticipate the development of more effective and robust visual-language models through model improvements and the application of novel technologies.

2.2   Fine-Grained Image Description Generation

Krause et al. [11] were the first to introduce the task of generating paragraph-level textual descriptions for images, and they made public the Image Paragraph Captioning dataset, which is currently the primary dataset used for fine-grained image description generation. They proposed a Hierarchical Recurrent Neural Network (HRNN) for this task, where the sentence-level RNN generates a sentence topic based on image region features, and the word-level RNN generates a sentence based on the sentence topic, thus forming a complete paragraph.

In fine-grained image description generation, images often contain multiple objects. It is a challenge to determine which objects need to be described. Krause et al. [11] used average pooling to encode region features into a global vector, then fed it into a Long Short-Term Memory (LSTM) network to generate the topic. However, this method may lose the inherent structural information between objects. To address this problem, Wang et al. [23] proposed a Convolutional Autoencoder (CAE) structure to generate image topics. The CAE abstracts and encodes the topic by performing convolution operations on region features. After that, it guides the deconvolutional decoder by reconstructing the topic to features, making the learned topics more representative.

To alleviate repetition issues and increase diversity in image descriptions, Melas et al. [18] proposed a repeat penalty mechanism. They were the first to use the SCST method in fine-grained image description generation. They incorporated a trigram repeat penalty to reduce repetition by lowering the likelihood of repeated words, thereby increasing the diversity of descriptions. Additionally, Kanani et al. [10] proposed a method that uses a language discriminator to enhance language diversity and reduce repetition by measuring word movement distance.

Existing methods for generating fine-grained image descriptions have optimized against repetitive descriptions, yet they still fall short of expectations. Moreover, there are no practical solutions to the problem of omitted descriptions. Consequently, we propose a fine-grained image description generation method based on joint objectives, aiming to mitigate both issues of repetition and omission in descriptions.

3 Method

To address the issues of repeated and omitted descriptions, we propose a Fine-grained Image Description Generation method based on Joint Objectives (FIDG-JO). As shown in Fig. 1, FIDG-JO consists of three main components: an object feature extraction module, a combined object module, and a language module. The innovation of FIDG-JO lies in its treatment of the objects related to the current sentence through the combined object module. It extracts features from the combined objects and excludes unrelated image content. Thus, it can maintain the relationship between the objects while extracting fine-grained information from the image, minimizing interference from other image content in the current sentence.

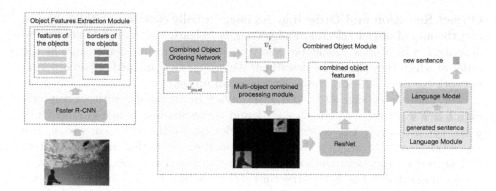

Fig. 1. FIDG-JO contains three modules: an object feature extraction module, a combined object module, and a language module.

3.1   Object Features Extraction Module

We denote the input image as I and its corresponding ground truth as y, comprised of S sentences. The ith sentence consists of N_i words, where $y_{i,j}$ indicates the jth word in the ith sentence.

Our object feature extraction module employs a pre-trained Faster R-CNN [20] for object detection, identifying K object regions $r = r_1, r_2, ..., r_K \in R^{4*K}$ from image I, where R^{4*K} represents a $4 * K$ dimensional space. Each $r_i = B_h, B_w, B_y, B_x$ is a 4D bounding box specifying the height (B_h), width (B_w), and top-left coordinates (B_y, B_x) of the object region. The associated visual features are denoted as $v = v_1, v_2, ..., v_k \in R^{H*K}$, where R^{H*K} represents an $H * K$ dimensional space, with H denoting the dimension of the visual features. In our experiments, we set $H = 2048$. The final visual feature v' for each object region is obtained by concatenating the object feature vector and the bounding box.

$$v' = Concat([v, r]) \tag{1}$$

3.2   Combined Object Module

"Combined objects" refers to collectively processing all M objects corresponding to a sentence y_i, thus forming a new sub-image of combined objects to extract visual features. We introduce the combined objects module to enhance the capture of inter-object relationships and reduce the interference of other irrelevant information in generating the current sentence.

The proposed combined objects module's workflow consists of three steps: (1) object selection and ordering, (2) object combination, and (3)feature extraction.

Object Selection and Ordering. An image usually contains multiple objects, and the aim of object selection and sorting is to learn which objects need to be described, which ones should be described within the same sentence, and the order in which they should be described. We propose a combined object ordering network to select and sort the K objects in an image.

For multiple objects $O = \{O_1, O_2, ..., O_K\}$ in an image, with corresponding object features $v' = \{v'_1, v'_2, ..., v'_k\}$ and corresponding image ground truth $y = \{y_1, y_2, ..., y_s\}$, the object regions relevant to the i-th sentence y_i are $sr_i = \{sr_{i,1}, sr_{i,2}, ..., sr_{i,Mi}\}$. We denote SO as the objects that have been sorted, and sr and sv' represent the sorted object regions and features, respectively.

As illustrated in Fig. 2, the structure of the combined object ordering network has two main inputs. On the left, it inputs the sequence of the combined object features $sv'_{past} = [sv'_1, sv'_2, ..., sv_t - 1']$ that have been generated for the first $t - 1$ sentences, where sv'_i represents the features of the object regions corresponding to the i-th sentence y_i. On the right, it inputs the object features $v' = v'_1, v'_2, ..., v'_k$ corresponding to the K objects in the image I. After passing through a fully connected layer, the decoder's output is fed into a softmax layer to predict the

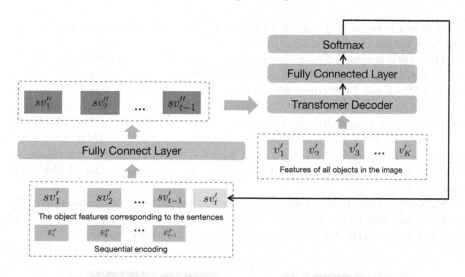

Fig. 2. The framework of combined object ordering network

probabilities of each object being the next object in the sequence. The calculation formula for p is as follows:

$$p = softmax(FC(logits)) \tag{2}$$

$$logits = Transformer(sv''_{past}|v') \tag{3}$$

where FC stands for a fully connected layer, and the left and right sections of "|" correspond to the two inputs for the Transformer decoder.

$$sv'' = W(sv' + E^p) + b \tag{4}$$

where E^p represents the positional encoding, and $W \in R^{(H+4)*(H+4)}, b \in R^{H+4}$ denote learned parameters.

Additionally, to mitigate the issue of redundant object descriptions, we introduce an object penalty mechanism that reduces the probability of an object being predicted as the next object based on the number of times it has already appeared.

$$logp_i = logp_i - \alpha log X_i \tag{5}$$

where p_i is the probability that object O_i is predicted as the next object, X_i is the number of times object O_i has already appeared, and α is a hyperparameter. When α equals 0, the object penalty mechanism is not utilized.

Object Combination. After determining the M objects through the combined object ordering network, we locate their corresponding regions in the image, retaining the information in these areas and filling other positions with zeros, forming a new combined object sub-image. This approach not only reduces interference from redundant information but also preserves the relative positional relationship between objects, enabling more effective processing of object relationships within the image.

The steps are as follows: Compute the dimensions of all object bounding boxes within the current batch, calculating the maximum height B_h^{max} and width B_w^{max} among the composite objects. Then we create a batch of composite object sub-images I^c with dimensions B_h^{max} and B_w^{max}, filled with zeros, and treat each composite object as an individual image. For the M objects $\{SO_1^i, SO_2^i, ..., SO_{M_i}^i\}$ corresponding to sentence y, we retrieve their pixel information from the original image, copy it into the combined object sub-image I^c, resulting in a combined object sub-image I^c corresponding to the M objects of sentence y.

Suppose the combined objects occupy a too-small area in the image, and the background (such as the black area) has a large proportion. In that case, we will appropriately enlarge the object area to enhance its visual features.

(a) Original image   (b)Combined objects: children, giraffe, cookies

(c) Original image   (d)Combined objects: Water,   (e)Combined objects:
                              pillar, chair   Motorcycle, pillar

Fig. 3. Example of two combined object sub-image

As shown in Fig. 3, Fig. 3(a) presents the original image, while Fig. 3(b) showcases the corresponding combined object sub-image. It can be seen that the combined object sub-image retains information about the objects themselves and their relative positional information while removing other redundant details from the image, thus emphasizing the information that "a child is feeding cookies to a giraffe." Similar roles can be observed in Figs. 3(c), 3(d), and 3(e).

Features Extraction. After constructing the combined object sub-image I^c, we used the pre-trained ResNet network [8] to extract visual features as combined object features v^c from the combined object sub-image.

$$v^c = ResNet(I^c) \tag{6}$$

where the combined object visual features $v^c \in R^{H' * K'}$, H' is the dimension of the visual features, and K' is determined by the size of the image and the ResNet.

3.3 Language Modules

Our language module adopts a sentence-by-sentence generation approach. It utilizes the visual features v_t^c of the t-th composite object sub-image I_t^c and the previously generated $t - 1$ sentences $y_1, y_2, ..., y_{t-1}$ to generate the next t-th sentence y_t. Our language model employs the VIRTEX method [5] and the SCST (w/rep.penalty) method [18].

VIRTEX Method. The method based on VIRTEX utilizes a Transformer decoder as its language model. The input to the decoder consists of two parts: (1) the combined object visual features corresponding to the current t-th sentence, extracted through the ResNet network, and (2) the previously generated $t - 1$ sentences. The output of the decoder is the current t-th sentence.

SCST(w/rep. Penalty) Method. The language module in the method based on SCST(w/rep. penalty) is composed of a top-down attention LSTM and a language LSTM. The top-down attention LSTM is used to assess the importance of each feature region, while the language LSTM decodes the image features into textual descriptions. The input for the top-down attention LSTM consists of three parts: (1)the previous output of the Language LSTM, (2)the average pooled object features, and (3)the encoding of the previously generated word. The input for the Language LSTM includes the output from the top-down attention LSTM, and the object features weighted through an attention mechanism. The language LSTM outputs the corresponding description of the image.

Contrary to the original model, which uses visual features based on all objects detected, our approach uses the combined object visual features extracted through the pre-trained ResNet. This adjustment allows our language model to filter out extraneous information, leading to a more compelling image description generation.

3.4 Aligning Objects and Sentences

For the implementation of our approach, the crucial prerequisite is the alignment of objects and sentences in the dataset. However, no public fine-grained image description generation dataset exhibits this alignment property between objects and sentences. To address this issue, we decide to align objects and sentences automatically.

Given that the labels of object detection and objects in sentences are not always identical but semantically similar, we cannot rely solely on whether a sentence contains the object label to determine relevance. To tackle this, we employ word embedding technology to compute the semantic similarity between the object label and sentence, thus aligning the object with the sentence.

BERT [6] is one of the most popular pre-trained language models, so we opted to use a pre-trained BERT to calculate the cosine similarity between the embedding of the object categories $E^O = E_1^O, E_2^O, ..., E_K^O$ and the word embedding in the sentence $E^w = E_1^w, E_2^w, ..., E_N^w$. With this semantic similarity, we can align the objects with the sentences.

4   Experiments

4.1   Dataset and Baseline Model

In these experiments, we utilize the Stanford Image Paragraph Captioning dataset [11]. This dataset, sourced from MS COCO [16] and the Visual Genome [12], is among the most popular for fine-grained image description generation research. It contains 19,551 images, each with at least one paragraph of description.

We selected several popular fine-grained image description generation models for benchmarking to facilitate comparison: CAVP [17], SCST w/rep.penalty [18], IMAP [27], IMG+LNG [9], VIRTEX [5], Regions-Hierarchical [11], and VTCM-Transformer [7]. These models have demonstrated strong competitiveness in fine-grained image description generation, with some even achieving state-of-the-art results.

4.2   Experiment Setup

In our experiments, Faster R-CNN employs a pre-trained model with the extracted object visual features having a dimension of 2048. In the method based on VIRTEX, both ResNet and Transformer decoders utilize pre-trained VIRTEX models without freezing the ResNet parameters. ResNet-50 is chosen for ResNet, with an output dimension of 2048. The parameters for the Transformer decoder are shown in the table. The training process involves a bidirectional Transformer decoder, whereas the generation process is unidirectional (Table 1).

Table 1. Main parameters of the Transformer in VIRTEX

Parameters	Size
Dimension of hidden layer	2048
Number of layers	1
Maximum length	150

For the method based on SCST (w/rep. penalty), ResNet utilizes a pre-trained ResNet-50 with frozen model parameters. The parameters for LSTM are detailed in the Table 2.

Table 2. Main parameters of LSTM

Parameters	Size
Dimension of hidden layer	1300
Number of layers	2

4.3 Evaluation Metrics

In addition to commonly used evaluation metrics in the field of fine-grained image description generation, such as BLEU [19], CIDEr [22], and METEOR [4], we propose new metrics based on the number of objects to more directly evaluate the performance of different methods in addressing issues of description repetition and omission. Expressly, we set four evaluation metrics based on the number of objects, which are:

(1) The number of described objects $|O_G|$: The average number of objects described per image in image description generation. A higher value indicates a more comprehensive image description, as it covers more objects.
(2) The number of objects Consistent with ground truth $|O_{G-Cap}|$: the average number of objects in a description that matches those in the ground truth. A higher value indicates the ability to describe more objects consistent with the ground truth.
(3) The coverage rate of described object RC_{Cap}: the ratio of $|O_{G-Cap}|$ to $|O_G|$. A higher value indicates a better ability to describe objects consistent with the ground truth.

$$RC_{Cap} = \frac{|O_{G-Cap}|}{|O_{Cap}|} \tag{7}$$

(4) $Rep - 4$: the number of objects in the fine-grained image description that appears four or more times (inclusive). A lower score in this metric is preferable, as repeating an object four times or more is usually considered excessive repetition.

The first three metrics assess the descriptions' comprehensiveness, while $Rep - 4$ gauges the repetition of descriptions.

4.4 Experimental Results and Discussions

Table 3 compares VIRTEX and SCST (w/rep.penalty), incorporating the FIDG-JO method against other models. With the introduction of FIDG-JO, VIRTEX has improved on all metrics, especially CIDEr, which has seen a significant rise from 15.90 to 23.19. CIDEr is an evaluation metric designed explicitly for image description generation tasks, and it is considered the most crucial metric for assessing the performance of fine-grained image description generation. After incorporating FIDG-JO, SCST (w/rep.penalty) has also seen improvements in most metrics, particularly in CIDEr, which increased from 25.73 to 29.42.

Table 3. Comparison with other methods on Image Paragraph Captioning dataset. The best results for each evaluation metric are marked in bold.

Methods	METEOR	CIDEr	BLEU-1	BLEU-2	BLEU-3	BLEU-4
IMG + LNG	11.28	26.04	24.96	13.82	8.04	4.6
IMAP	**17.13**	22.98	**44.02**	27.29	16.75	9.79
Regions-Hierarchical	15.95	13.52	41.9	24.11	14.23	8.69
CVAP	16.83	21.12	42.01	25.86	15.33	9.26
VTCM-Transformer	16.88	26.15	40.93	25.51	15.94	9.96
VIRTEX	14.56	15.9	33.24	19.68	12.12	7.44
VIRTEX + FIDG-JO(ours)	14.91	23.19	39.48	23.04	13.92	8.52
SCST (w/ rep.penalty)	16.28	25.34	42.11	29.51	17.36	**10.56**
SCST(w/ rep.penalty) + FIDG-JO(ours)	16.73	**28.46**	42.35	**29.57**	**18.21**	10.54

The experimental results show that FIDG-JO significantly improves the CIDEr metric, which suggests that, compared to other methods, the descriptions generated by FIDG-JO contain more keywords, pay attention to more information in the image, and provide a more comprehensive description.

Table 4. Experimental results based on object-based evaluation metrics

Methods and ground truth	$|O_G|$	$|O_{G-Cap}|$	RC_{cap}	$Rep-4$
Ground truth	6.38	-	-	-
VIRTEX	4.93	3.82	59.9	0.39
VIRTEX + FIDG-JO (ours)	7.31	5.22	81.8	0.18
SCST (w/ rep.penalty)	6.05	5.34	83.7	0.25
SCST (w/ rep.penalty) + FIDG-JO (ours)	**7.62**	**5.63**	**88.2**	**0.13**

Table 4 showcases the comparison of object-based evaluation metrics for VIRTEX and SCST (w/rep.penalty) before and after the introduction of FIDG-JO. It is noticeable that both VIRTEX and SCST (w/rep.penalty) have shown significant improvements in various metrics concerning description comprehensiveness after incorporating FIDG-JO, which indicates that the FIDG-JO can describe more objects and has a higher coverage rate for ground truth objects. At the same time, the metric of repeating the same object four times or more has noticeably decreased which fully illustrates that the FIDG-JO can effectively mitigate the problems of description repetition and omission.

4.5   Experimental Examples and Analyses

Figure 4 presents examples of image descriptions from VIRTEX, SCST (w/rep. penalty), and after incorporating FIDG-JO.

Image and Ground Truth	Methods	Descriptions
 The girl is looking at the camera and smiling. The sun is shining on the top and right hand side of the building. The green umbrella to the left is in the shade. The people are wearing numbers on their shirts.	VIRTEX	A man and woman are standing outside on a sunny day. The man is wearing a blue shirt and black shorts. The man is wearing a white shirt. The man is wearing a black shirt and black pants. The man is wearing a black shirt. The man is wearing a black shirt.
	VIRTEX + IDJO (ours)	A group of people are standing around a green umbrella on a sunny day. There is a large building in the background. The girl standing in front of the umbrella is wearing a blue shirt. There is a yellow and green umbrella. The man standing around the pole is wearing a green shirt and green pants.
 There are several people crossing the street. It is raining in the picture and they are holding umbrellas. There are also a lot of cars on the street. There is a building behind the people.	SCST (w/ rep.penalty)	A group of people are walking on a street. The street is white. There are people walking on the street. There are cars parked on the street. There is a man walking on the sidewalk. There is a building in the background.
	SCST (w/ rep.penalty) + IDJO (ours)	A group of people are walking on the street. Two of the man are carrying umbrellas. There is a black car parking on the street. A group of people are walking on the street. There is a building in the background.

Fig. 4. Examples of image descriptions generated by VIRTEX, SCST (w/rep. penalty), and after incorporating FIDG-JO

In the descriptions provided by VIRTEX, the number of objects consistent with the annotations is four, while for VIRTEX+FIDG-JO, the number is six, indicating that FIDG-JO can effectively enhance the coverage of annotated objects. VIRTEX tends to repeat objects at a higher rate, repeating the main subject (man) five times, and the shirt appears four times. With VIRTEX+FIDG-JO, the repetition is reduced, with the umbrella appearing three times and the shirt appearing two times. Analyzing the descriptions, we find that the occurrence of objects up to three times is relatively common and aligns with the logical description. In contrast, more frequent occurrences are abnormal and considered repetitions, which shows that FIDG-JO can significantly reduce the repetition in descriptions. VIRTEX frequently describes the subject as a man, while the image's subject should be female; VIRTEX+FIDG-JO accurately describes the subject as a girl. Also, VIRTEX has a lower accuracy rate for color recognition, while VIRTEX+FIDG-JO can recognize colors more accurately, indicating that FIDG-JO improves the accuracy of descriptions.

For SCST (w/rep. penalty), the number of objects consistent with the annotations is four. With SCST (w/rep. penalty) + FIDG-JO, it is five, suggesting that FIDG-JO can increase the annotation coverage. SCST (w/rep. penalty) includes one object inconsistent with the annotation, while SCST (w/rep. penalty) + FIDG-JO is entirely consistent with the annotation. SCST (w/rep. penalty) ignores the rain in the image, but SCST (w/rep. penalty) + FIDG-JO's description includes an umbrella, signifying that FIDG-JO can make the description more comprehensive. In SCST (w/rep. penalty)'s description, the word 'street' appears four times, creating an excessive repetition. With SCST (w/rep. penalty) + FIDG-JO, no descriptions exceed three repetitions, showing that FIDG-JO can reduce the redundancy in descriptions.

These experimental examples further confirm the effectiveness of FIDG-JO in solving the problems of repetitive and omitted descriptions.

5   Conclusion

To address the two primary challenges in fine-grained image description generation - description repetition and omission, we propose a Fine-grained Image Description Generation method based on Joint Objectives (FIDG-JO). FIDG-JO ingeniously integrates the advantages of image-level and object-level visual features, accurately capturing object information while excluding irrelevant image information. Additionally, we introduce an object penalty mechanism to limit the number of times an object is redundantly described. Experiments validate the effectiveness of FIDG-JO in mitigating description repetition and omission problems. Furthermore, since existing evaluation metrics cannot intuitively reflect the issues of description repetition and omission in descriptions, we propose object-based evaluation metrics. By examining the occurrence of objects, we can more intuitively reflect the method's performance.

Acknowledgment. This work is supported by the National Natural Science Foundation of China (No. 62076210, No. 81973752), the Natural Science Foundation of Xiamen city (No. 3502Z20227188) and the Open Project Program of The Key Laboratory of Cognitive Computing and Intelligent Information Processing of Fujian Education Institutions, Wuyi University (No. KLCCIIP2020203)

References

1. Brown, T., et al.: Language models are few-shot learners. Adv. Neural. Inf. Process. Syst. **33**, 1877–1901 (2020)
2. Chatterjee, M., Schwing, A.G.: Diverse and coherent paragraph generation from images. In: Proceedings of the European Conference on Computer Vision (ECCV), pp. 729–744 (2018)
3. Chen, Y.-C., et al.: UNITER: UNiversal image-TExt representation learning. In: Vedaldi, A., Bischof, H., Brox, T., Frahm, J.-M. (eds.) ECCV 2020. LNCS, vol. 12375, pp. 104–120. Springer, Cham (2020). https://doi.org/10.1007/978-3-030-58577-8_7
4. Denkowski, M., Lavie, A.: Meteor universal: Language specific translation evaluation for any target language. In: Proceedings of the ninth workshop on statistical machine translation. pp. 376–380 (2014)
5. Desai, K., Johnson, J.: Virtex: learning visual representations from textual annotations. In: Proceedings of the IEEE/CVF Conference on Computer Vision and Pattern Recognition, pp. 11162–11173 (2021)
6. Devlin, J., Chang, M.W., Lee, K., Toutanova, K.: Bert: pPre-training of deep bidirectional transformers for language understanding. arXiv preprint arXiv:1810.04805 (2018)

7. Guo, D., Lu, R., Chen, B., Zeng, Z., Zhou, M.: Matching visual features to hierarchical semantic topics for image paragraph captioning. Int. J. Comput. Vision **130**(8), 1920–1937 (2022)
8. He, K., Zhang, X., Ren, S., Sun, J.: Deep residual learning for image recognition. In: Proceedings of the IEEE Conference on Computer Vision and Pattern Recognition, pp. 770–778 (2016)
9. Ilinykh, N., Dobnik, S.: When an image tells a story: the role of visual and semantic information for generating paragraph descriptions. In: Proceedings of the 13th International Conference on Natural Language Generation, pp. 338–348 (2020)
10. Kanani, C.S., Saha, S., Bhattacharyya, P.: Improving diversity and reducing redundancy in paragraph captions. In: 2020 International Joint Conference on Neural Networks (IJCNN), pp. 1–8. IEEE (2020)
11. Krause, J., Johnson, J., Krishna, R., Fei-Fei, L.: A hierarchical approach for generating descriptive image paragraphs. In: Proceedings of the IEEE Conference on Computer Vision and Pattern Recognition, pp. 317–325 (2017)
12. Krishna, R., et al.: Visual genome: connecting language and vision using crowdsourced dense image annotations. Int. J. Comput. Vision **123**, 32–73 (2017)
13. Li, G., Duan, N., Fang, Y., Gong, M., Jiang, D.: Unicoder-vl: a universal encoder for vision and language by cross-modal pre-training. In: Proceedings of the AAAI Conference on Artificial Intelligence, vol. 34, pp. 11336–11344 (2020)
14. Li, X., Yin, X., Li, C., Zhang, P., Hu, X., Zhang, L., Wang, L., Hu, H., Dong, L., Wei, F., et al.: Oscar: Object-semantics aligned pre-training for vision-language tasks. In: Computer Vision-ECCV 2020: 16th European Conference, Glasgow, UK, August 23–28, 2020, Proceedings, Part 16. pp. 121–137. Springer (2020)
15. Liang, X., Hu, Z., Zhang, H., Gan, C., Xing, E.P.: Recurrent topic-transition gan for visual paragraph generation. In: Proceedings of the IEEE International Conference on Computer Vision, pp. 3362–3371 (2017)
16. Lin, T.-Y., Maire, M., Belongie, S., Hays, J., Perona, P., Ramanan, D., Dollár, P., Zitnick, C.L.: Microsoft COCO: common objects in context. In: Fleet, D., Pajdla, T., Schiele, B., Tuytelaars, T. (eds.) ECCV 2014. LNCS, vol. 8693, pp. 740–755. Springer, Cham (2014). https://doi.org/10.1007/978-3-319-10602-1_48
17. Liu, D., Zha, Z.J., Zhang, H., Zhang, Y., Wu, F.: Context-aware visual policy network for sequence-level image captioning. In: Proceedings of the 26th ACM International Conference on Multimedia, pp. 1416–1424 (2018)
18. Melas-Kyriazi, L., Rush, A.M., Han, G.: Training for diversity in image paragraph captioning. In: Proceedings of the 2018 Conference on Empirical Methods in Natural Language Processing, pp. 757–761 (2018)
19. Papineni, K., Roukos, S., Ward, T., Zhu, W.J.: Bleu: a method for automatic evaluation of machine translation. In: Proceedings of the 40th Annual Meeting of the Association for Computational Linguistics, pp. 311–318 (2002)
20. Ren, S., He, K., Girshick, R., Sun, J.: Faster r-cnn: towards real-time object detection with region proposal networks. Advances in neural information processing systems 28 (2015)
21. Sun, C., Myers, A., Vondrick, C., Murphy, K., Schmid, C.: Videobert: a joint model for video and language representation learning. In: Proceedings of the IEEE/CVF International Conference on Computer Vision, pp. 7464–7473 (2019)
22. Vedantam, R., Lawrence Zitnick, C., Parikh, D.: Cider: consensus-based image description evaluation. In: Proceedings of the IEEE Conference on Computer Vision and Pattern Recognition, pp. 4566–4575 (2015)

23. Wang, J., Pan, Y., Yao, T., Tang, J., Mei, T.: Convolutional auto-encoding of sentence topics for image paragraph generation. arXiv preprint arXiv:1908.00249 (2019)
24. Wang, P., et al.: Ofa: unifying architectures, tasks, and modalities through a simple sequence-to-sequence learning framework. In: International Conference on Machine Learning, pp. 23318–23340. PMLR (2022)
25. Wang, Z., Yu, J., Yu, A.W., Dai, Z., Tsvetkov, Y., Cao, Y.: Simvlm: simple visual language model pretraining with weak supervision. arXiv preprint arXiv:2108.10904 (2021)
26. Wu, S., Zha, Z.J., Wang, Z., Li, H., Wu, F.: Densely supervised hierarchical policy-value network for image paragraph generation. In: IJCAI, pp. 975–981 (2019)
27. Xu, C., Li, Y., Li, C., Ao, X., Yang, M., Tian, J.: Interactive key-value memory-augmented attention for image paragraph captioning. In: Proceedings of the 28th International Conference on Computational Linguistics, pp. 3132–3142 (2020)
28. Yang, H., Lin, J., Yang, A., Wang, P., Zhou, C., Yang, H.: Prompt tuning for generative multimodal pretrained models. arXiv preprint arXiv:2208.02532 (2022)
29. Zhang, P., et al.: Vinvl: revisiting visual representations in vision-language models. In: Proceedings of the IEEE/CVF Conference on Computer Vision and Pattern Recognition, pp. 5579–5588 (2021)

Analyzing Collective Intelligence Through Sentiment Networks in Self-organized Douban Communities

Tiantian Xie[1] and Xiaokun Wu[1,2]

[1] School of Journalism and Communication, South China University of Technology, Guangzhou 510006, Guangdong, China
wuxiaokun@scut.edu.cn
[2] Center for Data Analysis and Information Visualization, South China University of Technology, Guangzhou 510006, Guangdong, China

Abstract. Understanding the communication behaviors of online community users, particularly their crowd intelligence dynamics, has long been a focal point within network communication research. In this study, we present an approach integrating the BERTopic topic model, advanced Natural Language Processing (NLP) techniques, and Social Network Analysis, to meticulously dissect the intricate dynamics of emotion propagation and evolution within collective behaviors that unfold on social networks. Our investigation delves deeply into this complex landscape, exploring the relationships between the sentiment of the initial post and subsequent responses, the interplay between sentiment strength and activity levels, and the correlation between sentiment polarity and the intensity of activity. This study highlights the significance of harnessing the combined power of BERTopic, NLP, and social network methodologies to decode the subtleties of emotional propagation and transformation.

Keywords: Collective intelligence · BERTopic · Social Network Analysis · Natural Language Processing · Sentiment distribution

1 Introduction

Social anxiety disorder, often called "social fear," and its counterpart, the "social master" or "social cow," represent contrasting social traits in society. Social fear involves nervousness, discomfort, and social avoidance, while social masters excel in and enjoy socializing. In the Douban virtual community, these concepts offer an excellent opportunity for comparison. Both social fear and social cow groups in virtual communities share similarities. The former consists of individuals seeking support for social unease, while the latter includes those who thrive in social activities. This contrast forms a valuable framework for research, shedding light on community interaction behaviors. Through a careful comparative analysis, we gain insights into the emotional expressions and evolution of these traits in a networked environment. This research focuses on Douban, China's largest online interest-based community, with approximately 120,000 users, mainly aged 19 to 30. The Douban mobile app has around 12 million monthly and 3 million daily active users. We employ Bert topic modeling and semantic network analysis to construct comment interaction networks, uncovering virtual community dynamics. We analyze member contributions using a sentiment dictionary and conduct regression analysis to explore emotional changes during community engagement. The key contributions are as follows:

- By harnessing social network data from online community users, an opportunity arises to gain profound insights into the diffusion patterns and driving factors that underpin information flow within social networks. This fills a crucial void left by traditional social survey research, which often struggles to establish contact with specific demographic groups and comprehend the intricacies of their collective intelligence behaviors.
- Scrutinizing the intricacies of information dissemination within a particular community not only facilitates a grasp of the interconnections, patterns of association, and routes taken by information among group members, but also provides invaluable insights applicable to broader fields of social network research. These analytical outcomes serve as a point of reference for diverse areas of study.
- Social terror groups often coalesce into networks of mutual aid and solidarity within virtual communities. Delving into the dynamics of interactions and supportive bonds among community members unravels the intricacies of the social support network, affording comprehension of its evolution, composition, and influential factors. This analytical lens offers a foundation for investigating topics encompassing community dynamics, advocacy, mental well-being, and beyond.

2   Related Works

Previous research on social anxiety has largely focused on medical aspects, including cultural influences [9], educational backgrounds [6], social comparisons [11,13], and the psychological consequences [5]. NHowever, these studies often overlook the role of information interactions. To address this gap, our study collects data from two control communities and uses methods like social network analysis and topic modeling to uncover how information exchange and emotional convergence occur in virtual networks. We also examine factors shaping collective mentality in information dissemination. Our main goal is to reveal the mechanisms of swarm intelligence behavior in specific social contexts, an area less explored in existing studies.

To investigate collective intelligence in virtual communities, we utilize diverse tools and advanced technologies, including BERTopic, social network analysis, and sentiment analysis. Our objective is to comprehensively understand the emotions and behaviors within these virtual communities.

2.1   BERTopic Topic Modeling Method

BERTopic serves as a sophisticated topic modeling technique that extracts coherent topic representations by introducing a category-based variant of TF-IDF. It initiates the process by generating embeddings through a pre-trained model. Subsequently, the Unified Manifold Approximation and Projection (UMAP) methodology is applied to reduce the dimensionality of these embeddings. This reduction enhances the efficiency of document clustering. To finalize this clustering, the HDBSCAN algorithm, rooted in hierarchy and density-based principles [7], is employed.

UMAP is a nonlinear dimensionality reduction method that preserves local and global data relationships by creating a data domain, topology and refining low-dimensional representations. HDBSCAN is a density clustering algorithm for grouping data points into interconnected clusters while identifying varying densities and noise points. UMAP and HDBSCAN are prominent algorithms for data analysis and clustering. UMAP maps high-dimensional data to lower dimensions using topological insights and distance relationships. HDBSCAN organizes data points into closely related clusters, excelling with diverse datasets due to its adaptability to varying densities and noise.

BERTopic offers significant advantages over other topic modeling approaches by bridging the gap between density-based and center-based sampling methods. It excels in versatile data scenarios due to its unique ability to combine these strategies, enhancing its utility [2]. Furthermore, BERTopic's adaptability extends to various language models, enhancing its performance through co-optimization. This optimization improves accuracy and efficiency in topic modeling, as confirmed by studies [2]. Studies substantiate BERTopic's exceptional performance in language processing, increasing the General Language Understanding Evaluation (GLUE) score to an impressive 80.5%, reflecting a substantial improvement of 7.7% [2]. It outperforms alternatives by using pre-trained models, eliminating the need for data labeling and yielding context-infused embeddings for words and sentences, particularly beneficial for short text data [2].

2.2   User Sentiment Analysis Within Community Texts

Currently, sentiment analysis techniques within online communities can be broadly categorized into three main approaches: keyword-based sentiment analysis, machine learning-based sentiment analysis, and hybrid sentiment analysis techniques [15].

Keyword-based methods use dictionaries, requiring text preprocessing for accuracy. Sentiment words are extracted manually or from predefined dictionaries. Construction of these dictionaries is challenging and can incur costs [17]. Moreover, different types of texts demand distinct dictionaries, as employing the same dictionary for diverse text analyses may lead to various errors. Nonetheless, as artificially constructed dictionaries continue to improve, the accuracy of keyword-based sentiment analysis technology is expected to rise gradually.

Machine learning methods use labeled/unlabeled data and algorithms like SVM, decision trees, KNN, and Bayesian networks. They offer flexibility in choosing text features and classifiers for emotional text analysis. For instance, Md. Rafiqul Islam et al. used decision trees, SVM, KNN, and ensemble methods to analyze depression-related Facebook data, covering emotional characteristics, temporal attributes, and language style [10]. MICHAEL M. TADESSE et al. combined natural language processing and machine learning to uncover depression-related features in Reddit posts. SVM achieved 80% accuracy in extracting individual features, while the Multi-Layer Perceptron (MLP) excelled, reaching 91% accuracy with LIWC+LDA+bigram [20]. IGonzalo A. Ruz et al. used Bayesian networks to explore connections among sentiment words in Spanish datasets, enhancing sentiment analysis understanding [18].

In text sentiment analysis, neural network methods include single networks, hybrid models, attention-based approaches, and pre-trained models. They learn complex text features and context, improving understanding. For example, Zhou Yu et al. used a convolutional neural network with a Boltzmann machine for latent topic modeling and sentiment analysis [22]. However, deep learning methods require substantial data and time, limiting their effectiveness with smaller datasets and large-scale analysis.

Given the unique nature of our research sample, this study primarily employs sentiment analysis techniques based on sentiment dictionaries. Utilizing these artificially crafted lexicons, we compute the frequency of sentiment-infused words within the text and weigh them against other words to derive a sentiment index. It's worth noting that distinct texts necessitate the use of specific dictionaries, as applying a uniform dictionary to disparate texts may introduce varying errors. Nonetheless, as artificially constructed dictionaries continue to evolve and refine over time, the accuracy of keyword-based sentiment analysis technology has shown a progressive improvement.

3   Data and Methods

3.1   Data Collection

This study collects data from two virtual community groups on the Douban platform: the "Social Ability Rehabilitation Group" (Group 1) and the "Social OCD Group" (Group 2). Group 1 data was collected from January 17, 2021, to November 22, 2021, including 4,875 valid posts and 54,398 comments. Group 2 data covers September 7, 2021, to June 12, 2022, with 1,252 posts and 13,546 comments. Both groups were observed for approximately 10 months from their inception. This approach provides a comprehensive view of group dynamics and ample data for sentiment and social network analysis.

The dataset includes poster ID, post content, timestamps, responder IDs, reply content, and reply timestamps, forming a robust foundation for in-depth analysis of social interactions and emotional expressions.

3.2   Data Preprocessing

In this paper, we ensure data integrity, accuracy, and consistency. We first inspected crawled data for attributes and temporal gaps. We then conducted preprocessing, fixing missing, duplicate, and aberrant posts. Finally, we normalized the data for standardized format. These efforts yielded: Group 1 with 4,868 validated content posts and 54,120 comments, and Group 2 with 1,243 content posts and 15,450 comments.

To assess sentiment analysis precision, we sampled and manually annotated 200 entries from both groups. Two trained postgraduate students marked sentiment polarity as 1 for positive, -1 for negative, and 0 for no discernible sentiment. We compared and validated the labels, calculating accuracy (see Table 1).

Table 1. Accuracy of Dictionary-based Sentiment Evaluation

Data set	Posts of G1	Comments of G1	Posts of G2	Comments of G2
Accuracy	0.92	0.94	0.88	0.89

3.3   Data Analysis

Topic Model Analysis. In this study, we employed the BERTopic pre-training model for topic modeling analysis of the textual data. Our methodology involved several key steps:

- Stop Word Compilation: Initially, we merged three separate stop word lists, namely the Harbin Institute of Technology stop word list, Baidu stop word list, and a Chinese stop word list, into a single consolidated stop word list for subsequent processing. Word Compilation: Initially, we merged three separate stop word lists, namely the Harbin Institute of Technology stop word list, Baidu stop word list, and a Chinese stop word list, into a single consolidated stop word list for subsequent processing.
- Text Segmentation and Stop Word Removal: We utilized the jieba tokenizer to segment the text and effectively remove stop words. Additionally, to preserve specific fixed words, we excluded them from the word segmentation process.
- Dimensionality Reduction: Next, we employed the Unified Manifold Approximation and Projection (UMAP) technique to reduce the dimensionality of the word-segmented sentence vectors. This dimension reduction process aids in optimizing the embedding.
- Hierarchical and Density-Based Clustering: Subsequently, we applied the HDBSCAN algorithm, which is rooted in hierarchical and density-based principles, to perform clustering. This step enabled us to identify topics and the key feature words associated with these topics.
- Model Refinement: We made necessary adjustments and optimizations based on the modeling results to enhance the quality of our findings.

– Visualization and Output: Finally, we visualized and output the generated results, presenting the identified topics and their corresponding feature words through visualization techniques.

This comprehensive approach allowed us to effectively analyze and extract meaningful topics and insights from the text data under investigation.

Methods for optimal topic number determination in topic modeling include perplexity and topic similarity assessment. Perplexity, a language model quality measure, is inversely related to test set probability normalized by word count. Lower perplexity signifies better model performance. Typically, perplexity is used to compare topic modeling performance across different topic numbers in the same dataset [4]. Topic similarity evaluation gauges overall topic space distinctiveness and stability by measuring deviations between individual topics and their mean. Greater differences indicate higher topic distinctiveness and overall stability [16].

In our research, we combined perplexity curves with topic distinctiveness analysis. We compared the topic feature words when considering 5, 6, 7, 8, 9, and 10 topics. Eventually, we determined that the optimal number of topics was 8, as it maximized topic distinctiveness and allowed for clear description of the central themes through the topic feature words.

Semantic Network Construction. In text analysis, we employ BERT's methodology to construct semantic vectors for text content. Using the Transformer encoder unit and multi-head self-attention mechanism, we process and derive vector representations. These vectors undergo further processing through residual connections and normalization layers, followed by a feed-forward and residual network to extract semantic features.

For latent space representation, we use the K-means clustering algorithm to group semantically similar words without supervision. K-means initializes cluster centers based on the desired number of clusters (k) and iteratively minimizes the sum of squared errors, measuring distances between samples and cluster centers, as shown in formula (1).

$$J(c, u) = \sum_{i=1}^{M} \|x_i - \mu_{c_i}\|^2 \tag{1}$$

where x_i is the i sample, c_i is the cluster of x_i and μ_{c_i} is the center of cluster x_i, M is the total number of samples.

In this study, we use the Python-based TF-IDF algorithm to process main posts and comments in the clustered dataset. TF-IDF helps extract important keywords within each cluster, enhancing our understanding. The extracted data is then visualized and analyzed using Gephi software, creating informative maps that illustrate word connections and associations. These visual representations aid in in-depth analysis of word relationships within the textual data.

Sentiment Communication Analysis. To understand the spread of social anxiety online, we conducted emotion discrimination and contagion analyses on data from Group 1 and Group 2, using an emotion dictionary. Here are the steps:

- Construction of Sentiment Lexicon: We created a sentiment lexicon for supervised learning, including sentiment, negative, and degree words. We expanded an existing Chinese sentiment polarity dictionary with 200 additional emotional words.
- Processing of Main Posts and Texts: We systematically processed primary posts and text data to identify emotional words and compute their scores.
- Degree Word Consideration: We checked if the word before an emotional word was a degree word. If yes, we adjusted the emotional word's score accordingly.
- Negative Word Assessment: We examined if the word before an emotional word was negative. If an odd number of negative words were found, we multiplied the emotional word's score by -1. For a double negative, we multiplied by 1.
- Cumulative Score Calculation: We summed emotional word scores across all clauses in the post content to get the post's overall emotional score.

This comprehensive methodology allowed us to assess the emotional content of posts and gain insights into the propagation of social anxiety in the virtual community.

As a metric for gauging the impact of sentiment contagion within the network, we employ emotional shifts following the reception of information. Our approach involves computing the emotional score for each text by subtracting the negative emotional score from the positive emotional score. The sentiment change is calculated using the following formula:

$$S = S_P - S_N \tag{2}$$

where S_P is the positive emotion score while S_N represents the negative emotion score.

For measuring emotional transmission, we draw inspiration from Michela et al.'s research in Nature [1]. Their study explores how user sentiment and participation behavior transform community structure. We adopt a group dynamics perspective to quantify the interaction between user emotions and engagement. This involves analyzing changes in user emotional values during participation, assessing emotional transformation efficiency, and studying user emotional polarization. In alignment with Michela et al.'s approach, we have redefined three key indicators. These include:

Average Member Sentiment Value ($\sigma(i)$): This metric captures the average emotional disposition of a given community member i, where i represents the ith member, and σi denotes the average emotional value derived from all posts and comments authored by memberi.

Average Positive/Negative Comment Difference $n\rho(i)$: To compute this indicator, we assess the average disparity between positive and negative comments authored by member i.

Average User Sentiment Transformation($\rho(i)$): This indicator characterizes the emotional changes experienced by virtual community member i during their engagement in the community.

For the calculation of the average positive/negative review difference, we employ the following formula:

$$n\rho(i) = \frac{1}{T_i} \sum_{j=1}^{T_i} (Pos_j(i) - Neg_j(i)) \tag{3}$$

T_i is the number of days the user is active, $Neg_j(i)$ is the number of negative comments and posts issued by the user on day j, $Pos_j(i)$ is the number of positive comments and posts issued by the user on day j.

The formula for calculating the average user emotional polarization is expressed as:

$$\rho\sigma(i) = \frac{((N_i - 2k_i - h_i)(N_i - h_i))}{N_j^2} \tag{4}$$

where N_i, k_i, and h_i respectively refer to the number of total comments and posts, the number of negative comments and posts, and the number of neutral comments and posts.

4   Experimental Results

4.1   Results of BERTopic Topic Modeling Analysis

Using BERT and topic modeling, our aim is to identify topics in text data and group similar texts into categories. This helps us understand and structure extensive text data, uncover hidden topic patterns, and improve text analysis efficiency. We determine the number of topics based on perplexity and topic differentiation assessments, then cluster word vectors from the text accordingly. We reduce the dimensionality of these vectors for two-dimensional visualization. Our observation reveals that the clustering is clearest when using 8 clusters, as shown in Fig. 1. We applied BERTopic topic modeling to the combined text data from Group 1 and Group 2, revealing 8 distinct themes in each group. We thoroughly examined the results and present the topics and explanations for Group 1 and Group 2 in Table 2 below:

Distinctive patterns emerge in both Group 1 and Group 2. Group 1 focuses on interpersonal interaction, emotional support, and self-improvement. They emphasize empathy, problem-solving, and self-discovery. In contrast, Group 2 shares a similar emphasis on interpersonal engagement but leans towards empowerment, social interaction, and relationship dynamics, especially concerning opposite-sex interactions, reflecting their aspirations and relationship expectations.

To assess the comparability and distribution of topics across two virtual communities, we fed the sample data into the BERT model, resulting in the acquisition of topic word embeddings for each topic. To gauge topic similarity,

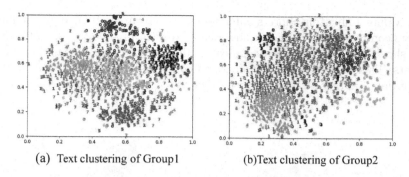

(a) Text clustering of Group1   (b)Text clustering of Group2

Fig. 1. Text clustering results divided by modules

Table 2. Induction of BERTopic Outputs

Topic model induction for G1	Topic model induction for G2
1) Interpersonal: involves interacting and communicating with other people	1) Interpersonal: involves interacting and socializing with other people
2) Blessing words: including blessings and good wishes	2) Contact with the opposite sex: Communication and interaction with the opposite sex
3) Emotional support: emotional support and comfort	3) Expressing expectations: deals with the topic of expressing expectations and expectations
4) Activities of Daily Living: Topics related to activities of daily living	4) Encouraging Others: Topics related to encouraging others and giving support
5) Group Belonging: involves a sense of belonging and group identity	5) Social Objects: Topics about social objects
6) Self-Escape: Topics related to escapism or self-preservation	6) Seeking Support: Topics that deal with seeking support and help from others
7) Improving the current situation: Topics about improving the current situation or seeking change	7) Emotional states: Topics related to emotions and affective states
8) Personality Type Testing: Topics related to testing and assessing an individual's personality type	8) Work life: Covers topics related to work and life

we computed the cosine similarity between all topic words within two topics, subsequently deriving the average similarity score. For the topic $\{A_1, \cdots, A_n\}$, each topic has m keywords, and for the i-th topic, the keywords are $\{w_1^j, \cdots, w_n^j\}$, the BERT model is f, and the similarity between the i-th and j-th topics is:

$$R_{ij} = \frac{1}{m^2} \sum_k \sum_t \frac{f(w_k^i)f(w_t^j)}{\|f(w_k^i)\|\|f(w_t^j)\|} \tag{5}$$

Figure 2 reveals a notable distinction in topic similarity between the two virtual communities. Specifically, the group 1 virtual community exhibits a topic similarity score of 0.256, indicating a comparatively higher degree of topic concentration within its posting content. Conversely, the group 2 virtual community records a topic similarity score of 0.223, signifying a relatively greater dispersion of topics within its content. Topic similarity values range from 0 to 1, with higher values indicating more similar topics. In Group 1, high topic similarity suggests common subject matter and focused discussions. Group 2, on the other hand, shows low topic similarity, indicating diverse discussions spanning various interests. This insight helps us understand community characteristics and topic distribution, guiding further research on member behavior and interactions.

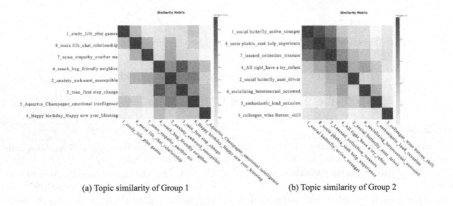

(a) Topic similarity of Group 1   (b) Topic similarity of Group 2

Fig. 2. Topic similarity Analysis

4.2   Output of Semantic Network Analysis

Based on our text topic analysis, we identified and defined 8 distinct clusters. Figure 3 visually displays high-frequency words in each cluster. To measure internal network cohesion, we used the modularity metric. Introduced by Newman and colleagues, modularity assesses network division quality. It's computed based on connection strengths among nodes and community partition consistency. Higher connection strength between nodes in the same community yields a greater modularity value.

Modularity values are typically bounded between -1 and 1, with values approaching 1 indicating stronger internal connections within communities and more effective community delineations. We first divide a social network in to k communities and defines a $k \times k$ matrix e, where e_{ij} represents the proportion of edges connecting community i and community j relative to the total number of edges. let $a_i = \sum_j e_{ij}$

$$Q = \sum_i (e_{ii} - a_i^2) = Tre - |||e^2|$$ (6)

Utilizing the aforementioned definition, we calculated the modularity scores for both group 1 and group 2, resulting in values of 0.565 and 0.541, respectively.With the above definition, we can obtain the modularity of group 1 and group 2, which is 0.565 and 0.541 respectively.

The semantic network analysis of Fig. 3 reveals complex relationships. In Group 1's network, prominent themes include "interpersonal" and "emotion." In the interpersonal network, scenarios like schools and companies are linked to emotional attributes like tension and dislike. While both Group 1 and Group 2 focus on "emotion" in their networks, there are notable differences in associated words. Group 2 includes positive terms like "happy," "courage," and "possess," whereas Group 1 uses more negative words like "introverted," "difficult," and "inferiority."

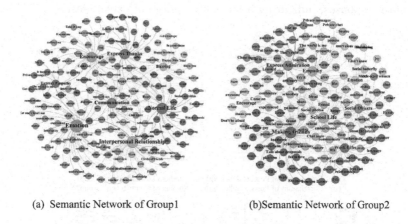

    (a) Semantic Network of Group1   (b)Semantic Network of Group2

Fig. 3. Semantic Network Visualization of Virtual Community Modules

Discourse analysis highlights family relationships' impact on teenage social anxiety, reflected in high-frequency words like "home," "parents," and "child." Frequent use of words such as "communication," "change," "try," "method," "way," "advice," "want to," and "chat" indicates active support-seeking and offering by members, including both information and emotions. In Group 2, interactions mainly involve strangers, evident in discussions related to unfamiliar individuals like "aunt," "driver," and unknown "middle-aged women." Group 2 members tend to engage with a broader social circle, contrasting with Group 1's behavior.

4.3   Outcomes of Sentiment Contagion

Sentiment contagion explores emotions' diffusion and impact in social networks, enhancing our grasp of online emotional dynamics. It describes how individuals or groups' moods are influenced by others, especially in social media, leading to emotional spread, creating emotional homophily [19]. Sentiment contagion is complex, influenced by factors like network evolution [21], individual suscepti-bility [3,14], user engagement levels [12], and the sway of opinion leaders [3]. Prior research [8] indicates that emotions expressed in main posts affect mem-bers' responses. This study explores how emotions like happiness and sadness in main posts trigger corresponding responses, impacting values, cognition, and behavior. It confirms the impact of main post sentiment on replies. Additionally, this study reveals that different emotional posts receive varying attention in Douban Forum. Posts with more replies exert a stronger influence due to platform mechanics. Thus, the study examines the relationship between main post emotions, reply count, and reply emotions, as depicted in Fig. 4.

The experimental findings reveal that in Group 1, no significant link is found between main post emotions and reply tones, implying rational discussions prevail. In contrast, Group 2's results highlight the impact of emotional value on response levels (R2 = 0.03, P<0.001). Positive emotions in Group 2 main posts elicit more responses, indicating a focus on emotional exchanges.

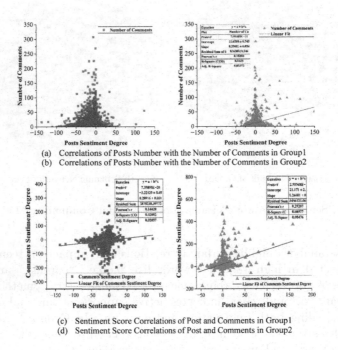

(a)   Correlations of Posts Number with the Number of Comments in Group1
(b)   Correlations of Posts Number with the Number of Comments in Group2

(c)   Sentiment Score Correlations of Post and Comments in Group1
(d)   Sentiment Score Correlations of Post and Comments in Group2

Fig. 4. Post and Comments index Relationship Diagram

Both groups display a meaningful positive correlation between reply and main post emotions. Negative main post sentiments lead to negative replies, showcasing sentiment contagion within social networks. Sentiment contagion occurred in both groups. In Group 2, positive main posts create a positive emotional environment, while Group 1's negative posts lead to a more pessimistic atmosphere.

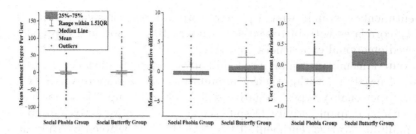

Fig. 5. Figure Distribution of three emotional indicators in Group 1 and Group 2

To enhance understanding of emotional differences, we introduce three sentiment indicators: average user sentiment, positive/negative comment difference,
and sentiment polarization, as shown in Fig. 5.

The analysis of Fig. 5 reveals Group 2's dominance over Group 1 in all three
emotional indicators. This suggests that while rational behavior is common to
both communities, Group 2 members are more influenced externally, evident in
their shifts from negativity to positivity. This susceptibility highlights Group
2's stronger sentiment contagion, possibly emphasizing community nature's role
over structure in emotional changes. Group 2's superior results across all three
indicators emphasize the prevalence of positive emotions, attributed to interaction patterns, emotional support, and reinforcement mechanisms. These findings
stress that a community's nature, culture, and values significantly impact emotional transformations in social networks.

This study reinforces the importance of community nature in shaping emotions within online communities. To understand the relationship between user
sentiment and activity, we analyzed the average user sentiment against the total
comments posted. Figure 6 depicts the results. A clear link between user activity
and their emotional state emerges. When users post fewer comments, their average sentiment tends to be lower. However, as they become more active, their aver-

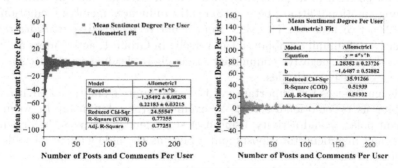

(a) Correlation between sentiment scores and number of comments in Group 1

(b) Correlation between sentiment scores and number of comments in Group 2

Fig. 6. Correlation analysis between sentiment scores and number of comments

age sentiment rises, indicating a positive correlation. This suggests that greater activity correlates with increased social interaction, emotional expression, and improved emotional experiences for users.

Group 1 members exhibit predominantly negative emotions, fostering the spread of negativity within their community. Group 2 is more varied, with two polarized personality types. Negative sentiment in Group 2 is somewhat correlated with participant activity. Despite the negativity, most active Group 2 members maintain positive sentiment. To explore the link between positive/negative comment sentiment difference and user activity, we analyze emotional shifts with total posts and replies as variables in Fig. 7 displays the findings.

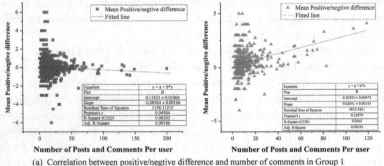

(a) Correlation between positive/negtive difference and number of comments in Group 1

(b) Correlation between positive/negtive difference and number of comments in Group 2

Fig. 7. Correlation Correlation analysis

Results revealed differing patterns in the two groups. In Group 1, increased engagement correlated with less efficient transitions from negative to positive attitudes. In contrast, Group 2 showed that higher activity linked to more efficient shifts from negative to positive attitudes. Group 1 active users tended to shift from positive to negative attitudes. This highlights that the community's prevailing emotional atmosphere significantly influences members' emotions. In Group 2, active users tend to shift from negative to positive attitudes due to the positive community ambiance. Conversely, in Group 1, active users are more influenced by the negative community atmosphere, leading to transitions from positive to negative attitudes.

This emphasizes the importance of the community's emotional environment in shaping users' emotional shifts. We examined the relationship between user sentiment polarity and activity, using user sentiment polarity as the dependent variable and members' total posts and replies as the independent variable. See Fig. 8 for results.

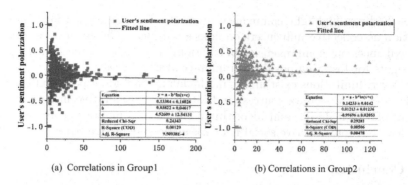

(a) Correlations in Group1   (b) Correlations in Group2

Fig. 8. Correlation Correlation between sentiment polarity and the total number of posts

Experimental results show that a sentiment polarity of 0 occurs when members balance positive and negative posts or share neutral content. As user activity increases, community members' sentiment polarity becomes more distinct. This emotional orientation results from a combination of community attributes and the prevailing atmosphere. In Group 1, where content leans negative, heightened activity corresponds to a more negative community sentiment. In Group 2, with initially positive sentiment polarity, increased activity tends to shift it towards neutrality. Further analysis of Group 2 reveals that beyond a certain threshold (n > 50 comments), sentiment polarity starts leaning positive with increased participation. This highlights the relationship between user activity and sentiment polarity. Community attributes and overall atmosphere play vital roles in shaping sentiment polarity among different groups.

5   Discussion and Conclusion

5.1   Discussion

This research leverages advanced technologies, including BERTopic, NLP, and social network analysis, to explore emotional communication and transformation in virtual communities. BERTopic aids in uncovering sentiment orientations and latent themes in social network data. By analyzing social media text, we reveal how user emotions spread and information flows in social networks.

We employ sentiment analysis algorithms to automatically detect and quantify emotional polarity in user posts and comments. Integrating social network methods with time series analysis helps us examine sentiment propagation's speed and impact. Text clustering techniques extract keywords and emotional discourse themes. This research delves into collective intelligence phenomena, providing a holistic understanding of emotional interactions and information dissemination. Challenges include handling diverse expressions and complex emotional nuances in social network texts.

The findings highlight community attributes, ambiance, activity, and participation as collective influencers on emotion diffusion in social networks. The study enhances our comprehension of emotional transmission mechanisms, offering insights for fostering positive community atmospheres.

However, limitations exist in this methodology, including potential for larger sample sizes, diverse data sources, and integrating qualitative methods. Investigating platform design and algorithmic effects on emotional communication could lead to more effective social network management strategies.

5.2 Conclusion

This study represents a comprehensive investigation into the intricate dynamics of emotion propagation and transformation within social networks. It highlights the value of combining BERTopic and NLP for sentiment analysis in social networks. Main posts significantly influence reply sentiments, while community atmosphere affects sentiment spread. User activity and emotional disposition are complexly linked; high activity often corresponds to negative emotions. BERTopic, NLP, and social network tech are vital for understanding emotional interactions and collective intelligence.

The implications of these findings extend beyond academic research. They hold practical relevance in the domains of emotion management and public opinion analysis within social network platforms, offering innovative methodologies to delve into the mechanisms governing the dissemination of emotions and the dynamics of collective intelligence behaviors within the realm of social networks.

References

1. Del Vicario, M., Vivaldo, G., Bessi, A., Zollo, F., Scala, A., Caldarelli, G., Quattrociocchi, W.: Echo chambers: emotional contagion and group polarization on facebook. Sci. Rep. **6**(1), 37825 (2016)
2. Devlin, J., Chang, M.W., Lee, K., Toutanova, K.: Bert: pre-training of deep bidirectional transformers for language understanding. arXiv preprint arXiv:1810.04805 (2018)
3. Doherty, R.W.: The emotional contagion scale: a measure of individual differences. J. Nonverbal Behav. **21**, 131–154 (1997)
4. Liu, G., Wang, T., H.T.K.W.Y.: Enhanced contextual neural topic model for short text. Computer Engineering and Applications, pp. 1–14 (2023)
5. Gómez-Ortiz, O., Roldán, R., Ortega-Ruiz, R., García-López, L.J.: Social anxiety and psychosocial adjustment in adolescents: relation with peer victimization, self-esteem and emotion regulation. Child Indic. Res. **11**, 1719–1736 (2018)
6. Gómez-Ortiz, O., Romera, E.M., Jiménez-Castillejo, R., Ortega-Ruiz, R., García-López, L.J.: Parenting practices and adolescent social anxiety: a direct or indirect relationship? Int. J. Clin. Health Psychol. **19**(2), 124–133 (2019)
7. Grootendorst, M.: Bertopic: neural topic modeling with a class-based tf-idf procedure. arXiv preprint arXiv:2203.05794 (2022)
8. Guangyang: An empirical analysis of social media network emotional contagion and clue influence mechanism. J. Shenzhen Univ. Humanities Soc. Sci. Edition **37**(6), 12 (2020)

9. Hofmann, S.G., Anu Asnaani, M., Hinton, D.E.: Cultural aspects in social anxiety and social anxiety disorder. Depress. Anxiety **27**(12), 1117–1127 (2010)
10. Islam, M.R., Kabir, M.A., Ahmed, A., Kamal, A.R.M., Wang, H., Ulhaq, A.: Depression detection from social network data using machine learning techniques. Health Inform. Sci. Syst. **6**, 1–12 (2018)
11. Jiang, S., Ngien, A.: The effects of instagram use, social comparison, and self-esteem on social anxiety: a survey study in Singapore. Soc. Media+ Soci. **6**(2), 2056305120912488 (2020)
12. Kramer, A.D., Guillory, J.E., Hancock, J.T.: Experimental evidence of massive-scale emotional contagion through social networks. Proc. Natl. Acad. Sci. U.S.A. **111**(24), 8788 (2014)
13. Melka, S.E., Lancaster, S.L., Adams, L.J., Howarth, E.A., Rodriguez, B.F.: Social anxiety across ethnicity: a confirmatory factor analysis of the fne and sad. J. Anxiety Disord. **24**(7), 680–685 (2010)
14. Meng, L.M., Duan, S., Zhao, Y., Lü, K., Chen, S.: The impact of online celebrity in livestreaming e-commerce on purchase intention from the perspective of emotional contagion. J. Retail. Consum. Serv. **63**, 102733 (2021)
15. Nor, N.M., Rahman, N.A., Yaakub, M.R., Zukarnain, Z.A.: Sentiment analysis on depression detection: a review. In: Science and Information Conference. pp. 718–726. Springer (2022)
16. Pengguan, Wang, F.: Research on the optimal topic number determination method of lda theme model in scientific and technological information analysis. Modern Library and Information Technology (9), 9 (2016)
17. Quinn, K.M., Monroe, B.L., Colaresi, M., Crespin, M.H., Radev, D.R.: How to analyze political attention with minimal assumptions and costs. Am. J. Political Sci. **54**(1), 209–228 (2010)
18. Ruz, G.A., Henríquez, P.A., Mascareño, A.: Sentiment analysis of Twitter data during critical events through bayesian networks classifiers. Futur. Gener. Comput. Syst. **106**, 92–104 (2020)
19. Schoenewolf, G.: Emotional contagion: Behavioral induction in individuals and groups. Modern Psychoanalysis (1990)
20. Tadesse, M.M., Lin, H., Xu, B., Yang, L.: Detection of depression-related posts in reddit social media forum. Ieee Access **7**, 44883–44893 (2019)
21. Xiong, X., Li, Y., Qiao, S., Han, N., Wu, Y., Peng, J., Li, B.: An emotional contagion model for heterogeneous social media with multiple behaviors. Phys. A **490**, 185–202 (2018)
22. Zhou, Y., Xu, R., Gui, L.: A sequence level latent topic modeling method for sentiment analysis via cnn based diversified restrict boltzmann machine. In: 2016 International Conference on Machine Learning and Cybernetics (ICMLC), vol. 1, pp. 356–361. IEEE (2016)

Similarity Metrics and Visualization of Scholars Based on Variational Graph Normalized Auto-Encoders

Guangtao Zhang, Xiangwei Zeng, Yu Weng, and Zhengyang Wu[✉]

South China Normal University, Guangzhou, Guangdong, China
{zhangguangtao,zengxiangwei,wengyu,wuzhengyang}@m.scnu.edu.cn

Abstract. With the rapid development of Internet technology and academic social media, it has become one of the important research directions of social networks to measure the similarity between scholars, which enables users to find scholars with similar research interests or similar backgrounds in the scholars' network and promote scientific research cooperation and communication. In this paper, we propose an algorithm for measuring the similarity of scholars based on variational graph normalized auto-encoders (VGNAE), which fuses the social relationship and attribute information of scholars, obtains the implicit feature representation of scholars through graph convolutional neural network encoding, and then compares different implicit feature vectors to measure the similarity of different scholars. In order to evaluate the effectiveness of this method, the SCHOLAT social network dataset is selected for experiments in this paper. The experimental results show that the model achieves the best performance on both the AUC and AP metrics on the task of measuring scholar similarity, with 98.7% and 98.8%, respectively, relative to other traditional widely used algorithms. In addition, by fusing the scholar similarity information into the scholar network visualization, users can access the connection between different scholars more intuitively and efficiently.

Keywords: Graph representation learning · Variational graph normalized auto-encoders · Scholar similarity · Visualization

1 Introduction

With the rapid development of Internet technology, academic social media has gradually become one of the main ways for scientists and scholars to communicate and collaborate on a daily basis. In recent years, the research of large-scale information networks has become a focus, in which how to learn node representations in information networks is now widely used in social network analysis, information retrieval, bioinformatics, recommender systems and other fields [1]. In academic social networks, the node objects are scholars. By analyzing the similarity degree among scholars in academic social networks in terms of research interests, research fields, academic achievements and work units, we can help scholars find potential partners in academic social platforms, and then exchange research ideas and improve research efficiency and quality, which is of great significance to promote the development and progress of academia.

Y. Sun et al. (Eds.): ChineseCSCW 2023, CCIS 2012, pp. 64–77, 2024.
https://doi.org/10.1007/978-981-99-9637-7_5

In recent years, graph neural network models have been devoted to mining relationships between similar objects in large-scale information networks to enrich the semantic representations of objects with good results [2]. In social networks, the similarity between users can be calculated by mapping each user's neighbor relationship and attribute information features into a low-dimensional vector space through graph representation learning. However, existing methods such as graph convolutional neural networks [3] and graph attention networks [4] use fixed graph convolution operators, and such methods are prone to overfitting problems during training, resulting in degraded model performance. To solve these problems, variational graph auto-encoders [5] introduce the variational idea in variational auto-encoders [6] to graphs, which can better fuse topological features and node attribute features of graphs to alleviate the overfitting problem and improve the robustness of models. However, the embedding of this approach is close to zero if the content features of isolated nodes are not considered. To overcome this problem, the variational graph normalization auto-encoders(VGNAE) [7] uses L2 normalization to enable better embedding of isolated nodes.

In order to more effectively utilize scholars' domain information for similarity metrics and incorporate similarity information into scholars' network visualizations, the main contributions of our work are as follows: (1) we use VGNAE to fuse scholars' attribute information with domain information to construct features in the latent space to measure similarity among scholars; (2) we chose the SCHOLAT social network dataset to conduct our experiments. The experimental results show that the model is superior to other traditional widely used algorithms in the task of measuring the similarity of scholars; (3) in order to better demonstrate the connection between scholars in the visualization of scholar migration, we designed a similarity-based scholar migration strategy, which selects the most similar scholar to the current scholar as the next migration target during the dynamic visualization process and intuitively displays the degree of similarity between the scholars and scores.

2 Related Work

2.1 User Similarity Metric

User similarity metric is a method used to measure the degree of similarity between two or more users and can be used to evaluate the connection between users. It is widely used in recommendation systems, where user similarity metrics are used to determine which users are similar to each other in order to provide more personalized recommendations for these users [8]. Lv et al. [9] addressed the problem of mining the similarity of users' long-term activities based on their trajectories by first extracting regular activities from their daily trajectories to capture their long-term patterns, and then calculating the similarity of users based on the extracted regular activities The similarity of users is then calculated based on the extracted regular activities in a hierarchical manner. Zhang Xu et al. [10] considered the missing display feedback data and cold start problem in collaborative filtering recommendation, and proposed a fused similarity user recommendation method, which computes the attribute similarity and behavior similarity of users using user attributes and implicit feedback data, respectively, and fuses the two similarities for prediction and user recommendation. Suhaim et al. [11] proposed a directional user similarity model for personalized recommendations in online social networks that uses a hybrid directional relational user similarity model (DRUSM) to match users' contexts using a diversity of subtle user behaviors and directional interactions. Li Kunlun et al. [12] proposed a collaborative filtering algorithm based on semi-supervised AP clustering and improved user similarity, which incorporates active user penalty factors and user rating trajectories in calculating user similarity to provide more information for similarity metrics to mitigate the impact of data sparsity. Ai et al. [13] designed a user-item link prediction algorithm based on resource assignment within a user similarity network, which calculates the similarity between users based on their historical ratings and constructs a similarity network between users by filtering the similarity results. Hawashin et al. [14] proposed a novel and effective hybrid similarity measure based on user interests for recommender systems, which mixes user interest-user interest similarity measure and user interest-item similarity measure to improve the current recommender systems. Su et al. [15] argued that the traditional collaborative filtering algorithm treats similarity as a scalar value, which causes some information loss, and proposed a new method to calculate user similarity, which uses a vector to measure user similarity in multiple dimensions and defines global similarity, local similarity, and meta-similarity to calculate vector similarity. Most of the current studies represent the relevant information of users as feature vectors, and then measure the similarity of users based on the feature vectors.

2.2 Variational Graph Normalized Auto-encoders

Auto-encoders (AE) [16] is an unsupervised neural network model, whose main idea is to compress and encode the input data, and then decode and restore the encoding result to the original data, so as to achieve self-reconstruction and feature extraction of the data, which is often applied to learn the low-dimensional representation of the data and realize the reduction and denoising of the data. Variational auto-encoders (VAE) [6] is an improved AE, which can better fit the distribution of data and generate more realistic samples by introducing hidden variables. In recent years, graph neural networks have been widely studied and applied. Compared with traditional deep learning methods, graph neural networks can better handle various different types of graph data, such as social networks, chemical molecules, circuit diagrams, etc. [17]. The earliest model of graph neural network is Graph Convolutional Neural Networks (GCN) [3], an operation that updates the representation of each node by passing information between local neighbor nodes, where the representation of each node is obtained by weighting and summing the representations of its neighbor nodes. However, this approach is prone to overfitting problems during the training process due to the fixed graph convolution algorithm, which leads to degradation of the model performance. In view of the development of the above techniques, researchers have started to explore the application of VAE to the task of representation learning of graph data. Kipf et al. [5] introduced VAE to graph neural networks and constructed variational graph auto-encoders (VGAE), which generated an independent potential representation for each node. This enables efficient representation learning of graph data. Subsequently, VGAE has been widely applied to tasks such as node classification, graph classification, link prediction, etc.

Zhang et al. [18] learned concept precondition relations from educational data by multi-headed attentional variational graph auto-encoders. Ding et al. [19] proposed a deep learning framework with variational auto-encoders for miRNA-disease association prediction (VGAE-MDA). Although VGAE can better address the drawbacks of using a fixed graph convolution algorithm, it cannot handle the embedding of isolated nodes well. Ahn et al. [7] built on the VGAE to enhance the embedding of isolated nodes by L2 normalizing the node features before obtaining the node embedding. The variational graph normalized auto-encoders (VGNAE) can capture the relationship between nodes in the network and map node embeddings into the low-dimensional space, thus in reducing the dimensionality of embeddings and improving the efficiency of the model; on the other hand, it can better handle isolated node embeddings. In social networks, it can further improve the accuracy of user representation and thus enhance the representation of users.

3 Scholar Similarity Metric Algorithm Based on Variational Graph Normalized Auto-encoders

3.1 Related Basic Definitions

Definition: homogeneous information network. An information network can be defined as a directed graph $G = \{V, E\}$, where V denotes entities (nodes), E denotes relationships (edges), and there exists a mapping relationship: $V \rightarrow A, E \rightarrow R$. An information network with the number of entity types $|A| = 1$ and the number of relationship types $|R| = 1$ is called a homogeneous information network or homogeneous graph.

3.2 VGNAE Model

Refer to Ahn and Kim's work [7], the VGNAE model used in this paper mainly consists of two modules, the encoder module and the decoder module, and the overall framework is shown in Fig. 1. First, in the encoder module, the mean and variance are calculated using Graph Normalized Convolutional Network (GNCN) and Graph Convolutional Network (GCN), respectively, followed by constructing a set of normal distributions and performing random sampling to obtain the embedding vectors of scholars in the potential space; then, in the decoder module, the feature vectors of different scholars in the potential space are compared to predict the probability of similarity among scholars; finally, the gap of model prediction is measured jointly by cross-entropy and KL divergence. Next, each module is described specifically.

Encoder Module. The encoder module consists of two graph convolutional neural networks. Firstly, GNCN normalizes the scholar features by L2 paradigm normalization and outputs the mean value by combining the scholar's adjacency, while GCN outputs the variance by directly combining the scholar's adjacency and feature matrix, and then constructs a set of normal distribution using these two parameters, and then performs random sampling from the normal distribution to generate the scholar's embedding vector in the potential space.

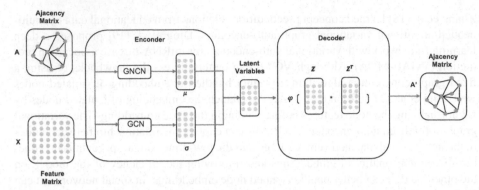

Fig. 1. VGNAE model framework

Suppose $G = (V, E)$ is an unweighted and undirected graph. The number of nodes is $N = |V|$, A is the $N \times N$ containing self-connected adjacency matrix in the input data, X is the feature matrix in the input data, then the encoder network of the VGNAE can be defined as:

$$q(Z|X, A) = \prod_{i=1}^{N} q(z_i|X, A) \tag{1}$$

where $q(z_i|X, A) = N(z_i|\mu_i, diag(\sigma_i^2))$. $\mu = GNCN(X, A, c)$ denotes the mean of the distribution in which the hidden variable Z is distributed, where $c \in R$ is a scaling constant representing the norm of the hidden feature being propagated; and $\log \sigma = GCN(X, A)$ denotes the value of the logarithm of the variance of the distribution in which the hidden variable Z is located. The GCN network can be concretely represented as $X_i = \tilde{A} X_{i-1} W_i$, where $\tilde{A} = D^{-1/2} A D^{-1/2}$ is a symmetrically normalized adjacency matrix, W_i denotes the parameter of the network of that layer, X_{i-1} denotes the embedded representation structure of the network of the previous layer, D is the degree matrix, which is denoted as $D_{i,j} = \sum_i A_{i,j}$, $A_{i,j}$ is 1 when there is a connection between node i and node j, and 0 otherwise.

Decoder Module. The task of the decoder module is to generate a similarity score between two scholars by comparing the similarity between different scholars from Z through inner product to reconstruct the adjacency matrix. The decoder network of VGNAE can be represented as:

$$p(A|Z) = \prod_{i=1}^{N} \prod_{j=1}^{N} p(A_{ij}|\vec{z_i}, \vec{z_j}) \tag{2}$$

where $p(A_{ij} = 1|Z) = \sigma\left(\vec{z_i}^T \vec{z_j}\right)$.

Loss Function. The ultimate goal of the VGNAE is to make the reconstructed graph as consistent as possible with the original graph, and its loss function consists of two parts, as shown in Eq. (3):

$$L = E_{q(Z|X,A)}\left[\log p(A|Z)\right] - KL[q(Z|X, A)||p(Z)] \tag{3}$$

where on the right, the first part uses cross entropy [20] to measure the gap between the reconstruction results and the original data, and the second part uses KL divergence

[21] to measure the gap between the predetermined prior distribution and the posterior distribution generated by the network.

4 Experiments and Analysis of Results

4.1 Experimental Data

Scholars' profiles usually have some meaningless words, so it is necessary to pre-process the profile text data, which includes word separation, deactivation, feature extraction and feature dimensionality reduction, etc. After these processes, the original data is put into the model for training. The text pre-processing flow chart is shown in Fig. 2.

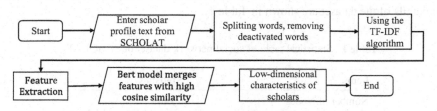

Fig. 2. Text pre-processing flow chart

After obtaining the scholar profile text from SCHOLAT, the Chinese text is sliced into word-based sequences using Python's jieba, followed by removing a large number of meaningless words such as inflections, conjunctions and pronouns, and the final obtained text is represented as:

$$j = [w_1, w_2, \ldots, w_n] \tag{4}$$

Firstly, the TF value of the word ($TF_{i,j}$) is obtained based on the number of occurrences of the word (w_i) in text j divided by the total number of words in text j. The formula is expressed as:

$$TF_{i,j} = \frac{n_{i,j}}{\sum_k n_{k,j}} \tag{5}$$

Next, the total number of texts is divided by the number of texts containing w_i in the text set, and then the resulting quotient is taken logarithmically to calculate the IDF value of the word (IDF_i). The formula is expressed as:

$$IDF_{i,j} = \log \frac{|D|}{|j:t_i \in d_j|} \tag{6}$$

Then, based on the results obtained from $TF_{i,j}$, IDF_i, the $TF - IDF_{i,j}$ values of the word w_i are computed for filtering the textual feature word (w_i), and the formula is expressed as:

$$TF - IDF_{i,j} = TF_{i,j} * IDF_{i,j} \tag{7}$$

After statistical analysis of all extracted user features, we found that there are 26,573 different features among the 27449 valid users of SCHOLAT. If the user feature matrix is directly constructed and input to the model for training, due to the excessive number of features, on the one hand this will make the training and testing of the model more difficult and time consuming, on the other hand the samples of the dataset will be edge very sparse and will lead to overfitting problems. Therefore, we need to reduce the number of existing features by using the Bert model to convert all feature keywords into word embeddings, calculate the cosine similarity between embeddings, and merge the feature keywords with similar features, and finally reduce the number of features to 1000.

Finally, we use a sparse matrix to construct the user social network and extract the relationships from the database. The binary of the relationship (u, v), representing the existence of a friend relationship between user u and user v, is added to the sparse matrix. The details of the dataset are shown in Table 1:

Table 1. Statistical table of social network dataset of SCHOLAT

Items	Statistics
Number of Nodes	27449
Number of relationships	52250
Node feature dimension	1000
Minimum Node Degree	0
Max Node Degree	1361
Average Node Degree	3.807

4.2 Parameter Setting

In the experiment, the Adam optimizer is used, the initial learning rate is set to 0.005, the data dimension of the input model is 1000, the GCN hidden layer dimension is 128, the number of training iterations is set to 300. The ratio of training set, validation set, and test set is 8:1:1. The number of positive samples is the same as the number of negative samples.

4.3 Evaluation Indicators

Whether two scholars are similar is defined as a second classification problem, and in the evaluation of the experimental results of the scholars' similarity metric, for the convenience of description and calculation, this paper defines two scholars similar as a positive sample and two scholars dissimilar as a negative sample, and the confusion matrix is used to calculate the indexes of the model, and the following indexes are mainly used to evaluate the prediction results: the area AP value of precision-recall (PR) curve of and the area AUC value of the receiver operating characteristic(ROC) curve.

The horizontal coordinate of the PR curve is Recall, which represents the proportion of the number of scholars predicted to be similar to the number of samples of all similar scholars, as shown in Eq. (8); the vertical coordinate is Precision, which represents the probability of the number of scholars predicted to be similar to the actual number of samples of similar scholars, as shown in Eq. (9).

$$Recall = \frac{TP}{TP+FN} \tag{8}$$

$$Precision = \frac{TP}{TP+FP} \tag{9}$$

The AP value represents the area under the PR curve and takes values between 0 and 1. Closer to 1 indicates better performance of the classifier and closer to 0 indicates worse performance of the classifier.

The horizontal coordinate of the ROC curve is the false positive rate (FPR), which represents the ratio of the number of samples of scholars incorrectly considered to be similar to the number of samples of all dissimilar scholars, as shown in Eq. (10); the vertical coordinate is the true positive rate (TPR), which represents the ratio of the number of samples of scholars predicted to be similar to the number of samples of all similar scholars, as shown in Eq. (11).

$$FPR = \frac{FP}{FP+TN} \tag{10}$$

$$TPR = \frac{TP}{TP+FN} \tag{11}$$

The closer the ROC curve is to the position where the horizontal coordinate is 0 and the vertical coordinate is 1, the better the prediction result of the classification network. The AUC value represents the area under the ROC curve, which takes values between 0 and 1. The closer it is to 1 indicates better performance of the classifier, and the closer it is to 0.5 indicates worse performance of the classifier, which is equivalent to random guessing [22].

4.4 Performance Comparison

The CN (Common Neighbors) algorithm [23] indicates the similarity between two nodes by calculating the number of common neighbors between them. AA (Adamic-Adar) model [24] assigns weights to the common neighbor algorithm based on the idea that nodes with higher degree in common neighbors are given lower weights and nodes with lower degree are given higher weights, thus emphasizing the role of neighbor nodes with lower degree. Jaccard coefficient [24] measures the similarity between two nodes by calculating the ratio of the number of common neighbor nodes to the total number of neighbor nodes between them. PA (Preferential Attachment) algorithm [24] assumes that the higher the number of neighbor nodes of a node, the higher its importance, thus defining the similarity of nodes as the product of their number of neighbor nodes. The RA (Resource Allocation) [25] model expresses the similarity between two nodes by calculating the reciprocal of the sum of the degrees of their common neighbors. The GCN (Graph Convolutional Network) model [3] maps the neighbor relationship between nodes and their own attribute information into a low-dimensional vector space, and converts the similarity between nodes into a similarity calculation between feature vectors, where the same weights are used for different neighbor nodes for fusion each time the convolution is done. The GAT (Graph Attention Network) model [4] introduces an attention mechanism on top of the graph convolutional neural network GCN, which uses different weights for different neighboring nodes for fusion. The experimental results are shown in Table 2:

Table 2. Comparison of experimental results

Method	AUC	AP
CN	0.889	0.930
Jaccard	0.888	0.891
PA	0.828	0.800
AA	0.888	0.925
RA	0.890	0.955
GCN	0.858	0.898
GAT	0.870	0.901
VGNAE	**0.987**	**0.988**

The experimental results show that the traditional neighbor relationship-based node similarity metric models CN, Jaccard, PA, AA and RA perform poorly in both AUC and AP metrics relative to VGNAE, with the RA model performing relatively well, because these methods are susceptible to noise interference in similarity metrics for sparse graphs due to fewer connections between nodes, resulting in less accurate. The GCN and GAT models also perform poorly in AUC and AP metrics compared to the VGNAE model because these algorithms use fixed global hidden variables, ignoring the randomness and uncertainty between nodes and edges in the graph, and different graph structures may require different hidden variable representations, which may not be well adapted to different graph structures and lead to degradation of the model performance due to overfitting problems. In contrast, VGNAE achieves uncertainty modeling by introducing random variables to describe the potential vectors of nodes, and uses random sampling and reparameterization trick to generate node representations, in addition to L2 paradigm normalization to better learn isolated node representations, thus alleviating the overfitting problem, improving the robustness of the model, and making the similarity measure of scholars more credible.

4.5 Encoder of Graph Convolution Types

To observe the effect of encoding with different graph convolution types on model performance, this experiment combines GAT, GCN and APPNP (Approximate Personalized Propagation of Neural Predictions) [26] combined with L2 paradigm normalization as encoders, respectively, where APPNP the core idea is to update the node's embedding vector by using an approximate personalized propagation process. The experimental results are shown in Table 3. The performance of the model encoded using GCN is somewhat better compared to APPNP, which can capture the global interactions between nodes to some extent, and its propagation process may make the information over-smoothed, leading to the loss or blurring of the node vector representation, which affects the performance of the model. In contrast, GCN can better capture the local structure and has higher efficiency on large-scale graph data. Compared with the model encoded using GAT, the GCN also performs better due to its better effectiveness in preserving the local structure of the graph.

Table 3. The type of graph convolution used for encoder

Method	AUC	AP
VGNAE-GAT	0.955	0.961
VGNAE-APPNP	0.978	0.983
VGNAE-GCN	**0.987**	**0.988**

5 Visualization of Scholar Migration Based on Similarity

Scholar migration visualization refers to the process of dynamically visiting scholars one by one in a network of scholars and displaying their business card information, and its visualization is shown in Fig. 3.

The existing access sequence is random, so that users cannot establish a continuous connection between scholars, which will reduce their understanding and awareness of the scholars' network as a whole. To solve the above problem, we calculate the similarity between scholars in the scholar network and determine the display sequence of scholars based on the similarity. Taking a scholar network containing four scholars as an example, its specific processing flow is shown in Fig. 4.

Specifically, the scholars in the set are first linked with all the remaining scholars to construct a scholar relationship matrix, and then the scholar relationship matrix and the scholar feature matrix are fed together into the trained VGNAE model to obtain the similarity scores of each scholar with other scholars in the set. Then, the conditional depth-first search algorithm is used to traverse the scholar similarity matrix, and the

Fig. 3. Scholar migration visualization

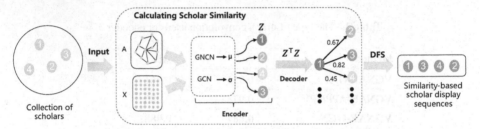

Fig. 4. Scholars demonstrate the acquisition process of sequences

scholars with the highest similarity scores with the current scholars are visited in priority each time, and finally the sequence of scholars display based on the similarity of scholars is constructed. According to the acquired sequences dynamically visit the scholars in the scholars' network and display the similarity with the previous scholars above the scholars' business cards, when the similarity is defined as mild similarity below 0.70, moderate similarity in 0.70–0.89, and high similarity in 0.90 and above. Different degrees of similarity are displayed using different colors, and the results are shown in Fig. 5.

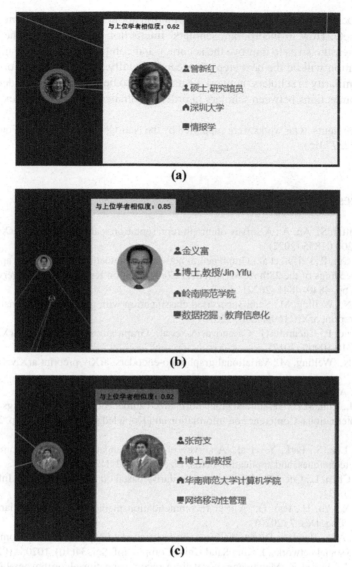

Fig. 5. (a) Mildly similar effect picture. (b) Moderately similar effect picture. (c) Highly similar effect picture

6 Conclusion

In this paper, we propose a scholar similarity measurement algorithm based on variogram normalized auto-encoder to better measure the similarity among scholars by fusing the attribute information of scholars with the network relationship structure to represent the characteristics of scholars' nodes. Experimental results on real datasets show that the proposed scholar similarity measurement algorithm in this paper performs well compared to other widely used traditional methods. However, scholars' interaction behaviors on academic social media can provide rich information about collaboration, common areas of interest, etc. How to incorporate scholars' interaction behaviors into the scholars' similarity measure so as to improve the accuracy and comprehensiveness of the similarity computation will be the next step of research. Finally, we apply the information of scholars' similarity in scholars' network visualization to better help users understand the potential connections between scholars in order to enhance the user visual experience.

Acknowledgements. Our works were supported by the National Natural Science Foundation of China (No. 62377015).

References

1. Khoshraftar, S., An, A.: A survey on graph representation learning methods. arXiv preprint arXiv:2204.01855 (2022)
2. Wu, L., Cui, P., Pei, J., et al.: Graph neural networks: foundation, frontiers and applications. In: Proceedings of the 28th ACM SIGKDD Conference on Knowledge Discovery and Data Mining, pp. 4840–4841 (2022)
3. Kipf, T.N., Welling, M.: Semi-supervised classification with graph convolutional networks. arXiv preprint arXiv:1609.02907 (2016)
4. Veličković, P., Cucurull, G., Casanova, A., et al.: Graph attention networks. arXiv preprint arXiv:1710.10903 (2017)
5. Kipf, T.N., Welling, M.: Variational graph auto-encoders. arXiv preprint arXiv:1611.07308 (2016)
6. Ilic, M.: Auto-encoding variational Bayes (2019)
7. Ahn, S.J., Kim, M.H.: Variational graph normalized autoencoders. In: Proceedings of the 30th ACM International Conference on Information and Knowledge Management, pp. 2827–2831 (2021)
8. Ko, H., Lee, S., Park, Y., et al.: A survey of recommendation systems: recommendation models, techniques, and application fields. Electronics 11(1), 141 (2022)
9. Lv, M., Chen, L., Chen, G.: Mining user similarity based on routine activities. Inf. Sci. 236, 17–32 (2013)
10. Zhang, X., Yu, H., Fan, G.: A user recommendation method based on similarity metric. Comput. Eng. Des. 7 (2020)
11. Suhaim, A.B., Berri, J.: Directional user similarity model for personalized recommendation in online social networks. J. King Saud Univ.-Comput. Inf. Sci. 34(10), 10205–10216 (2022)
12. Kunlun, L., Jiayao, Z., Mengmeng, W., et al.: A recommendation algorithm combining semi-supervised AP clustering and improved similarity. Small Microcomput. Syst. 42(7), 1396–1401 (2021)
13. Ai, J., Cai, Y., Su, Z., et al.: Predicting user-item links in recommender systems based on similarity-network resource allocation. Chaos Solitons Fractals 158, 112032 (2022)
14. Hawashin, B., Lafi, M., Kanan, T., et al.: An efficient hybrid similarity measure based on user interests for recommender systems. Expert. Syst. 37(5), e12471 (2020)
15. Su, Z., Zheng, X., Ai, J., et al.: Link prediction in recommender systems based on vector similarity. Physica A 560, 125154 (2020)
16. Bank, D., Koenigstein, N., Giryes, R.: Autoencoders. arXiv preprint arXiv:2003.05991 (2020)
17. Wu, Z., Pan, S., Chen, F., et al.: A comprehensive survey on graph neural networks. IEEE Trans. Neural Netw. Learn. Syst. 32(1), 4–24 (2020)

18. Zhang, J., Lin, N., Zhang, X., et al.: Learning concept prerequisite relations from educational data via multi-head attention variational graph auto-encoders. In: Proceedings of the Fifteenth ACM International Conference on Web Search and Data Mining, 1377–1385 (2022)

19. Ding, Y., Tian, L.P., Lei, X., et al.: Variational graph auto-encoders for miRNA-disease association prediction]. Methods **192**, 25–34 (2021)

20. De Boer, P.-T., et al.: A tutorial on the cross-entropy method. Ann. Oper. Res. **134**(1), 19–67 (2005)

21. Hershey, J.R., Olsen, P.A.: Approximating the KullbackLeibler divergence between Gaussian mixture models. In: 2007 IEEE International (2007)

22. Jie-yang, J., Zhao, Y., Ting, Z., et al.: Deep learning radiomics model accurately predicts hepatocellular carcinoma occurrence in chronic hepatitis B patients: a five-year follow-up. Am. J. Cancer Res. **11**(2), 576–589 (2021)

23. Ahmad, I., Akhtar, M.U., Noor, S., et al.: Missing link prediction using common neighbor and centrality based parameterized algorithm. Sci. Rep. **10**, 364 (2020). https://doi.org/10. 1038/s41598-019-57304-y

24. Liben-Nowell, D., Kleinberg, J.: The Link Prediction Problem for Social Networks (2004)

25. Zhou, T., Lü, L., Zhang, Y.C.: Predicting missing links via local information. Eur. Phys. J. B **71**, 623–630 (2009)

26. Gasteiger, J., Bojchevski, A., Günnemann, S.: Predict then propagate: graph neural networks meet personalized pagerank. arXiv preprint arXiv:1810.05997 (2018)

Scholar Influence Maximization via Opinion Leader and Graph Embedding Regression in Social Networks

Junjie Lin[1], Wanying Liang[1], Gangbin Chen[1], Guohua Chen[1,2(✉)], and Yong Tang[1,2]

[1] School of Computer Science, South China Normal University, Guangzhou, China
`{jjlin,sylvialaung,gbchan,chengh,ytang}@m.scnu.edu.cn`
[2] Pazhou Lab, Guangzhou, China

Abstract. The significance of influential nodes in information diffusion within scholar social networks has attracted increasing attention in the field of influence maximization problem. Most Existing influence maximization algorithms relying on scenario-specific centrality measures often underperform when applied to diverse social networks. Many influence maximization deep learning based algorithms use topological embedding to learn the global influence information. However, since most of these methods primarily focus on identifying high influence nodes to solve the influence maximization problem, they often suffer from poor performance due to the overlapping influence ranges among highly influential nodes within the seed set. In this paper, we propose a regression framework via opinion leaders and graph embedding, named Inf-LGR, to optimize the performance degradation problem caused by the highly overlapping influence ranges between the highly influential nodes in the seed set. Specifically, our framework first adopts an information diffusion model-based approach to obtain opinion leaders' tendency evaluation and meanwhile uses variational graph auto-encoders (VGAE) to encode it into low-dimensional vectors. Then we utilize an improved graph sample and aggregate (GraphSAGE) algorithm, whose aggregation based on the number of shortest paths, to generate the influence embedding of nodes. Finally, embedding results are fed into a regressor for predicting the influence score of each node. The top-K nodes with the highest scores are selected as the seed set of the influence maximization problem. Experimental results on four social networks demonstrate the proposed framework outperforms some of the recently proposed and classical influence maximization methods.

Keywords: Influence maximization · Social networks · Opinion leader · Data mining

1 Introduction

With the popularization of online communication tools, social media is gaining popularity in the academic community as a tool to facilitate research activi-

Y. Sun et al. (Eds.): ChineseCSCW 2023, CCIS 2012, pp. 78–92, 2024.
https://doi.org/10.1007/978-981-99-9637-7_6

ties, such as Scholat.com and Academia.edu. Efficiently identifying influential
spreader is crucial for accelerating the dissemination and communication of
research results, as well as fostering academic collaboration [33]. Witnessing
the power of influence analysis in every field, including opinion leaders [7], viral
marketing [13], disease epidemics [20] and other applications, influence maximization in social networks has caused great concern in the research community
[17]. Influence maximization is a task of selecting a set of k nodes from a complex graph $\mathcal{G}$ to maximize the expected number of influenced users under a given
information diffusion model [15]. Measuring node influence and selecting the top
k nodes as seeds in social networks are crucial tasks.

So far, numerous methods based on different centrality have been proposed to
solve influence maximization problem [6,18,21,30]. These prediction algorithms
are tailored to some particular networks, thus cannot be effectively generalized
to diverse network contexts [4]. To enhance adaptability, deep learning has been
introduce as a solution, including treating node influence in scholar social networks as a classification task to predict node influence. One example of such
an approach is DeepInf [23]. Moreover, treating node influence as a binary classification task that classifies nodes into high influence and low ones, as done
in InfGCN [31]. It may effectively predict local influence but lacks an intuitive
understanding of global influence and the quantification of the actual influence
of scholars in the network. Another recent work considers identifying influential
nodes as a regression problem, which is a graph convolution networks and convolution neural networks based algorithm called the RCNN algorithm was proposed
by Yu et al. [16]. Although the RCNN algorithm efficiently ranks influence, it
has unresolved issues in influence maximization. None of these methods of the
influence ranking proxy consider the influences of seeds, which have high-level
influence, have obvious overlaps.

The essential reason why the influence estimation would deviate significantly
from the actual spread of influence under the diffusion model is that the potential
tendency evaluation of opinion leaders is ignored. Generally, opinion leaders have
a significant impact on information diffusion in social networks due to their
influence on the opinions, decisions, and actions of other users [32]. And people
prefer to interact with their local opinion leaders from the perspective of social
identity [19]. Additionally, Lazarsfeld and Katz note that opinion leaders are
evenly distributed across various groups and classes in society, with each group
having its own opinion leaders. These opinion leaders typically have an equal
relationship with those they influence, rather than a hierarchical one [9]. Opinion
leaders are not necessarily the nodes with the highest global influence, but have
relatively high influence on nodes in a specific range. Thus, through making full
use of the potential tendency evaluation of the opinion leaders, we can optimize
the performance degradation problem caused by the highly overlapping influence
ranges between the highly influential nodes in the seed set.

In our works, we mine the opinion leaders of nodes by means of diffusion process based approach [1]. In addition, to embrace the properties of invariance of the graph neural network (GNN) in processing non-Euclidean data [14], we proposes an improved model GraphSAGE-SP based on GraphSAGE [5] to learn the embedding of nodes. Since the influence strengthens with the growth of the number of propagation path [2], the original GraphSAGE aggregation methods cannot satisfy the collective diffusion of influence information. Thus, the aggregation of GraphSAGE-SP improves the aggregation of influence information by incorporating a decay factor based on the number of shortest paths.

In this paper, we proposed an opinion leader and graph embedding based framework to identify influential nodes in social networks. The main contributions of this paper can be summarized as follows:

- We treat the influence prediction as a regression task, and consider the potential evaluation information of the opinion leaders to optimize the performance degradation problem caused by the highly overlapping influence ranges between the seeds.
- We propose an improved model, GraphSAGE-SP, which incorporates an influence decay factor based on the shortest path. GraphSAGE-SP generates embedding by considering the number of shortest paths. Finally, an influence score is generated for each node using an regressor.
- We run extensive experiments on four social networks and achieve impressive results. In particular, our framework outperforms recently proposed and classical algorithms for influence maximization.

2   Related Work

Researchers analyze broadly node influence from two perspectives: influence maximization and influential node ranking. Specifically, Node influence prediction is an integral part of the influence maximization problem. It involves selecting the top k nodes with the highest influence to serve as input for the information diffusion model, with the objective of maximizing the spread of influence. Ranking influential nodes is a natural approach in node influence analysis, where influence levels of nodes are determined by sorting their scores obtained through specific algorithms. In recent years, however, due to the expensive manual label verification for influence ranking, influence maximization in social network have been developed. These methods assign evaluation scores to nodes and select high-scoring nodes as seed nodes. These methods can be categorized as local feature-based, global feature-based, and random walk-based methods. Local methods for node influence analysis consider the local properties of nodes, such as degree centrality [6] and clustering coefficient [3]. However, these metrics often overlook the global network position of nodes. To address this limitation, global attribute-based methods, including betweenness centrality [21] and K-shell centrality [11], have been proposed. But centrality-based algorithms exhibit unstable performances in various complex networks due to their specificity. On the other hand, identifying influential nodes method based on random walk uses neighbors to describe node influence, such as HITS [12]. However, these methods overlook the intrinsic features of the nodes themselves.

To enhance adaptability, deep neural network approaches have also been proposed. Previous research in node influence analysis has focused on various network analysis tasks, including classification and regression. In the context of influence analysis, a common approach is to transform node influence prediction into a classification task, aiming to predict the status of nodes. A classic example of this approach is DeepInf [23]. The DeepInf model utilizes the local neighborhood and behavioral history of users to predict their future engagement in certain actions. For example, in a social platform, the model predicts whether a user will repost a message or a blog post on a specific topic based on the behavior of their immediate neighbors. However, treating the node influence problem as a binary classification task is not practical for predicting the entire set of affected users. Reapplying the model to each candidate inactive user in the network would result in high inference costs that are impractical to achieve. Thus, considering node influence prediction as a binary classification task fails to provide a comprehensive understanding of global influence and does not effectively quantify node influence in the network. So, introducing node influence identification as a regression task addresses this issue. A recent study proposed the RCNN algorithm, which uses a graph convolution network and a convolutional neural network, to solve the task of identifying influential nodes as a regression problem [16]. In this paper, we consider predicting node influence scores as a regression task. We selecting the top-k nodes based on their influence scores to solve the influence maximization problem. Our proposed framework provides quantifiable influence values for evaluating node influence and can be applied to solve the influence maximization problem.

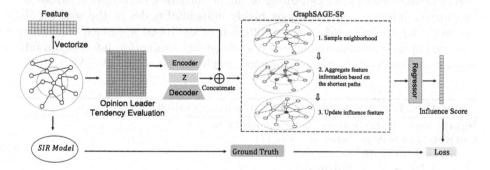

Fig. 1. The architecture of training the Inf-LGR framework.

3   Proposed Framework

In this section, we propose the Inf-LGR framework for selecting influential nodes as the seed set for influence maximization in social networks. A common approach is to rank nodes based on their influence scores and select the top-k nodes with high scores as the seed. In our framework, we treat the computation of node influence in social networks as a regression task, where the influence scores are continuous values. To perform supervised learning for regression, we require continuous ground truth influence scores for each node. These ground truth scores are generated through simulation using the susceptible-infected-recovered (SIR) model [24]. Figure 1 presents the architecture of the Inf-LGR framework. To leverage the potential tendency evaluation of opinion leaders, we encode their influence information into low-dimensional vectors using variational graph auto-encoders(VGAE) [10]. The combined feature of nodes, along with the adjacency matrix, is inputted into the GraphSAGE-SP model. The GraphSAGE-SP model utilizes shortest paths-based aggregation to generate node embeddings. The node embeddings are fed into a final regressor to obtain the influence score for each node. The influence scores are then ranked in descending order, and the top-k nodes with the highest scores are selected as the seed set for influence maximization. The algorithmic details of the Inf-LGR framework are described in the following subsections.

3.1   Extract Opinion Leader Tendency Evaluation

As mentioned above, opinion leaders are evenly distributed across various societal groups and classes. Each group possesses its own set of opinion leaders who maintain a relationship of equality with those they influence, rather than a hierarchical one [8]. By utilizing the potential tendency evaluation information of opinion leaders, we can mitigate the performance degradation caused by overlapping influence ranges among highly influential nodes in the seed set. In our work, we apply an information diffusion model-based approach to identify potential opinion leaders and encode their tendency evaluation information into low-dimensional vectors using variational graph auto-encoders (VGAE).

Algorithm 1. Extract opinion leader tendency evaluation

Input: Network (G), feature vector dimension (d)
Output: The feature vector of nodes (I)
 1: **for** node **in** G **do**
 2:      $Times_{node} \leftarrow$ SIR([node])
 3: **end for**
 4: $L \leftarrow$ Concat($Times_{node}$)
 5: $VGAE_{\text{trained}} \leftarrow$ VGAE(L^T, G)
 6: $I \leftarrow$ Encode($VGAE_{\text{trained}}, L, G$)
 7: **return** I

The pseudo-code of the proposed method is presented in Algorithm 1. Initially, each node alone will be set as an infected node, while the remaining nodes will be considered susceptible. Monte Carlo simulations are then conducted under the SIR model, where susceptible nodes can become infected by their neighbors whose state is infected with a probability of β. And the infected nodes will go into recovered with a probability of γ after simulation starting. We set the infection and recovery probability as the epidemic threshold β_{th} and one. It means that every infected node will not be re-infected in the next stage, because no one will retweet a message multiple times in a real social networks, except for trolls. The spreading process stops when there are no new infected nodes, and the times of infections of each node is recorded during the simulation. Given the varying outcomes of each simulation, we compute the average infection count $\mathcal{T}_i$ of each node across the 1000 runs. This average value represents the potential influence tendency of the node i on other nodes. By combining the average infection count $\mathcal{T}_i$, we calculate the transposition of the combination to formalize the potential tendency evaluation of opinion leaders as follows:

$$L = [\mathcal{T}_0, \ \mathcal{T}_1, \ ..., \ \mathcal{T}_{n-1}]^T \tag{1}$$

where the raw information of potential tendency evaluation of opinion leaders $L \in \mathbb{R}^{n \times n}$ and n is the number of nodes in the social network. And $\mathcal{T}_i \in \mathbb{R}^{1 \times n}$ denotes a vector which contains the average number of infected times for all nodes when set the node $i, i \in [0, n)$ as the seed alone. Using the obtained L values, we train a the most basic variational graph auto-encoders (VGAE) to integrate opinion leaders' potential tendencies and the topological structure in social networks. The VGAE outputs hidden representations for each node, which are utilized to predict their influence score.

3.2   Generating Embedding Using GraphSAGE-SP

The GraphSAGE algorithm consists of three steps: sample, aggregate, and update. To improve computational efficiency, a fixed number of neighbors are sampled for each node in the GraphSAGE model, rather than all neighbors. In the aggregation stage of GraphSAGE, the original aggregation methods are insufficient in capturing the collective influence diffusion. As the number of shortest paths increases, the influence tends to strengthen [2]. Thus, we introduce a decay factor based on the number of shortest paths between nodes in the aggregation function of the original GraphSAGE. This improved model called GraphSAGE-SP. Generally, nodes with more shortest paths to high-order neighbors tend to have a wider and stronger influence than those with fewer ones in a social network [28]. Relying solely on averaging, max pooling, or min pooling of influence features may not yield optimal results. This highlights the need for methods based on the shortest path to accurately capture and leverage varying strengths of influence across different numbers of propagation paths. Specifically, after preparing the final features for each node, we train a GraphSAGE-SP model consisting of two SAGE convolutional layers to generate node embedding. And the ReLU function is used as the activation function. The aggregation function is designed to consider the difference in the number of shortest paths between central node and its neighbors. As the number of shortest paths increases, the weight of the neighbor's influence feature information in the clustering process becomes greater. The decay factor η based on the number of shortest paths of neighbor node v is expressed as follows:

$$\eta_{v_i} = \text{normal}\left(\delta_{st}(v)\right) \tag{2}$$

$$\text{normal}\left(\delta_{st}(v)\right) = \frac{\delta_{st}(v) - \min(\delta_{st})}{\max(\delta_{st}) - \min(\delta_{st})} \tag{3}$$

where $\delta_{st}(v)$ donates the number of shortest paths from any two nodes that the source s to the destination t passing through the node v, and normal $\left(\delta_{st}(v)\right)$ indicates that a normalization can be performed without a loss of precision to prevent effectively gradient explosion. The aggregation operation used can be defined by the decay factor η:

$$h'_{\mathcal{N}_{v_i}} = \sum_{v_j \in \mathcal{N}_{v_i}}^{n} \eta_{v_j} h_{v_j} \tag{4}$$

where $\mathcal{N}_{v_i}$ is the neighbor node set of node v_i, η_{v_j} is the decay factor based on the number of shortest paths of neighbor node v_j, and h_{v_j} is the influence feature vector of neighbor node v_j before iteration. In other words, the aggregated node's influence feature is obtained by weighting the features of sampled neighbor nodes based on the decay factor. According to the original GraphSAGE [5], for a given central node v_i, the message passing update rule is: $h'_{v_i} = \sigma\left(W \cdot Concat(h_{v_i}, h'_{\mathcal{N}_{v_i}})\right)$. The node embeddings from the GraphSAGE-SP model are used as input to the final regressor for regression prediction.

3.3 Ground Truth Generation

The regression task in supervised learning requires continuous influence scores for each node as ground truth labels, generated using the susceptible-infected-recovered (SIR) model. Specifically, the SIR model, originally used to describe the spreading process of infectious diseases, is also applied to study the propagation of rumors, information and so on. SIR model splits nodes into susceptible S, infected I and recovered R states. Initially, all nodes, except for the designated seed nodes as infected I, are in the susceptible state S. Susceptible nodes will be infected by their infected neighbors transmit the infection with a probability of β. And Infected nodes transition to the recovered state R with a probability of γ. The SIR model assumes recovered nodes are immune and cannot be reinfected. Consequently, the spreading process terminates when no new infections occur. And the total number of infected nodes and recovered nodes is the final scales of the spreading as the influence of seeds. We set β and γ as β_{th} and 1 respectively, where $\beta_{th} = \frac{1}{d}$ is the critical threshold of infection probability and

$\bar{d}$ is the average degree of the social network. We compute the average diffusion influence scale of 1000 Monte-Carlo simulation as the label of each node due to the inherent randomness in the simulation results.

3.4   Prediction and Model Optimization

The final embedding of all nodes generated by the GraphSAGE-SP model will be used as input by the regressor for regression prediction of influence scores. It is worth noting that both the trainable parameters of the regressor and the GraphSAGE-SP model are optimized in the same optimizer. And then, the target scores for regression prediction will be fitted and regressed against the labels generated in Sect. 3.3. Furthermore, the loss function uses the square mean error (MSE) as follow:

$$\text{MSE} = \frac{1}{n} \sum_{i=1}^{n} \left(y_{v_i} - f(h_{v_i}) \right)^2 \tag{5}$$

where $f(h_{v_i})$ donates the final influence score of the node v_i, and y_{v_i} is the generated label. In general, the work of the regressor is to predict the influence score as a set of continuous values. The nodes are then ranked according to their predicted influence score. Ranking the influence score of nodes in descend order, the top-K nodes with high influence score will be selected as the seed set to begin information diffusion, with the aim of maximizing influence.

4   Experiments

4.1   Datasets

Table 1. Statistical cheatsheet of the social networks used.

Dataset	Nodes	Edges	$\bar{d}$	β_{th}
Hamster	2426	16631	13.71	0.072
LastFM	7624	27806	7.29	0.137
Email	1133	5451	9.62	0.104
Fb-TVshow	3892	17262	8.87	0.113

We applied our proposed framework on four real-world social networks to evaluate and compare its performance. The brief of the public social networks are as follows:

- Hamster [25]: A social network of the friendships and family links between users of the website www.hamsterster.com.
- LastFM [27]: It is a social network of LastFM users who from Asian countries. Nodes represent LastFM users and edges are friendships between them.

- Email [29]: An e-mail communication network of a large European research institution. Nodes indicate members of the institution. An edge between a pair of members indicates that they exchanged at least one email.
- Fb-TVshow [26]: The dataset represent blue verified Facebook page undirected networks of TV shows categories. Nodes represent the pages themselves, while edges represent mutual likes among them.

The statistical cheatsheet of the datasets are listed in Table 1. $\beta_{th} = \frac{1}{\bar{d}}$ is the epidemic threshold, where $\bar{d}$ is the average degree of the relevant social networks. All experiments of SIR model are run on the corresponded epidemic threshold β_{th} except otherwise stated. Additionally, in this paper, the used social networks considered are undirected and unweighted.

4.2   Evaluation Metrics

In this subsection, we introduce the evaluation metric for measuring the influence spreading capacity of seed sets in influence maximization algorithms as follow:

- **Influence scale** $N_{(k)}$:
  To evaluate the algorithm's performance in influence maximization, we use the SIR model. Ranking the influence score of nodes predicted by the algorithm in descend order, the top-k nodes with high influence score will be selected as the seed set. We can set the seed nodes to be infected and the others to be susceptible to estimate the influence of the seed nodes in the network. Infected nodes can infect its susceptible neighbors with a probability β, and will be recovered with a probability γ. For simplicity, the recovery probability γ set as one and the infection probability β set as the epidemic threshold β_{th}. $N_{(k)}$ represents the total number of infected and recovered nodes in the network after reaching a steady state in the spreading simulation, where the k denotes the initial seed set size. We denote the final infected scale of seed nodes as $N_{(k)}$ for the size of seed set k.
- **Average distance between seeds** D_{avg}:
  An ideal seed set is widely distributed throughout the network, as indicated by a higher value of D_{avg}. Additionally, it also shows whether there is a high overlap in the influence ranges of the seed set obtained by the algorithm. The Average distance between seeds D_{avg} is defined as:

$$D_{avg} = \frac{\sum_{v_i, v_j \in seed}^{k} D_{v_i v_j}}{C_k^2} \qquad (6)$$

where k denotes the size of the seed set, and $D_{v_i v_j}$ defined as the path length between any two nodes v_i and v_j in the seed set. Moreover, $C_k^2 = \frac{k(k-1)}{2}$ is the number of pairs of nodes in the seed set.

4.3 Experimental Results and Analysis

In this subsection, we present experimental results that demonstrate how our methods optimize the performance degradation caused by the overlapping influence ranges in the seed set. We compare our proposed framework with other approaches on four social networks. The comparison methods are M-RCNN [22], RCNN [16] and HITS [12].

Table 2. The average distance between seed nodes D_{avg} for different datasets using various algorithms. And the number of seed nodes is set to 2% of the total nodes in the networks.

Dataset	M-RCNN	RCNN	HITS	Inf-LGR
Hamster	1.42	1.45	1.53	**2.07**
LastFM	2.47	2.62	1.89	**3.17**
Email	1.60	1.71	1.61	**1.98**
Fb-TVshows	1.25	1.39	1.25	**2.27**

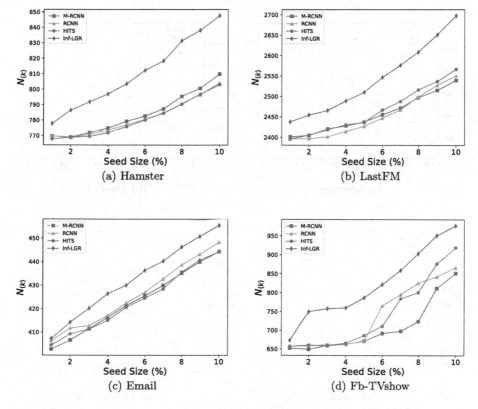

(a) Hamster   (b) LastFM

(c) Email   (d) Fb-TVshow

Fig. 2. Influence scale $N_{(k)}$ with different size of seed set value k obtained by various methods in different real social networks under SIR model. The infection probability β is set as the epidemic threshold β_{th} for the respective social networks.

Figure 2 shows the scale of influence of seed set obtained by various algorithm on all the chosen datasets with different seed set size under the SIR model. In all figures, the y-axis represents the size of the final infection scale, denoted as $N_{(k)}$, while the x-axis denotes the seed set size, ranging from 1% to 10% of the total number of network nodes in the dataset. The size of seed set in percentage terms ensures a fair comparison across social networks of different sizes. Moreover, the data points in all datasets are uniformly spaced with a step size of 1%. As mentioned above, the infection probability for each networks is taken as the epidemic threshold β_{th} which is different for each social networks. As for the result of the Hamster dataset in the Fig. 2a and the LastFM network in Fig. 2b, it is apparent that inf-LGR outperforms all other algorithms in terms of the final infection scale $N_{(k)}$ with different size of seed set. As depicted in Fig. 2c, it can be observed that although all algorithms exhibit similar performance, Inf-LGR still outperforms other algorithms. For Fb-TVshow dataset Fig. 2d, it clearly demonstrates the superior performance of Inf-LGR compared to other methods, reaffirming its superiority. It is worth noting that the classical algorithm HITS also tends to give competitive results as seeds size increases.

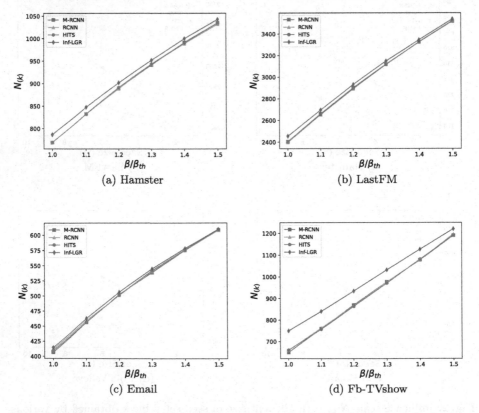

(a) Hamster

(b) LastFM

(c) Email

(d) Fb-TVshow

Fig. 3. Influence scale $N_{(k)}$ with different infect rate β value k obtained by various methods in different real social networks under SIR model.

Table 2 show the average path length D_{avg} between seeds obtained by various algorithm for all the datasets. The seed node count was fixed at 2% of the total nodes for all algorithms. Our approach consistently achieves optimal results in the evaluation metric D_{avg} across all networks, as shown in Table 2. The outstanding performance of Inf-LGR in this regard demonstrates that the selected nodes are opinion leaders distributed throughout the network rather than being concentrated in specific group and class. This can be attributed to the capability of Inf-LGR to identify opinion leaders across the network.

Table 3. The influence scale $N_{(k)}$ between different aggregation function for various datasets using Inf-LGR framework.

Dataset	mean	min	max	SP
Hamster	568	49	783	**786**
LastFM	2420	2417	2412	**2454**
Email	410	411	411	**414**
Fb-TVshows	661	666	655	**750**

Figure 3 shows that final infection scale $N_{(k)}$ is positively correlated with the infectious rates β. For the all algorithm, higher infection rates result in larger diffusion scale. While the results of other algorithms are competitive, Inf-LGR consistently performs slightly better.

In Table 3, the aggregation algorithm we proposed based on the number of shortest paths outperforms the simple aggregation of GraphSAGE. Our method utilizes the number of shortest paths to calculate node importance and aggregates the corresponding influence features accordingly. The stable performance of GraphSAGE-SP demonstrates the feasibility and effectiveness of the model in influence maximizing.

We can see from the result that performance of Inf-LGR is better than other algorithm in each network, demonstrating that the model via opinion leader and graph embedding framework improves the performance of solution in influence maximization problem. The reason is that some other purposed recently model does not consider the high overlap of the influence range between high-influence nodes, which leads to poor performance. Compared with other models, Inf-LGR not only selects the nodes with high global influence, but also selects the local opinion leader as its seed set, although the label value of the local opinion leader is not absolute great in the global network, in order to improve the performance of influence maximizing.

5   Conclusion

Solving the influence maximization problem based on identifying influential nodes, it is easily lead to poor performance caused by the highly overlapping influence ranges between the highly influential seed. To address this issue, we propose Inf-LGR, a regression framework via opinion leaders and graph embedding. Inf-LGR aims to optimize the performance degradation caused by the substantial overlap in influence ranges. Specifically, we use VGAE to encode the evaluation of opinion leaders into low-dimensional vectors, which are then used as node features in the subsequent steps. Additionally, we introduce GraphSAGE-SP, an improved GraphSAGE model based on the shortest path to generate the influence embedding of nodes. These embeddings are then used as input for a regressor to predict regression scores. The scores are subsequently ranked in descending order, and the top-k nodes with the highest scores are chosen as the seeds. The influence maximization effect of this seed set is evaluated using SIR model. Our framework achieves impressive performance, surpassing recently proposed and classical models, and making significant advancements in influence maximization.

Acknowledgements. This work was supported by National Natural Science Foundation of China No. U1811263.

References

1. Bamakan, S.M.H., Nurgaliev, I., Qu, Q.: Opinion leader detection: a methodological review. Expert Syst. Appl. **115**, 200–222 (2019)
2. Bao, Z.K., Ma, C., Xiang, B.B., Zhang, H.F.: Identification of influential nodes in complex networks: method from spreading probability viewpoint. Phys. A **468**, 391–397 (2017)
3. Berahmand, K., Bouyer, A., Samadi, N.: A new centrality measure based on the negative and positive effects of clustering coefficient for identifying influential spreaders in complex networks. Chaos, Solitons Fractals **110**, 41–54 (2018)
4. Fan, C., Zeng, L., Sun, Y., Liu, Y.Y.: Finding key players in complex networks through deep reinforcement learning. Nat. Mach. Intell. **2**(6), 317–324 (2020)
5. Hamilton, W., Ying, Z., Leskovec, J.: Inductive representation learning on large graphs. In: Advances in Neural Information Processing Systems, vol. 30 (2017)
6. Han, L., Zhou, Q., Tang, J., Yang, X., Huang, H.: Identifying top-k influential nodes based on discrete particle swarm optimization with local neighborhood degree centrality. IEEE Access **9**, 21345–21356 (2021)
7. Jain, L., Katarya, R.: Discover opinion leader in online social network using firefly algorithm. Expert Syst. Appl. **122**, 1–15 (2019)
8. Jain, L., Katarya, R., Sachdeva, S.: Opinion leader detection using whale optimization algorithm in online social network. Expert Syst. Appl. **142**, 113016 (2020)
9. Katz, E., Lazarsfeld, P.F.: Personal Influence, The Part Played by People in the Flow of Mass Communications. Transaction Publishers, Piscataway (1964)
10. Kipf, T.N., Welling, M.: Variational graph auto-encoders. arXiv preprint arXiv:1611.07308 (2016)
11. Kitsak, M., et al.: Identification of influential spreaders in complex networks. Nat. Phys. **6**(11), 888–893 (2010)
12. Kleinberg, J.M.: Authoritative sources in a hyperlinked environment. J. ACM (JACM) **46**(5), 604–632 (1999)

13. Leskovec, J., Adamic, L.A., Huberman, B.A.: The dynamics of viral marketing. ACM Trans. Web (TWEB) **1**(1), 5-es (2007)
14. Li, G., Xiong, C., Thabet, A., Ghanem, B.: DeeperGCN: all you need to train deeper GCNs. arXiv preprint arXiv:2006.07739 (2020)
15. Li, Y., Fan, J., Wang, Y., Tan, K.L.: Influence maximization on social graphs: a survey. IEEE Trans. Knowl. Data Eng. **30**(10), 1852–1872 (2018)
16. Yu, E.Y., Wang, Y.P., Fu, Y., Chen, D.B., Xie, M.: Identifying critical nodes in complex networks via graph convolutional networks. Knowl. Based Syst. **198**, 105893 (2020)
17. Li, Z., Ren, T., Ma, X., Liu, S., Zhang, Y., Zhou, T.: Identifying influential spreaders by gravity model. Sci. Rep. **9**(1), 8387 (2019)
18. Liu, H.L., Ma, C., Xiang, B.B., Tang, M., Zhang, H.F.: Identifying multiple influential spreaders based on generalized closeness centrality. Phys. A **492**, 2237–2248 (2018)
19. Liu, S., Jiang, C., Lin, Z., Ding, Y., Duan, R., Xu, Z.: Identifying effective influencers based on trust for electronic word-of-mouth marketing: a domain-aware approach. Inf. Sci. **306**, 34–52 (2015)
20. Malliaros, F.D., Rossi, M.E.G., Vazirgiannis, M.: Locating influential nodes in complex networks. Sci. Rep. **6**(1), 19307 (2016)
21. Maurya, S.K., Liu, X., Murata, T.: Fast approximations of betweenness centrality with graph neural networks. In: Proceedings of the 28th ACM International Conference on Information and Knowledge Management, pp. 2149–2152 (2019)
22. Ou, Y., Guo, Q., Xing, J.L., Liu, J.G.: Identification of spreading influence nodes via multi-level structural attributes based on the graph convolutional network. Expert Syst. Appl. **203**, 117515 (2022)
23. Qiu, J., Tang, J., Ma, H., Dong, Y., Wang, K., Tang, J.: DeepInf: social influence prediction with deep learning. In: Proceedings of the 24th ACM SIGKDD International Conference on Knowledge Discovery & Data Mining, pp. 2110–2119 (2018)
24. Qiu, L., Jia, W., Niu, W., Zhang, M., Liu, S.: SIR-IM: SIR rumor spreading model with influence mechanism in social networks. Soft. Comput. **25**, 13949–13958 (2021)
25. Rossi, R.A., Ahmed, N.K.: The network data repository with interactive graph analytics and visualization. In: AAAI (2015). http://networkrepository.com
26. Rozemberczki, B., Davies, R., Sarkar, R., Sutton, C.: GEMSEC: graph embedding with self clustering. In: Proceedings of the 2019 IEEE/ACM International Conference on Advances in Social Networks Analysis and Mining, pp. 65–72 (2019)
27. Rozemberczki, B., Sarkar, R.: Characteristic functions on graphs: birds of a feather, from statistical descriptors to parametric models. In: Proceedings of the 29th ACM International Conference on Information & Knowledge Management, pp. 1325–1334 (2020)
28. Song, C., Wang, B., Jiang, Q., Zhang, Y., He, R., Hou, Y.: Social recommendation with implicit social influence. In: Proceedings of the 44th International ACM SIGIR Conference on Research and Development in Information Retrieval, pp. 1788–1792 (2021)
29. Yin, H., Benson, A.R., Leskovec, J., Gleich, D.F.: Local higher-order graph clustering. In: Proceedings of the 23rd ACM SIGKDD International Conference on Knowledge Discovery and Data Mining, pp. 555–564 (2017)
30. Zhan, J., Gurung, S., Parsa, S.P.K.: Identification of top-K nodes in large networks using Katz centrality. J. Big Data **4**(1), 1–19 (2017)

31. Zhao, G., Jia, P., Zhou, A., Zhang, B.: InfGCN: identifying influential nodes in complex networks with graph convolutional networks. Neurocomputing **414**, 18–26 (2020)
32. Zhao, Y., Kou, G., Peng, Y., Chen, Y.: Understanding influence power of opinion leaders in e-commerce networks: an opinion dynamics theory perspective. Inf. Sci. **426**, 131–147 (2018)
33. Zhou, F., Xu, X., Trajcevski, G., Zhang, K.: A survey of information cascade analysis: models, predictions, and recent advances. ACM Comput. Surv. (CSUR) **54**(2), 1–36 (2021)

Incremental Inductive Dynamic Network Community Detection

Ling Wu[1,2(✉)], Jiangming Zhuang[1,2], and Kun Guo[1,2,3]

[1] College of Computer and Data Science, Fuzhou University, Fuzhou 350108, China
{gukn,wuling1985}@fzu.edu.cn
[2] Fujian Key Laboratory of Network Computing and Intelligent Information Processing, (Fuzhou University), Fuzhou 350108, China
[3] Key Laboratory of Spatial Data Mining and Information Sharing, Ministry of Education, Fuzhou 350108, China

Abstract. In order to address the problem of reconstruction and retraining time overhead in representation learning processing dynamic networks, this paper proposes an incremental inductive dynamic network community detection algorithm (IINDCD). First, the algorithm uses an attention mechanism to capture node neighborhood information and learn node representations by neighborhood aggregation induction while enhancing low-order structural representations. Second, the design uses random walking to capture high-order information and use it to construct node initial features for input into the attentional autoencoder, which effectively fuses high- and low-order structural features. Finally, the algorithm introduces the ideas of incremental update and model reuse for dynamic representation learning, constructs incremental node sets for updating the model, reduces training overhead, and quickly obtains node representation vectors for new moments of the network, then completing dynamic network community detection. IINDCD runs without reconstruction and with low retraining overhead.

Keywords: incremental dynamic network · neighborhood aggregation · the attention autoencoder

1 Introduction

As information becomes more complex, real-world networks are found to be constantly changing over time. As a result, scholars have extended their focus on static networks to dynamic networks, and dynamic network community detection has become the focus of research. The traditional incremental approach [1,5–7] is to design an adjustment strategy to update the current community division on the community structure of the snapshot network at the previous moment, and this type of approach achieves efficiency advantages but suffers from the error accumulation problem [2]. As for dynamic representation learning [3,9–12], it mostly adopts fusion of temporal information to embed dynamic networks, and

© The Author(s), under exclusive license to Springer Nature Singapore Pte Ltd. 2024
Y. Sun et al. (Eds.): ChineseCSCW 2023, CCIS 2012, pp. 93–107, 2024.
https://doi.org/10.1007/978-981-99-9637-7_7

although it achieves good results, its mining of historical temporal information makes the algorithm time overhead relatively large, leading to shortcomings in efficiency.

To address the above problems, this paper proposes an incremental dynamic network community detection algorithm based on neighborhood aggregation IINDCD. The overall framework is shown in Fig. 1. This paper optimizes the representation of low-order structures by combining attention coding with an autoencoder designed to embed information about key neighbors by applying attention to the neighborhoods of nodes. The feature vector generated by random walking containing high-order structure information is also used as the initial node features of IINDCD for encoding input to better fuse high- and low-order features. Dynamic representation learning community detection is two-stage [4] and cannot be directly processed using the traditional incremental approach. On the one hand, the algorithm in this paper introduces the core idea of incremental division of incremental node sets, unifying the set of nodes and edge sets that have changed, to the set of nodes that have changed, while expanding the first-order neighborhood of the set of changed nodes to the incremental node set. The incremental node set update training method is used to speed up the training of the model, and the model is reused in the dynamic representation process, and the community division is combined with the clustering algorithm whenever the new representation vector of the node is obtained at the current moment, and finally the dynamic network community detection is completed. On the other hand, the idea of neighborhood aggregation is used, which can solve the problem of representation learning of dynamic nodes. Our contributions can be summarized as follows.

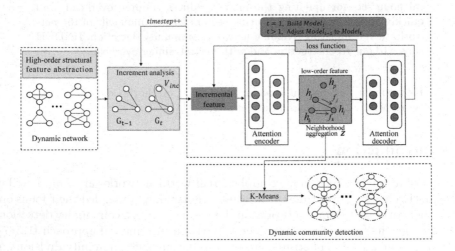

Fig. 1. IINDCD algorithm framework

1. High-order structural features abstraction based on random walk, unifying the dimensionality of input data to design dynamic network inductive representation learning model, which adapt dynamic networks with nodes vary and fix the issue of model reconstruction. Then kmeans clustering method was applied to detect communities on all these representation of vectors. The method can address the error accumulation problem.
2. Neighborhood aggregation with high-order structural features and low-order neighborhood features to learn the high quality representation vectors of nodes which vary in dynamic networks.
3. The incremental idea is introduced to design the incremental node set, and the network incremental calculation is used to partially update the model, which effectively reduces the training overhead.

The remainder of this paper is organized as follows: Sect. 2 represents the related work. The description of IINDCD algorithm is given in Sect. 3. We give the experimental results and the conclusion in Sects. 4 and 5 respectively.

2   Related Work

Incremental-based dynamic network community detection is the dominant approach among traditional dynamic network community detection algorithms because it better solves the time overhead problem. The incremental-based approach first divides the network community for the initial moment, and for subsequent moments, only the part of its change from the previous neighboring snapshot network is considered, and the community division is updated based on the previous community structure by computational analysis. Due to the reduction of computation, the incremental approach greatly improves the execution efficiency and better maintains the temporal smoothness. AFOCS (Adaptive Framework Overlapping Community Structure) [5] takes community density maximization as the objective function in dividing incremental nodes and edges to update community affiliation. For batch and small-scale incremental network structure changes, BatchInc [6] takes the previous moment network community structure as a priori knowledge and cyclically adjusts the nodes to get a new community division. ICNP (Incremental algorithm with Coherent Neighborhood Propinquity) [7] further improves the accuracy of dynamic network community detection by jointly considering node influence, association strength and belonging community affiliation for dynamic incremental updates to enhance the node influence range. BBTA [8] for detecting dynamic communities based on the tracking of backbones and bridges, using the rate of change of the network to assess the extent of network changes.

Representation learning-based dynamic network community detection contains two phases, namely dynamic representation learning and clustered community detection. With the rise of representation learning, more and more researchers have accomplished dynamic network community detection by combining representation learning. STWalk [9] fuses the current network structural path and the trajectory representation of the temporal path learning nodes generated by different time steps, and then uses Skip-Gram [10] to maximize the co-occurrence probability of nodes with their neighbors in the current moment to obtain a node representation containing information about a specific time window. DySAT [11] performs feature extraction in both spatio-temporal dimensions of the network based on recurrent neural networks. DySAT learns the spatio-temporal representation of nodes by efficiently fusing neighboring features based on recurrent neural networks and using adaptive attention networks. To solve the problem of imbalance between clustering accuracy and clustering drift in dynamic community recognition, jLDEC [12] learns jointly by integrating network embedding and clustering into an overall objective function, and the model extracts good graph representations guided by clustering, thus improving the clustering accuracy in reverse.

3   IINDCD Algorithm

The algorithmic framework of IINDCD is shown in Fig. 1 and consists of three parts: High-order structural features abstraction based on random walk, neighborhood aggregation with high- and low-order information and increment analysis.

3.1   High-Order Structural Features Abstraction Based on Random Walk

Random walk [13] uses each node in the network as the starting point to construct the wandering sample, and keeps randomly selecting the next hop nodes, repeating straight up to meet the sampling length, and finally inputting the Skip-Gram model to obtain the high-order structural features of the nodes for this algorithm, generating the initial feature vector of nodes with high-order features, and maximizing the following objective function during training to achieve according to Eq. (1):

$$L_{rw} = \log \sigma \left(v_j' \cdot v_i \right) - \sum_{k=1}^{K} \log \left(-\sigma \left(v_k' \cdot v_i \right) \right), \tag{1}$$

where v_i is the representation vector of node i, and v_j' denotes the contextual embedding vector of node j as the contextual node of other nodes, the contextual node as the positive sample, the goal is to maximize the similarity between the central node and the positive sample. k is the number of negative samples, selected from the negative sample $P_n(v)$, the goal is to minimize the similarity between the central node and the negative sample.

3.2   Neighborhood Aggregation with High- and Low-Order Information

The design of IINDCD representation learning uses an autoencoder architecture to aggregate features more accurately by using an attention-based two-layer encoder for learning node information and its deep relationships with neighboring nodes, for the low-order structure of nodes. Meanwhile, compared to the neighborhood information, the node vectors learned by random walking contain high-order structural information, so the algorithm in this paper uses random walk to construct initial features during encoding and add high-order features for embedding learning.

The attention encoding layer will calculate the attention coefficient e_{ij} between two neighboring nodes according to Eq. (2):

$$e_{ij} = a\left([Wh_i \parallel Wh_j]\right), \tag{2}$$

where h_i and h_j are the initial feature vectors of node i and node j, respectively, W is the weight matrix that can be learned during the linear transformation, and $\parallel$ is the vector splicing operation. a denotes a single-layer feed-forward neural network, which is generally designed as a parameter vector that needs to be involved in learning during training. For different nodes, the attention coefficients should be of the same order of magnitude to allow for more standard comparisons, so this paper uses the soft-max function to normalize the calculated attention coefficients e_{ij} to obtain t_{ij}, as shown in Eq. (3):

$$t_{ij} = \frac{\exp\left(LeakyRelu\left(e_{ij}\right)\right)}{\sum_{k \in N_i} \exp\left(LeakyRelu\left(e_{ik}\right)\right)}, \tag{3}$$

where LeakyRelu is the nonlinear activation function. After the different importance relationships between the target node and its neighboring nodes through attention extraction, the output of the coding layer is the weighted aggregation result of the attention coefficients of the neighboring nodes, and the final node representation vector is generated according to the following Eq. (4):

$$z_i = \sigma\left(\sum_{k \in N_i} t_{ik} W h_k\right), \tag{4}$$

where node k is a neighbor of node i, z_i obtains the node representation vector by aggregating h_k, and σ denotes the sigmoid function.

Since the encoder of the algorithm in this paper adopts the attention aggregation method, it is not necessary to know the overall structure of the network in advance, which is more adaptable to the dynamic changes of the network. Correspondingly, the decoder part is constructed by using a symmetric reversal encoder, which is calculated as shown in the following Eq. (5).

$$\hat{h}_i = \sigma\left(\sum_{k \in N_i} \hat{t}_{ik} \widehat{W} z_k\right), \tag{5}$$

where $\hat{h}_i$ is the reconstructed node feature vector of node i and $\widehat{W}$ is the weight matrix to be trained for the reconfiguration process. Encoding and decoding are several times of mapping the features, in which the embedding space changes subsequently, but the attention relationship between nodes should be fixed, so the attention coefficient $\hat{t}_{ik}$ of the decoder follows the attention coefficient of the encoder.

The loss function of IINDCD contains two aspects. First, since an attention-based encoder is used and the attention acts on the neighborhood, the algorithm in this paper maintains the low-order structure of the nodes by maximizing the local similarity, which is calculated as shown in Eq. (6).

$$L_l = -\sum_{i=1}^{N} \sum_{j \in N_I} \log \left(\frac{1}{1 + \exp\left(-z_i^T z_j\right)} \right), \tag{6}$$

This term is the local neighborhood loss, where z_i and z_j denote the representation vectors of two nodes i and j. If two nodes are neighbors of each other, the more similar the representation vectors between the two nodes should be.

Secondly, the input of the encoder is a feature vector generated by random walk with high-order feature information of the node, and the algorithm in this paper reconstructs its features and minimizes the difference between the original feature vector and the reconstructed feature vector, preserving the high-order structure of the node, as shown in Eq. (7).

$$L_h = \sum_{i=1}^{N} \left\| h_i - \hat{h}_i \right\|_2^2, \tag{7}$$

The high-order features in training are reconstructed as the initial features, and the closer the reconstructed features are to the initial features, the more complete the high-order information in the vector is preserved, and the better the quality of the vector is indicated.

Ultimately, the loss function of IINDCD includes the above two loss terms while optimizing the low-order structural features and preserving the high-order structural features, as shown in Eq. (8):

$$Loss = \sum_{i=1}^{N} \left\| h_i - \hat{h}_i \right\|_2^2 - \lambda \sum_{i=1}^{N} \sum_{j \in N_I} \log \left(\frac{1}{1 + \exp\left(-z_i^T z_j\right)} \right), \tag{8}$$

where the two loss terms are weighed by introducing the hyper-parameter λ.

3.3 Increment Analysis and Community Detection

In terms of topology, nodes and edges are the constituent elements of the network, so changes in the network can be classified into four cases: edge addition, edge disappearance, node addition and node disappearance. IINDCD is based on feature learning of nodes and thus obtaining the representation vector, so this paper unifies the changes in the network to the node perspective for incremental division. Compared to the previous moment, the nodes added or disappeared are naturally classified into the incremental set V_{inc}, while the edges added or disappeared are added to the set with their endpoints. To better consider the evolution of the network, this paper extends V_{inc} by further including the first-order neighbors of the nodes in the incremental part.

For the initial moment of the dynamic network, all nodes of the current network are added to V_{inc} since there is no previous moment, and the initial features are input to train the model to aggregate the representation vector; for non-initial moments, the algorithm updates V_{inc} according to its incremental change from the snapshot of the previous moment, inputs new initial features, and quickly adjusts them based on the model of the previous moment, and aggregates the same after training to obtain new representation vector of each node and combine with K-Means clustering to mine the current community structure of the network for dynamic community detection. In general, the dynamic process of IINDCD representation learning requires only some of the nodes to be involved in the incremental process, which greatly reduces the amount of training, and the model is reused at each moment instead of being rebuilt or retrained every snapshot, reducing the overhead.

The pseudocode of the IINDCD algorithm is shown in Algorithm 1, demonstrating the overall implementation steps of the algorithm.

Algorithm 1. IINDCD Algorithm Pseudocode

Input: $G = \{G_t | t = 1, 2, ..., T\}, \lambda, iter$
Output: $C = \{C_t | t = 1, 2, ..., T\}$

  for t in 1 to T do
    $X_t = Randomwalk(G_t)$
  end for
  $V_{inc} = \phi$
  for t in 1 to T do
    According to G_{t-1} and G_t to update V_{inc} by dividing the incremental part
    Extract the incremental part of the initial features X_t' according to V_{inc}
    $Z_t' = Encoder(G_t, V_{inc}, X_t')$
    $loss = Decoder(Z_t')$
    Update the parameters in the encoder using stochastic gradient descent
    Use Eq.4 as an aggregation function to generate Z_t
    Use Z_t combined with K-Means yielded C_t
  end for
  return $C = \{C_t | t = 1, 2, ..., T\}$

---

4   Experiments

To validate IINDCD, experiments are selected from real and artificial datasets, using two classical community detection metrics, compared with 8 baseline algorithms, which contain parametric experiments, accuracy experiments, and runtime experiments.

4.1 Datasets

Real-World Networks. As shown in Table 1, four real dynamic networks were selected for this experiment, including: Enron [14], AS-733 [15], Facebook [16], and Coauthor [17].

Table 1. Basic characteristics of the real dynamic networks

network	nodes	edges	snapshots	window	span
Enron	33377	69230	8	1 month	8 month
AS-733	33623	59623	10	10 day	100 day
Facebook	48516	61488	8	1 month	8 month
Coauthor	148118	235280	5	1 year	5 year

Artificial Networks. In this experiment, the artificial dynamic network is generated from a dynamic version of the LFR [18] benchmark network with a real community distribution. The main parameters of LFR are set as shown in Table 2. Among them are the number of nodes N, the community mixing parameter μ and the probability p of nodes exchanging community affiliation between two neighboring snapshot networks. The number of generated dynamic network snapshots is set to 10 for each group, and the remaining parameters are set according to the default values of the tool.

Table 2. Parameter settings for the LFR artificial dynamic network

Network	N	μ	p
D1	2000–10000	0.2	0.2
D2	2000	0.1–0.6	0.2
D3	2000	0.2	0.1–0.6
D4	2000	0.2	0.2

4.2 Baseline

To test the effectiveness of the IINDCD algorithm, eight comparison algorithms were selected for this experiment, among which the BatchInc [6], the LBTR [19], and the AFOCS [5] are traditional incremental dynamic network community detection algorithms. The DynGEM [20], the DynAE [21], and the DynRNN [21] are dynamic network representation learning algorithms, and the Node2Vec [22] and DAEGC [23] are static network representation learning algorithms, which are applied to each snapshot of the dynamic network for representation learning in this experiment.

4.3   Evaluation Metrics

This section introduces two classical community detection evaluation metrics: Normalized Mutual Information (NMI) [24] and Modularity [25].

Normalized Mutual Information (NMI) requires the community structure mined by the algorithm to be as consistent as possible with the real community segmentation, and the higher the consistency, the higher the score, which is an important measure of community detection. The NMI is calculated by the following Eq. (9):

$$NMI = \frac{-2 \sum_{i=1}^{C_A} \sum_{j=1}^{C_B} H_{ij} \log \left(\frac{H_{ij} \times N}{H_{i.} \times H_{.j}} \right)}{\sum_{i=1}^{C_A} H_{i.} \log \left(\frac{H_{i.}}{N} \right) + \sum_{j=1}^{C_B} H_{.j} \log \left(\frac{H_{.j}}{N} \right)}, \tag{9}$$

A and B are the real community division and the algorithmic community division, respectively, and C_A and C_B represent the number of communities. H is a mixing matrix, $H_{i.}$ is the sum of the elements of the ith row, and $H_{.j}$ is the sum of the elements of the jth column. H_{ij} represents the number of nodes in the same community under both divisions, and N is the total number of nodes.

Modularity (Q) is a metric proposed by Newman to evaluate the quality of community detection, and is widely used. This metric assumes that the communities delineated should satisfy as much cohesiveness and as little coupling as possible. The specific calculation of module degree is shown in Eq. (10):

$$Q = \frac{1}{2m} \sum_{uv} \left(A_{uv} - \frac{d_u d_v}{2m} \right) \delta \left(C_u, C_v \right), \tag{10}$$

where m denotes the total number of edges in the network, A is the adjacency matrix, d_* is the node degree, C_u and C_v denote the community belonging to nodes u and v, respectively, and $\delta \left(C_u, C_v \right)$ denotes the probability that nodes u and v belong to the same community.

4.4   Parameter Experiment

The parameter λ is used to control the weight of the low-order structural loss term in the loss function of the attention coding and decoding training process of the IINDCD algorithm. The larger the value of λ is, the greater the influence of local features on the algorithm, but if λ is too large, then the algorithm tends to ignore the high-order information thus leading to a decrease in the accuracy of subsequent community detection, so a suitable value of λ needs to be selected through experiment.

Figure 2 shows the effect of the parameter λ on dynamic networks in the D2 network group ($\mu = 0.1$, $\mu = 0.3$, $\mu = 0.5$), and the experimental results are the average of the algorithm's accuracy on 10 snapshots of each dynamic

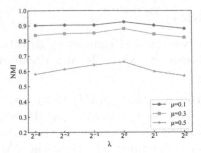

Fig. 2. Effect of parameter λ on the accuracy of the algorithm.

network. As shown in the figure, when $\lambda \leq 1$, the accuracy of the algorithm increases gradually with the increase of λ value to focus on the low-order features. However, when $\lambda > 1$, the accuracy of the algorithm tends to decline, and finally at $\lambda = 4$, the quality of the vectors obtained from node representation learning is deteriorated due to the over-reliance of the algorithm on the low-order structure, which leads to the lack of retention of high-order features, and thus the accuracy of community detection continues to decline. Therefore, $\lambda = 1$ is taken in all subsequent experiments.

4.5   Accuracy Experiment

Results on Real-World Networks. The experimental results of Q values of each algorithm on four real dynamic networks are shown in Fig. 3. Overall, the IINDCD algorithm outperforms the remaining three traditional incremental dynamic network community detection comparison algorithms on all four real dynamic networks, and achieves an advantage over both Node2Vec and DAEGC static representation learning algorithms on the community detection task as well. This is because the IINDCD algorithm uses random walking to construct an initial vector containing high-order structural features and incorporates an attention mechanism to optimize the capture of low-order structures during automatic encoding to jointly learn better quality node representations and improve the accuracy of subsequent community detection. Experimental results on Facebook show that the BatchInc algorithm and the LBTR algorithm on subsequent time slices The accuracy decreases faster because traditional incremental algorithms rely heavily on the quality of community segmentation in the previous moment snapshot, and potential missegmentation is passed to the next moment network over time, which cumulatively affects the accuracy of community detection.

Results on Artificial Networks. The artificial network is known to divide the real community and the experiments use NMI for a more objective evaluation. Figure 4 shows the accuracy experiments of each algorithm on the artificial dynamic network of group D1, where the value of parameter N increases continuously from 2000 to 10000, and the results of 10 time slices of the dynamic

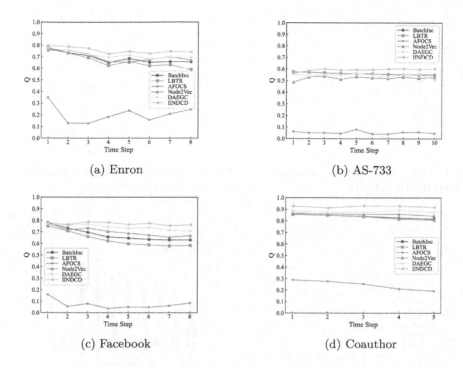

(a) Enron

(b) AS-733

(c) Facebook

(d) Coauthor

Fig. 3. Experimental results on the real dynamic network

network are averaged for each different value taken in the experiments. From the experimental results, it can be seen that the experimental accuracy does not show particularly large fluctuations due to the different number of nodes in the dynamic network, and the results are relatively stable, regardless of the IINDCD algorithm or the rest of the comparison algorithms. Meanwhile, the IINDCD algorithm performs the best on this group of artificial dynamic network.

Figure 5 shows the experimental results of NMI of each algorithm on the D2 artificial dynamic network, where the value of the parameter μ gradually increases from 0.1 to 0.6. As shown in the figure, the NMI of each algorithm decrease to a certain extent as the value of the parameter μ increases, because the larger the value of μ, the more blurred the community boundary is, and the more difficult it is to classify the algorithm. From the experimental results, it can be seen that the IINDCD algorithm achieves the highest values at different values of μ. This is because the IINDCD algorithm, by combining random walking and attention mechanisms, has better feature retention for both high-order and low-order characteristics of nodes, so the subsequent K-Means algorithm can mine the community structure relatively accurately.

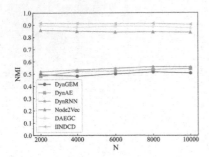

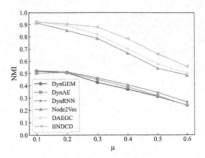

Fig. 4. NMI results with varying values of N on the D1 network

Fig. 5. NMI results with varying values of μ on the D2 network

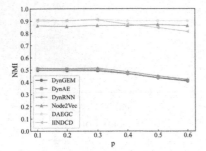

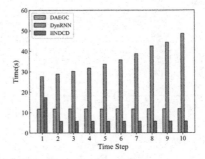

Fig. 6. NMI results with varying values of p on the D3 network

Fig. 7. Runtime results on the D4

Figure 6 shows the experimental results of NMI of each algorithm on the artificial dynamic network of group D3. The value of parameter p in this network increases continuously from 0.1 to 0.6, i.e., the evolutionary intensity of the dynamic network increases continuously. The accuracy of all the algorithms remains stable when p ≤ 0.3, and the dynamic evolution becomes more intense when p ≥ 0.4, and the accuracy of IINDCD and the three dynamic representation learning algorithms decreases to some extent, while the two static representation learning algorithms are basically unaffected and the results remain relatively stable. Overall, the IINDCD algorithm outperforms the remaining three dynamic representation learning algorithms on this network, and is almost comparable to the static representation learning algorithm in the case of increased evolution.

4.6 Runtime Experiment

In order to verify whether the incremental processing strategy of IINDCD can bring the improvement of running efficiency, this subsection selects the artificial dynamic dataset D4 for the time experiment, and the results are shown in Fig. 7.

Compared with DynRNN and DAEGC, the running time of IINDCD is the shortest because it takes into account the incremental changes of the network, which makes the volume of the model to be updated and trained greatly reduced, avoiding many unintentional repetitive calculations. Avoiding many meaningless repetitive calculations and effectively improving the overall running efficiency.

5   Conclusion

In this paper, we propose an incremental inductive dynamic network community detection. IINDCD incorporates an attention mechanism to aggregate neighborhood information and reuse the model, which effectively avoids model reconstruction and enhances generalization ability. Secondly, the incremental idea is introduced for dynamic representation learning, and the model update is completed by using incremental node sets, which reduces the retraining overhead. Meanwhile, it is combined with random walking to jointly learn the high and low-order features of nodes in order to improve the subsequent community detection accuracy. Experimental results on real and artificial dynamic network show that the proposed IINDCD algorithm has greater advantages in terms of accuracy and efficiency.

Acknowledgement. This work was supported in part by the National Natural Science Foundation of China under Grant 62002063, in part by the Fujian Natural Science Funds under Grant 2020J05112, in part by the Funds of Fujian Provincial Department of Education under Grant JAT190026, and in part by the Fuzhou University under Grant 510872/GXRC-20016, the National Natural Science Foundation of China under Grant No. 62002063 and No. U21A20472, in part by the National Key Research and Development Plan of China under Grant No. 2021YFB3600503, in part by the Fujian Collaborative Innovation Center for Big Data Applications in Governments, in part by the Fujian Industry-Academy Cooperation Project under Grant No. 2018H6010, in part by the Natural Science Foundation of Fujian Province under Grant No. 2020J05112, in part by the Fujian Provincial Department of Education under Grant No. JAT190026, in part by the Major Science and Technology Project of Fujian Province under Grant No. 2021HZ022007 and Haixi Government Big Data Application Cooperative Innovation Center and the China Scholarship Council under Grant 202006655008.

References

1. Wu, Z., Chen, J., Zhang, Y.: An incremental community detection method in social big data. In: Proceedings of the 5th IEEE/ACM International Conference on Big Data Computing Applications and Technologies, pp. 136–141 (2018)
2. Zhang, C., Zhang, Y., Wu, B.: A parallel community detection algorithm based on incremental clustering in dynamic network. In: Proceedings of the IEEE/ACM International Conference on Advances in Social Networks Analysis and Mining, pp. 946–953 (2018)
3. Xue, G., Zhong, M., Li, J., et al.: Dynamic network embedding survey. Neurocomputing **472**, 212–223 (2022)

4. Wang, S., Tang, J., Morstatter, F., et al.: Paired restricted Boltzmann machine for linked data. In: Proceedings of the 25th ACM International Conference on Information and Knowledge Management, pp. 1753–1762 (2016)

5. Nguyen, N.P., Dinh, T.N., Tokala, S., et al.: Overlapping communities in dynamic networks: their detection and mobile applications. In: Proceedings of the 17th Annual International Conference on Mobile Computing and Networking, pp. 85–96 (2011)

6. Chong, W.H., Teow, L.N.: An incremental batch technique for community detection. In: Proceedings of the 16th International Conference on Information Fusion, pp. 750–757 (2013)

7. Chen, N., Hu, B., Rui, Y.: Dynamic network community detection with coherent neighborhood propinquity. IEEE Access **8**, 27915–27926 (2020)

8. Long, H., Li, X., Liu, X., et al.: BBTA: detecting communities incrementally from dynamic networks based on tracking of backbones and bridges. Appl. Intell. **53**(1), 1084–1100 (2023)

9. Pandhre, S., Mittal, H., Gupta, M., et al.: STwalk: learning trajectory representations in temporal graphs. In: Proceedings of the ACM India Joint International Conference on Data Science and Management of Data, pp. 210–219 (2018)

10. Mikolov, T., Chen, K., Corrado, G., et al.: Efficient estimation of word representations in vector space. arXiv preprint arXiv:1301.3781 (2013)

11. Sankar, A., Wu, Y., Gou, L., et al.: DySAT: deep neural representation learning on dynamic graphs via self-attention networks. In: Proceedings of the 13th International Conference on Web Search and Data Mining, pp. 519–527 (2020)

12. Li, D., Lin, Q., Ma, X.: Identification of dynamic community in temporal network via joint learning graph representation and nonnegative matrix factorization. Neurocomputing **435**, 77–90 (2021)

13. Perozzi, B., Al-Rfou, R., Skiena, S.: Random Walk: online learning of social representations. In: Proceedings of the 20th ACM SIGKDD International Conference on Knowledge Discovery and Data Mining, pp. 701–710 (2014)

14. Klimt, B., Yang, Y.: The Enron corpus: a new dataset for email classification research. In: Boulicaut, J.-F., Esposito, F., Giannotti, F., Pedreschi, D. (eds.) ECML 2004. LNCS (LNAI), vol. 3201, pp. 217–226. Springer, Heidelberg (2004). https://doi.org/10.1007/978-3-540-30115-8_22

15. Leskovec, J., Kleinberg, J., Faloutsos, C.: Graphs over time: densification laws, shrinking diameters and possible explanations. In: Proceedings of the Eleventh ACM SIGKDD International Conference on Knowledge Detection and Data Mining, pp. 177–187 (2005)

16. Viswanath, B., Mislove, A., Cha, M., et al.: On the evolution of user interaction in Facebook. In: Proceedings of the 2nd ACM Workshop on Online Social Networks, pp. 37–42 (2009)

17. Zhuang, H., Sun, Y., Tang, J., et al.: Influence maximization in dynamic social networks. In: Proceedings of the 13th IEEE International Conference on Data Mining, pp. 1313–1318 (2013)

18. Greene, D., Doyle, D., Cunningham, P.: Tracking the evolution of communities in dynamic social networks. In: Proceedings of the International Conference on Advances in Social Networks Analysis and Mining, pp. 176–183 (2010)

19. Shang, J., Liu, L., Li, X., et al.: Targeted revision: a learning-based approach for incremental community detection in dynamic networks. Phys. A **443**, 70–85 (2016)

20. Goyal, P., Kamra, N., He, X., et al.: DynGEM: deep embedding method for dynamic graphs. arXiv preprint arXiv:1805.11273 (2018)

21. Goyal, P., Chhetri, S.R., Canedo, A.: dyngraph2vec: capturing network dynamics using dynamic graph representation learning[J]. Knowl.-Based Syst. **187**, 104816 (2020)

22. Grover, A., Leskovec, J.: node2vec: scalable feature learning for networks. In: Proceedings of the 22nd ACM SIGKDD International Conference on Knowledge Detection and Data Mining, pp. 855–864 (2016)

23. Wang, C., Pan, S., Hu, R., et al.: Attributed graph clustering: a deep attentional embedding approach. In: Proceedings of the Twenty-Eighth International Joint Conference on Artificial Intelligence, pp. 3670–3676 (2019)

24. Li, B., Pi, D.: Network representation learning: a systematic literature review. Neural Comput. Appl. **32**(21), 16647–16679 (2020)

25. Wang, D., Cui, P., Zhu, W.: Structural deep network embedding. In: Proceedings of the 22nd ACM SIGKDD International Conference on Knowledge Detection and Data Mining, pp. 1225–1234 (2016)

Er-EIR: A Chinese Question Matching Model Based on Word-Level and Sentence-Level Interaction Features

Yuyan Ying, Zhiqiang Zhang[✉], Haiyan Wu, and Yuhang Dong

College of Information Management and Artificial Intelligence, Zhejiang University of Finance and Economics, Hangzhou 310018, Zhejiang, China
{yyy_17,zqzhang,wuhy2020,yhdong}@zufe.edu.cn

Abstract. The semantic matching of questions is a fundamental aspect of retrieval-based question answering (QA) systems. Text representations containing rich semantic information are required to achieve a deeper understanding of question intent. While existing large pre-trained models can obtain character-based text representations with contextual information, the specificity of Chinese sentences makes word-based text representation superior to character-based text representation. In this paper, we propose a question semantic matching method based on word-level and sentence-level interaction features. We utilize a Bidirectional Long Short-Term Memory (BiLSTM) approach to enhance the contextual information of the word representations. Additionally, we incorporate a co-attention mechanism to capture the interaction information between sentence pairs. By comparing our model with several baseline models on a self-built dataset of university financial question pairs, we have achieved remarkable performance.

Keywords: Semantic Matching · Pre-trained Language Model · Co-attention Mechanism · University Finance QA

1 Introduction

With the advancement of artificial intelligence technology, automatic question answering (QA) has emerged as a research direction in the field of natural language processing, attracting significant attention and broad development prospects [1]. The automatic QA system can enable people to quickly and accurately retrieve the information they need from a vast amount of data. Based on the application field, automatic QA systems can be generally classified into open-domain and restricted-domain QA systems [2]. Open-domain QA systems typically use data from various fields on the Web to train models, imparting them with strong generalization ability. On the other hand, restricted-domain QA systems only apply to specific scenarios and require domain data to improve model expertise.

For instance, university members (faculty or staff) are often unfamiliar with financial rules and regulations, which can lead confusion. They consult the financial department staff or search for relevant documents to access the required information. In our investigation of existing financial consulting models within universities, we observed common consulting methods include telephone, WeChat, visiting the finance hall, etc. However, these methods have drawbacks such as delayed responses, time consumption, and high communication costs. To get over these issues, we collected real financial QA data from universities and planned to establish a financial QA system for universities, which enables faculty and staff to quickly and accurately obtain what they need from a variety of financial information anytime. The retrieval-based QA system takes natural language as input and output, matches user-entered questions with standard questions in the system, and outputs the answers with the highest matching degree [3]. In this process, the system requires a deep understanding of the semantics of questions and determine whether the semantics of two sentences match.

Since BERT [4] was introduced in 2018, many researchers have used it as a tool to obtain sentence embeddings. This is achieved by feeding sentences into the model, and the first token output by the model is used as the embedding of the entire sentence, which is deemed to integrate semantic information of individual words in the sentence. However, limited by two pre-training tasks, sentence embeddings obtained from the original BERT model do not perform well on sentence-pair tasks. Therefore, we decided to use the Erlangshen-SimCSE-Chinese [5] model trained by IDEA to obtain sentence embeddings. The model was retrained using a large number of unsupervised data and supervised data for contrastive learning [6] based on the model BERT-base-Chinese. Compared with the original BERT model, sentence embeddings obtained from the Erlangshen-SimCSE-Chinese model have better performance on sentence pair tasks.

The main contributions of this paper are summarized as follows: (1) We proposed a semantic matching model named **Er**langshen **E**nhanced **I**nteractive **R**epresentation (Er-EIR) for Chinese question pairs. This model comprises several key components, including a sentence embedding layer, contextual information enhancement layer, soft alignment layer, feature aggregation layer, and prediction layer. (2) After conducting field research, we obtained financial consulting QA pairs from a university and established a question semantic matching dataset consisting of 1021 Chinese financial question pairs through human annotation. (3) We conducted experiments on a real financial question pairs dataset and compared them with multiple baseline methods to demonstrate the effectiveness of the Er-EIR model.

2   Related Work

The QA system is an advanced information retrieval system that provides accurate and concise responses to users' queries in natural language. In 1966, Weizenbaum et al. [7] designed and implemented the first formal QA system, Eliza, which was applied to psychotherapy. In 2011, IBM launched the Watson QA system [8], which gained fame for beating human champions in the most popular quiz TV program in America. In 2014, Microsoft launched the Xiaoice intelligent chatbot [9], and subsequently, an increasing number of artificial intelligence assistants such as Siri, Xiaodu, and Xiaoai have achieved successful commercialized. In 2022, OpenAI released the ChatGPT based on GPT-3.5 architecture, which can not only realize casual conversation but also answer users' questions in various fields. The QA system, as a method of information access, has attracted increasing attention and investment from the public and industry players in related fields.

In the domain of financial automatic QA, Gao [10] employed part-of-speech tagging, syntactic parsing, and other natural language processing technologies to realize a university financial QA system. Chi [11] used deep learning to explore enterprise financial QA technology, incorporating an attention mechanism into enterprise financial research. This approach facilitated the creation of an enterprise financial QA system by calculating semantic similarity between users' questions and knowledge base's questions. Wang [12] implemented a knowledge graph-based QA system through entity recognition via multi-pattern matching AC algorithm and intention recognition based on question templates. Zhu et al. [13] established a QA benchmark on a hybrid of tabular and textual content in finance.

In existing retrieval-based automatic QA systems, the common method is to match user input questions with the questions already in the knowledge base, and the answer corresponding to the most similar question in the knowledge base is used as the answer to the input question [3]. In this process, how to catch on the meaning of questions and perform semantic matching is the key point. Some research works use statistical or machine learning methods to obtain semantic information of sentences by modeling the measured statistical features of words. And use the semantic information to realize question matching in QA systems [14, 15]. However, statistical features are not sufficient for the representation of questions in QA systems. Mikolov et al. [16] proposed a Word2Vec word vector training model to obtain a distributed representation of words containing semantic information. With the rapid development of deep learning, deep neural network models such as RNN [17], LSTM [18], and Transformer [19] have become more and more capable of mining and characterizing semantic information. The BERT using a bidirectional Transformer as a feature extractor can better integrate contextual information. Later, Gao et al. [6] proposed the SimCSE model, which used contrast learning to adapt the BERT pre-training model to optimize the effect of BERT in sentence embedding generation scenarios and achieved better performance on several similarity computation datasets.

3   Er-EIR Model

3.1   Task Definition

We first define the semantic matching task for Chinese sentences. The two Chinese sentences to be matched are denoted as $P = (p_1, p_2, ..., p_n)$ and $Q = (q_1, q_2, ..., q_m)$ respectively, where p_a and q_b denote the a-th and b-th Chinese characters in sentence P and Q, respectively. Meanwhile, n and m are the lengths of sentences P and Q, respectively. The goal of the task is to evaluate whether P and Q have the same semantic meaning by the proposed method. For each pair of sentences, we have a label $y \in \{0, 1\}$ where label 1 indicates that the two sentences have the same semantic meaning, while 0 on the contrary.

3.2 The Architecture of Er-EIR

A general overview of our proposed model is illustrated in Fig. 1. The whole model is composed of five layers: a word embedding layer, a contextual information enhancement encoding layer, a soft alignment layer, a feature fusion layer, and a prediction layer. Firstly, the word embedding layer converts Chinese sentences into sentence embeddings and word embeddings. The word embeddings are then fed into the BiLSTM for context information enhancement. The soft alignment layer uses an attention mechanism to extract word-level association information between two sentences. The feature fusion layer combines sentence-level interaction information and word-level interaction information and feeds them into the prediction layer to judge whether the sentence semantics match.

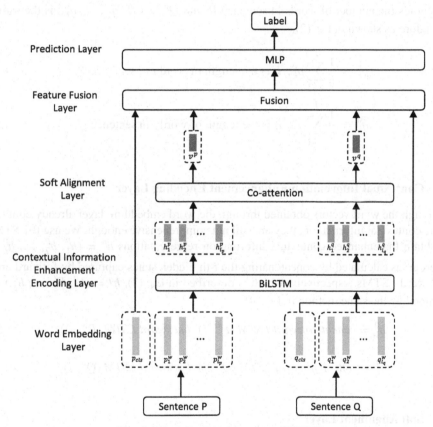

Fig. 1. The overall architecture of Er-EIR

3.3 Word Embedding Layer

To acquire embedding representations capable of capturing the deep semantics of sentences, we use an Erlangshen-SimCSE-Chinese model, which is based on a BERT-base architecture retrained through contrastive learning. This model outperforms BERT in extracting semantic information from Chinese sentences. We feed a Chinese sentence into this model and get sentence embedding and character embeddings from the last hidden state outputs. For a Chinese sentence P of length n, the model outputs vectors $([p_{cls}], p_1^c, p_2^c, ..., p_n^c)$ in which $[p_{cls}]$ token is considered to incorporate the semantic information of the full sentence and p_a^c is the vector corresponding to each character in the sentence. Since the smallest linguistic component in Chinese that can express complete semantic information is the word, we first segment the sentence P into words by using the Jieba tokenizer, which loaded with our self-built dictionary of the university finance field. And then average the vectors of characters that make up the word to obtain the word vector. The calculation is shown in Eq. (1). The word-based representation of a sentence is $P^w = (p_1^w, p_2^w, ..., p_{l_p}^w)$, p_i^w is the vector representation of the i-th word and l_p denotes the number of words in sentence P, and $Q^w = (q_1^w, q_2^w, ..., q_{l_q}^w)$ is the same procedure as shown in Eq. (2).

$$p_i^w = \frac{1}{l_i} \sum_{k=1}^{l_i} p_k^c, \ l_i \text{ is the length of word } i \text{ in sentence } P \tag{1}$$

$$q_j^w = \frac{1}{l_j} \sum_{z=1}^{l_j} q_z^c, \ l_j \text{ is the length of word } j \text{ in sentence } Q \tag{2}$$

3.4   Contextual Information Enhancement Encoding Layer

Although the word vectors obtained through the word embedding layer already contain some contextual information, they are still not comprehensive enough. We use BiLSTM to obtain the enhanced contextual information representations $h^P = (h_1^P, h_2^P, ..., h_{l_p}^P)$, where h_i^P is calculated by concatenating the i-th hidden states captured by forward and backward LSTMs respectively, which is described in Eq. (3), $h^q = (h_1^q, h_2^q, ..., h_{l_q}^q)$ is obtained by the same method in Eq. (4).

$$h_i^P = concat(forward\ LSTM\ (P^w, i); backward\ LSTM\ (P^w, i)) \tag{3}$$

$$h_j^q = concat(forward\ LSTM\ (Q^w, j); backward\ LSTM\ (Q^w, j)) \tag{4}$$

3.5   Soft Alignment Layer

The soft alignment layer extracts the association information of sentence pairs (P, Q) using the co-attention mechanism [20, 21]. For the i-th word in P, if it has a strong association with the j-th word in Q, the attention score $h_i^P h_j^{q^T}$ will be high. The shape of the attention score matrix $h^P h^{q^T}$ is $l_p \times l_q$, because of the unfixed length of sentences, the matrix shape of every sentence pair is different. In order to facilitate the calculation, we fix the shape to 30 × 30 by padding matrix with zero. And then transform the matrix linearly by inputting it to the 2-layer network without bias, in which the activation function is tanh. The computational process is shown in Eq. (5).

$$M = \tanh(h^p h^{q^T} W_1) W_2 \qquad (5)$$

Next, we use the softmax function to obtain the weight matrix. We then take a weighted sum over the other sentence to obtain $h_i^{p'}$ and $h_j^{q'}$. In detail, $h_i^{p'}$ represents the relevance information between the i-th word of sentence P and sentence Q, and $h_j^{q'}$ represents the relevance information between the j-th word of sentence Q and sentence P. Specifically, as shown in Eq. (6) and (7).

$$h_i^{p'} = \sum_{j=1}^{l_q} \frac{\exp(M_{ij})}{\sum_{r=1}^{l_q} \exp(M_{ir})} h_j^q \qquad (6)$$

$$h_j^{q'} = \sum_{i=1}^{l_p} \frac{\exp(M_{ij})}{\sum_{r=1}^{l_p} \exp(M_{rj})} h_i^p \qquad (7)$$

Finally, we input $h_i^{p'}$ into a linear layer with a ReLU activation function to obtain $h_i^{p''}$, and get the sentence representation v^p through averaging the new word representation. The process for obtaining v^q is the same. The v^p and v^q are given by Eq. (8) and (9).

$$v^p = \frac{1}{l_p} \sum_{i=1}^{l_p} h_i^{p''} \qquad (8)$$

$$v^q = \frac{1}{l_q} \sum_{j=1}^{l_q} h_j^{q''} \qquad (9)$$

3.6   Feature Fusion Layer

The feature fusion layer combines the p_{cls} and q_{cls} obtained from the word embedding layer with the association information v^p and v^q obtained from the soft alignment layer. Many studies [15, 20, 24, 27] have computed the representation vectors of two sentences and fed them into a classifier, and have demonstrated that the computed sentence representations perform better than directly using the representations of the two sentences in a sentence pair task. Therefore, we use element-wise multiplication and subtraction to get feature representations $p_{cls} \times q_{cls}$ and $|p_{cls} - q_{cls}|$ rather than directly using p_{cls} and q_{cls}. The final fusion feature is obtained by Eq. (10).

$$u = concat(|p_{cls} - q_{cls}|; p_{cls} \times q_{cls}; v^p; v^q) \qquad (10)$$

3.7 Prediction Layer

In the prediction layer, we use a 3-layer feedforward network (MLP) as a classifier to predict the matching label of the input sentence pairs, in which the first two layers' activation function is ReLU. The output of the classifier is a 2-dimensional vector, and label y is calculated by Eq. (11).

$$y = index(\text{argmax}(classifier(u))) \tag{11}$$

4 Experiment

We validate the effectiveness of the proposed model (Er-EIR) on a self-constructed dataset of question pairs in the field of university finance. Firstly, we describe the process of building the dataset, and then compare the baseline method with the proposed method to demonstrate the superiority of Er-EIR. Finally, ablation experiments are conducted to demonstrate the validity of the features and modules in Er-EIR.

4.1 Dataset

We initially obtained 1257 question-answer pairs from university financial question-answer WeChat group. We extracted the questions from these pairs and correct the typos and delete the special symbols in these questions. And manually parsed them to form 511 semantically identical question pairs. Additionally, we formed 510 semantically different question pairs through random selection. There are a total of 1021 question pairs in the dataset. Detailed information and examples are presented in Table 1 and Table 2, respectively.

Table 1. Experimental dataset

Dataset	Language	Scale (train/test)	Pos: Neg
University financial question pairs	Chinese	816/205	1:1

4.2 Experiment Setting

In our experiments, we randomly shuffle the dataset and divide the training set and test set in a 4:1ratio. The dimension of the word vector obtained from the word embedding layer is 768. In the contextual information enhancement encoding layer, the number of cells of the BiLSTM is set to 200, and the dropout rate is set to 0. In the prediction layer, we set the unit number of MLP to 1024, and the dropout rate is 0.3. For training, cross-entropy [22] is chosen as the loss function, and Adam [23] is the optimizer, and the initial learning rate is set to 0.0001. The hardware devices used for the experiments are as follows: Intel Core i9-12900K processor, 32 GB memory, and one NVIDIA GeForce RTX 3090 GPU.

Table 2. Examples in experimental dataset

Sentence pairs	Label
纵向课题省自科买一箱打印纸, 可以直接京东买吗? (EN: Zhejiang Provincial Natural Science Foundation vertical project, can directly buy printing paper on Jingdong?) 可以直接在网上买A4纸吗?纵向课题。 (EN: Can I buy A4 paper directly online for the vertical subject?)	1
请问横向课题可以报加油票吗? (EN: Can I reimburse the fuel invoice for the horizontal project?) 加油费可以在纵向课题里报吗? (EN: Can the fuel cost be reimbursed for the vertical project?)	0

4.3 Experimental Results

We validate the performance of our model by comparing it with several baseline methods, as described below:

1. ICE [24]: An effective model that combines character granularity and word granularity features got by Word2vec to perform sentence intention matching, and utilizes soft alignment attention to enhance the local information of sentences on the corresponding levels. We load its optimal parameters obtained by training on the dataset BQ [25] and fine-tune them using the self-built dataset.
2. Roberta [26]: The Roberta version in the experiment is Erlangshen-Roberta-110M-Similarity model [5] retrained by IDEA on the basis of Chinese-Roberta-WWM-ext-base model. The datasets used for retraining include 20 Chinese semantic matching datasets from different domains, and the model can directly predict whether the semantics of the input sentence pair are the same by an unsupervised method.
3. Roberta-MLP: We get the [CLS] token containing the sentence pair information from the last hidden state and feed it into a 3-layer feedforward network (MLP) to predict the label. The parameters in MLP are trained by our self-built dataset.
4. Erlangshen-Cosine: We calculate the cosine similarity of the [CLS] tokens of the two sentences output by model Erlangshen-SimCSE-Chinese, and determine whether the semantics of the two sentences match by the similarity. After several experimental comparisons, we set the threshold value to 0.72.
5. BERT-Cosine: We obtain the [CLS] tokens of the two sentences output by model BERT-base-Chinese and calculate the cosine similarity between them for judgment. We set the matching threshold to 0.85.

The results of the comparison experiment are shown in Table 3. The results show that Er-EIR outperforms several other baseline models in the university finance domain dataset. Compared with ICE, our method has an 8.29% improvement in accuracy, this probably because ICE focuses on local information of sentences and not enough on the association information between sentences. Different from that, our model utilizes a pre-trained language model to obtain dynamic word embeddings, and obtains the association information of sentence pairs through a soft alignment layer, and considers [CLS] that contains information about the entire sentence. In addition, our method has 19.72%, 6.34%, and 11.22% improvements compared to Roberta, Roberta-MLP, and Erlangshen-Cosine respectively. Besides, by comparing the experimental results of Roberta and Roberta-MLP, we can find that fine-tuning the pre-trained model by adding MLP can greatly improve the accuracy of prediction. The accuracy of method Erlangshen-Cosine is 13.17% percent higher than that of method BERT-Cosine, it is demonstrated that in the sentence pair task, model Erlangshen-SimCSE-Chinese can better understand the deep meaning of the sentence and performs better than the original BERT.

Table 3. Comparison experiment results

Methods	ACC.
ICE	81.95
Roberta	70.52
Roberta-MLP	83.90
Erlangshen-Cosine	79.02
BERT-Cosine	65.85
Er-EIR	**90.24**

The loss curves for ICE, Roberta-MLP, and Er-EIR throughout the training phase are shown in Fig. 2. It is notable that the loss curve of Er-EIR exhibits a smooth trajectory across the entire training process. Furthermore, Er-EIR displays a rapid initial decrease in loss during the early epochs, followed by successful convergence. This pattern of behavior signifies the effective acquisition of data features by the model, resulting in commendable performance on the university finance question semantic matching dataset.

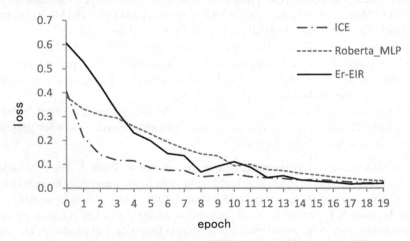

Fig. 2. The training loss curves of ICE, Roberta_MLP and Er-EIR

We present the predictive outcomes of each model for the two sentence pairs in Table 4, where "T → P" signifies the "True label → Predicted label". In the sentence pair (P1, Q1), both sentences share the intention of inquiring whether earphones be reimbursed from the research startup fund. However, sentence P1 incorporates an additional clause "请教计财处老师 (EN: may I ask the teacher from the Department of Finance)", that does not substantively contribute to conveying the actual intention. Only Er-EIR is correct in the prediction results of each model, showcasing the ability of our proposed model to mitigate the impact of irrelevant context. As for the sentence pair (P2, Q2), the primary differences lie in the phrases "评审费 (EN: review fee)" and "讲课费 (EN: lecture fee)", which possess distinct reimbursement criteria in university financial regulations. Only Er-EIR and Roberta produce accurate prediction results, demonstrating that Er-EIR can capture and distinguish the crucial information within the sentence pair. The above analyses demonstrate that our proposed model acquires a profound comprehension of the data features in the university financial question semantic matching dataset. Furthermore, the model proficiently identifies the similarities and differences within sentences.

Table 4. Examples of model prediction result comparison

Sentence pairs	Methods	T → P
P1: 请教计财处老师, 个人科研启动经费可以报销无线耳机吗? (EN: May I ask the teacher from the Department of Finance if I can claim reimbursement for wireless earphones from the personal research startup fund?) Q1: 科研启动金能报耳机吗? (EN: Can earphones be reimbursed from the research startup fund?)	ICE	1 → 0
	Roberta	1 → 0
	Roberta-MLP	1 → 0
	Erlangshen-Cosine	1 → 0
	BERT-Cosine	1 → 0
	Er-EIR	1 → 1
P2: 请问校外专家评审费单笔有限额么? (EN: Is there a limit on the single payment for external expert review fee?) Q2: 校外专家的讲课费有限制吗? (EN: Is there a limit on the lecture fees for external experts?)	ICE	0 → 1
	Roberta	0 → 0
	Roberta-MLP	0 → 1
	Erlangshen-Cosine	0 → 1
	BERT-Cosine	0 → 1
	Er-EIR	0 → 0

4.4 Ablation Experiment

We conducted ablation experiments to further demonstrate the validity of the various modules and features of our proposed model Er-EIR. Five sets of experiments are included, and the specific variations are shown as follows:

1. Er-EIR_char-base: We change the input granularity of the contextual information enhancement encoding layer from word to character. We no longer segment the input

sentences into words and directly use character vectors output from Erlangshen-SimCSE-Chinese model as the input of BiLSTM.

2. Er-EIR$^{-\text{BiLSTM}}$: The variant removes the contextual information enhancement encoding layer. We directly input the vector representations obtained from the word embedding layer into the soft alignment layer.

3. Er-EIR$^{-\text{soft}}$: The variant is similar to Er-EIR$^{-\text{BiLSTM}}$. It removes the soft alignment layer to highlight its effectiveness. We feed the output of the contextual information enhancement encoding layer directly into the feature fusion layer.

4. Er-EIR$^{-\text{BiLSTM, soft}}$: The variant removes both the contextual information enhancement encoding layer and the soft alignment layer and feeds only computed [CLS] features into the feature fusion layer.

5. Er-EIR$^{-\text{CLS}}$: The variant removes computed [CLS] features from the feature fusion layer and keeps only the output of the soft alignment layer.

The results of the ablation experiment are shown in Table 5. The experimental results show that each module of the model is important. We found that compared to char-based representation, word-based can capture the semantics of Chinese sentences more effectively. Er-EIR$^{-\text{BiLSTM}}$ tells us the BiLSTM can enhance contextual information, although the word vector representations output by the pre-trained model already contain some contextual information. In addition, the decrease in the accuracy of Er-EIR$^{-\text{soft}}$ demonstrates the effectiveness of the association information of sentence pair captured by the soft alignment layer. Finally, we found that the features $p_{cls} \times q_{cls}$ and $|p_{cls} - q_{cls}|$ can bring great improvement to the model. We think the interaction information of [CLS] tokens of sentence pair better reflects the semantic differences of sentence pair.

Table 5. Ablation experiment results

Methods	ACC.
Er-EIR_char-base	88.29
Er-EIR$^{-\text{BiLSTM}}$	88.78
Er-EIR$^{-\text{soft}}$	89.27
Er-EIR$^{-\text{BiLSTM, soft}}$	87.80
Er-EIR$^{-\text{CLS}}$	80.49
Er-EIR	**90.24**

5 Conclusion

We believe that establishing a QA system in the field of university finance can improve the current situation of consulting on university finance issues. Semantic matching of questions is the foundation of a retrieval-based QA system. We proposed a model based on sentence feature interaction for intelligent QA. In Er-EIR, we first obtain character-based sentence vector representations by a pre-trained language model, and then obtain word vector representations by averaging the character vectors within words. After that, we enhance the contextual information of the sentences by BiLSTM and obtain the word-level interaction information of the sentence pair through a soft alignment layer. Finally, we fuse the interaction information of sentence-level and word-level and use it to predict the label.

To evaluate the model's efficacy within the realm of university finance, we built a question semantic matching dataset. Firstly, we collected real university finance QA pairs. Then the questions were extracted from them, yielding a corpus comprising 511 positive and 510 negative question pairs, obtained by manual parsing. Experiments on this dataset demonstrate that Er-EIR outperforms baseline models such as Roberta. In the future, we plan to build a university financial QA system and deploy the model in the system to improve the efficiency of university faculty and staff in financial work. Currently, there is a scarcity of Chinese question matching datasets in the financial domain, particularly those focusing on the facet of university financial reimbursement. Our dataset is limited in size since it was collected from real scenarios, we would like to expand the dataset and conduct experiments on larger publicly semantic matching datasets to validate the robustness of our model.

Acknowledgments. This work was partly supported by the National Natural Science Foundation of China under Grant (61972336, 62073284), and Zhejiang Provincial Natural Science Foundation of China under Grant (LY23F020001, LY22F020027, LY19F030008).

References

1. Li, P., et al.: Dataset and neural recurrent sequence labeling model for open-domain factoid question answering. arXiv preprint arXiv:1607.06275 (2016)
2. Wang, D., Wang, W., Wang, S.: Research on domain-specific question answering system oriented natural language understanding: a survey. Comput. Sci. **44**(8), 1–41 (2017)
3. Yu, J., et al.: Modelling domain relationships for transfer learning on retrieval-based question answering systems in e-commerce. In: Proceedings of the Eleventh ACM International Conference on Web Search and Data Mining (WSDM), pp. 682–690. Association for Computing Machinery, New York, NY, USA (2018)
4. Devlin, J., Chang, M.W., Lee, K., Toutanova, K.: BERT: pre-training of deep bidirectional transformers for language understanding. arXiv preprint arXiv:1810.04805 (2018)
5. Wang, J., et al.: Fengshenbang 1.0: being the foundation of Chinese cognitive intelligence. arXiv preprint arXiv:2209.02970 (2022)
6. Gao, T., Yao, X., Chen, D.: SimCSE: simple contrastive learning of sentence embeddings. arXiv preprint arXiv:2104.08821 (2021)
7. Weizenbaum, J.: ELIZA—a computer program for the study of natural language communication between man and machine. Commun. ACM **9**(1), 36–45 (1966)
8. Ferrucci, D., Brown, E., Chu-Carroll, J., Fan, J., Gondek, D., Kalyanpur, A., et al.: Building watson: an overview of the deepqa project. AI Mag. **31**(3), 59–79 (2010)
9. Zhou, L., Gao, J., Li, D., Shum, H.Y.: The design and implementation of XiaoIce, an empathetic social chatbot. Comput. Linguist. **46**(1), 53–93 (2020)
10. Gao, T.: Design and implementation of university financial counseling question answering prototype system based on NLP (基于NLP的高校财务咨询问答原型系统设计与实现). Master's thesis, Beijing Jiaotong University (2020)

11. Chi, Y.: Research on question answering technology of enterprise financial audit based on deep learning (基于深度学习的企业财务审计问答技术研究). Master's thesis, Harbin Engineering University (2018)
12. Wang, Y.: Design and implementation of financial intelligent question answering system based on knowledge graph (基于知识图谱的财务智能问答系统的设计与实现). Master's thesis, Huazhong University of Science and Technology (2020)
13. Zhu, F., et al.: TAT-QA: a question answering benchmark on a hybrid of tabular and textual content in finance. arXiv preprint arXiv:2105.07624 (2021)
14. Zaib, M., Zhang, W.E., Sheng, Q.Z., Mahmood, A., Zhang, Y.: Conversational question answering: a survey. Knowl. Inf. Syst. **64**(12), 3151–3195 (2022)
15. Lu, X., Deng, Y., Sun, T., Gao, Y., Feng, J., Sun, X., et al.: MKPM: multi keyword-pair matching for natural language sentences. Appl. Intell. **52**(2), 1878–1892 (2022)
16. Mikolov, T., Chen, K., Corrado, G., Dean, J.: Efficient estimation of word representations in vector space. arXiv preprint arXiv:1301.3781 (2013)
17. Elman, J.L.: Finding structure in time. Cogn. Sci. **14**(2), 179–211 (1990)
18. Hochreiter, S., Schmidhuber, J.: Long short-term memory. Neural Comput. **9**(8), 1735–1780 (1997)
19. Vaswani, A., Shazeer, N., Parmar, N., et al.: Attention is all you need. In: Advances in Neural Information Processing Systems (NeurIPS), vol. 30, pp. 1-11 (2017)
20. Deng, Y., Li, X., Zhang, M., Lu, X., Sun, X.: Enhanced distance-aware self-attention and multi-level match for sentence semantic matching. Neurocomputing **501**, 174–187 (2022)
21. Parikh, A.P., Täckström, O., Das, D., Uszkoreit, J.: A decomposable attention model for natural language inference. arXiv preprint arXiv:1606.01933 (2016)
22. Su, J.: Text emotion classification (IV): better loss function (2017). https://spaces.ac.cn/arc hives/4293
23. Kingma, D.P., Ba, J.: Adam: a method for stochastic optimization. arXiv preprint arXiv:1412. 6980 (2014)
24. Zhang, X., Li, Y., Lu, W., Jian, P., Zhang, G.: Intra-correlation encoding for Chinese sentence intention matching. In: Proceedings of the 28th International Conference on Computational Linguistics (COLING), pp. 5193–5204. International Committee on Computational Linguistics, Barcelona, Spain (2020)
25. Chen, J., Chen, Q., Liu, X., Yang, H., Lu, D., Tang, B.: The BQ corpus: a large-scale domain-specific Chinese corpus for sentence semantic equivalence identification. In: Proceedings of the Conference on Empirical Methods in Natural Language Processing (EMNLP), pp. 4946–4951. Association for Computational Linguistics, Brussels, Belgium (2018)
26. Liu, Y., Ott, M., Goyal, N., Du, J., Joshi, M., Chen, D.: RoBERTa: a robustly optimized BERT pretraining approach. arXiv preprint arXiv:1907.11692 (2019)
27. Lu, W., et al.: Chinese sentence semantic matching based on multi-level relevance extraction and aggregation for intelligent human–robot interaction. Appl. Soft Comput. **131**, 109795 (2022)

MOOC Dropout Prediction Using Learning Process Model and LightGBM Algorithm

Hejing Nie[1], Yiping Wen[1,2(✉)], Buqing Cao[1], and Bowen Liang[1]

[1] School of Computer Science and Engineering, Hunan University of Science and Technology, Xiangtan 411201, China
ypwen81@gmail.com
[2] The 14Th Five-Year Plan" Research Base for Education Science, Education Informatization Research Base-Technology Application Direction, Hunan, China

Abstract. With the development and widespread application of Massive Open Online Courses (MOOC) platforms, the issue of reducing learners' dropout has become a challenge. Therefore, it is necessary to accurately predict whether a learner will complete the course or not. Existing researches mainly use machine learning methods to predict MOOC dropout, which still face challenges such as inadequate explanation and low prediction accuracy. In view of these problems, this paper proposes a MOOC dropout prediction method using learning process model and LightGBM algorithm. This method utilizes the learning process model to analyze learning behavior and generate feature vectors to provide a clear interpretation. Based on these feature vectors, the LightGBM algorithm is adopted to predict dropout. Compared to the related methods, the dropout prediction method proposed in this paper demonstrates improvements of 1.58%, 1.2%, 1.1%, and 0.864% in Recall, F1, Precision, and AUC respectively.

Keywords: MOOC · Dropout · Prediction · Feature Engineering

1 Introduction

With the popularity of Internet technology in the education industry, the online education industry is developing rapidly. Massive Open Online Courses (MOOCs) have gained significant popularity worldwide due to their unique advantages, such as course openness, material sharing, and educational autonomy. MOOCs address the limitations of traditional education methods and have attracted tens of thousands of learners globally [1]. However, the high degree of user selectivity and the absence of course monitoring mechanisms have contributed to a considerably high dropout rate among learners on MOOC platforms. This high dropout rate severely hampers the popularity and growth of these platforms [2]. To reduce the high dropout rate on MOOC platforms, a dropout prediction model is established by collecting relevant data such as learners' learning behavior and course information. Based on the prediction results, artificial reminders and interventions are implemented for learners who are likely to dropout. This has significant practical significance for addressing the issue of high dropout rates on MOOC platforms [3].

Y. Sun et al. (Eds.): ChineseCSCW 2023, CCIS 2012, pp. 121–136, 2024.
https://doi.org/10.1007/978-981-99-9637-7_9

Research on dropout prediction for MOOC platforms can be categorized into two groups. The first group consists of machine learning-based methods, where researchers manually select and extract factors that they believe are relevant to learner dropout. However, this introduces subjectivity, and the challenge lies in automatically identifying factors that truly impact learners' final outcomes based on data features. The second group focuses on deep learning prediction methods. However, these models are often considered black box models, limiting their interpretability. Current research methods face two primary issues: incomplete information expressed by feature modeling and a lack of interpretability.

We propose a learning process model in feature engineering that comprehensively analyzes learning behavior. This model bridges the issues of the above research methods. By incorporating parameters based on physical formulas, we characterize learners' learning progress through interpretable fluid flow processes. Moreover, we enhance prediction credibility by utilizing interpretable prediction algorithms. In summary, this paper makes the following significant contributions:

(1) We introduce the Learning Process Model (LPM) for the first time, which aims to explicitly model learners' learning behavior, enhancing the accuracy and interpretability of its representation.
(2) We propose a MOOC dropout prediction method that combines the LPM and LightGBM classification prediction method. This method achieves high prediction accuracy and interpretability.
(3) With the KDD CUP 2015 dataset, the experimental results demonstrate that the LPM-LightGBM method guarantees high overall prediction accuracy.

2   Related Work

In 2012, prestigious universities in the United States launched online MOOC platforms, providing free internet courses [2]. However, the growing popularity of MOOC platforms has highlighted the problem of high student dropout rates. To tackle this issue, researchers have extensively utilized machine learning and deep learning techniques to analyze learner behaviors and predict dropout likelihood [3].

Research on dropout prediction in machine learning typically involves using machine learning algorithms to predict whether learners will dropout or not. These methods are known for their simplicity and interpretability, making them accessible and easy to understand. For example, Nithya et al. [4] used feature selection techniques and various machine learning models such as SVM, LR, and DT for prediction. Kloft et al. [5] developed a clickstream-based SVM model to predict dropout in MOOCs. Lu et al. used an SVM model to predict certificate attainment in MOOC learners. Liang et al. constructed a gradient-boosted decision tree model to predict dropout rates with a high accuracy of 89%. Amnueyporsakul et al. analyzed submission behavior and learner interaction using data mining techniques and employed SVM for classification. Chen et al. [6] proposed a decision tree-based dropout prediction method for MOOCs, but faced challenges due to high-dimensional features and model complexity. Traditional machine learning methods rely heavily on data quality and require laborious feature engineering. Therefore, developing efficient feature sets through feature extraction and identification is a key focus of research.

Deep learning models have shown remarkable learning and adaptive capabilities compared to traditional machine learning methods. Researchers have explored the use of deep learning models for predicting learner learning outcomes. For instance, Shou et al. [7] developed a multi-scale convolution network with a variational information bottleneck technique to mitigate noise impact. Fu et al. [8] utilized convolutional neural networks and Bi-LSTM to extract high-dimensional and long-memory features. Basnet et al. [9] compared deep learning models with traditional machine learning models for MOOC dropout prediction. Zheng et al. [10] proposed the FWTS-CNN model, which filters and ranks behavioral features based on importance. Tang et al. [11] introduced an RNN-based prediction model with an AUC value of 88.1%. Wang et al. [12] proposed the E-LSTM model, effectively incorporating event and time information for dropout prediction. However, the interpretability and explicit modeling of learner behavioral features remain challenges for deep learning methods in feature construction and classification.

From the analysis conducted above, the previous methods have a limitation in that they do not explicitly model the learner's learning behavior. In this study, we aim to address this limitation by considering the impact of different types of learning behaviors and their corresponding time on dropout likelihood. We explicitly model the learning process and generate feature vectors that are highly interpretable. To achieve this, we combine the LPM with the LightGBM model. By utilizing LPM for in-depth analysis of learner behavior and employing LightGBM for dropout prediction, we construct an interpretable model for predicting MOOC dropouts.

3   Problem Description and Related Definition

This paper aims to address the problem of predicting dropout risk in online learning platforms. By analyzing learners' behavior logs and final learning outcomes, the objective is to generate effective features that represent their learning situations. These features are then used in a classification model to identify learners who are at risk of dropout. The definitions related to this problem are provided below:

Definition 1: Learning Behavior Logs. A learner's learning behavior log can be described as $B = <Id, T, B\_type>$. Among them, Id represents the unique registration number of the learner associated with the current learning behavior log. T represents the timestamp indicating the time when the current learning behavior log occurs. B_type represents the specific type of the current learning behavior log.

Definition 2: Learners and Learning Outcomes. Learners can be described by a set $S = \{s_1,...,s_n\}$. The learners' final learning outcomes, which means whether they complete the courses or not, can be divided into real learning outcomes and predictive learning outcomes, which are described as $\widehat{Y} = <Id, R>$ and $Y = <Id, R>$, respectively. Here, $R \in \{0,1\}$, where 0 represents not dropout and 1 represents dropout.

4 Proposed Method

4.1 Basic Idea of LPM-LightGBM

We propose a method named LPM-LightGBM for predicting learners' dropout. The method analyzes the learning behavior logs using the LPM, we generate a well-interpretable feature vector. These feature vectors are then combined with the LightGBM prediction algorithm to predict learners' dropout.

Specifically, the LPM-LightGBM method is described by Algorithm 1, which primarily comprises LPM construction, feature vector extraction, LightGBM model training, and dropout prediction. The crucial aspect of this method is the utilization of the LPM to analyze the learning behavior logs and extract the learning process feature vectors.

Algorithm 1: LPM-LightGBM

Inputs: B: Learner's learning behavior logs

$\quad\quad\quad$ S: All learners

$\quad\quad\quad$ $\hat{Y}$: Learners' real learning outcomes

Output: Y: Learners' predictive learning outcomes

1. $X = LearningProcess\ (B, S, \hat{Y})$
2. $F(X) = LightGBM\_training\ (X, \hat{Y})$
3. $Y = LPM\_LightGBM\_Predictor\ (F(X), B)$
4. *Return Y*

The LPM-LightGBM algorithm comprises the following main steps:

Step 1 (Line 1): LPM construction and feature vector extraction. We construct the LPM based on the learning behavior logs B. This analysis helps us derive the learning behavior feature vectors $X_i \in X$ for each learner $s_i \in S$, where X represents the set of learning behavior feature vectors of all learners.

Step 2 (Line 2): LightGBM model training. According to the learning behavior feature vector set X generated in step 1, the LightGBM model is trained until the preset training times are completed.

Step 3 (Lines 3–4): Dropout prediction. Using the trained LPM-LightGBM, we can predict the learning outcome of whether the learner chooses to dropout.

4.2 LPM Construction and Feature Vector Extraction

In the study of opinion formation in online social networks [13], three factors influence users' opinions: friends, public channels, and intrinsic views. These factors are represented as containers, with users, friends, public channels, and internal opinions being the entities. The fluid temperature within each container symbolizes opinions, while the fluid height remains constant. Pipes of varying cross-sectional areas simulate the impact of friends, public channels, and internal opinions on opinion formation. Fluid flow between containers models the process of opinion formation. Ultimately, the fluid temperature within a user's container represents their opinion, and the fluid volume indicates its persistence.

In this paper, the process of analyzing learners' learning behaviors is analogous to the process of analyzing users' opinions as discussed in the literature [13]. Consequently, we draw on the concepts such as containers, fluid temperature, and fluid volume. The learner's types of learning behaviors are represented by containers r_m, where the fluid temperature in container r_m reflects the influence of learning behavior time on learning outcomes. The cross-sectional area of pipes represents the degree of influence of the learning behavior type on learning outcomes. Blank containers $a_{m,i}$ recording the learner's learning process, where the fluid temperature in container $a_{m,i}$ represents temporal features of the learner's learning behavior and the fluid volume in container $a_{m,i}$ represents features related to the type and duration of the learning behavior. Table 1 summarizes the key concepts and parameters in the LPM.

Table 1. Concepts and notations related to LPM.

Concept	Notation	Description
Types of learning behaviors	B_type	Different types of learning behaviors
Time for learning behaviors	T	The time interval of learning behavior
Learning behavior container	r_m	Different types of learning behavior logs
Learner container corresponding to r_m and learner s_i	$a_{m,i}$	Record the learning process of learner s_i
Cross-sectional area of the pipe connecting r_m and $a_{m,i}$	$w_{ra,mi}$	Information gain of learning behavior type variables
Fluid temperature in container r_m	O_{rm}	Information gain of time variables of learning behavior
Fluid temperature in container $a_{m,i}$	$O_{am,i}$	The features of learners' learning behavior in time dimension
Fluid volume in container $a_{m,i}$	$H_{am,i}$	The features of learners' learning behavior in type and duration of learning
Time interval of knowledge forgetting	t_s	During the time interval t_s, learners do not engage in learning behavior, leading to a decline in their knowledge mastery
Fluid height reduction ratio	τ	The situation of learners' knowledge forgetting
Feature vector set	X	The fluid temperature and fluid volume in the containers $a_{m,i}$ from the analysis of learning behavior by LPM

The specific implementation of LPM construction and feature vector extraction is shown in Algorithm 2:

Algorithm 2: *LearningProcess*

Inputs: *B*: Learner's learning behavior logs

    S: All learners

    Ŷ: Learners' real learning outcomes

Output: *X*: Feature vector set

---

1. $w_{ra,mi}$=*InforGain* (*B_type*, *Ŷ*)

2. O_{rm}=*InforGain* (*T*, *Ŷ*)

3. *for each* $s_i{\in}S$ *do*

4. $a_{m,i}$=Ø

5.   *b*=*find* (s_i, *B*)

6.   *for each nonvoid subset of b corresponding to the same learning behavior do*

7.   *Capacity*=*Volume*$_{ra,mi}$ (H_{rm}, $w_{ra,mi}$)

8.   *if* $a_{m,i}{\neq}Ø$ *do*

9. $H_{am,i}$=*Volume*$_{am,i}^{(n)}$(*Volume*$_{am,i}^{(n-1)}$, *Capacity*)

10. $O_{am,i}$=*Temp* ($O_{am,i}^{(n-1)}$, O_{rm}, *Volume*$_{am,i}^{(n-1)}$, *Capacity*)

11.   *if* $b_j.T - b_{j-1}.T > t_s$ *do*

12. $H_{am,i}$=*Reduce* ($H_{am,i}$)

13. $X_i{\leftarrow}H_{am,i}$, $X_i{\leftarrow}O_{am,i}$

14. *return X*

The *LearningProcess* algorithm comprises the following main steps:

Step 1 (Lines 1–2): LPM construction. In this stage, in order to construct the cross-sectional area $w_{ra,mi}$ of the pipe connecting container r_m and container $a_{m,i}$ in Fig. 1, we begin by extracting various types of learning behavior $B\_type = \{b_t^1, b_t^2, ..., b_t^i, ...b_t^n\}$ and assess their degree of influence on the learning outcome using the information gain method. The degree of influence is quantified as $w_{ra,mi}$, and its calculation is described by Eqs. 1 and 2:

$$H(A) = -\sum\nolimits_{i=1}^{n} p(a_i)\log p(a_i) \tag{1}$$

$$H(D|A) = \sum\nolimits_{x{\in}X} p(a)H(D|A = a) \tag{2}$$

The information gain is computed as the difference between information entropy and conditional entropy. Equation 1 presents the formula for information entropy, where $p(a_i)$ represents the probability of random event A being a_i. Equation 2 illustrates the formula for conditional entropy, with $H(D|A)$ representing the uncertainty of random variable D under the condition that random variable A is known. When evaluating $w_{ra,mi}$, random variable A corresponds to the type of learning behaviors, while random variable D corresponds to the learner's actual outcome $\hat{Y}$.

For example, to determine the fluid temperature O_{rm} in the container r_m in Fig. 1, we analyze learning behaviors within different time intervals T. Previous studies [14] suggest a 10-day time window for effective feature generation in the prediction model.

Thus, we divide the occurrence time T of the learning behavior log into three intervals (t_1, t_2, t_3), each lasting 10 days. Information gain assesses the influence of T on learning outcomes, denoted as O_{rm}. Here, the random variable A represents the time of the learning behavior, while D represents the learner's actual learning outcome $\hat{Y}$.

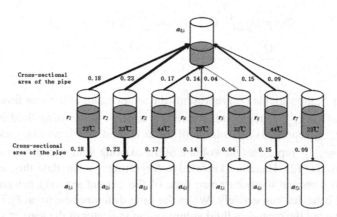

Fig. 1. An example of learning process model. The learning behavior containers r_m represent the different types of learning behavior logs. Learner containers $a_{m,i}$ corresponding to r_m and learner s_i represent record the learning process of learner s_i. The fluid temperature and fluid volume in the containers $a_{m,i}$ represents the feature vector generated by the LPM.

Step 2 (Lines 3–7): Analysis of learning behavior. we set containers $a_{m,i}$ to empty and find all the learned behaviors b of learner s_i. Then, we find the corresponding container r_m according to the B_type of b so that the fluid flows into the connected container $a_{m,i}$. The volume of the fluid is calculated using the function $Volume_{ra,mi}$. The function $Volume_{ra,mi}$ can be described using Eq. 3.

$$Volume_{ra,mi}(H_{rm}, w_{ra,mi}) = \sqrt{2gH_{rm}} \times w_{ra,mi} \times \Delta \qquad (3)$$

In the Eq. 3, Δ represents the duration of the fluid flow from container r_m to container $a_{m,i}$, which corresponds to the duration of the learning behavior. The formula for the velocity of fluid outflow from container r_m is denoted by $\sqrt{2gH_{rm}}$, while H_{rm} represents the height of the fluid in container r_m measured from the bottom of the container. Additionally, g denotes the acceleration of gravity, and $w_{ra,mi}$ represents the cross-sectional area of the pipe connecting container r_m to container $a_{m,i}$.

Step 3 (Lines 8–10): Analysis of the comprehensive learning situation of current learning behavior types. If container $a_{m,i}$ is not empty, we calculate the total volume of fluid in container $a_{m,i}$ after the new fluid inflow using the $Volume_{am,i}^{(n)}$ function, which can be described by Eq. 4.

$$Volume_{am,i}^{(n)}(Volume_{am,i}^{(n-1)}, Volume_{ra,mi}) = Volume_{am,i}^{(n-1)} + Volume_{ra,mi} \qquad (4)$$

We assume that the container $a_{m,i}$ already holds a volume of fluid denoted as $Volume_{am,i}^{(n-1)}$, and there is an inflow of new fluid with a volume of $Volume_{ra,mi}$. To simplify the calculations, we set the cross-sectional area of all containers to be 1. Thus, the volume of the fluid inside the containers and the height of the fluid are considered equivalent.

We calculate the temperature of the mixed fluid in container $a_{m,i}$ after the inflow of the new fluid using the *Temp* function. The *Temp* function can be expressed by Eq. 5.

$$Temp(O_{am,i}^{(n-1)}, O_{rm}, Volume_{am,i}^{(n-1)}, Volume_{ra,mi})$$
$$= \frac{O_{am,i}^{(n-1)} \times Volume_{am,i}^{(n-1)} + O_{rm} \times Volume_{ra,mi}}{Volume_{am,i}^{(n)}} \tag{5}$$

In the Eq. 5, the variable O_{rm} represents the temperature of the new fluid that flows into container r_m. $O_{am,i}^{(n-1)}$ represents the temperature of the existing fluid in container $a_{m,i}$. $Volume_{ra,mi}$ represents the volume of the new fluid that flows into container $a_{m,i}$. Lastly, $Volume_{am,i}^{(n-1)}$ represents the volume of the existing fluid in container $a_{m,i}$.

Step 4 (Lines 11–12): Handling knowledge forgetting. To simulate this, we use $b_j.T$ and $b_{j-1}.T$ to represent the occurrence time of the current learning behavior and the last learning behavior, respectively. When the time difference between $b_j.T$ and $b_{j-1}.T$ exceeds t_s, we use the change in fluid volume as an indicator of the learner's forgetting. The reduction in fluid volume is calculated using the $Reduce(H_{am,i})$ function, defined by Eq. 6.

$$Reduce(H_{am,i}) = H_{am,i} \times (1 - \tau) \tag{6}$$

In the Eq. 6, the variable τ represents the ratio of the reduction in fluid height in container $a_{m,i}$, while $H_{am,i}$ represents the original fluid volume in container $a_{m,i}$.

Step 5 (Lines 13–14): Generation of the feature vector set of learning behaviors. When the LPM analyzes all the learning behavior logs of learner s_i, the volume and temperature of the fluid in container $a_{m,i}$ of the LPM are returned as the learner's learning behavior feature vectors, denoted as X_i.

4.3   LightGBM Model Training

LightGBM is an improved algorithm derived from GBDT (Gradient Boosting Decision Tree), offering fast computation and high accuracy [15]. In this paper, we employ Light-GBM to process the learning behavior feature vectors generated by LPM and predict learner dropout likelihood. The training process is outlined in Algorithm 3, which is utilized to construct the LightGBM_training method in Algorithm 1.

Algorithm 3: *LightGBM_training*

Inputs: X: Feature vector set

　　　　$\hat{Y}$: Learners' real learning outcomes

Output: $F(X)$: A strong learner

1. $Y=Predict(X)$

2. $loss=Loss\ (Y,\hat{Y})$

3. $f_i(X)=DecisionTree(loss)$

4. $F(X)=IntegratedDecisionTree\ (f_i(X))$

5. ***return*** $F(X)$

Step 1 (Line 1): Prediction of learners' learning outcomes. According to the LPM, we generate a set of learning behavior feature vector set $X = \{x_1, x_2,\ldots, x_i,\ldots, x_n\}$ to predict the learning outcome. Here, $x_i \in \mathbb{R}^d$ represents the feature vector representation of the learner, and d represents the dimension of the vector. We use the *Predict* function to forecast the learning outcome, which can be described by Eqs. 7 and 8.

$$Y = \sum_{k=1}^{K} f_k(X), f_k \in \Gamma \tag{7}$$

$$\Gamma = \{f(X) = \omega_{q(X)}\}(q: R^m \rightarrow T, \omega \in \mathbb{R}^T) \tag{8}$$

In the Eqs. 7 and 8, Y represents the predicted value indicating whether a learner will dropout. K represents the number of regression trees, and f_k represents an independent tree structure that can be mapped to the corresponding leaf node T. Each regression tree is part of the same regression tree space Γ, and ω represents the leaf weight.

Step 2 (Line 2): Calculation of the loss function. Upon obtaining the predicted values in step 1, we calculate the loss function of LightGBM using the *Loss* function. The calculation process of the *Loss* function can be described by Eqs. 9 and 10, which consist of two parts: the loss value and the regularization term.

$$Loss = \sum_{i=1}^{n} l\left(\hat{Y}, Y\right) + \sum_{k=1}^{K} \Phi(f_k) \tag{9}$$

$$\Phi(f_k) = \gamma T + \frac{1}{2}\lambda|\omega|^2 \tag{10}$$

In the Eqs. 9 and 10, $l\left(\hat{Y}, Y\right)$ represents the loss function, $\hat{Y}$ represents the learner's real dropout outcome, and $\sum_{k=1}^{K} \Phi(f_k)$ represents the regularization term, which is shown in Eq. 9. In Eq. 10, γ represents the penalty term coefficient. After regularization can control the complexity of the model and prevent overfitting. To simplify the calculation of the loss value, Eq. 9 is further simplified, and its second-order Taylor expansion can be obtained.

$$Loss_i^{(t)} \approx \sum_{i=1}^{n} l(Y, Y^{(t)}) + \sum_{i=1}^{t} \Phi(f_i)$$

$$= \sum_{i=1}^{n} l\left(Y, Y^{(t-1)} + f_t(x_i)\right) + \Phi(f_t) + constant \qquad (11)$$

$$= \sum_{i=1}^{n} [l(Y, Y^{(t-1)}) + g_i f_t(x_i) + \tfrac{1}{2} h_i f_t^2(x_i)] + \Phi(f_t) + constant$$

In the Eq. 11, $g_i = \partial_{Y^{(t-1)}i} l(Y, Y^{(t-1)})$ represents the first-order derivative of the previous round of predictions and $h_i = \partial^2_{Y^{(t-1)}i} l(Y, Y^{(t-1)})$ represents the second-order derivative of the Loss function. Equation 11 can be simplified as follows.

$$Loss_i^{(t)} \approx \sum_{j=1}^{T} [(\sum_{i \in I_j} g_i) \omega_j + \frac{1}{2} (\sum_{i \in I_j} h_i + \lambda) \omega_j^2] + \gamma T \qquad (12)$$

Step 3 (Line 3): Construction of a decision tree. We construct a decision tree based on the obtained loss function from step 2, as shown in Eq. 13.

$$f_i(X) = f_{i-1}(X) + \sum_{j=1}^{T} [(\sum_{i \in I_j} g_i) \omega_j + \frac{1}{2} (\sum_{i \in I_j} h_i + \lambda) \omega_j^2] \qquad (13)$$

Step 4 (Line 4): Integration of decision trees. We partition the decision tree by calculating the importance of the features. Through iteration, we aim to find the decision tree with the optimal structure $F(X)$. The decision trees generated in each round are then linearly summed to obtain the final regression tree structure, as illustrated in Eq. 14. The process of creating new decision trees is stopped either when the information gain is below a certain threshold or when the maximum depth of the tree is reached [16].

$$F(X) = \partial_0 f_0(X) + \partial_1 f_1(X) + \cdots + \partial_m f_m(X) \qquad (14)$$

In the Eq. 14, $F(X)$ represents a strong learner, $f_m(X)$ represents a weak learner, ∂_m represents the weight coefficient of the m-th weak learner, and its value is denoted as γT.

5   Experimental Evaluation

5.1   Dataset

The dataset used in this paper is the KDD CUP 2015 dataset sourced from "Xuedang Online," China's largest MOOC platform. It includes 39 courses, 120,543 registered learners, and 8,157,277 learning behavior logs recorded between 2013 and 2014. The dataset captures the learning behaviors of learners for over 40 days. For this study, we utilized the learning behavior logs from the first 30 days as model inputs. The last 10 days of learning behavior logs were used to determine if the learner dropped out or continued. Learners without recorded behavior in the last 10 days were marked as dropouts, while those with recorded behavior were labeled as continuing learners.

In this paper, we randomly selected 50,000 learners and their 2,958,710 learning behaviors for the experiment. We analyzed the logs of learning behaviors and generated feature vectors using the LPM. These feature vectors were then inputted into the LightGBM for dropout prediction.

5.2 Evaluation Metrics

In the experiment, we utilize the AUC value, recall rate (Recall), F1 value, and accuracy (Precision) as evaluation metrics to assess the prediction performance of the LPM-LightGBM. The calculation formulas for these four evaluation indicators are presented as follows (Eqs. 15–18). In the Eq. 15, $AUROC$ represents the area below the ROC curve.

$$AUC = (2 \times AUROC) - 1 \qquad (15)$$

$$Recall = \frac{\text{The sample size of learners correctly classified as dropputs}}{\text{The sample size of dropout learners}} \qquad (16)$$

$$Precision = \frac{\text{The sample size of learners correctly classified as dropputs}}{\text{The sample size of learners identified as dropouts}} \qquad (17)$$

$$F1 = \frac{2 \times Precision \times Recall}{Precision + Recall} \qquad (18)$$

5.3 Experimental Results and Analysis

This paper analyzes the effects of different types of learning behaviors and key parameters. For simplicity, we only list the results of *Precision* values on the dataset. Table 2 presents the *Precision* values for all learning behavior types, as well as the *Precision* value when one learning behavior type is ignored. The main findings are as follows:

(1) Each learning behavior type has its influence, and ignoring any one learning behavior type leads to a decrease in the *Precision* value. This indicates that each learning behavior type plays a role in improving the prediction results.
(2) Among the different learning behavior types, accessing coursework other than videos and assignments b_t^2 has the greatest impact on learner outcomes. Conversely, accessing the course Wikipedia b_t^3 has the least impact on learner outcomes.

In this paper, we conducted univariate experiments on the DoT = 20% dataset to investigate the effects of specific hyperparameters on the performance of the LPM-LightGBM model. The hyperparameters examined were the knowledge forgetting time interval (t_s) with values of 5, 7, 10, and 15, and the ratio of fluid height reduction (τ) with values of 0.2, 0.15, 0.1, and 0.05.

(1) Knowledge forgetting time interval (t_s): The t_s parameter represents the decline in learners' knowledge mastery when there is no learning behavior within a specific time interval. Increasing the t_s value appropriately can capture the learner's forgetting process. However, setting t_s too high may deviate from the real situation. From the experimental results shown in Table 3(a), it can be concluded that the LPM-LightGBM achieves the best performance when $t_s = 10$.
(2) Ratio of fluid height reduction (τ): The τ parameter represents the extent to which learners have forgotten knowledge. Higher values of τ indicate greater knowledge loss. However, both excessively small and large values of τ do not accurately reflect learners' forgotten knowledge. Based on the experimental results in Table 3(b), the best performance of the LPM-LightGBM is obtained when $\tau=0.1$.

Table 2. The influence of learning behavior types on the performance of the LPM-LightGBM

Learning behavior types	Precision
b_t^1, b_t^2,b_t^3, b_t^4, b_t^5,b_t^6, b_t^7	88.80%
b_t^2,b_t^3, b_t^4, b_t^5,b_t^6,b_t^7	88.00%
b_t^1,b_t^3, b_t^4, b_t^5,b_t^6,b_t^7	87.73%
b_t^1,b_t^2, b_t^4, b_t^5,b_t^6,b_t^7	88.20%
b_t^1,b_t^2, b_t^3, b_t^5,b_t^6,b_t^7	88.07%
b_t^1,b_t^2, b_t^3, b_t^4,b_t^6,b_t^7	87.79%
b_t^1,b_t^2, b_t^3, b_t^4,b_t^5,b_t^7	87.97%
b_t^1, b_t^2,b_t^3, b_t^4, b_t^5,b_t^6	87.82%

Table 3. Performances of the LPM-LightGBM with different parameter values

(a) Knowledge forgetting time interval		(b) Ratio of fluid height reduction	
The value of t_s	Precision	The value of τ	Precision
5	87.1%	0.2	87.6%
7	88.3%	0.15	87.9%
10	88.8%	0.1	88.8%
15	88.2%	0.05	88.5%

The paper utilizes the LPM-LightGBM to predict whether learners will choose to dropout. The evaluation of the experiment includes several performance metrics: AUC value, recall rate (Recall), F1 value, and accuracy rate (Precision). The results of the final dropout prediction are as follows: AUC value of 88.5%, Recall of 98.58%, Precision of 88.8%, and F1 value of 93.4%.

The dataset for this experiment was divided into training and test sets in an 8:2 ratio. To enhance the performance of the LightGBM, the following adjustments were made to its parameters: (1) To prevent overfitting, the maximum depth of the training tree was set between 8 and 12, with a step size of 1. The number of leaf nodes was set between 10 and 50, with a step size of 10. (2) The learning rate was set to 0.07, which was determined to be the optimal value through a grid search. (3) To reduce model complexity, the data sampling used in the iteration process was set between 0.7 and 1, with a step size of 0.1. (4) The default values of the other model parameters were used. The optimal parameters of the final model are presented in Table 4.

Table 4. Setting of the parameter values on the LightGBM

Notation	Parameter	Value
num_leaves	The number of leaf nodes	10
learning_rate	The learning rate	0.07
bagging_fraction	Data sampling	0.9
max_depth	The maximum depth of the training tree	11
n_estimators	The maximum number of iterations	150

5.4 Comparative Experiment I

To further validate the effectiveness of the LPM-LightGBM method proposed in this paper, we compared it with the following methods used in other studies. The experimental results comparison is shown in Table 5.

(1) SVM [4]: This method uses real-time data to extract features for predicting early learners' dropout rate with SVM. However, SVM may not capture nonlinear relationships well, and the dropout problem is not necessarily linear. In contrast, the proposed LPM-LightGBM method effectively models the nonlinear relationship between learning behavior and dropout behavior using LightGBM.

(2) AdaBoost [9]: This method fits a classifier on the dataset and multiple replicas, adjusting weights for misclassified instances. However, manual feature and parameter selection limit its flexibility. In contrast, the proposed LPM-LightGBM method automatically analyzes learner's learning behavior logs and generates features based on the LPM.

(3) CLSA [8]: This pipeline model uses learner behavioral data, employing convolutional neural networks to extract local high-dimensional features and Bi-LSTM to capture hidden long-term memory features in the time series. The attention mechanism assigns weights to enhance performance.

(4) MFCN-VIB [7]: This method uses a multiscale fully convolutional network to extract features from student behavior time-series data, suppressing noise with the variational information bottleneck. However, it lacks differentiation of the importance of different learning behaviors. In contrast, the proposed method in this paper calculates information gain to reduce noise and distinguish the significance of learning behaviors.

(5) FCA [17]: This method evaluates classification by mining time rules at different confidence levels and time slots. However, it only considers the time dimension of learning behavior. In contrast, the proposed method in this paper considers both time and the impact of different learning behavior types.

(6) LightGBM [15]: This method directly applies LightGBM for dropout prediction without utilizing the LPM. Its performance is inferior to the proposed LPM-LightGBM due to the lack of in-depth analysis of learning behavior.

Based on the above analysis, the LPM-LightGBM proposed in this paper outperforms the baseline method in four evaluation indicators. When compared to the best method

Table 5. Results of comparative experiment I

Method	AUC	Recall	F1	Precision
SVM [4]	85%	97%	91%	86%
AdaBoost [9]	87.636%	92.4%	89.9%	86.3%
CLSA [8]	87.6%	86.5%	86.9%	87.4%
MFCN-VIB [7]	87.2%	96.0%	92.2%	87.7%
FCA [17]	87.32%	96.41%	86.2%	84.58%
LightGBM [15]	86.2%	94.3%	89.9%	86.0%
LPM-LightGBM	**88.5%**	**98.58%**	**93.4%**	**88.8%**

in the control group, the Recall index improved by 1.58%, the AUC index improved by 0.864%, the F1 index improved by 1.2%, and the Precision index improved by 1.1%.

Traditional methods often rely on subjective domain expertise for manual feature selection, resulting in information loss and decreased model performance. Deep learning, while powerful, is often seen as a black box with limited interpretability. In contrast, this paper introduces the LPM-LightGBM, which considers the importance of learning behavior types and time during feature engineering. By utilizing a LPM with strong physical meaning and incorporating parameters derived from physical formulas, this method achieves both accuracy and interpretability.

5.5 Comparative Experiment II

To validate the effectiveness of the LPM in extracting feature vectors, we conduct experiments using the number of learners' learning behaviors commonly used in previous studies. These feature vectors are then utilized in six machine learning methods (Light-GBM, RF, Logistic, Tree, GBDT, and AdaBoost) to predict learners' dropout status. The experimental results can be found in Table 6.

Comparing the experimental results, the result of dropout prediction using the learning behavior feature vector generated by the LPM proposed in this paper is better than that of directly using the learner's learning behavior times as the feature vector. The combination of the LPM with LightGBM achieves the highest performance, with an AUC of 88.5%, Recall of 98.58%, Precision of 88.8%, and F1 of 93.4%. Feature engineering without the LPM improves AUC by 2.3%, recall by 4.28%, precision by 3.5%, and F1 by 2.8%. When using RF, Logistic, Tree, GBDT, and AdaBoost for classification, feature engineering with the LPM outperforms without it. RF shows improvements of 2.6% in AUC, 3.4% in F1, 2.7% in recall, and 3.6% in precision. GBDT exhibits the smallest improvement with a 1.5% increase in AUC, 1% in recall, 0.6% in F1, and 2.4% in precision.

The experimental results indicate that the LPM incorporates the timing and type of learning behavior, extracting meaningful information to create a comprehensive feature vector. This feature vector effectively captures the learners' learning situation and enhances the accuracy of classification predictions.

Table 6. Results of comparative experiment II

Method	AUC	Recall	F1	Precision
RF	82.9%	83.5%	82.0%	82.0%
LPM-RF	**85.5%**	**86.2%**	**85.4%**	**85.6%**
Logistic	84.2%	84.3%	83.1%	84.0%
LPM-Logistic	**85.8%**	**86.6%**	**85.4%**	**85.2%**
Tree	76.8%	78.0%	78.7%	77.5%
LPM-Tree	**78.9%**	**79.4%**	**79.9%**	**79.8%**
GBDT	84.5%	85.4%	84.9%	84.0%
LPM-GBDT	**86.0%**	**86.4%**	**85.5%**	**86.4%**
AdaBoost	83.9%	84.6%	83.5%	82.0%
LPM-AdaBoost	**85.8%**	**86.7%**	**86.8%**	**85.9%**
LightGBM	86.2%	94.3%	89.9%	86.0%
LPM-LightGBM	**88.5%**	**98.58%**	**93.4%**	**88.8%**

6   Summary and Outlook

To tackle the issue of high dropout rates among learners on MOOC platforms, we propose the LPM-LightGBM method for predicting learner dropout. This method leverages the LPM to generate comprehensive learning behavior characteristics based on the analysis of learners' behaviors and corresponding timestamps. By employing LightGBM, we accurately classify dropout likelihood. Evaluation of the LPM-LightGBM method demonstrates its effectiveness across metrics such as AUC, Recall, F1, and Precision. Future work involves exploring the impact of learning modules and behavior sources on final outcomes while enhancing dropout prediction accuracy.

Acknowledgment. This work was supported by the National Natural Science Foundation of China (No. 62177014), and Research Foundation of Hunan Provincial Education Department of China (No.20B222).

References

1. Wang, W., Zhao, Y., Wu, Y.J., et al.: Factors of dropout from MOOCs: a bibliometric review. Libr. Hi Tech **41**(2), 432–453 (2023)
2. Zhang, S., Che, S.P., Nan, D., et al.: MOOCs as a research agenda: changes over time. Int. Rev. Res. Open Distrib. Learn. **23**(4), 193–210 (2022)
3. Chen, J., Fang, B., Zhang, H., et al.: A systematic review for MOOC dropout prediction from the perspective of machine learning. Interact. Learn. Environ. 1–14 (2022)
4. Nithya, S., Umarani, S.: Comparative analysis of the learning on KDD Cup 2015 dataset. Webology **19**(1), 705–717 (2022)

5. Kloft, M., Stiehler, F., Zheng, Z., et al.: Predicting MOOC dropout over weeks using machine learning methods. In: Proceedings of the EMNLP 2014 Workshop on Analysis of Large Scale Social Interaction in MOOCs, pp. 60–65 (2014)
6. Chen, J., Feng, J., Sun, X., et al.: MOOC dropout prediction using a hybrid algorithm based on decision tree and extreme learning machine. Math. Probl. Eng. (2019)
7. Shou, Z., Chen, P., Wen, H., et al.: MOOC dropout prediction based on multidimensional time-series data. Math. Probl. Eng. 1–12 (2022)
8. Fu, Q., Gao, Z., Zhou, J., et al.: CLSA: a novel deep learning model for MOOC dropout prediction. Comput. Electr. Eng. **94**, 107315 (2021)
9. Basnet, R.B., Johnson, C., Doleck, T.: Dropout prediction in MOOCs using deep learning and machine learning. Educ. Inf. Technol. **27**(8), 11499–11513 (2022)
10. Zheng, Y., Gao, Z., Wang, Y., et al.: MOOC dropout prediction using FWTS-CNN model based on fused feature weighting and time series. IEEE Access **8**, 225324–225335 (2020)
11. Tang, C., Ouyang, Y., Rong, W., Zhang, J., Xiong, Z.: Time series model for predicting dropout in massive open online courses. In: Penstein Rosé, C., et al. (eds.) AIED 2018. LNCS (LNAI), vol. 10948, pp. 353–357. Springer, Cham (2018). https://doi.org/10.1007/978-3-319-93846-2_66
12. Wang, L., Wang, H.: Learning behavior analysis and dropout rate prediction based on MOOCs data. In: International Conference on Information Technology in Medicine and Education (ITME), pp. 419–423. IEEE (2019)
13. Jiang, W., Wu, J.: Active opinion-formation in online social networks. In: IEEE International Conference on Computer Communications, pp. 1–9. IEEE (2017)
14. Qiu, L.: Investigating a dropout prediction model for MOOCs learners using behavioral data. Central China Normal University (2019). (in Chinese)
15. Ke, G.L., Meng, Q., Finley, T., et al.: LightGBM: A highly efficient gradient boosting decision tree. In: Proceedings of the 31st Conference on Neural Information Processing Systems, pp. 3149–3157 (2017)
16. Tang, G.Y., Zhu, S.L., Zhou, W.F., Yang, S.G.: Inversion of Indian ocean subsurface temperature based on Gaussian mixture clustering and LightGBM algorithm. J. Qingdao Univ. Sci. Technol. Nat. Sci. Ed. **44**(2), 116–126 (2023). (in Chinese)
17. Blundo, C., Fenza, G., Fuccio, G., et al.: A time-driven FCA-based Approach for identifying students' dropout in MOOCs. Int. J. Intell. Syst. **37**(4), 2683–2705 (2022)

Nonnegative Matrix Factorization Based on Topology-and-Attribute-Matching Degree for Community Detection

Ruolan Zeng[1,2,3], Zhanghui Liu[1,2,3], and Kun Guo[1,2,3]($\boxtimes$)

[1] College of Computer and Data Science, Fuzhou University, Fuzhou 350108, China
gukn@fzu.edu.cn
[2] Fujian Key Laboratory of Network Computing and Intelligent Information Processing, Fuzhou University, Fuzhou 350108, China
[3] Key Laboratory of Spatial Data Mining and Information Sharing, Ministry of Education, Fuzhou 350108, China

Abstract. Community detection is widely used in network analysis, which seeks to divide network nodes into distinct communities based on the topology structure and attribute information of the network. Due to its interpretability, nonnegative matrix factorization becomes an essential method for community detection. However, it decomposes the adjacency matrix and attribute matrix separately, which do not tightly incorporate topology and attributes. And in the problem of division inconsistency based on topology and attributes caused by the mismatch between the topology similarity and attribute similarity of paired nodes, it ignores the difference in the matching degree of each attribute and each node. In this paper, we propose a nonnegative matrix factorization algorithm for community detection (MTACD) based on the matching degree between topology and attribute. First, we employ an attribute embedding mechanism to enhance the node-attribute relationship. Second, we design an attribute matching degree and a node topology-and-attribute matching degree in order to resolve the mismatch between topology and attribute similarity. Experiments on both real-world and synthetic networks demonstrate the effectiveness of our algorithm.

Keywords: Communtity detection · Attributed network · Nonnegative matrix factorizatioin

1 Introduction

With the development of various types of complex networks, such as circles of acquaintances in social networks, proteins with similar functions, etc., community structure has become more pervasive. Community detection is widely used in network analysis, which seeks to divide network nodes into distinct communities by mining information that reflects potential network structures and patterns. In recent years, network representation learning has also been extensively utilized in community detection, which embeds network nodes into low-dimensional vectors by preserving network topology, node attributes, and other data.

© The Author(s), under exclusive license to Springer Nature Singapore Pte Ltd. 2024
Y. Sun et al. (Eds.): ChineseCSCW 2023, CCIS 2012, pp. 137–151, 2024.
https://doi.org/10.1007/978-981-99-9637-7_10

Nonnegative matrix factorization [2] constrains decomposition matrices to be nonnegative, thus they can be understood as node community membership matrices and used for one-stage community detection. But community detection algorithms based on nonnegative matrix factorization in attributed networks have two limitations. First, the attribute matrix and adjacency matrix are decomposed separately. However, the relationship between a node and an attribute should not be deemed irrelevant if the values of the majority of the node's topology neighbors on the attribute are 1 but the node's own value is 0. Second, in community detection, there are situations in which topology and attributes lead to distinct community partitions, such as near topological distances between nodes with dissimilar attributes or considerable topological distances with similar attributes. Some work [13, 15] has been proposed to solve the problem by an adaptive trade-off parameter between topology and attributes or focusing on one kind of information but they disregard the fact that the topology-and-attribute-matching degree of each node may be different.

In this paper, we propose a nonnegative matrix factorization algorithm based on the matching degree between topology and attribute for community detection (MTACD) to address the limitations above. The attribute information embedding mechanism combines the topology information with the attribute matrix to be decomposed in order to incorporate more information regarding the relationship between nodes and attributes than decomposing the topology proximity matrix and attribute matrix separately. In addition, an attribute matching degree is designed to construct the node-attribute matrix that will be decomposed. And a topology-and-attribute-matching degree of each node is designed to limit the similarity of the community division of each node based on its topology and attributes. The contributions of this paper can be summarized as follows:

1. An attribute information embedding mechanism adds topology information to the attribute matrix to enhance the node-attribute relationship.
2. An attribute matching degree for each attribute and a topology-and-attribute matching degree for each node are designed to take into consideration the difference between each node and each attribute in order to resolve the mismatch between topology and attribute similarity.
3. Experiments on both real-world and synthetic networks show the effectiveness of our algorithm.

2   Related Work

In this section, we introduce related work on network representation learning based on matrix factorization and community detection based on nonnegative matrix factorization.

2.1   Network Representation Learning Based on Matrix Factorization

Network representation learning algorithms generate community partitions in two stages in the community detection task. The node embeddings are generated first, and then a clustering algorithm, such as KMeans, is employed to derive the node community partition. Yang et al. [3] proposed the TADW algorithm, which decomposes a high-order topology proximity matrix into a decomposed attribute matrix and other matrices and concatenates them as node embeddings. Huang et al. [4] proposed the AANE algorithm, which decomposes the cosine similarity matrix of node attributes into the product of the node embedding matrix and its transpose matrix, and employs a constraint to increase the similarity of nodes and their neighbors in the topology structure. Qiu et al. [5] proposed the NetMF algorithm, which proposes that three earlier pure structure network representation learning algorithms based on random walks, DeepWalk [6], Line [7] and Node2vec [8] are equivalent to imposing Singular Value Decomposition (SVD) on the high-order random walk matrix to obtain the node embedding matrix.

2.2 Community Detection Based on Nonnegative Matrix Factorization

Community detection algorithms generate community partitions in one stage. Some consider community detection in networks without attributes. Wang et al. proposed the M-NMF [9] algorithm, which employs a constraint term that maximizes modularity and asymmetrically decomposes the second-order proximity matrix and the community membership matrix. Ye et al. [10] proposed the DANMF algorithm, which introduced a deep autoencoder structure into community detection to reconstruct the adjacency matrix from the community membership matrix and project the adjacency matrix into the community membership matrix. And Some algorithms work in attributed networks. Wang et al. proposed the SCI [11] algorithm, which decomposes the adjacency matrix symmetrically into the community membership matrix and reconstructs the community membership matrix using the product of the attribute matrix and the attribute community matrix. Li et al. [12] proposed the CDE algorithm, which decomposes a structure matrix and the attribute matrix, and adds a constraint to reduce interference from unimportant attributes for each community.

Among the community detection algorithms based on nonnegative matrix factorization, some work considers the problem of mismatch of topology and attribute similarity, which leads to the inconsistency of division based on topology and attributes. Qin et al. proposed the ASCD [13] algorithm, which adaptively modifies the trade-off parameter of topology and attribution in each iteration based on the mismatching degree of the community partition between topology and attributes and prioritizes topological information. Zhao et al. proposed the ANMF [14] algorithm, which adaptively modifies the trade-off parameter between topology and attributes based on the modularity of their partition in each iteration and decomposes the adjacency matrix using the idea of encoder-decoder. Qin et al. [15] proposed the DHCD algorithm, which employs two matrix decomposition forms to accommodate two cases of networks in which topology has the dominant effect and attributes have the dominant effect. These algorithms consider the topology and attribute information as two components to be weighted by a hyperparameter but ignore the difference in the matching degree of each attribute and each node.

3   Preliminaries

3.1   Problem Definition

Given an attributed network $G = (V, E, \mathbf{A}, \mathbf{X})$, where $V = \{v_1, \ldots, v_n\}$ is the set of n nodes, E is the set of e edges, $\mathbf{A}$ is the adjacency matrix, $\mathbf{A}_{ij} = 1$ if $(v_i, vj) \in E$ and 0 otherwise. $\mathbf{X}$ is the attribute matrix where f denotes the number of attributes. $\mathbf{X}_{ij}$ denotes the value of j-th attribute of node i.

Community detection is to divide the node set V of a network G into k disjoint groups $C = \{c_1, \ldots, c_k\}$, where each node belongs to only one community.

3.2   Non-negative Matrix Factorization

Symmetric nonnegative matrix factorization and asymmetric nonnegative matrix factorization are two common types of Nonnegative matrix factorization in community detection; the former decomposes a matrix into two identical matrices, while the latter decomposes a matrix into two different matrices.

Symmetric Nonnegative Matrix Factorization. Given a proximity matrix $\mathbf{D}$, symmetric nonnegative matrix factorization reconstructs $\mathbf{D}$ from the community membership matrix $\mathbf{U}$ and its transpose matrix. And $\mathbf{U}_{ic}$ represents the probability that node i is a member of the community c. We can divide each node i into the community to which it belongs with the highest probability. The symmetric nonnegative matrix factorization is as follows, where $\| \cdot \|_F$ denotes the Frobenius norm.

$$\min_{\mathbf{U} \geq 0} \|\mathbf{D} - \mathbf{U}\mathbf{U}^T\|_F^2 \tag{1}$$

Asymmetric Nonnegative Matrix Factorization. Given an attribute matrix $\mathbf{D}$ denoting the relationship between the nodes and attributes, asymmetric non-negative matrix factorization decomposes it into the community membership matrix $\mathbf{U}$ and the attribute community membership matrix $\mathbf{V}$.

$$\min_{\mathbf{U} \geq 0, \mathbf{V} \geq 0} \|\mathbf{D} - \mathbf{U}\mathbf{V}^T\|_F^2 \tag{2}$$

4   The Proposed Algorithm

4.1   Framework of MTACD

The framework of MTACD consists of the four steps illustrated in Fig. 1. First, in the step of topology information embedding, a high-order proximity matrix $\mathbf{T}$ is constructed using the adjacency matrix. Second, in the step of the attribute information embedding mechanism, we combine topology information with the attribute matrix by utilizing the product of the high-order proximity matrix and attribute matrix. Third, in the step of computation of attribute matching degree and node matching degree, we construct a node-attribute matrix $\mathbf{B}$ based on the attribute matching degree and the node choice weight to model the relationship between nodes and attributes. And we design the constraint term based on the topology-and-attribute-matching degree of each node. Finally, in the step of objective function optimization, the constructed matrices are decomposed using the multiplicative update rule.

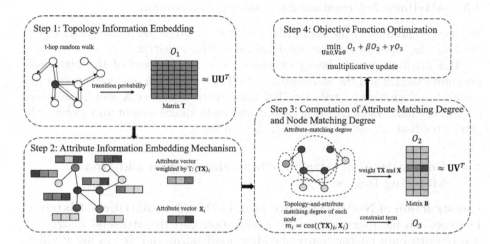

Fig. 1. Framework of MTACD

4.2 Topology Information Embedding

We construct a high-order proximity matrix from the adjacency matrix by random walk. Then we use symmetric nonnegative matrix factorization to decompose it into a community membership matrix.

As the proof in [5], the implicit matrix of DeepWalk is

$$(\mathbf{A}_0)_{ij} = log(\frac{e}{t}\sum_{r=1}^{t}\mathbf{P}^r\mathbf{D}^{-1}) \tag{3}$$

where $\mathbf{D} = diag\,(d_1,\ldots,d_n)$, d_i is the degree of node i, $\mathbf{P} = \mathbf{D}^{-1}\mathbf{A}$ is the matrix of one-step transition probability of nodes, t is the window size of random walk.

We decompose the similarity of nodes in topology based on the transition probability of nodes; the higher the transition probability between two nodes, the greater the topology similarity between them. Therefore, we construct a symmetric high-order proximity matrix $\mathbf{T}$ to be decomposed based on $\mathbf{A}_0$.

$$\mathbf{T}_{ij} = \frac{(\mathbf{A}_0)_{ij} + (\mathbf{A}_0)_{ji}}{2\sum_{j=1}^{n}(\mathbf{A}_0)_{ij}} \tag{4}$$

The first term of the objective is as follows, where $\mathbf{T}$ is decomposed symmetrically into a community membership matrix $\mathbf{U}$:

$$O_1 = \|\mathbf{T} - \mathbf{U}\mathbf{U}^T\|_F^2 \tag{5}$$

4.3   Attribute Information Embedding Mechanism

We use the product of the high-order proximity matrix and attribute matrix to combine the topology information into the attribute matrix.

The attribute matrix based on topology is the product of the high-order proximity matrix and the attribute matrix $\mathbf{TX}$ whose each row corresponds to a node's topology-based attributes. $\mathbf{TX}$ and attribute matrix $\mathbf{X}$ will be weighted by the attribute matching degree and the node choice weight to combine the attributes that mismatch and match the topology.

4.4   Computation of Attribute Matching Degree and Node Matching Degree

Construction of Node-Attribute Matrix Based on Attribute Matching Degree. To incorporate topology information into the attribute matrix, we use the attribute information embedding mechanism and design an attribute matching degree to construct the node-attribute matrix to be decomposed.

First, inspired by assortativity [16] and modularity [17], we define the matching degree of each attribute with topology as the density of edges between nodes with similar attribute values.

We normalize the adjacency matrix to get the fraction matrix, where e is the number of edges:

$$(\mathbf{A}_1)_{ij} = \frac{\mathbf{A}_{ij}}{e} \tag{6}$$

Definition 1: For 0-1 binary attribute m, the attribute matching degree is

$$r_m = \frac{1}{2}\left(\frac{e_{11} + e_{00} - a_1 b_1 - a_0 b_0}{1 - a_1 b_1 - a_0 b_0} + 1\right) \tag{7}$$

where e_{11}, e_{00} denote the sum of fractions among the nodes that the value of attribute m is 1 and 0, respectively, and a_i and b_i denote the fractions of the end of an edge that is attached to nodes with attribute value i, i is in $\{0, 1\}$.

In matrix form, the e_{11}, e_{00}, a_1, a_0, b_1, b_0 are calculated as

$$e_{11} = \mathbf{X}_{\cdot m}^T \mathbf{A}_1 \mathbf{X}_{\cdot m}, e_{00} = \overline{\mathbf{X}}_{\cdot m}^T \mathbf{A}_1 \overline{\mathbf{X}}_{\cdot m} \tag{8}$$

$$a_1 = \mathbf{X}_{\cdot m}^T \mathbf{A}_1 \mathbf{1}, a_0 = \overline{\mathbf{X}}_{\cdot m}^T \mathbf{A}_1 \mathbf{1}, b_1 = \mathbf{1}^T \mathbf{A}_1 \mathbf{X}_{\cdot m}, b_0 = \mathbf{1}^T \mathbf{A}_1 \overline{\mathbf{X}}_{\cdot m} \tag{9}$$

where $\mathbf{X}_{.m}$ denotes the m-th column vector of attribute matrix $\mathbf{X}$, which means the value of attribute m of each node, $\mathbf{1}$ is a n-dimensional column vector with each element equal to 1, and $\overline{\mathbf{X}}_{.m} = \mathbf{1} - \mathbf{X}_{.m}$. As for attribute vectors with real-value attributes, a Min-Max Normalization is performed on attribute vectors prior to executing Eq. (7). The attribute matching degree constructs a diagonal matrix $\mathbf{R} = diag\,(r_1, \ldots, r_f)$. And $(\mathbf{I}_f - \mathbf{R})$ denotes the mismatching degree of attributes, where $\mathbf{I}_x$ is an x-dimensional identity matrix.

Second, we construct the node-attribute matrix to be decomposed. The attributes that match the topology are $\mathbf{TXR}$, and that do not match are $\mathbf{X}(\mathbf{I} - \mathbf{R})$. The weights of the choice of each node between match attributes and mismatch attributes form a diagonal matrix $\mathbf{W} = diag\,(w_1, \ldots, w_n)$, where w_i indicates the strength of the relationship between node i and the attributes matching the topology. The node-attribute matrix $\mathbf{B}$ is defined as follows:

$$\mathbf{B} = \mathbf{WTXR} + (\mathbf{I}_n - \mathbf{W})\,\mathbf{X}\,(\mathbf{I}_f - \mathbf{R}) \tag{10}$$

In this paper, w_i is defined as the connection strength between a node and its topology neighbors. To construct a graph based on attributes, edges are added for node i and the d_i nodes with the greatest cosine similarity of attributes with node i on the set of nodes, where d_i is the degree of node i. $s_{ij} = \frac{cos(i,j)}{\sum_{r=1}^{n} cos(i,j)}$ is the normalized cosine similarity between the attribute vectors of node i and j. $\mathcal{N}\,(i)$ is the set of neighbors of node i, and $\mathcal{N}_a\,(i)$ is the set of neighbors of node i on the graph based on attributes. We use Softmax to smooth the difference in the connection strength of the attribute that matches and mismatches the topology in the following manner:

$$w_i = \frac{e^{\sum_{j \in \mathcal{N}(i)} \mathbf{T}_{ij}}}{e^{\sum_{j \in \mathcal{N}(i)} \mathbf{T}_{ij}} + e^{\sum_{j \in \mathcal{N}(i) - \mathcal{N}_a(i)} s_{ij}}} \tag{11}$$

The second term of the objective is as follows, where $\mathbf{U}$ is the community membership matrix and $\mathbf{V}$ is the attribute membership matrix:

$$O_2 = \|\mathbf{B} - \mathbf{U}\mathbf{V}^T\|_F^2 \tag{12}$$

Constraint Term Based on Topology-and-Attribute-Matching Degree.
We define a topology-and-attribute-matching degree for each node to constrain the community membership matrix based on topology and attribute.

Definition 2: The topology-and-attribute-matching degree of node i is

$$m_i = cos\,((\mathbf{TX})_i\,, \mathbf{X}_i) \tag{13}$$

where the subscript i means the i-th row of the matrix, and $cos\,(\cdot)$ means the function of cosine similarity. The topology-and-attribute-matching degree is defined as the similarity of its topology-based attributes and attributes of itself.

The topology-based community membership matrix is denoted by $\mathbf{PU}$, where the i-th row represents the linear combination of the community membership vectors of the topology neighbors of node i. And the attribute-based community membership matrix is defined as $\mathbf{X_0 V}$, where i-th row represents the linear combination of the attribute membership vectors of attributes of node i, and $\mathbf{X_0}$ represents the normalized attribute matrix $\mathbf{X}$, whose each column sums to 1. The higher the matching degree of a node is, the closer its topology-based community membership vector and its attribute-based community membership vector should be. The matching degree matrix is $\mathbf{M} = diag\,(m_1, \ldots, m_n)$. The constraint term is as follows:

$$O_3 = m_i \sum_{i=1}^{n} \| (\mathbf{PU})_i - (\mathbf{X_0 V})_i \|_2^2 = \| \mathbf{M}\,(\mathbf{PU} - \mathbf{X_0 V}) \|_F^2 \tag{14}$$

4.5   Objective Function Optimization

We combine the aforementioned three components into a unified objective function and use the multiplicative update rule [2] to optimize it.

The unified objective function of MTACD is defined as follows, where β and γ are two hyperparameters

$$\begin{aligned} \min_{\mathbf{U} \geq 0, \mathbf{V} \geq 0} L(\mathbf{U}, \mathbf{V}) &= \min_{\mathbf{U} \geq 0, \mathbf{V} \geq 0} O_1 + \beta O_2 + \gamma O_3 \\ &= \min_{\mathbf{U} \geq 0, \mathbf{V} \geq 0} \|\mathbf{T} - \mathbf{UU}^T\|_F^2 + \beta\|\mathbf{B} - \mathbf{UV}^T\|_F^2 \\ &\quad + \gamma\|\mathbf{M}\,(\mathbf{PU} - \mathbf{X_0 V}) \|_F^2 \end{aligned} \tag{15}$$

Using the multiplicative update rule, the update of matrix $\mathbf{U}$ in the $(l+1)$-th iteration is as follows, where $(-)_{ij}$ and $(+)_{ij}$ denote the element in i-th row and j-th column of the terms with negative and positive coefficients of the partial derivative of $\mathbf{U}$ in the objective function, respectively.

$$\mathbf{U}_{ij}^{(l+1)} \leftarrow \mathbf{U}_{ij}^{(l)} \frac{(-)_{ij}}{(+)_{ij}} \tag{16}$$

With $\mathbf{V}$ fixed, update $\mathbf{U}$ by the rule above:

$$\frac{\partial L}{\partial \mathbf{U}} = 4\mathbf{UU}^T\mathbf{U} - 2\left(\mathbf{T} + \mathbf{T}^T\right)\mathbf{U} + 2\beta\mathbf{UV}^T\mathbf{V} - 2\beta\mathbf{BV} + 2\gamma\mathbf{P}^T\mathbf{M}^T\mathbf{M}\,(\mathbf{PU} - \mathbf{X_0 V}) \tag{17}$$

$$\mathbf{U}_{ij}^{(l+1)} \leftarrow \mathbf{U}_{ij}^{(l)} \frac{\left(\left(\mathbf{T} + \mathbf{T}^T\right)\mathbf{U} + \beta\mathbf{BV} + \gamma\mathbf{P}^T\mathbf{M}^T\mathbf{MX_0 V}\right)_{ij}}{\left(2\mathbf{UU}^T\mathbf{U} + \beta\mathbf{UV}^T\mathbf{V} + \gamma\mathbf{PM}^T\mathbf{MPU}\right)_{ij}} \tag{18}$$

Similarly, with $\mathbf{U}$ fixed, $\mathbf{V}$ is updated as follows:

$$\frac{\partial L}{\partial \mathbf{V}} = 2\beta\mathbf{VU}^T\mathbf{U} - 2\beta\mathbf{B}^T\mathbf{U} + 2\gamma\mathbf{X_0}^T\mathbf{M}^T\mathbf{M}\,(\mathbf{X_0 V} - \mathbf{PU}) \tag{19}$$

$$\mathbf{V}_{ij}^{(l+1)} \leftarrow \mathbf{V}_{ij}^{(l)} \frac{\left(\beta \mathbf{B}^T \mathbf{U} + \gamma \mathbf{X}_0^T \mathbf{M}^T \mathbf{MPU}\right)_{ij}}{\left(\beta \mathbf{V} \mathbf{U}^T \mathbf{U} + \gamma \mathbf{X}_0^T \mathbf{M}^T \mathbf{MX}_0 \mathbf{V}\right)_{ij}} \tag{20}$$

Update $\mathbf{U}$ and $\mathbf{V}$ alternately until the objective function converges or the iteration reaches a specified number. Normalization of each row of $\mathbf{U}$ and $\mathbf{V}$ is performed in addition to each iteration in order to make the community membership of each node sum to 1.

5   Experiments

First, we introduce the dataset and baseline algorithms, and evaluation metrics. Second, we conduct the parameter, ablation, and accuracy experiments to verify the validity of MTACD. The results show the effectiveness of MTACD.

5.1   Datasets

We evaluate the effectiveness of MTACD using five real-world networks (Cora, CiteSeer, BlogCatalog, Wiki, and Flickr) and synthetic networks. Table 1 contains detailed network information, where n is the number of nodes, f is the number of attributes, e is the number of edges, and k is the number of communities. The synthetic networks with 1000 nodes and 20 communities are generated by LFR [18] and the attributes generated by [19]. We vary the parameter μ from 0.2 to 0.6, which regulates the mixing of network topology and community. As μ increases, the topology structure becomes more confusing.

Table 1. The description of real-world networks

Network	n	f	e	k
Cora	2708	1433	5278	7
Citeseer	3327	3708	4732	6
BlogCatalog	5196	8189	171743	6
Wiki	2405	4973	17981	19
Flickr	7575	12047	239738	9

5.2   Baseline Algorithms

The first five baselines are network representation learning algorithms, which generate node embeddings and obtain the community division by KMeans, and the rest are community detection algorithms based on nonnegative matrix factorization.

DeepWalk [6] learns the node embeddings based on random walk.

Node2Vec [8] uses a biased random walk to explore the neighbors of each node by depth and breadth.

NetMF [5] decomposes an implicit DeepWalk matrix to generate the node embeddings.

TADW [3] decomposes a high-order topology proximity matrix into a decomposed attribute matrix and other matrices and concatenates the matrices as the node embeddings.

AANE [4] decomposes the cosine similarity matrix of node attributes into the node embeddings and increases the similarity of nodes and their neighbors.

DANMF [10] introduces a deep autoencoder structure into community detection to construct the relationship of the adjacency matrix and community membership matrix.

DHCD [15] uses two matrix decomposition forms to accommodate two cases of networks: DHCD T-A denotes the form that topology has the dominant effect, and DHCD A-T denotes the form that attributes have the dominant effect.

ANMF [14] adaptively modifies the trade-off parameter between topology and attribute by the modularity of their partition in each iteration and decomposes the adjacency matrix using the idea of encoder-decoder.

5.3   Experimental Settings

For Deepwalk and Node2Vec, the number of walks started from each node is set to 80, the walk length to 40, and the window size to 10. For NetMF, the window size of random walk is set to 10. For TADW, the harmonic factor to balance the decomposition and penalty terms is set to 0.9 due to the stability of the parameter in the classification experiment in its paper. The parameters for AANE, DANMF, and ANMF are set according to the recommendations of their paper. For DHCD, the optimal parameter value balancing the importance of topology and attributes is searched in $[0, 10]$. The number of iterations of MTACD is set to 300, and the window size of random walk is set to 5.

5.4   Evaluation Metrics

Three widely used metrics [20] are used to evaluate the accuracy of algorithms.

Normalized Mutual Information (NMI) of two partitions $X = \{X_1, \ldots, X_a\}$ and $Y = \{Y_1, \ldots, Y_b\}$ is defined as follows:

$$NMI(X, Y) = \frac{-2 \sum_{i=1}^{a} \sum_{j=1}^{b} \mathbf{C}_{ij} log\left(\mathbf{C}_{ij} n / \mathbf{C}_i \mathbf{C}_j\right)}{\sum_{i=1}^{a} \mathbf{C}_i log\left(\mathbf{C}_i / n\right) + \sum_{j=1}^{b} \mathbf{C}_j log\left(\mathbf{C}_j / n\right)} \tag{21}$$

where the $\mathbf{C}_{ij}$ denotes the number of the nodes in X_i that occur in Y_j, $\mathbf{C}_i$ is the sums of row i of $\mathbf{C}$ and $\mathbf{C}_j$ is the sum of column j of $\mathbf{C}$.

Adjusted Rand Index (ARI) is defined as follows:

$$ARI = \frac{RI - E(RI)}{max(RI) - E(RI)} \tag{22}$$

where $E(RI)$ and $max(RI)$ is the expected and maximal values of RI.
Micro F1-score (F1) is defined as follows:

$$Precision = \frac{TP}{TP + FP}, Recall = \frac{TP}{TP + FN} \tag{23}$$

$$F1 = \frac{2 \cdot Precision \cdot Recall}{Precision + Recall} \tag{24}$$

The higher values of the three metrics above indicate the higher accuracy of a community detection algorithm.

5.5 Parameter Experiment

We vary the parameter β in $[0.2, 2]$ with γ set to 2 to modify the weight of the attribute information of the objective function within the interval β less than 1 and β greater than 1. Then, we fix β, which corresponds to the highest NMI value on different networks, and vary the γ in $[1, 5]$ to modify the weight of the match information constraint of the objective function by searching in a range that makes γ more significant (Fig. 2).

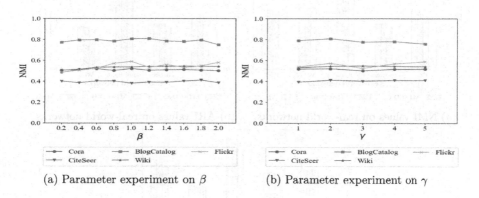

(a) Parameter experiment on β (b) Parameter experiment on γ

Fig. 2. Parameter experiment on β and γ on NMI

The parameters of the remaining experiments are fixed to which the highest NMI value corresponds on each network, which are summarized in Table 2.

Table 2. The optimal values of β and γ on real networks

Parameter	Cora	CiteSeer	BlogCatalog	Wiki	Flickr
β	0.6	1.8	0.4	1.8	1.0
γ	2	5	2	2	5

5.6 Ablation Experiment

The ablation experiment evaluates the effectiveness of the attribute information embedding mechanism and the constraint term based on topology-and-attribute-matching degree, respectively.

MTACD-B removes the attribute information embedding mechanism and the attribute matching degree, which means changing the O_2 into $\|\mathbf{X} - \mathbf{U}\mathbf{V}^T\|_F^2$.

MTACD-C removes O_3, the constraint base on topology-and-attribute matching degree of each node.

As shown in Fig. 3, compared with MTACD-B and MTACD-C, the accuracy of MTACD is the highest, with the exception of MTACD-B on CiteSeer by less than 2% over MTACD. In the majority of networks, it demonstrates the effectiveness of the node-attribute matrix based on the attribute information embedding mechanism and the attribute matching degree and the effectiveness of the constraint term based on the topology-and-attribute-matching degree.

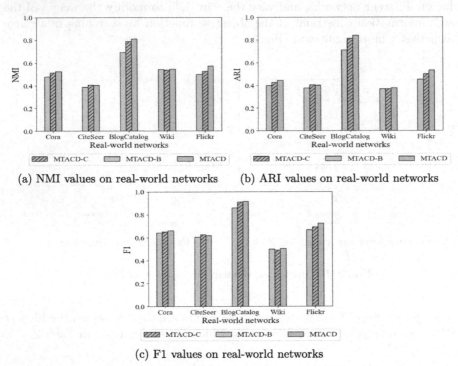

(a) NMI values on real-world networks   (b) ARI values on real-world networks

(c) F1 values on real-world networks

Fig. 3. Results of ablation experiment

5.7 Accuracy Experiment

As shown in Fig. 4, MTACD outperforms the baseline with the exception of TADW on CiteSeer and the NMI value of TADW on Cora. This is due to the fact that TADW can utilize the matching information between topology and attributes more effectively on networks where topology plays a crucial role, such as Cora and CiteSeer. In the remaining real-world networks where attributes are significant, MTACD outperforms the baseline, demonstrating that the node-attribute matrix based on the attribute information embedding mechanism can more effectively incorporate the topology and attribute information. On synthetic networks, as μ increases, the performance of MTACD remains the best while the performance of the baseline declines more significantly. It demonstrates that nodes with the higher topology-and-attribute-matching degree can make the community membership based on topology more similar to the community membership based on attributes to resolve the mismatch between topology and attribute similarity and preserve accuracy.

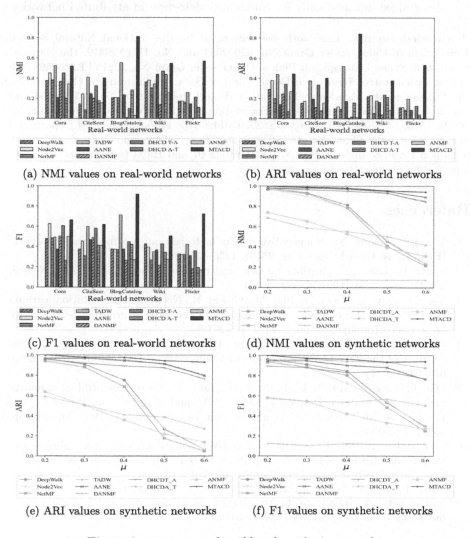

(a) NMI values on real-world networks   (b) ARI values on real-world networks

(c) F1 values on real-world networks   (d) NMI values on synthetic networks

(e) ARI values on synthetic networks   (f) F1 values on synthetic networks

Fig. 4. Accuracy on real-world and synthetic networks

6 Conclusions

In this paper, we propose a nonnegative matrix factorization algorithm based on the matching degree between topology and attribute for community detection. First, an attribute information embedding mechanism adds topology information to the attribute matrix to enhance the node-attribute relationship. Second, an attribute matching degree for each attribute and a topology-and-attribute matching degree for each node are designed to take into consideration the difference between each node and each attribute in order to resolve the mismatch between topology and attribute similarity. Experiments on both real-world and synthetic networks show the effectiveness of our algorithm. In the future, we will study the methods based on nonnegative matrix factorization with the parameters determined automatically for community detection in attributed networks.

Acknowledgements. This work was supported by the National Natural Science Foundation of China under Grant No. 62002063 and No. U21A20472, the National Key Research and Development Plan of China under Grant No. 2021YFB3600503, the Fujian Collaborative Innovation Center for Big Data Applications in Governments, the Fujian Industry-Academy Cooperation Project under Grant No. 2017H6008 and No. 2018H6010, the Natural Science Foundation of Fujian Province under Grant No. 2022J01118, No. 2020J05112 and No. 2020J01420, the Fujian Provincial Department of Education under Grant No. JAT190026, the Major Science and Technology Project of Fujian Province under Grant No. 2021HZ022007 and Haixi Government Big Data Application Cooperative Innovation Center.

References

1. Wang, Y., Zhang, Y.: Nonnegative matrix factorization: a comprehensive review. IEEE Trans. Knowl. Data Eng. **25**(6), 1336–1353 (2012)
2. Seung, D., Lee, L.: Algorithms for non-negative matrix factorization. Adv. Neural. Inf. Process. Syst. **13**, 556–562 (2001)
3. Yang, C., Liu, Z., Zhao, D., Sun, M., Chang, E.: Network representation learning with rich text information. In: Proceedings of the 24th International Conference on Artificial Intelligence, pp. 2111–2117 (2015)
4. Huang, X., Li, J., Hu, X.: Accelerated attributed network embedding. In: Proceedings of the 2017 SIAM International Conference on Data Mining (SDM), pp. 633–641 (2017)
5. Qiu, J., Dong, Y., Ma, H., Li, J., Wang, K., Tang, J.: Network embedding as matrix factorization: unifying DeepWalk, LINE, PTE, and Node2vec. In: Proceedings of the 11th ACM International Conference on Web Search and Data Mining, pp. 459–467 (2018)
6. Perozzi, B., Al-Rfou, R., Skiena, S.: DeepWalk: online learning of social representations. In: Proceedings of the 20th ACM SIGKDD International Conference on Knowledge Discovery and Data Mining, pp. 701–710 (2014)
7. Tang, J., Qu, M., Wang, M., Zhang, M., Yan, J., Mei, Q.: Line: large-scale information network embedding. In: Proceedings of the 24th International Conference on World Wide Web, pp. 1067–1077 (2015)

8. Grover, A., Leskovec, J.: node2vec: scalable feature learning for networks. In: Proceedings of the 22nd ACM SIGKDD International Conference on Knowledge Discovery and Data Mining, pp. 855–864 (2016)
9. Wang, X., Cui, P., Wang, J., Pei, J., Zhu, W., Yang, S.: Community preserving network embedding. In: Proceedings of the AAAI Conference on Artificial Intelligence, vol. 31 (2017)
10. Ye, F., Chen, C., Zheng, Z.: Deep autoencoder-like nonnegative matrix factorization for community detection. In: Proceedings of the 27th ACM International Conference on Information and Knowledge Management, pp. 1393–1402 (2018)
11. Wang, X., Jin, D., Cao, X., Yang L., Zhang, W.: Semantic community identification in large attribute networks. In: Proceedings of the AAAI Conference on Artificial Intelligence, vol. 30 (2016)
12. Li, Y., Sha, C., Huang, X., Zhang, Y.: Community detection in attributed graphs: an embedding approach. In: Proceedings of the AAAI Conference on Artificial Intelligence, vol. 32 (2018)
13. Qin, M., Jin, D., He D, Gabrys, B., Musial, K.: Adaptive community detection incorporating topology and content in social networks. In: Proceedings of the 2017 IEEE/ACM International Conference on Advances in Social Networks Analysis and Mining 2017, pp. 675–682 (2017)
14. Zhao, Z., Ke, Z., Gou, Z., Guo, H., Jiang, K., Zhang, R.: The trade-off between topology and content in community detection: an adaptive encoder-decoder-based NMF approach. Expert Syst. Appl. **209**, 118230 (2022)
15. Meng, Q., Kai, L.: Dual-channel hybrid community detection in attributed networks. Inf. Sci. **551**, 146–167 (2021)
16. Newman, M.E.J.: Mixing patterns in networks. Phys. Rev. E **67**(2), 026126 (2003)
17. Newman, M.E.J., Girvan, M.: Finding and evaluating community structure in networks. Phys. Rev. E **69**(2), 026113 (2004)
18. Lancichinetti, A., Fortunato, S., Radicchi, F.: Benchmark graphs for testing community detection algorithms. Phys. Rev. E **78**(4), 046110 (2008)
19. Huang, B., Wang, C., Wang, B.: NMLPA: uncovering overlapping communities in attributed networks via a multi-label propagation approach. Sensors **19**(2), 260 (2019)
20. Chakraborty, T., Dalmia, A., Mukherjee, A., Ganguly, N.: Metrics for community analysis: a survey. ACM Comput. Surv. (CSUR) **50**(4), 1–37 (2017)

Unsupervised Multi-population Evolutionary Algorithm for Community Detection in Attributed Networks

Junjie Wu[1,2], Lin Wu[1,2,3], and Kun Guo[1,2,3(✉)]

[1] College of Computer and Data Science, Fuzhou University, Fuzhou 350108, China
wujunjie1008@qq.com, {wuling1985,gukn}@fzu.edu.cn
[2] Fujian Key Laboratory of Network Computing and Intelligent Information
Processing (Fuzhou University), Fuzhou 350108, China
[3] Key Laboratory of Spatial Data Mining and Information Sharing, Ministry of
Education, Fuzhou 350108, China

Abstract. Community detection on attributed networks is a method to discover community structures within attributed networks. By applying community detection on attribute networks, we can better understand the relationships between nodes in real-world networks. However, current algorithms for community detection on attribute networks rely on hyper-parameters, and it is difficult to obtain an ideal result when facing networks with inconsistent attributes and topology. Consequently, we propose an Unsupervised Multi-population Evolutionary Algorithm (UMEA) for community detection in attributed networks. This algorithm adds edges between nodes based on attribute similarity, allowing it to combine attribute information during the process of community detection. In addition, this algorithm determines the optimal number of added edges autonomously through communication and learning between multiple populations. Furthermore, we propose a series of strategies to accelerate population convergence for the locus-based encoding. Experiments have demonstrated that our algorithm outperforms the benchmark algorithms in both real and artificial networks.

Keywords: Evolutionary algorithm · Community detection · Attributed networks · Attribute similarity

1 Introduction

An attributed networks is a graph structure consisting of multiple nodes and edges, as well as the node attributes [1]. These graph structures can be used to represent a variety of real networks, including social networks, cross-referencing networks, etc. Performing community detection on nodes in attributed networks can help us understand complex relationships, such as society and biology, and can be applied in fields like recommendation systems and protein recognition. Therefore, this study aims to detect communities in attributed networks efficiently.

© The Author(s), under exclusive license to Springer Nature Singapore Pte Ltd. 2024
Y. Sun et al. (Eds.): ChineseCSCW 2023, CCIS 2012, pp. 152–166, 2024.
https://doi.org/10.1007/978-981-99-9637-7_11

Evolutionary algorithms (EAs) have gained popularity in community detection in recent years. Current community detection algorithms based on evolutionary algorithms, which optimize structure and node attribute information, demonstrate the benefits of combining the two approaches. Nonetheless, they still face the following issues: First, when confronting the problem of community structure and attribute mismatch in attributed networks, it remains difficult to find a satisfactory solution. Certain algorithms use attribute information to add edges between nodes based on the original network to address this issue. However, they often set the number of added edges as a hyper-parameter. We believe this strategy leads to an excessive reliance on hyper-parameter settings, and once the network alters, the initial hyper-parameter settings become ineffective. Second, community detection algorithms based on evolutionary computation typically represent solutions with label-based encoding and locus-based encoding. Label-based encoding, however, requires prior knowledge of the number of communities, whereas locus-based encoding struggles to partition nodes into the same community in graphs with low edge density. As a result, achieving an optimal solution becomes difficult for the algorithm. We believe that utilizing locus-based encoding throughout the iteration process will ensure that the number of communities is no longer fixed during solution revisions.

To solve these problems, we propose an Unsupervised Multi-population Evolutionary Algorithm (UMEA) for community detection in attributed networks. The algorithm includes a Normally Distributed Edge Addition (NDEA) strategy that randomly adds edges between nodes and a Local Structure Update (LSU) strategy for locus-based encoding. Specifically, the following is a summary of the article's key innovations:

1. Different populations in UMEA can perform unsupervised learning of the number of edges to be added during the iteration and make corresponding adjustments to the network of each population. It eliminates the need for manual reconfiguration of hyper-parameters when dealing with different networks, thereby enhancing the accuracy and robustness of the algorithm.
2. The NDEA adds edges to the original network based on the similarity of attribute vectors of each node. This approach addresses the issue of poor performance of locus-based encoding when encountering low edge density. Moreover, it permits the algorithm to combine both topology and attribute information for community detection.
3. LSU, based on edge connections, can prevent the generation of useless solutions during iterations that may occur with locus-based encoding, thus accelerating solution convergence.

2 Related Work

In this section, we will introduce the relevant work from two aspects: evolutionary algorithm for community detection and community detection in attributed networks.

2.1   Evolutionary Algorithm for Community Detection

Shi et al. [2] proposed a multi-objective optimization framework for community detection. The framework combines multiple objective functions that have been or may be used for community detection. It introduces the concept of correlation between objective functions to characterize the relationship between them. Zhang et al. [3] designed a multi-objective evolutionary algorithm for community detection. Their approach incorporates a network reduction method, which merges nodes that may belong to the same community into a single node in subsequent iterations. This technique accelerates the convergence speed of the algorithm without sacrificing its accuracy. He et al. [4] employed a statistical significance measure for each attribute of a vertex to perform community detection. They adopted a strategy that searches for communities with maximum connectivity saliency and minimum saliency between any two communities in the network. Additionally, they introduced a replication process consisting of special crossover and mutation operators to accelerate the evolution process. Sun et al. [5] proposed a graph neural network coding method for multi-objective evolutionary algorithms (MOEAs) by combining evolutionary computation with neural networks. Their method represents the edges of nodes as continuous variables and introduces two objective functions for evaluating the attribute homogeneity of community nodes in single attribute and multi-attributed networks, respectively. Experimental results have demonstrated the effectiveness of their proposed graph neural network encoding method.

2.2   Community Detection in Attributed Networks

Wang et al. [6] applied automatic encoders to community detection. They proposed an edge-based graph convolutional network that disrupts the content of network nodes, allowing node attributes to interact with network features. The destroyed features are then learned in the context of a graph self-encoder to obtain graph feature representation. Finally, spectral clustering is used to partition the communities. Li et al. [7] defined attribute community detection as a non-negative matrix factorization optimization problem. They designed iterative update rules to transform the nodes of the attribute graph into embedding vectors for clustering. Naderipour et al. [8] proposed an evaluation index that combines the structural information and attribute information of the network. This index evaluates the effectiveness of community division without requiring real community division. Experimental results demonstrate that the clustering algorithm using this index can accurately predict the number of communities. Kakisim et al. [9] addressed the sparsity of the attribute space by capturing high-order semantic relationships between attributes through random walks on the network. They learned embeddings in a joint space composed of both network structure and attributes. This approach enables the method to discover potential attribute representations of objects.

3   Preliminaries

In this section, we will discuss attributed network, community detection based on EAs and objective function, which are fundamental to our work.

3.1   Attributed Networks

An attributed network can be defined as $G(V, E, F)$, where $V = \{V_1, V_2, V_3, ..., V_n\}$ is a set containing n nodes, $E = \{E_1, E_2, E_3, ..., E_m\}$ is a set containing m edges, $F = (F_{ij})_{n \times k}$ is a matrix containing n node attribute vectors of dimension k. A community is a group of related nodes. For example, $C_i = (V_i, E_i, F_i)$ represents the ith community of G. In no-overlapping community detection, $V = \bigcup_{i=1}^{c} V_i$ and $V_i \cap V_j = \emptyset$ when $i \neq j$. Attributed networks community detection needs to satisfy two requirements: ensuring tight connections and maximizing the prevalence of common attributes among nodes within the community [10].

3.2   Community Detection Based on EAs

In EAs for community detection, each solution is represented by a vector x, where $x = [x_1, x_2, ..., x_n]$. This vector represents a community detection result. In locus-based encoding, each element of the vector typically represents a node in the network. If the value of the i-th element of the solution is j, it indicates an edge between the i-th and j-th nodes, representing their belonging to the same community. The set of all feasible candidate solutions for an optimization problem is known as the decision space. Each solution updates and iterates in accordance with a predefined strategy until the maximum number of updates is reached or the population's optimal solution remains unchanged. Additionally, a fitness function must be defined to evaluate the quality of population solutions. Frequently, the fitness function is defined as the optimization objective of the problem.

3.3   Objective Function

Modularity [11] is a standard metric for evaluating the community structure of complex networks. The equation for calculation is as follows:

$$Q = \frac{1}{2M} \sum_{ij} \left(C_{ij} - \frac{k_i k_j}{2M} \right) \delta(c_i, c_j) \tag{1}$$

where M represents the number of edges on the network, C_{ij} is the value of the combined adjacency matrix, $\delta(c_i, c_j)$ indicates whether the community of node i and the community of node j are the same. If they belong to the same community, $\delta(c_i, c_j) = 1$, otherwise, $\delta(c_i, c_j) = 0$, k_i represents the degree of node i.

4   Proposed Algorithm

This paper proposes a new unsupervised multi-population evolutionary algorithm for community detection in complex networks. The framework of UMEA is shown in Fig. 1.

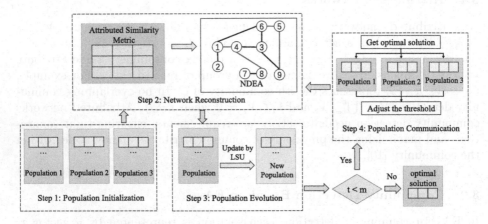

Fig. 1. Framework of UMEA

Step 1: We initialize multiple populations. Step 2: We calculate the attribute similarity between nodes and add edges to the original networks of different populations based on NDEA. Step 3: We revise and iterate the candidate solutions in the population according to the LSU. Step 4: Once the iteration reaches a certain threshold, populations communicate to determine the number of edges that must be added. Steps 2, 3 and 4 are repeated until $t > m$. $t > m$ indicates that the algorithm has reached its maximum iteration. When $t > m$, the algorithm will select the global optimal solution as its final result and output. We will now introduce UMEA's specifics.

4.1   Population Initialization

To accelerate the convergence speed of the algorithm, we have incorporated a heuristic rule into the initialization process. Specifically, during initialization, the i-th element of each solution randomly selects a neighboring node number of node i as its value.

4.2   Network Reconstruction

Calculate Attribute Similarity. Cosine similarity is used to determine the attribute similarity between two nodes. The range of the cosine similarity metric is -1 to 1. A value of 1 indicates that the attributes of the two nodes are identical, whereas a value of -1 indicates that the attributes are entirely distinct. The equation for calculating cosine similarity is as follows:

$$\cos(F_i, F_j) = \frac{F_i \cdot F_j}{\|F_i\| \, \|F_j\|} \tag{2}$$

In the equation, F_i represents the attribute vector of the i-th node.

Normally Distributed Edge Addition Strategy. Each node v_i calculates the attribute similarity with other nodes in the network using Eq. 2, and then sorts the obtained attribute similarities in descending order to create a set $AN(v_i)$. And for each node in the set $AN(v_i)$, select n nodes with similar attributes as new neighbors.

$$N(v_i) = \{AN(v_i) \,|\, 0 < l < t\} \tag{3}$$

where t is a random number with a normal distribution, and the number of attribute edges added by each node is different. This reduces the impact of noise nodes with similar attribute vectors on the algorithm results. The average μ and standard deviation σ of t are calculated as follows:

$$\mu = p \times n \tag{4}$$

$$\sigma = \frac{1}{3} \times p \times n \tag{5}$$

Among them, n represents the number of nodes in the dataset, and p represents a decimal value within the range of $[0, 0.1]$. During population iteration, the value of p will be learned adaptively. We believe that the proportion of nodes with attribute-related connections to other nodes does not exceed ten percent of the entire network. The range of p is therefore set between 0 and 0.1.

According to the above calculation equation, the adjacency matrix $\mathbf{A}$ of the network attribute can be obtained:

$$\mathbf{A}_{ij} = \begin{cases} 1, & j \in N(v_i) \\ 0, & others \end{cases} \tag{6}$$

Then, the union of attribute adjacency matrix $\mathbf{A}$ and topological adjacency matrix $\mathbf{T}$ is used as the combined adjacency matrix $\mathbf{S} = \mathbf{A} \cup \mathbf{T}$ for the subsequent iterations of the algorithm.

4.3   Population Evolution

Due to revisions to the locus-base encoding, there may be instances in which the value of element i is changed from node j to node k within the same community, with no change to the detection result. These updates are referred to as meaningless updates. As shown in Fig. 2(b), the first element of the solution has changed from 2 to 4, and the third element has changed from 9 to 8, but the overall community structure remains unchanged. We believe that meaningful updates should be like Fig. 2(c), where the third element of the solution changes from 9 to 6, and the seventh element changes from 8 to 7. In this change, nodes 3, 7, 8, and 9 no longer belong to the same community.

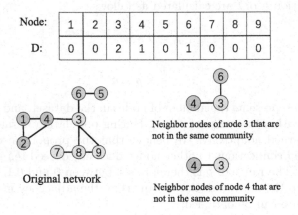

(a) Original network   (b) Invalid update   (c) Effective update

Fig. 2. Solution updating

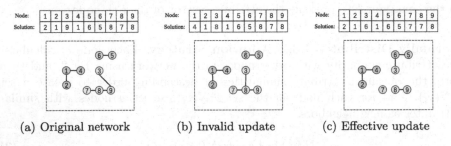

Original network

Fig. 3. Node output degree calculation

Therefore, we incorporate LSU into the solution's update procedure to ensure that each update is effective and to accelerate the algorithm's convergence speed. First, as a result of EAs learning global optimal solution mechanism, each element of the solution has a certain probability of becoming an element in the same position in the global optimal solution. This can accelerate the convergence of the solution. Second, we calculate the number of neighbors, denoted as d, that are not in the same community for each node. We refer to this as the **output degree**. Then, we obtain O, which represents the set of nodes where d is not equal to 0. Third, to accomplish the goal of altering the community structure, we change the corresponding elements in the node-set by randomly selecting a neighbor who is not in the same community as the new element value. As shown in Fig. 3, the selected node set is $O = 3, 4$. During the solution update process, if the fitness function of a solution exceeds that of the optimal global solution, the optimal global solution will be updated. The solution update process is as Algorithm 1, where $random(a, b)$ means to randomly select a number in the interval $[a, b]$; CalculateModularity() represents the calculation of modularity for the community detection result according to Eq. 1.

Algorithm 1: UpdateIndividual()

Input: S: The combined adjacency matrix; NG_i: The network after expanding the edge of the i-th population; P_i: The i-th population; g_i: The individual with the highest modularity in P_i; N_p: The size of each population; I: The s-th individual of the population; C_s: The community detection of the s-th individual; r: The learning rate to global optimal solution;

Output: NP_i: The i-th updated population;

1 $s = 1$;
2 **while** $s \leq N_p$ **do**
3   **foreach** n in V **do**
4   **if** Random(0, 1) $< r$ **then**
5              $I_n = g_i(n)$;
6   **else**
7   **foreach** m in V **do**
                // when the neighbor m is not in the same community with n
8   **if** $S_{n,m} = 1$ and $C_s(n, m) = 0$ **then**
9                      $B = B \cup m$;
10   **end**
11                 $I_n = $ RandomSelect(B);
12   **end**
13   **end**
14   Q_s=CalculateModularity(ind_s);
15   Q_g=CalculateModularity(g_i);
16   **if** $Q_s > Q_g$ **then**
17         $g_i = I_n$;
18   **end**
19   **end**
20     $s = s + 1$;
21     $NP_i = NP_i \cup I_n$;
22 **end**
23 **return** NP_i;

4.4   Population Communication

Regarding the threshold p in Sect. 4.2, we believe that the optimal global solution found by multiple populations during the evolution process can be used as the learning basis for the population's threshold p. First, we refer to the threshold range in Sect. 4.2 and set the initial values of p_i for each population as 0, 0.05, and 0.1, respectively. When the population iteration reaches a certain number of rounds, we calculate the community's internal attribute similarity SA of the optimal global solution in each population using Eq. 7:

$$SA = \frac{\sum_{k=1}^{c} \sum_{i,j \in k, i<j} 2\cos(F_i, F_j)}{\sum_{k=1}^{c} n_k (n_k - 1)} \tag{7}$$

Among them, c represents the total number of communities, n_k represents the total number of nodes in the k-th community, and F_i represents the attribute vector of the i-th node. In terms of community detection, SA indicates whether there is a close connection in terms of attributes within a community.

Then, each population utilizes the updated threshold, as per the NDEA in Sect. 4.2, to reconstruct a new combined adjacency matrix based on the original network. After multiple iterations and exchanges, this population communication strategy enables all populations to converge the p threshold to a range close to the optimal solution. The pseudo-code of the algorithm is as follows, where random(a, b) means to randomly select a number in the interval $[a, b]$; CalculateSA() means to calculate the SA of the global optimal solution for each population based on formula 7; $\max(sa_1, sa_2, sa_3)$ means to obtain the maximum SA and its corresponding threshold p.

Algorithm 2: PopulationCommunication()

Input: p: The threshold for the populations; g: The globally optimal individual of the populations;

Output: np: The new threshold for the populations;

1 sa_1, sa_2, sa_3=CalculateSA(g_1, g_2, g_3);
2 $sa_{max}, p_{max} = \max(sa_1, sa_2, sa_3)$;
3 $t = 1$;
4 **while** $t \leq 3$ **do**
5      $mp_t = (p_{max} + p_t)/2$;
6   **if** $mp_t > p_t$ **then**
7 | np_t=random(p_t, mp_t);
8   **end**
9   **if** $mp_t < p_t$ **then**
10 | np_t=random(mp_t, p_t);
11   **end**
12     $t = t + 1$;
13 **end**
14 **return** np;

As shown in Algorithm 3, we first initialize three populations. During the iteration process, we update and find the globally best individual among the three populations. Once the iteration reaches a predetermined threshold, population communication occurs,the cosine similarity of attribute vectors for all nodes is calculated and the NDEA is used to modify the network. Here, CalAttrCos-Similarity(F) represents calculating the cosine similarity of attribute vectors for all nodes according to Eq. 2; FindBestIndividual(Ch_i) denotes finding the best individual from the population.

Algorithm 3: UMEA

Input: $G = (V, E, F)$: The attributed networks; T_i: The adjacency matrix of the i-th population; N_p: The size of population; c: The number of generations intervals between which the population begins to communicate; m: the maximum number of generations; n: the number of node;

Output: R: The final obtained result of community detection;

1 $P_1, P_2, P_3 =$ InitializePopulation(T);
2 $t = 1$;
3 **while** $t \leq m$ **do**
4   **for** i to 3 **do**
5          $Ch_i=$UpdataIndividual(P_i, Np);
6          $g_i =$ FindBestIndividual(Ch_i);
7   **end**
8   **if** $t\%c = 0$ **then**
9   PopulationCommunication();
10   N = CalAttrCosSimilarity(F);
         // NDEA
11   **for** i to 3 **do**
12   **for** j to n **do**
13   **for** k to N_k **do**
14                     $T_i(j, k) = 1$;
15   **end**
16   **end**
17   **end**
18   **end**
19     $t = t + 1$;
20 **end**
21 $P = P_1 \cup P_2 \cup P_3$;
22 $R =$ FindBestIndividual(P);

---

5   Experiments

In this section, we will introduce the dataset, evaluation metrics, and comparison algorithms. In addition, we provide experimental results demonstrating the efficacy of UMEA in terms of accuracy and convergence.

5.1 Datasets

The real-world networks we used are six networks with node attributes in the real world: Texas, Washington, Wisconsin, Cornell, Cora, and CiteSeer. The scale of these networks is shown in Table 1. n, M, and c represent the number of nodes, edges, and communities, respectively, while K represents the number of features in each node.

Table 1. Real-World networks

Dataset	n	m	K	c
Texas	187	328	1703	5
Washington	230	446	1703	5
Wisconsin	265	530	1703	5
Cornell	195	304	1703	5
Cora	2708	5429	1433	7
CiteSeer	3327	4723	3073	6

The synthetic network dataset is generated based on the LFR [12] benchmark. When generating a network, there are several parameters: N represents the number of nodes, k represents the average node degree, k_{max} represents the maximum degree of nodes, c_{min} represents the minimum community size, c_{max} represents the maximum community size, and μ represents the community structure of the network. The larger the value of μ, the more ambiguous the community structure of the network. The networks are shown in Table 2.

Table 2. Synthetic networks

Dateset	N	μ	k	k_{max}	c_{min}	c_{max}
G1	2000	0.5	20	50	10	100
	4000	0.5	20	50	10	100
	6000	0.5	20	50	10	100
	8000	0.5	20	50	10	100
	10000	0.5	20	50	10	100
G2	1000	0.1	20	50	10	100
	1000	0.2	20	50	10	100
	1000	0.3	20	50	10	100
	1000	0.4	20	50	10	100
	1000	0.5	20	50	10	100
	1000	0.6	20	50	10	100

5.2 Evaluation Metrics

Normalized Mutual Information (NMI) [13] is used to measure the similarity between real communities and algorithm results. The greater the effectiveness of the algorithm, the closer the NMI value is to 1. The calculation equation for NMI is as follows:

$$NMI\left(C_t, C\right) = \frac{-2\sum_{i=1}^{c1} \sum_{j=1}^{c2} H_{ij} log\left(\frac{n \times H_{ij}}{H_{i\cdot} \cdot H_{\cdot j}}\right)}{\sum_{i=1}^{c1} H_{i\cdot} log\left(\frac{H_{i\cdot}}{n}\right) + \sum_{j=1}^{c2} H_{\cdot j} log\left(\frac{H_{\cdot j}}{n}\right)} \tag{8}$$

where C_t represents the real community, C represents the community obtained by the algorithm, H_{ij} represents the number of nodes shared by the i-th community, n represents the number of nodes, c_1 and c_2 represent the number of communities in the two results of detection.

5.3 Baseline Algorithms

Our baseline algorithms are sourced from different domains, including: random walks, auto-encoder, matrix factorization, modularity, and evolutionary algorithms.

1. **DeepWalk** [14]: It is an algorithm base on random walks. This algorithm can learn the hidden information of the network and represent the nodes in the graph as a vector.
2. **node2Vec** [15]: An algorithm model inherited from Deepwalk. It can maintain node neighbor information and is easy to train.
3. **MGAE** [6]: It is an automatic edge map encoder. It transforms the adjacency matrix of a graph into an embedding vector and then clusters the nodes.
4. **Louvain** [16]: A semi-supervised graph clustering algorithm that uses modularity as a constraint to measure the quality of the results.
5. **SCI** [17]: It is a novel nonnegative matrix factorization (NMF) model. The use of node attributes improves community detection and provides a semantic interpretation to the resultant network communities.
6. **vGraph** [18]: It is a matrix factorization model. It learns community membership and node representation collaboratively.
7. **RMOEA** [3]: A multi-objective evolutionary algorithm based on network reduction. During the iteration, some closely related nodes are merged into one node to accelerate algorithm convergence.
8. **MOEA-SA** [19]: A multi-objective evolutionary algorithm based on structural and attribute similarity.

5.4 Accuracy Experiment

We compared the accuracy of UMEA with baseline algorithms on real-world networks and synthetic networks. Table 3 presents the NMI values of the community detection results obtained by different algorithms across six real-world

Table 3. NMI on real-world networks

Algorithm	Texas	Washington	Wisconsin	Cornell	Cora	CiteSeer
Deepwalk	0.0325	0.0752	0.0447	0.1030	0.3616	0.1087
node2vec	0.0321	0.0538	0.0477	0.1021	0.3882	0.1836
MGAE	0.2330	0.1933	0.1740	0.2586	0.4554	**0.4036**
Louvain	0.0825	0.1168	0.1113	0.1310	**0.4615**	0.3302
SCI	0.2197	0.2096	0.1852	0.1520	0.1780	0.0922
vGraph	0.0809	0.0649	0.0852	0.0803	0.3445	0.1030
RMOEA	0.0948	0.1351	0.1262	0.1776	0.3213	0.2999
MOEA-SA	0.1410	0.1690	0.170	0.1780	0.3940	0.3330
UMEA	**0.3448**	**0.3971**	**0.3956**	**0.4182**	0.3832	0.3410

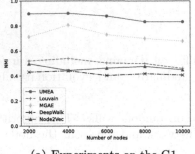

(a) Experiments on the G1

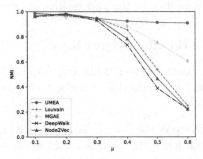

(b) Experiments on the G2

Fig. 4. NMI on synthetic networks

networks. From the table, it can be observed that UMEA demonstrates certain advantages in most networks. It is because the core and Citeseer networks have a higher edge density, and relying on topological information alone is sufficient to establish node connections. Once attribute information is introduced, it leads to decreased accuracy. As a result, UMEA is 0.06 lower than the best result. However, in other networks, many nodes do not have neighbors and need to establish connections with other nodes through attribute information. Therefore, NDEA can effectively combine attribute information and outperform other best algorithms by 0.17 on different datasets.

Figure 4 illustrates that our algorithm performs satisfactorily as the community size and μ increases. Even when the community structure becomes ambiguous, UMEA's algorithm maintains an NMI of 0.8 or above. Other baseline algorithms show a decline in NMI values after μ exceeds 0.4. Even when μ is set to 0.6, the best-performing algorithm, MGAE, only achieves an NMI of around 0.6. UMEA is more effective than other algorithms at integrating network attribute information for community detection when network topology information is ambiguous. UMEA improves the connectivity between nodes that should belong to the same community by adding edges to the original network based on the attribute information. In subsequent iterations, there is a greater tendency to allocate them to the same community, thereby enhancing the precision of community detection.

6   Conclusions

We propose an unsupervised multi-population evolutionary algorithm for community detection in attributed networks. This algorithm allows various populations to learn from one another and add new edges between nodes based on the attribute information of the original network, thereby dividing the community more accurately. Moreover, the updated strategies can hasten the convergence of solutions. The experimental results demonstrate that UMEA outperforms baseline algorithms on various datasets. We will continue our research in the feature to enable this algorithm to perform community detection on overlapping attributed networks.

Acknowledgement. This work was supported by the National Natural Science Foundation of China under Grant No. 62002063 and No. U21A20472, the National Key Research and Development Plan of China under Grant No.2021YFB3600503, the Fujian Collaborative Innovation Center for Big Data Applications in Governments, the Fujian Industry-Academy Cooperation Project under Grant No. 2017H6008 and No. 2018H6010, the Natural Science Foundation of Fujian Province under Grant No.2022J01118, No.2020J05112 and No.2020J01420, the Fujian Provincial Department of Education under Grant No.JAT190026, the Major Science and Technology Project of Fujian Province under Grant No.2021HZ022007 and Haixi Government Big Data Application Cooperative Innovation Center.

References

1. Ma, H., Liu, Z., Zhang, X., Zhang, L., Jiang, H.: Balancing topology structure and node attribute in evolutionary multi-objective community detection for attributed networks. Knowl.-Based Syst. **227**, 107169 (2021)
2. Shi, C., Yan, Z., Cai, Y., Wu, B.: Multi-objective community detection in complex networks. Appl. Soft Comput. **12**(2), 850–859 (2012)
3. Zhang, X., Zhou, K., Pan, H., Zhang, L., Zeng, X., Jin, Y.: A network reduction-based multiobjective evolutionary algorithm for community detection in large-scale complex networks. IEEE Trans. Cybern. **50**(2), 703–716 (2018)
4. He, T., Chan, K.C.: Evolutionary community detection in social networks. In: IEEE Congress on Evolutionary Computation (CEC), vol. 2014, pp. 1496–1503. IEEE (2014)
5. Sun, J., Zheng, W., Zhang, Q., Xu, Z.: Graph neural network encoding for community detection in attribute networks. IEEE Trans. Cybern. **52**(8), 7791–7804 (2021)
6. Wang, C., Pan, S., Long, G., Zhu, X., Jiang, J.: MGAE: marginalized graph autoencoder for graph clustering. In: Proceedings of the 2017 ACM on Conference on Information and Knowledge Management, pp. 889–898 (2017)

7. Li, Y., Sha, C., Huang, X., Zhang, Y.: Community detection in attributed graphs: an embedding approach. In: Proceedings of the AAAI Conference on Artificial Intelligence, vol. 32, no. 1 (2018)
8. Naderipour, M., Zarandi, M.H.F., Bastani, S.: A fuzzy cluster-validity index based on the topology structure and node attribute in complex networks. Expert Syst. Appl. **187**, 115913 (2022)
9. Kakisim, A.G.: Enhancing attributed network embedding via enriched attribute representations. Appl. Intell. **52**(2), 1566–1580 (2022)
10. Bothorel, C., Cruz, J.D., Magnani, M., Micenkova, B.: Clustering attributed graphs: models, measures and methods. Netw. Sci. **3**(3), 408–444 (2015)
11. Newman, M.E.: Modularity and community structure in networks. Proc. Natl. Acad. Sci. **103**(23), 8577–8582 (2006)
12. Lu, D.-D., Qi, J., Yan, J., Zhang, Z.-Y.: Community detection combining topology and attribute information. Knowl. Inf. Syst. **64**(2), 537–558 (2022)
13. Amelio, A., Pizzuti, C.: Is normalized mutual information a fair measure for comparing community detection methods? In: Proceedings of the 2015 IEEE/ACM International Conference on Advances in Social Networks Analysis and Mining, vol. 2015, pp. 1584–1585 (2015)
14. Perozzi, B., Al-Rfou, R., Skiena, S.: DeepWalk: online learning of social representations. In: Proceedings of the 20th ACM SIGKDD International Conference on Knowledge Discovery and Data Mining, pp. 701–710 (2014)
15. Grover, A., Leskovec, J.: node2vec: scalable feature learning for networks. In: Proceedings of the 22nd ACM SIGKDD International Conference on Knowledge Discovery and Data Mining, pp. 855–864 (2016)
16. Blondel, V.D., Guillaume, J.-L., Lambiotte, R., Lefebvre, E.: Fast unfolding of communities in large networks. J. Stat. Mech: Theory Exp. **2008**(10), P10008 (2008)
17. Wang, X., Jin, D., Cao, X., Yang, L., Zhang, W.: Semantic community identification in large attribute networks. In: Proceedings of the AAAI Conference on Artificial Intelligence, vol. 30, no. 1 (2016)
18. Sun, F.-Y., Qu, M., Hoffmann, J., Huang, C.-W., Tang, J.: vgraph: a generative model for joint community detection and node representation learning. In: Advances in Neural Information Processing Systems, vol. 32 (2019)
19. Li, Z., Liu, J., Wu, K.: A multiobjective evolutionary algorithm based on structural and attribute similarities for community detection in attributed networks. IEEE Trans. Cybern. **48**(7), 1963–1976 (2017)

Parallel High Utility Itemset Mining Algorithm on the Spark

Chengyan Li, Lei Zhang$^{(\boxtimes)}$, and Anqi Sun

Harbin University of Science and Technology, Harbin 150080, China
1752198319@qq.com

Abstract. In the field of efficient utility itemset mining, considering both internal and external utility values provides a more comprehensive approach compared to traditional frequency-based methods. However, the increased complexity of computations and the generation of numerous candidate itemsets pose challenges for efficient mining on large-scale datasets. To address these challenges, this paper proposes a parallel mining algorithm based on the Spark framework. The algorithm leverages a vertical dataset structure to efficiently store and process the data. A utility table is utilized to store the data items along with their corresponding transaction utility values. By utilizing the utility table, the algorithm can directly access transaction utility values, simplifying the computation process and reducing overhead. To further enhance efficiency, the algorithm combines a prefix partitioning strategy with a minimum utility threshold. By employing this strategy, the generation of candidate itemsets is effectively reduced, resulting in a smaller search space and enhancing the efficiency of the mining process. The algorithm is implemented on the Spark framework, leveraging its capabilities in parallel processing and scalability. By leveraging the distributed computing capabilities of Spark, the algorithm can efficiently mine efficient utility frequent item-sets from large-scale datasets. Experimental results demonstrate the effectiveness and efficiency of the proposed algorithm in performing efficient utility itemset mining. It surpasses traditional approaches and showcases its ability to handle large-scale datasets while maintaining high performance.

Keywords: Data mining · Spark framework · Parallel computing · Efficient utility item-sets

1 Introduction

Association analysis is an essential data mining process with diverse applications, encompassing the mining of frequent itemsets from a database and the discovery of association rules. Traditional algorithms for frequent itemset mining, such as the Apriori algorithm and the FP-Growth algorithm, focus primarily on item frequency, neglecting other essential factors like item significance or profitability [1]. As a result, these algorithms tend to extract only highly frequent itemsets, potentially over-looking less frequent itemsets that could be highly profitable.

© The Author(s), under exclusive license to Springer Nature Singapore Pte Ltd. 2024
Y. Sun et al. (Eds.): ChineseCSCW 2023, CCIS 2012, pp. 167–181, 2024.
https://doi.org/10.1007/978-981-99-9637-7_12

Liu, et al. [2] introduced HUIM algorithms to address these limitations. These algorithms are widely used in real-world scenarios, including analyzing shopping basket data, website clickstream data, and biomedical applications [3]. HUIM algorithms overcome the shortcomings of traditional frequent itemset mining by considering additional attributes of transaction items, such as internal and external utility.

Due to the absence of the downward closure property, HUIM algorithms employ alternative pruning techniques for efficient mining of high-utility itemsets [4]. The Two-Phase algorithm, an extension of the Apriori algorithm [5], incorporates the concepts of transaction-weighted utility and the downward closure property to perform high-utility itemset mining in two distinct stages.

To address the efficiency and scalability issues encountered in the Two-Phase algorithms, researchers have proposed single-phase algorithms that aim to overcome these challenges [6]. By eliminating the need for a separate first phase for candidate set generation, these algorithms streamline the mining process and improve overall efficiency. HUI-Miner and UP-Growth are single-phase algorithms that address the efficiency and scalability challenges of the Two-Phase algorithms by streamlining the mining process into a single step [7]. HUI-Miner employs a utility list data structure to efficiently store utility information associated with transaction items. This enables the algorithm to generate high-utility frequent itemsets by efficiently scanning and processing the utility list [8].

However, single-phase algorithms are typically designed for single-machine systems [9], limiting their ability to mine large datasets due to memory constraints. To enable efficient high-utility itemset mining in large-scale datasets, researchers have proposed extending these algorithms to distributed big data platforms [10]. The PHUI-Growth algorithm, designed for the Hadoop platform, achieves parallel high-utility itemset mining using the Hadoop MapReduce framework [11]. Nonetheless, the inherent limitations of the Hadoop platform result in significant overhead during the mapping iterations [12]. In contrast, the Spark platform offers faster in-memory processing higher iteration efficiency [13], and greater flexibility compared to the Hadoop MapReduce framework. Leveraging these advantages, the PKU (Parallel top-k High Utility Item Mining) algorithm has been proposed to run on the Spark platform. Although the PKU algorithm achieves high mining efficiency [14], the continuous adjustment of boundary values to obtain a specified number of high-utility itemsets may generate numerous intermediate low-utility item-sets [15], leading to increased memory consumption and time complexity.

In order to overcome these challenges, we have developed a parallel algorithm for mining high-utility itemsets. This algorithm takes advantage of the Spark framework, enabling efficient and scalable processing of large-scale datasets. The algorithm utilizes a vertical data format [16] for mining, stores and computes utility information using utility tables, incorporates pruning techniques through prefix partitioning and a minimum utility threshold, and achieves fast high-utility itemset mining in a parallel manner within the Spark framework.

2 Relevant Definitions

The transaction database $D = \{T1, T2,\ldots, Tm\}$ is composed of a set of transactions. Each transaction T belonging to the database D has a unique identifier TID. $I = \{i1, i2,\ldots, in\}$ is a finite set of n items from D. For each transaction T, an itemset $X \subseteq I$ is a finite collection of items. Each item is associated with positive values of both internal utility (e.g., purchase quantity) and external utility (e.g., unit profit). Table 1 provides an example transaction database containing five transactions, which will be used for illustrative purposes. Transaction T3 contains items a, c, d, e, and g with internal utility values of 2, 3, 4, 1, and 1, respectively. Table 2 presents the external utility values for all items.

Definition 1 (Internal Utility of an Item): Let T_j represent a transaction, i denote an item, and X represent an itemset. The internal utility of an item i in transaction T_j, denoted as $q(i, T_j)$, signifies the quantity of the item sold[2].

Definition 2 (External Utility of an Item):The external utility of an item i represents the profit obtained from selling a single unit of the item. It is denoted as p(i)[2].

Definition 3 (Utility of an Item):The utility of item i in transaction T_j[2], denoted as $u(i, T_j)$[2], is defined as follows:

$$u(i, T_j) = p(i) \times q(i, T_j) \tag{1}$$

For example, the utility value of item a in transaction T_1 is obtained by multiplying the internal utility of item a in transaction T_1 with the external utility of item a. Therefore, $u(a,T_1) = p(a) \times q(a,T_1) = 5 \times 1 = 5$.

Definition 4 (Utility of an Itemset in Transaction T_j):The utility of an itemset X in transaction T_j [2], denoted as $u(X, T_j)$, is defined as follows:

$$u(X,T_j) = \sum_{i \in X} u(i, T_j) \tag{2}$$

For example, the utility of item a in T_4 is calculated as $u(a,T_4) = 3 \times 5 = 15$. The utility of itemset {a, c} in T_1 is calculated as $u(\{a,c\},T_1) = u(a,T_1) + u(c,T_1) = 1 \times 5 + 3 \times 3 = 6$. The utility of itemset {c, d} is calculated as $u(\{c,d\}) = u(\{c,d\},T_2) + u(\{c,d\},T_3) + u(\{c,d\},T_4) = u(c,T_2) + u(d,T_2) + u(c,T_3) + u(d,T_3) + u(c,T_4) + u(d,T_4)$.

Definition 5 (Transaction Utility, TU): The utility of transaction T_j, denoted as $TU(T_j)$, is the sum of the utility values of all items in that transaction [2]. It can be calculated using the following formula:

$$TU(T_j) = \sum_{i \in T_j} u(i, T_j) \tag{3}$$

For example, let's consider transaction T4. The calculation of its transaction utility is as follows: $TU(T_4) = u(a,T_4) + u(c,T_4) + u(d,T_4) + u(e,T_4) + u(g,T_4) = 15 + 3 + 4 + 6 + 3 = 31$.

Definition 6 (Transaction Weighted Utility, TWU): The transaction weighted utility [2], TWU(X), is defined as follows:

$$TWU(X) = \sum_{T_j \in g(X)} TU(X, T_j) \tag{4}$$

where g(X) is the set that contains X.

For example, TWU(a), the transaction weighted utility of item a, is calculated as $TWU(a) = TU[T_1] + TU[T_2] + TU[T_3] + TU[T_4] = 19 + 21 + 25 + 31 = 96$. Table 3 displays the transaction weighted utility (TWU) of each item in the database.

Definition 7 (Minimum Utility Threshold): The minimum utility threshold (minutl) is a user-defined threshold greater than 0. It is used as a filtering condition during the mining process of high-utility itemsets.

Definition 8 (High-Utility Itemset): High Utility Itemsets (HUIs) refer to sets of items for which the user-defined utility exceeds the minimum utility threshold [2]. An itemset X is considered a high-utility itemset if its weighted utility TWU(X) is not less than minutl. Otherwise, it is considered a low-utility itemset.

For example, when setting the minimum utility threshold (minutl) to 60, in the example database, the high utility frequent 1-itemsets are {a}, {c}, {d}, and {e}, with transaction weighted utilities of 94, 105, 77, and 65, respectively. The frequent 2-itemsets are {a, d}, {a, c}, {c, d}, and {c, e}, with transaction weighted utilities of 77, 69, 77, and 65, respectively. The high utility frequent 3-itemset is {a, c, d}, with a transaction weighted utility of 77.

Table 1. Example database table.

TID	Transaction	TU
T_1	(a,1)(b,3)(c,3)	19
T_2	(a,1)(b,4)(c,2)(d,3)	21
T_3	(a,2)(c,3)(d,4)(e,1)(g,1)	25
T_4	(a,3)(c,3)(d,2)(e,2)(g,3)	31
T_5	(b,2)(c,1)(e,1)(f,2)	9

Table 2. Transaction external utility table.

Item	a	b	c	d	e	f	g
External Utility	5	2	1	2	3	1	1

Table 3. Item transaction weighted utility table.

Item	a	b	c	d	e	f	g
TWU	94	49	105	77	65	9	56

Definition 9 (Item Utility Table): It is a storage structure that stores the vertical data, consisting of data items and their corresponding Transaction IDs (TIDs).

Definition 10 (Transaction Utility Table): It is a storage structure that stores the transaction numbers and their corresponding Transaction Utility (TU) values for each transaction in the database.

Definition 11 (High-Utility Prefix): Given a high-utility itemset $\{i_1, i_2, i_3, \ldots, i_n, i_{n+1}\}$ consisting of n + 1 data items, the high-utility prefix refers to the remaining data items $\{i_1, i_2, i_3, \ldots, i_n\}$ after excluding the last data item, i_{n+1}.

3 Algorithm Introduction

3.1 Data Preprocessing

The algorithm utilizes the vertical dataset format and employs bitmap-based TidSets for storing and managing TIDs associated with items. This approach facilitates efficient retrieval of TIDs, simplifies TWU (Transaction Weighted Utility) calculation, eliminates redundant dataset reading, improves algorithm efficiency, and saves computational space. Therefore, this paper's algorithm utilizes a vertical dataset format and employs bitmaps for item storage, making the algorithm process more straightforward. The process of transforming a horizontal efficient utility dataset into a vertical dataset is illustrated in Fig. 1.

TID	Items
T1	(a,1)(b,3)(c,3)
T2	(a,1)(b,4)(c,2)(d,3)
T3	(a,2)(c,3)(d,4)(e,1)(g,1)
T4	(a,3)(c,3)(d,4)(e,2)(g,3)
T5	(b,2)(c,1)(e,1)(f,2)

Item	TIDs
a	(1,1)(2,1)(3,2)(4,3)
b	(1,3)(2,4)(5,2)
c	(1,3)(2,2)(3,3)(4,3)(5,1)
d	(2,3)(3,4)(4,2)
e	(3,1)(4,2)(5,1)
f	(5,2)
g	(3,1)(4,3)

Fig. 1. Diagram illustrating the process of converting a horizontal dataset to a vertical dataset.

3.2 Initialize Utility Table

The processed vertical dataset is read and stored by leveraging the vertical format of the data. To enhance the computation speed and efficiency of the algorithm, and to leverage the vertical storage format, utility tables are used to store and access data during the algorithmic process. In this paper's algorithm, two utility tables are established to store and retrieve data, namely the item utility table and the transaction utility table.

The storage format of the item utility table is shown in Table 4. Item {a} is present in transactions 1, 2, 3, and 4, with corresponding transaction IDs (TIDs) {1, 2, 3, 4}. In the map(), {a} is stored as the key, and the TIDs are stored as the value in the bitmap.

The storage format of the Transaction Utility Table is shown in Table 5. Each transaction has a unique transaction utility (TU) value associated with it. For example, transaction 1 has a computed TU value of 19, so the key-value pair of transaction number 1 and its TU value of 19 is stored in the map().

Table 4. Data item utility table.

Item	TIDs
a	1,2,3,4
b	1,2,5
c	1,2,3,4,5
d	2,3,4
e	3,4,5
f	5
g	3,4

Table 5. Transaction utility table.

TID	TU
1	19
2	21
3	25
4	31
5	9

To calculate the transaction-weighted utility for itemsets, it is necessary to retrieve the set of transaction IDs associated with the particular item or itemset from the item utility table. By accessing the corresponding transaction IDs, the transactions involved can be identified. Leveraging the transaction utility table, the transaction utilities relevant to the item or itemset are obtained. These utilities are then summed to compute the transaction-weighted utility. Utilizing the utility table to store and access data simplifies the algorithm's implementation process and enhances computation speed.

3.3 Computation of Efficient Utility Frequent 1-itemsets

In Fig. 2, we compute high utility frequent 1-itemsets with a minimum threshold of 60. Using the data item utility table and TIDs, TU values are fetched from the transaction utility table for each transaction. Transaction-weighted utility is calculated by summing these TUs and compared to the threshold to spot high utility frequent itemsets. For instance, data item {a} in transactions 1, 2, 3, and 4 has a TWU of 94—above the 60 threshold. {a} and its TIDs update the transaction-item utility table. However, data item {b} has a utility of 49, below the high utility limit, and is excluded. After processing all items, high utility frequent 1-itemsets are determined and the table is updated accordingly.

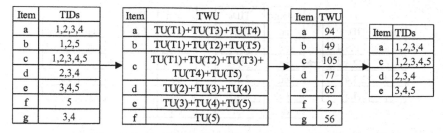

Fig. 2. Depicts the generation process of frequent 1-itemsets with high utility.

Algorithm 2	Calculate frequent 1-itemsets
Input	The Data utility table、 The Transaction utility table
Output	Frequent 1-items fre_1
1	fre_1←new HashMap
2	str[]←item,bitset
3	tag←item
4	TWU←0
5	for i <=str[].length do
6	str1←item,bitset←TIDs
7	TWU+=tuMap.get(str1[0])
8	if TWU >=minutl
9	fre_1.put(tag,bitset)
10	return fre_1

3.4 Computation of Efficient Utility Frequent 2-itemsets

After obtaining high utility frequent 1-itemsets using the updated data item utility table, the algorithm proceeds to compute frequent 2-itemsets. By leveraging TIDs from both transaction item utility and transaction utility tables, the algorithm retrieves itemset TUs, computes TWU, and filters out low utility itemsets against minutl. This process yields high utility frequent 2-itemsets, updating the data item utility table. Figure 3 depicts this process. Resulting high utility candidate 2-itemsets are stored in a new transaction item utility table. This table holds itemsets and corresponding TIDs. The algorithm then fetches TUs for each candidate itemset, computes TWU, and discards low utility itemsets. Remaining itemsets satisfying high utility conditions are deemed high utility frequent 2-itemsets and are stored.

In the specific implementation of generating high utility frequent 2-itemsets, we employ an updated Item_table2, which acts as a repository for the high utility frequent 1-itemsets and is implemented using a HashMap(). The termination condition for the loop is determined by the length of the 1-itemsets, ensuring that we iterate through all the relevant elements.

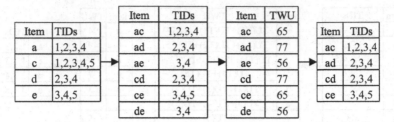

Fig. 3. Illustration of generating high utility frequent 2-itemsets.

These steps collectively contribute to the extraction of high utility frequent 2-itemsets, showcasing the importance and profitability of these itemsets in the dataset under examination. The pseudocode outlining the algorithm for generating fre_2 is presented in Algorithm 3.

Algorithm 3	Calculate frequent 2-itemsets
Input	Frequent 1-items
Output	Frequent 2-items fre_2
1	Item_table3←new hasMap()
2	for i<fre_1.size() do:
3	iterator←fre_1.values().iterator()
4	while iterator.hasNext() do
5	bitSet←TIDs
6	bitSet3←bitSet&&bitSetClone
7	if !bitSet3.isEmpty() do
8	TWU=TU(bitSet3)
9	if TWU>=minutl
10	fre_2.put(key,bitSet3)
11	return fre_2

3.5 Computation of Efficient Utility Frequent k(k > 2)-Itemsets

In the process of computing high utility frequent k (k > 2)-itemsets, we employ a strategy known as prefix partitioning to effectively reduce the exploration space.

To illustrate this process, we can refer to Fig. 4. In the depicted example, we start by extracting prefixes from the high utility frequent 2-itemsets. These prefixes are then evaluated for potential matches. In the case of {ac} and {ad}, we observe that both of them share the same prefix {a}. This discovery allows us to perform an intersection operation on the corresponding TIDs associated with {c} and {d}, ultimately resulting in the identification of the item {cd} along with its set of TIDs {2, 3, 4}.

Furthermore, we proceed to merge the extracted prefix {a} with the item {cd}. This merging operation enables us to form a candidate 3-itemset {a, c, d}, suggesting a potentially high utility frequent itemset. The set of TIDs {2, 3, 4} is retained as the associated transaction identifiers for this candidate itemset.

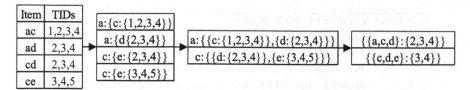

Fig. 4. Prefix partitioning illustration.

The process for generating frequent k-itemsets is depicted in Fig. 8. We performed calculations on the candidate itemsets obtained after employing the prefix partitioning strategy. By retrieving the corresponding Transaction ID Utility (TU), we computed the Transaction-Weighted Utility (TWU) values for {acd} and {cde} as 77 and 56, respectively. Considering our minimum utility threshold set at 60, we excluded {cde} as it did not meet the threshold criteria. However, the item {acd} satisfied the threshold condition and was consequently stored in the set of high utility frequent 3-itemsets (Fig. 5).

Item	TIDs
acd	2,3,4
cde	3,4

Item	TWU
acd	77
cde	56

Item	TIDs
acd	2,3,4

Fig. 5. Illustration of the generation process of high utility Frequent k-itemsets.

During the computation of fre_k, we still utilize iterators to extract and store the transaction IDs (TIDs) from the transaction item utility table.

Next, a combination of action operators and transformation operators is employed to perform the prefix partitioning process, resulting in a candidate itemset. By combining this candidate itemset with the transaction item utility table, we calculate the Transaction-Weighted Utility (TWU) and obtain a row in fre_k. This entire process is executed within a larger loop, continuing until the updated transaction item utility table from the previous stage has been traversed k times. The pseudocode for this stage is presented in Algorithm 4.

Algorithm 4	Calculate frequent k-itemsets
Input	Frequent(k-1)-items
Output	Frequent k-items
1	Item_table(k)←new hasNext()
2	iteratori1←Item_table(k).keySet,iterator i2←Item_table(k).value
3	while i1.hasNext() && i2.hasNext()
4	if i<k
5	str[]←i1.split(",")
6	while i<k
7	String str_i=str[k-1]
8	map1.put(str_1,bitSet)
9	map2.put(str_2,map1)
10	JavaRDD←sc.parallerlizePairs(map2).reduceKey(item,bitSet)
11	map.put(item,bitSet)
12	if !bitSet.Empty()
13	TWU←TU(bitSet)
14	if TWU>=minutl
15	fre_k.put(key,bitSet)
16	return fre_k

3.6 Pruning Process

The algorithm combines prefix partitioning and a minimum utility threshold to efficiently prune candidate itemsets, reducing itemset generation and search space. For high-utility frequent k-itemsets, we retrieve prior (k-1)-itemsets and their transaction sets. Prefixes are formed by extracting (k-2) sub-items and merging with remaining sub-items to create 2-itemsets. These merge with prefixes to generate candidate k-itemsets.Fig. 6 depicts the pruning process to generate high-utility frequent 3-itemsets from high-utility frequent 2-itemsets. In the diagram, there are 4 high-utility frequent 2-itemsets: {ac}, {ad}, {cd}, and {ce}, each with corresponding transaction IDs (TIDs). After prefix extraction, remaining items are intersected pairwise to form 2-itemsets. These merge with prefixes to create high-utility candidate 3-itemsets. By calculating utility and comparing with the threshold, we identify the high-utility frequent 3-itemset {acd}.

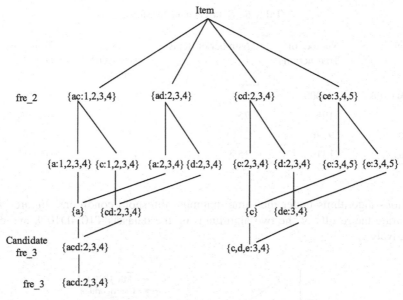

Fig. 6. Pruning process illustration.

4 Experiment

4.1 Experimental Design

To evaluate the performance of the algorithm, we considered two crucial factors that significantly influence the efficiency of the utility itemset mining algorithm:

Dataset: We assigned utility values to the items in these datasets to obtain the desired efficient utility datasets. We also selected both sparse and dense datasets for conducting the algorithm experiments.

Minimum Utility Threshold: We conducted experiments to investigate the influence of the minimum utility threshold on the HUIM algorithm's performance. By adapting this threshold, determined by dataset characteristics, we measured runtime across different threshold values.

4.2 Experimental Dataset

In our evaluation of the algorithm's time efficiency, we utilized a total of six datasets obtained from the FIMI website. The characteristics of each dataset are detailed in Table 6.

4.3 Comparison of Algorithm Runtime Efficiency

To evaluate the algorithm's time efficiency across different platforms, we performed multiple runs using different datasets and decreasing minimum utility thresholds. For each dataset, we collected five sets of comparative data to measure the execution times

Table 6. Dataset characteristics.

Dataset	Number of Transactions	Number of Items	Average Transaction Length	Transaction Density
T10I4D100k	100000	870	10	1.16%
chess	3196	75	37	49.33%
pumsb	49046	2113	74	3.5%
foodmart	4141	1559	4.42	0.28%

of various algorithms under the same minimum threshold conditions. Figures 7 and 8 illustrate the results of the two algorithms on the datasets T10I4D100k and chess, respectively.

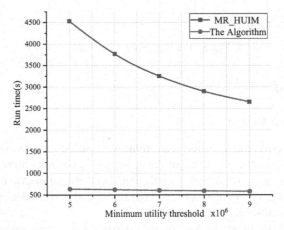

Fig. 7. Efficiency comparison of algorithm execution time on the T10I4D100k dataset.

As illustrated in Fig. 7 and Fig. 8, In the T10I4D100k dataset, the algorithm's execution time exhibits a relatively stable In the context of sparse dataset T10I4D100k and dense dataset chess, the algorithm is executed with varying threshold values. The performance evaluation demonstrates the algorithm's effectiveness in both sparse and dense datasets, showcasing its consistent performance across diverse threshold settings. This finding confirms the superiority of the proposed efficient high-utility itemset mining algorithm on the Spark platform compared to algorithms utilized in the MapReduce framework on the Hadoop platform. The algorithm not only outperforms its counterpart in terms of performance but also exhibits higher mining efficiency.

On the Spark platform, we performed concurrent executions of the UP-Growth algorithm, HUI-Miner algorithm, and the proposed algorithm on the foodmart and pumsb datasets. This allowed us to measure the execution times of each algorithm across different minutls. By systematically varying the minutl and analyzing the corresponding

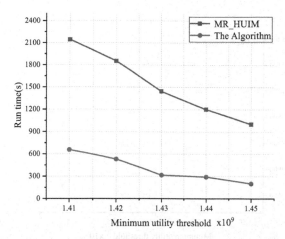

Fig. 8. Efficiency comparison of algorithm execution time on the chess dataset.

execution times, we obtained precise insights into the performance characteristics of these algorithms. This rigorous evaluation provides a solid foundation for comparing their efficiency, scalability, and suitability for mining high utility itemsets on diverse datasets.

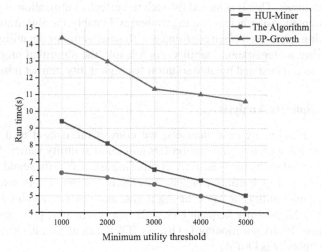

Fig. 9. Efficiency comparison of algorithm execution time on the Foodmart dataset.

Figures 9 and 10 show a comparison of execution times for three efficient high utility itemset mining algorithms on the foodmart and pumsb datasets. In the foodmart dataset, the proposed algorithm demonstrates lower time consumption than the UP-Growth algorithm and the HUI-Miner algorithm, all operating under the same minimum utility threshold. Specifically, the proposed algorithm takes about half the time of the HUI-Miner algorithm. Moreover, as the minimum utility threshold decreases, the time

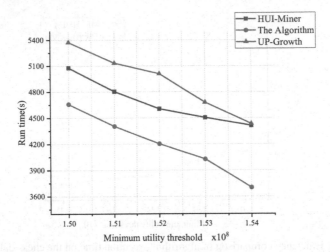

Fig. 10. Efficiency comparison of algorithm execution time on the pumsb dataset.

consumption difference between the proposed algorithm and the UP-Growth and HUI-Miner algorithms becomes more pronounced.

Based on the comprehensive analysis of experimental results, it can be concluded that the algorithm proposed in this paper showcases exceptional performance when applied to large-scale datasets. This is achieved through the effective utilization of utility tables and the implementation of efficient pruning strategies. Notably, the algorithm maintains a consistent mining speed even when confronted with smaller minimum utility thresholds, thus underscoring its remarkable stability. As a result, the algorithm proposed in this paper emerges as a robust and reliable solution for high utility itemset mining tasks.

4.4 Time Complexity Analysis

To compute high-utility frequent itemsets, we convert the dataset to a vertical format, associate items with their transaction IDs and internal utility values. We calculate transaction-weighted utility for 1-itemsets, comparing against the threshold. Complexity for this is $O(n^2)$. For high-utility frequent 2-itemsets, we iterate 1-itemsets, calculate transaction-weighted utility for co-occurring items, and generate candidate sets. Complexity is $O(n^3)$. High-utility frequent k ($k > 2$)-itemsets involve prefix extraction and TWU calculation. Prefix partitioning is $O(n^3)$, TWU calculation is $O(n)$. Combined, k-itemsets' complexity is $O(n^4)$.

5   Conclusion

In this paper, we perform high-utility itemset mining in a single pass over the database. We use a utility table to store dataset utility information, which is dynamically updated during execution to reduce memory usage and computational load. We employ a high-utility prefix partitioning strategy for pruning, minimizing utility tables and saving computational space. The algorithm is implemented on the Spark distributed cluster, enabling efficient mining of large-scale datasets. It improves mining speed, addresses memory overflow in single-machine mining, and demonstrates fast execution, stability, and effectiveness even with low minimum utility thresholds.

Acknowledgements. This work was supported in part by: Natural Science Foundation of Heilongjiang Province (Nos. LH2021F032).

References

1. Kumar, S., Mohbey, K.K.: High utility pattern mining distributed algorithm based on spark RDD. In: Bhateja, V., Satapathy, S.C., Travieso-Gonzalez, C.M., Flores-Fuentes, W. (eds.) Computer Communication, Networking and IoT. LNNS, vol. 197, pp. 367–374. Springer, Singapore (2021). https://doi.org/10.1007/978-981-16-0980-0_34
2. Liu, Y., Liao, W.-K., Choudhary, A.: A two-phase algorithm for fast discovery of high utility itemsets. In: Ho, T.B., Cheung, D., Liu, H. (eds.) PAKDD 2005. LNCS (LNAI), vol. 3518, pp. 689–695. Springer, Heidelberg (2005). https://doi.org/10.1007/11430919_79
3. Cheng, Z., Fang, W., Shen, W., et al.: An efficient utility-list based high-utility itemset mining algorithm. Appl. Intell. **53**, 6992–7006 (2023)
4. Pushp, Chand, S.: Mining of high utility itemsets for incremental datasets. In: International Conference on Electrical, Computer, Communications and Mechatronics Engineering (ICECCME). IEEE (2021)
5. Dam, T.-L., Li, K., Fournier-Viger, P., Duong, Q.-H.: CLS-Miner: efficient and effective closed high-utility itemset mining. Front. Comput. Sci. **13**(2), 357–381 (2018). https://doi.org/10.1007/s11704-016-6245-4
6. Zida, S., Fournier-Viger, P., Lin, C.W., et al.: EFIM: a fast and memory efficient algorithm for high-utility itemset mining. Knowl. Inf. Syst. **51**(2), 1–31 (2017)
7. Yildirim, I., Celik, M.: Mining high-average utility itemsets with positive and negative external utilities. New Gener. Comput. **38**(1), 153–186 (2019). https://doi.org/10.1007/s00354-019-00078-8
8. Dong, X., Wang, M., Liu, Y., Xiao, G., Huang, D., Wang, G.: An efficient spatial high-utility occupancy frequent item mining algorithm for mission system integration architecture design using the MBSE method. Aerosp. Syst. **5**, 1–16 (2021). https://doi.org/10.1007/s42401-021-00126-6
9. Kumar, R., Singh, K.: A survey on soft computing-based high-utility itemsets mining. Soft. Comput. **26**(13), 6347–6392 (2022)
10. O'reilly: Learning spark lightning-fast big data analysis. Oreilly & Associates Inc, (2015)
11. Saleti, S.: Incremental mining of high utility sequential patterns using MapReduce paradigm. Clust. Comput. **25**(2), 805–825 (2021). https://doi.org/10.1007/s10586-021-03448-4
12. Zhang, F., Liu, M., Gui, F., et al.: A distributed frequent itemset mining algorithm using spark for big data analytics. Cluster Comput. **18**, 1493–1501 (2015)
13. Wu, J.M.-T., Srivastava, G., Wei, M., Yun, U., Chun-Wei Lin, J.: Fuzzy high-utility pattern mining in parallel and distributed Hadoop framework, Inf. Sci., 31–48 (2021)
14. Sathyavani, D., Sharmila, D.: Retraction note to: an improved memory adaptive up-growth to mine high utility itemsets from large transaction databases. J. Ambient Intell. Hum. Comput. **14**(Suppl 1), 229 (2023)
15. Ganesan, M., Shankar, S.: High utility fuzzy product mining (HUFPM) using investigation of HUWAS approach. J. Ambient Intell. Hum. Comput. **13**, 3271–3281 (2022)
16. Ishita, S.Z., Ahmed, C.F., Leung, C.K.: New approaches for mining regular high utility sequential patterns. Appl. Intell. **52**, 3781–3806 (2022)

ABCD-HN: An Artificial Network Benchmark for Community Detection on Heterogeneous Networks

Junjie Liu[1,2,3], Kun Guo[1,2,3(✉)], and Ling Wu[1,2,3]

[1] Fujian Provincial Key Laboratory of Network Computing and Intelligent Information Processing, Fuzhou University, Fuzhou 350108, China
gukn@fzu.edu.cn
[2] College of Computer and Data Science/College of Software, Fuzhou University, Fuzhou 350108, China
[3] Key Laboratory of Spatial Data Mining and Information Sharing, Ministry of Education, Fuzhou 350108, China

Abstract. Community detection is essential for identifying cohesive groups in complex networks. Artificial benchmarks are critical for evaluating community detection algorithms, offering controlled environments with known community structures. However, existing benchmarks mainly focus on homogeneous networks and overlook the unique characteristics of heterogeneous networks. This paper proposes a novel artificial benchmark, called ABCD-HN (Artificial Network Benchmark for Community Detection on Heterogeneous Networks), for community detection in heterogeneous networks. This benchmark enables the generation of artificial heterogeneous networks with controllable community quantity, node quantity, and community complexity. Additionally, an evaluation framework for artificial heterogeneous networks is proposed to assess their effectiveness. Experimental results demonstrate the effectiveness and usability of ABCD-HN as a benchmark for artificial heterogeneous networks.

Keywords: artificial benchmark · community detection · heterogeneous network

1 Introduction

Community detection refers to identifying groups of nodes with intrinsic and tight connections within complex networks. In the field of community detection, artificial benchmarks are crucial tools. These networks possess known community structures and topological properties, making them suitable for testing and evaluating various community detection algorithms. In the early stages of community detection research, artificial benchmarks were primarily constructed based on random graph models and generative models, such as the ER model

(Erdős-Rényi model) [2] and the BA model (Barabási-Albert model) [3]. However, these models had limitations in capturing the complex social network structures in the real world. To overcome these issues, researchers began developing more complex and realistic artificial benchmarks, such as the GN benchmark (Girvan-Newman benchmark) [4] and the LFR benchmark (Lancichinetti-Fortunato-Radicchi benchmark) [5]. These benchmarks consider the complexity of real social networks and exhibit better interpretability and applicability.

As research progressed, more benchmark tests were proposed to evaluate the performance of community detection algorithms in different types of networks, dynamic networks, and complex scenarios with overlapping communities. However, these artificial benchmarks were all based on homogeneous networks, where the nodes and edges in the network are the same types. Although there are some manually constructed artificial heterogeneous networks for specific purposes, they lack generality. The existing benchmarks designed for homogeneous networks cannot be readily adapted to heterogeneous networks due to the individual heterogeneity of such networks. Therefore, there is a need to design a specialized artificial benchmark for community detection in heterogeneous networks that can generate controllable artificial heterogeneous networks in terms of network size and community complexity. Additionally, no dedicated evaluation framework is currently available for assessing artificial heterogeneous networks.

This paper proposes an artificial benchmark for heterogeneous networks called ABCD-HN (Artificial Network Benchmark for Community Detection on Heterogeneous Networks). ABCD-HN allows construction of artificial networks with different node quantities, community quantities, and community complexities according to user requirements. Additionally, we introduce an evaluation framework to validate the effectiveness of this benchmark by comparing the performance of heterogeneous network community detection algorithms on both real-world and artificial networks. The contributions of this paper are as follows:

1. We are the first to propose an artificial benchmark for heterogeneous networks that can generate artificial heterogeneous networks with specified node quantities, community quantities, and community complexities.
2. We propose an evaluation framework for comparing the performance of heterogeneous network community detection algorithms on real-world and artificial networks to validate the effectiveness of the artificial benchmark.
3. The experimental results demonstrate the effectiveness of the proposed artificial benchmark for heterogeneous networks.

2 Related Work

Many scholars have made significant contributions to the research on artificial benchmarks. The works of Erdős and Rényi [2], Barabási and Albert [3], Girvan and Newman [4], and others have laid the foundation for the study of artificial benchmarks. Subsequently, numerous scholars have expanded this field by proposing various benchmark generation methods. For example, Lancichinetti and Fortunato [5,6] introduced generation methods based on scale-free network models, while Orman et al. [7] proposed more practical benchmark generation methods. Furthermore, methods focus on generating dynamic communities (Granell et al., [8]; Rossetti, [9]), overlapping communities (Sengupta et al., [11]), and large-scale networks (Hamann et al., [12]), among other features. In recent years, new benchmark generation methods have emerged. For example, Kamiński et al. [17] introduced the fast random graph model ABCD for generating networks with community structures. Citraro and Rossetti [18] developed the X-Mark benchmark based on node attributes. Additionally, methods focus on hypergraphs (Kamiński et al., [19]) or generating benchmark networks with specific features (Meena and Tokekar, [20]).

These emerging benchmark generation methods give researchers more choices and possibilities for evaluating and studying community detection algorithms. However, there is currently no specific artificial benchmark available for heterogeneous networks.

3 Preliminaries

This section provides the preliminary definitions of heterogeneous graph and community detection.

Definition 1 (Heterogeneous Graph). *A heterogeneous graph is defined as $G = (V, E, A, R)$ with a node type mapping function $\phi : V \to A$ and an edge type mapping function $\psi : E \to R$, where V, E, A, and R correspond to the set of nodes, edges, node types, and edge types, respectively. Each node $v \in V$ and each edge $e \in E$ belong to one specific type in A and R, i.e., $\phi(v) \in A$ and $\psi(e) \in R$. Each heterogeneous graph has multiple node or edge types such that $|A| + |R| > 2$.*

Definition 2 (Community Detection). *Community detection aims to partition the nodes of an undirected graph $G = (V, E)$, where V represents the set of nodes and E represents the set of edges. The objective is to find a partition $C = \{C_1, C_2, ..., C_k\}$, where C_i is a subset of the graph G. This partition satisfies the following conditions: each subset C_i is non-empty ($C_i \neq \emptyset$), the subsets C_i are pairwise disjoint ($C_i \cap C_j = \emptyset$ for $i \neq j$), and the union of all subsets C_i covers the entire set of nodes (i.e., $\cup C_i = V$).*

4 ABCD-HN

4.1 Framework for ABCD-HN

Figure 1 illustrates the framework of ABCD-HN, composed of two steps.

Step 1: Construct Fundamental Edges (CFE) - Generate an initial network based on the given parameters, where $\mu \in [0, 1]$ controls the community complexity of the entire network. A smaller value of μ makes the community structure more prominent, and the initial graph is constructed with community partitions.

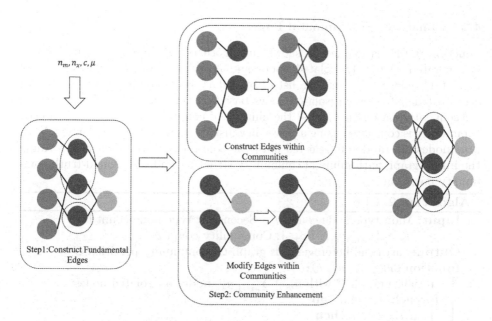

Fig. 1. Framework For ABCD-HN

Step 2: Community Enhancement - This step consists of two sub-steps: Construct Edges within Communities (CEC) and Modify Edges within Communities (MEC). These sub-steps aim to enhance the community structure of the network further.

Finally, the user obtains an artificial heterogeneous network and community partitions. The details of each component will be discussed in the subsequent sections.

Algorithm 1: ABCD-HN

Input: Main type node count n_m, Secondary type node count list
$n_x = \{n_{x_1}, n_{x_2}, ..., n_{x_n}\}$, Community count c, Complexity
parameter μ

Output: artificial heterogeneous graph G, community partition C

1   $G, C \leftarrow \text{CFE}(n_m, n_x, c)$; // Construct Fundamental Edges

2   **foreach** n_{x_i} *in* n_x **do**

3   **if** $n_{x_i} > n_m$ **then**

4       $G \leftarrow \text{MEC}(G, C, n_{x_i}, \mu)$;
      // Modify Edges within Communities

5   **else**

6       $G \leftarrow \text{CEC}(G, C, n_{x_i}, \mu)$;
      // Construct Edges within Communities

7   **return** G, C;

4.2 Construct Fundamental Edges

Function "CFE" is defined as shown in Algorithm 2. Firstly, an initial graph is generated with only isolated nodes and no edges based on the number of main type nodes, n_m, and the list of secondary node counts, n_x. Then, edges are constructed between isolated nodes based on the quantities of n_m and n_{x_i}. Subsequently, based on n_m and the number of communities, c, the size of each community is computed using a power-law distribution probability density. Main type nodes are randomly selected until the community size is reached, forming the initial graph with minimal community structure and the ground-truth community partition.

Algorithm 2: CFE

Input: Main type node count n_m, Secondary type node count list
$n_x = \{n_{x_1}, n_{x_2}, ..., n_{x_n}\}$, Community count c

Output: artificial heterogeneous graph G, community partition C

1 **function** CFE(n_m, n_x, c):
2   Initialize graph G with $n_m + \sum_{i=1}^{n} n_{x_i}$ nodes as isolated nodes;
3   **foreach** n_{x_i} in n_x **do**
4   **if** $n_{x_i} > n_m$ **then**
5              $n_1 = n_{x_i}$ and $n_2 = n_m$;
6   **else**
7              $n_1 = n_m$ and $n_2 = n_{x_i}$;
         // Let V_1 be the n_1 node set, V_2 be the n_2 node set
8   **foreach** v_s in V_2 **do**
9   Select a node v_e from V_1 with probability $P(v_e) = \frac{1}{|V_1|}$;
10   Add the edge (v_s, v_e) to graph G;
11   Remove v_e from V_1;
12   **foreach** v_s in V_1 **do**
13   Select a node v_e from V_2 with probability $P(v_e) = \frac{1}{|V_2|}$;
14   Add the edge (v_s, v_e) to graph G;

     // Let V_m be the main type nodes set
15     $C \leftarrow []$ // [
16   l]Create an empty community partition list $\alpha = 0.6$;
17   **for** $i = 1$ to c **do**
18         $s_i = \lceil \alpha \cdot i^{\alpha-1} \cdot n_m \rceil$; // Calculate the community size
19         $c_i \leftarrow []$; // Create an empty community list
20   **for** $j = 1$ to s_i **do**
21   Select a node v_s from V_m with probability $P(v_s) = \frac{1}{|V_m|}$;
22   Add v_s to c_i;
23   Remove v_s from V_m;
24   Add c_i to C;
25   **return** G, C;

4.3   Community Enhancement

For initial graphs with minimal community structure, we utilize parameter-controlled edge construction and edge modification operations to enhance the visibility of community structures.

Construct Edges Within Communities. The edge construction operation is suitable when the number of secondary type nodes exceeds the number of main type nodes. In such cases, each secondary type node is connected to only one main type node without creating connections between the main type nodes. Hence, we establish connections between nodes within the community by constructing edges, enhancing the visibility of the community structure. The edge construction function, called 'CEC,' is presented in Algorithm 3.

Algorithm 3: CEC

Input: Artificial heterogeneous graph G, Community partition C,
   Secondary type node count list $n_x = \{n_{x_1}, n_{x_2}, ..., n_{x_n}\}$,
   Complexity parameter μ
Output: artificial heterogeneous graph G

1 **function** CEC(G, C, n_x, μ):
   // Let s_i be the size of community c_i in C
2   **for** $\lceil i = 1 \ to \ (1.1 - \mu) \times n_x \rceil$ **do**
3   Select a community c_i from C with probability $P(c_i) = \frac{s_i}{\sum_{j=1}^{|C|} s_j}$;
4   Select a node n_s from c_i with probability $P(n_s) = \frac{degree(n_s)}{\sum_{n \in c_i} degree(n)}$;
       // Let N_x be the set of x type neighbors of n_s
5   Select a node n_m from N_x with probability $P(n_m) = \frac{1}{|N_x|}$;
6   Randomly select a node n_e from $c_i \setminus n_s$ with probability
         $P(n_e) = \frac{1}{|c_i|-1}$;
7   Add the edge (n_m, n_e) to graph G;
8   **return** G;

Modify Edges Within Communities. The edge modification operation is applied when the number of secondary type nodes is fewer than the number of main type nodes. In such cases, each secondary type node is connected to multiple main type nodes, creating connections between the main type nodes and blurring the community structure. Therefore, we employ a dictionary structure to record the occurrence count of each secondary type node in each community, adjusting the edge connections and refining the relationships between nodes within the community to enhance the visibility of the community structure. After the edge modification operation is completed, we proceed to the edge construction operation. The edge modification function, referred to as 'MEC,' is presented in Algorithm 4.

Algorithm 4: MEC

Input: Artificial heterogeneous graph G, Community partition C,
Secondary type node count list $n_x = \{n_{x_1}, n_{x_2}, ..., n_{x_n}\}$,
Complexity parameter μ

Output: artificial heterogeneous graph G

1 **function** MEC(G, C, n_x, μ):
2   Initialize an empty dictionary D_c ;
3   **foreach** c_i *in* C **do**
4   Initialize an empty dictionary D_x ;
5   **foreach** v *in* c_i **do**
            // Let N_v be the set neighbors of v
6   **foreach** u *in* N_v **do**
7   **if** u *is type* x **then**
8                      $D_x[u] += 1$;
9          $D_c[c_i] = D_x$;
10   **for** $i = 1$ *to* $n_m \times n_m \div n_x \times (1.1 - \mu)$ **do**
11   Select a community c_i from C with probability $P(c_i) = \frac{s_i}{\sum_{j=1}^{|C|} s_j}$;
12   Select a node v_s from c_i with probability $P(v_s) = \frac{1}{|c_i|}$;
            // Let N_x be the set of type x neighbors of v_s
13   Select a node v_m from N_x with probability $P(v_m) = \frac{1}{|N_x|}$;
14   **if** $degree(v_m) \geq 2$ **then**
15   Remove the edge (v_s, v_m) from graph G;
16   Select a node v_n from keys of $D_c[c_i]$ with probability
        $P(v_n) = \frac{D_c[c_i][v_n]}{\sum_{k \in D_c[c_i]} D_c[c_i][k]}$;
17   Add the edge (v_s, v_n) to graph G;
18     $G \leftarrow$ CEC(G, C, n_x, $n_m \times (1.1 - \mu)$);
19   **return** G;

---

5 Evaluation Framework for Artificial Heterogeneous Network

We have developed an evaluation framework based on the artificial heterogeneous network benchmark introduced in Sect. 4 to standardize and simplify the evaluation of artificial heterogeneous networks. Figure 2 provides an overview of our evaluation framework. This framework assesses the effectiveness of artificial heterogeneous networks by evaluating the performance of different algorithms on both real-world networks and artificial networks.

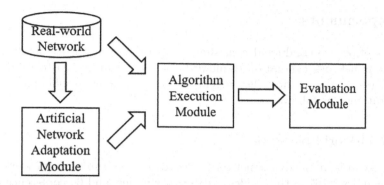

Fig. 2. Evaluation Framework For Artificial Heterogeneous Network

5.1 Artificial Network Adaptation Module

This module extracts the number of nodes and community information for each node type in a real-world network. The parameter n_m in ABCD-HN is set to the number of nodes in the community type, n_x to the number of nodes in other types, and c to the number of communities. This adjustment of parameters in ABCD-HN aligns it with the real-world network, ensuring the comparability of experimental results. By varying the parameter μ, networks of different complexities are generated for subsequent modules.

5.2 Algorithm Execution Module

This module transforms the received real-world network and artificial heterogeneous network formats into the input formats required by each algorithm in the algorithm set A, such as edge lists and adjacency matrices, to obtain the input set I. Each $i \in I$ will be inputted to $a \in A$ to obtain the output set O, which will be passed to the next module.

5.3 Evaluation Module

This module receives the output set O and computes the corresponding Normalized Mutual Information (NMI) [1] metric. NMI is a measure of the similarity between two clusterings of a dataset. It is defined as the mutual information between the two clusterings divided by the average entropy of the clusterings. NMI ranges between 0 and 1, where 0 indicates no mutual information, and 1 indicates perfect agreement between the clusterings.

The NMI metric is calculated using the following formula:

$$NMI(O) = \frac{I(O)}{\sqrt{H(C_1) \cdot H(C_2)}}$$

where $I(O)$ is the mutual information between the two clusterings C_1 and C_2, and $H(C_1)$ and $H(C_2)$ are the entropies of C_1 and C_2 respectively.

6   Experiments

In this section, we conducted consistency experiments using the artificial heterogeneous network evaluation framework mentioned in Sect. 5 to validate the effectiveness of the artificial heterogeneous network. The specific experimental configuration is as follows.

6.1   Real-World Network

ACM. ACM is an academic network. We extracted a sub-network from ACM, which includes 7,167 author nodes, 4,019 paper nodes, and 60 conference nodes. The paper nodes are labeled to represent three different research fields. We use the labeled paper nodes as the target for the community detection task.

Yelp. Yelp is an online review and rating platform where users can rate and write reviews for businesses, restaurants, service providers, and more. We extracted a sub-network from Yelp, which includes 2,614 business nodes, 1,286 user nodes, two state nodes, two review nodes and nine tip nodes. The business nodes are labeled to represent three different research fields. We use the labeled business nodes as the target for the community detection task.

6.2   Algorithms

The detailed introduction of the algorithm set A used in the evaluation framework is as follows:

1. **Metapath2vec** [21]: Metapath2vec is a method for learning node embeddings in heterogeneous networks. It guides the random walk process using meta-paths to capture the structural information in the heterogeneous network. Then, models like Word2Vec are used to learn vector representations of the nodes, where nodes with similar contexts are closer in the embedding space.
2. **MetaGraph2vec** [22]: MetaGraph2vec is a node embedding method based on meta-path-guided hierarchical attention networks. It uses meta-paths to define the contextual relationships between nodes and leverages hierarchical attention mechanisms to aggregate the information of neighboring nodes. This approach captures the multi-level structure and important meta-path information in heterogeneous networks, resulting in node embeddings.
3. **HeteSpaceyWalk** [23]: HeteSpaceyWalk generates node sequences in heterogeneous networks. It generates node sequences by performing random walks on the heterogeneous network and randomly selecting neighboring nodes along meta-paths. This method preserves the structural information of the heterogeneous network and provides input data for subsequent node embedding learning.

4. **HAN** [24]: HAN (Heterogeneous Attention Network) is a graph neural network model for heterogeneous networks. It utilizes meta-paths to define the neighborhood relationships between nodes and employs hierarchical attention mechanisms to aggregate the information of neighboring nodes. HAN learns the importance of different meta-paths and generates high-dimensional embedding representations for each node.
5. **DHNE** [25]: DHNE (Deep Heterogeneous Network Embedding) is a deep learning method for generating node embeddings in heterogeneous networks. It maps the heterogeneous network to a low-dimensional continuous vector space while preserving the structural and semantic information between nodes. DHNE learns embedding vectors by maximizing node similarity and minimizing heterogeneity.
6. **HeGAN** [26]: HeGAN (Heterogeneous Graph Adversarial Networks) is a generative adversarial network model for heterogeneous networks. It learns node embeddings in the heterogeneous network through adversarial training of a generator and a discriminator. HeGAN effectively captures node similarity and structural information in the heterogeneous network and generates high-quality node embeddings.

6.3   Experimental Setup

In the experiments, the parameters for each algorithm were set as follows: For algorithms that output node representation vectors, the dimension of the vectors was set to 64. The node representation vectors generated by each algorithm were obtained using the clustering algorithm K-means for community assignment, with the number of clusters K set to the respective number of true communities in the network. For algorithms that utilized random walks (such as Metapath2vec and HeteSpaceyWalk), the number of walks w_n, walk length w_l, and window size w_w were set to 5, 10, and 5, respectively. For algorithms that utilized metapaths (such as Metapath2vec, MetaGraph2vec, DHNE, HeGAN, and HAN), the recommended metapaths from the respective papers were used. Lastly, the remaining parameters for the comparison algorithms were set according to the recommendations of their respective authors.

6.4   Consistency Experiment

In this section, we present the results of the evaluation framework.

Table 1. NMI Values of Algorithms on ACM and Artificial Heterogeneous Networks

Algorithm	ACM	μ					
		0.0	0.2	0.4	**0.6**	0.8	1.0
DHNE	0.265	0.6608	0.5914	0.5739	**0.2741**	0.0546	0.0015
HAN	0.267	0.3435	0.6018	0.3676	**0.263**	0.0036	0.0608
HeGAN	0.2076	0.0657	0.0313	0.0094	**0.0037**	0.0026	0.0021
HeteSpaceyWalk	0.4305	0.8245	0.7459	0.7308	**0.4351**	0.2529	0.0078
MetaGraph2vec	0.4392	0.8664	0.7861	0.7447	**0.4403**	0.2589	0.0024
Metapath2vec	0.1927	0.0255	0.0185	0.0041	**0.0034**	0.0034	0.0002

The results of the consistency experiment between ABCD-HN and the real-world network ACM are shown in Table 1. When ABCD-HN's μ parameter is set to 0.6, most algorithms exhibit similar performance on both ABCD-HN and ACM. However, Metapath2vec performs worse on ABCD-HN compared to ACM. This problem may be because the algorithm focuses on the influence of author nodes on communities by using the meta-path "p-a-p" At the same time, ABCD-HN does not emphasize the information of each minor type node equally, resulting in poor performance of Metapath2vec. Metapath2vec as pre-training embeddings in HeGAN also contributes to its suboptimal performance. Future research could assign different importance levels to each secondary type. Additionally, the table shows that as μ increases, the performance of all algorithms gradually decreases, indicating that the parameter μ effectively controls the complexity of the artificially generated heterogeneous network by ABCD-HN.

Table 2. NMI Values of Algorithms on Yelp and Artificial Heterogeneous Networks

Algorithm	Yelp	μ					
		0.0	0.2	0.4	0.6	0.8	1.0
HAN	0.3866	0.6683	0.5879	0.5488	0.5388	0.5026	0.1126
HeGAN	0.0124	0.9047	0.8975	0.2037	0.1813	0.0104	0.002
HeteSpaceyWalk	0.0101	0.6356	0.5658	0.0601	0.0311	0.0098	0.0004
MetaGraph2vec	0.0106	0.9292	0.892	0.8417	0.8155	0.7586	0.1651
Metapath2vec	0.0162	0.5554	0.3883	0.08	0.03	0.0088	0.0002

Table 2 presents the consistency experiment results of ABCD-HN with the real-world network Yelp. Yelp is a real-world network with edge weights, and algorithms may exhibit poor performance when they cannot effectively utilize edge weight information. In contrast, ABCD-HN generates artificial networks without edge weights. Therefore, extending the benchmark to heterogeneous networks with edge weights is a future research direction. From the table, it can be observed that as μ increases, the performance of the algorithms gradually decreases. This phenomenon indicates that the parameter μ effectively controls the complexity of the artificial heterogeneous networks generated by ABCD-HN. There are notable performance drops for certain algorithms in specific μ settings, such as MetaGraph2vec's performance on $\mu = 0.8$ and $\mu = 1.0$ artificial networks. This problem suggests that the complexity control provided by μ may need to be smoother, potentially due to a lack of significant influence from a small number of nodes of secondary types. Assigning different levels of importance to each secondary type is another future research direction.

7   Conclusions

We propose an artificial network benchmark for community detection on heterogeneous networks called ABCD-HN, which allows for generating artificial networks with specified node quantities, community counts, and community complexities. Additionally, we propose an evaluation framework to validate its effectiveness. Through experiments, we demonstrate the effectiveness of the proposed ABCD-HN. In future work, the benchmark can be extended to more complex scenarios, such as having different levels of importance for various secondary types, heterogeneous networks with edge weights, and community detection based on secondary rather than main type.

Acknowledgements. This work was supported by the National Natural Science Foundation of China under Grant No. 62002063 and No. U21A20472, the National Key Research and Development Plan of China under Grant No. 2021YFB3600503, the Fujian Collaborative Innovation Center for Big Data Applications in Governments, the Fujian Industry-Academy Cooperation Project under Grant No. 2017H6008 and No. 2018H6010, the Natural Science Foundation of Fujian Province under Grant No. 2022J01118, No. 2020J05112 and No. 2020J01420, the Fujian Provincial Department of Education under Grant No. JAT190026, the Major Science and Technology Project of Fujian Province under Grant No. 2021HZ022007, the Hong Kong RGC TRS T41-603/20R and Haixi Government Big Data Application Cooperative Innovation Center.

References

1. Danon, L., Díaz-Guilera, A., Duch, J., Arenas, A.: Comparing community structure identification. J. Stat. Mech: Theory Exp. **2005**(09), P09008 (2005)
2. Erdős, P., Rényi, A.: On the evolution of random graphs. Publ. Math. Inst. Hung. Acad. Sci. **5**, 17–60 (1960)
3. Barabási, A.L., Albert, R.: Emergence of scaling in random networks. Science **286**(5439), 509–512 (1999)
4. Girvan, M., Newman, M.E.J.: Proc. Natl. Acad. Sci. U.S.A. **99**, 7821 (2002)
5. Lancichinetti, A., Fortunato, S., Radicchi, F.: Phys. Rev. E **78**(4), 046110 (2008)
6. Lancichinetti, A., Fortunato, S.: Phys. Rev. E **80**(1), 016118 (2009)
7. Orman, G.K., Labatut, V., Cherifi, H.: Towards realistic artificial benchmark for community detection algorithms evaluation, arXiv (2013). https://doi.org/10.1504/IJWBC.2013.054908

8. Granell, C., Darst, R.K., Arenas, A., et al.: Phys. Rev. E **92**(1), 012805 (2015)
9. Rossetti, G.: RDyn: graph benchmark handling community dynamics (2017)
10. Yang, Z., Perotti, J.I., Tessone, C.J.: Phys. Rev. E **96**(5), 052311 (2017)
11. Sengupta, N., Hamann, M., Wagner, D.: Benchmark generator for dynamic overlapping communities in networks. In: 2017 IEEE International Conference on Data Mining (ICDM) (2017)
12. Hamann, M., Meyer, U., Penschuck, M.: et al.: I/O-efficient generation of massive graphs following the LFR benchmark (2017)
13. Le, B.D., Nguyen, H.X., Shen, H., et al.: GLFR: a generalized LFR benchmark for testing community detection algorithms. In: 2017 26th International Conference on Computer Communication and Networks (ICCCN), pp. 1–9 (2017)
14. Muscoloni, A., Cannistraci, C.V.: Leveraging the nonuniform PSO network model as a benchmark for performance evaluation in community detection and link prediction. New J. Phys. **20**(6), 063022 (2018)
15. Pasta, Q., Zaidi, F.: Model to generate benchmark graphs based on evolution dynamics. In: 2018 IEEE/ACM International Conference on Advances in Social Networks Analysis and Mining (ASONAM), pp. 1223–1231 (2018)
16. Liu, D., Liu, G., Meng, K., et al.: Benchmark snapshots for testing social network evolving algorithms. Procedia Comput. Sci. **147**, 228–232 (2019)
17. Kamiński, B., Praat, P., Théberge, F.: Artificial Benchmark for Community Detection (ABCD): Fast Random Graph Model with Community Structure (2020)
18. Citraro, S., Rossetti, G.: X-Mark: a benchmark for node-attributed community discovery algorithms. Soc. Netw. Anal. Min. **11**(1), 1–14 (2021)
19. Kamiński, B., Prałat, P., Théberge, F.: Hypergraph Artificial Benchmark for Community Detection (h-ABCD), arXiv preprint arXiv:2210.15009 (2022)
20. Meena, S.S., Tokekar, V.: A model to generate benchmark network with community structure. In: Zhang, Y.D., Senjyu, T., So-In, C., Joshi, A. (eds.) SmartCom 2022. LNNS, vol. 396, pp. 235–244. Springer, Singapore (2022). https://doi.org/10.1007/978-981-16-9967-2_23
21. Dong, Y., Chawla, N.V., Swami, A.: metapath2vec: scalable representation learning for heterogeneous networks. In: Proceedings of the 23rd ACM SIGKDD International Conference on Knowledge Discovery and Data Mining, pp. 697–706 (2017)
22. Zhang, Y., Tang, J., Chawla, N.V.: Meta-graph based recommendation fusion over heterogeneous information networks. In: Proceedings of the 24th ACM SIGKDD International Conference on Knowledge Discovery and Data Mining, pp. 135–144 (2018)
23. Shi, C., Zhang, Q., Cheng, X., Cheng, J.: HeteSpaceyWalk: a general metapath based embedding framework for heterogeneous information networks. IEEE Trans. Knowl. Data Eng. **32**(12), 2346–2359 (2019)
24. Wang, X., et al.: Heterogeneous graph attention network. In: Proceedings of the 25th ACM SIGKDD International Conference on Knowledge Discovery and Data Mining, pp. 793–803 (2019)
25. Fu, Y., Dong, Y., Zhu, J., Hicks, Y.A., Chawla, N.V.: Deep heterogeneous network embedding with information diffusion. In: Proceedings of the 25th ACM SIGKDD International Conference on Knowledge Discovery and Data Mining, pp. 1194–1203 (2019)
26. Liu, H., Zhao, L., Zhou, X., Li, L., Zhang, X.: HeGAN: heterogeneous graph adversarial networks for heterogeneous network representation learning. IEEE Trans. Knowl. Data Eng. **33**(8), 3273–3286 (2020)

A Multi-behavior Recommendation Based on Disentangled Graph Convolutional Networks and Contrastive Learning

Jie Yu[1], Feng Jiang[1], JunWei Du[1], and Xu Yu[2](✉)

[1] Qingdao University of Science and Technology, Qingdao, China
[2] China University of Petroleum, Qingdao, China
yuxu0532@upc.edu.cn

Abstract. Traditional recommendation models typically rely on a single type of user-item interaction data, which presents a serious challenge due to data sparsity. Multi-behavior recommendation models leverage various available user behaviors in the recommendation scenario as auxiliary data to assist in predicting user-item interaction. However, existing multi-behavior recommendation models do not take into account potential factors that affect multi-behavior interaction, or the differences that exist between different types of behaviors. In this paper, we propose a Multi-Behavior Recommendation Based on Disentangled Graph Convolutional Networks and Contrastive Learning (DCMBR). Specifically, we construct subgraphs for new dissatisfied behavior, and use disentangled convolution networks to separate potential factors that affect interaction between users, items, and behaviors, so as to reconstruct node features for users under different behaviors. Then, users' multi-behavior characteristics are aggregated using contrastive learning to achieve personalized multi-behavior information aggregation. Experimental results on two datasets demonstrate that DCMBR can effectively leverage multi-behavioral data, and significantly improve recommendation performance compared to the optimal baseline.

Keywords: Multi-behavior recommendation · Disentangled graph convolutional network · Contrastive learning

1 Introduction

As the Internet continues to evolve, people have gone from an era of information scarcity to one of information overload, which not only brings convenience to their lives, but also presents the challenge of difficult decision-making. Recommendation systems [9,15] primarily rely on a user's historical behavior records to recommend products and services that they may like, providing a personalized recommendation process that effectively alleviates the problem of information overload.

© The Author(s), under exclusive license to Springer Nature Singapore Pte Ltd. 2024
Y. Sun et al. (Eds.): ChineseCSCW 2023, CCIS 2012, pp. 195–207, 2024.
https://doi.org/10.1007/978-981-99-9637-7_14

Traditional recommendation models [6] only use one type of user-item interaction data, namely, a single association between a user and an item, which we call a single-behavior recommendation model. In a single purchase behavior, a new user may not have had any previous purchasing behavior, resulting in the problem of sparse data which can fail to capture the user's true preferences and may result in poor recommendation performance. In real scenarios, users have more than one type of behavior. The platform can collect other user behaviors that are easy to occur, such as search, browse, click, and favorite behaviors, using these behaviors as auxiliary behaviors to help predict the user's future interaction with the target behavior [1,12]. We call this type of recommendation model multi-behavior recommendation. Multi-behavior recommendation can effectively alleviate the data sparsity and cold-start problems and significantly enrich the construction of user interest preferences. The types of behaviors vary in different contexts, for example, in e-commerce systems, users click, add to cart, and purchase behaviors for items, and in social recommender systems, users can like, share, and comment behaviors. In this paper, we take e-commerce systems as the background for research, and consider the purchase behavior as the target behavior and the rest of the behaviors as auxiliary behaviors, so that we can use the easily accessible auxiliary behaviors to help users interact with the target behaviors, which effectively improves the recommendation performance.

In recent years, the multi-behavior recommendation model initially used the simplest approach, modeling all types of behaviors and applying them to single-behavior recommendation models [4], without considering the differences between different behaviors. With the development of deep learning, many neural network techniques have been proposed to enhance the collaborative filtering architecture [2], and to model complex interaction patterns between users and items. Inspired by the success of graph neural networks, Jin et al. [7] proposed using graph relationship encoders to model user-item interactions, and used attention mechanism models to capture high-order relationships between users and items. However, graph neural networks usually adopt a holistic representation learning approach, where the learned node representations ignore the subtle differences between user embedding vectors under different behaviors. The preferences expressed by a user in different behaviors reflect a certain aspect of the user's preferences, and the preferences expressed by a user in a single behavior must be included in the user's overall preferences, which is not taken into account by most multi-behavior recommendation models.

Existing multi-behavior recommendation models face certain challenges that must be addressed:

The Potential Factors that Influence the Interaction Among Users, Items, and Behaviors in Multi-behavior Data have not been Taken into Account. The factors influencing user-item interactions in real-life scenarios are complex and diverse, users may click on items based on their appearance or bookmark them based on their style. Learning about the underlying factors that induce user-item interactions within specific behavior types is not a capability of the current multi-behavior recommendation models. Learning why a user interacts with an item for a specific type of behavior also enables the model to learn additional information that is not learned by existing models. For example, a user clicking on a product but not having the rest of the behavior occur can enable the model to learn what prevents the user from engaging in the targeted behavior.

The Models do not Take into Account the Differences Between Various user Behaviors. There are coarse-grained commonalities and fine-grained differences between user-item interactions under different behaviors. Coarse-grained commonality means that all types of behaviors reflect user preferences in some way. Fine-grained differences mean that different behaviors indicate different levels of user preferences. There is a priority between the target behavior and other behaviors, with clicks occurring before the rest of the behaviors, and clicks being much more frequent than purchases. We can consider items that are clicked but not purchased as more difficult negative samples that can allow the model to learn what prevents the user from purchasing. Capturing these commonalities of multiple behaviors can be used to enhance the representation of embedding under the target behavior.

To address the aforementioned challenges, we propose a Multi-Behavior Recommendation Based on Disentangled Graph Convolutional Networks and Contrastive Learning (DCMBR). DCMBR can leverage potential factors underlying user-item interactions in specific behavior types and enhance user's feature representation during the convolution process, thereby accounting for the differences between different behaviors and alleviating the data sparsity issue in the target behavior. Specifically, we introduce a novel subgraph for dissatisfied behavior and use a disentangled convolutional network to separate the potential factors influencing user-item-behavior interactions in each subgraph, enabling the reconstruction of user node features across different behaviors. Subsequently, the multi-behavior feature of the user is achieved through contrastive learning to facilitate personalized aggregation of multi-behavioral information.

The main contributions of our work are as follows:

1. We introduce a novel subgraph for dissatisfied behavior (only involves a single auxiliary behavior and no other auxiliary behaviors), it can enhance user feature representation and account for the differences between different behaviors.
2. We propose a disentangled graph convolutional network to learn the feature representation of user nodes. This network can separate the potential factors influencing user-item-behavior interactions in each subgraph and improve the generalization ability and robustness of the features.
3. We conduct extensive experiments on a dataset, and the results demonstrate that the proposed model outperforms the best-performing baseline models.

The rest of the paper is organized as follows: In Sect. 2, we review related work. In Sect. 3, we introduce our proposed approach. After conducting experiments in Sect. 4, we summarize the paper in Sect. 5.

2 Related Work

2.1 Multi-behavior Recommendation

Multi-behavior recommendation utilizes other types of behaviors as auxiliary activities to enhance the representation ability and assist in predicting users' future interactions with the target behavior, thereby improving the effectiveness of the target behavior recommendation [2]. Most multi-behavior recommendation models are based on heterogeneous graph neural networks or attention models. For example, Xia et al. [12] uses self-attention to encode the pairwise correlations between different types of behaviors and predict the target behavior. Jin et al. [7] proposes a multi-behavior recommendation model based on heterogeneous graphs, which aggregates the interaction modes of user-item pairs under the same behavior to learn behavior influence weights and capture behavior semantics.

However, these methods fail to take into account the high-order information implicit in the graph. To address this limitation, Xia et al. [13] proposes a knowledge-enhanced hierarchical graph transformation network that dynamically learns the high-order multi-relationships between users-items and items-items through a time encoding strategy. Yang et al. [14] introduces a mutual relation encoder that adaptively learns complex structural relationships related to the graph and potential cross-type dependencies among behaviors under different interaction patterns. Moreover, Gori et al. [3] combines meta-learning and graph neural networks to extract meta-knowledge regarding users-items and behavior types, generating customized network parameters to obtain user-item features.

2.2 Graph Neural Networks

In recent years, the use of graph neural networks (GNNs) to solve the recommendation problem has become an extremely important research topic [3], deep learning methods on GNNs are committed to mining the hidden information contained in the graph, but there is a large amount of unstructured data in real life, such as based on the recommendation of the social network, the knowledge graph. In particular, graph convolutional neural networks (GCNs) have been widely used to deal with non-Euclidean data, which can capture the higher-order similarities and structural connectivity between the user's items, and has a strong ability to learn the representation. Most existing recommendation methods utilizing Convolutional Neural Networks are based on spatial-based approaches, such as Light Graph Convolution Network(LightGCN) [5] learning user and item embeddings, calculating the weighted sum of embeddings across all layers as the final embedding.

Existing graph neural networks usually use holistic representation learning methods, ignoring subtle differences between domains. Disentangled Representation Learning has gained extensive attention. Disentangled Graph Convolutional Networks(DisenGCN) [8] proposes a new neighborhood routing mechanism to dynamically identify potential factors that may lead to the edge between nodes and their neighbors, learning node representations. Wang et al. [11] proposes a disentangled graph collaborative filtering model to model the distribution of each user-item interaction intention, extracting relevant information for each intention.

3   Our Proposed Method

3.1   Problem Definition

Assuming that this model is developed for recommendation on an e-commerce platform, let's first introduce key symbols. We define the user-item interaction graph as $G_u = (U, V, E_u)$, Where $U = \{u_1, ..., u_i, ..., u_I\}$ is the set of user nodes, $V = \{v_1, ..., v_j, ..., v_J\}$ is the set of item nodes, E is the behavior type of the user-item interaction (such as purchase, add to cart, etc.), and E^k is the score for the k-th behavior type of the user-item interaction. In the user-item interaction graph G_u, if there is an interaction between user u_i and item v_j under behavior type k, there exists an edge, $e_{i,j}^k = 1$. Conversely, if there is no interaction, $e_{i,j}^k = 0$.

Input: Graph of user-item interactions G_u.

Output: The probability of interaction between user u_i and item v_j under the target behavior type k is denoted as r_{ij}.

3.2   Overall Framework

Construction of Subgraphs. Initially, we constructed a user-item interaction graph $G_u = (U, V, E_u)$, which includes nodes representing users node and items node, as well as edge E_k denoting different types of behaviors. We partitioned the user-item interaction graph based on the types of edges to form multiple subgraphs $G_k = (U, V, E_k)$, thus transforming a heterogeneous graph to multiple homogeneous ones for modeling.

There exists substitutability among different behaviors, such as the add-to-cart behavior and the favorite behavior, which have a similar impact on the purchase behavior. Therefore, we choose the purchase as the target behavior and regard other behaviors such as the click and the add-to-cart as auxiliary behaviors. There also exists a certain degree of ordering among different behaviors, with the click behavior occurring much more frequently than the purchase behavior. The click behavior represents the user's initial preference for the item, while the occurrence of the purchase behavior indicates the user's strong preference. Additionally, we classify the behavior of clicking on an item but not performing any other subsequent action as a "dissatisfied" behavior, and construct a dissatisfied subgraph to analyze the reasons behind why users are not interested in the item, highlighting the differences among behaviors. Finally, we use the purchase, add-to-cart, and dissatisfied subgraphs as inputs to the model.

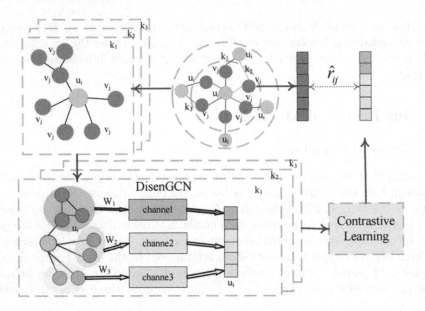

Fig. 1. Architecture diagram of the model.

Node Representation Learning. The overall structure is illustrated in Fig. 1. We obtain the user's feature vector for each behavior subgraph by decoupling the graph convolution operation for each subgraph, which is represented by hidden factors entangled under the behavior. Taking the purchase behavior as an example, we assume that there are m latent factors that influence whether users make a purchase. We map them to m latent spaces and obtain m latent factors that affect user-item interactions through graph convolution. We concatenate the m latent factors together to finally obtain the user's feature vector for the purchase behavior. The same operation is applied to obtain feature vectors for other behaviors.

The key aspect of graph neural networks (GNNs) lies in learning a function f that takes node and edge features as inputs and output the feature information of each node. Embedding vectors $p_i^{(0)} \in R^d$ and $q_j^{(0)} \in R^d$ are introduced to represent a user or an item. Given the feature information of the user node p_u and its neighboring nodes $q_v : (u, v) \in G$, the output is:

$$\hat{p}_u = f(p_u, \{q_v : (u, v) \in G\}). \tag{1}$$

The most significant difference between disentangled graph convolution and regular graph convolutional networks is the multi-channel convolutional layer. The convolutional layer of disentangled graph convolution performs a new neighborhood routing mechanism that dynamically identifies potential factors that may lead to edges between a node and its neighbors and assigns the neighbors to a channel accordingly. This mechanism infers potential factors within a channel by iteratively analyzing the cluster of potential subspaces formed by the node and its neighbors and projecting it into multiple subspaces.

There are m channels in the disentangled graph convolution layer, and we consider c_m to be the final output of the first channel, then $p_u = [c_1, c_2, ..., c_m]$, where $c_m \in R^{d_{in} \times \frac{d_{out}}{M}}$ denotes the hidden factor affecting the occurrence of the behavior. First assume that when given a single node, m channels can extract different features by projecting the feature vector g to different subspaces:

$$c_{i,m} = \frac{\sigma(W_m^T \hat{p}_i + b_m)}{||\sigma(W_m^T \hat{p}_i + b_m)||_2}, \tag{2}$$

which $W_m \in R^{d_{in} \times \frac{d_{out}}{M}}$ and $b_m \in R^{\frac{d_{out}}{M}}$ are the parameters of the channel, $\sigma(\cdot)$ is the nonlinear activation function, and $z_{i,m}$ approximates the aspect of node associated with the m-th factor.

Let $f^{(l)}(\cdot)$ be the DisenConv layer of the Lth layer and let $\hat{p}_u^{(l)} \in R$ be the output of that layer. ReLU is used as the activation function. Then, the output of the L-th layer can be expressed as

$$\hat{p}_u^{(l)} = dropout(f^{(l)}(\hat{p}_u^{(l-1)}, \{\hat{p}_v^{(l-1)} : (u, v) \in G\})), \tag{3}$$

which $1 \leq l \leq L$, dropout operation is appended after each layer and is enabled only during training. The last layer is a fully connected layer:

$$\hat{p}^{(L+1)} = W^{(L+1)^T} \hat{p}^{(L)} + b^{(L+1)}. \tag{4}$$

After obtaining the user feature vectors p_u^k for each subgraph, we aim to aggregate the user feature vectors across multiple behaviors. To effectively model personalized multi-behavior diversity among different users, we introduce a contrastive learning framework. By learning the contrast among users' behaviors, we can achieve personalized multi-behavior information aggregation.

Contrast learning is an unsupervised learning method used to learn useful representations based on the establishment of similarity relationships between samples. The goal of contrast learning is to learn high-quality representations so that the distances of different samples in the embedded space can express the semantic differences between them, that is, samples with similar semantics have similar embedding distances in the embedded space, while samples with different semantics have longer embedding distances in the embedded space. The key is to find positive and negative pairs, and the different behaviors of the same user must be closer than the behaviors of different users. We regard the different behaviors of the same user as positive pairs, and the behaviors of different users as negative pairs, and calculate the comparative loss, so as to achieve the maximum mutual information.

In this paper, the add-to-cart behavior features obtained from the subgraphs are used as positive samples and uninterested behavior features are used as negative samples. We constrain the purchase behavior features to be as close as possible to the positive samples and far away from the negative samples in the feature space.

$$L_{contrastive} = -\sum_{u \in U} \log \frac{\exp\{(\hat{p}_{uk})^T \hat{p}_{u+k'}/\tau\}}{\exp\{(\hat{p}_{uk})^T \hat{p}_{u-k''}/\tau\}}, \tag{5}$$

which parameter τ denotes the temperature coefficient, τ determines the degree of dependency on negative samples

Objective Loss. The objective loss of DCMBR is comprised of two components: the contrastive loss and the cross-entropy loss. These components can be expressed mathematically as follows:

$$L = -\sum_{p_i \in U} \sum_{q_j \in V} r_{ij} \log(\hat{r}_{ij}) + (1 - r_{ij}) \log(1 - \hat{r}_{ij}) + L_{contrastive}, \tag{6}$$

which $\hat{r}_{ij}$ is the inner product of the multi-behavioral features of the user and the item features, denoted as $\hat{r}_{ij} = \hat{p}_i \cdot q_j.r_{ij}$ is the original scoring matrix, obtained from $r_{ij} = p_i \cdot q_j$.

4 Experimental Results and Analysis

4.1 Data Description

This paper examines e-commerce platforms as a context, we conducted extensive experiments using the Tmall and Online Retail datasets to evaluate the proposed method and compared it with relevant models.

1) Tmall: This is a public dataset from the Tmall e-commerce platform that includes four types of user behaviors: clicks, adding to cart, adding to favorites, and purchases where the latter is the target behavior and the former are auxiliary behaviors.
2) Online Retail: Explicit multi-type user-item interactions were used in an online retail scenario in the real world, including page views, adding to cart, adding to favorites, and purchases where the latter is the target behavior and the former are auxiliary behaviors.

Table 1. Statistics of experimented datasets.

Dataset	User	Item	Interaction	Interactive Behavior Type
Tmall	147894	99037	7.6× 106	{Page View, Favorite, Cart, Purchase}
Online Retail	805506	584050	6.4 × 107	{Page View, Favorite, Cart, Purchase}

4.2 Evaluation Metrics

In our experiments, we employed two evaluation metrics: Normalized Discounted Cumulative Gain (NDCG) and Hit Ratio (HR). HR focuses on the accuracy of the model's recommendations and determines whether the user's requirement items are included in the model's recommendations or not.NDCG takes into account the recommendation order of the items in the recommendation list, the higher the better. A higher HR and NDCG indicate better performance of the model. The HR and NDCG formula is as follows:

$$HR = \frac{1}{S} \sum_{i=1}^{S} hit(i) \tag{7}$$

$$NDCG = \frac{1}{S} \sum_{i=1}^{S} \frac{1}{\log_2(p_i + 1)} \tag{8}$$

which S is the number of samples, $hit(i)$ is whether the i-th demand item is included in the model list, 1 if it is included and 0 if it is not. $p(i)$ is the position of the i-th demand in the re-recommended items list and 0 if it is not in the recommended list.

4.3 Baseline Models

In this experiment, we compared our proposed method to multiple single-behavior models and multi-behavior models used as baselines.

The single-behavior models:

NCF [6]:A neural collaborative filtering-based recommendation model that replaces the inner product with a neural architecture that can learn arbitrary functions from data to simulate higher-order interactions, enabling nonlinear feature interactions.

NGCF [10]:A collaborative filtering model based on graph neural networks explicitly modeling higher-order connectivity between user items to enhance embedding.

LightGCN [5]:A recommendation model based on graph convolutional neural network, which is considered as an optimization and improvement of NGCF, performs graph convolution, aggregates neighboring features using a simple weighted summation, and discards feature transformations and nonlinear activation complex structures.

The multi-behavior models:

MATN [12]:Self-attention was used to encode two-by-two correlations between different types of behaviors, preserving cross-type behavioral synergy signals and type-specific behavioral context information, and explicitly encoding multi-behavioral relational structures.

MBGCN [7]:A heterogeneous graph-based multi-behavioral recommendation model that learns behavioral influence weights and captures behavioral semantics by aggregating the way user items interact under the same behavior.

MBRec [14]:An interrelational encoder is proposed to adaptively learn the complex relational structure of graphs of interest in different interaction modes as well as potential cross type behavioral interdependencies

By comparing our proposed method to these baseline models, we can evaluate its effectiveness and advantages in the field of recommendation tasks.

4.4   Performance Comparison

We first compared our model with other models, and after conducting experiments on two datasets, the results are shown in Table X. The table shows the performance of each model at different Recall@k and NDCG@k values, where k is 20 and 40 respectively. It can be seen that our model, DCMBR, outperforms the other six models in terms of all recall and NDCG@k values. On the Tmall and Online Retail datasets, our DCMBR model has Recall@20 values of 0.156 and 0.168, respectively, which are far superior to the other models.

The analysis of experimental results shows that using multi-behavioral data to analyze user preferences is better than using single row as data, which indicates that adding multi-behavioral information can effectively alleviate data sparsity. In this paper, we design the disentangled graph convolution module and the contrastive learning module, which play an important role in capturing the commonalities and dissimilarities among behaviors, mining user behavior patterns, and discovering users' fine-grained preferences.

Table 2. Performance of the method in this paper with the baseline model on Tmall and Online Retail.

	Datasets	Tmall				Online Retail			
	Method	Recall@20	NDCG@20	Recall@40	NDCG@40	Recall@20	NDCG@20	Recall@40	NDCG@40
Single-behavior	NCF	0.132	0.116	0.144	0.118	0.147	0.133	0.157	0.135
	NGCF	0.133	0.116	0.145	0.119	0.147	0.133	0.158	0.135
	LightGCN	0.13	0.114	0.141	0.116	0.145	0.131	0.155	0.133
Multi-behavior	MATN	0.143	0.114	0.162	0.122	0.156	0.132	0.173	0.138
	MBGCN	0.141	0.119	0.157	0.123	0.154	0.136	0.169	0.139
	MBRec	0.125	0.111	0.137	0.113	0.141	0.128	0.152	0.13
Our model	DCMBR	0.156	0.124	0.182	0.129	0.168	0.14	0.19	0.145

4.5   Ablation Study

The model in this paper mainly relies on two modules, disentangled graph convolution as well as contrastive learning, to enhance the user embedding representation, and in this section we explore the importance of the two modules in the model. Specifically, we design two model variants according to the model, one is to model the user directly using graph convolution without the disentangled graph convolution module, and the other is to stitch together the vector representations of the user under different behaviors directly without the contrastive learning module.

Without Using Disentangled Graph Convolution Module. The DCMBR model using disentangled graph convolution has improved Recall@k and NDCG@k values on both datasets compared to those without disentangled graph convolution, demonstrating the important role of disentangled graph convolution for performance improvement of multi-behavior recommendation tasks. This is because disentangled graph convolution is able to separate potential factors affecting the interaction between users, items and behaviors in multiple subgraphs to better reconstruct the node features of users under different behaviors, thus improving the generalization and robustness of features.

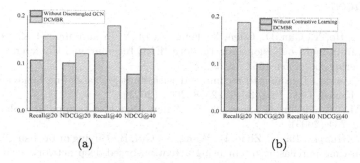

(a)   (b)

Fig. 2. Comparison of results without disentangled graph convolution module and contrastive learning

Without Using the Contrastive Learning Module. The DCMBR model using contrastive learning also has improved Recall@k and NDCG@k values on both datasets compared to those without contrastive learning, indicating the importance of contrastive learning in mitigating data sparsity of target behaviors and capturing the co-variance among different behaviors of users. This may be due to the fact that contrastive learning can better exploit the user's features under multiple behaviors, thus enabling the aggregation of user personalized multi-behavior information.

In summary, the results of these two ablation experiments show that disentangled graph convolution and contrastive learning have an important impact on the performance of the DCMBR model in a multi-behavior recommendation task, and can improve the model's recommendation effect in real recommendation systems.

5   Conclusion

In this work, we focus on the potential factors of multi-behavior interactions that are not considered by existing multi-behavior recommendations and the variability that exists among different behaviors. We effectively separate the representation of highly entangled potential factors of user, item and behavior types by disentangled graph convolutional networks, and construct a user disinterest subgraph to achieve user personalized multi-behavior information aggregation through inter-behavior contrastive learning. Experimental results on a diverse real-world dataset demonstrate that our model can significantly improve recommendation on target behaviors. In our future work, we will continue to work on multi-behavior recommendation systems to improve the interpretability of the model.

References

1. Gao, C., He, X., Gan, D., Chen, X., Feng, F., Li, Y.: Neural multi-task recommendation from multi-behavior data. In: 35th IEEE International Conference on Data Engineering, pp. 1554–1557 (2019)
2. Gao, C., et al.: Learning to recommend with multiple cascading behaviors. IEEE Trans. Knowl. Data Eng. **33**(6), 2588–2601 (2021)
3. Gori, M., Monfardini, G., Scarselli, F.: A new model for earning in raph domains, pp. 729–734 (2005)
4. Guo, L., Hua, L., Jia, R., Zhao, B., Wang, X., Cui, B.: Buying or browsing?: predicting real-time purchasing intent using attention-based deep network with multiple behavior. In: Proceedings of the 25th ACM SIGKDD International Conference on Knowledge Discovery, pp. 1984–1992 (2019)
5. He, X., Deng, K., Wang, X., Li, Y., Zhang, Y., Wang, M.: Lightgcn: simplifying and powering graph convolution network for recommendation. In: SIGIR, pp. 639–648. (2020)
6. He, X., Liao, L., Zhang, H., Nie, L., Hu, X.: Neural collaborative filtering, pp. 173–182. ACM (2017)
7. Jin, B., Gao, C., He, X., Jin, D., Li, Y.: Multi-behavior recommendation with graph convolutional networks. In: Proceedings of the 43rd International ACM SIGIR Conference on Research and Development in Information Retrieval, pp. 659–668 (2020)
8. Ma, J., Cui, P., Kuang, K., Wang, X., Zhu, W.: Disentangled graph convolutional networks, pp. 4212–4221. In: Proceedings of the 36th International Conference on Machine Learning (2019)
9. Smith, J.B., Smith, F.D., Malone, T.W.: Grouplens: an open architecture for collaborative filtering of netnews, pp. 175–186. ACM (1994)
10. Wang, X., He, X., Wang, M., Feng, F., Chua, T.S.: Neural graph collaborative filtering, pp. 165–174. ACM (2019)
11. Wang, X., Jin, H., Zhang, A., He, X., Xu, T., Chua, T.S.: Disentangled graph collaborative filtering, pp. 1001–1010. ACM (2020)
12. Xia, L., Huang, C., Xu, Y., Dai, P., Zhang, B., Bo, L.: Multiplex behavioral relation learning for recommendation via memory augmented transformer network, pp. 2397–2406 (2021)
13. Xia, L., et al.: Knowledge-enhanced hierarchical graph transformer network for multi-behavior recommendation. In: Thirty-Fifth AAAI Conference on Artificial Intelligence, pp. 4486–4493 (2021)

14. Yang, Y., Huang, C., Xia, L., Liang, Y., Yu, Y., Li, C.: Multi-behavior hypergraph-enhanced transformer for sequential recommendation. In: KDD, pp. 2263–2274 (2022)
15. Yuan, F., He, X., Karatzoglou, A., Zhang, L.: Parameter-efficient transfer from sequential behaviors for user modeling and recommendation, pp. 1469–1478 (2020)

How Hypergraph-to-Graph Conversion Affects Cooperative Working Visualization: A Multi-metric Evaluation

Zhihan Xiong[1,2,3], Ruixin Mu[1,2,3], Chongshen Yang[1,2,3], Wenjun Xie[1,2,3], and Qiang Lu[1,3,4(✉)]

[1] Key Laboratory of Knowledge Engineering with Big Data (Hefei University of Technology), Ministry of Education, Hefei 230009, China
{xiongzhihan,muruixin,prometheus}@mail.hfut.edu.cn,
{wjxie,luqiang}@hfut.edu.cn
[2] School of Software, Hefei University of Technology, Hefei 230601, China
[3] Intelligent Interconnected Systems Laboratory of Anhui Province (Hefei University of Technology), Hefei 230009, China
[4] School of Computer and Information, Hefei University of Technology, Hefei 230601, China

Abstract. It is commonplace to use hypergraphs to represent cooperative work since hypergraphs explicitly capture complex interactions and connections, enabling researchers to analyze with ease. Nonetheless, hypergraphs are usually chaotic due to sophisticated relations between vertices. Therefore, it is necessary to look into which method prevails over other methods in specific circumstances. In our study, we propose an appraisal framework in which we use six quantitative and five qualitative metrics to assess the performance of each conversion method in terms of layout quality and effectiveness. The results show that while no method is ideal for all situations, certain methods, such as Centroid-single, perform well. Researchers can use our experiment results to select the optimal method tailored to their specific dataset and circumstances. This paper serves researchers and practitioners in choosing the most suitable conversion method for their research.

Keywords: Hypergraph evaluation · Hypergraph conversion · Cooperative working · Multi-metric evaluation

1 Introduction

Cooperation means working together for a common goal. Visualization helps collaboration by making complex data easier to understand. Hypergraphs are a visualization technique that can show data with intricate relationships. They reduce high-dimensional data to two or three dimensions so people can grasp data features and connections. Hypergraphs differ from regular graphs, where each edge links only two vertices. Hypergraphs can merge multiple vertices with one hyperedge. Hypergraphs are helpful in many fields, such as biochemistry, circuit representation, databases, and machine learning. However, visual clutter and low comprehensibility limit their use in cooperation visualization as work gets complicated.

Table 1. 12 Conversion Methods (Categorized in 4 Types).

Split methods	Aggregate methods	Centroid methods	Expansion methods
△ Split-clique	⌒ Aggregate-collapse	△ Centroid-single	△ Line-expansion
⌒ Split-path	△ Aggregate-summarize	△ Centroid-aggregate-summarize	△ Line-expansion-aggregate-summarize
⬠ Split-cycle	△ Aggregate-relationship-summarize	△ Centroid-aggregate-relationship-summarize	△ Line-expansion-aggregate-relationship-summarize

To overcome the visual clutter issue in hypergraphs, the hypergraph's layout has been well studied in visualization [20,27] . The majority of proposed hypergraph layout techniques rely on conversing the hypergraph into a graph [1], and in this paper, the term "conversion" is used to refer to the process of creating a graph $G1 = (V_1, E)$ from a hypergraph G = (V, H) . **Figure** 1 illustrates how this conversion optimizes the process of hypergraph visualization. Based on the evaluation metrics we defined, subjective experiments were conducted to explore the merits and drawbacks of each conversion method. This paper focuses on exploring each conversion method, and the impact of each method on the performance and quality of the final hypergraph visualization. We analyzed twelve methods as listed in Table 1.

Three datasets, with varying visual clutter for hypergraph visualization, were presented in this paper. In pre-study, 40 participants, invited by us, select colors and layout algorithm. During main study, 18 participants attended five experiments to compare conversion methods. Finally, their subjective experiences, through a subjective questionnaire, were studied by us. The code and appendix are at https://github.com/Hypergraph-to-graph/Hypergraph-to-graph.

2   Related Work

2.1   Visualization of Hypergraphs

Various hypergraph visualization methods, have been surveyed by us. They are mainly two types: subset-based and node-link-based. Subset-based methods, such as QUAD [18] and Euler diagrams [21], use rectangles or points to show set relations. Node-link-based methods, such as MetroSets [14], 3D layout [16], and radial layout [17], use links or curves to connect nodes. Other methods include timeline-based [25] and matrix-based [22] approaches, but they have limitations in filtering, interaction, or scalability.

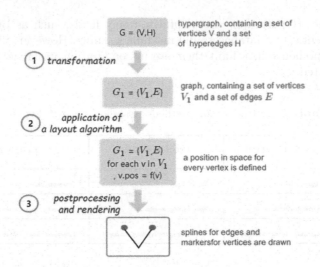

Fig. 1. Steps to be taken from hypergraph definition to drawing.

This paper uses Euler diagrams to visualize hypergraphs based on data categories, the emphasis of us. Since Euler diagrams are visually attractive, easy to understand, and space-efficient, they are a suitable tool for hypergraph analysis and exploration.

3   Evaluation Landscape

3.1   Selection of Conversion Methods

Papers, on hypergraph conversion from IEEE TVCG, IEEE VIS, PacificVis, and EuroVis in the last 10 year, are surveyed by us. Besides, Google Scholar and ChatGPT are used to find relevant papers. Finally, 5 methods are found, via reviewing relevant papers.

As relatively few methods have been proposed in this field, several new methods have been developed and tested by us, in addition to the original methods as listed in Table 2. The specific definitions, formulas, diagrams, and post-processing steps for each conversion method are included in the appendix.

3.2   Selection of Datasets

Methods on datasets from previous works, which produced hypergraphs with various features, have been thoroughly studied by us, such as size, density, and subgraph number.

Three datasets ,with different cooperative patterns, also, have been used by us, including: Southern Women, which recorded 18 women's social interactions in 14 events over 9 months (18 vertices and 14 hyperedges) [7]; DBLP, which

Table 2. References, features, worst-case complexities of conversion, and post-processing of our conversion methods. VC refers to the conversion in which the vertices are changed after the conversion, $|I|$ indicates the maximum number of vertices incident to a single hyperedge. $|H|$ indicates the number of hyperedges. $|V|$ indicates the number of vertices.

Conversion method	References	VC	Converse	Post-processing
Split-clique	[3]		$O(|H|*|I|^2)$	$O(|H|*|I|)$
Split-path	[3]		$O(|H|*|I|)$	$O(|H|*|I|)$
Split-cycle	[1,2]		$O(|H|*|I|)$	$O(|H|*|I|)$
Aggregate-collapse	[3]	✓	$(|H|^2*|I|^2)$	$O(|H|^2*|I|^2)$
Aggregate-summarize	[3]	✓	$O(|H|^2*|I|^2)$	$O(|V|^2)$
Aggregate-relationship-summarize	[2,5]	✓	$O(|H|*|I|*|V|^2)$	$O(|V|^2)$
Centroid-single	[3]	✓	$O(|H|*|I|)$	$O(|H|*|I|)$
Centroid-aggregate-summarize	[3]	✓	$O(|H|^2*|I|^2)$	$O(|H|*|I|*|V|)$
Centroid-aggregate-relationship-summarize	[2,3,5]	✓	$O(|H|^2*|I|^2)$	$O(|H|*|I|*|V|)$
Line-expansion	[26]	✓	$O(|H|^2*|I|^2)$	$O(|H|*|I|*|V|)$
Line-expansion-aggregate-summarize	[3,26]	✓	$O(|H|^2*|I|^2)$	$O(|H|*|I|*|V|)$
Line-expansion-aggregate-relationship-summarize	[2,26] , [5]	✓	$O(|H|*|I|*|V|^2)$	$O(|V|^2)$

selected the top 15 papers on visualization from IEEE VIS (1990–2018) and added related papers by the same authors (68 vertices and 30 hyperedges) [19]; and Coauthor Network, which explored the network of authors in information-retrieval with H-index of 40 or higher (114 vertices and 120 hyperedges) [23]. See Figure 2 for details.

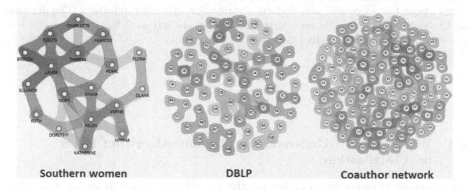

Southern women   **DBLP**   **Coauthor network**

Fig. 2. Datasets select for our evaluation. Here are the output hypergraphs of three datasets using the Centroid-single method.

3.3   Selection of Evaluation Metrics

Through comprehensive research, we defined evaluation metrics from both quantitative and qualitative aspects. Six metrics, summarized from literature, were employed by us to evaluate the quantitative aspects of the trials, bar time and accuracy: (1) concavity, the number of nonconvex edges, lower values indicate better aesthetics [1]; (2) planarity, the number of edge crossings, lower values reduce clutter and ambiguity [1]; (3) coverage rate, the formula is in the appendix, higher values mean better canvas utilization [1]. The canvas size was fixed at 860 × 860 pixels.(4) regularity, which refers to the evenness of the distance between the connections of vertices, is quantified by the variance of the lengths of the edges connecting vertices. The larger the evenness, the more uniform the distribution of vertices [1]; These metrics often appear under different names in papers evaluating graph layouts [10]. Figure 3 illustrates the impact of each evaluated metric on hypergraph visualization very well. We surveyed users on various aspects of each trial and output hypergraph. The survey is in the appendix. We used six quantitative and five qualitative metrics. These metrics help us evaluate the conversion methods and their scenarios. See Figure 4 for the metric system.

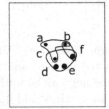 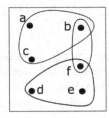

Fig. 3. Two drawings of hyperedgesa,b,c,b,f,d,e,f.The drawing on the left has a concave shape, poor Coverage and non-uniform distribution of vertices(clutter), The drawing on the right is aesthetically superior to the one on the left as it has no concavity, less crossings, comparatively better Coverage and Regularity.

4   Pre-Study

4.1   Experiment 1: Understanding Layout Algorithm Effect on Visualization

The purpose is to specify a choice for the formal study: which layout algorithm should be used for the data layout of graphs in the formal study. Several layout algorithms have been proposed for common graphs in previous research, and we selected four algorithms from the most commonly used force-directed layout algorithms: forceAltas2 [15], Fruchterman [1,6,8], CompoundSpringEmbedder-Graph(CoSE) [4,12,13], and the original force algorithm coming from prefuse(a software framework) [9,11,24].

Trial and Procedure. Having conducted three experiments with datasets of equal size but different content, we applied four layout algorithms to each dataset

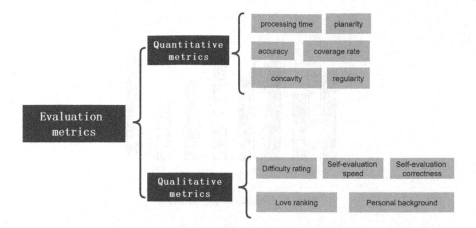

Fig. 4. The metric system for evaluation.

and showed the resulting graphs to participants. They rated each algorithm on a 5-point scale based on two criteria: 1) how well points in the same category clustered together, and 2) how well points in different categories spread apart. Each experiment took about 10 min.

Participants and Apparatus. We ran an experiment with 40 computer science students (28M, 12F, 18–30 years old). They had different levels of familiarity with visualization: 25 very, 10 moderate, 5 low. We used a web prototype (appendix) and a $1,920 \times 1,080$ screen resolution.

Results. Considering that each layout algorithm performs differently on datasets of different sizes, we chose the layout algorithm with the highest average score, which was Fruchterman. As shown in Figure 5, the average score of Fruchterman was significantly higher than the other three algorithms, and it performed well on both small and medium-sized graphs. One participant said, *"The graph generated by Fruchterman is more helpful for me to distinguish different classes."*Therefore, we decided to use the Fruchterman layout algorithm in the formal study to optimize the visualization effects.

5   Formal Study

5.1   Hypotheses

Formal study aims to evaluate the performance of 12 conversion methods based on whether they can optimize the following five visual metrics: concavity, planarity, the coverage rate of the plane, regularity, and the cognitive capacity of data; above-mentioned five metrics, inarguably, play an vital role in hypergraph conversion methods; in order to fathom out their relationship with hypergraph conversion, five hypotheses, therefore, were formulated to guide the experimental design.

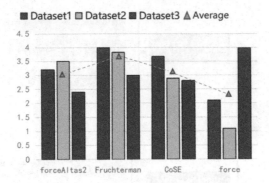

Fig. 5. Results of pre-study.

H1: In terms of reducing concavity, the user perception of the Centroid-aggregate-relationship-summarize method outperforms other conversion methods.

H2: In terms of improving planarity, the user perception of Split-path and Split-cycle methods perform better.

H3: In terms of improving coverage, the user perception of Line-expansion method performs better compared to other methods.

H4: In terms of improving regularity, the user perception of the performance of other conversion methods is worse than that of the Line-expansion-aggregate-relationship-summarize method.

H5: In terms of improving the cognitive capacity of data, users experience the shortest completion time and the highest accuracy in the Line-expansion and Centroid-aggregate-relationship-summarize methods.

5.2   Experiments

Guided by the five hypotheses (H1-H5), we designed five experiments (E1-E5). Note that E1-E5 were controlled experiments.

E1: Perception of concavity reduction. The experiment tests how well different methods can make graphs look less concave. Participants ranked 12 graphs from most to least concave, based on the number of non-convex superedges. For three datasets, one question, coupled with 12 graphs corresponding to 12 conversion methods, is generated. Overall, 3 trials have been prepared for each participant.

E2: Perception of planarity increases. This experiment tests how different conversion methods affect planarity perception. Participants ranked 12 graphs by planarity, from least to most superedge crossings. Each question had 12 graphs for one dataset. There were 3 trials per participant, one for each dataset.

E3: Perception of the coverage rate of the plane increase. The experiment aims to compare how different conversion methods affect visual perception of coverage. Participants ranked 12 graphs by coverage rate and answered one question for each dataset. 3 trials in total, one for each dataset, waited for participants to solve.

E4: Perception of regularity increases. The experiment tests how different conversion methods affect the uniformity of vertex distances. Participants ranked 12 graphs by vertex distance evenness for each of three datasets. Each dataset had one question and 12 graphs. Three trials in total waited to be solved.

E5: Perception of cognitive capacity of data improvement. This paragraph aims to assess how various conversion methods can improve users' data categorization skills in visual perception. Users answer hypergraph-based questions on data categorization. Each method has one question for each output hypergraph. There are 36 trials in total for users, with 12 conversion methods and 3 datasets.

5.3 Participants, Apparatus and Testing Data

Participants. Our formal study invited 18 computer-related participants (14 males, 4 females, aged 11–30). Their familiarity with visualization varied: 10 were familiar, 5 were moderately familiar, and 3 were unfamiliar. All had normal or corrected vision and no color vision problems.

Apparatus. The experiments were conducted online through a website(Figure 6), in which participants were required to visit it remotely on the Chrome browser and finish the experiment on a screen with a resolution of $1{,}536 \times 864$. After finishing our experiment, they would share their screen with us in attempt to enable remote monitoring.

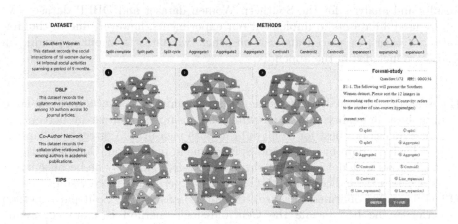

Fig. 6. Formal Study Website.

5.4 Procedure

The experiment had two phases: training and testing. The training explained the experiment and concepts (e.g. concavity). Participants could ask questions to understand better. They started testing after confirming their comprehension. They had a 5-minute break before each experiment. They gave background and basic information before, and rated, using the Likert 5-point scale, and suggested evaluation metrics after. Each participant spent about an hour.

6   Experimental Results

6.1   Analysis Approach

Objective measurements were recorded for E1-E5 and the accuracy and completion time for each trial were documented.

The user-selected and the best-performing conversion methods were compared by us for sorting problems (E1-E4) and analyzed how they affected the user's perception, difficulty, speed and accuracy. For the judgment problem (E5), having calculated and analyzed the accuracy and completion time of each method, we identified the best one. Finally, the results, on the basis of the questionnaire, are correlated by us, with the participants' backgrounds, to understand the suitability and applicability of the method.

6.2   Results Analysis

Results and analysis for the Southern Women dataset and DBLP dataset (we totally used 3 datasets to implement our experiments; however, due to the limitation of pages, we placed analysis on other two datasets in our appendix) in E1-E4 are included in the appendix.

H1 is partly supported: Centroid-aggregate-summarize converts medium-sized data best in reality and Aggregate-relationship-summarize in perception. Line-expansion is best for small data in both measures. Aggregate-collapse is best for large data in reality and Split-clique in perception. Completion time in E1 grows with data size, but shrinks in E2-E4. This may be because larger data makes the indicators of the last three experiments more visible.

H2 is partially confirmed because, for small datasets, the Split-path method performs the best, while the Centroid-single method is more commonly known among users; for medium-sized datasets, the Centroid-single method is both the best in actual results and user perception; for large datasets, the Aggregate-relationship-summarize method has the best actual results, while the Centroid-aggregate-relationship-summarize method is more commonly known among users.

H3 is rejected because for small datasets, the Aggregate-collapse method has the best actual results, but most users are familiar with the Centroid-aggregate-summarize method. For medium-sized datasets, both the Centroid-single method and user perception are the best. The results and user perception are best with the Split-path method for large datasets.

H4 is rejected because for small datasets, the Centroid-single method has the best actual results, but most users are familiar with the Line-expansion method. For medium-sized datasets, both the actual results and user perception are the best with the Aggregate-relationship-summarize method. For large datasets, both the actual results and user perception are best with the Centroid-aggregate-relationship-summarize method.

H5 is rejected because Split-path method has the highest accuracy and Aggregate-relationship-summarize method has the shortest time. Figure 8, 9 shows the results for each conversion method in E5.

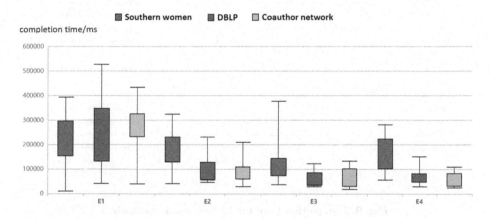

Fig. 7. The average completion time of the three datasets in Experiments 1 to 4.

Takeaways: Centroid-single works well for medium datasets, especially for planarity and coverage. Aggregate-relationship-summarize is better for regularity. For large datasets, Split-path gives higher coverage, while Centroid-aggregate-relationship-summarize gives higher regularity. Line-expansion helps users classify data accurately and quickly.

6.3   Important Visual Metrics

The average ratings(shown in Figure 10) for regularity, planarity, and concavity were 4.32, 4.1, and 4.03. The high ratings confirm that the evaluated metrics are common issues of concern in hypergraph visualization. Furthermore, we found differences among participants with different backgrounds (detailed data and analysis can be found in the appendix): users familiar with visualization are

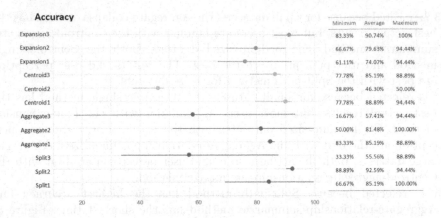

Accuracy

	Minimum	Average	Maximum
Expansion3	83.33%	90.74%	100%
Expansion2	66.67%	79.63%	94.44%
Expansion1	61.11%	74.07%	94.44%
Centroid3	77.78%	85.19%	88.89%
Centroid2	38.89%	46.30%	50.00%
Centroid1	77.78%	88.89%	94.44%
Aggregate3	16.67%	57.41%	94.44%
Aggregate2	50.00%	81.48%	100.00%
Aggregate1	83.33%	85.19%	88.89%
Split3	33.33%	55.56%	88.89%
Split2	88.89%	92.59%	94.44%
Split1	66.67%	85.19%	100.00%

Fig. 8. Accuracy for 12 conversion methods.

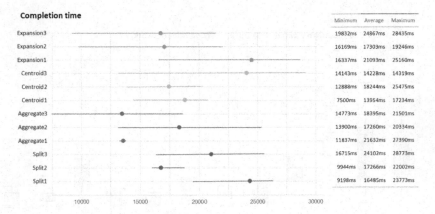

Completion time

	Minimum	Average	Maximum
Expansion3	19832ms	24867ms	28435ms
Expansion2	16169ms	17303ms	19246ms
Expansion1	16337ms	21093ms	25160ms
Centroid3	14143ms	14228ms	14319ms
Centroid2	12888ms	18244ms	25475ms
Centroid1	7500ms	13954ms	17234ms
Aggregate3	14773ms	18395ms	21501ms
Aggregate2	13900ms	17260ms	20334ms
Aggregate1	11837ms	21632ms	27390ms
Split3	16715ms	24102ms	28773ms
Split2	9944ms	17266ms	22002ms
Split1	9198ms	16485ms	23773ms

Fig. 9. Completion time for 12 conversion methods.

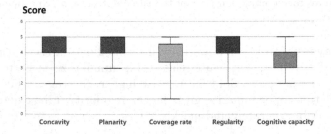

Fig. 10. The score of evaluation metrics.

more concerned about regularity and improving their cognitive capacity of data categories, while participants with a research focus on visualization or software engineering are more interested in reducing concavity compared to those in the computer vision field. In the interviews conducted after the experiment, participants proposed new evaluation metrics, such as color, the degree of cohesion within the same class, and the degree of dispersion between different classes.

7 Conclusion and Future Work

Hypergraph conversion methods, from a perceptual perspective, were empirically evaluated by us. 12 methods, 6 quantitative metrics, and 5 qualitative metrics, with five hypotheses and experiments, have been proposed by us. Moreover, a pre-study determines the layout algorithm for graph conversion has been conducted to identify the most optimal method to convert hypergraph. The results offer practical guidance for choosing conversion methods and visualization methods for cooperative work.

This paper has some limitations and suggestions for improvement. It does not examine how the dataset's vertex and hyperedge numbers affect hypergraph visualization. It also does not address the color overlap problem that may bias the data classification. Future work should explore these issues, compare the conversion methods for different datasets, and find ways to assign unique colors to overlapping hyperedges. Moreover, this paper uses a limited dataset, so more datasets with larger and diverse scopes are needed for thorough analysis.

Acknowledgement. This work was supported in part by the Open Foundation of the Key lab (center) of Anhui Province Key Laboratory of Intelligent Building & Building Energy Saving (IBES2022KF03), and the Scientific and Technological Achievement Cultivation Project of Intelligent Manufacturing Institute of HFUT (IMIPY2021022).

References

1. Arafat, N.A., Bressan, S.: Hypergraph drawing by force-directed placement, pp. 387–394 (08 2017). https://doi.org/10.1007/978-3-319-64471-4_31
2. Bannister, M.J., Eppstein, D., Goodrich, M.T., Trott, L.: Force-directed graph drawing using social gravity and scaling. CoRR abs/1209.0748 (2012). http://arxiv.org/abs/1209.0748
3. Di Bartolomeo, S., Pister, A., Buono, P., Plaisant, C., Dunne, C., Fekete, J.D.: Six methods for transforming layered hypergraphs to apply layered graph layout algorithms. Comput. Graph. Forum **41** (2022). https://doi.org/10.1111/cgf.14538
4. Dogrusoz, U., Belviranli, M.E., Dilek, A.: Cise: a circular spring embedder layout algorithm. IEEE Trans. Visual Comput. Graph. **19**, 953–966 (2013)
5. Ducournau, A., Bretto, A., Rital, S., Laget, B.: A reductive approach to hypergraph clustering: An application to image segmentation. Pattern Recogn. **45**, 2788–2803 (07 2012). https://doi.org/10.1016/j.patcog.2012.01.005
6. Frickey, T., Lupas, A.: Clans: a java application for visualizing protein families based on pairwise similarity. Bioinformatics (Oxford, England) **20**, 3702–4 (01 2005). https://doi.org/10.1093/bioinformatics/bth444
7. Fuller, C.: Caste, race, and hierarchy in the american south. J. Royal Anthropol. Inst. **17**, 604–621 (08 2011). https://doi.org/10.1111/j.1467-9655.2011.01709.x

8. Gajdo, P., Ježowicz, T., Uher, V., Dohnalek, P.: A parallel fruchterman-reingold algorithm optimized for fast visualization of large graphs and swarms of data. Swarm Evol. Comput. **26** (08 2015). https://doi.org/10.1016/j.swevo.2015.07.006

9. Ágg, B., et al.: The entoptlayout cytoscape plug-in for the efficient visualization of major protein complexes in protein-protein interaction and signalling networks. Bioinformatics (Oxford, England) **35**, 4490–4492 (11 2019). https://doi.org/10.1093/bioinformatics/btz257

10. Haleem, H., Wang, Y., Puri, A., Wadhwa, S., Qu, H.: Evaluating the readability of force directed graph layouts: a deep learning approach. CoRR abs/1808.00703 (2018), http://arxiv.org/abs/1808.00703

11. Heer, J., Card, S., Landay, J.: Prefuse: a toolkit for interactive information visualization, pp. 421–430 (04 2005). https://doi.org/10.1145/1054972.1055031

12. Herman, I., Melançon, G., Marshall, M.: Graph visualization and navigation in information visualization: a survey. IEEE Tran. Visual. Comput. Graph. **6**, 24–43 (02 2000). https://doi.org/10.1109/2945.841119

13. Hu, Y.: Efficient and high quality force-directed graph drawing. Math. J. 10, 37–71 (01 2005)

14. Jacobsen, B., Wallinger, M., Kobourov, S., Nöllenburg, M.: Metrosets: visualizing sets as metro maps. IEEE Trans. Visualization Comput. Graph. **PP**, 1–1 (10 2020). https://doi.org/10.1109/TVCG.2020.3030475

15. Jacomy, M., Venturini, T., Heymann, S., Bastian, M.: Forceatlas2, a continuous graph layout algorithm for handy network visualization designed for the gephi software. PloS one **9**, e98679 (06 2014). https://doi.org/10.1371/journal.pone.0098679

16. Kapec, P.: Hypergraph-based software visualization. In: International Workshop on Computer Graphics, Computer Vision and Mathematics, GraVisMa 2009 - Workshop Proceedings, pp. 149–153 (01 2009)

17. Kerren, A., Jusufi, I.: A novel radial visualization approach for undirected hypergraphs (01 2013). https://doi.org/10.2312/PE.EuroVisShort.EuroVisShort2013.025-029

18. Kritz, M., Perlin, K.: A new scheme for drawing hypergraphs. Int. J. Comput. Math. **50**(3-4), 131–134 (Jan 1994). https://doi.org/10.1080/00207169408804250, copyright: Copyright 2015 Elsevier B.V., All rights reserved

19. Ley, M.: Dblp.uni-trier.de: Computer science bibliography. http://dblp.uni-trier.de/ (1993)

20. Qu, B., Zhang, E., Zhang, Y.: Automatic polygon layout for primal-dual visualization of hypergraphs. CoRR abs/2108.00671 (2021). https://arxiv.org/abs/2108.00671

21. Riche, N., Dwyer, T.: Untangling euler diagrams. IEEE Trans. Visual Comput. Graph. **16**(6), 1090–1099 (2010). https://doi.org/10.1109/TVCG.2010.210

22. Streeb, D., Arya, D., Keim, D.A., Worring, M.: Visual analytics framework for the assessment of temporal hypergraph prediction models (2019)

23. Tang, J., Zhang, J., Yao, L., Li, J., Zhang, l., Su, Z.: Arnetminer: extraction and mining of academic social networks, pp. 990–998 (08 2008). https://doi.org/10.1145/1401890.1402008

24. Thawonmas, R., Kurashige, M., Chen, K.T.: Detection of landmarks for clustering of online-game players. IJVR **6**, 11–16 (01 2007)

25. Valdivia, P., Buono, P., Plaisant, C., Dufournaud, N., Fekete, J.D.: Analyzing dynamic hypergraphs with parallel aggregated ordered hypergraph visualization. IEEE Trans. Visualization Comput. Graph. **PP**, 1–1 (08 2019). https://doi.org/10.1109/TVCG.2019.2933196

26. Yang, C., Wang, R., Yao, S., Abdelzaher, T.F.: Hypergraph learning with line expansion. CoRR abs/2005.04843 (2020). https://arxiv.org/abs/2005.04843
27. Zhou, Y., Rathore, A., Purvine, E., Wang, B.: Topological simplifications of hypergraphs. CoRR abs/2104.11214 (2021). https://arxiv.org/abs/2104.11214

Vessel Traffic Flow Prediction and Analysis Based on Ship Big Data

Tong Wang, Xiaoyang Gai, Songming Liu[✉], Shan Gao, Min Ouyang, and Liwei Chen

Harbin Engineering University, Harbin 150001, People's Republic of China
lsming926@hrbeu.edu.com

Abstract. In the face of the development of the waterway collaboration transportation, the big data analysis of the waterborne transport has become a hot topic in the field of transportation. Due to the nonlinear and not obvious periodic space-time characteristics of ship traffic flow, it is a great challenge to accurately predict it. In this paper, a CNN-BiLSTM prediction model based on residual fitting network and attention mechanism is proposed, which considers the temporal and spatial characteristics of ship flow, and the extraction analysis of the ship big data and short-term ship flow prediction of sea port. The model extracts the multi-dimensional features of traffic with the help of one-dimensional convolution layer, obtains information mining on the forward and backward sequential data of the two-way long and short time memory network. Besides, the attention mechanism is used to enhance the learning of important features and residual fitting is used to enhance the fit of results. In this paper, we collected the AIS data in waters near New York Harbor, and the multi-segment regional traffic flow dataset is constructed by dividing regions. By comparison with ARIMA, LSTM, GRU, BiLSTM, CNN-LSTM and Attention-BiLSTM models, the proposed prediction model has higher prediction accuracy and a higher degree of fitting with the real value of ship flow.

Keywords: Ship big data · AIS data · Ship traffic flow prediction

1 Introduction

In recent years, with the growth of traffic data and the development of intelligent transportation, the era of traffic big data has been entered. As a research direction of big data analysis, data-driven traffic calculation based on traffic prediction has attracted extensive attention from scholars. With the continuous development of global port and navigation technology, big data of water transportation has become a research hotspot in the field of transportation. With the development of satellite positioning and waterway collaboration technology, a large number of ship historical data and track information can be obtained by various ways such as radar satellite and Automatic Identification System (AIS) as the basic data of water transportation. How to excavate its useful information has significant research value and significance for ship flow prediction in the field of water transport.

© The Author(s), under exclusive license to Springer Nature Singapore Pte Ltd. 2024
Y. Sun et al. (Eds.): ChineseCSCW 2023, CCIS 2012, pp. 222–239, 2024.
https://doi.org/10.1007/978-981-99-9637-7_16

Waterway traffic and road traffic belong to the field of traffic research, there are some differences and connections between them. 1) The main body of road traffic is vehicle, while that of waterway traffic is ship. The differences in ship speed and size of different types of ships will affect the prediction of waterway traffic flow. 2) Road traffic lines are directly visible, and the flow direction, aggregation and congestion of traffic volume can be clearly seen. On the contrary, water traffic lines converge, disperse and cross each other, which makes the prediction of traffic flow more complicated. 3) The road traffic flow is relatively dense and stable, which has obvious periodicity, while the waterway traffic flow has poor stability and great volatility affected by data collection methods, water traffic conditions, changeable water speed and wind direction on the waterway, which brings great difficulty to the prediction of the waterway traffic flow based on big data.

With the development of maritime traffic, the flow of ships in maritime waters increases sharply, and the port traffic becomes more and more congested. Due to ship congestion on the route, some ports which are constrained by natural geographical environment and navigation conditions may decrease navigation efficiency and even cause waterway traffic accidents. How to guarantee the efficiency of port navigation and the safety of ship navigation puts forward higher requirements for ship flow prediction. Accurate and efficient ship flow prediction can provide important basis for navigation management, early warning for navigation safety and ship channel planning, which is beneficial to improve navigation efficiency and ensure safety, and is of great significance for the construction of water transportation based on big ship data.

In this paper, we separate the forecasting task from the road traffic field under big data to establish the application scenario of sea port. The ship flow dataset was collected, and a ship flow prediction model was established to forecast ship flow changes. We aim to make the following four contributions to the research field of ship traffic prediction work of sea port:

(1) AIS data in the vicinity of New York port was collected and a ship traffic dataset with temporal and spatial characteristics was constructed by means of regional division. Our model was trained and model performance was tested based on this dataset.

(2) Based on convolutional neural network, cyclic neural network and residual fitting method, a CNN-BiLSTM ship flow prediction model based on residual prediction network and attention mechanism is proposed. The network considers the nonlinear characteristics and spatial-temporal characteristics of ship flow data, and is used to predict the short-term changes of ship flow in port.

(3) In our proposed model, convolution operation was added to extract the temporal and spatial features between traffic data, BiLSTM was used to capture the two-way long and short term features, and attention mechanism was introduced to obtain the influence of different regional traffic on characteristics of data. The use of residual fitting reduces the influence of excessive prediction error caused by the rapid change of ship flow, and improves the prediction accuracy of ship flow change.

(4) The proposed model was compared with ARIMA, LSTM, GRU, BiLSTM, CNN-LSTM and Attention-LSTM models, and the effectiveness and robustness of the proposed method were verified.

2 Related Work

For the research of ship traffic flow prediction, the proposed methods are mainly divided into the traditional statistical theory method, machine learning method and deep neural network model method. The methods based on statistical theory mainly include linear time series model, nonlinear parameter regression model and wavelet theory model. ARIMA(Autoregressive Integrated Moving Average model) [1] is a typical time series method with parametric models, which established regression models for traffic flow prediction by checking the periodicity of traffic flow. The disadvantage of it is that the parametric model depends on prior conditions. The nonparametric model K-nearest neighbor algorithm (K-NN) can directly conduct complex nonlinear modeling of ship flow data, assuming that it does not depend on the characteristics of traffic flow [2]. SARIMA model (Seasonal Autoregressive Integrated Moving Average model) [3] is an improved differential autoregressive moving average model with good forecasting effect for obvious seasonal ship flow in waterways. Liu [4] established Markov model based on grey theory and applied it to ship traffic flow prediction to improve model fitting and prediction accuracy. These methods are simple and fast, but has low precision, and it is unable to deal with the unexpected situation in practical application, so it is difficult to reach the application level. In addition, nonlinear methods [5] based on wavelet analysis and chaos theory have good performance in dealing with complex problems, but they are not effective in practical prediction applications.

With the progress of machine learning algorithms, many scholars begin to use relevant algorithm models to study traffic prediction. Machine learning models can learn from large amounts of data to better predict nonlinear complex systems. Wang et al. [6] adopted BP neural network model to overcome the shortcomings of linear regression and forecast ship flow effectively. Feng et al. [7] applied the support vector regression model to ship flow prediction, which improved the prediction accuracy and robustness. Zhang et al. [8] combined the particle swarm optimization algorithm with BP neural network to optimize the network parameters and improve the convergence rate of the model. Jiang et al. [9] proposed a traffic flow prediction model combining random forest and cuckoo search algorithm, and verified the accuracy of the model. However, the current machine learning algorithm has the weakness of complex structure, low learning efficiency and easy fitting, which can not be widely used.

In recent years, with the development of artificial intelligence methods, deep learning methods have been widely used in the field of traffic prediction, which has become a research hotspot. RNN (Recurrent Neural Network) uses sequence data as input, connects recurrent units in chain, which can well extract nonlinear features between data. Long Short Term Memory Network (LSTM), as an improved network of RNN, is easy to automatically extract features through end-to-end modeling, and can effectively solve the problem of gradient disappearing explosion by maintaining long-term memory. As its advantages in processing time series, LSTM has become a popular time series model framework. Ma et al. [10] adopted LSTM network for the first time and used roadside sensors to collect vehicle speed data to predict road traffic speed. Ji et al. [11] used LSTM network to forecast the ship traffic flow of Qingdao Port, it is verified that it has more advantages than traditional models such as ARIMA. Yan et al. [12] obtained the temporal and spatial characteristics of the traffic flow through CNN and combined it with the LSTM model to realize the short-term prediction of the traffic flow. Liu et al. [13] proposed a prediction method based on Conv-LSTM model in order to analyze the spatio-temporal and periodic characteristics of traffic data. Suo et al. [14] compared the GRU model with the multi-layer sparse self-decoder(SAEs) and LSTM model, it is proved that the adopted model has better effect in the traffic flow prediction of Gulei Port area in Fujian, China. Yang et al. [15] introduced the attention mechanism into the LSTM model to solve the problem that the error would be increased over time. Wen et al. [13] used genetic algorithm to improve the network parameters of LSTM, optimized the number of hidden layers and training times, which made the optimization speed of the model faster and the prediction performance better. Su et al. [16] proposed a short-term ship flow prediction method based on two-way long-term and short-term memory network and attention mechanism, which has higher prediction accuracy. Liu et al. [17] took DTW, a dynamic time adjustment algorithm, as a model loss function and proposed CNN-LSTM-DTW combined model algorithm to study ship traffic flow, which improved the efficiency of feature extraction and prediction accuracy.

At present, the traffic prediction model in the field of waterway transport is mostly based on the road traffic prediction model. Nevertheless, due to the complex and changeable weather conditions of the water area, the irregular changes of ship routes and the volatility of port traffic data, the performance of most of the traffic prediction models in the port flow prediction degrades. Therefore, how to establish a traffic prediction model with better adaptability for water transport scenarios according to the characteristics of water transportation is a major problem to be solved in the field of waterway port traffic prediction.

3 Methodologies

3.1 LSTM Networks

LSTM network has great advantages in capturing long-term information and extracting time series features. As shown in Fig. 1, LSTM network is mainly composed of three gate structures: input gate i_t, forgetting gate f_t and output gate o_t. The input gate determines the amount of information passing through, the forgetting gate determines the amount of information to be discarded, and the output gate controls the proportion of cell state to be outputed. Equations (1)–(3) provide the specific calculation processes of three gates. Equations (4)–(5) show the calculation processes of cell storage units and hidden states.

$$f_t = Sigmoid(W_f \cdot [h_{t-1}, X_t] + b_f) \tag{1}$$

$$i_t = Sigmoid(W_i \cdot [h_{t-1}, X_t] + b_i) \tag{2}$$

$$C_t = f_t \cdot C_{t-1} + i_t \cdot \tanh(W_c \cdot [h_{t-1}, X_t] + b_c) \tag{3}$$

$$o_t = Sigmoid(W_o \cdot [h_{t-1}, X_t] + b_o) \tag{4}$$

$$h_t = o_t \cdot \tanh(C_t) \tag{5}$$

where, X_t represents the input data at the current time. W_f, W_i, W_o, W_c are the weight matrices of forgetting gate, input gate, output gate and cell state respectively, and b is the bias vector of each gate structure.

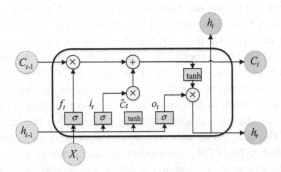

Fig. 1. LSTM network structure diagram.

The cell storage unit is used to transmit information sequence, so that the characteristic information of the early unit can be transferred to the later unit. In this way, the LSTM network can remember the information of the long time series.

3.2 CNN Networks

CNN(convolutional neural network) is a multi-layer neural network used for supervised learning. As shown in Fig. 2, it is composed of input layer, convolutional layer, pooling layer, fully connected layer and output layer.

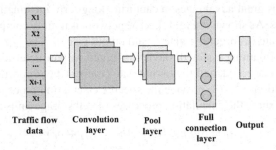

Fig. 2. CNN network structure diagram.

The convolutional layer extracts features from the input data, and the number of features extracted depends on the convolution sum number and convolution sum size parameters. Pooling layer carries on the reduction and quadratic feature extraction for the features obtained from the convolution operation. The calculation of convolution layer and pooling layer can be expressed as Eqs. (6) and (7). The data characteristics after the aggregation pooling operation of the full connection layer can achieve regression prediction.

$$Y_c = f(W_c \otimes X_c + b_c) \tag{6}$$

$$P_c = \max \text{Pool}(Y_c) \tag{7}$$

where, Y_c represents the output of the convolutional layer, W_c represents the weight vector, X_c represents the input data, b_c represents the bias parameter, and f represents the excitation function. P_c indicates the output of the pooling layer, and *maxpool* indicates the maximum pooling function.

3.3 CNN-BiLSTM Model Based on Residual Fitting and Attention Mechanism

In order to overcome the shortcomings that CNN and LSTM models can only obtain local features and one-way time information, and to solve the problem of excessive residual prediction caused by abnormal data changes, this paper proposes a CNN-BiLSTM prediction model based on residual fitting and attention mechanism, which we call it as R-ATT-CNN-BiLSTM model.

Model Input

The original ship flow data is used as model input after data preprocessing and standardization. The input sequence of data can be expressed as $X = [x_1, x_2, ..., x_{t-1}, x_t]^T$, $X \in R^{t \times d}$, where t is the number of time steps, x_t is the data vector at current time, which contains d feature dimensions. In order to better obtain the features of time series data and generate corresponding training samples, sliding window with fixed width and fixed step length are used to generate training sets. The processing data of sliding window is shown in Fig. 3.

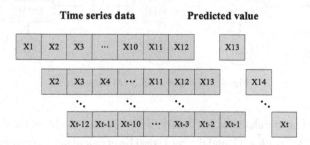

Fig. 3. Data processing using a sliding window.

Convolutional Layer

Convolution layer is used to extract temporal and spatial features of input data. In this paper, one-dimensional convolution layer is used to extract local features of data. Batch normalization is adopted to eliminate data distribution differences with feature vectors and generate data distribution with mean value 0 and variance 1. Then, the normalized data is reconstructed and adjusted to restore original feature distribution for network feature learning at the next layer. Equations (8)-(9) show the calculation process of the normalization and reconstruction.

$$\hat{x}_k = \frac{x_k - \overline{x_k}}{\sqrt{\dfrac{1}{n}\sum_{k=1}^{n}(x_k - \overline{x_k})^2}} \tag{8}$$

$$y_k = \alpha_k \hat{x} + \beta_k \tag{9}$$

where, x_k is the data unit for convolution, $\overline{x_k}$ is its average value, $\hat{x}_k$ is the normalized value of x_k, α_k and β_k are the data reconstruction parameter.

BiLSTM Layer
LSTM network can only obtain one-way features of time series data, and will ignore the impact of future data on the current state. In this paper, BiLSTM (Bi-directional Long Short-Term Memory) is used to extract correlation between sequences and bidirectional information features. As shown in Fig. 4, BiLSTM network is composed of forward LSTM layer and backward LSTM layer. A reverse chronological connection is added between hidden layers, and the two reverse LSTM networks are combined into a connection group of hidden layer.

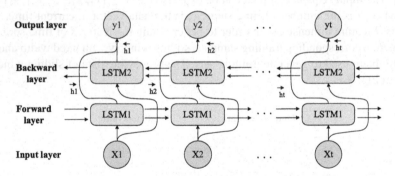

Fig. 4. Structure o BiLSTM network.

The forward layer calculates for the forward sequence to obtain the forward hidden state $\overrightarrow{h}_t = LSTM(x_t, \overrightarrow{h}_{t-1})$, and the backward layer calculates the reverse propagation for the reverse time series to obtain the backward hidden state $\overleftarrow{h}_t = LSTM(x_t, \overleftarrow{h}_{t-1})$. By combining the results of the forward and backward hidden states, the output hidden state value h_t of BiLSTM model can be obtained.

Because BiLSTM network uses forward information and backward information, it is favorable to obtain bidirectional long and short term characteristics of time series data. Predictably, it will perform better than LSTM.

Attention Layer

In the ship time series, time and space characteristics on the change of ship flow such as the characteristics of different times, different days, and different flow change in different regions, have diverse influences on the output results. We add attention mechanism to learn the influence of different features of data on the results, whose core is to use a weighting scheme to highlight the influence of key features on the target and extract the significantly feature information. The structure and composition diagram is shown in Fig. 5.

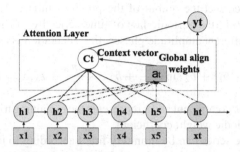

Fig. 5. Structure of attention mechanism.

The implementation process is as follows:

Step1: Calculate the attention score value e_i of the hidden unit at each moment according to the value of the hidden unit, as shown in Eq. (10).

$$e_i = \tanh(Wh_i + b) \tag{10}$$

Step2: Normalize the Attention score to get the of attention weight a_i, , as shown in Eq. (11).

$$a_i = \frac{\exp(e_i)}{\sum\limits_{j=1}^{T} \exp(e_j)} \tag{11}$$

Step3: Multiply the attention weight of each moment by the corresponding hidden state h_t to get the context vector c_t of the current moment, as shown in Eq. (12).

$$c_t = \sum\limits_{i=1}^{T} a_i h_i \tag{12}$$

Step4: Use activation function *tanh* to activate the context vector of each moment and get the attention vector of the prediction model, as shown in Eq. (13).

$$a_t = f(c_t, h_t) = \tanh(W_c[c_t; h_t]) \tag{13}$$

where, W and b are the weight and bias coefficient, h_i is the hidden unit status value.

By calculating the feature weight of the output hidden layer of the BiLSTM layer through the Attention layer, the influence of important features on the output results is highlighted, so that the features with prominent influence on the prediction results can get higher attention, which is effective to improve the prediction accuracy.

Residual Fitting Prediction Model Based on Periodic Function
Due to the nonlinearity and poor periodicity of ship flow data, the abnormal change of flow in some time periods may have a large fluctuation, which will cause a large flow prediction error. Therefore, this paper adopts the residual fitting method based on periodic function to correct the output of the previous model. The fitting method of periodic function is to fit the periodic law of time series by superposition of sine and cosine functions of different amplitude phases, the calculation is as Eq. (14).

$$g(x) = b_0 + b_1 x + b_2 \sin \frac{2\pi x}{L} + b_3 \cos \frac{2\pi x}{L} + \varepsilon_x, x = 1, 2, \ldots, n \qquad (14)$$

where, L is the periodic component and ε represents the remaining trigonometric function term, and b is the periodic weight coefficient.

In theory, the time series can be infinitely fitted according to the periodicity of the data to make the results more accurate, but high fitting order will increase the uncertainty of the prediction and reduce the convergence of the algorithm. In this paper, the second order sine and cosine trigonometric function is used to construct the residual fitting function, which is calculated as Eq. (15).

$$\hat{r}(t+1) = \hat{b}_0 + \hat{b}_1 k + \hat{b}_2 \sin \frac{2\pi t}{L} + \hat{b}_3 \cos \frac{2\pi t}{L}, t = 1, 2, \ldots. \qquad (15)$$

Since ship flow data is significantly affected by month, so we set the parameter L to 12 in this paper. Weight coefficient $\hat{b}_0, \hat{b}_1, \hat{b}_2, \hat{b}_3$ can be obtained by least square method, and is calculated as shown in (16):

$$[\hat{b}_0, \hat{b}_1, \hat{b}_2, \hat{b}_3]^T = (B^T B)^{-1} B^T R_n \qquad (16)$$

where, B is the periodic regular matrix of trigonometric function, and R_n is the sequence of inverse residual matrix. Equations (17)-(18) shows the calculation of B and R_n.

$$B = \begin{bmatrix} 1 & 1 & \sin \frac{2\pi}{L} & \cos \frac{2\pi}{L} \\ 1 & 2 & \sin \frac{4\pi}{L} & \cos \frac{4\pi}{L} \\ \vdots & \vdots & \vdots & \vdots \\ 1 & n-1 & \sin \frac{2(n-1)\pi}{L} & \cos \frac{2(n-1)\pi}{L} \end{bmatrix} \qquad (17)$$

$$R_n = [r(2), r(3), \ldots r(n)]^T. \qquad (18)$$

The predicted value at each moment after residual fitting is shown in Eq. (19).

$$\begin{aligned} \hat{x}_{pre}(t) &= x(t), t = 1 \\ \hat{x}_{pre}(t) &= x(t) + \hat{r}(t), t = 2, 3, \ldots, \end{aligned} \qquad (19)$$

where, $\hat{x}_{pre}(t)$ represents the sequence of prediction results after residual fitting of trigonometric function.

Global Model Architecture

The overall structure of R-ATT-CNN-BiLSTM model is illustrated in Fig. 6.

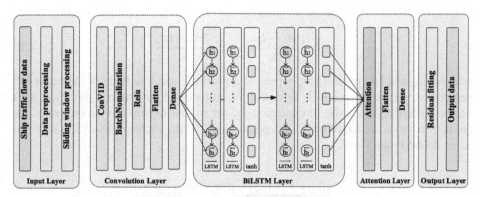

Fig. 6. Structure of R-ATT-CNN-BiLSTM prediction model.

In the network, the input layer first normalizes the two-dimensional spatio-temporal data of ships, and a sliding window with fixed width is adopted to generate training samples. The spatial and temporal characteristics of input data are obtained by the convolutional layer, and the correlation and bidirectional data information between sequences are extracted by the BiLSTM layer. In order to enhance the network learning ability, CNN and BiLSTM layers are stacked in this paper, CNN layer reduces training parameters by pooling, and a Dropout layer is appended to the BiLSTM layer to prevent overfitting. The Attention layer is introduced to extract the influence of key features in time space on model output, and the connection function is added to fuse the features. Finally, the residual fitting model was used to retrain and fit the pre-output to improve the accuracy of the prediction results.

4   Experiments and Analysis

4.1   Datasets

In the experiment, we use AIS ship data provided by the online platform of the United States Oceanic Administration [17]. We select AIS data of ships in waters near New York Harbor (74°00.72 'W ~ 74°01.92' W, 40°42.90 'N ~ 40°44.10' N) for a total of 24 months from 00:00 on January 1, 2020 to 24:00 on December 30, 2021 as the experimental data. AIS data mainly includes MMSI code (aquatic service identification code), ship length, ship type, draft depth, longitude, latitude, course, speed and other dynamic data. Dynamic navigation information in AIS data is selected as the basic data, and incomplete or abnormal data with outliers, null values and repeated values are removed to prevent them from affecting the accuracy of traffic data.

Since there is no fixed ship route in the selected port waters and the ship flow is large, it is very difficult to predict the regional statistical ship flow and analyze the temporal and spatial distribution characteristics in a large area. In this paper, the selected port sea area is divided into $a \times b$ grids, and each grid represents a sub-prediction area. The upper left $p_h = (lon_h, lat_h)$ and lower right $p_l = (lon_l, lat_l)$ vertices of the original prediction region were used to determine the range, which was divided into $a \times b$ grid regions with length m and width n. Equation (20) displays the calculation for grid division.

$$m = \frac{lon_h - lon_l}{b}, \ n = \frac{lat_h - lat_l}{a} \tag{20}$$

where, lon_h and lat_h respectively represent the latitude and longitude of the upper left vertex, lon_l and lat_l respectively represent the latitude and longitude of the lower right vertex. According to the size of the region and the volume of ship flow, in our paper, the prediction region is divided into 2×2 grid regions, which are respectively ①, ②, ③ and ④, as shown in the Fig. 7.

Fig. 7. The division of prediction area.

According to the ship MMSI code, the discrete track points of filtered AIS data are drawn into continuous navigation track lines, and the intersection algorithm is used to determine whether it intersects with each sub prediction region, and the ship flow of each region in different time periods is calculated according to the time when it crosses the sub region. The discrete trajectory points and navigation trajectory diagrams obtained in the experiment are shown in Fig. 8. And Fig. 9. In the experiment, ship flow in each area was counted at intervals of every 6h, 8h and 12h, 3068, 2301 and 1534 samples were obtained as datasets respectively.

4.2 Experimental Setup

In order to set the parameters of the dataset, the data of the first 20 months is taken as the training set, and the data of the last 4 months is taken as the test set for data division. Meanwhile, the last 5% of the training data set is taken as the verification set to verify the performance of the model. The characteristic dimension of the input data and the output data is 6, which are the data time, the traffic flow in the area ① to ④, and the total traffic

Fig. 8. Scatter diagram of ship data.

Fig. 9. The track diagram of ship data.

flow of the area. The experimental test shows that when the sliding window width is 12, the model evaluation index is optimal. Therefore, we select the sliding window with a fixed width of 12 and a fixed step size of 1 to process data to generate the training set. We set the training parameters and construction parameters of the model by referring to the optimal parameters in the previous literature and by comparing the parameters for several times in the experiment. The learning rate of our model and its comparison model was set as 0.001, the sample number of one training was 64, and a total of 600 rounds of epochs iteration were carried out. After comparing different training optimizers, adam optimizer is selected in model training. The number of convolutional nuclei in CNN layer is set to 16, the number of neurons in LSTM layer is set to 64, and the number of neurons in BiLSTM layer is set to 128.

In order to evaluate the effectiveness of the model proposed in this paper, root mean square error (RMSE), mean absolute error (MAE), mean square error (MSE), mean absolute percentage error (MAPE) and determination coefficient (R2) were selected as evaluation indexes to quantitatively evaluate the prediction effect of the model.

4.3 Analysis of Experimental Results

To verify the effectiveness of our proposed model, the ARIMA model [1], LSTM model [10], GRU model [14], BiLSTM model [16], CNN-LSTM model [12] and ATT-BiLSTM (Attention-BiLSTM) model [15] were chosen as baseline models to compare and analyze the results with R-ATT-CNN-BiLSTM model. The visualization result of the output flow data was illustrated. Figure 10, Fig. 11 and Fig. 12 provide the comparison between the predicted value and the real value obtained by each model from September to October 2021 at intervals of every 6h, 8h and 12h.

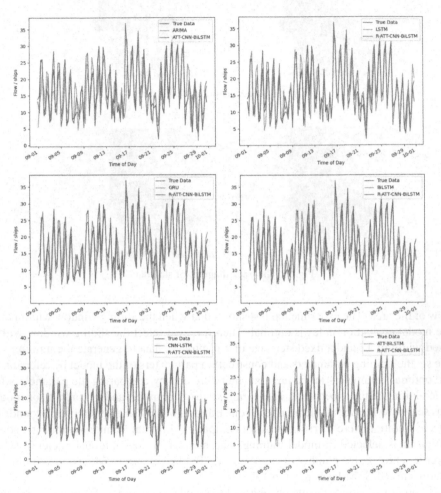

Fig. 10. The prediction results between basic model and R-ATT-CNN-BiLSTM model at 6 h interval.

It can be shown that the ship traffic flow of the selected segment can roughly show a periodic trend, and the predicted results given by the models used in the experiment are generally consistent with the change trend of the real traffic flow value. Compared with other models, the prediction curve of the proposed model is closer to the true value in most time periods, and the degree of fitting between it and the true value curve of ship flow at peak and trough is higher than that of other models. Due to the addition of the CNN layer and the attention mechanism, the model can better extract the global and local characteristics of the data, which makes the influence on the prediction of traffic

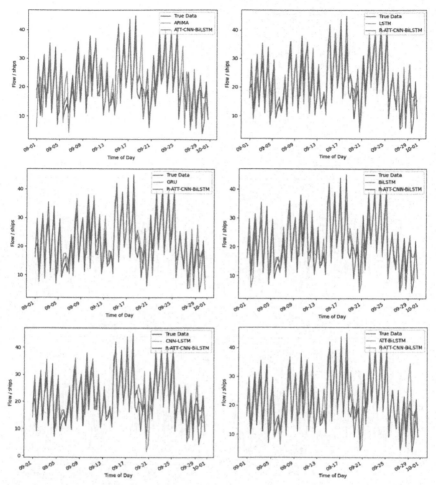

Fig. 11. The prediction results between basic model and R-ATT-CNN-BiLSTM model at 8 h interval.

changes over a long period of time smaller. When the traffic flow changes suddenly increase or decrease, it can also predict the results more accurately.

In order to more vividly represent the degree of fitting between the predicted results of each model and the real results of traffic flow, this paper makes a visual comparison between the predicted value and the real value by residual operation. As shown in Fig. 13, the three figures from left to right are the residual comparison of the prediction results of 6 h, 8 h and 12 h. It can be seen from the residual results that the residual results of our proposed model are smaller than those of other models, therefore, it has a higher degree of fitting with the real value of ship flow.

To further demonstrate the prediction performance of our model, the prediction errors under different evaluation indexes of six baseline models and the proposed model is shown in Table 1, Table 2 and Table3. It can be seen that the prediction accuracy

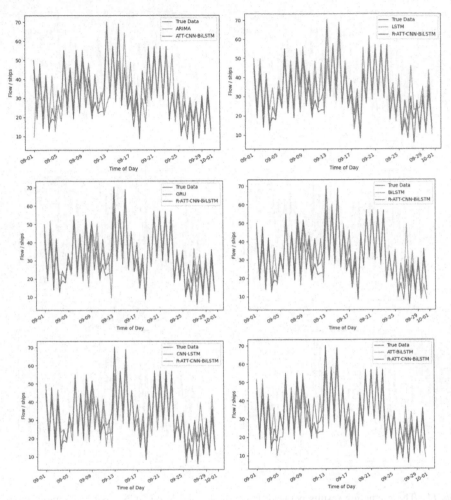

Fig. 12. The prediction results between basic model and R-ATT-CNN-BiLSTM model at 12 h interval.

of traditional ARIMA method is relatively low under each index, while the prediction accuracy of LSTM and GRU method is relatively high. The prediction performances of CNN-LSTM, BiLSTM and ATT-BiLSTM are better, but are not stable. The prediction error of our method is lowest in each index and it has better performance than other models.

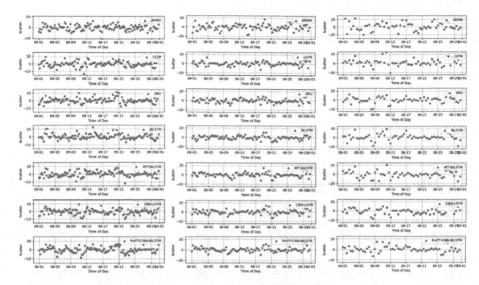

Fig. 13. Residual comparison of predicted and true values

Table 1. The comparison of evaluation index results of each model(6 h interval)

Model	MAE	MAPE	MSE	RMSE	R2
ARIMA	3.28	49.48	17.82	4.22	0.7166
LSTM	2.01	26.39	8.91	2.98	0.8160
GRU	2.00	25.70	9.11	3.01	0.8119
BiLSTM	2.02	25.30	9.13	3.02	0.8115
CNN-LSTM	1.97	27.62	8.74	2.95	0.8195
ATT-BiLSTM	2.01	24.21	8.84	2.97	0.8223
Our model	1.95	19.72	7.43	2.72	0.8623

Table 2. The comparison of evaluation index results of each model(8 h interval)

Model	MAE	MAPE	MSE	RMSE	R2
ARIMA	3.81	37.16	24.33	4.93	0.7037
LSTM	2.58	22.33	13.44	3.66	0.8252
GRU	2.48	21.52	13.18	3.63	0.8286

(*continued*)

Table 2. (*continued*)

Model	MAE	MAPE	MSE	RMSE	R2
BiLSTM	2.54	20.69	13.41	3.66	0.8256
CNN-LSTM	2.45	21.50	13.29	3.64	0.8272
ATT-BiLSTM	2.56	21.14	13.57	3.68	0.8236
Our model	2.19	15.90	10.98	3.31	0.8602

Table 3. The comparison of evaluation index results of each model(12 h interval)

Model	MAE	MAPE	MSE	RMSE	R2
ARIMA	5.76	30.83	62.94	7.93	0.7028
LSTM	4.21	29.19	33.12	5.75	0.8120
GRU	4.07	27.30	31.66	5.42	0.8169
BiLSTM	3.34	17.35	29.32	5.41	0.8336
CNN-LSTM	3.11	15.92	24.92	4.87	0.8498
ATT-BiLSTM	3.87	21.35	31.44	5.61	0.8215
Our model	2.53	14.06	21.34	4.62	0.8801

5 Conclusion

On account of the complexity and variability of waterway, the irregularity of ship routes and the volatility of port traffic data bring tough difficulties to the ship flow prediction problem of port waters. In order to overcome the shortcomings of existing models, such as weak feature extraction ability of nonlinear data and low prediction accuracy, a CNN-BiLSTM prediction model based on residual fitting and attention mechanism was proposed in this paper to achieve applicability in waterway prediction. In our model, CNN is used to capture the spatial characteristics of input data, BiLSTM is used to obtain the correlation and bidirectional characteristics between input sequences, in addition, attention mechanism is introduced to obtain the influence of flow characteristics of different regions on ship flow variation. On the basis of paying attention to the global information, the local features of the flow data in time and space can be better extracted. Finally, through residual fitting, the periodic rule extracted from the data can be used to reduce the prediction error to the greatest extent and reduce the impact of the dramatic changes of ship data on the prediction results. The experimental results show that compared with other models, the ship flow prediction model proposed in this paper has higher prediction accuracy and better model performance, and it has the lowest error in all kinds of evaluation indicators.

In the future, the work of this study can be applied in other prediction fields such as social media and power field, and can provide some help and support for port flow forecast and waterway ship cooperation. In addition, we will conduct multi-segment and multi-port flow prediction ablation experiments to further verify the performance of the model under big ship data.

References

1. Liu, R.W., Chen, J., Liu, Z.: Vessel traffic flow separation-prediction using low-rank and sparse decomposition. In: 2017 IEEE 20th International Conference on Intelligent Transportation Systems (ITSC). IEEE (2017)
2. Liu, Y., Yu, H., Fang, H.: Application of KNN prediction model in urban traffic flow prediction. In: 2021 5th Asian Conference on Artificial Intelligence Technology (ACAIT), pp. 389–392. Haikou, China (2021)
3. Kumar, V., Vanajakshi, L.: Short-term traffic flow prediction using seasonal ARIMA model with limited input data. Eur. Transp. Res. Rev. 7(3), 1–9 (2015)
4. Liu, C.Y., Chen, S.Z.: Prediction of vessel traffic flow based on grey Markov model. Navig. China 41(3), 98–103 (2018)
5. Huang, Q.F.: Research on Forecasting Method Based on Wavelet Transform and Neural Network. Xiamen University, Xiamen (2020)
6. Wang, C., Zhang. X., Chen. X.: Vessel traffic flow forecasting based on BP neural network and residual analysis. In: 2017 4th International Conference on Information, Cybernetics and Computational Social Systems (ICCSS), pp. 350–354. IEEE (2017)
7. Feng, H., Kong, F., Xiao, Y.: Vessel traffic flow forecasting model study based on support vector machine. In: Shen, G., Huang, X. (eds.) ECWAC 2011. CCIS, vol. 143, pp. 446–451. Springer, Heidelberg (2011). https://doi.org/10.1007/978-3-642-20367-1_72
8. Zhang, Z., Yin, J., Wang, N.: Vessel traffic flow analysis and prediction by an improved PSO-BP mechanism based on AIS data. Evol. Syst. 10(3), 397–407 (2019)
9. Hongren, J.: A random forest model based on parameter optimization using cuckoo search algorithm for ship traffic flow forecasting. In: Proceedings of the 34th Chinese Control and Decision Conference (CCDC), pp. 4960–4964 (2022)
10. Ma, X.L., Tao, Z.M., Wang, Y.H.: Long short-term memory neural network for traffic speed prediction using remote microwave sensor data. Transp. Res. Part C: Emerg. Technol. 54, 187–197 (2015)
11. Ji, Z., Wang, L., Zhang, X.B.: Ship traffic flow forecast of Qingdao port based on LSTM. In: 2021 6th International Conference on Electromechanical Control Technology and Transportation (ICECTT 2021), vol. 12081, pp.1208124-1–1208124-9 (2022)
12. Yan, Z., Yu, C.C., Han, L.: Short-term traffic flow prediction method based on CNN+LSTM. Comput. Eng. Design 40(9), 2620–2624 (2019)
13. Liu, Y.P., Zheng, H.F., Feng, X.X.: Short-term traffic flow prediction with Conv-LSTM. In: 2017 9th International Conference on Wireless Communications and Signal Processing (WCSP), pp. 23–31. IEEE (2017)
14. Suo, Y.F., Chen, W.K., Yang, S.H.: Prediction of ship traffic flow based on deep neural network. J. Jimei Univ. (Natural Science) 25(6), 430–436 (2020)
15. Yang, B.L., Sun, S.L., Li, J.Y.: Traffic flow prediction using LSTM with feature enhancement. Neurocomputing 332, 320–327 (2019)
16. Su, W.J., Liu, M.J.: Short term ship flow prediction based on whale algorithm optimized attention-BiLSTM model. J. Wuhan Univ. Technol. 44(05), 34–39 (2022)
17. Liu, J.X., Gao, G.X.: Short-term water traffic flow prediction with convolutional neural network and long short-term memory network. Navig. China 45(2), 56–61 (2022)
18. MarineCadastre.gov. https://marinecadastre.gov/accessais/

TGPPN: A Transformer and Graph Neural Network Based Point Process Network Model

Qing Qi[1], Shitong Shen[1], Jian Cao[1(✉)], Wei Guan[1], and Shiyu Gan[2]

[1] Department of Computer Science and Engineering, Shanghai Jiao Tong University, Shanghai, China
cao-jian@sjtu.edu.cn
[2] Shanghai E & P International Inc., Shanghai, China

Abstract. The Temporal Point Process (TPP) is applicable in various fields including healthcare, device failure prediction, and social media. It allows for the precise modeling of event occurrences and their associated types, as well as timestamps. Although recent studies have integrated deep learning and reinforcement learning techniques into TPP, most of them focus only on the event sequence without incorporating other fundamental information such as time series information. Moreover, the majority of these studies only predict the information of the next event, which may not be sufficient for practical applications that needs predicting multi-step events. Therefore, we propose the TGPPN model, which employs a Transformer structure to address the multi-step forecasting task, and a graph neural network to handle multi-variable time series in conjunction with event sequences. Our experiments on real-world datasets demonstrate the effectiveness of our proposed model.

Keywords: temporal point process · attention mechanism · graph neural network · multi-step forecasting

1 Introduction

Temporal Point Process (TPP) is a powerful tool for modeling the latent mechanisms that govern the occurrence of random events observed over time. In particular, these models can be used as predictive models, that are capable of specifying the timing of future events. The precise modeling of event occurrences and their associated types and timestamps is a critical aspect of TPP, which distinguishes it from other temporal modeling techniques. Traditional TPP models rely on prior knowledge about the dynamics of an event sequence to determine the appropriate form of the intensity function for predicting future events. For example, the Hawkes process [1] assumes that past events have an incentive effect on future events, while the self-correcting process assumes that past events suppress future events [2]. In contrast, the Poisson point process [3] assumes that the occurrence of events is independent of past events.

Traditional TPP models are limited in their ability to capture complex patterns in data, prompting the development of many neural network-based TPP

Y. Sun et al. (Eds.): ChineseCSCW 2023, CCIS 2012, pp. 240–251, 2024.
https://doi.org/10.1007/978-981-99-9637-7_17

models in recent years. These models include RMTPP, which leverages the learning ability of recurrent neural networks to model complex dependencies among historical events [4], and THP, which employs a Transformer Encoder structure to extract event relations [5]. Xiao et al. also introduced two LSTM models to process event sequence and time series data, respectively [6]. Their subsequent work combined two RNN models to model the exogenous and endogenous intensity [7]. As a result, recent studies on temporal point processes have primarily focused on deep neural network-based models, which offer improved universality and reduced dependence on domain knowledge.

An event is typically composed of multiple attributes, resulting in a multivariate time-series for each event type. Thus, an event sequence can be represented by multiple multivariate time-series. However, current TPP models only utilize event type information and timestamps to predict future event types, disregarding event attribute information. To address this limitation, we propose the TGPPN model, which employs a transformer and a graph neural network to model the temporal point process and multiple multivariate time-series, respectively. The TGPPN model is specifically designed for multi-step prediction problems as it provides more reference information than single-step forecasting, enabling better decision-making.

The rest of the paper is organized as follows: Sect. 2 presents the related work. The detail of TGPPN is introduced in Sect. 3. Section 4 introduces the experiment and discusses the results. Finally, Sect. 5 is the conclusion.

2   Related Work

In this section, we will introduce the preliminary of TPP, followed by an introduction to several traditional TPP models and neural network methods.

2.1   Preliminary

Temporal Point Process (TPP) is a random process used for modeling event sequences like $\mathcal{S} = \{(t_i, k_i)\}_{i=1}^{L}$. The core concept of TPP is the intensity function [8]:

$$\lambda^*(t) = \lambda(t|H_t) = \lim_{h \to 0^+} \frac{P(t \leq T \leq t + h|T \geq t)}{h} = \frac{f^*(t)}{1 - F^*(t)} \tag{1}$$

which is defined as the probability of event occurrence at infinitesimal time interval given the history event sequence. The form of intensity function varies with the assumption of event triggering relation. Essentially, the probability function is a function that is piece-wise in nature and changes when a new event occurs. It can be obtained by transforming the intensity function:

$$f^*(t) = f(t|H_t) = \lambda^*(t) \exp(-\int_{t_i}^{t} \lambda^*(s)ds) \tag{2}$$

where t_i is the occurrence time of the latest event before t.

Given an event sequence, to estimate the parameters of an assumed probability distribution, the likelihood is defined as:

$$L = \left(\prod_{i=1}^{n} \lambda^*(t_i, k_i) \right) \exp\left(- \int_0^T \lambda^*(s)ds\right) \tag{3}$$

To simplify the computation process, likelihood functions are often logarithmically transformed, converting the product term into a sum term.

$$logL = \sum_{i=1}^{n} \log\lambda_{k_i}^*(t_i) - \int_0^T \lambda^*(s)ds \tag{4}$$

2.2   Traditional Temporal Point Process Model

Conventional TPP models typically rely on prior knowledge to establish the interdependence among event sequences, and the parameter form of the intensity function is subsequently determined. Here are three typical models:

Poisson Process [3]: The Poisson process assumes that the rate at which events occur is independent of previous events. The intensity function is a constant parameter. The Poisson process is commonly employed in queuing theory.

Self-correcting Process [2]: In contrast to the Poisson process, the self-correcting process assumes that the occurrence of past events decreases the likelihood of future events. Therefore, its intensity function increases over time but decreases with the occurrence of past events. The self-correcting process is well-suited for scenarios where the likelihood of an event decreases after it has occurred, such as when purchasing similar items.

Hawkes Process [1]: In contrast, the Hawkes process assumes that the occurrence of past events increases the likelihood of future events.

2.3   Neural Temporal Point Process

Neural network-based temporal point processes have gained popularity [9] because the flexible form of the intensity function helps address the problem of form misspecification. Recurrent neural networks (RNNs) have been widely used in neural temporal point processes [4,7]. However, RNNs may encounter the catastrophic forgetting problem when handling long sequences. To address this problem, long short-term memory (LSTM) networks implement input, forget, and output gates to retain important information while discarding insignificant ones [10]. Xiao et al. used two LSTMs to model the dynamics of event sequences [6], while Mei et al. implemented a continuous-time LSTM for TPP [11].

Transformers [12] are attention-based models that can compute the relationship between different positions, regardless of their sequential distance. Du et al. were the first to combine transformers with temporal point processes [5], and Yeung et al. used transformers to analyze football match events [13]. Furthermore, Erfanian et al. implemented the transformer decoder structure to perform multi-step forecasting for TPP [14].

3   TGPPN: A Transformer and Graph Neural Network Based Point Process Network Model

TGPNN amied to tackle the task of multi-step temporal point process prediction. Given an event sequence $\mathcal{S} = (t_i, k_i)i = 1^L$, our goal is to predict the output sequence $\mathcal{S}out = (t_i, k_i)_{i=L+1}^{L+L'}$, where L and L' denote the lengths of the input and output sequences. We first employ an event embedding layer to convert the event sequences into hidden vectors. These vectors are then fed into the encoder module, which is responsible for identifying complex relationships between events. The decoder module generates the hidden vectors of the multi-step future events in an autoregressive manner. The graph neural network module is used to extract essential information from the multi-variate time series. Finally, the intensity layer integrates these components to produce the prediction results for multiple future steps. Figure 1 shows the structure of TGPPN.

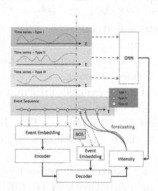

Fig. 1. Structure of TGPPN

3.1   Event Embedding Layer

To preserve the relative position information of event sequences, the event embedding layer utilizes positional encoding. Specifically, for an event $e_i = (t_i, k_i)$, its positional encoding is defined as follows:

$$[PE(i)]_j = \begin{cases} sin(i/10000^{\frac{j}{d_{model}}}), & j \text{ is even} \\ cos(i/10000^{\frac{j-1}{d_{model}}}), & j \text{ is odd} \end{cases} \tag{5}$$

where d_{model} is the dimension of the positional encoding vector, i is the relative position of event e_i in sequence. The trigonometric function guarantees the same distance for $PE(z)$ and $PE(z + o)$ given offset o regardless of the start position z. At the same time, we train a weight w_t for the event timestamp, and an embedding matrix $\mathbf{U} \in \mathbb{R}^{(d_{model}-1) \times K}$ to represent the event type, where K

represents the number of event types. We denote that the one-hot encoding of event type k_i as $\mathbf{k}_i$ and the event embedding vector of e_i is defined as: $[\mathbf{E}]_i = [w_t t_i, PE(i) + \mathbf{U}\mathbf{k}_i]$, where $\mathbf{E} \in \mathbb{R}^{L \times d_{model}}$ is the event embedding matrix of the event sequence S and L is the length of sequence.

3.2 Encoder

The encoder module is composed of several encoder layers that contain both multi-head self-attention mechanism and feed-forward neural network.

$$self\_attn\_weight = Softmax(\frac{\mathbf{Q}_h\mathbf{K}_h^T}{\sqrt{\mathbf{M}_K}}), \mathbf{S}_h = self\_attn\_weight \times \mathbf{V}_h \quad (6)$$

$$\mathbf{Q}_h = \mathbf{E}\mathbf{W}_h^Q, \quad \mathbf{K}_h = \mathbf{E}\mathbf{W}_h^K, \quad \mathbf{V}_h = \mathbf{E}\mathbf{W}_h^V$$

where $\mathbf{Q}_h, \mathbf{K}_h, \mathbf{V}_h$ are the query, key and value matrix of the h-th head respectively. $\mathbf{W}_h^Q, \mathbf{W}_h^K \in \mathbb{R}^{d_{model} \times M_K}, \mathbf{W}_h^V \in \mathbb{R}^{d_{model} \times M_V}$ represent their corresponding linear transformation matrix. $self\_attn\_weight(i, j)$ represents the relation weight of event e_i and e_j, and $\mathbf{S}_h \in \mathbb{R}^{M_V}$ is the output matrix. Specifically, to guarantee the correct representations of temporal relationship of the events in the sequence, so as to ensure previous events' encoding is not generated from future events' information, we use masks to fill the corresponding weights $self\_attn\_weight(i + 1, i)$, $self\_attn\_weight(i + 2, i)$, $\cdots$, $self\_attn\_weight(i + 1, i)$ by 0. The H heads will concurrently encode the sequence, and their outputs are then concatenated as $\mathbf{S} = [\mathbf{S}_1, \mathbf{S}_2, ..., \mathbf{S}_{n_{heads}}]\mathbf{W}^O$.

Finally, the output of the multi-head self-attention mechanism S will be passed to the feed-forward neural network $\mathbf{H} = ReLU(\mathbf{S}\mathbf{W}_1 + b_1)\mathbf{W}_2 + b_2$.

After l_{enc} encoder layers' processing, we get the encoder's output $\mathbf{M} \in \mathbb{R}^{L \times d_{model}}$ and the i-th row of $\mathbf{M}$ represents the encoding of event e_i.

3.3 Decoder

The encoder module is to extract the complex relationships within the input sequence. Similarly, the decoder module consists of multiple decoder layers, each with a multi-head self-attention mechanism, a feed-forward neural network, and a multi-head cross-attention mechanism. The first two components are identical to the encoder layer and are used to process the output sequence into $\mathbf{H}_{out} \in \mathbb{R}^{L' \times d_{model}}$. The multi-head cross-attention mechanism is then used to extract the complex relationships between the input and output sequences, defined as:

$$cross\_attn\_weight = Softmax(\frac{\mathbf{Q}_h\mathbf{K}_h^T}{\sqrt{M_K}}), \mathbf{S}_h = cross\_attn\_weight \times \mathbf{V}_h \quad (7)$$

$$\mathbf{Q}_h = \mathbf{H}_{out}\mathbf{W}_h^Q, \quad \mathbf{K}_h = \mathbf{M} \times \mathbf{W}_h^K, \quad \mathbf{V}_h = \mathbf{M} \times \mathbf{W}_h^V$$

where $cross\_attn\_weight(i, j)$ represents relation weight between input sequence's event e_i and output sequence's event e_j. The decoder module is designed to generate the embedding of the multi-step output sequence by absorbing information from the event sequence. After l_{dec} layers of computation, the decoder output $\mathbf{O} \in \mathbb{R}^{L' \times d_{model}}$ is obtained, similar to the encoder.

3.4   Graph Neural Network

Inspired by Wu's work [15], we have designed a graph neural network to extract basic information from multivariate time series $\mathcal{X} = (x_{1,t}, x_{2,t}, ..., x_{K,t})t = 1^T$. First, we employ a time series layer to obtain the embedding of each variable using LSTM, resulting in the corresponding representations $H_1, H_2, ..., H_K \in \mathbb{R}^{dlstm}$. The relation between variables is denoted by an adjacency matrix, which is learned using the graph structure learning layer and defined as:

$$\mathbf{M_1} = tanh(\alpha \mathbf{Z}\theta_1), \mathbf{M_2} = tanh(\alpha \mathbf{Z}\theta_2),$$
$$\mathbf{A} = ReLU(tanh(\alpha(\mathbf{M_1}\mathbf{M_2}^T - \mathbf{M_2}\mathbf{M_1}^T))) \tag{8}$$

where $\mathbf{A} \in \mathbb{R}^{K \times K}$ is the adjacency matrix and $\mathbf{Z} \in \mathbb{R}^{K \times d_{model}}$ is embedding for each variable of time series. The $ReLu$ activation function ensures that the adjacency matrix $\mathbf{A}$ is unidirectional. The structure of the graph convolution module employs two mix-hop propagation layers to handle the inflow and outflow information from nodes. Mix-hop propagation layer aims to incorporate the interdependent relationships of each variable with its neighboring variables. The layer comprises of two phases, namely information propagation and selection, as depicted in Fig. 2. Initially, the input $\mathbf{H}_{in} = [H_1, H2, ..., HK]$ is fed into the layer. In the propagation phase, the updating approach at each hop is defined as: $\mathbf{P}^{(k)} = \beta \mathbf{H}_{in} + (1 - \beta)\mathbf{A}\mathbf{P}^{(k-1)}$, where β controls the weight of original information and $\mathbf{H}_{in}$ is the concatenation of LSTM embeddings of the variables.

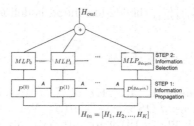

Fig. 2. Structure of mix-hop propagation layer

If the critical information tends to fade away during the propagation process, the information selection phase is devised to isolate essential information. The selection phase is defined as: $\mathbf{H}_{out} = \sum_{k=0}^{g_{depth}} \mathbf{P}^{(k)}W^{(k)}$, where $\mathbf{H}_{out} \in \mathbb{R}^{d_{model}}$ is the output of mix-hop propagation layer, $\mathbf{W}^{(k)}$ is the filter weight of k-th hop, and g_{depth} is the depth of information propagation. The final output of the graph neural network module, denoted as $\mathbf{G} \in \mathbb{R}^{d_{model}}$, is obtained by adding the outputs of two mix-hop propagation layers.

3.5   Intensity Layer

Once the modules have processed the input, we obtain the embedding information for the output event sequence and the multivariate time series, denoted as $\mathbf{O} \in \mathbb{R}^{d_{model}}, \mathbf{G} \in \mathbb{R}^{d_{model}}$, respectively. To generate the prediction, we begin by representing them as an intensity function, which is defined as follows:

$$\lambda_k^j(t|H_t) = f_k(\underbrace{\alpha_k \frac{t-t_{j-1}}{t_{j-1}}}_{current\ influence} + \underbrace{w_k^T[\mathbf{O}]_j}_{event\ sequence} + \underbrace{u_k^T\mathbf{G}}_{time\ series}) \qquad (9)$$

where $\lambda_k^j(t|H_t)$ represents the intensity function of event type k at j-th step and $1 \le j \le L'$, $f_k(\cdot)$ is a hard threshold activation function that ensures both the convergence of the training process and the positivity of the intensity.

Then, the total intensity function is obtained by summing up the intensity functions of all event types. And the prediction for event type and timestamp is generated using the following equation:

$$\hat{k}_{j+1} = \arg\max_k \frac{\lambda_k^j(t_{j+1}|H_t)}{\lambda^j(t_{j+1}|H_t)}, \hat{t}_{j+1} = \int_{t_j}^{\infty} t \cdot f^j(t|H_t)dt \qquad (10)$$

where $f^j(t|H_t)$ can be transformed from $\lambda^j(t|H_t)$ by Eq. (2). To improve the efficiency of parameter learning, neural network-based methods are employed in practice to perform event time prediction [5]: $\hat{t}_{j+1} = \mathbf{W}_2^{time}(\mathbf{W}_1^{time}[[\mathbf{O}]_j, \mathbf{G}])$, where $\mathbf{W}_1^{time} \in \mathbb{R}^{d_{time} \times 2d_{model}}$, $\mathbf{W}_2^{time} \in \mathbb{R}^{d_{time}}$ represent the weight matrices of the fully connected neural network.

3.6   Learning Method

For sequence $\mathcal{S} = \{(t_i, k_i)\}_{i=1}^L$, the log-likelihood is defined as:

$$ll(\mathcal{S}) = \sum_{j=1}^{L} \log\lambda_{k_j}^j(t_j|H_{t_j}) - \sum_{j=1}^{L-1} \int_{t_j}^{t_{j+1}} \lambda^j(s|H_{t_j})ds \qquad (11)$$

Our goal is to maximize the $ll(\mathcal{S})$ for all $\mathcal{S}$ in training dataset. Hence, the loss function is defined as: $LOSS = -\sum ll(\mathcal{S})$. We leverage FLAML (a fast and lightweight AutoML library) [16] to automatically search for the optimal hyperparameters by optimizing the loss function. The search space is outlined in Table 1. During training, we also use the teacher forcing method to ensure parallel computing and prevent the accumulation of deviation.

4   Experiments

We evaluated TGPPN using real-world data and compared with several models. Results show that our model has excellent event sequence modeling capabilities.

Table 1. TGPPN hyper parameter search space

hyper parameter	search space	hyper parameter	search space
d_{model}	(32, 64, 128, 256)	d_{lstm}	(32, 64, 128)
d_{ffn}	(32, 64, 128, 256)	g_{depth}	(1, 2, 3)
$dropout$	(0.1, 0.2, 0.3)	α	(2, 3, 4)
l_{enc}	(1, 2, 3, 4)	β	(0.05, 0.1, 0.15)
l_{dec}	(1, 2, 3, 4)	d_{time}	(16, 32, 64, 128, 256)
n_{heads}	(2, 4, 8)		

4.1   Experiment Datasets

We utilized six datasets that were generated from real-world scenarios, including **StackOverflow** [17], **Retweet** [18], **911 calls**[1], **DJIA**[2], **Football**[3] and **Shopping**[4]. Table 2 shows the statistical information for these 6 datasets.

Table 2. Dataset statistical information

Dataset	number of event types	number of events
StackOverFlow	22	442349
Retweet	3	2394581
911-Calls	3	663229
DJIA	31	76310
Football	11	941009
Shopping	4	1314545

To mitigate the slow convergence of training caused by the extremely large numbers in the UNIX time format, and to facilitate the universal evaluation of model prediction across datasets with different magnitudes of timestamps, we scale the timestamps of each event sequence to the range [0, 1]. This approach, as used in TPP-NRI [19], helps to make the timestamp a less dominant factor in the intensity function.

4.2   Comparative Models

We employed a recursive multi-step forecast strategy [20] for our study. This method uses the previous step's forecast result as the input for the next step's

---

[1] https://www.kaggle.com/datasets/mchirico/montcoalert.
[2] https://www.kaggle.com/datasets/szrlee/stock-time-series-20050101-to-20171231.
[3] https://www.kaggle.com/datasets/secareanualin/football-events.
[4] https://www.kaggle.com/datasets/mkechinov/ecommerce-events-history-in-cosmetics-shop.

prediction. We compared different models to evaluate their multi-step forecasting abilities in event timestamp, type classification, and sequence modeling domains. The evaluation metrics we used were RMSE, Macro-F1, and log-likelihood, respectively. Here are the models we compared:

RMTPP [4]: RMTPP (Recurrent Marked Temporal Point Process) uses RNN to learn the relationship between events.

NHP [11]: NHP (Neural Hawkes Process) employs a continuous-time LSTM network to model event sequences. It uses the recurrent neural network's hidden state to predict future events based on the past event stream.

SAHP [21]: SAHP (Self-attentive Hawkes Process) applies a self-attention mechanism to model event sequence relations while also considering the time interval information using the positional encoding method.

THP [5]: THP (Transformer Hawkes Process) is based on the Transformer-encoder structure. It uses a multi-head self-attention mechanism to address the problem of mining long sequence relations.

TGPPN': To evaluate the utility of the graph neural network module, we conducted an ablation experiment. We only used the Transformer encoder-decoder structure for prediction.

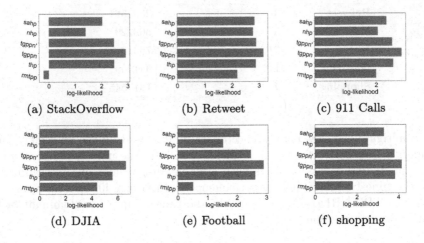

Fig. 3. Log-likelihood

4.3   Results

We conducted a comparative analysis of the log-likelihood, Macro-F1, and RMSE for the aforementioned models, and the results are presented in Fig. 3 and Fig. 4.

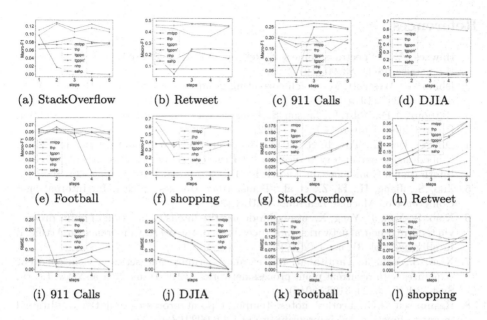

(a) StackOverflow   (b) Retweet   (c) 911 Calls   (d) DJIA

(e) Football   (f) shopping   (g) StackOverflow   (h) Retweet

(i) 911 Calls   (j) DJIA   (k) Football   (l) shopping

Fig. 4. Macro-F1 and RMSE

Our experimental results demonstrate that our model outperforms its counterparts in terms of log-likelihood, and the ablation experiment reveals that the graph neural network module of our model helps to enhance the event sequence modeling ability. Concerning the prediction of event timestamps, our model outperforms its ablation version, while obtaining a moderate level of performance compared to its counterparts. On the other hand, our model achieves the best prediction effect for event type classification. In general, our model demonstrates good multi-step forecasting ability for future event timestamps and event type classification, and is capable of effectively modeling the event sequence.

5   Conclusion

Our paper presents a new model called TGPPN, which tackles the challenges of multi-variable time series forecasting and multi-step temporal point process forecasting. Our experiments demonstrate that our model is effective and can improve event sequence modeling and prediction with the use of a graph neural network module.

Acknowledgement. This work is partially supported by the Program of Technology Innovation of the Science and Technology Commission of Shanghai Municipality (Granted No. 21511104700 and 21DZ1205000). This work is also supported by China National Science Foundation (Granted Number 62072301).

References

1. Hawkes, A.G.: Spectra of some self-exciting and mutually exciting point processes. Biometrika **58**(1), 83–90 (1971)
2. Isham, V., Westcott, M.: A self-correcting point process. Stochast. Process. Appl. **8**(3), 335–347 (1979)
3. Barbour, A.D., Holst, L., Janson, S.: Poisson Approximation, vol. 2. The Clarendon Press, Oxford University Press (1992)
4. Du, N., Dai, H., Trivedi, R., et al.: Recurrent marked temporal point processes: Embedding event history to vector. In: Proceedings of the 22nd ACM SIGKDD International Conference on Knowledge Discovery and Data Mining (2016)
5. Zuo, S., Jiang, H., Li, Z., et al.: Transformer Hawkes process. In: International Conference on Machine Learning. PMLR (2020)
6. Xiao, S., Yan, J., Yang, X., et al.: Modeling the intensity function of point process via recurrent neural networks. In: Proceedings of the AAAI Conference on Artificial Intelligence, vol. 31, no. 1 (2017)
7. Xiao, S., Yan, J., Farajtabar, M., et al.: Learning time series associated event sequences with recurrent point process networks. IEEE Trans. Neural Netw. Learn. Syst. **30**(10), 3124–3136 (2019)
8. Rasmussen, J.G.: Lecture notes: temporal point processes and the conditional intensity function. arXiv preprint arXiv:1806.00221 (2018)
9. Shchur, O., Caner Türkmen, A., Januschowski, T., et al.: Neural temporal point processes: a review. arXiv preprint arXiv:2104.03528 (2021)
10. Hochreiter, S., Schmidhuber, J.: Long short-term memory. Neural Comput. **9**(8), 1735–1780 (1997)
11. Mei, H., Eisner, J.M.: The neural Hawkes process: a neurally self-modulating multivariate point process. In: Advances in Neural Information Processing Systems, vol. 30 (2017)
12. Ashish, V., Shazeer, N., Parmar, N., et al.: Advances in Neural Information Processing Systems, vol. 30, pp. 5998–6008 (2017)
13. Yeung, C.C.K., Sit, T., Fujii, K.: Transformer-based neural marked spatio temporal point process model for football match events analysis. arXiv preprint arXiv:2302.09276 (2023)
14. Erfanian, N., Segarra, S., de Hoop, M.: Neural multi-event forecasting on spatio-temporal point processes using probabilistically enriched transformers. arXiv preprint arXiv:2211.02922 (2022)
15. Wu, Z., Pan, S., Long, G., et al.: Connecting the dots: multivariate time series forecasting with graph neural networks. In: Proceedings of the 26th ACM SIGKDD International Conference on Knowledge Discovery & Data Mining (2020)
16. Wang, C., Qingyun, W., Weimer, M., et al.: FLAML: a fast and lightweight AutoML library. Proc. Mach. Learn. Syst. **3**, 434–447 (2021)
17. Leskovec, J., Krevl, A.: SNAP datasets: Stanford large network dataset collection (2014)
18. Zhao, Q., Erdogdu, M.A., He, H.Y., et al.: Seismic: a self-exciting point process model for predicting tweet popularity. In: Proceedings of the 21th ACM SIGKDD International Conference on Knowledge Discovery and Data Mining (2015)
19. Zhang, Y., Yan, J.: Neural relation inference for multi-dimensional temporal point processes via message passing graph. In: IJCAI (2021)

20. Bontempi, G., Ben Taieb, S., Le Borgne, Y.-A.: Machine learning strategies for time series forecasting. In: Aufaure, M.-A., Zimányi, E. (eds.) eBISS 2012. LNBIP, vol. 138, pp. 62–77. Springer, Heidelberg (2013). https://doi.org/10.1007/978-3-642-36318-4_3
21. Zhang, Q., Lipani, A., Kirnap, O., et al.: Self-attentive Hawkes process. In: International Conference on Machine Learning. PMLR (2020)

Attention and Time Perception Based Link Prediction in Dynamic Networks

Li Wang[✉], Mingliang Zhang, Xiaoya Xu, and MD Masum Billa Shagar

College of Data Science, Taiyuan University of Technology, Jinzhong 030600, Shanxi, China
wangli@tyut.edu.cn

Abstract. There are numerous applications that could be modeled as networks and predicting their relationships within their evolution process is an important task. The continuous changing of the network makes link prediction challenge, but its structure and temporal information will give clues to support this task. Inspired by this, we proposed a novel link prediction model that incorporates attention and time-awareness mechanisms to extract the latent pattern from the spatial and temporal information. A Transformer model is introduced to capture the long-time dependencies between nodes, combined with link similarity coding to capture the correlation between links in dynamic networks, while neighbour weights are calculated based on temporal differences to aggregate neighbour information. Ultimately, a classifier is employed for link prediction. Comprehensive experiments on real-world datasets demonstrate the superior performance of proposed model than other baselines.

Keywords: Link Prediction · Dynamic Network · Network Embedding

1 Introduction

Network is an important model that can demonstrate various real application systems, in which the node is entity and the edge is linkage relationship between entities. All the thing is evolving and predicting the future relationship is a common basic task in many scenarios, which is dynamic network link prediction problem. It has become an important research topic and attracted many academics to focus on it.

Earlier link prediction methods usually evaluated the network topology to get the nodes similarity such as common neighbors method [1], Jaccard similarity coefficient method [2], and local paths-based method [3]. The higher the node pair's similarity is, the higher the probability of generating link is. Word2vec [4] offered a way for word representing firstly and then DeepWalk [5], node2vec [6] with skip-gram of Word2vec were put forward for node embedding. With the development of Graph Neural Network (GNN), Graph Convolutional Network (GCN) [7] and Graph Attention Network (GAT) [8] have been powerful tools for mining high-dimensional graph structures. But they usually deal with static networks and for dynamic networks, accurately acquiring temporal information is still a challenge task.

Y. Sun et al. (Eds.): ChineseCSCW 2023, CCIS 2012, pp. 252–262, 2024.
https://doi.org/10.1007/978-981-99-9637-7_18

Over the past few years, recurrent neural networks such as Long Short-Term Memory (LSTM) [9] and Gate Recurrent Unit (GRU) [10] have been increasingly employed to model the evolving characteristics of networks. Transformer [11] uses self-attention mechanism to encode and learn the representation of input sequence, which have significant advantages in processing long sequences and large-scale data.

For dynamic network link prediction problem, existing methods often pay more attention to the whole network evolution but ignore the time information on the edge and the temporal information on local structures is always neglected, resulting in the inability to extract the temporal differences between nodes. In this paper we propose a dynamic network link prediction model with attention and time-awareness mechanism, in which a Transformer-based model is introduced to capture long sequence information, a link similarity coding is combined to capture the correlation between links. The time-aware module is built to perform time-weighted aggregation of the neighbors of a node, which effectively captures local structural and temporal information to compensate for Transformer.

The contributions of this paper can be summarized as the three points:

- A link representation is proposed without slicing the dynamic network.
- A link prediction model in dynamic network is designed that builds an attention mechanism combining link similarity coding and time-aware aggregation to improve prediction performance.
- Extensive experiments on real datasets are done and the results show our method better performances than others.

2 Related Work

2.1 Topological Similarity Methods

Traditional link prediction methods operate on the assumption that greater similarity implies a higher probability of connection. These methods always rely on node attributes and do not take into account network structure information. Newman et al. introduced a node similarity calculation method based on common neighbors. Jaccard proposed a similarity coefficient, which is the ratio of shared neighbors between nodes to the total number of neighbors. Pairs of nodes with a high Jaccard similarity coefficient are considered more likely to establish links. Adam et al. also contributed to this field by proposing a novel node similarity metric for networks.

2.2 Attention Mechanism

With the emergence of attention mechanism, researchers have used attention to capture evolutionary patterns. Sankar et al. proposed a dynamic self-attention network DySAT [12] that calculates node representations with self-attention mechanisms across two dimensions: structural neighborhood and temporal dynamics. A multilayer GAT and self-attention are used to construct structural and temporal encoders for the DySAT model. Subsequently, Min et al. put forward a graph neural network framework, Spatial-Temporal Graph Social Network (STGSN) [13] that aimed to model dynamic networks from both spatial and temporal aspects. This method assigns different weights to different parts of the network from multiple perspectives, which makes it more flexible to deal with dynamic networks. However, it cannot accurately differentiate and weight information with different time, which affects the performance of prediction.

2.3 Recurrent Neural Network

Most discrete dynamic networks use Recurrent Neural Networks (RNN) to capture temporal features, GCN to capture spatial features. Taking inspiration from high-resolution video prediction techniques with Generative Adversarial Networks (GAN), Qin et al. proposed GCN-GAN [14] for weighted dynamic network link prediction, which combines encoder-decoder framework with GAN to generate predictions for weighted time slices. Recently, Goyal et al. [15] proposed a deep architecture to learn network temporal evolution by building structural and temporal encoders from Multilayer Perceptron (MLP) and LSTM respectively. EvolveGCN [16] uses a multilayer encoder architecture, where a GCN based encoder is for structural representation and a RNN-based encoder for temporal representation. In addition, the temporal encoder uses the RNN to directly evolve the parameters of GCN, rather than dealing with potential embedding captured by each time slice.

3 Methodology

3.1 Problem Formulation

In this study, the dynamic network link prediction problem is defined as a binary classification problem that determines whether a link exists or not. This is conducted on an evolving network, which comprises nodes and links with timestamps. Given a network $G = (V, E_T, T)$ that consists of node set V, link set E_T and time set T, where $v_i \in V$ denotes node i in the network, and $e_{ij}^t \in E$ denotes the relationship between node i and node j happened at the time t, $t \in T$ and each edge has a timestamp t. Dynamic network link prediction aims to predict when $t > t_0$ whether new links will be generated between v_i, v_j.

3.2 Model

In this paper, we propose a new dynamic network link prediction model ATTP and its framework is as in Fig. 1. It can be divided into three modules: time-aware module, sequence evolution module and link prediction module.

Time-aware Module. In a dynamic network, the structural and temporal information of the network is important for prediction. Temporal information is the timing information in the network, such as the time sign and the difference between time signs. Graph neural network brought an effective method for node representation by aggregating their neighbors and GCN is a popular graph neural network, where the representation of node $v_i \in V$ at layer l can be obtained by the following equation:

$$z_v^l = \sigma \left(W_l \sum_{u \in N(v) \cup v} \frac{\vec{z}_u^{l-1}}{\sqrt{|N(u)||N(v)|}} \right) \tag{1}$$

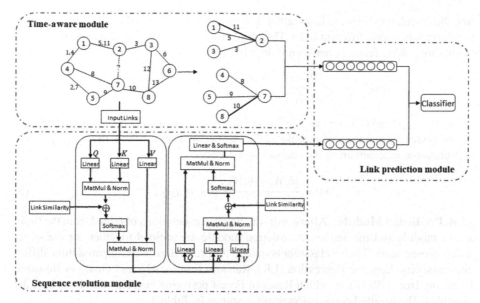

Fig. 1. General framework of the ATTP

where σ is the nonlinear activation function, and $N(v)$ is the aggregation of neighbors of node v, and W represents the weight matrix that can be learned.

For dynamic networks link prediction, we wish to capture the evolutionary process in the network, such as the time difference between edges. We assigned weights to edges according to time that help aggregation neighbourhood information from temporal aspect and network topology aspect. Therefore, we build the time-aware module with the following formula:

$$z_v^k = \sigma\left(\sum_{u \in N_t(v) \cup v} \alpha_{vu}^t W z_u^{k-1}\right) \tag{2}$$

where σ is the nonlinear activation function, W is the learnable weight matrix, k is the layer number, and z_u^{k-1} denotes the node representation of the previous layer. The initial node representation is denoted as $z_v^0 = x_v$, and the weights α_{vu}^t can be calculated as follows:

$$\alpha_{vu}^t = \frac{e^{t-t_{v,u}}}{\sum_{u \in N_t(v) \cup v} e^{t-t_{v,u}}} \tag{3}$$

where $t_{v,u}$ denotes the time on the edges formed by node v and node u.

Sequence Evolution Module. Transformer uses self-attention mechanism as a core component to deal with the relationships and dependencies between different positions. Its powerful sequence modelling capabilities can be used to effectively model the network link prediction problem.

Another key technique in Transformer is positional encoding, which allows the model to capture the position of words in a sentence. However, the link prediction task aims to find the correlation between links rather than between nodes, and there may be structural similarities between different links. Therefore, a link similarity encoding was developed to capture similar features between links with the following formula:

$$\varphi(l_i, l_j) = \frac{\left|N(v_{i1}) \cap N(v_{j1})\right|}{\left|N(v_{i1})\right| + \left|N(v_{j1})\right|} + \frac{\left|N(v_{i2}) \cap N(v_{j2})\right|}{\left|N(v_{i2})\right| + \left|N(v_{j2})\right|} \tag{4}$$

where (v_{i1}, v_{i2}) and (v_{j1}, v_{j2}) are the links of the nodes l_i and l_j, and $N(v_{i1})$ is the neighbor set of nodes v_{i1}, and an adjustable scalar is specified as a bias term $b_{\varphi(l_i, l_j)}$ in the self-attention mechanism of the encoder and decoder,

$$A_{ij} = \frac{(h_i W_Q)(h_j W_K)^\top}{\sqrt{d}} + b_{\varphi(l_i, l_j)} \tag{5}$$

Link Prediction Module. Afterwards, the link representations obtained from the time-aware module and the sequence evolution module are spliced together for the target link representation. Then a classifier is trained for prediction. We compared three different classifiers, Logistic Regression (LR), Random Forest (RF) and Gradient Boosting Decision Tree (GBDT), in which Random Forest performs best and we chose it as the classifier. The detailed comparison result is shown in Table 4.

4 Experiments

4.1 Datasets

We selected four real-world network datasets with different scenarios from the web repository [17] for our experiments, and the statistical information is shown in Table 1.

Table 1. Statistics of datasets.

Dataset	Nodes	Edges	Average degree	Density
Enron	151	50.5K	669.8	4.44
Sfhh	403	70.3K	348	0.87
Invs	95	394.2K	8.3K	88.30
Fb-forum	899	33.7K	75.0	0.08

- Enron: An Email network that comprises emails exchanged among Enron employees from 2002.2 to 2004.2.
- Sfhh: A network of human connections that consists of the communication records of a set of wireless sensor nodes in a laboratory environment from 2008 to 2014.
- Invs: A human-computer interaction network that includes data from four different social scenarios from 2009 to 2013, which was collected by the Social Networks research team at the French National Centre for Scientific Research (CNRS).
- Fb-forum: An online social network that consists of the interactions between students on a Facebook-like-forum during about 5 months in 2004.

4.2 Baselines

- Common Neighbours (CN): It proposed that two nodes tend to connect if the ratio of common neighbors between them is high.
- Node2vec: It utilized depth-first walk sampling to capture structure characteristics in the network and breadth-first walk sampling to capture homogeneity in the network.
- CTDNE [18]: It utilized temporal random walks to incorporate time information into the node embedding for prediction.
- E-LSTM-D [19]: This model consists of an encoder-decoder framework, an attention mechanism and dense connectivity to improve prediction accuracy and model robustness based on LSTM networks.
- DySAT: It integrates the features of the network using both the structural self-attention layer and the time self-attention layer.
- EvolveGCN: The algorithm employs a genetic algorithm-based approach to adaptively tune the parameters of the convolutional layer to dynamically changing graph structures.
- TGAT [20]: It develops a temporal embedding technique based on the classical Bochner theorem of harmonic analysis.
- GC-LSTM [21]: It embedded GCN into LSTM network in order to capture the structural and temporal information.
- RWTA [22]: It combines time-constrained stochastic wandering and temporal aggregation processes and using binary operations to obtain link representations for link prediction.

4.3 Experimental Results

Performance Comparison. We compare ATTP and other baselines on four datasets. The AUC and AP values for all methods are presented in Tables 2 and 3, and the best and suboptimal results, which are averaged over ten replicated experiments, are marked in bold and underlined.

We can see that the ATTP model outperformed all baseline methods on most datasets. In detailed, for AUC ATTP model improved by 0.4%, 4.5%, 0.4%, and -2% respectively relative to the suboptimal model, and although the method did not perform optimally on the Invs dataset, it was still suboptimal. Meanwhile, a similar improvement in AP values was observed.

The significant improvement in dynamic network link prediction methods compared to static network link prediction methods is due to their consideration of the temporal ordering of links, which better captures the evolution of links in the network. In comparison with the three methods using recurrent neural networks, E-LSTM-D, EvolveGCN and GC-LSTM, our method has a good enhancement because the Transformer can capture the sequence information effectively. From the results, it can be seen that the time-aware module has some advantages over the attention mechanism in dealing with dynamic networks because the attention mechanism generates node representations weighted by the relationships between nodes and does not directly consider the timing information. While the time-aware module takes into account the difference in timestamps and better captures the dynamic evolution of the network.

Table 2. AUC values of different methods on datasets

Methods	Enron	Sfhh	Invs	Fb-forum
CN	0.891	0.874	0.912	0.713
Node2vec	0.831	0.802	0.837	0.823
CTDNE	0.854	0.829	0.866	0.756
E-LSTM-D	0.915	0.918	0.931	0.855
DySAT	0.878	0.863	0.903	0.821
EvolveGCN	0.896	0.855	0.894	0.803
TGAT	0.786	0.846	0.882	0.878
GC-LSTM	0.843	0.915	0.874	0.902
RWTA	0.953	0.926	0.919	**0.944**
ATTP	**0.957**	**0.968**	**0.935**	0.924

Table 3. AP values for different methods on datasets

Methods	Enron	Sfhh	Invs	Fb-forum
CN	0.876	0.887	0.913	0.704
Node2vec	0.826	0.786	0.824	0.801
CTDNE	0.836	0.773	0.862	0.746
E-LSTM-D	0.904	0.893	0.919	0.822
DySAT	0.855	0.859	0.835	0.803
EvolveGCN	0.848	0.795	0.861	0.798
TGAT	0.774	0.817	0.866	0.831
GC-LSTM	0.861	0.901	0.848	0.897
RWTA	0.921	0.916	0.908	**0.923**
ATTP	**0.943**	**0.952**	**0.927**	0.915

Table 4. AUC values for different classifiers

Classifiers	LR	RF	GBDT
Enron	0.921	**0.957**	0.934
Sfhh	0.945	**0.968**	0.942
Invs	0.907	**0.935**	0.913
Fb-forum	0.886	**0.924**	0.901

Ablation Study. To illustrate the effectiveness of the submodels of ATTP, ablation studies were designed to investigate the effects of the sequence evolution module and the time-aware module on the experimental results. The results of the ablation experiments on all datasets are shown in Fig. 2, and only the AUC evaluation metrics are compared in this section. The details of the two model variants are described below:

- w/o sequence evolution: A variant of ATTP that removes the sequence evolution module and does not take into account the sequence information of the dynamic network.
- w/o time-aware: A variant of ATTP that removes the time-aware module and does not take into account local structural and temporal information.

It can be obtained from Fig. 2, the ATTP model has superior performance over the two variants on all four datasets, indicating that the simultaneous consideration of sequential and temporal information can be very helpful in improving the dynamic network link prediction task.

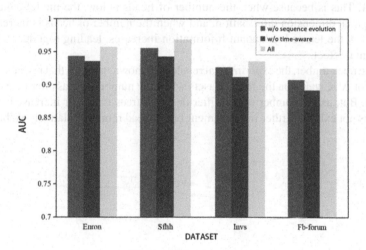

Fig. 2. Ablation study

As can be seen from the figure, the results of the variant with time-aware removed are worse compared to the variant with sequence evolution removed, indicating that the time-aware module has a greater impact on the model. Therefore, the time-aware module can capture both local structural and temporal information to get a better node representation.

Parameter Sensitivity Experiments. We gave the parameter sensitivity analysis of the ATTP model on the four datasets. Specifically, the effects of two parameters, the number of heads of multi-head attention and the number of classifier decision trees, on the model performance are explored and the results are shown in Fig. 3.

In experiments, we set the head in multi-head attention be 1, 2, 4, and 8. The results show that with the increase of the number of heads in multi-head attention, the AUC

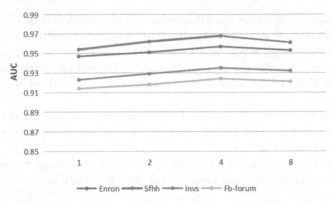

Fig. 3. Performance for different number of attention heads

value of the model on the four datasets shows a general trend of increasing first and then decreasing. The accuracy of the model reaches its highest when the number of heads is set to 4. This is because when the number of heads is low, the model cannot learn enough spatial dimension information, and when the number of heads is increased to a certain level, the learned redundant information increases, leading to a decrease in the experimental effect.

For the tree number, the experimental results are shown in Fig. 4, that reveals a gradual increase for AUC value on the four datasets when the number of classifier decision trees increased. But, as the number of classifier decision trees is further increased, the AUC value does not exhibit further improvement but instead remains relatively stable.

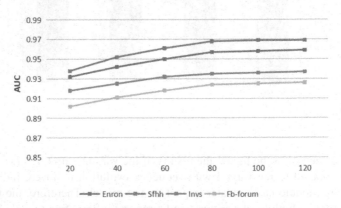

Fig. 4. Performance of different decision trees

5 Conclusion

In this paper, a dynamic network link prediction model is designed, which mainly consists of three modules:time-aware model that captures local structural and temporal information, sequence evolution module that captures sequence information through an improved Transformer,a random forest classifier for prediction. Experiments conducted on four datasets demonstrate our method the superior performance than other approaches. In the future we will explore more sophisticated technologies to improve the prediction performance.

Acknowledgment. This work was supported by the National Key Research and Development Program of China (No. 2021YFB3300503), Regional Innovation and Development Joint Fund of National Natural Science Foundation of China (No. U22A20167).

References

1. Newman, M.E.J.: The structure and function of complex networks. SIAM Rev. **45**(2), 167–256 (2003)
2. Liben-Nowell, D., Kleinberg, J.: The link prediction problem for social networks. In: Proceedings of the Twelfth International Conference on Information and Knowledge Management, pp. 556–559 (2003)
3. Lü, L., Jin, C.H., Zhou, T.: Similarity index based on local paths for link prediction of complex networks. Phys. Rev. E **80**(4), 046122 (2009)
4. Mikolov, T., Chen, K., Corrado, G., et al.: Efficient estimation of word representations in vector space. arXiv preprint arXiv:1301.3781 (2013)
5. Perozzi, B., Al-Rfou, R., Skiena, S.: DeepWalk: online learning of social representations. In: Proceedings of the 20th ACM SIGKDD International Conference on Knowledge Discovery and Data Mining, pp. 701–710 (2014)
6. Grover, A., Leskovec, J.: node2vec: scalable feature learning for networks. In: Proceedings of the 22nd ACM SIGKDD International Conference on Knowledge Discovery and Data Mining, pp. 855–864 (2016)
7. Kipf, T.N., Welling, M.: Semi-supervised classification with graph convolutional networks. arXiv preprint arXiv:1609.02907 (2016)
8. Veličković, P., Cucurull, G., Casanova, A., et al.: Graph attention networks. arXiv preprint arXiv:1710.10903 (2017)
9. Graves, A.: Long short-term memory. In: Graves, A. (ed.) Supervised sequence labelling with recurrent neural networks, pp. 37–45. Springer, Berlin, Heidelberg (2012). https://doi.org/10.1007/978-3-642-24797-2_4
10. Cho, K., Van Merriënboer, B., Gulcehre, C., et al.: Learning phrase representations using RNN encoder-decoder for statistical machine translation. arXiv preprint arXiv:1406.1078 (2014)
11. Vaswani, A., Shazeer, N., Parmar, N., et al.: Attention is all you need. In: Advances in Neural Information Processing Systems 30 (2017)
12. Sankar, A., Wu, Y., Gou, L., et al.: DySAT: deep neural representation learning on dynamic graphs via self-attention networks. In: Proceedings of the 13th International Conference on Web Search and Data Mining, pp. 519–527 (2020)
13. Min, S., Gao, Z., Peng, J., et al.: STGSN—a spatial-temporal graph neural network framework for time-evolving social networks. Knowl.-Based Syst. **214**, 106746 (2021)

14. Lei, K., Qin, M., Bai, B., et al.: GCN-GAN: a non-linear temporal link prediction model for weighted dynamic networks. In: IEEE INFOCOM 2019-IEEE Conference on Computer Communications, pp. 388–396. IEEE (2019)
15. Yang, M., Liu, J., Chen, L., et al.: An advanced deep generative framework for temporal link prediction in dynamic networks. IEEE Trans. Cybern. **50**(12), 4946–4957 (2019)
16. Pareja, A., et al.: EvolveGCN: evolving graph convolutional networks for dynamic graphs. Proc. AAAI Conf. Artif. Intell. **34**(04), 5363–5370 (2020). https://doi.org/10.1609/aaai.v34 i04.5984
17. Rossi, R., Ahmed, N.: The network data repository with interactive graph analytics and visualization. In: Proceedings of the AAAI Conference on Artificial Intelligence, vol. 29, issue 1 (2015).https://doi.org/10.1609/aaai.v29i1.9277
18. Nguyen, G.H., Lee, J.B., Rossi, R.A., et al.: Continuous-time dynamic network embeddings. In: Companion Proceedings of the Web Conference, pp. 969–976 (2018)
19. Chen, J., Zhang, J., Xu, X., et al.: E-LSTM-D: a deep learning framework for dynamic network link prediction. IEEE Trans. Syst. Man, Cybern. Syst. **51**(6), 3699–3712 (2019)
20. Xu, D., Ruan, C., Korpeoglu, E., et al.: Inductive representation learning on temporal graphs. arXiv preprint arXiv:2002.07962 (2020)
21. Chen, J., Wang, X., Xu, X.: GC-LSTM: graph convolution embedded LSTM for dynamic network link prediction. Appl. Intell., 1–16 (2022)
22. Zhang, M., Xu, B., Wang, L.: Dynamic network link prediction based on random walking and time aggregation. Int. J. Mach. Learn. Cybern., 1–9 (2023)

Users' Emotional Diffusion and Public Opinion Evolution Under Public Health Emergencies: Taking the Community Group Purchasing on Zhihu as an Example

Xin Feng[1]([⊠]), Jiangfei Chen[2], Juan Du[3], and Wenrui Wang[2]

[1] Shijiazhuang Tiedao University, Shijiazhuang 050043, Hebei, China
1731046381@qq.com
[2] Yanshan University, Qinhuangdao 066004, Hebei, China
[3] Hebei GEO University, Shijiazhuang 050031, Hebei, China

Abstract. COVID-19 closures forced community residents to organize daily supply group purchasing for anti-epidemic needs. Public service satisfaction constitutes an important public health emergency governance indicator. Analyzing community group purchasing satisfaction emotional diffusion assists governments in timely, comprehensively grasping mass needs, resolving main public opinion development contradictions across stages, and maintaining stability amid special periods. User comment text spanning December 19, 2019 to August 2, 2021 was captured for five related Zhihu community topics. After cleaning, 2,034 items were utilized to calculate user emotional tendency scores. Ebbinghaus forgetting curves were then introduced for interpolation fitting to form complete community purchasing satisfaction time series. Regional influence on time series patterns was studied using three city Zhihu data. Autoregressive integrated moving average (ARIMA) models constructed with Wuhan and Shijiazhuang outbreak phase data predicted public opinion evolution regarding community purchasing satisfactio. Wuhan demonstrated "flat before, medium, tight and slow" characteristics. Shijiazhuang exhibited "low middle and high sides". Guangzhou showed cyclical "steady-decreasing-rising" tendencies. Emotions gradually became cyclical and smooth. The research examines real-time public community group purchasing needs amid public health emergencies like epidemics from the public stance. Analyzing digital traces of public sentiments during crises provides data-driven insights to guide responsive governance. Further research should expand datasets across platforms and issues while refining techniques to extract signals from noise. Findings can illuminate universal public opinion dynamics to better predict future trajectories. Integrating computational social science, data science and psychology can strengthen collective resilience.

Keywords: Public health emergency · COVID-19 · Community group purchasing · Emotional diffusion · Evolution of public opinion · Sentiment analysis · Time series analysis

1   Introduction

Public health emergencies like COVID-19 can prompt anxiety, stress, and fear [1]. As a discussion platform, social media allows information exchange while serving as a barometer of public sentiment [2]. During COVID-19 closures, the Chinese Q&A site Zhihu enabled essential information sharing about community needs. Capturing sentiment values by analyzing hot topics can elucidate sentiment diffusion dynamics on social media [3].

Home isolation imbalances caused supply shortages, prompting community group purchasing and discussion on social media. These interactive Q&As involved product quality judgments, sector predictions, and commentary on companies like Meituan and Orange Heart. Research into emotion diffusion and opinion evolution on community purchasing can help government address public needs and opinion contradictions during emergencies.

While research exists on community purchasing cost optimization, information asymmetry, and quality impacts, few studies utilize Zhihu data or predict sentiment diffusion with ARIMA models. This research combines ARIMA and SnowNLP sentiment analysis of Zhihu "community group purchasing" topics to forecast trends and inform prevention and control (Fig. 1).

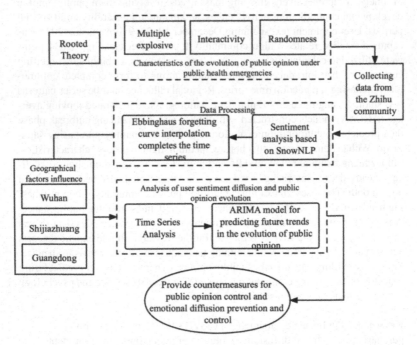

Fig. 1. Images of research ideas

2 Overview of the Theoretical Basis

Public health emergencies like COVID-19 are uncertain and disruptive, complicating response as online attention prompts rapid public opinion evolution. Three characteristics shape shifts:

1. Multiple outbreaks - External stimuli like resurgences transform declining trends into outbreaks, causing multiple opinion outbreaks.
2. Randomness - Unpredictable user dynamics on myriad platforms alter opinion field directions randomly.
3. Interactivity - Social media enables user and information interactions, generating copious topics and opinions [4].

Sentiment analysis extracts affective tendencies from subjective texts by classifying emotional attitudes, enabling predictive social media opinion analysis. Lexicon-based SnowNLP sentiment analysis is employed to examine community purchasing satisfaction shifts during COVID-19.

Time series analysis elucidates indicator change patterns for prediction. While LDA modeling is common, it does not resolve invalid word impacts on interpretability [5]. However, ARIMA models effectively fit and forecast emergent opinion formation and shifts, responding better to prediction value changes [6]. Therefore, ARIMA is leveraged to analyze and predict "community group purchasing" opinion progression, improving predictive accuracy for other emergencies.

3 Data Collection and Processing

3.1 Data Collection

This study examined user comments on five pertinent Zhihu topics – "community group purchasing", "group purchasing", "group purchasing websites", "group purchasing mode", and "group purchasing products" - from the January 2020 Wuhan outbreak through August 2021 Guangzhou epidemic conclusion. In total, 2,051 data points were obtained, with 2,034 valid text data pieces following cleaning. To ensure representativeness and validity, user ratings were weighted by like counts, granting higher weights for highly liked articles and comments in overall sentiment calculations. This yielded frequently appearing keywords in community group purchasing evaluations (Table 1). The most common words in community group purchasing assessments were group purchase, community, Meituan, platform, interconnection, and networking. This suggests most community users conducted online community group purchasing through platforms like Meituan during the December 2019 to August 2021 epidemic.

3.2 Data Processing

3.2.1 Sentiment Analysis Based on SnowNLP

This research used SnowNLP sentiment analysis to rapidly extract polarity from text by assigning sentiment scores [7].

Table 1. High-frequency keywords in topic evaluation

Keywords	Number of occurrences	Keywords	Number of occurrences	Keywords	Number of occurrences
group purchasing	1322	marketplace	132	e-commerce	100
communal	1034	head of a delegation	132	capital	94
American group	289	tycoon	129	development	94
platforms	208	preferential	129	spend	92
interconnections	156	mode	124	industry	90
network	154	businessmen	118	No. 1	83
the Internet	154	answer	101	company	81

First, SnowNLP accuracy was evaluated by comparing its scores for 100 random examples against subjective assessments. Alignment with human judgment demonstrated applicability.

Second, overall sentiment analysis determined user affective tendencies. SnowNLP scores below 0.4 are negative, 0.4–0.6 are neutral, and above 0.6 are positive. Of 2,034 valid comments, 1,401 (68.88%) were positive, 581 (28.56%) were negative, and 52 (2.56%) were neutral, indicating overall positivity towards community purchasing despite some negativity (Table 2).

Table 2. Distribution of comment attributes

Comment on the type of emotion	Positive emotion	Neutral emotion	negative emotion
Number of comments	1401	52	581

Third, subjective scoring validated results. Descriptive statistics on assigned emotions showed a mean of 0.70 and median of 1.00, evidencing highly positive sentiments, with few low outliers reducing the mean. Most comments were positive, reflecting broad user satisfaction (Table 3).

Table 3. Statistical distribution of topic evaluation descriptions

	Count	Mean	Standard deviation	Box plot min	Box plot Q1(25%)	Box plot Q2(50%)	Box plot Q3(75%)	Box plot max
Corresponds score	2034.00	0.70	0.44	0.00	0.07	1.00	1.00	1.00

3.2.2 Ebbinghaus Forgetting Curve Interpolation Complements the Time Series of Community Group Purchasing Emotional Diffusion

In early 2020, attention to community group purchasing on Zhihu was low, so user sentiment ratings were initially sparse. Missing data impedes later sentiment prediction. To ensure data continuity, this research completes the time series based on the Ebbinghaus forgetting curve, which describes gradual memory decline over time.

Some scholars have applied this theory to model user interest changes over time [8]. The forgetting curve characterizes nonlinear data memorability. For a time series, "long-term memory" means observations are non-independent, so earlier data affects later data (Fig. 2).

The Ebbinghaus curve prescribes residual memory rates daily after an event. Interpolating these rates completed the purchasing sentiment diffusion time series. Introducing the forgetting curve ensured data continuity and credibility [9], enabling time series construction and laying the groundwork for further research (Table 4).

Table 4. Table of the daily corresponding residual rate value in the Ebbinghaus forgetting curve

Day n after memory	The first day	The second day	The third day	The fourth day	The fifth day	The sixth day	The seventh day
Corresponding residual rate	40%	25%	22%	18%	15%	13%	10%

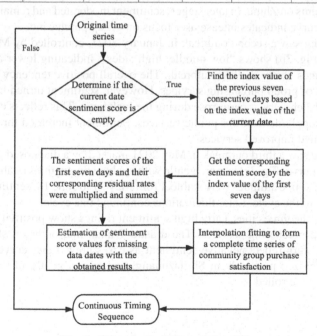

Fig. 2. Flow chart of interpolation fitting

4 Analysis of Public Opinion Evolution

The area where the epidemic broke out is different, and the situation in each area is also different. This article combines sentiment analysis with the time series images of the three cities based on geographical factors, clearly analyzes the spread and attention of user community group purchasing emotions in different regions, and judges the overall sentiment trend of users. In addition, the ARIMA model is constructed to better predict the evolution of public opinion on the spread of community group purchasing sentiment, and relevant departments can use this to understand the people's demand for community group purchasing when the epidemic repeats.

4.1 Analysis of the Difference of Time Series Images of Emotional Diffusion Under the Influence of Regional Factors

The community group purchasing time series is divided into three phases based on major outbreak locations - Wuhan, Shijiazhuang, and Guangdong. Plots have date on the x-axis and sentiment rating on the y-axis. Drastic image changes reflect high user attention; smooth changes reflect lower attention and fluctuation. Sentiment values indicate community satisfaction with group purchasing services.

Wuhan saw the initial domestic outbreak and control. Sentiment trends showed "flat beginning, dramatic middle, and soothing end" (Fig. 3a). Despite early fluctuations, satisfaction was stable and positive with lower attention initially. During opinion evolution, rising global impact kept supply concerns high, prompting surging negative group purchasing comments on Zhihu. In later stages, sentiment moderated and remained positive. The dramatic curve indicates intense user focus on group purchasing.

Shijiazhuang saw a second outbreak in January 2021, controlled by May. The sentiment curve (Fig. 3b) shows "low middle, high sides", indicating lower attention and moderate changes versus the first outbreak. The overall positive tendency reflects public recognition of group purchasing services. However, sentiment turned negative from January to mid-February as cases rose during the lockdown. This reflects changing attitudes toward supply/demand for public services. Sentiment increased through May as residents affirmed improved services.

Guangdong saw a third outbreak in May 2021 marked by a diagnosed grandmother. The sentiment curve (Fig. 3c) is more gentle with cyclical fluctuations (stable-declining-rising). Early positive attitudes were stable. From May 31 to June 14, sentiment dropped then rose back to the cycle. Later fluctuations continued this cycle.

Comparing the three cities, early high sentiment ratings show positivity about post-outbreak group purchasing services. The drastic Wuhan mid-outbreak shift and Shijiazhuang downturn reflect negative sentiment as cases grew. Later curves moderated in Wuhan, stabilized positively in Shijiazhuang, and cycled gently in Guangdong as outbreaks were controlled.

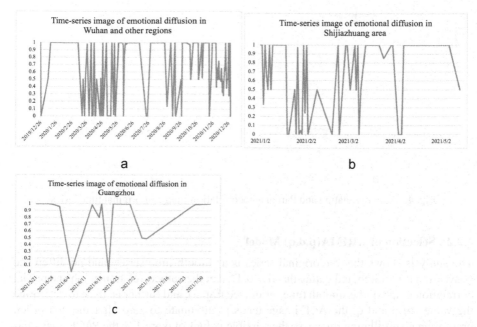

Fig. 3. Time series image of emotional diffusion in Wuhan、 Shijiazhuang and Guangzhou in the three stage

4.2 Constructing an ARIMA Model to Predict User Sentiment Diffusion and Public Opinioevolution Trend

4.2.1 Screening and Processing of Time Series Data

By observing the time series plots, attention to "community group purchasing" decreased over epidemic progression. Wuhan and Shijiazhuang saw the most comments and intense attitude changes, providing meaningful research data. Thus, ARIMA modeling was applied to predict public opinion evolution on group purchasing satisfaction in these cities during the outbreak periods.

To construct an accurate ARIMA model, the text data was subdivided. Data from January 4, 2020 to February 28, 2021 was used as the training set, and data from March 1, 2021 to March 11, 2021 as the testing set. The ARIMA model predictions were then tested against the actual testing set data.

Before ARIMA modeling, the training data time series was checked for smoothness - no systematic variation in mean or variance, and no periodic fluctuations. The ADF test gave p = 0.00 < 0.05, indicating the series was smooth.

The ARIMA(p,d,q) model was applied, with parameters for autoregression, differencing, and moving average orders. Autocorrelation and partial autocorrelation analyses showed neither autocorrelation nor partial autocorrelation in the series. Noise testing gave p = 0.54 > 0.05, indicating a non-white noise series (Fig. 4).

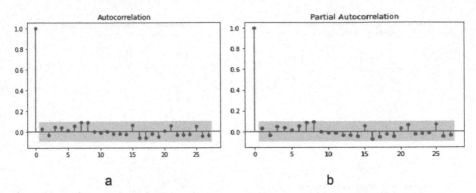

Fig. 4. Auto correlation and Partial autocorrelation image of original time series

4.2.2 Selection of ARIMA(p,d,q) Model

The analysis shows that the original series is a smooth time series, and no difference conversion is required, indicating that $d = 0$. Detect the autocorrelation graph and partial correlation graph of the smooth time series (see Fig. 5), and further analyze to determine the values of p and q: the ACF image tends to attenuate to zero after the first order, presenting an oscillating image, so the possible values of q are 1,2; the PACF image has a tendency of attenuation to zero after the 7th order, and does not show an oscillating image, so the possible values of pare 7,8.

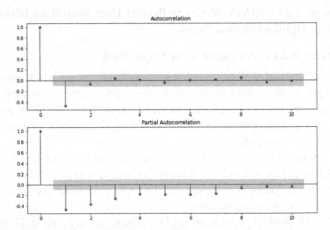

Fig. 5. Autocorrelation graph and partial correlation graph of smooth time series

Based on the above, the four mobile models of ARIMA (8,1), ARIMA (8,2), ARIMA (7,1), and ARIMA (7,1) were initially selected. In order to select the model with the best effect, compare and analyze the residual graphs of the four group models, it is found that the theoretical hypothesis value in the ARIMA (8,1) model fits best with the actual value of the sample, and the D-W test result value of the model is 1.9953. Compare the actual data in the test set with the results predicted by the ARIMA (8,1) model. The inspection situation is as follows (Table 5).

Table 5. Error statistics for actual data and predicted results

Date	Actual value	Predicted value	Inaccuracies	Date	Actual value	Predicted value	Inaccuracies
2021.3.1	0.5	0.4914	0.0086	2021.3.7	0.45	0.4895	−0.0395
2021.3.2	0.5	0.4582	0.0418	2021.3.8	0.5	0.5051	−0.0051
2021.3.3	0.6586	0.4573	0.2013	2021.3.9	0.5	0.4714	0.0286
2021.3.4	0.45	0.3922	0.0578	2021.3.10	0.8	0.4665	0.3335
2021.3.5	0.43	0.4177	0.0123	2021.3.11	0.44	0.4664	−0.0264
2021.3.6	0.34	0.4261	−0.0861				

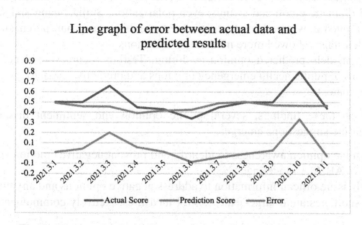

Fig. 6. Line graph of error between actual data and predicted results

The error line chart (Fig. 6) clearly and intuitively indicates changes between actual data and prediction errors over the 11-day timeframe. Except for larger differences on March 3 and 10, absolute errors were ≤ 0.3335, evidencing an overall good fit between predicted and actual sentiment values with relatively stable trends. Predicted scores were generally low (≤0.5), while actual sentiment fluctuated above and below the neutral 0.5 score.

With vaccine introduction and reasonable government control, China's COVID-19 outbreak developed positively, with gradual relaxation of city and community lockdowns. As predicted by the ARIMA model, the reopening of purchasing choices intensified competition between group purchasing and supermarkets/online shopping, exposing group purchasing weaknesses. Public satisfaction decreased, showing an overall negative trend. However, with outbreak control and met purchasing needs, satisfaction with public services became more positive, making actual sentiment scores higher than predicted. This reflects public affirmation of government epidemic governance capabilities.

However, some negative scores remind the government to further improve group purchasing shortcomings, promptly understand and meet public service needs, and better maintain social stability. Overall, the ARIMA(8,1) model demonstrated high accuracy, good sentiment prediction, and applicability for public health emergency opinions.

5 Conclusions and Discussion

The COVID-19 pandemic represents a major public health crisis. Analyzing community group purchasing satisfaction provides practical insights into public response during outbreaks, informing policymaking for public health emergencies. This paper examined public opinion shifts using Zhihu commentary text and sentiment analysis. Regional analysis revealed sentiment magnitude changes and trajectories. ARIMA modeling of Wuhan and Shijiazhuang text elucidated opinion dissemination patterns.

1. Regional time series showed low initial attention, limited fluctuations, and positive stability after outbreaks. Amid escalation, attention and opinions increased. Wuhan showed dramatic emotional swings, even polarization. Shijiazhuang and surroundings exhibited downtrends and negative sentiments about group purchasing. Later controlled stages showed more moderate fluctuations.
2. ARIMA models predicted opinion evolution. Testing accuracy evidenced robust reflections of public health emergency opinions and predictive capacities extendable to other contexts.

Based on these findings, several public opinion and sentiment dissemination countermeasure suggestions emerge:

1. Raise online opinion awareness to identify and prevent negative emotion spread via predictive ARIMA modeling.
2. Promptly issue official information to address negative opinions and anxieties about supply shortages amid large-scale control measures. Actively communicate supply status.
3. Refine community group purchasing services based on public demands, improving management and safeguarding interests to heighten satisfaction.
4. Expand analysis to more geographic areas to boost ARIMA accuracy.

Analyzing public discourse provides critical insights into collective crisis response, enabling ethical, effective policymaking.

References

1. Laato, S., Islam, A.K.M., Islam, M.N.: Why do people share misinformation during the Covid-19 pandemic? (2020). arXiv preprint arXiv:2004.09600
2. Zhao, R.Y., Chang, R.R., Chen, Z.: Research on the theme evolution of public health emergencies based on Zhihu. J. Inf. Resour. Manag. 11(02), 52–59 (2021)
3. Ma, X.Y., Sun, M.F.: Research on the Diffusion of Ethnic Cultures Integrating the Theme Evolution of Hot Events Library and information service, pp.106–117 (2022)
4. Cui, L., Wang, T., Zhu, T.: Information dissemination and public opinion evolution analysis based on complex network models. Physica A A **517**, 125–136 (2019)

5. Cao, J., Xia, T., Li, J., Zhang, Y., Tang, S.: A systematic comparison of LDA and LDA-based topic models with application to news analysis. Proc. AAAI Conf. Artifi. Intell. **34**(05), 7888–7895 (2020)

6. Yue, C., Morstatter, F., Shafiq, Z., Ferrara, E., Liu, H.: ARIMA-based forecasting of COVID-19 dynamics using Google Trends. Appl. Netw. Sci. **6**(1), 1–22 (2021)

7. Zhang, S., Yao, L., Sun, A., Tay, W.: Sentiment Analysis: A Literature Review. In Applied Computing in Medicine and Health, pp. 109–116. Springer, Cham (2021)

8. Yang, F., Liu, Y., Yu, X., Yang, Q.: Modeling the evolution of user interests in social media. ACM Trans. Inf. Syst. **39**(3), 1–33 (2021)

9. Chao, S., Cui, Y., Feng, J.: Data processing of intelligent IoT devices based on blockchain and edge computing. IEEE Internet Things J. **8**(7), 5188–5197 (2021)

Mobile Edge Computing Offloading Strategy Based on Deep Reinforcement Learning

Xu Hui[1], Ma Ningling[1,2], Hu Wenting[4], and Zhu Xianjun[2,3(✉)]

[1] Nanjing University of Aeronautics and Astronautics, Nanjing 210016, China
[2] Jinling Hospital, Nanjing 210002, China
691825308@qq.com
[3] Jinling Institute of Technology, Nanjing 211169, China
[4] Jiangsu Open University, Nanjing 210036, China

Abstract. Edge computing is a very good choice to solve the shortage of computing power of mobile devices (MD), the bandwidth resources and computing power of edge servers are also limited, therefore, efficient task offloading strategies and resource scheduling can reduce task computing time, reduce system energy consumption and improve user experience. In this study, a three-layer network architecture is proposed, namely a "end-edge-cloud" three-layer network architecture. Secondly, considering the maximum tolerance delay of user service, a comprehensive optimization model for task offloading and resource allocation aiming at the minimum energy consumption of the system is designed. The model clearly defines the state space, action space and reward function of Markov stochastic process, and adopts the simulation based on double Q-network (DDQN) and dueling deep Q-network (Dueling DQN). Experimental results show that the proposed scheme is better than multiple baseline algorithms and the original DQN algorithm.

Keywords: Mobile edge computing · Task offloading · Resource allocation · System energy consumption · Deep Reinforcement Learning (DRL)

1 Introduction

With the rapid development of communication technology and the Internet of Things technology, the number of connected devices such as smart devices and tablets is showing an explosive growth trend, and mobile applications are becoming increasingly complex New applications require high latency and energy consumption, and the existing network structure cannot meet users' requirements for real-time performance and low energy consumption [1–3]. Cloud computing data centers are usually far away from mobile devices, and the interaction process between mobile devices and the central cloud not only has a long time delay. In 2014, the European telecommunications standards institute (ETSI) proposed a new computing paradigm - Mobile edge computing (MEC) technology [4, 5].

In recent years, with the widespread application of artificial intelligence (AI) technology, deep reinforcement learning (DRL) combining deep learning and reinforcement learning (RL) has achieved good performance in dynamic environments. The problem of computing offload in mobile edge computing involves resource allocation and task scheduling between multiple mobile devices and edge servers and cloud servers, which is a typical decision-making problem. The DRL algorithm can learn the optimal strategy and behavior through the interaction between agents and the environment, thereby solving the problem.

In this article mainly optimizes the task offloading decision and resource allocation of the MEC system, with the goal of minimizing the energy consumption of the entire MEC system. This study is organized as follows: Sect. 2 reviews related work. The MEC system model and problem definition in Sect. 3. MEC calculation offloading scheme based on the DRL algorithm shown on Sect. 4. And, Sect. 5 shows the results of experiment,

2 Related Work

Scholars have conducted a series of studies on how mobile devices can efficiently make offloading decisions and how servers can reasonably allocate resources.

Minimize latency: Many scholars have conducted research on delay. Yu et al. [6] integrated an OFDMA based system with cloud and MEC servers. Wang et al. [7] proposed a lightweight heuristic algorithm to achieve fast scheduling, although considering the direct transmission delay of MEC servers. **Minimize energy consumption:** Wei et al. [8] used reinforcement learning method DQN to solve unloading decisions to minimize energy consumption. **Balancing energy consumption and latency:** Wang et al. [9] proposed an offloading strategy based on dynamic perception hybrid artificial fish school algorithm. Reference [10] constructed an unloading scheme based on Markov Decision Process (MDP), and obtained the optimal unloading strategy through the optimal value of the MDP model's value function.

3 System Model and Problem Formalization

Firstly, introduce the network structure adopted in this article, and then conduct a detailed analysis of the structural model, including communication model and computational model.

1)Network Model: As shown in Fig. 1, an end edge cloud MEC system with multiple users and edge servers, consisting of multiple base stations (BS) and a cloud data center. Define the task as a triplet $S_i = (D_i, C_i, \tau_i^{max})$, $i \in N$, where D_i represents the input data size for task processing, C_i represents the computing resources required to process the task (Fig. 2).

3.1 Communication Model

The transmission rate from mobile device n to MEC server node i can be obtained by Shannon's theorem. Then OFDMA technology to reduce signal interference:

$$R_{ni} = w_n log_2 \left(1 + \frac{p_n h_{ni}^2 (r_i^s)^{-\alpha}}{N_0 + \sum_{k \neq i} (p_k h_k^2 (r_k^s)^{-\alpha})} \right) \tag{1}$$

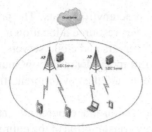
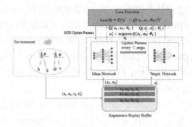

Fig. 1. Computing system model of end-edge-cloud

Fig. 2. The flowchart of DDQN algorithm

3.2 Calculation Model

There are three ways to process the task:

1) Local computing model: The time spent by mobile device i processing tasks locally t_i^{loc}, the energy consumed by mobile device i to complete tasks locally is E_i^{loc}.

$$T_n^{loc} = \sum_{n=1}^{N} \frac{C_i}{f_n^{loc}} \bullet x_n^l \tag{2}$$

$$E_n^{loc} = \sum_{n=1}^{N} \sigma \bullet \left(f_n^{loc}\right)^2 \bullet C_i \bullet x_n^l \tag{3}$$

2) Edge unloading model: The system overhead will include the following three processes: uploading the task to the server.

$$T_n^{edge} = \sum_{n=1}^{N} y_{nm}^e \left(t_n^e + 2t_{n,m}^e\right) \tag{4}$$

$$E_n^{edge} = \sum_{n=1}^{N} \left(E_n^e + E_{n,idle}^e + E_{n,m}^e\right) \tag{5}$$

3) Cloud offloading model: If device i chooses to unload the task to the cloud server, first select the channel with the best channel status to upload the task to the cloud server:

$$T_n^{cloud} = \sum_{n=1}^{N} z_n^c \left(\frac{D_i}{R_{ic}} + \frac{C_i}{f_n^{cloud}}\right) \tag{6}$$

$$E_n^{cloud} = \sum_{n=1}^{N} \left(\frac{D_i}{C_i} \cdot p_i + C_i \cdot \omega_c + \left(\frac{D_i}{R_{ic}} + \frac{C_i}{f_n^{cloud}}\right) \cdot p_w\right) \tag{7}$$

Based on the delay and energy consumption formulas for various calculation modes mentioned above, the total cost of mobile devices in the entire system is:

$$T_{total} = T_n^{loc} + T_{n,m}^{edge} + T_n^{cloud} \tag{8}$$

$$E_{total} = E_n^{loc} + E_{n,m}^{edge} + E_n^{cloud} \tag{9}$$

3.3 Problem Definition

This article proposes an end-to-end cloud structure, explores the impact of multiple variables on system energy consumption, and optimizes the total energy consumption of MEC systems. This article jointly optimizes the unloading decision with the goal of optimal energy consumption in MEC systems $\Phi_i=[x_i^l, y_{i,j}^e, z_i^c]$, channel bandwidth resource ω_i and edge server computing resources f_{ij}, while meeting the maximum tolerance delay limit for each task, the problem Q_1 is defined as follows:

$$Q_1 : \min_{\phi_i, \omega_i, f_{ij}} E_{total} \tag{10}$$

s.t.

$$C1 : x_i^l \left(t_i^{loc} \right) + \sum_{j=1}^{M} (y_{i,j}^e \left(t_i^e + t_{i,j}^e + \right) + z_i^c \left(T_i^{cloud} \right) \le \tau_i^{max}$$

$$C2 : \sum_{i=1}^{N} f_{i,j}^{edge} y_{ij}^m \le F_{jmax}^{edge}$$

$$C3 : \sum_{i=1}^{N} w_{ij} \le W_j, \forall j \in M$$

$$C4 : 0 \le w_i \le W_i, \forall i \in N$$

$$C5 : 0 \le f_{i,j}^{edge} \le F_{jmax}^{edge}, \forall j \in M, \forall i \in N$$

$$C6 : x_i^l + \sum_{j=1}^{M} y_{i,j}^e + z_i^c = 1$$

$$C7 : x_i^l, y_{ij}^e, z_i^c \in \{0, 1\}$$

4 Algorithm Design

This article proposes (MDP model based on reinforcement learning, and provides a computing offloading and resource allocation scheme based on Double DQN and Dueling DQN.

4.1 MDP Model

Markov Decision Process (MDP) can be defined as a five tuple (S, A, R, P, γ) To solve the unloading problem. State: The system state has six components, including the states of time slot $s_t \in S$ is defined as $(\ominus, sc, sw, ac, aw, cw)$. Among them, χ: Device task offloading decision vector; Sc: The allocated computing resources for the current task; Sw: bandwidth information allocated to the task; AC: Remaining computing resources of edge servers; Aw: The remaining bandwidth resources of the edge server; Cw: The size of the remaining bandwidth resource state space dimension of the cloud server is.

$(N * (1 + M + 1) + N + N + 1 + M + 1 + M + 1)$. Action: In this scenario, the action space consists of three parts: the offloading location of the task, the computing resources allocated by the server, and the bandwidth resources allocated, where $a_t \epsilon A$ is defined as. Reward function: in each time slot t, in a certain s_t. After the agent takes action, the environment provides a feedback value R (s_t, a_t) to the agent. In this article, the reward function is designed as follows:

$$r_t = \begin{cases} +100, \ E_t < E_t^{best} \\ +1, \ E_t = E_t^{best} \\ -100, \ E_t > E_t^{best} \end{cases} \tag{11}$$

4.2   Mobile Edge Computing Offload Scheme Based on DRL Algorithm

1) Mobile edge computing offload scheme based on dual depth Q network.

The DQN algorithm uses the same Q network to evaluate actions and update state action values, and the corresponding objectives of DQN iterative learning are:

$$Q_t = R_t + \gamma \max_{a_t} Q(S_{t+1}, a_t; \theta_t) \tag{12}$$

The algorithm flowchart of DDQN, and the selection of actions still uses online updated weights θ_t use another set of weights θ_t' to evaluate the effectiveness of this strategy:

$$Q_t = R_l + \gamma Q(S_{(t+1)}, \underset{a_t}{argmax} \, Q(S_{(t+1)}, a_t; \theta_t); \theta_{t'}) \tag{13}$$

2) Mobile edge computing Offload Scheme Based on Dual Q Network.

Q (s, a) represents the value of action a in states. Due to the condition of states, this value cannot fully represent the value of this action. Therefore, in order to measure the respective values of state and action, Decoupling the network structure of DQN is called dual networks.

$$Q(s, a; \omega^A, \omega^V) = V(s; \omega^V) + (A(s, a; \omega^A) - \underset{a' \in |A|}{max} A(s, a'; \omega^A)) \tag{14}$$

5   Analysis of Simulation Results

This article uses Python and TensorFlow to implement the algorithm proposed.

5.1 System Parameter Settings

The number edge servers is $M = 3$, and the MD is randomly dispersed within the range of [200m, 500m] of the AP, and the number of MDs is $N = 10$. The computing power and bandwidth resources of MEC servers are different F_{max}^{edge} follows a uniform distribution on [4GHZ/sec, 8GHZ/sec], W_{max}^{edge} follows a uniform distribution on [10MHz, 15MHz], with the CPU frequency locally calculated for each MD set to a uniform distribution on [0.5GHZ/sec, 1.5GHZ/sec], $\sigma=10^{-26}$, set the power of the MD transmission task and the idle waiting power to p_n=500mW and p_w=200mW. Assuming the data size D of the device uninstallation task D_n satisfies a uniform distribution of [16Mbit, 30Mbit] and the number of CPU cycles required to complete the task C_n follows the uniform distribution of [200 3500].

5.2 Performance Analysis

Introduce the following baseline scheme in the application scenario of this article: 1) Local Execution. 2) Full Offloading to Edge. 3) Full Offloading to Cloud. 4) Natural DQN. This article first verifies the impact of the proposed algorithm on the system under different learning rates. Figure 3 studies the loss values of the proposed algorithm under different learning rates, i.e., 0.01, 0.05, 0.005, and 0.0001, respectively. After 900 iterations, the loss value gradually becomes stable (Fig. 4).

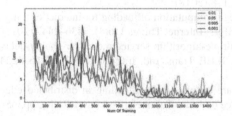
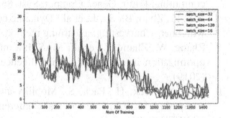

Fig. 3. Change of loss value under different learning rates

Fig. 4. Explores the batch size of multiple samples,

6 Conclusion

This paper combines and optimizes cloud computing and mobile edge computing modes to form a cloud edge collaborative computing model: end edge cloud architecture. A model for task offloading and resource allocation was established with the goal of minimizing energy consumption in the MEC system. Then, an MDP model was designed and a computing offloading and resource allocation scheme based on DRL for DDQN and Dueling DQN was proposed. Finally, simulation experiments showed that the algorithm proposed in this paper can effectively reduce system energy consumption compared to various baseline algorithms.

Acknowledgment. This work was supported in part by China Postdoctoral Science Foundation, Special Fund for Epidemic prevention and control of COVID-19 Fund (No. 2020T130129ZX), the Postdoctoral Research Fund of Jiangsu Province (No. 2019K086),the High-Level Talent Foundation of Jinling Institute of Technology (No.JIT-B-201703, JIT-RCYJ-201802), 2019 school-level research fund incubation project (No. Jit-fhxm-201912), the Postdoctoral Research Fund of Jiangsu Province (No. 2019K086), "Qinglan Project" of Jiangsu Province.

References

1. LNCS Homepage. http://www.springer.com/lncs. Accessed 20 Jul 2023
2. Shi, W., Cao, J., Zhang, Q., et al.: Edge computing: vision and challenges. IEEE Internet Things J. **3**(5), 637–646 (2018)
3. Leduc, S., Cantor, Z., Kelly, P., et al.: LO15: Paramedic and allied health professional interventions at long-term care facilities to reduce emergency department visits: systematic review. Can. J. Emerg. Med. **22**(S1), S12–S12 (2020)
4. Mach, P., Becvar, Z.: Edge computing: a survey on architecture and computation offloading. IEEE Commun. Surv. Tut. **19**(3), 1628–1656 (2017)
5. Liu, B., Liu, C., Peng, M.: Resource allocation for energy-efficient MEC in NOMA-enabled massive IoT networks. IEEE J. Sel. Areas Commun. **39**(4), 1015–1027 (2021)
6. Li, Y., Wang, X., et al.: Learning-aided computation offloading for trusted collaborative mobile edge computing. IEEE Trans. Mobile Comput. **19**(12), 2833–2849 (2020)
7. Wang, Z., Zhao, Z., Min, G., et al.: User mobility aware task assignment for mobile edge computing. Futur. Gener. Comput. Syst. **85**, 1–8 (2018)
8. Wei, Z., Zhao, B., Su, J., et al.: Dynamic edge computation offloading for internet of things with energy harvesting: a learning method. IEEE Internet Things J. **6**(3), 4436–4447 (2018)
9. Zhang, W., Zhang, Z., et al.: MASM: a multiple-algorithm service model for energy-delay optimization in edge artificial intelligence. IEEE Trans. Ind. Informat. **15**(7), 4216–4224 (2019)
10. Jeon, Y., Baek, H., Pack, S.: Mobility-aware optimal task offloading in distributed edge computing. In: 2021 International Conference on Information Networking (ICOIN), pp. 65–68. IEEE (2021)

Study of Mental Model in Human-Computer Interaction Based on EEG Signal Data

Jiaping Chen[1], Ruoxi Zhang[1], Yaming Liu[2], Xuan Zhou[3], Zhijing Wu[1],
Hanzhen Ouyang[1(✉)], and Weihui Dai[1(✉)]

[1] School of Management, Fudan University, Shanghai 200433, China
{20307100001,20307100127,zhijingwu20,ouyanghanzhen,
whdai}@fudan.edu.cn
[2] School of Mechanical and Automotive Engineering, South China University of Technology,
Guangzhou 510006, China
[3] Guanghua Law School, Zhejiang University, Hangzhou 310008, China

Abstract. Mental model refers to the internal cognitive structure and reasoning mechanism in the human brain, and its influence on users' psychological preferences and behavior decisions mainly occurring at the subconscious level, which is difficult to comprehensively and accurately evaluated by subjective self-reports in the conscious state. Taking human-computer interaction tasks and scenarios in e-commerce shopping as the background, this study makes an exploratory study on the classification and characteristics of users' mental models based on EEG signal data. It was found that the parameters of α wave, β wave and cognitive load in EEG signal can better reflect the mental model differences of users in the aforementioned interaction process. On this basis, the clustering method and optimal classification of typical mental models are analyzed, and the comparative analysis shows that the K-means method can yield optimal results for refining the typical mental models of the users. The study provides a new basis and reference for the design of human-computer interaction system.

Keywords: Human-Computer Interaction · Mental Model · EEG · Online Shopping · Clustering Analysis

1 Introduction

In the process of human-computer interaction, how to design the interactive interface according to users' perceptive and cognitive characteristics as well as their behavior habits is of great significance for improving user experience and interactive efficiency, which has become a prominent research focus in recent years [1, 2]. Existing studies have indicated that the above users' perceptive and cognitive characteristics and behavioral habits are largely influenced by their mental models [2–4]. For instance, when the mental model of the system designer is quite different from that of the user; it may negatively impact user experience and consequently affects the effectiveness of human-computer interaction [4].

Y. Sun et al. (Eds.): ChineseCSCW 2023, CCIS 2012, pp. 281–288, 2024.
https://doi.org/10.1007/978-981-99-9637-7_21

The aforementioned mental models refer to the inherent cognitive structures and reasoning mechanisms in the human brain, which mainly influence individuals' psychological preferences and behavioral decisions at a subconscious level, and are difficult to be comprehensively and precisely evaluated through subjective self-reports in conscious states [6, 7]. The development of modern neuroscience technologies, for example EEG (electroencephalogram) signals, has provided effective means for in-depth observation of neural activities and mental model study at the subconscious level [8–10].

E-commerce online shopping system is a human-computer interaction system composed of a series of web pages, software functions and databases. The design of the interaction interfaces and operation steps of the system has important impacts on users' experiences, purchasing behaviors and shopping efficiencies [11, 12]. This study aims to explore the user-based mental model characteristics from EEG signal data under that online shopping background and the contexts, so as to provide a new basis and reference for the design of human-computer interaction system.

2 Experimental Test

2.1 Online Shopping Process

This study is based on the online shopping APP of Taobao (www.taobao.com), a mobile e-commerce platform. Portable EEG recording devices were used to primarily observe participants' frontal neural activity. The main interface and human-computer interaction process of online shopping is illustrated in Fig. 1.

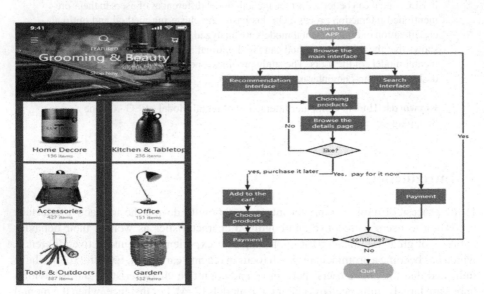

Fig. 1. The main interface and interactive process of online shopping.

In the given process, when users open the APP, the main interface contains many functional modules, such as searching and scanning keys, functional partition, etc., as well as the information of the recommended products. During the shopping process, users may choose to enter the searching interface to search for the products they want, or select suitable products on the recommendation page. After the appropriate product is selected, users will generally go to the details page of the product to view its details. If they wish to purchase the product, they can either add it to their shopping cart or buy it directly. If they have no intention to buy, they can return to the list of items to choose another one. On the shopping cart page, users can select the items they want to purchase and proceed to check out, and then return to the main interface to continue browsing or exit the APP.

2.2 EEG Data Acquisition

This study conducted the test tasks under four situations: static interface perception (Static test), product selection from recommendation page (Situation A test), product selection from searching page (Situation B test), and product selection from shopping cart (Situation C test). A total of 13 participants took part in the test, all of whom were college students between 21 and 25 years old with more than 3 years' online shopping experience. After checking the test process and collected data, we confirmed that 10 of them were valid subjects.

During the whole process of online shopping, the EEG signal data of subjects were recorded with a wearable acquisition device. Through a comparative analysis of the users with different behavior habits, combined with the interview of their perceptions and cognitions, it was found that the parameters of subjects' α wave, β wave, and cognitive load can reflect the differences of users' mental models significantly. For example, the β waveforms of two subjects with different mental models are shown in Fig. 2 and Fig. 3 respectively.

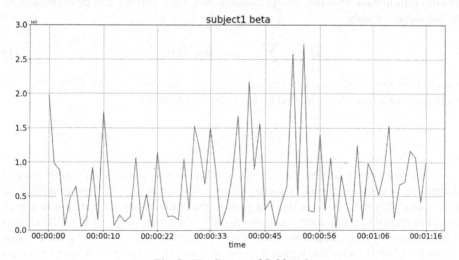

Fig. 2. The β wave of Subject 1

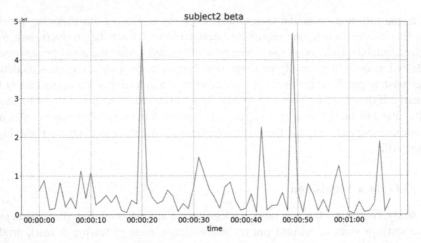

Fig. 3. The β wave of Subject 2

3   Mental Model Study

3.1   Feature Indicators

The following two EEG indicators can better reflect the characteristics of neural activities in the subconscious and conscious states of the brain, and were adopted as the basic feature indicators for mental model analysis in the study.

(1) β wave entropy, which reflects the degree of disorder/orderliness and complexity of signal energy, thereby capturing the fluctuation characteristics of the signals. Higher β wave entropy indicates stronger fluctuation and greater attention of subjects to the specific information stimulus. The calculation of β wave entropy can be expressed by the following formula:

$$H = -\sum_{k=1}^{N} p(c_k) log_2[p(c_k)] \tag{1}$$

where, N is the length of the signal, $p(c_k)$ is the probability of the *K-th* β wavelet coefficient, which can be estimated by the following formula:

$$p(c_k) = \frac{|c_k|}{\sum_{i=1}^{N} |c_i|} \tag{2}$$

(2) Energy ratio of β wave and α wave: β wave often appears in the mental state of excitement, tension and stress, α wave usually occurs in the relaxed and quiet mental state, and Eβ/Eα reflects the activity degree of the brain. When subjects are in a high degree of mental concentration, excitement and tension, the energy of the EEG signals should be mainly concentrated on the β waves, while the energy carried by the α waves should be relatively less. The higher the energy ratio of β wave and α wave to a certain information, the subject is in a state of increased stress, the brain cognitive load is more complex with deeper concentrative thinking.

3.2   Clustering Analysis

Due to the different lengths of the EEG signals recorded by each subject, the traditional distance calculation methods are difficult to effectively calculate the unaligned time series signals. Therefore, based on the extracted wave parameters from EEG signal data, the study adopted the FASTDTW (Fast Dynamic Time Warping) algorithm to calculate the distance matrix between different subjects as follows:

$$D(i,j) = Dist(i,j) + \min\{D(i-1,j), D(i,j-1), D(i-1,j-1)\} \tag{3}$$

DTW measures the similarity between two time series using the sum of the distances between similar points, called WPD(Warp Path Distance). When implementing DTW, we adopt the idea of dynamic programming, where $D(i, j)$ represents the integration path distance between two time series of length i and j. Due to the high complexity of DTW algorithm, this study used the improved algorithm of FASTDTW to realize the fast calculation by reducing the data space and data abstraction.

The distance matrix data between different subjects calculated by FASTDTW algorithm are used for clustering analysis. In order to compare the performances of different commonly-used clustering methods, the study took the contour coefficient as the assessment index, which can be calculated by the following formula:

$$S(i) = \frac{b(i) - a(i)}{\max\{a(i), b(i)\}} \tag{4}$$

where, $a(i)$ represents the average degree of dissimilarity between vector i and other points in the same cluster, $b(i)$ represents the minimum of the mean dissimilarity of vector i to the other clusters. The closer the contour coefficient is to 1, the better the clustering result is. The contour coefficients of the commonly-used clustering methods, hierarchical clustering, DBSCAN (Density-Based Spatial Clustering of Applications with Noise), K-means, and AP (Affinity Propagation) clustering, are compared as in Table 1.

Table 1. The contour coefficients of different clustering methods.

Test tasks	Hierarchical clustering	DBSCAN	K-means	AP clustering
Static test	0.546	0.148	0.540	0.528
Situation A test	0.802	0.220	0.802	0.533
Situation B test	0.621	0.259	0.694	0.621
Situation C test	0.798	0.118	0.787	0.738
Mean value	0.692	0.186	0.706	0.605

The comparative analysis shows that K-means method can yield optimal results for refining the typical mental models of the users. Therefore, the users' psychological preferences and behavior habits corresponding to each type of mental models can be considered for improving the design of human-computer interface and operation procedures.

Based on the clustered results by K-means method, the study categorized the 10 subjects into the following three mental model groups:

(1) Meticulous Selection Group: These users are cautious and meticulous during the selection phase, paying attention to various details and comparisons of products. They take a longer time to make decisions. During the purchasing phase, they are rational and thrifty, repeatedly calculating the prices of different product combinations to save expenses. This group includes users 1, 4, 7, and 10.

(2) Clear Objective Group: These users are quick and decisive during the selection phase, having clear purchasing goals and specific needs. They don't waste time on irrelevant products. During the purchasing phase, they are efficient and confident, selecting suitable product combinations based on their plans and budgets without hesitation or regret. This group includes users 2, 3, and 8.

(3) Casual Browsing Group: These users browse products casually and without specific purchasing goals or needs during the selection phase. They simply explore products for entertainment or inspiration. During the purchasing phase, they are spontaneous and random, deciding whether to make a purchase based on their mood and budget, without excessive consideration or calculations. This group includes users 5, 6, and 9.

On this basis, this study proposed the following improvements on the design of human-computer interactions for those users with the corresponding mental models:

First, for the Meticulous Selection Group, provide additional filtering, sorting, comparison, and bookmarking functions to help them easily find desired products and save their selections. Additionally, display more relevant product information such as ratings, sales volume, and coupons on the recommendation page to enhance their trust. Offer more promotional information, such as discounts, deductions, and loyalty points, on the shopping cart page to stimulate their purchasing desire.

Next, for the Clear Objective Group, offer faster search, navigation, and payment functions to help them quickly complete their purchasing tasks and provide a better user experience. Show more personalized product information, such as "You May Like" or "Recommended for You," on the recommendation page to increase their satisfaction. Provide more assurance information, such as returns and exchanges, after-sales services, and invoices, on the shopping cart page to enhance their sense of security.

Lastly, for the Casual Browsing Group, provide more interactive, social, and entertaining features to allow them to enjoy the process of browsing products and gain inspiration. Display more novelty product information, such as new arrivals, bestsellers, and limited-time offers, on the recommendation page to pique their curiosity. Offer more psychological cues, such as limited stock, high popularity, or last day reminders, on the shopping cart page to create a sense of urgency.

4   Conclusion and Discussion

This study raised the question of the impacts of mental models on human-computer interaction, and made exploration on the feature indicators and clustering analysis of users' mental models based on EEG signal data. Through the EEG experimental test analysis of human-computer interactions in e-commerce online shopping tasks and scenarios, it was found that the parameters of α wave, β wave and cognitive load can better reflect the mental model differences, and K-means method can yield optimal results for refining the typical mental models of the users. According to the clustered typical mental models, the study proposed improvements on the design of human-computer interactions.

However, as an exploratory study, the findings and the proposed method needs to be further verified by more experimental test subjects. Besides, EEG signals are subject to the interferences from many aspects, and how to accurately extract the feature indicators related to mental models still needs to be further thought and tested. In addition, the subjects' attention, emotional changes, and other useful indicators may also be considered for the clustering analysis of mental models. Furthermore, the users' perceptive and cognitive characteristics as well as their behavior habits with different mental models are worth in-depth study under more situations.

Acknowledgements. This study was supported by the Undergraduate Program of Fudan University (No. 22530). Jiaping Chen, Ruoxi Zhang, Yaming Liu and Xuan Zhou are the joint first authors who made equal contributions, Weihui Dai and Hanzhen Ouyang are the joint corresponding authors. Many thanks to Dr. Jian Wang from Shanghai International Studies University for completing the translation work.

References

1. Hibbein, M., Jenkins, J.L., Schneider, C., et al.: How is your user feeling? Inferring emotion through human-computer interaction devices. MIS Q. **41**(1), 1–22 (2017)
2. Yamaoka, T., Doi, T., Nishizaki, Y.: A proposal of a user-interface index that corresponds with mental model structural elements. Theor. Issues Ergon. Sci. **13**(2), 135–145 (2012)
3. Xiong, Z.: Theory and Application of Mental Models. Huazhong Agricultural University, Wuhan (2012)
4. Yang, M.M., Yang, F.F., Cui, T.R., Cheng, Y.C.: Analysing the dynamics of mental models using causal loop diagrams. Aust. J. Manag. **44**(3), 495–512 (2019)
5. Zhang, W.Y., Yu, S.H., Liu, Z.: Intelligent robot service design based on mental model measurement. Mech. Des. **35**(5), 105–110 (2018)
6. Treur, J.: Mental models in the brain: on context-dependent neural correlates of mental models. Cogn. Syst. Res. **69**, 83–90 (2021)
7. Bara, B.G., Bucciarelli, M., Lombardo, V.: Model theory of deduction: A unified computational approach. Cogn. Sci. **25**(6), 839–901 (2021)
8. Wang, W.L.: Application of EEG Monitoring in the Evaluation of Consciousness Disorders. Tianjin University, Tianjin (2023)
9. Yu, Y.Q., Yang, N.F.: Research on neuromarketing based on consumer's subconscious mind. Mod. Econ. Inf. **2018**(4), 149–150 (2018)
10. Wang, D., Miao, D.Q.: Monitoring Brain Activity - EEG Decoding and Its Application Research. Tongji University Press, Shanghai (2017)

11. Wen, H.J., Chen, H.G., Hwang, H.G.: E-commerce Web site design: strategies and models. Inf. Manag. Comput. Secur. **9**(1), 5–12 (2013)
12. Wu, J.N., Liu, L., Cui, T.: What drives consumer website stickiness intention? The role of website service quality and website involvement. Int. J. Serv. Technol. Manage. **27**(3), 189–208 (2021)

Collaborative Mechanisms, Models, Approaches, Algorithms and Systems

A Scholarly Information Retrieval System Incorporating Recommendation with Semantic Similarity

Yangbo Lan, Ronghua Lin[(✉)], and Chengjie Mao

South China Normal University, Guangzhou, Guangdong, China
{yblan,rhlin}@m.scnu.edu.cn

Abstract. The scholarly information retrieval systems help us to access a broader range of information. However, the currently available systems do not always ensure data authenticity and real-time. To solve these problems, we propose a Scholar Think Tank System based on an actual scholar database from SCHOLAT to build a high-quality and reliable database. Our system ensures the authenticity and real-time data through data synchronization and manual information collection from scholars not registered to SCHOLAT. In addition, users may be interested in scholars based more on common research content, which reminds us that we need to pay attention to the similarity between scholars. With this inspiration, we have developed a semantic similarity-based scholar recommendation service. We use the pre-training language model SBERT to calculate the similarity between scholars through their profiles and devise an incremental update algorithm to reduce the use of computing resources. Our system has been developed and online.

Keywords: Scholarly information retrieval · Recommendation system · Semantic similarity · SCHOLAT

1 Introduction

The advent of scholarly information retrieval systems has facilitated scholars in connecting with their peers and accessing a broader range of academic resources, thereby enhancing the efficacy and level of their research. Previous studies [14,16,25,28] have shown that the emergence of these systems helps get more scholarly information. We can search for structured information on scholars through SCHOLAT [22], Google Scholar, Academia, ResearchGate, AMiner [23], etc. Sometimes, we can get some recommended information.

In this paper, we try to address these challenges by proposing a new system. We propose a Scholar Think Tank System. Leveraging SCHOLAT's extensive repository of actual scholarly data, we establish a high-quality and reliable database for our system. In order to ensure real-time information, we devise a data synchronization algorithm to extract valuable data from SCHOLAT. More

© The Author(s), under exclusive license to Springer Nature Singapore Pte Ltd. 2024
Y. Sun et al. (Eds.): ChineseCSCW 2023, CCIS 2012, pp. 291–302, 2024.
https://doi.org/10.1007/978-981-99-9637-7_22

than relying on one data source alone is undoubtedly required, which can lead to a lack of breadth in our data. We also collect more information from other sites and strictly review the reality of the data.

Many information recommendation services in social networks [7–9,11,24] are based on users' social relationships. These social relationships reflect possible common hobbies or common backgrounds among users and can therefore be used as recommendations. However, for academic circles, the scholars that users may be interested in are based more on their common research interests or common workplace. This observation inspired us to focus on the similarity of the textual information in the scholar's profile. The advent of BERT [4] has brought a dramatic change to Semantic Textual Similarity (STS). Then a series of improved models [5,12,13,21,29] based on BERT have been proposed. However, a significant drawback of the BERT network structure lies in its inability to independently compute sentence embedding, posing challenges when deriving sentence embedding from BERT. SBERT [19] used the pre-trained BERT and RoBERTa [15] network and only fine-tune it to yield useful sentence embedding.

We use the pre-trained language model SBERT to extract embeddings of crucial information about scholars and calculate the similarity between these embeddings. With similarity, we give the user a practical scholar recommendation service. The system has been successfully developed and is presently online.

The main contributions of this paper are summarized as follows: (1) We implement a system that could provide high-quality and reliable scholarly information. (2) We devise a data synchronization algorithm for the system to extract data from SCHOLAT. It enables us to take full advantage of the vast amount of scholarly information on SCHOLAT. (3) We build a scholar recommendation service by pre-training language model SBERT.

The rest of the paper is arranged as follows. Related works are summarized in Sect. 2. The proposed system is shown in Sect. 3. The conclusion is drawn in Sect. 4.

2   Related Work

In this section, we first introduce scholarly information retrieval system and then discuss semantic similarity-based recommendation.

2.1   Scholarly Information Retrieval System

We review some common scholar information retrieval systems on the Internet that provide users convenient ways to find information about scholars. SCHOLAT [22] is a comprehensive academic social networking platform designed for reliable data sharing. Google Scholar is a widely used academic search engine that provides a comprehensive search function for academic resources. But Chen et al. [3] also points out that Google Scholar has less information about scholars. ResearchGate and Academia are two well-known academic social networking platforms where researchers can post and share research results and communicate and collaborate with other scholars.By using these scholarly information retrieval system, we can easily access scholars' profiles, published papers, citations, and other relevant information.

Regarding these information systems, Bastopcu et al. [1] mentioned the need to focus on the frequency and weight of information updates. Walters [27] studied the coverage of numerous academic information databases, and the comprehensiveness of information is also an important indicator in evaluating an information retrieval system.

2.2   Semantic Similarity-Based Recommendation

The Semantic similarity-based recommendation system is to learn the text feature representation of users or items by some algorithms or models. And then calculate their semantic similarity, taking the user or item with the highest similarity as the recommendation result. Huang et al. [10] proposed a new deep latent semantic model that map queries and documents into a shared low-dimensional space, allowing easy computation of document relevance to a given query based on their distance. Shen et al. [20] proposed latent semantic model integrates a convolutional-pooling structure over word sequences to acquire low-dimensional, semantic vector representations for search queries and Web documents. Elkahky et al. [6] designed a content-based recommendation system that addresses both recommendation quality and system scalability.

The advent of BERT [4] has brought a dramatic change to this task. The advantages of pre-trained language models are obvious. Devlin et al. proposed BERT, which is a pre-trained transformer [26] network and set a new state-of-the-art performance on the Semantic Textual Semilarity (STS) benchmark [2]. It is a good choice to use it in a semantic similarity-based recommendation system. However, a significant drawback of the BERT network structure lies in its inability to independently compute sentence embedding, posing challenges when deriving sentence embedding from BERT. To overcome these limitations, researchers have devised methods [17,18,30] to address this issue by passing individual sentences through BERT and subsequently deriving a fixed-sized vector. This can be achieved through techniques such as averaging the outputs or utilizing the output of the special CLS token. Reimers et al. [19] used the pre-trained BERT and RoBERTa [15] network and only fine-tune it to yield useful sentence embedding. We attempts to introduce SBERT into our scholar recommendation service with scholars' profiles.

3   Scholar Think Tank System

Searching on a trusted data platform can yield more relevant results when searching for information about scholars and academic information. As mentioned in Sect. 1, finding such information in academic social networks is difficult due to the increase in unreal information. In addition, results are limited when we use only

Fig. 1. The home page of Scholar Think Tank System.

one platform with a tiny data source. To deal with these problems, we propose a Scholar Think Tank System. The home page of the system is shown in Fig. 1. Based on the massive amount of real scholarly information from SCHOLAT, we regularly synchronize high-value scholars to ensure the authenticity and real-time of our information. We will continuously collect publicly available information online to further solve the problem of insufficient data coverage. We also provide a scholar recommendation service. Specifically, we measure the similarity among scholars in the semantic space. We calculate the similarity between scholars by extracting the textual features from their profiles. Scholars with high similarity will be recommended to users.

Fig. 2. The information of scholar in Scholar Think Tank System.

The architecture of our system is shown in Fig. 3. At first, in order to collect scholarly information, we used SCHOLAT's database and publicly available information online as the data source. For SCHOLAT, we devise a data synchronization algorithm. We process publicly available information through crawlers or manual entry. And then, we use scholars' profiles as input to the pre-training model SBERT and get the sentence embedding as the representation of the scholars. The similarity between scholars is obtained by calculating the cosine similarity between sentence embedding. The similarity is a basis for the recommendation. Finally, we put the scholars' profiles and recommendation results into the online application. We will introduce the details in the remaining parts of the section.

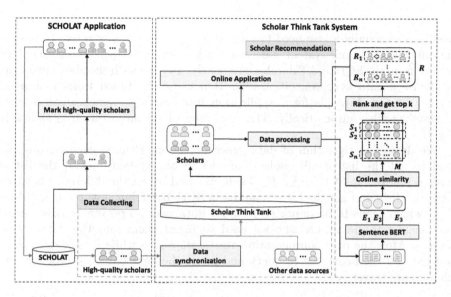

Fig. 3. The architecture of Scholar Think Tank System. Collecting data from SCHOLAT and the Internet. With the help of the collected data, SBERT was used to obtain the scholars' representations and calculate the cosine similarity between scholars. Finally, ranking and recommendation are based on similarity.

3.1   Data Collecting

The first work that needs to be finished is data collection, which we summarize in two ways: collecting from SCHOLAT and collecting online.

Collecting from SCHOLAT. Although SCHOLAT is an academic social network, it attracts many non-scholar users. It has accumulated many users and is an essential data source for our system. However, to ensure the quality of scholarly information in our system, we will not import all users into our database. We manually mark high-quality users and import them into Scholar Think Tank System.

We will mark high-quality users from time to time. These newly marked scholars will be synced to our database. Also, marked scholars may update their

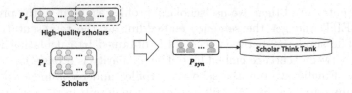

Fig. 4. Synchronizing Data from SCHOLAT.

profiles occasionally, so we need to remind our system administrators to update the information in our system. Therefore, it is essential to synchronize scholars' profiles from the SCHOLAT database regularly. To cope with the above problem, we devise a data synchronization algorithm using the timed tasks module of Spring Boot, a Java platform application framework, to synchronize marked scholars' profiles automatically. The brief step of synchronization is shown in Fig. 4.

We devise an algorithm of data synchronization. Before synchronizing, we need to get the list of all scholars' profiles in our system P_t and the list of marked scholars in SCHOLAT P_s. Then, we need to get the difference between these two lists and get the list of marked in SCHOLAT but not in our database P_{syn}, which needs to be imported into our database. To prevent synchronizing too much data simultaneously, we need to insert them into the database in batches. After the insertion operation starts, we wait a while for the data to be inserted and then continue to query and insert the next batch of data until all scholars are traversed.

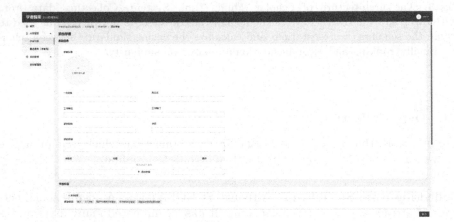

Fig. 5. The add scholar function in the management system.

Collecting Online. Collecting online. We will search for scholars from the official websites of universities or research institutions. Generally, these sites are rich in information about scholars, so we use this as one of the data sources for our system. The data in SCHOLAT is structured data, which is also stored in the structured database. Therefore, we could copy these structured data to our system. Instead of importing from the database, we provide a management system for the administrator to manage our data. The administrator can add scholarly information through the management system. The add scholar function in the management system is shown in Fig. 5.

During the entry process, some fields are required, while others can be optional. The details of the fields are shown in Table 1. In addition to these fields, we provide a way to fill in custom fields. For example, a scholar provides a work email address, but we do not provide a field for the email address. At this point, we can add the email for this scholar using a custom field. The custom field is stored with a JSON structure. It is displayed the same way as the other fields, and the users will not see any difference.

In addition, we also record the websites from which this information originates, as appropriate. Users can see the source of information on the scholar's personal home page, which further ensures the authenticity of our information. We will also try to record the scholars' study and work experiences. This information will not necessarily be shown to users, but we can produce more exciting work by recording this information for backup, perhaps.

Table 1. Fields to be collected.

Field	Data type	Required	Example
avatar url	String	False	/
Chinese name	String	True	/
English name	String	False	/
work unit	String	False	/
work apartment	String	False	/
title	String	False	Professor, Associate professor
degree	String	False	Bachelor, Master, PhD
custom field	JSON	False	/

These two ways of data collecting focus on different angles of our data management. They complement each other and can build a more comprehensive database of scholarly information. Our system currently includes more than 1,300 high-quality scholars, most of whom are from SCHOLAT. These scholars cover a wide range of disciplines and come from a variety of research institutions. The following section will introduce how to use them to build scholar recommendation service.

3.2   Scholar Recommendation

One of the essential functions of our system is to recommend scholars for users. The idea is that if a user browses a scholar, then he will be interested in the same workplace or similar research interests of that scholar. In order to obtain better recommendation results, we use the information of scholars' research fields and work units as the recommendation basis, combine with the SBERT model to obtain fixed-size embedding $E = \{E_1, E_2, ..., E_n\}$ of the information text about scholars, and then calculate the cosine similarity between these embedding.

Fig. 6. The recommendation result for the scholar in Fig. 2. His research interests of are data intelligence, social network computing, educational big data and knowledge graph for scholars

For any two scholars' representation p_u and p_v, we have:

$$s_{uv} = sim\left(E_u, E_v\right) = \frac{\sum_{i=1}^{n}\left(e_{u_i} \cdot e_{v_i}\right)}{\sqrt{\sum_{i=1}^{n}\left(e_{u_i}\right)^2} \cdot \sqrt{\sum_{i=1}^{n}\left(e_{v_i}\right)^2}} \tag{1}$$

The output s_{uv} is the similarity of the two scholars. Furthermore, we use this similarity as a basis for scholar recommendation, prioritizing recommending scholars with high similarity to a scholar when the user browses the information of that scholar. With such a recommendation, we can provide more personalized recommendation services to users, which will help them find scholars they are interested in Scholar recommendation is based on the calculation of SBERT sentence embedding cosine similarity, which also needs to consider the real-time recommendation and scholars' update, so the primary process of this module is divided into two stages: offline calculation and incremental update.

Offline Calculation. Firstly, we preprocess the scholars' profiles, retaining only the three information of scholar id, research field, and work unit, and using the research field and work unit as the scholars' feature texts. Then we use the pre-training model SBERT to calculate the sentence embedding of each scholar feature text and then calculate the similarity between scholars by the Eq. 1. At this time, we can get a similarity matrix M, for the scholar u and the scholar v, we have:

$$m_{uv} = s_{uv}, m_{uv} \in M$$

According to the similarity matrix M, for scholar u, we can get a list S_u of similarities about scholar u:

$$S_u = \{s_{u1}, s_{u2}, ..., s_{un}\}$$

Finally, the similarities between scholars are ranked, and the top k scholars with the most similarity to each scholar are taken as the final recommendation results. We can get the recommendation results R_u for the scholar u:

$$R_u = \{r_{u_1}, r_{u_2}, ..., r_{u_k}\}$$
$$r_{u_k} = \{n, s_{uk}\} \tag{2}$$

Suppose there are five scholars with high similarity to scholar u, and the k is their index are $[1, 3, 5, 7, 9]$. Then r_u can be expressed explicitly as:

$$R_u = \{\{1, s_{u1}\}, \{3, s_{u3}\}, \{5, s_{u5}\}, \{7, s_{u7}\}, \{9, s_{u9}\}\}$$

If the user visits the scholar u's profile, we will recommend scholars in r_u to the user. The results of the offline calculation need to be saved for the next incremental update part. There are two results that must be stored, which are E and R.

Incremental Update. New scholars are constantly added to our system, and new scholars do not exist in the current recommendation results. The system neither recommends similar scholars for new scholars nor recommends new scholars until the similarity is recalculated. For this reason, we devise an incremental update module, which only calculates similarity for new scholars and does not recalculate it among existing scholars. Our approach is more efficient than the full update and saves computational resources.

When new scholars are joined, we use SBERT to compute their embedding E^n. Then we load the previous scholars' embedding E^h and combine the newly computed embedding to obtain a full embedding E^f. We need to compute the similarity S^n between the new scholars and the current full scholars using Eq. 1. For each newly joined scholar, we can get their recommendation results based on

---

Algorithm 1. Incremental Update for Scholar Recommendation

Input: newly joined scholars' embedding $E^n = \{E_1^n, E_2^n, ..., E_n^n\}$, previous scholars' embedding $E^p = \{E_1^p, E_2^p, ..., E_n^p\}$, previous recommendation results $R^p =$
   $\{R_1^p, R_2^p, ..., R_n^p\}$.
Output: full scholars' embedding E^f, full recommendation results R^f
1: $E^f \leftarrow E^n + E^p$
2: $M^n \leftarrow \text{Sim}(E^n, E^f)$
3: **for** all u in newly joined scholars **do**
4:     $S_u^n \leftarrow \text{GetTopK}(S_u^n), S_u^n \in M^n$
5:     $R_u^n \leftarrow \{\{1, s_{u1}^n\}, \{2, s_{u2}^n\}, ..., \{k, s_{uk}^n\}\}, R_u^n \in R^n$
6: **end for**
7: **for** all v in previous scholars **do**
8:     $S_v^p \leftarrow \text{GetSimFromRec}(R_v^p)$
9:     $r_{v_n}^p \leftarrow \{n, \text{GetTopK}(S_v^p + S_v^n)\}, r_v^p \in R_v^p$
10: **end for**
11: $R^f \leftarrow R^p + R^n$
12: **return** E^f, R^f

---

the newly computed similarity. We get recommendation results for the additional
scholars, and we just need to calculate it according to Eq. 2.

Now we load the previous recommendation results R^h. For scholars v that
already existed in the database, after adding new scholars, there may be new
scholars that are more similar to the original scholars v. We need to update the
recommendation results. For each previous scholar, we can get the corresponding similarity from the previous recommendation results. We merge the newly
calculated similarities with the previous similarities and reorder them to take
the top ones. Then we get the updated recommendation results.

Then we merge the new recommendation result R^n with R^h. Finally, we get
a full recommendation result R^f. Similarly, two results must be stored for the
next incremental update: E^f and R^f.

The recommendation for scholar is shown in Fig. 6. The research interests of
the scholars in Fig. 2 are data intelligence, social network computing, educational
big data and knowledge graph for scholars. From the recommendation results,
their research directions are relatively related, mainly focusing on social networks
and big data. Clicking on a scholar will take users to their personal page, where
users can view the scholar's details. The recommendation algorithm comprehensively considers the available information about scholars without information
about their social networks.

4   Conclusion

In this paper, we propose a Scholar Think Tank System that could provide high-
quality and reliable scholarly information for users. Its data comes from the
academic social network SCHOLAT and Internet public information. Users can
retrieve much more information about scholars that is useful to them through our

system, reducing the time they spend on gathering information. For the database of SCHOLAT, we implement a data synchronization algorithm that helps ensure real-time system performance. In addition, we offer a scholar recommendation service based on the pre-training language model SBERT, which can better help users find scholars of interest and related academic information. Moreover, our incremental update algorithm effectively reduces the amount of computation. In future work, we will include more scholars in our system to build a comprehensive scholar network to support more research and applications.

Acknowledgements. This work was supported by National Natural Science Foundation of China No. U1811263.

References

1. Bastopcu, M., Ulukus, S.: Who should google scholar update more often? In: IEEE INFOCOM 2020-IEEE Conference on Computer Communications Workshops (INFOCOM WKSHPS), pp. 696–701. IEEE (2020)
2. Cer, D., Diab, M., Agirre, E., Lopez-Gazpio, I., Specia, L.: SemEval-2017 task 1: semantic textual similarity-multilingual and cross-lingual focused evaluation. arXiv preprint arXiv:1708.00055 (2017)
3. Chen, Y., Ding, C., Hu, J., Chen, R., Hui, P., Fu, X.: Building and analyzing a global co-authorship network using google scholar data. In: Proceedings of the 26th International Conference on World Wide Web Companion, pp. 1219–1224 (2017)
4. Devlin, J., Chang, M.W., Lee, K., Toutanova, K.: BERT: pre-training of deep bidirectional transformers for language understanding. arXiv preprint arXiv:1810.04805 (2018)
5. Dong, L., et al.: Unified language model pre-training for natural language understanding and generation. In: Advances in Neural Information Processing Systems, vol. 32 (2019)
6. Elkahky, A.M., Song, Y., He, X.: A multi-view deep learning approach for cross domain user modeling in recommendation systems. In: Proceedings of the 24th International Conference on World Wide Web, pp. 278–288 (2015)
7. Fan, W., Derr, T., Ma, Y., Wang, J., Tang, J., Li, Q.: Deep adversarial social recommendation. arXiv preprint arXiv:1905.13160 (2019)
8. Fan, W., et al.: Graph neural networks for social recommendation. In: The World Wide Web Conference, pp. 417–426 (2019)
9. Fan, W., Ma, Y., Yin, D., Wang, J., Tang, J., Li, Q.: Deep social collaborative filtering. In: Proceedings of the 13th ACM Conference on Recommender Systems, pp. 305–313 (2019)
10. Huang, P.S., He, X., Gao, J., Deng, L., Acero, A., Heck, L.: Learning deep structured semantic models for web search using clickthrough data. In: Proceedings of the 22nd ACM International Conference on Information & Knowledge Management, pp. 2333–2338 (2013)
11. Jamali, M., Ester, M.: A matrix factorization technique with trust propagation for recommendation in social networks. In: Proceedings of the fourth ACM Conference on Recommender Systems, pp. 135–142 (2010)
12. Joshi, M., Chen, D., Liu, Y., Weld, D.S., Zettlemoyer, L., Levy, O.: SpanBERT: improving pre-training by representing and predicting spans. Trans. Assoc. Comput. Linguist. **8**, 64–77 (2020)

13. Lan, Z., Chen, M., Goodman, S., Gimpel, K., Sharma, P., Soricut, R.: ALBERT: a lite BERT for self-supervised learning of language representations. arXiv preprint arXiv:1909.11942 (2019)

14. Liu, J., Ren, J., Zheng, W., Chi, L., Lee, I., Xia, F.: Web of scholars: a scholar knowledge graph. In: Proceedings of the 43rd International ACM SIGIR Conference on Research and Development in Information Retrieval, pp. 2153–2156 (2020)

15. Liu, Y., et al.: RoBERTa: a robustly optimized BERT pretraining approach. arXiv preprint arXiv:1907.11692 (2019)

16. Lopes, G.R., Moro, M.M., Wives, L.K., de Oliveira, J.P.M.: Collaboration recommendation on academic social networks. In: Trujillo, J., Dobbie, G., Kangassalo, H., Hartmann, S., Kirchberg, M., Rossi, M., Reinhartz-Berger, I., Zimányi, E., Frasincar, F. (eds.) ER 2010. LNCS, vol. 6413, pp. 190–199. Springer, Heidelberg (2010). https://doi.org/10.1007/978-3-642-16385-2_24

17. May, C., Wang, A., Bordia, S., Bowman, S.R., Rudinger, R.: On measuring social biases in sentence encoders. arXiv preprint arXiv:1903.10561 (2019)

18. Qiao, Y., Xiong, C., Liu, Z., Liu, Z.: Understanding the behaviors of BERT in ranking. arXiv preprint arXiv:1904.07531 (2019)

19. Reimers, N., Gurevych, I.: Sentence-BERT: sentence embeddings using Siamese BERT-networks. arXiv preprint arXiv:1908.10084 (2019)

20. Shen, Y., He, X., Gao, J., Deng, L., Mesnil, G.: A latent semantic model with convolutional-pooling structure for information retrieval. In: Proceedings of the 23rd ACM International Conference on Conference on Information and Knowledge Management, pp. 101–110 (2014)

21. Song, K., Tan, X., Qin, T., Lu, J., Liu, T.Y.: MASS: masked sequence to sequence pre-training for language generation. arXiv preprint arXiv:1905.02450 (2019)

22. Tang, F., Zhu, J., He, C., Fu, C., He, J., Tang, Y.: SCHOLAT: an innovative academic information service platform. In: Cheema, M.A., Zhang, W., Chang, L. (eds.) ADC 2016. LNCS, vol. 9877, pp. 453–456. Springer, Cham (2016). https://doi.org/10.1007/978-3-319-46922-5_38

23. Tang, J., Zhang, J., Yao, L., Li, J., Zhang, L., Su, Z.: ArnetMiner: extraction and mining of academic social networks. In: Proceedings of the 14th ACM SIGKDD International Conference on Knowledge Discovery and Data Mining, pp. 990–998 (2008)

24. Tang, J., Hu, X., Liu, H.: Social recommendation: a review. Soc. Netw. Anal. Min. **3**, 1113–1133 (2013)

25. Thelwall, M., Kousha, K.: ResearchGate articles: age, discipline, audience size, and impact. J. Am. Soc. Inf. Sci. **68**(2), 468–479 (2017)

26. Vaswani, A., et al.: Attention is all you need. In: Advances in Neural Information Processing Systems, vol. 30 (2017)

27. Walters, W.H.: Google scholar coverage of a multidisciplinary field. Inf. Process. Manage. **43**(4), 1121–1132 (2007)

28. Yan, W., Zhang, Y., Hu, T., Kudva, S.: How does scholarly use of academic social networking sites differ by academic discipline? A case study using researchgate. Inf. Process. Manage. **58**(1), 102430 (2021)

29. Yang, Z., Dai, Z., Yang, Y., Carbonell, J., Salakhutdinov, R.R., Le, Q.V.: XLNet: Generalized autoregressive pretraining for language understanding. In: Advances in Neural Information Processing Systems, vol. 32 (2019)

30. Zhang, T., Kishore, V., Wu, F., Weinberger, K.Q., Artzi, Y.: BERTScore: evaluating text generation with bert. arXiv preprint arXiv:1904.09675 (2019)

DAG-Based Task Scheduling Optimization in Heterogeneous Distributed Systems

Chen Chen[1] and Jie Zhu[1,2]([✉])

[1] Nanjing University of Posts and Telecommunications, Nanjing 210003, China
{1221045528,zhujie}@njupt.edu.cn
[2] State Key Laboratory Chinese of Computer Architecture, Institute of Computing Technology, Academy of Sciences, Beijing 100864, China

Abstract. The scheduling of tasks with limited resources in cloud computing systems has been a popular research topic. One approach to addressing this problem is to employ dynamic voltage and frequency scaling (DVFS) techniques to further constrain energy consumption. In this paper, we investigate the scheduling of directed acyclic graph (DAG) tasks in heterogeneous distributed systems while considering both resource and energy constraints. We aim to decrease the duration required for task scheduling. To accomplish this, we propose a task scheduling framework that takes into account energy constraints, which provides an initial solution at the start. Additionally, we introduce a heuristic, the firefly algorithm, to further enhance the initial solution. Finally, we conduct experiments with various settings and parameters, and the experimental statistics demonstrate our suggested method exhibits a performance gain that is at least twice as significant as that of other benchmark algorithms.

Keywords: directed acyclic graph · heterogeneous distributed systems · task scheduling optimization framework · firefly algorithm

1 Introduction

As the scope of computer applications continues to expand, traditional single-core computer system are inadequate for meeting the increasingly growing computational and resource demands. The properties of heterogeneous distributed systems address, to some extent, the problems and challenges of computer system performance. The evolution from single-core systems to distributed computing systems has shown that as the number of processors or cores increases, there is a greater increase in performance while maintaining energy efficiency [3]. However, the increasing number of computing and data-intensive tasks has greatly increased the system's energy consumption. High energy consumption brings problems such as high temperatures, electromagnetic interference, environmental degradation, and global economy, which are important obstacles to the sustainable progress and development of computer systems [16]. Therefore, the issue of how to reduce energy consumption is of particular relevance. In the commonly employed techniques for reducing system energy consumption, dynamic voltage and frequency scaling (DVFS) stands out as one of the most prevalent methods [11]. The primary concept for conserving energy is to dynamically tune the clock frequency and voltage in order to achieve a balance between energy cost and effectiveness.

The energy consumption research of heterogeneous computer systems primarily encompasses two types: one aims to achieve minimum energy consumption while meeting some performance indicators, and the other is to achieve maximum or minimum of some indicators under energy consumption constraints, such as time and reliability. Our research topic belongs to the second type, which is to minimize task scheduling length under energy consumption constraints. In recent years, there have been many similar researches, and they all share the common feature of preallocating the energy consumption of each task to meet the energy consumption limit of the entire application. Among them, Xiao et al. [13] proposed the minimum scheduling length for energy-constrained computing (MSLECC) algorithm, which allocates the minimum energy consumption for each task. However, because energy is allocated to high-priority tasks first, low-priority tasks receive very little energy, so they choose low-power processors and lower frequencies, which leads to an increase in the overall scheduling length of the application. Based on this problem, researchers have proposed the independent set-based allocation for energy-constrained computing (ISAECC) algorithm in [9], which allocates energy based on the energy weight of each task, thereby avoiding some of the shortcomings of the MSLECC algorithm. These two algorithms are heuristics. In this paper, we propose neighborhood search algorithms to further optimize these heuristics. Specifically, we use a metaheuristic algorithm, the firefly algorithm, to iteratively search the solution space to obtain the optimal scheduling length, randomly selecting the firefly's movement direction using the roulette algorithm during the iteration process, and constantly interfering with the sequence of the temporary optimal solution to avoid getting trapped in a local optimal solution. Our application program is described by a directed acyclic graph (DAG) and includes multiple sub-tasks. Task scheduling based on DAG poses an exceptionally challenging problem as it is classified as an NP-hard problem [5].

The main contributions of this paper include: (1) Based on the ISAECC algorithm, we propose a method that uses the firefly algorithm to iteratively explore the solution domain to obtain the optimal scheduling length, while using the roulette algorithm to randomly select the firefly's movement direction during the iteration process and constantly interfering with the position of the optimal firefly to avoid falling into a local optimal solution. (2) We propose an energy-constrained task scheduling framework that obtains the shortest task scheduling length by optimizing the initial solution under certain energy constraints. (3) We use actual parallel applications to evaluate our algorithm, and the experimental results show that our algorithm has superior performance.

This paper is structured as follows. The related work is discussed in Sect. 2. The problem under consideration is formulated in Sect. 3. Section 4 introduces an task scheduling optimazation framework and an improved algorithm based on the firefly algorithm. Section 5 present and evaluate the experimental results, while Sect. 6 concludes the findings.

2   Related Work

The concept of energy-efficient design methodologies utilizing Dynamic Voltage and Frequency Scaling (DVFS) was initially introduced in the publication [12]. Subsequently, a multitude of studies have been undertaken to enhance energy efficiency within this framework. In [6], the authors partitioned the scheduling issue into three sub issues concerning precedence constraints, task scheduling, and power supply. They then presented a method for achieving energy-efficient scheduling of sequential tasks with precedence constraints in multi-processor systems. In [8], the authors proposed a hierarchical task scheduling algorithm which uses a two-level allocation strategy for time, energy, and power. Additionally, [7] proposed a list scheduling algorithm for task scheduling and a list placement algorithm for speed determination. The objective of all these research was to address the challenge of minimizing the scheduling length while considering energy limits, or minimizing energy consumption while considering scheduling time constraints. However, these studies primarily focused on homogeneous systems with data center networks or shared memory, which differ from the heterogeneous systems examined in this paper. There have been several studies related to energy savings in heterogeneous system environments. Some studies use the method of reclaiming slack time between tasks. For instance, [18] used a global slack reclamation approach that enables tasks to be transferred to slacks in other processors to achieve minimum energy consumption per processor. The authors also implemented an energy-efficient scheduling algorithm by combining global DVFS and non-DVFS. Another important energy-saving technique is processor merging, which achieves energy savings by powering down certain specific processors. In order to reduce the amount of energy used by several real-time processes on a cyber-physical system, [17] proposed a global energy-efficient algorithm for multiple processes and a method for combining processors based on deadlines. Moreover, [2] proposed a bifurcated energy-efficient scheduling algorithm, which reduces static energy consumption by opening the most energy-efficient processor through the idea of bifurcation, and reduces dynamic energy consumption with DFVS. All of these algorithms aim to obtain the minimum energy consumption under certain metric constraints, which is the opposite of what we are studying in this paper.

The strategy of energy preallocation was first applied in reference [13], where the core idea was to preallocate the remaining energy to tasks that are not scheduled to processors according to a certain ratio while passing the energy consumption constraint of the whole application to each task. Nevertheless, in [13] the author pre-assign the minimum energy consumption for each task, which is pessimistic and affects the energy consumption allocation of low-priority tasks, resulting in unfairness for low-priority tasks. As a result, subsequent studies improved the preallocation strategy. For example, [10] used the average energy preallocation technique to distribute the remaining energy equally. [4] used a timely preallocation technique based on [10]. Additionally, [9] employed a weighted energy preallocation technique, which preallocates according to the decision of the average energy consumption of each task. The authors [14] introduced a rate-based energy preallocation technique designed for customising individual task. Moreover, [3] suggested a way to categorize the assignment of weights according to task levels. While these works use models similar to ours, they employ different preallocation methods. Their algorithms are heuristic algorithms that efficiently generate feasible solutions within reasonable time and space constraints, but they do not guarantee optimum solutions or quantify the divergence from optimality and therefore have significant limitations. In contrast, our work employs a meta-heuristic algorithm-based method for searching the optimal task ordering and proposes a method for task execution frequency adjustment to help mitigate the adverse consequences of becoming trapped in local optima.

3   Problem Description

This paper focuses on three main subjects: the application model, energy model, and execution model. The primary elements defined in the application model are the mapping relationships between tasks and processors, as well as the transfer and reliance relationships between tasks. The energy model aims to ascertain the total energy consumption of the application system. The execution model outlines the limitations and objectives for optimizing issues, and it defines the execution plan as a five-tuple.

3.1   Application Model

Suppose there are m processors in the system, which can be denoted as the set $\mathbb{P} = \{p_i | i = 1, \ldots, m\}$. The processors are utilized for task processing, with each processor possessing a distinct processing capacity. The application is depicted by a directed acyclic graph (DAG) $G = <\mathbb{T}, \mathbb{W}, \mathbb{E}, \mathbb{C}>$ as illustrated in Fig. 1. The symbol $\mathbb{T}$ denotes the collection of nodes in graph G, with each node representing a task. Let's assume that the application has n tasks which is denoted as $\mathbb{T} = \{t_i | i = 1, \ldots, n\}$. We have a matrix $\mathbb{W}$ with dimensions $|\mathbb{T}| \times |\mathbb{P}|$, where $w_{i,j} \in \mathbb{W}$ indicates the execution time of task t_i on processor p_j at the maximum frequency. $\mathbb{E}$ denotes the collection of edges connecting two nodes in G. Each edge $e_{i,j} \in \mathbb{E}$ symbolizes the dependency connection between task t_i and task t_j. The symbol $\mathbb{C}$ denotes the collection of communication times for each edge. Here, $c_{i,j} \in \mathbb{C}$ indicates the communication time from task t_i to task t_j for the edge $e_{i,j}$. When two tasks are allocated to the same processor, there is no time spent on communication between them. The collection of direct predecessor tasks for each task can be denoted as $pred(t_i)$ and defined as $\{t_{i'} | <t_{i'}, t_i> \in \mathbb{E}\}$. The collection of direct successor tasks can be denoted as $succ(t_i)$ and defined as $\{t_{i'} | <t_i, t_{i'}> \in \mathbb{E}\}$. The application consists of a single entry task, denoted as t_{entry}, and a single exit task, denoted as t_{exit}. The entry task has no direct predecessor tasks, i.e., $pred(t_{entry}) = \emptyset$. The exit task has no direct successor tasks, i.e., $succ(t_{exit}) = \emptyset$.

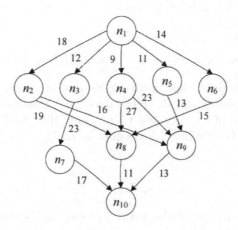

Fig. 1. An example of a Directed Acyclic Graph (DAG)-based application

3.2   Energy Model

The power model described in Quan's study [9] is utilized to assess the energy consumption of processors. The processors can function at varying frequency. The power consumption of processor p_j at frequency f_j is calculated using Eq. (1).

$$P(p_j, f_j) = \rho_j + cp_j \times f_j^{\varepsilon_j} \tag{1}$$

The variables ρ_j, cp_j, and ε_j represent frequency-independent power consumption, effective capacitance parameter, and dynamic power exponent, respectively. The processor v_j can have its frequency f_j adjusted within the range of f_j^{min} to f_j^{max}. It is crucial to acknowledge that although DVFS might decrease energy consumption, it results in longer completion times for the application when operating at lower frequencies. Therefore, low frequencies may not consistently provide the most optimal choice for energy conservation at the system level. Therefore, f_j^{min} must satisfy $f_j^{min} \geq \varepsilon_j \times \sqrt{\frac{\rho_j}{(\varepsilon_j-1) \times c_j}}$ as stated in [15].

Equation (2) may be employed to compute the energy consumption of the processor for a given task at a particular frequency, where $w_{i,j}$ represents the execution time of task t_i on processor v_j at its highest frequency.

$$E(t_i, p_j, f_j) = P(p_j, f_j) \times w_{i,j} \times \frac{f_j^{max}}{f_j} \tag{2}$$

3.3 Execution Model

In order to make the problem description more concise, we may represent the allocation of a task t_i as a tuple $<s_{i,j}, e_{i,j}, p_{i,j}, f_{i,j}, w_{i,j,f_{i,j}}>$. $s_{i,j}$ and $e_{i,j}$ represent the earliest start time and earliest end time of task t_i on processor $p_{i,j}$, respectively. $p_{i,j}$ represents the assignment of task t_i to processor p_j, $f_{i,j}$ represents the frequency at which p_j occurs during the processing of t_i, whereas $w_{i,j,f_{i,j}}$ reflects the time it takes to process task t_i on $p_{i,j}$ at frequency $f_{i,j}$. $s_{i,j}$ can be defined by Eq. (3).

$$s_{i,j} = \max\left\{ \text{available}[m], \max_{t_{i'} \in \text{pre}(t_i)} \left\{ aft(t_{i'}) + c'_{i',i} \right\} \right\} \tag{3}$$

where available$[m]$ is the earliest available time of processor p_m, $aft(t_{i'})$ is the actual end time of task $t_{i'}$ and $c'_{i',i}$ represents the communication time between $t_{i'}$ and t_i. The value of $c'_{i',i}$ is equal to $c_{i',i}$ only if $t_{i'}$ and t_i are allocated to distinct processors. Otherwise, $c'_{i',i}$ is equal to 0. Then, $e_{i,j}$ can be defined by Eq. (4).

$$e_{i,j} = s_i + w_{i,j} \times \frac{f_{i,j}^{max}}{f_{i,j}} \tag{4}$$

The scheduling scheme of the entire system can be represented by a set $S = \{a_i | i = 1, \ldots, m\}$, where s_i represents the scheduling arrangement of task t_i. To achieve a feasible scheduling scheme, the following constraints must be satisfied:

(1) Precedence constraint: A task can commence execution only after all of its predecessor tasks have completed and their data has been transmitted to the task. The constraint can be expressed using Eq. (5).
(2) No overlap constraint: The duration of two tasks being processed on the same processor cannot overlap, meaning that a processor cannot handle two tasks at the same time. We can express this condition of non-overlapping constraints using Eq. (6).
(3) Energy consumption constraint: The overall energy consumption of the application must not above a specific threshold $E_{given}(G)$. The constraint can be expressed using Eq. (7).

$$s_{i,j} \geq \max\{e_{i',j'} + c_{i',i} | t_{i'} \in pred(t_i)\}, \forall t_i \in \mathbb{T} \tag{5}$$

$$min\{e_{i,j}, e_{i',j}\} \leq max\{s_{i,j}, s_{i',j}\}, \forall t_i, t_{i'} \in \mathbb{T} \tag{6}$$

$$\sum_{a_i \in S} E(t_i, p_{i,j}, f_{i,j}) \leq E_{given}(G) \tag{7}$$

The primary goal of this challenge is to reduce the total time it takes to complete the full application, which is sometimes referred to as the makespan. The total duration of the whole application may be computed using Eq. (8).

$$C_{max}(S) = \max\{e_i | a_i \in S\} \tag{8}$$

4   Proposed Methods

This study introduces the firefly algorithm (FA) as a solution to our task scheduling challenge. Our algorithm is called FA-based energy-constrained task scheduling (FETS) algorithm. At the same time, we have designed an algorithm framework called firefly-based task scheduling optimization framework (FTSOF) as shown in Algorithm 1, and our algorithm works within this framework.

Algorithm 1: Firefly-based task scheduling optimization framework (FTSOF)

---

1 Apply the *Variable Initialization Methodology* to compute variables associated with energy.
2 Apply the *Generating Viable Solutions Methodology* to create a schedule S that is possible to implement.
3 Apply the *Solution Enhancement Methodology* to enhance S and achieve the local optimal solution S^*.
4 **return** S^*.

This framework mainly consists of three constituent components, which will be detailedly introduced in the following text.

The energy consumption range of task t_i, represented by $E_{min}(t_i)$ and $E_{max}(t_i)$, may be calculated by evaluating the energy consumption of the task at various processors and frequencies using Eq. (9) and (10).

$$E_{min}(t_i) = \min\{E(t_i, p_j, f_j)|p_j \in \mathbb{P}, f_j \in [f_j^{min}, f_j^{max}]\} \qquad (9)$$

$$E_{max}(t_i) = \max\{E(t_i, p_j, f_j)|p_j \in \mathbb{P}, f_j \in [f_j^{min}, f_j^{max}]\} \qquad (10)$$

The average energy consumption of task t_i, represented as $E_{avg}(t_i)$, can be computed using Eq. (11).

$$E_{avg}(t_i) = \frac{E_{max}(t_i) + E_{min}(t_i)}{2} \qquad (11)$$

The application's minimal and maximum energy consumptions are represented as $E_{min}(G)$ and $E_{max}(G)$, respectively. These values may be computed using Eq. (12) and (13), respectively.

$$E_{min}(G) = \sum_{i=1,...,n} E_{min}(t_i) \qquad (12)$$

$$E_{max}(G) = \sum_{i=1,...,n} E_{max}(t_i) \qquad (13)$$

The average energy consumption of the application, represented as $E_{avg}(G)$, can be computed using Eq. (14).

$$E_{avg}(G) = \sum_{i=1,\ldots,n} E_{avg}(t_i) \tag{14}$$

This paper presents a strategy for assigning energy to individual tasks in advance, using the energy consumption ratio of the application as a basis. This strategy aims to mitigate the inequitable distribution of energy allocation to some degree. The pre-allocated energy of task t_i, represented as $E_{pre}(t_i)$, can be defined using Eq. (15).

$$E_{pre}(t_i) = \min\{E_{max}(t_i), (E_{max}(G) - E_{min}(G)) \times \frac{E_{avg(t_i)}}{E_{avg}(G)} + E_{min}(t_i)\} \tag{15}$$

The restriction on energy use $E_{given}(x_{[i]})$ for task $x_{[i]}$ in the provided task sequence $x = (x_{[1]}, \ldots, x_{[n]})$ may be specified using Eq. (16).

$$E_{given}(x_{[i]}) = E_{given}(G) - \sum_{x=1}^{i-1} E(x_{[i]}, p_{[i],j}, f_{[i],j}) - \sum_{y=i+1}^{n} E_{pre}(x_{[i]}) \tag{16}$$

Generating viable solutions methodology(GVSM) is similar to ISAECC algorithm to get the feasible solution of task sequence x_0. The FSGM is described by Algorithm 2.

The primary concept of this algorithm is to sequentially go through the task sequence, processors, and processor frequencies, consistently updating the earliest end time of the tasks while adhering to the energy limitations of the tasks, and then determining the ideal arrangement of the tasks.

(1) In Line 1, we initialize the tasks arrangement S to be empty.
(2) In Lines 2–4, we sequentially examine each task, initialize all the elements of the task arrangement, and compute the energy consumption restriction for the task.
(3) In Lines 5–13, we iterate through the processors and frequencies in order to identify the most efficient tasks schedule, which is then appended to S.
(4) In Line 14, we get the best solution for all tasks.

We suggest utilizing the firefly algorithm (FA) as a means to enhance the GVSM. The fundamental concept of the firefly algorithm is that each firefly will gravitate towards a firefly that emits a brighter light than itself. The firefly with the highest luminosity indicates the ideal solution. Consequently, the fireflies gradually converge to discover the optimal solution through iterative processes.

We use a roulette wheel strategy to move in the direction of movement, and the brightest firefly will make a random position movement after each iteration, which enhances the randomness and avoids the disadvantage of the firefly algorithm in entering the local optimum. The process of FA can be presented by Algorithm 3.

Algorithm 2: GVSM($x = (x_{[1]}, \ldots, x_{[n]})$)

---

1 $S \leftarrow \varnothing$;
2 **for** $x_{[i]} \in x$ **do**
3 $\quad$ $e^*_{[i],j} \leftarrow \infty$; $s^*_{[i],j} \leftarrow NULL$; $p^*_{[i],j} \leftarrow NULL$; $f^*_{[i],j} \leftarrow NULL$;
   $\quad$ $w^*_{[i],j,f_{[i],j}} \leftarrow NULL$;
4 $\quad$ Calculate $E_{given}(x_{[i]})$; // Eq. (16)
5 $\quad$ **for** $p_j \in \mathbb{P}$ **do**
6 $\quad\quad$ **for** $f_j \in [f_j^{min}, f_j^{max}]$ **do**
7 $\quad\quad\quad$ **if** $E(x_{[i]}, p_j, f_j) <= E_{given}(x_{[i]})$ **then**
8 $\quad\quad\quad\quad$ Calculate $s_{[i],j}$; // Eq. (3)
9 $\quad\quad\quad\quad$ Calculate $e_{[i],j}$; // Eq. (4)
10 $\quad\quad\quad\quad$ **if** $e_{[i],j} < e^*_{[i],j}$ **then**
11 $\quad\quad\quad\quad\quad$ $e^*_{[i],j} \leftarrow e_{[i],j}$; $s^*_{[i],j} \leftarrow s_{[i],j}$; $p^*_{[i],j} \leftarrow p_j$; $f^*_{[i],j} \leftarrow f_{[i],j}$;
   $\quad\quad\quad\quad\quad$ $w^*_{[i],j,f_{[i],j}} \leftarrow w_{[i],j,f_{[i],j}}$;
12 $\quad$ $a_{[i]} \leftarrow <s^*_{[i],j}, e^*_{[i],j}, v^*_{[i],j}, f^*_{[i],j}, w_{[i],j,f_{[i],j}}>$;
13 $\quad$ $S \leftarrow S \cup \{a_{[i]}\}$;
14 **return** S.

Algorithm 3: FA

---

1 Randomly generate n fireflies $F = \{x_i | i = 1, \ldots, n\}$;
2 Calculate Light intensity I_i at x_i calculated by $GVSM(x_i)$;
3 Determine light absorption cofficient γ;
4 $I_{max} = -\infty$;
5 $x_{max} = NULL$;
6 $S^* = NULL$;
7 **while** $t < MaxGeneration$ **do**
8 $\quad$ **for** $i=1$:n **do**
9 $\quad\quad$ **for** $j=1$:n **do**
10 $\quad\quad\quad$ **if** $I_i < I_j$ **then**
11 $\quad\quad\quad\quad$ Compute the attractiveness β_j with the distance r via $exp[-\gamma r]$
   $\quad\quad\quad\quad$ and record;
12 $\quad$ Select the firefly move to using the roulette method and move;
13 $\quad$ **if** $I_i > I_{max}$ **then**
14 $\quad\quad$ $I_{max} = I_i$; $x_{max} = x_i$; $S^* = FSGM(x_i)$;
15 $\quad$ Randomly change x_{max};
16 **return** S^*.

---

5 Experimental Evaluation

The methods presented and evaluated in this paper are implemented utilising the JAVA programming language and the IDEA 2019 integrated development environment. The tests are performed on a PC including an AMD Ryzen 7 5800H CPU working at a clock speed of 3.20 GHz, 16 gigabytes of RAM, and running on a 64-bit Windows 10 Home Edition.

We conducted a comparative analysis of our suggested method with the MSLECC method [13] and the ISAECC method [9], all of which have investigated the identical topic.

The settings of tasks and processors are generated arbitrarily from the specified ranges: $p_{i,j}^{max} \in [10, 100]$, $c_{i,i'} \in [10, 100]$, $\rho_j \in [0.03, 0.07]$, $c_j \in [0.8, 1.2]$, $\varepsilon_j \in [2.5, 3.0]$. The processor frequency is set with an accuracy of 0.01 Hz.

The DAGs is created by the use of a stochastic algorithm [1], with the task number n and the order strength (OS) serving as input variables. In order to accommodate DAGs that include many tasks at the beginning and end, we include a fictitious task at the beginning and another at the end of the DAG. These fictitious tasks have a processing time of 0. Furthermore, the FA is limited to a maximum of 100 iterations.

In order to assess the experimental findings, we employ the average relative percentage deviation (ARPD) metric, which is calculated using Eq. (17).

$$ARPD = \frac{C_{max}^{ALG}(S) - C_{max}^*(S)}{C_{max}^*(S)} \times 100 \tag{17}$$

Here, $C_{max}^*(S)$ denotes the optimal makespan achieved by all methods being compared, whereas $C_{max}^{ALG}(S)$ indicates the makespan achieved by the specific method being considered. A lower ARPD number signifies superior method effectiveness.

The threshold for the overall energy consumption of a arrangement, denoted as $E_{given}(G)$, is determined by evaluating Eq. (18).

$$E_{given}(G) = E_{min}(G) + \frac{\theta}{223} \times (E_{max}(G) - E_{min}(G)) \tag{18}$$

The integer energy factor θ is defined as follows: $[1, 222]$.

We evaluate four instance parameters: task size (n), number of processors (m), order strength (OS), and energy factor (θ). The value of n ranges from 10 to 50, m ranges from 2 to 10, OS ranges from 0.2 to 0.8, and θ ranges from 8 to 40. As a result, there are a total of 500 variations of testing cases. For every permutation, we employ a random process to create 5 test examples and evaluate 3 methods on each instance, yielding a cumulative of 7500 experimental outcomes.

The ARPD comparison of different methods with several instance parameters is presented detailed in Table 1. It is evident that FETS has superior average relative percentage differences (ARPDs) compared to all other methods, despite its higher execution time.

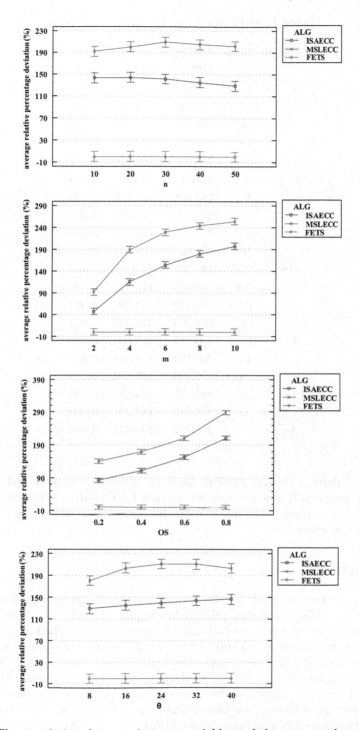

Fig. 2. The associations between instance variables and the contrasted approaches

Table 1. ARPD comparison of different methods

Param.	Value	ARPD(%)		
		MSLECC	ISAECC	FETS
n	10	191.672	143.258	0.000
	20	200.139	144.013	0.000
	30	208.952	141.505	0.000
	40	204.749	135.373	0.000
	50	201.708	129.225	0.000
m	2	92.641	47.522	0.000
	4	188.858	115.120	0.000
	6	228.774	154.040	0.000
	8	243.310	179.759	0.000
	10	253.637	196.932	0.000
OS	0.2	139.490	81.416	0.000
	0.4	168.543	110.878	0.000
	0.6	209.479	152.096	0.000
	0.8	288.263	210.309	0.000
θ	8	180.314	129.068	0.000
	16	203.183	135.364	0.000
	24	210.499	139.154	0.000
	32	210.189	143.556	0.000
	40	203.036	146.231	0.000
Avg.		201.022	145.641	0.000

Figure 2 depicts the associations between instance variables and the contrasted approaches. It is worth mentioning that FETS outperforms the ISAECC and MSLECC methods by a large margin and maintains stability under different instance parameters.

6   Conclusion

Our paper involves determining the optimal processor and operating frequency for each task, while considering priority constraints. To achieve our objective of minimizing the execution time of all tasks, we employ a task scheduling optimization framework known as FTSOF. The FTSOF involves determining a viable solution and calculating the energy-related parameter. Subsequently, the FETS method is employed to provide a solution that is locally optimal. We utilise the GVSM heuristic algorithm to generate the first tasks scheduling scheme. Through extensive testing, we have found that our approach consistently outperforms two more advanced algorithms, MSLECC and ISAECC, in various task scheduling circumstances.

Our paper specifically examines a static task scheduling problem in which all tasks are simultaneously received by the processor. However, in practical situations, tasks typically come one after another, and certain tasks may need to be addressed immediately because of time-sensitive limitations. Hence, as a component of our next endeavours, we want to investigate dynamic and preemptive task scheduling systems.

References

1. Demeulemeester, E., Vanhoucke, M., Herroelen, W.: RanGen: a random network generator for activity-on-the-node networks. J. Sched. **6**(1), 17–38 (2003). https://doi.org/10.1023/A:1022283403119
2. Gao, N., Xu, C., Peng, X., Luo, H., Wu, W., Xie, G.: Energy-efficient scheduling optimization for parallel applications on heterogeneous distributed systems. J. Circ. Syst. Comput. **29**(13), 2050203 (2020). https://doi.org/10.1142/S0218126620502035
3. Huang, K., Jing, M., Jiang, X., Chen, S., Liu, Z.: Task-level aware scheduling of energy-constrained applications on heterogeneous multi-core system. Electronics **9**(12), 2077 (2020). https://doi.org/10.3390/electronics9122077
4. Li, J., Xie, G., Li, K., Tang, Z.: Enhanced parallel application scheduling algorithm with energy consumption constraint in heterogeneous distributed systems. J. Circ. Syst. Comput. **28**(11), 1950190 (2019). https://doi.org/10.1142/S0218126619501901
5. Li, J., et al.: Multiobjective oriented task scheduling in heterogeneous mobile edge computing networks. IEEE Trans. Veh. Technol. **71**(8), 8955–8966 (2022). https://doi.org/10.1109/TVT.2022.3174906
6. Li, K.: Scheduling precedence constrained tasks with reduced processor energy on multiprocessor computers. IEEE Trans. Comput. **61**(12), 1668–1681 (2012). https://doi.org/10.1109/TC.2012.120
7. Li, K.: Energy and time constrained task scheduling on multiprocessor computers with discrete speed levels. J. Parallel Distrib. Comput. **95**, 15–28 (2016). https://doi.org/10.1016/j.jpdc.2016.02.006
8. Li, K.: Power and performance management for parallel computations in clouds and data centers. J. Comput. Syst. Sci. **82**(2), 174–190 (2016). https://doi.org/10.1016/j.jcss.2015.07.001
9. Quan, Z., Wang, Z.J., Ye, T., Guo, S.: Task scheduling for energy consumption constrained parallel applications on heterogeneous computing systems. IEEE Trans. Parallel Distrib. Syst. **31**(5), 1165–1182 (2019). https://doi.org/10.1109/TPDS.2019.2959533
10. Song, J., Xie, G., Li, R., Chen, X.: An efficient scheduling algorithm for energy consumption constrained parallel applications on heterogeneous distributed systems. In: 2017 IEEE International Symposium on Parallel and Distributed Processing with Applications and 2017 IEEE International Conference on Ubiquitous Computing and Communications (ISPA/IUCC), pp. 32–39 (2017). https://doi.org/10.1109/ISPA/IUCC.2017.00015
11. Tian, Z., Chen, L., Li, X., Feng, J., Xu, J.: Multi-core power management through deep reinforcement learning. In: 2021 IEEE International Symposium on Circuits and Systems (ISCAS), pp. 1–5. IEEE (2021)

12. Weiser, M., Welch, B., Demers, A., Shenker, S.: Scheduling for reduced CPU energy. In: Imielinski, T., Korth, H.F. (eds.) Mobile Computing. The Kluwer International Series in Engineering and Computer Science, vol. 353, pp. 449–471. Springer, Boston (1994). https://doi.org/10.1007/978-0-585-29603-6_17
13. Xiao, X., Xie, G., Li, R., Li, K.: Minimizing schedule length of energy consumption constrained parallel applications on heterogeneous distributed systems. In: 2016 IEEE Trustcom/BigDataSE/ISPA, pp. 1471–1476. IEEE (2016). https://doi.org/10.1109/TrustCom.2016.0230
14. Xie, G., Huang, J., Li, Y.L.R., Li, K.: System-level energy-aware design methodology towards end-to-end response time optimization. IEEE Trans. Comput.-Aided Design Integr. Circ. Syst. 1 (2019). https://doi.org/10.1109/TCAD.2019.2921350
15. Xie, G., Jiang, J., Liu, Y., Li, R., Li, K.: Minimizing energy consumption of real-time parallel applications using downward and upward approaches on heterogeneous systems. IEEE Trans. Industr. Inf. **13**(3), 1068–1078 (2017). https://doi.org/10.1109/TII.2017.2676183
16. Xie, G., Xiao, X., Peng, H., Li, R., Li, K.: A survey of low-energy parallel scheduling algorithms. IEEE Trans. Sustain. Comput. **7**(1), 27–46 (2021). https://doi.org/10.1109/TSUSC.2021.3057983
17. Xie, G., Zeng, G., Jiang, J., Fan, C., Li, R., Li, K.: Energy management for multiple real-time workflows on cyber-physical cloud systems. Futur. Gener. Comput. Syst. **105**, 916–931 (2020). https://doi.org/10.1016/j.future.2017.05.033
18. Xie, G., Zeng, G., Xiao, X., Li, R., Li, K.: Energy-efficient scheduling algorithms for real-time parallel applications on heterogeneous distributed embedded systems. IEEE Trans. Parallel Distrib. Syst. **28**(12), 3426–3442 (2017). https://doi.org/10.1109/TPDS.2017.2730876

A Distributed Cross-Layer Protocol for Sleep Scheduling and Data Aggregation in Wireless Sensor Networks

Zhenxiong Xia[✉] and Jingjing Li

College of Computer Science, South China Normal University, Guangzhou, China
2021023262@m.scnu.edu.cn

Abstract. We propose a Cross-layer Protocol for Sleep scheduling and Data aggregation (CPSD) in Wireless Sensor Networks (WSNs) to improve the performance in WSNs. Data aggregation and sleep scheduling have shown good performance in reducing energy consumption and improving network lifetime. A lot of past studies about sleep scheduling focused on scheduling exactly once for each node, without long-term solutions. In this paper, we combine data aggregation and sleep scheduling for improving network lifetime and supporting the long-term operation of the network. We propose the Maximum Lifetime Minimum Hop Path Aggregation Tree Problem (MLMHPATP) with the probability of each node sending in a cycle, and divide it into the Maximum Lifetime Parent-Child Matching Problem (MLPCMP). We also define the Time Slot Scheduling Problem (TSSP) in bipartite graphs based on the SINR interference model. We use the Q-learning algorithm to solve the MLPCMP and solve the MLMHPATP bottom-up based on it. As for TSSP, we propose a distributed approach for it. We propose a novel cycle structure for the data transmission phase, which staggers three kinds of time frames at nodes with adjacent levels. The simulation results show that CPSD protocol has good performance in terms of throughput, energy consumption, aggregation delay, and network lifetime.

Keywords: Wireless sensor networks (WSNs) · Distributed cross-layer protocol · Data aggregation · Sleep scheduling · Q-learning

1 Introduction

Wireless sensor networks (WSNs) consist of small, low-cost sensors that are easy to deploy and can sense surroundings through sensing elements. These sensors periodically detect a series of events and generate data, which is sent through one or multiple hops to the sink node. Data aggregation is one of the main techniques for eliminating duplicate data and reducing energy consumption in WSNs [1]. All received packets, along with its own packet, can be merged into one packet by some logical or mathematical operation for data compression purposes.

Most sensors in WSNs are battery-powered, which means that energy consumption needs to be minimized or balanced to extend the network lifetime.

Y. Sun et al. (Eds.): ChineseCSCW 2023, CCIS 2012, pp. 317–332, 2024.
https://doi.org/10.1007/978-981-99-9637-7_24

Idle listening is one of the primary sources of energy waste in WSNs. In this paper, we focus on sleep scheduling [2] as an effective energy-saving strategy in WSNs. A sensor node is able to switch to the sleeping state, turning off the communication module, to reduce the energy waste in idle listening. There are several challenges to implementing sleep scheduling in data aggregation WSNs. First, data transmission is only possible when both the sender and receiver nodes are in active state, which means that nodes must wait for their next hop nodes in active state before transmitting. Secondly, it is essential for sleep scheduling strategies to be continuously applied in WSNs.

The CPSD protocol proposed in this paper is divided into topology setup and data transmission phases. In the topology setup phase, we determine the level of each node. Besides, the maximum lifetime minimum hop path aggregation tree construction and time slot scheduling are done. In the data transmission phase, we divide the lifetime of nodes into three kinds of time frames and stagger these time frames at nodes with adjacent levels to complete data aggregation and collection in a novel cycle structure. Our main contributions are as follows.

1. We define the lifetime of a node and the Maximum Lifetime Minimum Hop Path Aggregation Tree Problem (MLMHPATP), and divide it into the Maximum Lifetime Parent-Child Matching Problem (MLPCMP). We propose a solution using the reinforcement learning algorithm Q-learning for MLPCMP, on which MLMHPATP is solved bottom-up based.
2. We define the Time Slot Scheduling Problem (TSSP) based on SINR interference model and propose a distributed approach for it that provides collision-free transmission schedule.
3. We propose a novel cycle structure that provides each node an opportunity to receive data packets from all child nodes and send a packet to its parent node in one cycle. By dividing three kinds of time frames and staggering them at nodes with adjacent levels, data are forwarded in a pipeline.

We have evaluated the performance of CPSD by simulations. Simulation results show the better performance of CPSD in terms of data aggregation delay, throughput, energy consumption and network lifetime.

2   Related Work

There are several studies that utilize reinforcement learning algorithms for optimizing routing policies in wireless networks. A. F. E. Abadi et al. [6] proposed an energy-efficient control and routing protocol for WSNs that uses reinforcement learning for energy management and optimizing routing policies. O. Al-Jerew et al. [7] proposed a data collection algorithm based on Q-learning method called bounded hop count-reinforcement learning approach (BHC-RLA). The reward function is used to select cluster heads to balance the energy and data collection delay of the mobile base station. W. -K. Yun et al. [4] defined sensor-type-dependent aggregation rewards and proposed a Q-learning-based data-aggregation-aware energy-efficient routing algorithm, which to determine the optimum path that maximizes the rewards by sensor-type-dependent data aggregation level of the neighbor node, communication cost and hop count to sink. S. Redhu et al. [5] used Reinforcement Learning (RL) methods for learning network behavior by calculating the adaptive halt-times of a mobile sink based on the number of active nodes in each cluster. The above RL schemes focus more on routing in specific scenarios rather than constructing a data aggregation tree with the goal of maximizing the lifetime based on the probability of a node becoming a source node which can be built once and applied for a long time.

The studies of sleep scheduling aim to adjust the ratio of active time to sleeping time in the cycle to reduce latency and save energy. In synchronous wake-up strategies, two nodes in direct communication need to wake up simultaneously. S. J. Philip et al. [8] proposed an optimization heuristic that classifies nodes into two roles, relay nodes and leaf nodes, based on the type of action in terms of forwarding packets. The leaf nodes go to sleep during the active period of the work cycle, thus reducing packet overhead and saving energy consumption. JRAM, a cross-layer protocol proposed by R. Singh et al. [9], uses a novel cycle structure that provides multiple scheduling opportunities for each node in a cycle.

There are a few researches combined sleep scheduling with data aggregation in WSNs. The wake-up scheduling scheme proposed by Y. Wu et al. [10] uses TDMA as MAC protocol. In this scheme, nodes wake up only twice in a cycle: once for receiving from all child nodes and once for transmitting. The weight of nodes is defined as the time of reception, to which wake-up scheduling is performed according. Q. Chen et al. [11] proposed a Distributed non-Structure based data Aggregation algorithm for Duty-cycle networks (DSAD), which generate aggregation trees and collision-free transmission scheduling simultaneously. The above sleep scheduling schemes are less likely to design a sleep scheme based on the network topology, and do not propose a sleep scheduling scheme that maximizes the lifetime of the WSN to support long network operation.

3   Network Model and Problem Definition

3.1   Basic Model

Consider a multi-hop WSN containing n sensor nodes and a sink node denoted by an undirected graph $G(V, E)$, where V is the set of sensor nodes along with the sink node, and E is the edge set. Each sensor node has the same transmission range R. If node u and node v have Euclidean distance $d_{uv} \leq R$, they are within each other's transmission range and can communicate with each other, and an undirected edge (u, v) exists between them. We assume the transmission distance is equal to the interference distance of radio transmission, and sensor nodes cannot transmit and receive simultaneously due to their half-duplex communication feature.

3.2   Energy Model

In this paper, we use the first-order energy model [3] as the energy model of the sensor nodes. In the first-order energy model, there are two sources of energy for the sensor to transmit data, one is the transmission circuit and the other is the amplifier. The energy consumption for transmitting a k-bit message at a distance of d can be calculated as:

$$E_T(k, d) = E_{elec} \cdot k + \epsilon_{amp} \cdot k \cdot d^2, \tag{1}$$

where E_{elec} denotes energy consumed for transmitting or receiving a per bit data, and ϵ_{amp} denotes energy consumption of the amplify circuit. The energy consumption for receiving k-bit messages is expressed as:

$$E_R(k) = E_{elec} \cdot k. \tag{2}$$

In this paper, we assume that the nodes consume the same energy in receiving mode and idle mode [12]. Additionally, the energy consumed in the sleep mode is usually negligible, as reported in [13].

3.3 Interference Model

In this paper, we consider the SINR-based interference model [14]. A successful transmission of the link (u, v) requires that the Signal to Interference plus Noise Ratio (SINR) of it satisfies that:

$$SINR(u, v) = \frac{\frac{L_u}{d_{uv}^{\zeta}}}{\eta + \sum_{i \in NB(v) \backslash u} \frac{L_i}{d_{iv}^{\zeta}}} \geq \beta, \tag{3}$$

where L_u and L_i are the transmission powers in Watt of node u and node i respectively, $\frac{1}{d_{uv}^{\zeta}}$ is the propagation attenuation of the signal from node u to node v, ζ is the path-loss exponent, $NB(v)$ is the neighbor node set of node v and η is the environment noise power in Watt, β is a threshold value that denotes the lowest signal power level that allows a receiver to detect and decode the information in the signal. In this paper, we assume that the node can obtain the distances to its neighbor nodes by the ranging algorithm and the transmission powers of nodes are uniform.

3.4 Data Aggregation Tree Construction Problem

In this section, we introduce the construction of a minimum hop path data aggregation tree with the goal of maximizing the network lifetime. A node's high-level neighbors refer to its neighbors whose minimum hops to sink node are one hop closer than itself, while the low-level neighbors are the opposite.

The energy consumption of nodes mainly originates from data receptions and data transmissions. We define the lifetime of the node v as the total number of cycles v can run, where a cycle refers to receiving data from all child nodes and sending packet to the parent node. The lifetime of v can be calculated as:

$$l(T, v) = \frac{E(v)}{E_R(k) \cdot |CH(T, v)| + E_T(k, \overline{D_h(v)}) \cdot P_t(T, v)}, \tag{4}$$

where T denotes a specific minimum-hop path data aggregation tree, $E(v)$ is the remaining energy of v, $CH(T, v)$ is the set of child nodes of v in T, $D_h(v)$ denotes the average distance from v to all its high-level neighbors, and $P_t(T, v)$ is the probability that v send a data packet in each cycle under T. A node's data are derived from the child nodes and itself. $P_t(T, v)$ can be expressed by:

$$P_t(T, v) = \begin{cases} P_s(v) + (1 - P_s(v)) \cdot [1 - \displaystyle\prod_{u}^{CH(T,v)} (1 - P_t(T, u))], & |CH(T, v)| > 0 \\ P_s(v), & |CH(T, v)| = 0, \end{cases}$$

(5)

where $P_s(v)$ is the probability of v being a source node in each cycle. We assume that $P_s(v)$ satisfies a Poisson distribution with expectation μ, and it can be setup in advance by prior knowledge or deployment personnel according to the actual situation. We define the lifetime of the WSN as the time from the start of network running to the depletion of the first node.

Problem 1 (MLMHPATP). *Given a WSN $G(V, E)$, $P_s(v)$ and $E(v)$ for $v \in V$, the problem is to find a Maximum Lifetime Minimum Hop Path Aggregation Tree T_{opt} in G, which can be formulated formally as:*

$$T_{opt} = arg \max_{T \in MHPT} l(T) = arg \max_{T \in MHPT} \min_{v \in V} l(T, v),$$

(6)

where $MHPT$ denotes the set of Minimum Hop Path Tree in G and $l(T)$ is the lifetime of the network with the aggregation tree T.

Theorem 1. *For each node, changing the set of its child nodes only affects the lifetimes of itself and other nodes at the same level.*

Proof. From the Eq. (5), v's the lifetime is only affected by its child nodes and their probability of sending a data packet in each cycle. Since the candidate child nodes of each node are its low-level neighbors, the conflict in child node assignment only happen among the nodes with the same level. This indicates that changing the lifetime of a node by changing its set of child nodes only affects the lifetimes of the other nodes at the same level.

Theorem 1 demonstrates that the assignment of child nodes is independent for each level of nodes and we can solve MLMHPATP at each level independently. We denote the set of nodes at level i as V_i, $i = 1, 2, 3, \ldots, ml$, where ml is the maximum level in the network. The lifetime of a specific minimum-hop path aggregation tree is the minimum lifetime of all levels, which can expressed by:

$$l(T) = \min_{i \in [1, ml]} l(T, V_i) = \min_{i \in [1, ml]} \min_{v \in V_i} l(T, v).$$

(7)

The analysis above indicates that the MLMHPATP can be divided into sub-problems below.

Problem 2 (MLPCMP). *Given a bipartite graph $G_i = (V_i \cup V_{i-1}, E_i)$, $E(v)$, $E_T(k, \overline{D_h(v)})$, $P_s(v)$ for $v \in V_{i-1}$, and $P_t(M_{i+1}, u)$ for $u \in V_i$, where V_i is the set of child nodes, V_{i-1} is the set of parent nodes, and $E_i \subseteq V_i \times V_{i-1}$. We define a set $M_i \subseteq E_i$ as a **parent-child matching** if each node $u \in V_i$ is incident to exactly one edge in M_i. The lifetime of M_i is the minimum lifetimes of nodes in V_{i-1}. The problem is to find an Maximum Lifetime Parent-Child Matching M_i in G_i such that $l(M_i)$ is maximized.*

Theorem 2. *The MLPCMP is NP-complete.*

Proof. Firstly, a non-deterministic algorithm just need to check in polynomial time if the minimum lifetime among parent nodes is no less than a specific real number q in a specific parent-child matching, which indicates problem is in NP. LBSMP [18] is to find a semi-matching in a bipartite graph that maximizes the minimum load among the V-vertices. The contribution of node weights to the load in MLPCMP is not identical, so MLPCMP is a more complex problem than LBSMP. LBSMP is NP-complete, thus MLPCMP is also NP-complete.

3.5   Time Slot Scheduling Problem

In this paper, time slot scheduling involves assigning a time slot for each node to enable collision-free transmission. Since we stagger the time frames of adjacent level nodes mentioned in Sect. 4.4, the sleeping time frame enables us to focus only on the current-level nodes and the high-level neighbors for each node during time slot scheduling.

Problem 4 (TSSP). *Given a bipartite graph $G_b = (X \cup Y, E_P \cup E_N)$, L_z for $z \in X \cup Y$ and d_{xy} for $x \in X$ and $y \in Y$, where X is the transmitting nodes set, Y is the receiving nodes set, E_P denotes the parent-child edge set, E_N denotes the neighbor edge set. For each $x \in X$, there is exactly one edge in E_P. $E_N \subseteq X \times Y$ and $E_P \cap E_N = \emptyset$. Let $p(x)$ denotes the parent node of x. The Time Slot Scheduling Problem (TSSP) is to find an available time slot assignment $ts(x)$ for each $x \in X$ that achieves two goals: 1) there is no transmission collision under the SINR-based interference model and 2) the maximum time slot is minimized.*

4   CPSD Protocol

The CPSD protocol is divided into two phases: topology setup phase and data transmission phase (DTP). In the topology setup phase, each node is assigned a parent node and a time slot. During the DTP, the network runs according to the novel cycle structure we proposed, conducting data transmission.

4.1   Node Level Division Phase

In this phase, the levels of nodes is determined and neighbors information is collected. We define the level of nodes as the minimum number of hops from the sink, which is initialized to infinity.

Algorithm 1. The Proposed Distributed Approach for MLPCMP

Step 1: Initialization

1: Each node $u \in V_i$ initializes the Q-table with zeros
2: $t \leftarrow 0$

Step 2: Taking Action

1: u selects a temporary parent node with the maximum Q-value
2: **if** $t < \rho$ **then**
3:　　u sends an ACTION message containing $P_t(M_{i+1}, u)$ to the selected temporary parent node
4: **else**
5:　　u selects the temporary parent node as matched parent node and broadcasts an SELECT message to high-level neighbors
6:　　Exit
7: **end if**

Step 3: Rewarding for Action

1: Each node $v \in V_{i-1}$ receives all ACTION messages from nodes selecting v as temporary parent node denoted temporary child nodes of v
2: v calculates the rewards for each temporary child node of v based on Eq. (9)
3: v sends a REWARD message containing rewards to v's temporary child nodes

Step 4: Updating Q-table

1: u receives the REWARD message from v.
2: Update the Q-value of node v in the Q-table based on Eq. (8)
3: $t \leftarrow t + 1$
4: Skip to Step 2

This phase is started by sink broadcasting a control packet with level 0. Each node receiving the control packet save the information into the neighbor table. Then check whether the neighbor's level is smaller than its own level minus one. If so, it set its own level to that neighbor's level plus one and broadcast a new control packet containing information about itself. By this way, each node finally obtains the minimum hops to the sink node.

4.2 Data Aggregation Tree Construction Phase

In this paper, we use Q-learning [20] approach to solve the MLPCMP. In CPSD, each sensor node is an agent with only one state. We call the matching during the iteration of the algorithm as temporary matching, and the nodes of temporary matching also is temporary parent-child relationship with each other. Different actions denote different selection of temporary parent node. In MLPCMP, for each node $u \in V_i$, the Q-function in this paper is:

$$Q(t, v_t) = (1 - \alpha) \cdot Q(t, v_t) + \alpha \cdot (R(t, v_t, u) + \gamma \cdot \max_{v_{t+1}} Q(t + 1, v_{t+1})), \qquad (8)$$

where v_t is the node chosen as u's temporary parent node at round t, $R(t, v_t, u)$ denotes the reward after u choosing v_t as temporary parent node at round t.

Algorithm 2. Time Slot Assignment Process

Input: $F2T(x_1)$, $L_{max}^{x_1}$ and $L_{min}^{x_1}$ lists in all time slot
Output: $ts(x_1)$

1: $ts(x_1) = -1$
2: flag $\leftarrow$ **true**
3: **while** flag $\leftarrow$ **true do**
4:     $ts(x_1) \leftarrow ts(x_1) + 1$
5:     flag $\leftarrow$ **false**
6:     **if** $ts(x_1) \in F2T(x_1)$ or $L_{x_1} > L_{max}^{x_1}(ts(x_1))$ or $L_{x_1} < L_{min}^{x_1}(ts(x_1))$ **then**
7:         flag $\leftarrow$ **true**
8:     **end if**
9: **end while**

Algorithm 3. The Proposed Time Slot Scheduling Approach

Step 1: Time Slot Assignment

1: Each node $x_1 \in X$ calculate $ts(x_1)$ according to Algorithm 2
2: x_1 broadcasts AM $= [x_1, ts(x_1), L_{x_1}]$

Step 2: Time Slot Assignment Feedback

1: Each node $y \in Y$ receiving x_1's AM produces a FM
2: y broadcasts FM $= [ts(x_1), \text{TYPE}, \text{constraint value}]$

Step 3: Processing FM

1: Each node $x_2 \in X$ processes the FM from y
2: **if** x_2 is the child node of y and TYPE of FM is 1 **then**
3:     $F2T(x_2) \leftarrow F2T(x_2) \cup ts(x_1)$
4: **else if** x_2 is not the child node of y and TYPE of FM is 1 **then**
5:     $L_{max}^{x_2}(ts(x_1)) \leftarrow min(S_{max}^y \cdot d_{yx_2}^\zeta, L_{max}^{x_2}(ts(x_1)))$
6: **else if** x_2 is the child node of y and TYPE of FM is 2 **then**
7:     $L_{min}^{x_2}(ts(x_1)) \leftarrow max(S_{min}^y \cdot d_{yx_2}^\zeta, L_{min}^{x_2}(ts(x_1)))$
8: **end if**

In each round, a node adopts the greedy strategy to select a temporary parent node, i.e. u take the action with maximum Q-value. Since the matching problem requires considering more immediate rewards, i.e., the efficiency of the current matching is immediately known, we consider setting the discount factor γ to 0. We define the reward function as follows:

$$R(t, v, u) = l_t(M_{tmp}(t), v) - l_{exp}(v) - d_{u,v}^2, \tag{9}$$

where $l_t(M_{tmp}(t), v)$ is the lifetime of v under the temporary matching at round t, $l_{exp}(v)$ is the lifetime expectancy of v, and $d_{u,v}$ is the Euclidean distance between u and v. In CPSD, $l_t(M_{tmp}(t), v)$ is calculated by equation (4) according to the temporary child node set of v in round t. $l_{exp}(v)$ is a pre-defined value and is identical for all nodes. The distance between two nodes is added to the reward function to distinguish different nodes in V_i.

We propose a distributed approach for MLPCMP, constructing a maximum lifetime minimum hop path aggregation tree from the bottom up. The specific steps of it are shown in Algorithm 1, where ρ denotes the number of iterative rounds of the Q-learning algorithm. For each node, the execution of the approach starts only after it receives the SELECT messages from all its low-level neighbors. Thus, this approach completes the MLPCMP level by level and eventually constructs a minimum hop path data aggregation tree in the network.

4.3   Time Slot Scheduling Phase

In the time slot scheduling phase, we assign a time slot to each node such that there is no transmission collision under SINR-based interference model. We propose a time slot scheduling approach for TSSP as shown in Algorithm 3, and the steps are as follows:

1. Node $x_1 \in X$ calculates an available time slot through Algorithm 2 and broadcasts the Assignment Message (AM), containing x_1's ID, $ts(x_1)$ and L_{x_1}, to the high-level neighbors. In Algorithm 2, $F2T(x_1)$ denotes the time slots forbidden to transmit in, $L_{max}^{x_1}(ts(x_1))$ and $L_{min}^{x_1}(ts(x_1))$ denote the maximum and minimum power constraint in time slot $ts(x_1)$ respectively.
2. Each node $y \in Y$ that receives AM of x_1 return a Feedback Message (FM). The content of the FM includes a time slot, message type (TYPE) and constraint value. The two message types are shown as follows:
   (a) *TYPE = 1:* It means y is the parent of x_1, y calculates the constraint value S_{max}^y that is equal to the maximum interference signal and is expressed by the SINR function as below:

   $$S_{max}^y = \frac{L_{x_1}}{\beta d_{yx_1}^\zeta} - \eta - \sum_{i \in X_{ts(x_1)}} \frac{L_i}{d_{iy}^\zeta}, \qquad (10)$$

   where $X_{ts(x_1)}$ denotes the neighbors of y in X whose scheduled time slot is equal to $ts(x_1)$.
   (b) *TYPE = 2:* If y is the not parent of x_1, y calculates the constraint value S_{min}^y that is equal to the minimum transmission signal and is expressed as below:

   $$S_{min}^y = \beta(\eta + \sum_{i \in X_{ts(x_1)}} \frac{L_i}{d_{iy}^\zeta}). \qquad (11)$$

3. Each node $x_2 \in X$ that receives FM from y processes the FM depending on different situations.

4.4   Data Transmission Phase

In CPSD protocol, time synchronization [15] is required, which mainly relies on three parameters: clock offset, clock skew, and clock drift [16]. In CPSD, we use the LDSP [17] synchronization protocol and regard the sink node as a reference node for the time of other sensor nodes.

In DTP, we propose a novel cycle structure that enables nodes to perform level-based pipe-lined data transmissions. In the node with adjacent levels, those three different time frames are staggered, as shown in Fig. 1, the arrows indicate the direction of data transmission. The first time frame of all nodes with level of $3k+3$ is TTF, while that of all nodes with level of $3k+2$ is RTF. In this way, nodes in adjacent levels can complete data transmission. In addition, all nodes with level of $3k+1$ keep sleeping in their first time frame, i.e., STF.

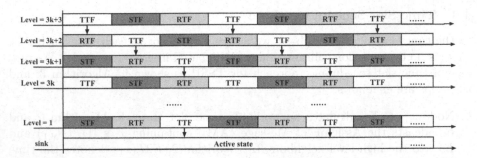

Fig. 1. The proposed cycle structure overlapping time frames of different grade nodes

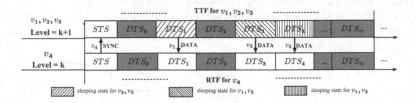

Fig. 2. Sample of TTF and RTF

Figure 2 gives a sample of transmission process in adjacent levels, where the white and gray time slots indicate the active and sleeping states respectively, the shaded time slots represent the sleeping state of specific nodes and m denotes the maximum time slot in the network. v_1, v_2 and v_3 wake up to transmit data in their respective data time slots (DTSs), while v_4 wakes up to receive data in those time slots. Additionally, all nodes wake up during the synchronization time slot (STS) for time synchronization and remain in a sleeping state in time slots where no transmission or reception is required.

5   Simulation Results

We evaluate the performance of CPSD by simulation. We use the network simulator NS3 for the simulation to evaluate the performance of these distributed algorithms. The monitoring area is 100 m × 100 m. The communication range of each sensor is 15 m. The probability of each node becoming a source node in each cycle satisfies a Poisson distribution with $\mu = 0.4$.

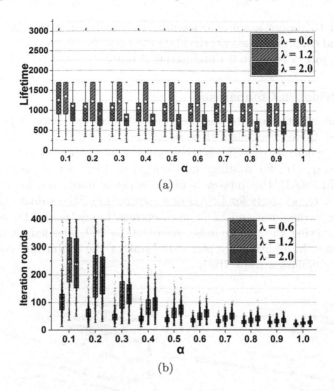

Fig. 3. The boxplots with different learning rate α of Q-learning algorithm under different λ about (a) lifetime of matching and (b) the number of iteration rounds to converge

5.1 Parameter Analysis

In this paper, there are two parameters to be analyzed, which are the learning rate α and the number of iteration rounds ρ of the Q-learning algorithm used to solve the MLPCMP. We evaluate the maximum lifetime of the parent-child matching and the number of iterations to reach convergence with different α. We vary the α from 0.1 to 1.0, and set λ to 0.6, 1.2, and 2.0 as comparison, where λ denotes the ratio of $|V_{i-1}|$ to $|V_i|$.

After the algorithm has converged, the lifetime of matching with different α under different λ is presented in the boxplot with dot overlap, as shown in Fig. 3(a). In Fig. 3, white dots indicate the average value, and discrete small black dots indicate data points. It is evident to see that as α increases, the lifetime of the matches gradually decreases, both in terms of the mean and the overall distribution. Figure 3(b) shows the number of iteration rounds for the Q-learning algorithm to reach convergence with different α. It is obvious that as α increases, the number of iteration rounds required to reach convergence decreases.

We need to choose a suitable learning rate to balance the lifetime of the matching and communication overhead. In the performance evaluation of CPSD, the learning rate α is set to 0.4 and iteration rounds ρ is set to 200.

5.2 Performance Comparison

To verify the effectiveness of our proposed protocol in terms of performance, we compared three other algorithms or protocols: DSAD [11], JRAM [9], and A_{SM1}+CLS, where A_{SM1}+CLS is the protocol that combines the semi-matching algorithm A_{SM1} [19] for routing and Contiguous Link Scheduling (CLS) algorithm [21]. In DSAD, the duty-cycle of the nodes is fixed, and we set $C = 15\%$ and $C = 30\%$ respectively for DSAD as a comparison. We evaluate throughput, average energy consumption (AEC), data aggregation delay (DAD) and network lifetime by varying the node number from 120 to 200. The length of time slot is set to 0.02 s. In addition, we placed the sink at the center and corner of the area for the simulation respectively.

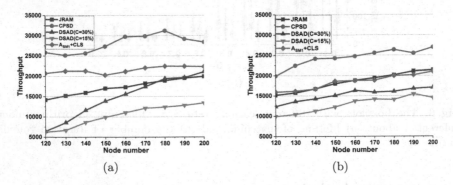

(a)   (b)

Fig. 4. Throughput with different number of nodes (a) Sink at center (b) Sink at corner

We define throughput as the number of data packets successfully transmitted throughout the network during a certain time in the data transmission phase. Figure 4 depicts the total network throughput within 200s as the number of nodes increases. It is evident that the CPSD protocol outperforms the other algorithms and protocols no matter if sink is in the center or corner. The better throughput performance of CPSD is due to that the cycle structure allows about one-third of the nodes to complete data transmission within one time frame.

In Fig. 5, it is observed that as the number of nodes increases, the AEC of nodes in the network remains almost constant over 200 s. This is because the increase in network size does not significantly affect the duty cycle of the nodes. The AEC performance of the CPSD protocol is slightly worse than that of A_{SM1}+CLS, but better than the other protocols. In CLS, we set the interval between two schedule to the maximum scheduling time, which results in the low duty-cycle and energy consumption.

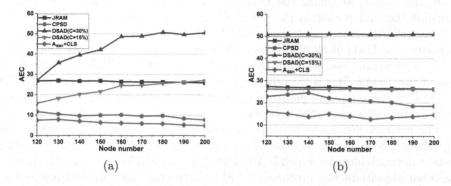

Fig. 5. AEC with different number of nodes (a) Sink at center (b) Sink at corner

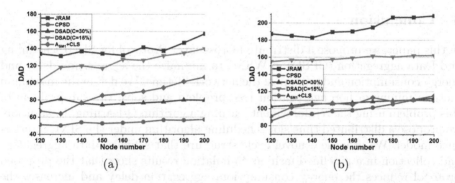

Fig. 6. Data aggregation delay with different number of nodes (a) Sink at center (b) Sink at corner

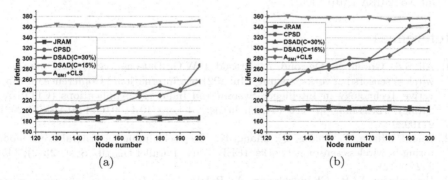

Fig. 7. Network lifetime with different number of nodes (a) Sink at center (b) Sink at corner

In this paper, we define the DAD as the number of time slots required to transmit the first packet in the network, with each node sending exactly one packet, until the last packet is received by the sink node. As the network size increases, the DAD of all algorithms and protocols increases as well, as shown in Fig. 6. It is observed that the DAD performance of the CPSD is better than that of the others. This is the advantage of pipeline scheduling, where the DAD of CPSD is theoretically equal to the product of the time frame length and the total number of levels in the network.

The network lifetime is defined as the time from the start of network to the appearance of the first dead node. As shown in Fig. 7, DASD ($C = 15\%$) has the highest network lifetime, which is attributed to its fixed low duty-cycle. Among the other algorithms and protocols, CPSD has the best network lifetime performance. A_{SM1} is a semi-matching algorithm used to build data aggregation trees with the goal of maximizing network lifetime. Therefore, its network lifetime performance is also good.

6 Conclusion

In this paper, we propose a distributed Cross-layer Protocol for Sleep scheduling and Data aggregation (CPSD) in WSNs, to minimize the aggregation delay and energy consumption and maximize the network lifetime. We define the maximum lifetime minimum hop aggregation tree problem and solve the sub-problem of this problem using the reinforcement learning algorithm Q-learning. In addition, we propose a distributed time slot scheduling algorithm under the SINR interference model. We propose a novel cycle structure that achieves data aggregation and collection in a pipelined fashion. Simulation results show that the proposed protocol reduces the energy consumption, aggregation delay and increases the throughput and network lifetime in comparison with the existing schemes.

Acknowledgment. This work was supported by the Key Project of Science and Technology Innovation 2030 supported by the Ministry of Science and Technology of China (Grant No. 2018AAA0101300).

References

1. Ali, S.S., Giweli, N., Dawoud, A., Prasad, P.W.C.: Data aggregation techniques in wireless sensors networks: a survey. In: 2021 6th International Conference on Innovative Technology in Intelligent System and Industrial Applications (CITISIA), Sydney, Australia, pp. 1–9 (2021). https://doi.org/10.1109/CITISIA53721.2021.9719939
2. Guo, P., Jiang, T., Zhang, Q., Zhang, K.: Sleep scheduling for critical event monitoring in wireless sensor networks. IEEE Trans. Parallel Distrib. Syst. **23**(2), 345–352 (2012)
3. Heinzelman, W.R., Chandrakasan, A., Balakrishnan, H.: Energy-efficient communication protocol for wireless microsensor networks. In: Proceedings of the 33rd Annual Hawaii International Conference on System Sciences, Maui, HI, USA, vol. 2, p. 10 (2000)

4. Yun, W.-K., Yoo, S.-J.: Q-learning-based data-aggregation-aware energy-efficient routing protocol for wireless sensor networks. IEEE Access **9**, 10737–10750 (2021)
5. Redhu, S., Garg, P., Hegde, R.: Joint mobile sink scheduling and data aggregation in asynchronous wireless sensor networks using Q-learning. In: 2018 IEEE International Conference on Acoustics, Speech and Signal Processing (ICASSP), Calgary, AB, Canada, pp. 6438–6442 (2018). https://doi.org/10.1109/ICASSP.2018.8461561
6. Abadi, A.F.E., Asghari, S.A., Marvasti, M.B., Abaei, G., Nabavi, M., Savaria, Y.: RLBEEP: reinforcement-learning-based energy efficient control and routing protocol for wireless sensor networks. IEEE Access **10**, 44123–44135 (2022)
7. Al-Jerew, O., Bassam, N.A., Alsadoon, A.: Reinforcement learning for delay tolerance and energy saving in mobile wireless sensor networks. IEEE Access **11**, 19819–19835 (2023). https://doi.org/10.1109/ACCESS.2023.3247576
8. Philip, S.J., Peng, C., Cao, X.: Role based medium access control in wireless sensor networks. In: 2019 IEEE 5th International Conference on Computer and Communications (ICCC), Chengdu, China, pp. 624–628 (2019). https://doi.org/10.1109/ICCC47050.2019.9064319
9. Singh, R., Rai, B.K., Bose, S.K.: A joint routing and mac protocol for transmission delay reduction in many-to-one communication paradigm for wireless sensor networks. IEEE Internet Things J. **4**(4), 1031–1045 (2017)
10. Wu, Y., Li, X.-Y., Liu, Y., Lou, W.: Energy-efficient wake-up scheduling for data collection and aggregation. IEEE Trans. Parallel Distrib. Syst. **21**(2), 275–287 (2010)
11. Chen, Q., Gao, H., Cai, Z., Cheng, L., Li, J.: Distributed low-latency data aggregation for duty-cycle wireless sensor networks. IEEE/ACM Trans. Netw. **26**(5), 2347–2360 (2018)
12. Lin, D., Wang, Q., Min, W., Xu, J., Zhang, Z.: A survey on energy-efficient strategies in static wireless sensor networks. ACM Trans. Sen. Netw. **17**(1), 1–48 (2020). Article 3
13. Shih, E., et al.: Physical layer driven protocol and algorithm design for energy-efficient wireless sensor networks. In: Proceedings of the 7th Annual International Conference on Mobile Computing and Networking (MobiCom 2001), pp. 272–287. Association for Computing Machinery, New York (2001). https://doi.org/10.1145/381677.381703
14. Halldórsson, M.M., Holzer, S., Markatou, E.A., Lynch, N.: Leader election in SINR model with arbitrary power control. Theor. Comput. Sci. **811**, 21–28 (2019)
15. Wu, Y.-C., Chaudhari, Q., Serpedin, E.: Clock synchronization of wireless sensor networks. IEEE Signal Process. Mag. **28**(1), 124–138 (2011)
16. Geetha, D.D., Tabassum, N.: A survey on clock synchronization protocols in wireless sensor networks. In: International Conference on Smart Technologies for Smart Nation (SmartTechCon), Bengaluru, India, pp. 504–509 (2017). https://doi.org/10.1109/SmartTechCon.2017.8358424
17. Huang, H., Yun, J., Zhong, Z.: Scalable clock synchronization in wireless networks with low-duty-cycle radio operations. In: 2015 IEEE Conference on Computer Communications (INFOCOM), pp. 2011–2019 (2015)
18. Low, C.P.: On load-balanced semi-matchings for weighted bipartite graphs. In: Cai, J.-Y., Cooper, S.B., Li, A. (eds.) TAMC 2006. LNCS, vol. 3959, pp. 159–170. Springer, Heidelberg (2006). https://doi.org/10.1007/11750321_15
19. Luo, D., Zhu, X., Wu, X., Chen, G.: Maximizing lifetime for the shortest path aggregation tree in wireless sensor networks. In: 2011 Proceedings IEEE INFO-

COM, Shanghai, China, pp. 1566–1574 (2011). https://doi.org/10.1109/INFCOM.
2011.5934947

20. Jang, B., Kim, M., Harerimana, G., Kim, J.W.: Q-learning algorithms: a comprehensive classification and applications. IEEE Access **7**, 133653–133667 (2019). https://doi.org/10.1109/ACCESS.2019.2941229

21. Ma, J., Lou, W., Li, X.-Y.: Contiguous link scheduling for data aggregation in wireless sensor networks. IEEE Trans. Parallel Distrib. Syst. **25**(7), 1691–1701 (2014). https://doi.org/10.1109/TPDS.2013.296

Time Split Network for Temporal Knowledge Graph Completion

Changkai You, Xinyu Lin, Yuwei Wu, Sirui Zhang, Fuyuan Zhang,
and Jingbin Wang[✉]

College of Computer and Data Science, Fuzhou University, Fuzhou 350108, Fujian,
China
wjb@fzu.edu.cn

Abstract. Temporal Knowledge Graphs (TKGs), represented by quadruples, describe facts with temporal relevance. Temporal Knowledge
Graph Completion (TKGC) aims to address the incompleteness issue
of TKGs and has received extensive attention in recent years. Previous approaches treated timestamps as a single node, resulting in incomplete parsing of temporal information and the inability to perceive temporal hierarchies and periodicity. To tackle this problem, we propose a
novel model called Time Split Network (TSN). Specifically, we employed a
unique approach to handle temporal information by splitting timestamps.
This allows the model to perceive temporal hierarchies and periodicity,
while reducing the number of model parameters. Additionally, we combined convolutional neural networks with stepwise fusion of temporal features to simulate the hierarchical order of time and obtain comprehensive temporal information. The experimental results of entity link prediction on the four benchmark datasets demonstrate the superiority of the
TSN model. Specifically, compared to the state-of-the-art baseline, TSN
improves the MRR by approximately 2.6% and 1.3% on the ICEWS14 and
ICEWS05-15 datasets, and improves the MRR by approximately 33.5%
and 34.6% on YAGO11k and Wikidata12k, respectively.

Keywords: Temporal knowledge graph · Temporal knowledge graph
completion · Convolutional neural network

1 Introduction

Knowledge graphs (KGs) utilise triple structures to describe real-world knowledge, improving the accuracy and efficiency of downstream tasks such as question answering, recommendation systems, etc., by offering valuable background
information. However, KGs still suffer from incompleteness. Knowledge graph
completion (KGC) is the process of filling in these missing pieces of information,
such as entities or relations.

In the field of static knowledge graphs, KGC methods use structured or
unstructured information to improve the representation of entities and relations,
but only for facts that remain the same over time. Temporal Knowledge Graphs
(TKGs), including ICEWS, YAGO, and Wikidata, add a time dimension to

Y. Sun et al. (Eds.): ChineseCSCW 2023, CCIS 2012, pp. 333–347, 2024.
https://doi.org/10.1007/978-981-99-9637-7_25

the static KGs, using a quadruple representation to describe facts relevant to time. For instance, (*Trump, President, USA, 2017-01-20*) represents Trump's presidency on *2017-01-20*. TKGs also have an issue of incompleteness, which Temporal Knowledge Graph Completion (TKGC) aims to resolve.

The TKGC model typically employs two methods to model time information. The first method involves dividing different snapshots by timestamp, with each snapshot including events with the same timestamp. Model examples of this method are HyTE [1], which dedicates a hyperplane to project the entities and relations in each snapshot. The second method uses timestamp embedding, with models such as TComplEx [2] and TeRo [3] creating a dedicated embedding for each timestamp. Nevertheless, this method requires a large number of additional parameters.

A clear hierarchical structure exists among timestamps containing year, month, and day. Specifically, the year plays the primary role in establishing context and temporal background for the occurrence of months. As the second largest unit, the month provides more specific and accurate time information about seasonal changes. The day, as the smallest unit, introduces variability of facts in relation to the same context. This is exemplified by (*Presidential Executive Order, issued by, Donald Trump*) having been effective solely from *2017-01-20* to *2021-01-20*, which suggests its sensitivity to the year's temporal information. Conversely, "Farmers sow soybeans" generally takes place in the spring, indicating sensitivity to the month's temporal information. Within TKGs, entities and relations have different sensitivities to time at different levels. Therefore, considering time information from a hierarchical perspective can better understand the contextual background in which events occur. In addition, in the real world, there are many periodic events, such as the Olympics held every four years and credit card bills sent monthly. These events occur periodically within specific time periods and present regularity and cyclical patterns [4]. Therefore, considering periodicity is very useful as it can provide clues to the development of these events.

The current methods of modeling time in TKGC treat timestamps as a single node, which results in incomplete time information analysis, ignores the hierarchical structure and fails to distinguish the sensitivity of entities and relations to different levels of time. Moreover, by considering each timestamp as independent, these methods only focus on predicting event information during the current or nearby times, disregarding the periodicity.

In this paper, we propose a novel model called Time Split Network (TSN) to improve TKGC by capturing the hierarchical structure and periodicity of time. TSN incorporates two key modules, namely Temporal Feature Generator (TFG) and Hierarchical Order Convolutional Network (HCN). To capture the hierarchical structure and periodicity of time, TFG splits each timestamp into year, month, and day sequences and utilizes the Long Short-Term Memory (LSTM) mechanism to capture temporal dynamics and extract reliable features for HCN. In addition, TSN shares temporal features to identify periodic patterns, uncover regularity at different time granularities, and substantially reduce the model complexity. To capture the hierarchical structure of time, we devise HCN to simulate the evolution of entities and relations by integrating temporal features in a step-by-step manner. Specifically, entities and relations have distinct temporal contexts and histories at various stages. By conditioning on the historical information, the HCN module can evolve entities and relations under the constraint of high-level temporal information, leading to comprehensive time-aware embeddings and precise semantic extraction. The contributions of our work can be summarized as follows:

1. We present a novel method for processing temporal information, which addresses the limitations of previous TKGC models in capturing the hierarchical structure and periodicity of time while also reducing the complexity of the models.
2. We combine convolutional neural networks with step-by-step fusion of temporal features to simulate the hierarchical order of time and obtain complete time information, thereby improving the model's comprehension and semantic extraction accuracy.
3. Comprehensive experiments on multiple temporal knowledge graph completion datasets demonstrate that our proposed model outperforms state-of-the-art methods by a significant margin.

2   Related Work

Since the emergence of Knowledge Graphs, many static KGC models have been developed, which can be broadly classified into three categories: translation-based, tensor factorization, and neural network models. The first translation-based model that was proposed by Bordes et al. [5] is called TransE. It uses a distance function to model the interaction between entities and relations, and models the reliability of the triple through the difference between the subject entity, relation, and object entity. However, complex relations cannot be accurately modeled using TransE, and in order to mitigate this issue, scholars have proposed a series of TransE-based models such as TransH [6], TransR [7], and TransD [8]. Other tensor factorization models, such as RESCAL [9], DistMult [10], and ComplEx [11] have also garnered widespread attention, as these models decompose entities and relations into low-dimensional matrices or tensors for the purpose of completing triples. The approach of translation and tensor factorization-based models has been criticized by Dettmers et al. [12]. They believed that these models only learn shallow features, and proposed a new model called ConvE, which is based on a multi-layer convolutional neural network that calculates output vectors using convolutional filters on reshaped embeddings of entities and relations. In addition to ConvE, the InteractE [13] model is another neural network-based method that generates various feature matrices by permuting the different dimensions of the entity and relation representation vectors. The model utilizes circular convolution on the resulting permuted 2D matrix, thereby enhancing the interaction between the relation and entity representation, ultimately improving the link prediction performance. However, these static KGC methods do not efficiently perceive temporal information.

Several early methods attempted to extend static KGC models to TKGC tasks using temporal information. TTransE [14] was the first KGC model that modeled temporal information and extended the TransE model to TKGC by introducing time constraints. Specifically, TTransE defined three time-constraint characteristics: temporal sequence, temporal exclusion, and span. Since TTransE did not explicitly introduce a time embedding, HyTE [1] defined a hyperplane for each point in time, and projected entities and relations onto the hyperplane at each time point. HyTE obtained a fusion of entity and relation embedding representations with time-awareness. TA-DistMult [15] processed temporal information into a time sequence, and then used a Long Short-Term Memory neural network (LSTM) to learn the features between the relations and time sequence. TComplEx [2] extended ComplEx [11] by using fourth-order tensor decomposition and a new regularized scheme. TeLM [16]improved TComplEx by performing tensor decomposition of TKG using a linear time regularizer and multi-vector embedding. TuckERTNT [17] incorporated prior knowledge into the tensor decomposition model using cosine similarities, contrastive learning, and other methods. The core tensor was also constrainedly used to avoid overfitting problems. TeRo [3] introduced a specific embedding for each timestamp and defined the time evolution of entity embedding as a rotation in the complex vector space from the initial time to the current time. BoxTE [18] captured cross-temporal reasoning patterns and modeled relation information for specific times by introducing embeddings for timestamps and extending the static BoxE model. These TKGC models generally treat timestamps as separate nodes, ignore the hierarchical structure of time, and have difficulty capturing the periodic information.

3   Problem Definition

A Temporal Knowledge Graph (TKG) can be represented as a set of quadruples $\mathcal{G} = \{(s, r, o, \tau) \mid s, o \in \mathcal{E}, r \in \mathcal{R}, \tau \in \mathcal{T}\}$, where $\mathcal{E}$, $\mathcal{R}$, $\mathcal{T}$ represent the set of entities, relations, and timestamps. Each quadruple represents the fact of the relation (r) between the subject entity (s) and the object entity (t) at the specified timestamp (τ). Given a quadruple (s, r, o, τ), $\mathbf{e_s}$, $\mathbf{e_r}$, and $\mathbf{e_o}$ are respectively embeddings corresponding to subject entity, relation, and object entity, where $\mathbf{e_s}, \mathbf{e_s}, \mathbf{e_o} \in \mathbb{R}^d$, d is the embedding dimension. while $\mathbf{t_y}, \mathbf{t_m}, \mathbf{t_d} \in \mathbb{R}^d$ are embeddings corresponding to the year, month, and day obtained by splitting the timestamp τ.

Temporal Knowledge Graph Completion(TKGC) aims to predict missing facts (s, r, o, τ) based on known temporal facts , i.e., predicting o given $(s, r, ?, \tau)$, or predicting s given $(?, r, o, \tau)$. TKGC usually trains a model to predict the missing facts, which can learn a scoring function to calculate the probability score of the predicted new facts.

4   Methodology

To effectively address the task of completing a temporal knowledge graph, it is often necessary to incorporate time information into the embedding model. Nevertheless, the timestamps possess a clear sequence and dependency relationship among the year, month, and day. Therefore, directly integrating time embeddings into the model may not capture the semantic and periodic knowledge of entities and relations over time with high precision.

We propose the Time Split Network (TSN) model to effectively model time's hierarchical structure and periodicity to enhance TKGC performance. The TSN model is composed of two modules, i.e., Temporal Feature Generator (TFG) and Hierarchical Sequence Convolutional Neural Network (HCN), shown in Figs. 1 and 2, respectively. The TFG module splits timestamps into year, month, and day components following their hierarchical structure. A timestamp is considered as a time embedding sequence, and a LSTM is utilized to capture its variability and generate reliable temporal features. The HCN module integrates the three types of temporal features into the feature representation before the convolution operation to simulate time's hierarchical structure, and it obtains periodicity information by sharing the same timestamp's embedding. The HCN feature map is then flattened and passed through fully connected layers to obtain an embedding representation of the entity, relation, and time. Finally, the model's prediction score is obtained by multiplying the embedding representation with the tail entity set and passing the result through the sigmoid function.

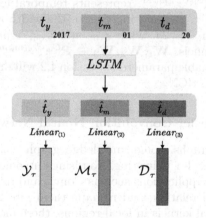

Fig. 1. An illustration of Temporal Feature Generator (TFG). TFG splits the timestamp τ into year, month, and day, and generates the corresponding time features $\mathcal{Y}_\tau$, $\mathcal{M}_\tau$, and $\mathcal{D}_\tau$. In this example, τ is 2017-01-20.

4.1   Temporal Feature Generator

We split the timestamp into a combination of year, month, and day embeddings to perceive the hierarchical structure of time. Sharing the same parts within the combination allows us to model periodic facts and significantly reduce the number of parameters. For instance, the embeddings for *05-01* is shared between the timestamps *2015-05-01* and *2016-05-01*, conveying periodic information at the year level. Please refer to Sect. 5.3 for a detailed analysis of the parameter reduction. Because there is an obvious time order and dependency between year, month, and day, they are arranged in a sequence and inputted into the LSTM model to reduce the discreteness of time information and enhance its ability to capture dynamic trends of time series, then obtain evolved time embeddings $\hat{t}_y, \hat{t}_m, \hat{t}_d$. Formally, this approach can be expressed as follows:

$$\hat{t}_y, \hat{t}_m, \hat{t}_d = \text{LSTM}\left(t_y, t_m, t_d\right), \tag{1}$$

where $\hat{t}_y, \hat{t}_m, \hat{t}_d \in \mathbb{R}^d$ respectively represent the evolved embedding of year, month, and day at timestamp τ. Furthermore, we will map these embeddings to generate temporal features:

$$\begin{aligned}
\mathcal{Y}_\tau &= \hat{t}_y \mathbf{W}_1^{\mathrm{T}} + \mathbf{b}_1, \\
\mathcal{M}_\tau &= \hat{t}_m \mathbf{W}_2^{\mathrm{T}} + \mathbf{b}_2, \\
\mathcal{D}_\tau &= \hat{t}_d \mathbf{W}_3^{\mathrm{T}} + \mathbf{b}_3,
\end{aligned} \tag{2}$$

where $\mathcal{Y}_\tau, \mathcal{M}_\tau, \mathcal{D}_\tau \in \mathbb{R}^{C_{\text{in}} C_{\text{out}} m_w m_h}$ represents temporal feature in year, month, and day at timestamp τ. m_w and m_h denote the width and height of the feature map, where $m_h m_w = 2d$. while C_{in} and C_{out} represent the number of input and output channels. $\mathbf{W}_1, \mathbf{W}_2, \mathbf{W}_3 \in \mathbb{R}^{C_{\text{in}} C_{\text{out}} m_w m_h \times d}$ and $\mathbf{b}_1, \mathbf{b}_2, \mathbf{b}_3 \in \mathbb{R}^{C_{\text{in}} C_{\text{out}} m_w m_h}$, are trainable parameters. Section 4.2 will discuss how to use temporal feature vectors in HCN.

4.2   Hierarchical Order Convolution Neural Network

In static knowledge graphs, some knowledge graph completion models have attained satisfactory results, delivering promising outcomes on 2D convolutional neural network (CNN) applications such as ConvE and InteractE. These models concatenate entity and relation, and reshape them into 2D matrices as input. By sliding convolutional kernels in local regions, these models can extract local features to enhance the interaction between entitiy and relation.

The Hierarchical Order Convolution Neural Network (HCN) retains the benefits of the models mentioned previously in regards to feature extraction. The integration of temporal information is associated with the depth of the convolutional layer to capture the dynamic evolution of entities and relations. Firstly, the interaction between entities and relations is amplified, resulting in a fused feature representation that is input into a 1×1 convolution layer to enhance feature expression. Secondly, Temporal features obtained from TFG are integrated into the feature map before each convolutional layer in the order of years, months, and days. This integration allows the model to gain a more accurate perception of the temporal awareness.

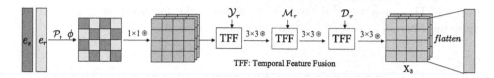

Fig. 2. This diagram showcases a Hierarchical Order Convolutional Neural Network (HCN) that fused temporal features in the order of year, month, and day. For a more detailed explanation of the temporal feature fusion process, please refer to Sect. 4.2 and Fig. 4.

Taking inspiration from prior research [13], our study employs Feature Permutation and Checkered Reshaping to better capture the interaction between entities and relations and enhance model expressiveness. Afterwards, we define the input matrix as:

$$A = \phi(\mathcal{P}(\mathbf{e_s}), \mathcal{P}(\mathbf{e_r})), \tag{3}$$

where $\mathcal{P}$ and ϕ represent the operations of Feature Permutation and Checkered Reshaping, respectively. $\mathcal{P}$ randomly shuffles the embeddings, while ϕ arranges the shuffled dimensions of $\mathbf{e_s}$ and $\mathbf{e_r}$ sequentially, and finally reshapes them into a matrix. As shown in Fig. 3, for example, given an 8-dimensional subject entity $\mathbf{e_s} = \{s^1, s^2, s^3, s^4, s^5, s^6, s^7, s^8\}$, where s^i represents the embedding of this subject entity in the i-th dimension, the output entity representation after $\mathcal{P}$ could be $\mathbf{e_s} = \{s^7, s^2, s^8, s^5, s^3, s^6, s^4, s^1\}$. Then, applying ϕ yields the input feature matrix A, where $A \in \mathbb{R}^{m_h \times m_w}$.

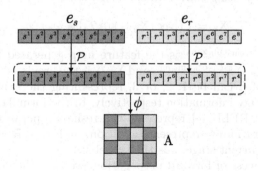

Fig. 3. A depiction of the method known as Feature Permutation and Checkered Reshaping.

To further enhance the feature expression, the augmented feature representation of entities and relations is passed through a 1×1 convolutional layer,

$$\overline{A} = f\left(A \circledast \omega_{1\times 1}\right),\qquad(4)$$

where $\circledast$ is the convolution operator, f represent the nonlinear activation function RELU, and $\overline{A} \in \mathbb{R}^{C_{in} \times C_{out} \times m_h \times m_w}$ denotes the feature map generated by applying filter $\omega_{1\times 1} \in \mathbb{R}^{C_{in} \times C_{out}}$ to the input matrix A.

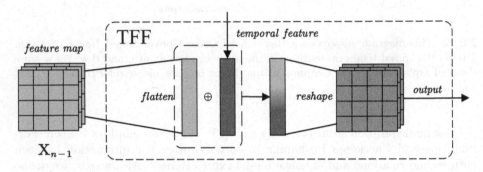

Fig. 4. Temporal feature fusion (TFF) process employed by HCN, the temporal feature was from TFG.

We merge temporal features in hierarchical order: year, month, and day, and use convolutional filters to extract semantic information, the method of fusing temporal features is shown in Fig. 4. We first flatten the input feature map to obtain a feature vector with dimensions equivalent to those of the temporal feature. The next step involves adding the flattened feature vector to the temporal feature to merge them, and resulting in a merged feature map that is reshaped to align with the original feature map. Finally, we obtain the feature map for the current stage by using convolutional operations,

$$X_n = f\left(\left[\text{vec}\left(X_{n-1}\right) \oplus \mathcal{T}_n\right] \circledast \omega_n\right),\qquad(5)$$

where $X_n \in \mathbb{R}^{C_{in} \times C_{out} \times m_h \times m_w}$ is the feature map generated by fusing current temporal feature $\mathcal{T}_n \in \mathbb{R}^{C_{in} C_{out} m_w m_h}$, and X_{n-1} is the previously obtained feature map. The value of n can be 1, 2, or 3, representing the stages of integrating year, month, and day information respectively. In the formula, f represents the nonlinear function RELU, $[\cdot]$ represents the reshape operation, $\text{vec}(\cdot)$ denotes the flattening operation, $\oplus$ represents addition, and $\omega_n \in \mathbb{R}^{C_{in} \times C_{out} \times k \times k}$ is the filter used in the current stage, k is the kernel size.

During the process of forward propagation, we take the enhanced representation feature map $\overline{A}$ as the initial input X_0 before fusing time, and then we sequentially fuse the temporal feature $\mathcal{T}_n$ obtained from TFG into the feature map according to the time hierarchy split by the timestamp, where $\mathcal{T}_1 = \mathcal{Y}_\tau$, $\mathcal{T}_2 = \mathcal{M}_\tau$, $\mathcal{T}_3 = \mathcal{D}_\tau$. By processing the feature map via the convolutional layer, we eventually acquire a fully integrated feature map X_3 that contains complete temporal features.

HCN can share periodic knowledge by utilizing the same temporal features, but typically, historical events have a minor effect on current events. Distant events can increase noise levels and therefore have a negligible impact. To solve this problem, we utilized the LSTM mechanism in TFG (Sect. 4.1) to consider changing factors and ensure that the model not only shares periodic knowledge but also detects variations. This way, the model can manage complex time series data more efficiently and enhance its generalizability.

4.3   Training and Optimization

The final output feature map of HCN is flattened, and then this vector is projected into the embedding space $\mathbb{R}^d$, and matched with the object embedding $\mathbf{e_o}$ via a dot product. Formally, the scoring function used in TSN is defined as follows:

$$\psi(s, r, o) = f\left(\text{vec}\left(\text{HCN}(\mathbf{e_s}, \mathbf{e_r})\right) \mathbf{W}\right) \mathbf{e_o}, \tag{6}$$

where $\text{vec}(\cdot)$ denotes the flattening operation, $\mathbf{e_o}$ represents the object entity embedding matrix and $\mathbf{W}$ is a trainable weight matrix.

The predicted probability $p(o_i \mid s, r, t)$ for the selected object entity as the answer is obtained by applying the logistic sigmoid function to the scores. To train the model parameters, we minimize the binary cross-entropy loss defined as follows:

$$\mathcal{L}(y, p) = -\tfrac{1}{N} \sum_{i=1}^{N} \left(y_i \log p\left(o_i \mid s, r, t\right) + (1 - y_i) \log\left(1 - p\left(o_i \mid s, r, t\right)\right)\right),$$

$$y_i = \begin{cases} 1 & \text{if } (s, r, o_i, t) \in \mathcal{G}, \\ 0 & \text{if } (s, r, o_i, t) \in \mathcal{G}', \end{cases} \tag{7}$$

where N is the number of entities, y_i represents the label of positive or negative quadruples, $\mathcal{G}$ is the set of positive quadruples, and $\mathcal{G}'$ is the set of negative quadruples obtained by randomly replacing the subject or object entities.

5   Experiments

5.1   Experimental Setup

Datasets. This paper assesses the performance of the TSN model on four commonly used public datasets, namely, ICEWS14, ICEWS05-15, YAGO11k, and Wikidata12k. ICEWS14 [15] and ICEWS05-15 [15] datasets are derived from the Integrated Crisis Early Warning System, which tracks significant events related to politics, economy, security, and society for the years 2014 and 2005–2015, respectively. YAGO11k [1] and Wikidata12k [1] are large-scale knowledge graphs constructed using Wikipedia as a source, containing various contents including personal relationships, birthplace relationships, and work relationships. Refer to

Table 1 for detailed dataset information. The YAGO11k dataset offers annotations on time that are measured in days. Following the previous study conducted by [1], this paper deals exclusively with annual tasks on time range and omits information on month and date. To resolve the issue of imbalance in YAGO11k and Wikidata12k, we established time levels and minimum thresholds.

Table 1. Statistics of datasets.

Dataset	#Entities	#Relations	#Training	#Validation	#Test	Time Interval
ICEWS14	6,869	230	72,826	8,941	8,963	day
ICEWS05-15	10,094	251	368,962	46,275	46,092	day
YAGO11k	10,623	10	16,406	2,050	2,051	year
Wikidata12k	12,554	24	32,497	4,062	4,062	year

Evaluation Metrics. For each test sample, the model will provide a set of candidate entities. MRR considers the position of the correct entity in the ranking of candidate entities. This metric is obtained by adding the reciprocal of the ranking of the correct entity in all test samples and dividing by the total number of test samples. Hit@N (N = 1, 3, 10) is used to evaluate whether the model includes the correct entity in the top N candidate entities. The final evaluation metric is the mean score of Hit@N for all test samples.

Baselines. In this study, we compare the performance of static KGC and TKGC models. The static KGC models investigated in this study consist of TransE [5], DistMult [10], RotatE [19], and InteractE [13] while the TKGC models comprised TTransE [14], HyTE [1], TA-TransE [15], TA-DistMult [15], DE-SimplE [20], TComplEx [2], TeRo [3], TeLM [16], TuckERTNT [17], and BoxTE [18]. It is worth noting that the source codes and experimental findings of models such as TuckERTNT have not been publicly released for the YAGO11k and Wikidata12k datasets. As such, this study only includes a comparison of the models on the ICEWS14 and ICEWS05-15 datasets.

Implementation Details. The TSN model was implemented in PyTorch, using an NVIDIA GeForce RTX 3090 for all experiments. The Adam optimizer was used for optimization, employing a learning rate set to 0.001. For all datasets, the embedding dimension d was 300, and the number of convolution filters was set at 128. The ICEWS14 and ICEWS05-15 datasets employed a convolution kernel size of 3, while the YAGO and Wikidata12K datasets utilized a convolution kernel size of 5.

5.2 Link Prediction

Link prediction is the most significant task in knowledge graph completion, aiming to predict subject/object entities or relations that are missing based on existing knowledge. Tables 2 and 3 illustrate the prediction results of entities in link prediction, the best results are shown in bold and the second best are shown underlined.

Table 2. Link prediction results on ICEWS14 and ICEWS05-15. *: the result is obtained from TeRo [3]. ♣: the result is obtained by applying the source code to a new dataset. Other results are from the original papers.

Model	ICEWS14				ICEWS05-15			
	MRR	Hit@1	Hit@3	Hit@10	MRR	Hit@1	Hit@3	Hit@10
TransE*	28.0	9.4	–	63.7	29.4	9.0	–	66.3
DistMult*	43.9	32.3	–	67.2	45.6	33.7	–	69.1
RotatE*	41.8	29.1	47.8	69.0	30.4	16.4	35.5	59.5
InteractE♣	48.2	36.4	54.6	71.3	48.7	36.8	54.9	71.9
TTransE*	25.5	7.4	–	60.1	27.1	8.4	–	61.6
HyTE*	29.7	10.8	41.6	65.5	31.6	11.6	44.5	68.1
TA-TransE*	27.5	9.5	–	62.5	29.9	9.6	–	66.8
TA-DistMult*	47.7	36.3	–	68.6	47.4	34.6	–	72.8
TComplEx	61.0	53.0	66.0	77.0	66.0	59.0	71.0	80.0
TeRo	56.2	46.8	62.1	73.2	58.6	46.9	66.8	79.5
TeLM	<u>62.5</u>	<u>54.5</u>	<u>67.3</u>	<u>77.4</u>	<u>67.8</u>	<u>59.9</u>	<u>72.8</u>	<u>82.3</u>
TuckERTNT	<u>62.5</u>	54.4	<u>67.3</u>	77.3	67.5	59.3	72.5	81.9
BoxTE	61.3	52.8	66.4	76.3	66.7	58.2	71.9	82.0
TSN	**64.1**	**56.1**	**69.1**	**78.7**	**68.7**	**60.3**	**74.2**	**83.9**

The TSN model proposed in this paper achieved the best performance among other models in this task, demonstrating its advantages. Compared to the optimal baseline, TSN improves the MRR by approximately 2.6% and 1.3% on the ICEWS14 and ICEWS05-15 datasets, and improves the MRR by approximately 33.5% and 34.6% on YAGO11k and Wikidata12k, respectively.

Using temporal information to distinguish timely facts is advantageous for TKG link prediction in most TKGC models, which are typically more effective than static KGC models. TSN, unlike InteractE [13] which uses convolutional neural networks, integrates the time embedding generated time characteristics into the convolutional process, enabling it to perceive the semantic information of entities and relations that change over time. It worth noting that TSN outperformed all other models in all link prediction indicators. In comparison with other TKGC models like the TuckERTNT [17] and BoxTE [18], the TSN model decomposes each timestamp embedding into year, month, and day, allowing it to capture semantic information at various time levels. Additionally, by sharing the same year, month, or day temporal features at various times, the TSN model models periodic information and thereby significantly improves the model's feature extraction and expression abilities.

Table 3. Link prediction results on YAGO11k and Wikidata12k. *: the result is obtained from TeRo [3]. ♣: the result is obtained by applying the source code to a new dataset. Other results are from the original papers.

Model	YAGO11k				Wikidata12k			
	MRR	Hit@1	Hit@3	Hit@10	MRR	Hit@1	Hit@3	Hit@10
TransE*	10.0	1.5	13.8	24.4	17.8	10.0	19.2	33.9
DistMult*	15.8	10.7	16.1	26.8	22.2	11.9	23.8	46.0
RotatE*	16.7	10.3	16.7	30.5	22.1	11.6	23.6	46.1
InteractE♣	14.7	9.4	14.9	26.1	23.7	14.4	25.5	43.2
TTransE*	10.8	2.0	15.0	25.1	17.2	9.6	18.4	32.9
HyTE*	10.5	1.5	14.3	27.2	18.0	9.8	19.7	33.3
TA-TransE*	12.7	2.7	16.0	32.6	17.8	3.0	26.7	42.9
TA-DistMult*	16.1	10.3	17.1	29.2	21.8	12.2	23.2	44.7
TComplEx	18.5	12.7	18.3	30.7	33.1	_23.3_	35.7	53.9
TeRo	18.7	12.1	_19.7_	31.9	29.9	19.8	32.9	50.7
TeLM	_19.1_	_12.9_	19.4	_32.1_	_33.2_	23.1	_36.0_	_54.2_
TSN	**25.5**	**18.8**	**26.3**	**40.0**	**44.7**	**35.1**	**49.1**	**64.2**

5.3   Timestamp Embedding Space Complexity

Table 4 summarizes several scoring functions and the timestamp tmbedding space complexities based on the TKGC method and . The variables n_y, n_m, and n_d correspond to the number of years, months, and days, respectively. d represents the dimension of the timestamp embedding. In ICEWS14, TSN splits the timestamp *2014-05-27* into three embeddings: the year *2014*, the month *05*, and the day *27*. The dataset includes all timestamps from 2014, and the traditional TKGC model necessitates approximately 365 timestamp embeddings. In contrast, our combined model only needs 44 embeddings, one each for the year and thirty one for the dates, and twelve for the months. This indicates a nearly ten-fold reduction in parameters. Suppose we apply this method to a larger dataset such as ICEWS05-15. In that case, the effect will be more remarkable, with a parameter decrease of almost 100 times.

5.4   Ablation Study

In this study, ablation experiments were performed on the ICEWS05-15 dataset to examine the effectiveness of TSN's key modules, as displayed in Table 5.

Table 4. Comparison of TSN with several baseline models for scoring function and timestamp embedding space complexity.

Model	Scoring Function	Timestamp embedding Space Complexity
TransE	$\|s + r - o\|$	–
TTransE	$\|s + r + \tau - o\|$	$\mathcal{O}\left((n_y n_m n_d)d\right)$
HyTE	$\|P_t(s) + P_t(r) - P_t(o)\|$	$\mathcal{O}\left((n_y n_m n_d)d\right)$
TeRo	$\|s_t + r - \bar{o}_t\|$	$\mathcal{O}\left((n_y n_m n_d)d\right)$
TSN	$f\left(\text{vec}\left(\text{HCN}(e_s, e_r)\right) W\right) e_o$	$\mathcal{O}\left(n_y d + n_m d + n_d d\right)$

Among them, TSN (-T) represents the non-fusion of temporal features in the convolution process, that is, the removal of time information; TSN (-TS) represents the embedding that does not split the timestamp into "year", "month", and "day", and sets a separate embedding representation for each timestamp; TSN (-HC) represents that the features generated by the convolution of the year, month, and day are concatenated and fused as the final output, regardless of the hierarchical order. The experimental results show that the performance of TSN significantly decreased after removing the time information (T), timestamp split (TS), and hierarchical order (HC), indicating that these modules are important components of TSN. Specifically, after eliminating timestamp split and hierarchical convolution, the performance of TSN decreased significantly, and the MRR were reduced by 5.5% and 1.6%, respectively, because these two modules can perceive the hierarchical structure and periodicity information of time, and model the evolution process of entities and relations in the hierarchical structure. In addition, after eliminating time information, the performance of TSN decreased significantly, and the MRR was reduced by 29.8%. The elimination of this module will hinder the modeling ability of TSN for knowledge that changes over time, thereby limiting the expressive power of the model, which emphasizes the importance of time information in knowledge graph completion.

Table 5. Results of the ablation study on ICEWS05-15 dataset.

Model	ICEWS05-15			
	MRR	Hits@1	Hits@3	Hits@5
TSN(-T)	48.2	36.0	54.5	72.2
TSN(-TS)	64.9	55.8	70.8	81.4
TSN(-HC)	67.6	58.8	73.4	83.6
TSN	**68.7**	**60.3**	**74.2**	**83.9**

6   Conclusion and Future Work

In this paper, we propose a novel model called TSN for temporal knowledge graph completion. Unlike the previous TKGC method, TSN is capable of capturing the time hierarchy and periodicity, thus overcoming their limitation. Utilizing Temporal Feature Generator and Hierarchical Order Convolutional Network, TSN captures the hierarchy and periodicity of time, and possesses a more comprehensive time awareness. Additionally, TSN minimizes the number of model parameters. The experiment results indicate that TSN outperforms the baseline model in comprehensibility, semantic extraction accuracy, and overall performance on multiple datasets. In future research, we will focus on exploring the extrapolation ability of TSN.

Acknowledgements. This work was supported by the Natural Science Foundation of Fujian, China (No. 2021J01619).

References

1. Dasgupta, S.S., Ray, S.N., Talukdar, P.P.: HyTE: hyperplane-based temporally aware knowledge graph embedding. In: EMNLP, pp. 2001–2011 (2018)
2. Lacroix, T., Obozinski, G., Usunier, N.: Tensor decompositions for temporal knowledge base completion. arXiv preprint arXiv:2004.04926 (2020)
3. Xu, C., Nayyeri, M., Alkhoury, F., Yazdi, H.S., Lehmann, J.: TeRo: a time-aware knowledge graph embedding via temporal rotation. arXiv preprint arXiv:2010.01029 (2020)
4. Wang, J., et al.: GLANet: temporal knowledge graph completion based on global and local information-aware network. Appl. Intell. 1–17 (2023)
5. Bordes, A., Usunier, N., Garcia-Duran, A., Weston, J., Yakhnenko, O.: Translating embeddings for modeling multi-relational data. In: Advances in Neural Information Processing Systems, vol. 26 (2013)
6. Wang, Z., Zhang, J., Feng, J., Chen, Z.: Knowledge graph embedding by translating on hyperplanes. In: Proceedings of the AAAI Conference on Artificial Intelligence, vol. 28 (2014)
7. Lin, Y., Liu, Z., Sun, M., Liu, Y., Zhu, X.: Learning entity and relation embeddings for knowledge graph completion. In: Proceedings of the AAAI Conference on Artificial Intelligence, vol. 29 (2015)
8. Ji, G., He, S., Xu, L., Liu, K., Zhao, J.: Knowledge graph embedding via dynamic mapping matrix. In: Proceedings of the 53rd Annual Meeting of the Association for Computational Linguistics and the 7th International Joint Conference on Natural Language Processing (Volume 1: Long Papers), pp. 687–696 (2015)
9. Nickel, M., Tresp, V., Kriegel, H.-P., et al.: A three-way model for collective learning on multi-relational data. In: ICML, vol. 11, pp. 3104482–3104584 (2011)
10. Yang, B., Yih, W., He, X., Gao, J., Deng, L.: Embedding entities and relations for learning and inference in knowledge bases. arXiv preprint arXiv:1412.6575 (2014)
11. Trouillon, T., Welbl, J., Riedel, S., Gaussier, É., Bouchard, G.: Complex embeddings for simple link prediction. In: International conference on machine learning, pp. 2071–2080. PMLR (2016)

12. Dettmers, T., Minervini, P., Stenetorp, P., Riedel, S.: Convolutional 2D knowledge graph embeddings. In: Proceedings of the AAAI Conference on Artificial Intelligence, vol. 32 (2018)
13. Vashishth, S., Sanyal, S., Nitin, V., Agrawal, N., Talukdar, P.: InteractE: improving convolution-based knowledge graph embeddings by increasing feature interactions. In: Proceedings of the AAAI Conference on Artificial Intelligence, vol. 34, pp. 3009–3016 (2020)
14. Leblay, J., Chekol, M.W.: Deriving validity time in knowledge graph. In: Companion Proceedings of the the Web Conference 2018, pp. 1771–1776 (2018)
15. García-Durán, A., Dumančić, S., Niepert, M.: Learning sequence encoders for temporal knowledge graph completion. arXiv preprint arXiv:1809.03202 (2018)
16. Xu, C., Chen, Y.-Y., Nayyeri, M., Lehmann, J.: Temporal knowledge graph completion using a linear temporal regularizer and multivector embeddings. In: Proceedings of the 2021 Conference of the North American Chapter of the Association for Computational Linguistics: Human Language Technologies, pp. 2569–2578 (2021)
17. Shao, P., Zhang, D., Yang, G., Tao, J., Che, F., Liu, T.: Tucker decomposition-based temporal knowledge graph completion. Knowl.-Based Syst. **238**, 107841 (2022)
18. Messner, J., Abboud, R., Ceylan, I.I.: Temporal knowledge graph completion using box embeddings. In: Proceedings of the AAAI Conference on Artificial Intelligence, vol. 36, pp. 7779–7787 (2022)
19. Sun, Z., Deng, Z.-H., Nie, J.-Y., Tang, J.: RotatE: knowledge graph embedding by relational rotation in complex space. arXiv preprint arXiv:1902.10197 (2019)
20. Goel, R., Kazemi, S.M., Brubaker, M., Poupart, P.: Diachronic embedding for temporal knowledge graph completion. In: Proceedings of the AAAI Conference on Artificial Intelligence, vol. 34, pp. 3988–3995 (2020)

Deep Q-Learning Based Circuit Breaking Method for Micro-services in Cloud Native Systems

Xuan Sun, Bo Cui, and Zhicheng Cai[✉]

School of Computer Science, Nanjing University of Science and Technology,
Nanjing 210094, China
caizhicheng@njust.edu.cn

Abstract. More and more modern applications are being deployed on cloud-native systems. High concurrent requests that exceed the processing capacity lead to service failures, and the failure of a single microservice result in the entire application unavailable. Currently, most existing methods rely on manual adjustment of microservice's circuit breaking strategies based on empirical experience. It is very complex to select an appropriate circuit breaking strategy, considering the processing capacity, ect. In this paper, a reinforcement learning-based method is proposed which tries to select optimal circuit breaking strategy by interacting with the system continuously. The proposed method is evaluated on a real Kubernetes and Istio based cluster. Experimental results demonstrate that our approach achieves a successful service rate of 92.6% for requests while 7.4% of requests experience failures. In contrast, the static circuit breaker achieves an average of 48.4% successful service and 51.6% failure rate.

Keywords: Cloud Computing · Microservices · Istio · Reinforcement Learning · Circuit Breaking

1 Introduction

It is important to select appropriate circuit breaking strategies for microservices in a cloud-native environment. Cloud native based micro-service architecture has increased the complexity of software operating. Cloud-native mesh microservice, a new type of microservices architecture, typically uses service mesh to handle communication and routing between services [1]. Under high workload, the number of request connections between microservices may exceed their resource limits, leading to performance degradation or system failures. Circuit breaking is a technique for handling inevitable faults and exceptions in microservices architecture [2]. In Istio, circuit breaking is an important traffic management policy. When a target service experiences anomalies or the request load exceeds a predefined threshold, Istio automatically triggers the circuit breaking mechanism,

Y. Sun et al. (Eds.): ChineseCSCW 2023, CCIS 2012, pp. 348–362, 2024.
https://doi.org/10.1007/978-981-99-9637-7_26

halting invocations between services and providing customized fallback strategies to prevent cascading failures. When the number of container resources is fixed, setting a small limit on the maximum number of connections for microservice requests can result in a low number of requests, thereby preventing the container resources from fully utilizing their performance and leading to resource waste. On the other hand, setting a large limit on the maximum number of connections for microservice requests can render flow control operations ineffective. Therefore, the goal of this paper is to proposed an algorithm that can dynamically adjust the connection limits of microservices based on real-time workload. This algorithm enables effective resource management and improves system stability.

Due to the complexity, dynamism, and diversity of microservices architecture, the parameter setting of circuit breaking strategies becomes complex. Multiple factors should be considered comprehensively to adjust these parameters considering real time conditions. Most existing methods for microservices circuit breaking strategies belong to manual adjustments [3]. However, manual adjustment methods are often static and cannot adapt to workload and system changes dynamically. Additionally, manual adjustment methods suffer from subjective bias, affecting the consistency and stability of strategies. Therefore, some research has focused on automated and intelligent circuit breaking strategy configuration and adjustment. For example, some research utilize the exponential smoothing method to construct a circuit breaking [4] which adjusts the threshold of the request wait queue online dynamically and aims to keep the response time of services below as a specified threshold. However, this method relies on historical data to calculate the current average and system state, making it less sensitively to workload changes and unable to fully prevent system anomalies during significant fluctuations in requests.

In this paper, a deep Q-learning [5,6] based circuit breaking algorithm (DQCB) is proposed, which adjusts the maximum request connection limit of microservices with fixed resources dynamically. DQCB utilizes Jaeger and Elasticsearch to collect, store, and preprocess the invocation chains and metrics of microservices. DQCB can continuously interact with the system and utilize collected data to train its internal deep neural network, achieving the approximation of the non-linear Q function. The main contributions of this paper are as follows.

(1) An intelligent algorithm based on deep Q Learning is proposed to dynamically set the connection limits of microservices.
(2) A controller including the intelligent circuit breaking algorithm is implemented as a plugin of the Kubernetes and Istio based system.

The remaining sections of this paper are organized as follows. Section 2 provides a literature review on circuit breaking in the context of Istio. Section 3 describes the problem statement and formulation in detail. Section 4 presents the details on the proposed algorithm for intelligent setting of the maximum request connection limit. Section 5 discusses the experimental setup and presents the results obtained from the experiments. Finally, Sect. 6 concludes the paper by summarizing the main findings and contributions.

2   Related Work

In a microservices architecture, the circuit breaking is one of the crucial components that ensure system stability. Hence, numerous research efforts have been devoted to improving the performance and effectiveness of circuit breaking. The existing research in this field is surveyed from circuit breaking controllers' strategies.

Existing fault handling methods are composed of: retry, fallback strategy, and circuit breaker. The retry mechanism allows for retrying failed requests, with the number of retries specified by the retry attempts parameter and the retry interval set by the retry timeout parameter, to achieve reliable communication between microservices. For example, Mendonca et al. [7] conducted continuous-time Markov chain analysis of circuit breaker behavior and retry mechanism patterns in single-layer architectures.

The fallback strategy provides alternative responses or actions when a service is unavailable or encounters a problem. Saleh et al. [3] conducted research on circuit breaking and fallback strategies in Istio, revealing the impact of these strategies in microservices through the setting of static parameters.

Istio [2] has the advantages of integration, centralized management, and a unified control plane [8], making the configuration and management of circuit breaking strategies more convenient. As the application of Istio becomes more widespread, its circuit breaking and rate limiting functionalities play important roles. Rate limiting is a mechanism for controlling the traffic flow within a system. By restricting the number or rate of requests, it helps prevent system overload and resource exhaustion. On the other hand, the circuit breaker [9] is a mechanism to monitor and manage service invocations. It monitors the state and performance of services and automatically isolates them in case of failures or performance degradation. Here are some studies on fault localization and fault recovery using circuit breaking. Meina et al. [10] proposed a microservice tracing system based on Kubernetes and Istio to monitor and collect invocation information among microservices in a distributed system. The sloution handles tracing information by separating the network proxy layer, minimizing modifications. Fanfei et al. [11] proposed a workflow based on a reinforcement learning model to achieve fault recovery capability in service networks. It is capable of predicting the most critical fault recovery behaviors at the network application layer. In addition, there are also some studies on how to implement circuit breaking strategies. Lennart et al. [12] discussed how Istio and Traefik achieve disconnection at the infrastructure level, using Resilience4j as an example. The combination of circuit breaking and edge computing [13] has also been explored in research studies. Ganguli et al. [14] combined service mesh architecture with edge computing [15,16] to explore the complexities of deploying service mesh in edge environment. There is only several works on rate limiting. For example, Mohammad et al. [4] proposed an adaptive circuit breaker collector that uses an exponential smoothing function to dynamically adjust the threshold of the request queue, controlling the service response time to be below a specified threshold.

In total, many existing methods use fixed thresholds to determine whether to open or close the circuit breaker and lack dynamism. Our algorithm is applied as a plugin to control the connection limits of microservices based on Istio dynamically.

3 Problem Description

Kubernetes [17,18] is a container orchestration platform used for automating the deployment, scaling, and management of containers. By defining and managing various components of containerized applications such as Pods, Deployments, and Services, Kubernetes provides a flexible and reliable way to run and manage distributed applications. Istio [19], built on top of Kubernetes, is an open-source service mesh platform that comprehensive service governance capabilities for microservice architectures [20]. By injecting proxies (Enovy) between services, Istio enables fine-grained control and management of service-to-service communication. The combination of Kubernetes and Istio offers a complete containerization solution for microservice architectures. Microservice applications typically consist of multiple microservices, with each microservice containing multiple Pods (typically comprising a business container and an accompanying Istio container). Figure 1 shows the microservice architecture based on Kubernetes and Istio. The "Bookinfo" provided by the Istio website is a sample application, which consists of four microservices: Productpage, Details, Ratings, and Reviews [21]. These microservices provide an online platform for book review and browsing collaboratively. Istio's Pilot component is responsible for traffic management and policy configuration across the entire service mesh. It communicates with Kubernetes API to dynamically understand the location and availability of services. Meanwhile, Jaeger is utilized as a distributed tracing system to comprehensively visualize and monitor traffic in the microservice architecture. The functionalities such as distributed tracing, performance analysis, and anomaly tracking could be performed based on trace data collected by Jaeger. Finally, Elasticsearch is used as a solution for logging, metrics collection, storage, and visualization. Elasticsearch is an open-source distributed search and analytics engine [22] that can be used for log collection and storage, metrics collection and monitoring, as well as data visualization and analysis. The objective of this paper is to leverage this tracing data to obtain performance and resource metrics for different services and design a circuit breaker controller.

In a microservice architecture, the failure or latency of one service can impact the performance and availability of the entire system. The Istio architecture provides many features and capabilities that contribute to the design and implementation of a circuit breaking controller. These include centralized traffic management and control plane, rich observability and monitoring capabilities, and support for custom traffic strategies and rules. It is necessary to design a intelligent controller that dynamically adjusts the connection limits of microservices and rejects all requests beyond the acceptable range when a microservice is overload. The decision maker servers as a core component responsible for making circuit breaking decision based on real-time information and policies. Its

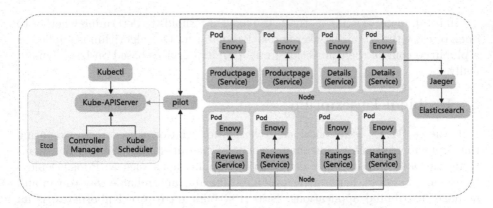

Fig. 1. The architecture of a real system environment.

primary objective is to monitor and assess the performance and reliability of microservices and dynamically adjust the circuit breaking strategy to maintain system stability and availability.

For implementing the circuit breaking controller, an intelligent circuit breaking algorithm is proposed for the controller in Kubernetes and Istio architectures. The controller consists of three modules: the log collection module, the log processing module, and the control center module. Figure 2 depicts the architecture of the controller. The user access traces are monitored by the Istio-Ingressgateway load balancer running at the service mesh boundary. In the log collection module, Jaeger is utilized as the request tracing system, and the tracing information is sampled by configuring the zipkin attribute and sampling rate in Istio's configuration files. The traced request link information is persistently stored in the Elasticsearch backend storage system. The logs are analyzed by the log processing module, and the processed logs are stored in the local file system. The control center retrieves the processed parameterized log information every 15 s, including metrics such as request count, arrival rate, response time, CPU utilization, Memory utilization, and successful request count. Based on the actions provided by the algorithm, the maximum connection count for requests is determined and dynamically adjusted by the adaptive control system.

Our goal is to develop an intelligent algorithm for this decision maker. The algorithm enables the controller to make informed and adaptive circuit breaking decision based on the collected information and system state. Assuming a microservice system contains N services, where each service has a maximum concurrent connection count of C_i, where $i \in [1, N]$. To describe the system state, the following metrics are defined: T_i denotes the average response time of the ith service. P_i denotes the current load of the ith service, i.e. the sum of existing connections. S_i denotes the success request of the ith microservices. Our objective is to determine the maximum connection count C_i for each microservices in order to maximises the system throughput while maintaining stability and reliability. The objective function is express in the following equation:

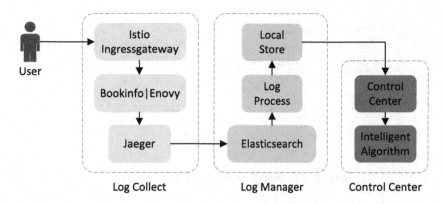

Fig. 2. The architecture of the controller.

$$\max_{C_i} \sum_{i=1}^{N} \frac{S_i}{P_i} \tag{1}$$

Therefore, an algorithm that intelligently sets the maximum connection count C_i for each microservice using historical request data and system state to optimise the objective function mentioned above is required to optimize the above objectives.

4   Proposed Deep Q-Learning Based Circuit Breaking Method

The deep Q-learning [23] based circuit breaking (DQCB) is proposed for the controller to set the connection limits of microservices intelligently. The controller automatically learn and decide the optimal number of requests, adapting to different system loads and service demands.

4.1   The Architecture of DQCB

The reason for choosing the DQN algorithm is that deep Q-learning allows for autonomous learning of complex strategies through interaction with the environment and enables the selection of appropriate thresholds based on dynamic factors such as workload and processing capabilities. Traditional static circuit breakers often rely on predefined rules and thresholds to determine the circuit breaking strategy, which cannot dynamically adjust based on real-time system status and load conditions, and it is challenging to find the optimal circuit breaker configuration. Therefore, an intelligent approach is needed to adaptively adjust the request connection limit of microservices.

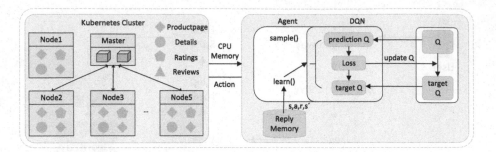

Fig. 3. The flowchart of the DQN algorithm.

The overall idea of DQN is to learn and make decisions on the optimal request connection number by continuously interacting with the system, in order to adapt to different system loads and service requirements. The flowchart of the DQN algorithm is shown in Fig. 3. In this problem, the DQCB algorithm takes the system's state information, such as CPU utilization and memory utilization, as input, and outputs the decision on the request connection number. Through interaction with the environment, DQN selects actions based on the observed system state and updates the Q-value function of the neural network based on the rewards and feedback signals obtained from the chosen actions. By learning through trial and error, the controller gradually optimizes its strategy to achieve the best performance and resource utilization.

4.2   State and Action Spaces

The CPU utilization and Memory utilization are used as input for the DQN algorithm because they provide a direct reflection of the system's current processing capability. In the experiment, a state space S is defined which includes the CPU utilization and Memory utilization of the microservice. In terms of the action space, an action space A is defined which represents the maximum number of connections to be set by the microservices. The dimension of the action space action_dim is defined as 3. By defining these three actions, different scenarios and requirements are able to be covered. The optimal action could be find to achieve the best system performance and resource utilization through training and learning. In this experiment, each action is transformed into the number of requested connections, respectively "10-1-1", "10-1-5", "10-1-10". The first number indicates the value of the property of the $maxConnection$, and the second number indicates the value of the property of the $maxRequestsPerConnection$, and the last number indicates the value of the property of the $http1MaxPendingRequests$, all of which can be defined and changed in the destination rules.

4.3   Reward Function and Loss Function

The reward function Rwd based on the success rate of requests is used to evaluate the system's performance, which can be defined as:

$$Rwd_t = \begin{cases} -1 + rate_t \, , \, rate_t < 0.8 \\ rate_t \, , \, rate_t \geq 0.8 \end{cases} \tag{2}$$

where $rate_t$ represents the success rate of obtained requests, and Rwd_t denotes the reward obtained by performing action a_t in state s_t.

When the threshold of a microservice is set to a larger value, more requests can successfully enter the system through the Ingress Gateway. This means that within the processing capacity of the Pod, the system can handle a higher number of requests, resulting in a high request success rate. Conversely, if the threshold is set to a smaller value, only a limited number of requests can be accepted, potentially causing a decrease in the system's load capacity. This may lead to some requests being rejected, resulting in a low request success rate. When the success rate of requests is greater than or equal to 0.8, a positive reward is given. The magnitude of the reward is equal to the success rate of the requests. When the success rate of requests is less than 0.8, a penalty is given. The magnitude of the penalty is adjusted based on the level of the success rate. A higher success rate results in a lower penalty, while a lower success rate results in a higher penalty.

After defining the state space, action space, and reward function. To evaluate the goodness of each state, a value function $Q(s, a)$ is defined to represent the long-term payoff of choosing action a in state s. In DQN, a deep convolutional neural network is used to estimate this value function [24]. Generally, an objective function is used to update the value function, which can be defined as:

$$Q_{target}(s, a) = r + \gamma \max_{a'} Q(s', a') \tag{3}$$

where r is the immediate payoff at the current moment, γ is the discount factor, s' is the next state to enter after selecting action a, $\max_{a'} Q(s', a')$ is the maximum value that can be obtained in the next state.

The mean square error is used as the loss function, which can be defined as:

$$L(\theta) = \frac{1}{2} \left[Q_{target}(s, a) - Q(s, a; \theta) \right]^2 \tag{4}$$

where θ is a parameter of the neural network and $Q(s, a; \theta)$ is an estimate of the value function under the current state and action.

4.4   Formal Description

A DQN-based algorithm for intelligently setting the number of microservice requests is based on the Istio and Kubernetes platform. In this algorithm, the agent is responsible for giving a policy for adjusting the maximum number of request connections by a microservice.

An action is chosen based on a certain policy at each time step after defining the state and action spaces, the reward function, the loss function and initializing the weights and parameters of the neural network. The chosen action is applied to the environment, and the feedback from the environment, including the reward and the next state, is observed. The experiences of each time step, including the state, action, reward, and next state, are defined as a quadratic $t(s, a, r, s')$ which is stored in an experience replay cache D. A batch of experiences is randomly sampled from the experience replay buffer for training the neural network. The objective is to minimize the loss function using the sampled experiences for training the neural network.

The Stochastic Gradient Descent (SGD) is used to update the parameters of the neural network θ to minimize the loss function $L(\theta)$, with the following parameter update formula:

$$\theta_{t+1} = \theta_t - \alpha \nabla_\theta L(\theta) \tag{5}$$

where α is the learning rate and $\nabla_\theta L(\theta)$ is the gradient of the loss function $L(\theta)$ with respect to the parameter θ.

4.5   Implementation of the Intelligent Controller

In the implementation process of the intelligent controller, several aspects need to be considered, including the format of trajectory data, handling of trajectory data by the intelligent controller, and adjusting thresholds based on given actions.

The data obtained from the Elasticsearch backend database is in JSON format and includes fields such as traceID, spanID, operationName, startTimeMillis, and tags. Table 1 shows the format of log data in Elasticsearch. The spanID is a unique identifier used to represent specific operations or activities within a request or transaction. The traceID is a unique identifier that represents a series of spans associated with a particular request or transaction. Each traceID corresponds to multiple spanIDs, indicating the relationship between them. The "operationName" field indicates the name of the operation or activity for each span. The "startTimeMillis" field records the start time of each span and the "tags" field provides additional labeling information, including whether the request was successful or not.

Table 1. The Format of Log Data in Elasticsearch.

Key	Value
traceID	ee6e5ad8bac3228ca606db51adbd15ab
spanID	6031a37387f28940
operationName	reviews.default.svc.cluster.local:9080/*
startTimeMillis	1678414964471
tags	http.status_code=200

DestinationRules is a custom resource type in Istio that is used to define traffic between services. With DestinationRules, we can define traffic distribution ratios, failure retry mechanisms, load balancing strategies, and more for different service versions. The configuration file for DestinationRules is shown in Fig. 4. The experiment is based on the trafficPolicy field to define the traffic policies for the service. The tls field is used to specify the TLS mode for the traffic. The connectionPool field is used to specify the connection pool settings for TCP and HTTP protocols. The maxConnections field in the tcp section is used to specify the maximum number of allowed connections. The http1MaxPendingRequests field in the http section is used to specify the maximum number of pending requests. The maxRequestsPerConnection field is used to specify the maximum number of requests per connection. For the threshold adjustment problem in the intelligent controller, since Istio uses a custom resource type called DestinationRules to define traffic rules between services, the patchClusterCustomObject method provided by the Kubernetes Java Client is used to modify the custom resource.

```
apiVersion: networking.istio.io/v1alpha3
kind: DestinationRule
metadata:
    name: productpage
spec:
    host: productpage
    subsets:
     - name: v1
      labels:
        version: v1
    trafficPolicy:
        tls:
            mode: ISTIO_MUTUAL
        connectionPool:
            tcp:
                maxConnections: 10
            http:
                http1MaxPendingRequests: 3
                maxRequestsPerConnection: 1
        outlierDetection:
            consecutive5xxErrors: 1
            interval: 1s
            baseEjectionTime: 3m
            maxEjectionPercent: 100
```

Fig. 4. The configuration of DestinationRules.

5   Experiments

In this section, the proposed DQN-based circuit breaking method is compared with manual static circuit breaking approaches. Table 2 shows three configurations of manual static circuit breaking methods. The three configurations of the manual static circuit breaker are named as "10-1-1", "10-1-3", and "10-1-5". When the circuit breakers are set as static configurations, these three values respectively represent the maximum connection limit, maximum requests per connection, and maximum pending requests allowed when using the HTTP/1.1 protocol for the target service.

Table 2. The three configurations of manual static circuit breaking methods.

Configuration	10-1-1	10-1-3	10-1-5
maxConnecions	10	10	10
maxRequestsPerConnection	1	1	1
http1MaxPendingRequests	1	3	5

Algorithms are evaluated on a real Kubernetes and Istio based platform. The Kubernetes cluster consists of a master node and five slave nodes. The master node consists of an 8-Core CPU and 8 G of Memory, and the remaining node consists of an 5-Core CPU and 5 G of Memory. The Wikibench [25] dataset is a collection of Wikipedia article edit history records. Such data is used to validate the algorithm's ability to handle fluctuating workloads because the history of Wikipedia exhibits fluctuating patterns. JMeter requests are generated per second based on the arrival rate of historical Wikipedia access data.

The platform collects the CPU utilization, Memory utilization, load and the number of successful requests of the productpage every 15 s. In this experiment, the batch_size of the experience replay buffer is set to 256, the learning rate α of the agent is set to 0.0003, and the discount factor γ is set to 0.99. In the modal training, the algorithm samples a random batch of experience samples from the experience replay buffer, which is used to calculate the loss, and updates the parameters of the neural network by gradient descent. In the evaluation phase, the DQCB is applied to a real environment for testing. By observing the behavior of the agent in the test environment, three metrics are selected to evaluate the effectiveness and performance of the algorithm, namely the number of successful requests (200 HTTP status condes), the number of failed requests (503 HTTP status codes) and the rate of success requests.

5.1   Experimental Results

In the experiment, each training episode lasted for 3 h, and system data was collected every 15 s. In total, 720 sets of training data are collected during each

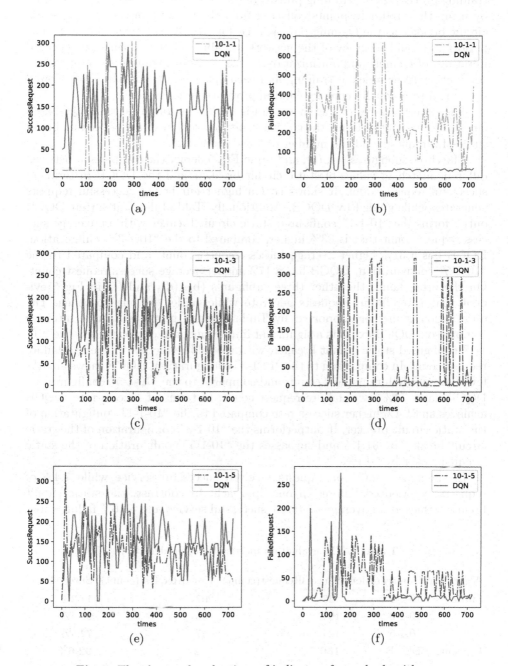

Fig. 5. The charts of evaluations of indicators for each algorithm

training process. In the training process of the DQN network, the offline training by using the 2160 data points collected from the training process of the static circuit breaker as the training data is used for the DQN network initially. The performance and accuracy of the network are able to improve through repeated iterations of training and optimization. Next, the online training is employed by conducting 12 episodes of training and each episode lasts for 3 h. This allowed the model to gradually converge and improve its performance.

The experiment results, as shown in Fig. 5, demonstrate that the DQN-based circuit method outperforms the static circuit breakers in terms of the number of successful requests and the number of failed requests.

The three subfigures (a), (c), and (e) in Fig. 5 depict the comparison between different matching values of static circuit breakers and the DQCB in terms of successful request count. It shows that a higher number of successful requests generates while guided by DQCB. Additionally, Table 3 illustrates that DQCB outperforms the "10-1-1" configured static circuit breaker with an average success request count that is 83% higher, compared to the "10-1-3" configuration, DQCB has a 31% higher average success request count, and compared to the "10-1-5" configuration, DQCB has a 17% higher average success request count. On the other hand, the other three subfigures (b), (d), and (f) in Fig. 5 evident that fewer failure requests generate while guided by our approach. The observation is further supported by Table 3, which provides a more intuitive comparison. DQCB exhibits a significant improvement in comparison to the "10-1-1" configured static circuit breaker, with a 5-fold reduction in average failure request count. In comparison to the "10-1-3" configuration, DQCB shows an 81% lower average failure request count, and compared to the "10-1-5" configuration, DQCB has a 74% lower failure request count. In terms of success rate, DQCB achieves an 81.4% higher success rate compared to the "10-1-1" configuration of the static circuit breaker. It outperforms the "10-1-3" configuration of the static circuit breaker by 31.1% and surpasses the "10-1-5" configuration of the static circuit breaker by 20.1%.

In summary, 92.6% of requests received successful service while 7.4% of requests experienced failures in our approach. In contrast, the static circuit breaker achieved an average of 48.4% successful service and 51.6% failure rate.

Table 3. The evaluation metrics for each algorithm.

Algorithm	Configuration	SuccessRequest(count)	FailedRequest(count)	SuccessRate
Static	10-1-1	26	207	11.2%
	10-1-3	104	65	61.5%
	10-1-5	124	47	72.5%
Dynamic	DQCB	**150**	**12**	**92.6%**

6   Conclusion

This article proposes a DQN-based circuit breaking method based on the Kubernetes and Istio platforms, using the DQN algorithm to address the challenge of adjusting circuit-breaking methods in resource-constrained environments. The objective of this work is to design an adaptive circuit breaker to overcome the limitations of static circuit breakers. The proposed method is evaluated through a 36-hour experiment with over 6 million requests. The experimental results demonstrate that the circuit breaker which is guided by our approach, outperforms static circuit breakers with different configurations. It generates more successful requests and achieves a higher success rate. Current research mainly focuses on optimizing the circuit-breaking strategies with a fixed number of resources. However, in real-world environments, the quantity of resources may vary. Therefore, for future work, we intend to investigate the coordination between circuit-breaking strategies and resource quantity. Additional circuit-breaking strategies and algorithms need to be explored to enhance the performance and reliability of microservice architectures.

Acknowledgements. This work is supported by the National Natural Science Foundation of China (Grant No. 61972202, 61973161, 61991404), the Fundamental Research Funds for the Central Universities (No. 30919011235).

References

1. Zhang, W.: Improving microservice reliability with Istio (2020)
2. Sharma, R., Singh, A., Sharma, R., Singh, A.: Istio virtualservice. In: Getting Started with Istio Service Mesh: Manage Microservices in Kubernetes, pp. 137–168 (2020)
3. Saleh Sedghpour, M.R., Klein, C., Tordsson, J.: An empirical study of service mesh traffic management policies for microservices. In: Proceedings of the 2022 ACM/SPEC on International Conference on Performance Engineering, pp. 17–27 (2022)
4. Sedghpour, M.R.S., Klein, C., Tordsson, J.: Service mesh circuit breaker: from panic button to performance management tool. In: Proceedings of the 1st Workshop on High Availability and Observability of Cloud Systems, pp. 4–10 (2021)
5. Fan, J., Wang, Z., Xie, Y., Yang, Z.: A theoretical analysis of deep q-learning. In: Learning for Dynamics and Control, pp. 486–489. PMLR (2020)
6. Gu, S., Lillicrap, T., Sutskever, I., Levine, S.: Continuous deep Q-learning with model-based acceleration. In: International conference on machine learning, pp. 2829–2838. PMLR (2016)
7. Mendona, N.C., Aderaldo, C.M., Cámara, J., Garlan, D.: Model-based analysis of microservice resiliency patterns. In: IEEE International Conference on Software Architecture (ICSA 2020) (2020)
8. Ponomarev, K.Y.: Attribute-based access control in service mesh. In: 2019 Dynamics of Systems, Mechanisms and Machines (Dynamics), pp. 1–4. IEEE (2019)
9. Montesi, F., Weber, J.: Circuit breakers, discovery, and API gateways in microservices. arXiv preprint arXiv:1609.05830 (2016)

10. Song, M., Liu, Q., Haihong, E.: A mirco-service tracing system based on Istio and kubernetes. In: 2019 IEEE 10th International Conference on Software Engineering and Service Science (ICSESS), pp. 613–616. IEEE (2019)
11. Meng, F., Jagadeesan, L., Thottan, M.: Model-based reinforcement learning for service mesh fault resiliency in a web application-level. arXiv preprint arXiv:2110.13621 (2021)
12. Potthoff, L.: Vergleich von circuit-breaker-implementierungen in service-meshes. Abschlussbericht FEP **2022**, 49 (2022)
13. Larsson, L., Tärneberg, W., Klein, C., Kihl, M., Elmroth, E.: Towards soft circuit breaking in service meshes via application-agnostic caching. arXiv preprint arXiv:2104.02463 (2021)
14. Ganguli, M., Ranganath, S., Ravisundar, S., Layek, A. Ilangovan, D., Verplanke, E.: Challenges and opportunities in performance benchmarking of service mesh for the edge. In: 2021 IEEE International Conference on Edge Computing (EDGE), pp. 78–85. IEEE (2021)
15. Cao, K., Liu, Y., Meng, G., Sun, Q.: An overview on edge computing research. IEEE Access **8**, 85714–85728 (2020)
16. Mao, Y., You, C., Zhang, J., Huang, K., Letaief, K.B.: A survey on mobile edge computing: the communication perspective. IEEE Commun. Surv. Tutor. **19**(4), 2322–2358 (2017)
17. Sayfan, G.: Mastering Kubernetes. Packt Publishing Ltd. (2017)
18. Santos, J., Wauters, T., Volckaert, B., De Turck, F.: Towards network-aware resource provisioning in kubernetes for fog computing applications. In: 2019 IEEE Conference on Network Softwarization (NetSoft), pp. 351–359. IEEE (2019)
19. Harabi, R.: Managing microservices with Istio service mesh (2019)
20. Calcote, L., Butcher, Z.: Istio: Up and Running: Using a Service Mesh to Connect, Secure, Control, and Observe. O'Reilly Media (2019)
21. Zhou, J., Li, X., Wang, Q., Qin, X., Miao, W., Tian, J.: Balancing load: an adaptive traffic management scheme for microservices. In: 2022 IEEE 28th International Conference on Parallel and Distributed Systems (ICPADS), pp. 641–648. IEEE (2023)
22. Kononenko, O., Baysal, O., Holmes, R., Godfrey, M.W.: Mining modern repositories with elastic search. In: Proceedings of the 11th Working Conference on Mining Software Repositories, pp. 328–331 (2014)
23. Osband, I., Blundell, C., Pritzel, A., Van Roy, B.: Deep exploration via bootstrapped DQN. In: Advances in Neural Information Processing Systems, vol. 29 (2016)
24. Elfwing, S., Uchibe, E., Doya, K.: Sigmoid-weighted linear units for neural network function approximation in reinforcement learning. Neural Netw. **107**, 3–11 (2018)
25. van Baaren, E.-J.: Wikibench: a distributed, Wikipedia based web application benchmark. Master's thesis, VU University Amsterdam (2009)

FRS4CPP: A Fair Recommendation Strategy Considering Interests of Users, Providers and Platform

Haiyan Zhao[1], Ping Zhou[1], Jian Cao[2(✉)], and Nengjun Zhu[3]

[1] University of Shanghai for Science and Technology, Shanghai, China
[2] Shanghai Jiaotong University, Shanghai, China
cao-jian@sjtu.edu.cn
[3] Shanghai University, Shanghai, China
zhu_nj@shu.edu.cn

Abstract. Currently, the research on the fairness of recommender systems has expanded beyond considering only the interests of users and product providers. However, the stakeholders of recommender systems go beyond just users and product providers; the platform that provides the recommendation service is also an important player whose interests are currently overlooked in the recommendation algorithm. In this study, we address this gap by considering the potential gains of the platform in addition to recommendation quality and fairness among providers. We analyze the theoretical relationships between recommendation quality, fairness among providers, and the platform's potential gains. Subsequently, we propose a fair recommendation strategy that takes into account the interests of all three parties. Through experiments conducted on a real-world dataset, we demonstrate that our models successfully achieve the desired design goals.

Keywords: three-sided interests · fairness of recommendation · fairness among providers · platform's potential gains

1 Introduction

The objective of a personalized recommender system is to provide recommendations to users (customers) by understanding their preferences. Studies have shown that recommendations significantly impact user decision-making and contribute to a positive user experience [20]. However, it is important to note that recommender systems involve multiple stakeholders [1–3]. Apart from users, there are also product providers, the platforms that operate the recommender system, and other participants.

Users aim to have personalized recommendations that cater to their individual needs, which is a fundamental objective of existing recommendation algorithms [20]. Simultaneously, the recommended products originate from various providers. Typically, products ranked higher in the recommendation list tend

© The Author(s), under exclusive license to Springer Nature Singapore Pte Ltd. 2024
Y. Sun et al. (Eds.): ChineseCSCW 2023, CCIS 2012, pp. 363–377, 2024.
https://doi.org/10.1007/978-981-99-9637-7_27

to gather more attention. Consequently, if provider A consistently receives lower rankings compared to provider B, it leads to a situation where provider A obtains fewer sales due to reduced exposure of their products in the recommendations [23]. Thus, it is crucial to ensure fairness in the exposure of products among providers to prevent dissatisfaction and potential attrition of providers from the platform.

The platform serves as a mediator by offering recommendation services that facilitate transactions between providers and users [18]. The platform derives benefits from charging for product exposure and clicks [6,14,23]. However, if the platform prioritizes its own revenue generation too heavily, it may lean towards granting superior positions to products whose providers can afford to pay more. Unfortunately, such a approach not only diminishes fairness among providers but also negatively impacts user satisfaction. Ultimately, this results in the loss of users and the departure of providers from the platform.

It is evident that the objective of recommender systems must expand beyond solely ensuring user satisfaction to encompass the interests of multiple stakeholders. Currently, there are limited studies focusing on enhancing fairness among users or providers within recommender systems. Some research, such as [4,9], addresses fairness among users, while others, such as [17,21,22], tackle fairness among product providers. Furthermore, a few studies simultaneously consider fairness among both parties, i.e., users and product providers, in the recommender system. For example, [15,16] examine the fairness among both product providers and users.

We introduce a novel fair recommendation strategy that considers the interests of multiple stakeholders simultaneously, including users, providers, and the platform. This approach represents the first attempt to address the concerns of all parties involved. Specifically, users' interests are assessed based on recommendation quality, providers' interests are captured through fairness in the exposure of their products, and the platform's interests are reflected by the revenue generated from users' clicks on the recommended products from providers.

Our contributions can be summarized as follows:

1) We analyze the interrelationships among recommendation quality, fairness among providers, and the platform's potential gains. Additionally, we propose the fair recommendation problem, which, for the first time, considers the interests of users, providers, and the platform.
2) We propose the Fair Recommendation Strategy considering the interests of users, providers, and the platform (FRS4CPP). FRS4CPP dynamically adjusts the user's recommended list while ensuring recommendation quality, thus promoting individual fairness among providers and serving the interests of the platform. To implement FRS4CPP, we design three algorithms.
3) We conduct experiments using a real-world dataset of user behaviors on the Taobao platform, incorporating simulated pay-per-click information. The experimental results demonstrate that our strategy effectively upholds the interests of all stakeholders involved.

2   Related Work

The fairness of recommender systems can be classified from various perspectives [23]. Individual fairness emphasizes equal treatment for each individual, while group fairness focuses on equal treatment among groups with specific attributes. In terms of the number of recommendations, fairness can be divided into cumulative recommendation fairness and single round recommendation fairness. Regarding the stage at which fairness is ensured within the recommender system, algorithms can be classified into three categories: pre-processing [7], in-processing [4], and post-processing [12,13,19]. Depending on the stakeholders within the system, the fairness of recommender systems can be further divided into three main categories: user-side fairness, provider-side fairness, and fairness for other stakeholders [2,3].

Currently, most research on recommendation fairness primarily focuses on a single stakeholder's perspective, with only a few studies examining fairness from the viewpoints of both users and product providers.

In terms of user-side fairness, researchers primarily focus on investigating whether there are systematic differences in the quality or types of recommended products for different users [1,23]. For instance, [9] addresses the issue of varying recommendation quality for users with different levels of activity, both at the individual and group levels, within the context of knowledge graph recommendations. They aim to eliminate or mitigate this unfair phenomenon. Another study, [4], mitigates unfairness to users by learning a set of adversarial filters and removing user-sensitive attribute information from graph embeddings. Additionally, [10] considers user preferences from an Envy-Free perspective [5,8], ensuring that users with similar product preferences are presented with similar recommendations.

Regarding provider-side fairness, the focus is mainly on exploring how providers can obtain fair opportunities for selection and whether their products meet fairness requirements within user recommendation lists. For example, [21] proposes explaining the unfair treatment of product providers using non-sensitive attributes and employs causal graphs to assess unfair treatment. In [22], provider-side fairness in top-k ranking is quantified by analyzing the distribution of products in user recommendation lists. The fairness of recommendation based on provider exposure is considered in [17].

A few studies take into account both user-side fairness and provider-side fairness. In [15], the FairRec algorithm is introduced to maximize the exposure of most product providers while ensuring envy-free fairness among users. Regarding the impact of platform updating algorithms on the fairness of product exposure, [16] proposes an integer linear programming (ILP) based algorithm that guarantees stable exposure rates for product providers after algorithm updates, while ensuring each user's minimum utility.

The aforementioned studies primarily focus on user-side fairness or provider-side fairness within recommender systems. However, there is limited research that considers the interests of other stakeholders. For the first time, we consider the simultaneous inclusion of recommendation quality, provider-side fairness, and the platform's interests in our study.

3   Fair Recommendation for the Interests of Users, Providers, and Platform

We consider the application scenario of top-k recommendation, where recommendations are generated based on users' historical behavior. To ensure a balance among recommendation quality, fairness among product providers, and the potential gains of the platform, we propose to reorder the original recommendation list. Specifically, we employ nDCG [11] as a measure of recommendation quality. Additionally, we quantify the benefits of product providers using Click-Through Rate (CTR), and Pay-Per-Click (PPC) [14] serves as the basis for providers to pay the platform.

3.1   Notations

We introduce the following notations:

- $U = \{u_1, u_2, \ldots, u_m\}$ denotes the set of users.
- $P = \{p_1, p_2, \ldots, p_n\}$ denotes the set of providers.
- $I = \{i_1, i_2, \ldots, i_s\}$ denotes the set of recommended items.
- $L^{ori} = \{l_{u_1}^{ori}, l_{u_2}^{ori}, \ldots, l_{u_m}^{ori}\}$ represents the set of original recommendation lists.
- $L^{rec} = \{l_{u_1}^{rec}, l_{u_2}^{rec}, \ldots, l_{u_m}^{rec}\}$ represents the set of recommendation lists outputted to customers.
- $i^p = \{i_1^p, i_2^p, \ldots, i_l^p\}$ represents the set of items provided by provider p.
- $i^{p,u} = \{i_1^{p,u}, i_2^{p,u}, \ldots, i_t^{p,u}\}$ represents the set of recommended items provided by provider p in the recommendation list of customer u.
- $v_{u,i}$ denotes the relevance between user u and item i.

3.2   Recommendation Quality

Ideally, in a recommendation algorithm, a user's recommendation list should be sorted based on their preferences, reflecting the relevance between the user and the recommended products. However, when other objectives are introduced, such as fairness considerations, the item rankings in the list may be adjusted. As a result, some items with lower relevance may be ranked higher, leading to a potential decline in the recommendation quality. Therefore, we use the original recommendation list l_u^{ori} as a baseline to evaluate the recommendation quality after adjustments.

To quantify the recommendation quality, we employ two classic metrics from information retrieval: Discount Cumulative Gain (DCG) and Normalized Discount Cumulative Gain (nDCG).

3.3   Fairness Among Product Providers

Previous studies on provider fairness mainly focused on measuring the fairness based on the exposure of products. However, exposure alone does not fully capture the economic benefits that product providers can potentially gain. In e-commerce, Click-Through Rate (CTR) is commonly used to measure the economic gains of product providers [17]. Therefore, we utilize CTR as a metric to quantify the possible economic benefits of product providers.

CTRs of Products and Providers. The position of a product in the recommendation list significantly influences its CTR. We assume that the higher a product is ranked in the list, the higher its CTR will be. Although there are other factors that can affect CTR, such as product images displayed on the platform, we consider the position as the sole factor influencing CTR in this research.

CTR represents the click probability of a product at each position in the recommendation list and is calculated as follows:

$$CTR\left(i_x^{p,u}\right) = \frac{1}{\log_2 x + 1}. \tag{1}$$

Since each provider typically has multiple products on the platform, we introduce the concept of CTRs of providers. Let T_R denote the total number of recommendations, and T_R^p represent the total number of times provider p appears in the recommendation lists. The CTRs of provider p are calculated by summing the CTRs of its products and dividing by T_R^p:

$$CTR^p = \frac{\sum_{j=1}^{|U|} \sum_{x=1}^{|i^{p,u_j}|} CTR(i_x^{p,u_j})}{T_R^p} \tag{2}$$

Fairness of CTRs Among Providers. A fair recommendation system aims to achieve consistency in the CTRs among product providers. In other words, the recommendation is fair if the CTRs of all providers are equal:

$$CTR^{p_i} = CTR^{p_j}, \forall p_i, p_j \in P \tag{3}$$

To measure the level of fairness among providers, we calculate the average of all providers' CTRs as the baseline:

$$CTR_{avg} = \frac{\sum_{j=1}^{|P|} \sum_{s=1}^{|U|} CTR(i^{p_j,u_s})}{T_R}. \tag{4}$$

The difference between the baseline and a provider's CTR is defined as:

$$PCF^p = CTR_{avg} - CTR^p. \tag{5}$$

When $PCF^p > 0$, it indicates that the CTR of product provider p is lower than the average level, which is unfair to product provider p. Conversely, when $PCF^p < 0$, it implies that the CTR of product provider p is higher than the average, which is unfair to other product providers.

Furthermore, we use the variance of all providers' CTRs to evaluate the overall fairness level among product providers.

3.4 Potential Gains of the Platform

Pay-Per-Click (PPC) is a common pricing model used by platforms to charge product providers, and it is widely adopted by companies such as Taobao, Google, and Baidu [14]. Therefore, we utilize PPC as a metric to estimate the total potential gains of the platform.

The PPC can vary for different providers as it is negotiated between the providers and the platform. Let $value^p$ denote the PPC for provider p. The expected gains from a position can be calculated as follows:

$$TC(i_x^p) = CTR(i_x^p) * value^p \tag{6}$$

When the platform prioritizes its own potential gains, it tends to promote products with higher PPC rankings to increase its revenue. The total potential gains of the platform can be estimated using the following equation:

$$Gains = \sum_{y=1}^{|P|}\sum_{x=1}^{|i^{p_y}|} CTR(i_x^{p_y}) * value^{p_y}. \tag{7}$$

3.5 Relations Among Recommendation Quality, Provider Fairness, and Platform Gains

Experimental studies [20] have shown that when a recommender system perfectly aligns with users' preferences, it often leads to unfairness among product providers. Additionally, the potential gains of the platform are closely related to the PPC. When we make adjustments to the rankings to achieve fairness among product providers or maximize platform gains, the following three observations can be made:

Observation 1: Any recommendation that prioritizes objectives other than user preferences will result in lower recommendation quality compared to the original recommendation list l_u^{ori}, which is designed to best match users' preferences.

When the system modifies the original recommendation lists to enhance fairness among product providers' CTRs, the $nDCG\,(l_u^{rec})$ value becomes less than 1. However, the PPC of a provider remains independent of their CTRs, and the platform's interests do not exhibit any systematic changes. Hence, we observe:

Observation 2: Strategic adjustments made to the recommendation list l_u^{ori} to improve fairness among providers lead to a decrease in recommendation quality and random changes in the platform's interests.

When the system modifies the original recommendation lists to increase the platform's potential gains, the rankings of products from providers with higher PPCs are promoted, causing $nDCG\,(l_u^{rec})$ to become less than 1. However, the fairness among providers remains unchanged since the CTRs of each position are independent of the PPCs of individual providers. Therefore, we have:

Observation 3: As the potential gains of the platform increase, recommendation quality decreases, while fairness among providers' CTRs remains unaffected.

Based on the above observations, achieving fairness in recommendations for the interests of all three stakeholders requires sacrificing recommendation quality in order to enhance fairness among providers and maximize platform gains.

4   FRS4CPP: The Fair Recommendation Strategy Considering Interests of Customers, Providers, and Platform

Based on the analysis in Sect. 3.5, we have devised the strategy for fair recommendation that takes into account the interests of users, product providers, and platforms.

4.1   Strategy Design

To achieve fairness among product providers or maximize platform gains, it is necessary to lower the recommendation quality. However, we aim to minimize the impact on recommendation quality. Therefore, we combine all these objectives into a single value:

$$Value_{FRS4CPP} = w_1 * v_{rq} + w_2 * v_{fp} + w_3 * v_{PG} \tag{8}$$

Here, v_{rq}, v_{fp}, and v_{PG} represent utilities related to recommendation quality, fairness among providers, and potential gains of the platform, respectively.

As analyzed in Sect. 3, this problem can be reduced to a knapsack problem, which is known to be NP-complete even when considering the interests of only two sides. For instance, when considering recommendation quality and provider fairness, the length of the recommendation list can be considered as the knapsack capacity, the products to be recommended as the items to be placed in the knapsack, and maximizing provider fairness as the objective. The problem becomes more complex when the potential gains of the platform are taken into consideration. Hence, we propose heuristic fairness recommendation strategies to address this problem.

4.2   Algorithms for Implementing the Strategy

We employ three algorithms to implement FRS4CPP.

Overall Score-Based Algorithm (OSA). OSA calculates a synthetic score for each product in each position of the list and selects the products with the highest score for each position, starting from the highest position and moving downward. The score of a product for position x is computed using Eq. 7:

$$score_x^i = \frac{v_{i,u}}{\log_2(x+1)} + \alpha * PCF^p + \beta * value^p \tag{9}$$

The factors influencing recommendation quality are the relevance between users and products. The fairness among providers PCF^p represents the cumulative fairness of an individual provider over multiple rounds of recommendations, thus affecting the system's dynamic adjustment of the current recommendation list. The main factor influencing the potential gains of the platform is the pc^p

of product provider p. We assign weights to PCF^p and $value^p$ according to the following rules: 1) to account for magnitude differences among the three interest measurements and 2) to adjust the relative importance of the three interest measurements. If the system emphasizes recommendation quality, the values of α or β should be reduced. If the fairness among product providers or the potential gains of the platform are given more attention, the values of α or β can be correspondingly increased.

OSA reorders the original list l_u^{ori} only if $score_{x-1}^{i_{x-1}} < score_x^{i_x}$. In this case, the original list l_u^{ori} is modified, and PCF_x^p or the platform's potential gains increase.

Two-Round Reordering Algorithm (2RA). The 2RA strategy consists of two steps:

Step 1: We calculate the benefit score for both recommendation quality and fairness among providers by weighting and evaluating the factors. Each product's score for a given position in the top-k ranking is determined, and the product with the highest score is selected for each position, from highest to lowest, as the first round of recommendation results. The calculation method for both sides is presented in Eq. 10:

$$score_x^i = \frac{v_{i,u}}{\log_2(x+1)} + a * PCF^p. \tag{10}$$

Step 2: The recommendation list obtained in the first step is fine-tuned to maximize the platform's potential gains. We compare the price per click of adjacent products in the recommendation list obtained from the first step. If the difference between the products at positions x and $x - 1$ exceeds a threshold value ($\triangle price$), we exchange the products at these positions.

In the first step, we adjust the list based on the interests of both sides. In the original list l_u^{ori}, for products ranked at positions x and $x - 1$, where $v_{x-1} \geq v_x$, we change the list l_u^{ori} only if the fairness among providers' click-through rates (CTRs) satisfies $PCF_x^p > PCF_{x-1}^p$. As a result, the position of the provider with a lower CTR rises, increasing the fairness of provider CTRs.In the second step, the products at positions x and $x - 1$ are exchanged when the following condition is met:

$$value_x^p - value_{x-1}^p > \triangle value. \tag{11}$$

This leads to an increase in the platform's potential gains. The value of $\triangle price$ determines the extent to which the second step influences the first step.

Tree-Round Reordering Algorithm (3RA). 3RA determines the final list of recommendations through three rounds of selection and sorting. We select the products in the order of the original list to guarantee the user's recommendation quality:

The 1st Round: The products whose providers' CTRs are lower than fair CTR ($PCF > 0$), and whose PPC are lower than the average of PPC ($value_i^p > \overline{value}$) are listed in the recommended list l_u^{rec}.

The 2nd Round: The products whose product providers' CTRs are lower than fair CTR ($PCF > 0$), or whose PPCs are lower than the average CTR ($value_i^p > \overline{value}$) are still listed in the recommended list l_u^{rec}.

The 3rd Round: The remaining products are sequentially added to the list based on their relevance, taking into account the recommendation quality.

In the 3RA strategy, the three rounds of selection are conducted in a sequential manner, following the original order, with each round considering the recommendation quality during reordering. In the first round, the emphasis is on prioritizing products that enhance fairness among providers and maximize the platform's potential gains. The ranking of products that align with the interests of all three parties is placed at the forefront of the list, ensuring the maximum alignment of interests. In the second round, the focus is on selecting and sorting products that further improve fairness among providers or increase the platform's potential gains. Products that cater to the interests of the user and either the provider or the platform are given secondary priority. This ensures a certain degree of alignment between the interests of the two sides. The first two rounds of reordering already include products that significantly enhance fairness among providers or maximize the platform's potential gains. Therefore, in the third round of reordering, only the recommendation quality is considered, as the primary objective.

4.3   Time Complexity Analysis

In OSA, the algorithm calculates the scores of each product in each position, selects the product for each position based on the scores, and updates the CTRs of providers. In the worst-case scenario, the time complexity is $O(k^2 + kn)$. However, in practice, the number of providers (n) is typically greater than the length of the recommendation list (k), resulting in a time complexity of $O(kn)$ for OSA. Similarly, in the first step of 2RA, the algorithm calculates the scores of each product in each position, selects the product for each position based on the scores, and then fine-adjusts the product's position in the second step using click values. Finally, it updates the providers' CTRs. Therefore, the time complexity of 2RA is also $O(kn)$. In 3RA, the algorithm updates the CTRs of providers after three rounds of selection. Thus, the time complexity of 3RA is also $O(kn)$.

5   Experiments

5.1   Datasets and Metrics

To conduct our experiments, we utilize a desensitized dataset from Taobao. The original dataset comprises behavior data from 1.14 million users over a span of 8 days. For our experiment, we extract behavior data from 10,782 users to create a new dataset.

To generate the original recommendation lists, we employ the ALS algorithm to match users with products. However, obtaining the PPC (Pay-Per-Click) information for each provider is challenging, if not impossible, due to its confidential nature. To simulate the PPC information, we generate random numbers between 0 and 1, following a normal distribution, to represent the PPC values.

For evaluating the recommendation quality, fairness among product providers, and potential gains of the platform, we utilize the metrics introduced in Sect. 3.

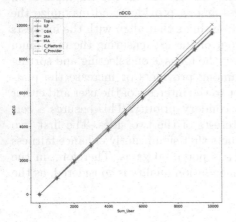

Fig. 1. Cumulative Value of nDCG

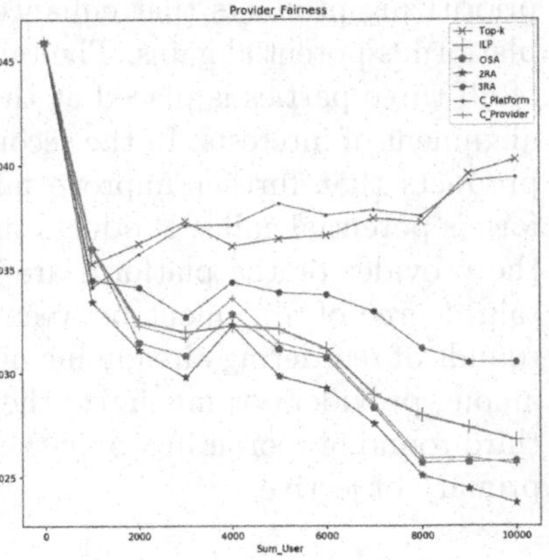

Fig. 2. Variance of CTRs of Providers

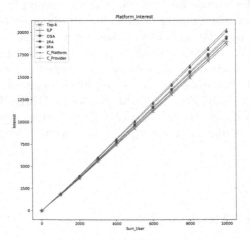

Fig. 3. Cumulative Potential Gains of Platform

5.2   Compared Approaches

In our comparative analysis, we evaluate our proposed approach against the following algorithms:

1) *Top-k.* This algorithm is based on item-based collaborative filtering and directly recommends the top-k items, focusing solely on maximizing recommendation quality.
2) *An ILP-based fair ranking mechanism.* This algorithm utilizes Integer Linear Programming (ILP) to ensure Quality Weighted Fairness in provider exposure. It aims to minimize the absolute difference between the two cumulative values while considering recommendation quality as a constraint.
3) *C-Provider.* This algorithm considers only recommendation quality and provider fairness, without any deliberate bias towards specific providers. We utilize the result of the first step of the 2RA algorithm to generate a recommendation list.
4) *C-Platform.* This algorithm considers only recommendation quality and the platform's potential gains, without favoring any specific providers. We utilize the second step of the 2RA algorithm to generate a recommendation list.

5.3   Experimental Results

Figures 1, 2 and 3 present the experimental results, demonstrating that the three algorithms trade off a portion of the recommendation quality to improve fairness among providers and increase the potential gains of the platform.

Table 1. The Result of the Experiment Considering Two side Interests

Algorithms	nDCG	Variance of CTRs	Platform Gains
Top-k	10782	0.0404	20000
C-Platform	10503	0.0398	21808
C-Provider	10300	0.0234	20180

It can be observed that the cumulative nDCGs of the post-processed recommendation results, denoted as the sum of cumulative nDCGs, are lower than the sum of cumulative nDCGs in $l_u^o ri$ (the original list) when considering the objectives of platform potential gains and fairness among providers. This confirms the validity of Observation 1.

Table 1 presents the experimental results of the C-Provider algorithm. It can be seen that when the system considers the goals of recommendation quality and fairness among providers, the platform's potential gains in the C-Provider algorithm (20180) only slightly deviate from the original list $l_u^o ri$ of the Top-k algorithm (20000). Therefore, Observation 2 is supported. Similarly, the experimental results of the C-Platform algorithm demonstrate that when the system considers recommendation quality and platform's potential gains, the variance of providers' CTRs (0.0398) is slightly lower compared to the original list $l_u^o ri$ (0.0404). This supports Observation 3.

Furthermore, the results of the ILP-based fair ranking mechanism highlight that while the algorithm ensures recommendation quality and fairness among providers, it performs poorly in terms of platform potential gains.

Experiment Results of OSA. In the OSA algorithm, this experiment involves adjusting the weight coefficient α of PCF (Provider Cumulative Fairness) and the weight coefficient β of the potential gains of the platform. The results of adjusting α are presented in Fig. 4:

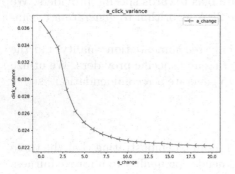

Fig. 4. The Change of CTRs of Providers

Fig. 5. The Change of Potential Gains of Platform

As the weight coefficient α gradually increases from 0 to 20, the variance of the provider's CTRs shows a decreasing trend and eventually stabilizes. This indicates that when the system prioritizes the fairness among providers, the level of unfairness among them gradually diminishes but cannot be completely eliminated.

The experimental results of adjusting β are depicted in Fig. 5. As β increases from 0 to 10, the platform's potential gains demonstrate an upward trend and eventually stabilize. Assuming that the recommended products are sorted in descending order of PPCs (Pay-Per-Click), the platform's potential gains reach their maximum. However, in practice, the achieved potential gains may not reach the absolute maximum due to other constraints and factors.

It is evident that while the OSA algorithm experiences a decrease in recommendation quality to some extent, both the fairness among providers and the platform's potential gains are improved.

Experiment Results of 2RA. To examine the impact of $\triangle price$ on the first step and its influence on the platform's potential gains, this study adjusts the value of $\triangle price$.

To investigate the effect of the algorithm on recommendation quality, we introduce a binary weight Q to represent the consideration of recommendation quality in the first step of scoring. When $Q = 1$, the algorithm takes recommendation quality into account. As presented in Table 2, as $\triangle price$ gradually decreases, the platform's potential gains increase, the fairness among providers improves, and the recommendation quality decreases. When $Q = 0$, indicating that recommendation quality is not considered, the nDCG (Normalized Discounted Cumulative Gain) for recommendation quality is 9845. In the case of $Q = 1$, as $\triangle price \rightarrow 0$, the second step has the most significant impact on the outcome of the first step, resulting in cumulative nDCGs of 10100, which surpass the result when recommendation quality is not considered. Hence, even when $\triangle price \rightarrow 0$, the influence of the second step on the recommendation quality of the first step remains limited, and the 2RA algorithm can ensure recommendation quality.

Table 2. The Result of the Experiment on 2RA

$\triangle price$	Q	a	nDCG	Variance of CTRs	Platform Gains
1	1	5	10300	0.0234	20277
0.5	1	5	10286	0.0223	20313
0.25	1	5	10205	0.0214	20636
0.1	1	5	10160	0.0211	20736
0.01	1	5	10106	0.0211	20891
0.001	1	5	10100	0.0212	20900
0.0001	1	5	10100	0.0212	20900
0.00001	1	5	10100	0.0212	20900
0.25	0	5	9845	0.0208	20501
0.25	1	0	10503	0.0398	21808

Regarding the 2RA algorithm, as depicted in Fig. 1, compared to the Top-k algorithm, there is a certain decrease in recommendation quality. However, there are noticeable improvements in both the fairness among providers and the platform's potential gains.

Experiment Results of 3RA. When the recommendation quality is not considered, as in the case of $Q = 0$, an experiment called CFPRM is conducted. The results of the CFPRM algorithm and 3RA are presented in Table 3. The result indicates that 3RA ensures a certain level of recommendation quality.

Table 3. The Result of the Experiment on 3RA

Algorithms	nDCG	Variance of CTRs	Platform Gains
Top-k	10782	0.0404	20000
CPFRM	9845	0.0208	20501
3RA	10266	0.0291	21520

It can be found from the results that the 3RA manages to control the decrease in recommendation quality to a certain extent, while simultaneously improving both the fairness among providers and the potential gains of the platform.

6   Conclusions

This paper aims to address the interests of users, providers, and the platform by improving fairness among providers, maximizing the potential gains of the platform, and ensuring recommendation quality. To achieve this goal, we propose a fair recommendation strategy and design three algorithms to implement it.

In this paper, we process the original top-k recommendation list through post-processing methods (reordering) to obtain a recommendation list that satisfies all three objectives. In the future, we can explore in-processing approaches, where we directly revise the recommendation algorithm itself to achieve these objectives.

References

1. Abdollahpouri, H., et al.: Multistakeholder recommendation: survey and research directions. User Model. User-Adap. Inter. **30**(1), 127–158 (2020)
2. Abdollahpouri, H., Burke, R.: Multi-stakeholder recommendation and its connection to multi-sided fairness (2019)
3. Abdollahpouri, H., Burke, R., Mobasher, B.: Recommender systems as multistakeholder environments. In: Proceedings of the 25th Conference on User Modeling, Adaptation and Personalization, pp. 347–348. ACM, New York (2017)
4. Bose, A.J., Hamilton, W.L.: Compositional fairness constraints for graph embeddings (2019)
5. Budish, E.: The combinatorial assignment problem: approximate competitive equilibrium from equal incomes. J. Polit. Econ. **119**(6), 1061–1061 (2010)
6. Burke, R.: Multisided fairness for recommendation (2017)
7. Calmon, F.P., Wei, D., Vinzamuri, B., Ramamurthy, K.N., Varshney, K.R.: Optimized pre-processing for discrimination prevention. In: Proceedings of the 31st International Conference on Neural Information Processing Systems, pp. 3995–4004. Curran Associates Inc., Red Hook (2017)
8. Do, V., Corbett-Davies, S., Atif, J., Usunier, N.: Online certification of preference-based fairness for personalized recommender systems. In: Proceedings of the AAAI Conference on Artificial Intelligence, vol. 36, no. 6, pp. 6532–6540 (2022)

9. Fu, Z., et al.: Fairness-aware explainable recommendation over knowledge graphs. In: Proceedings of the 43rd International ACM SIGIR Conference on Research and Development in Information Retrieval, pp. 69–78. Association for Computing Machinery, New York (2020)

10. Ilvento, C., Jagadeesan, M., Chawla, S.: Multi-category fairness in sponsored search auctions. In: Proceedings of the 2020 Conference on Fairness, Accountability, and Transparency, FAT* 2020, pp. 348–358. Association for Computing Machinery, New York (2020). https://doi.org/10.1145/3351095.3372848

11. Järvelin, K., Kekäläinen, J.: Cumulated gain-based evaluation of IR techniques. ACM Trans. Inf. Syst. **20**(4), 422–446 (2002)

12. Karako, C., Manggala, P.: Using image fairness representations in diversity-based re-ranking for recommendations. In: Adjunct Publication of the 26th Conference on User Modeling, Adaptation and Personalization, pp. 23–28. Association for Computing Machinery, New York (2018). https://doi.org/10.1145/3213586.3226206

13. Liu, W., Burke, R.: Personalizing fairness-aware re-ranking (2018)

14. Liu Peng, W.C.: Advertising Computing: Market and Technology of Realizing Internet Business. Posts & Telecom, Beijing (2019)

15. Patro, G.K., Biswas, A., Ganguly, N., Gummadi, K.P., Chakraborty, A.: FairRec: two-sided fairness for personalized recommendations in two-sided platforms. In: Proceedings of The Web Conference 2020, pp. 1194–1204. ACM, New York (2020). https://doi.org/10.1145/3366423.3380196

16. Patro, G.K., Chakraborty, A., Ganguly, N., Gummadi, K.: Incremental fairness in two-sided market platforms: on smoothly updating recommendations. In: Proceedings of the AAAI Conference on Artificial Intelligence, vol. 34, no. 01, pp. 181–188 (2020)

17. Singh, A., Joachims, T.: Fairness of exposure in rankings. In: Proceedings of the 24th ACM SIGKDD International Conference on Knowledge Discovery and Data Mining, pp. 2219–228. ACM, New York (2018). https://doi.org/10.1145/3219819.3220088

18. Sühr, T., Biega, A.J., Zehlike, M., Gummadi, K.P., Chakraborty, A.: Two-sided fairness for repeated matchings in two-sided markets: a case study of a ride-hailing platform. In: the 25th ACM SIGKDD International Conference, pp. 3082–3092 (2019)

19. Wu, C., Wu, F., Wang, X., Huang, Y., Xie, X.: FairRec: fairness-aware news recommendation with decomposed adversarial learning (2020)

20. Wu, Y., Cao, J., Xu, G., Tan, Y.: TFROM: a two-sided fairness-aware recommendation model for both customers and providers. In: Proceedings of the 44th International ACM SIGIR Conference on Research and Development in Information Retrieval, pp. 1013–1022. Association for Computing Machinery, New York (2021)

21. Wu, Y., Zhang, L., Wu, X.: On discrimination discovery and removal in ranked data using causal graph. In: Proceedings of the 24th ACM SIGKDD International Conference on Knowledge Discovery and Data Mining, pp. 2536–2544. ACM, New York (2018). https://doi.org/10.1145/3219819.3220087

22. Yang, K., Stoyanovich, J.: Measuring fairness in ranked outputs. In: Proceedings of the 29th International Conference on Scientific and Statistical Database Management (2017). https://doi.org/10.1145/3085504.3085526

23. Zhao, H.Y., Zhou, P., Chen, Q.K., Cao, J.: Fairness evaluation methods in recommender system: current research and prospects. J. Chin. Comput. Syst. **43**(3), 456–465 (2022)

Accelerating Unsupervised Federated Graph Neural Networks via Semi-asynchronous Communication

Yuanming Liao[1,2,3], Duanji Wu[1,2,3], Pengyu Lin[1], and Kun Guo[1,2,3(✉)]

[1] College of Computer and Data Science, Fuzhou University, Fuzhou 350108, China
[2] Fujian Key Laboratory of Network Computing and Intelligent Information
Processing, Fuzhou University, Fuzhou 350108, China
gukn@fzu.edu.cn
[3] Key Laboratory of Spatial Data Mining and Information Sharing,
Ministry of Education, Fuzhou 350108, China

Abstract. Graph neural networks have shown excellent performance in many fields owing to their powerful processing ability of graph data. In recent years, federated graph neural network has become a reasonable solution due to the enactment of privacy-related regulations. However, frequent communication between the coordinator and participants in federated graph neural network results in longer model training time and consumes many communication resources. To address this challenge, in this paper, we propose a novel semi-asynchronous federated graph learning communication protocol that simultaneously alleviates the negative impact of stragglers(slow participants) and accelerate the training process in the unsupervised federated graph neural network scenario. First, the weighted enforced synchronization strategy is intended to preserve the information carried by stragglers while preventing their stale models from harming the global model update. Second, the adaptive local update strategy is developed to make the local model of the participant with poor computing performance as close as possible to the global model. Experiments combine federated learning with graph contrastive learning. The results demonstrate that our proposed protocol outperforms the existing protocols in real-world networks.

Keywords: Federated learning · Graph contrastive learning ·
Communication protocol · Semi-asynchronous communication · Graph
neural network

1 Introduction

In the Internet era, many graph data composed of nodes and edges are generated daily. Moreover, the growing awareness of the need to protect data privacy makes it more challenging to collect graph data. As a distributed machine learning method, federated learning enables participants to generate a globally

© The Author(s), under exclusive license to Springer Nature Singapore Pte Ltd. 2024
Y. Sun et al. (Eds.): ChineseCSCW 2023, CCIS 2012, pp. 378–392, 2024.
https://doi.org/10.1007/978-981-99-9637-7_28

shared model under the coordination and control of the coordinator without sharing local data. Graph neural networks (GNNs) can aggregate node attribute information in a graph into node embeddings based on topological similarity, supporting downstream tasks such as community detection and traffic flow prediction [30]. Federated graph neural network (FedGNN), which combines federated learning and GNN, is expected to solve the contradiction between model training data requirements and user data privacy protection [6]. However, due to the network bandwidth limitation and the need for participants and the coordinator to exchange numerous model parameters during the training process, the communication cost becomes the primary bottleneck of FedGNN.

At present, synchronous, asynchronous, and semi-asynchronous communication protocols are the primary methods of mitigating the problem caused by communication overhead. (1) In synchronous communication protocols, such as FedProx [12], stragglers determine the duration of each round of federated learning. If randomly selected participants crash before submitting their local model parameters, continuing the global training process will be difficult. (2) In asynchronous communication protocols, such as FedAsync [27], although they can mitigate the negative effect of stragglers by performing global aggregation as soon as the local model parameters of each participant is received, this can lead to unnecessary version differences. When the number of participants is large, the communication overhead may not be reduced because the coordinator frequently receives and sends model parameters. (3) In the semi-asynchronous communication protocols, such as WKAFL [31], SAFA [26], even though the coordinator will wait some time before aggregating the received local models, it is still inevitable that some participants will train their local models based on the stale global model in the later stage. They not only lower the speed of global model training but also affect its accuracy. Although an enforced synchronization strategy can be adopted to allow the stragglers to train with the latest global model, it would make the global model lose the information carried by stragglers. We aim to retain the information carried by stragglers while avoiding training with stale global model. In addition, these methods aim to solve supervised federated learning. In some fields where the data often appear in graphs, such as social networks and traffic flow prediction, their label information is difficult to obtain.

In this paper, we propose a Semi-asynchronous protocol with Weighted Enforced synchronization and Adaptive Local updaTe (SWESALT) for FedGNN to address the above issues. SWESALT includes three steps. In the first step, the adaptive local update (ALU) strategy is used to specify the local iteration number of participants. In the second step, the coordinator performs global aggregation based on the local model parameters received and sends the latest global model parameters to the corresponding participants. The third step employs weighted enforced synchronization (WES) to provide stragglers with the latest global model parameters. The main contributions of our work are summarized as follows:

- The weighted enforce synchronization strategy can further improve the training speed and accuracy of the unsupervised FedGNN by giving stragglers the latest global model parameters proportionally, which solves the problem of discarding the information carried by the straggler to prevent the negative impact of the stale model.

- The adaptive local update strategy can reduce the possibility of stragglers by allocating fewer local iterations to participants with weak computational performance, which solves the problem that too many stragglers lead to slow convergence speed and low global model accuracy.
- Experiments that combine graph contrastive learning with federated learning are conducted on real-world networks to validate the performance of SWE-SALT in terms of training runtime and prediction accuracy on a community detection task.

2   Related Work

In this section, we present three approaches to federated learning to solve the communication overhead problem.

2.1   Federated Learning Based on Synchronous Communication

In federated learning based on synchronous communication protocol, during each iteration, the coordinator samples a subset of participants for local training. The coordinator must receive model parameters uploaded by all sampled participants before performing a global update. In 2017, FedAvg, proposed by McMahan et al. [18], combined local stochastic gradient descent with a server that performs model averaging, and the local iteration results were sent to the server through multiple iterations of local updates. In 2020, Li et al. [12] proposed FedProx, a method that dynamically adjusts the number of local iterations required by different participants in each round, eliminating the need for participants to perform a unified number of iterations during each update. In 2022, Bibikar et al. [1] proposed a federated learning framework called FedDST, which introduced dynamic sparse training into federated learning. In 2022, Dai et al. [3] proposed DisPFL to use personalized sparse masks to customize sparse local models on edge devices in a decentralized scenario. Yi et al. [28] proposed QSFL to use a sparse cyclic sliding segment algorithm to compress the model to be uploaded by devices to the central server.

When training on graph data, the embedding calculation of a node usually requires the information of its recursive neighbors from several hops away. In practice, a graph's number of nodes and edges is vast. For example, the OGB dataset [11] contains about 100 million nodes, so neighbor sampling for generating node embeddings will require large network bandwidth and lead to excessively long training time until convergence. In 2022, Pan et al. [19] proposed FedWalk as the first algorithm for node-level federated unsupervised graph embedding vectors, saving communication time to the $(i + 1)$th element by directly building a path from the ith element to the $(i + 2)$th element. In 2022,

Du et al. [4] proposed an algorithm for determining the neighbor sampling interval in federated graph learning, which concluded the optimal neighbor sampling interval based on the trade-off between convergence error and actual running time to reduce the communication overhead caused by cross-device neighbor sampling. Currently, federated learning on graph data is mainly based on synchronous communication protocol, and research on asynchronous and semi-asynchronous communication protocols is rare.

2.2 Federated Learning Based on Asynchronous Communication

In federated learning based on asynchronous communication protocol, as soon as the coordinator receives a local model, it executes the global aggregation and sends the latest global model to the corresponding participants without waiting for other participants to upload the model. At the same time, other participants can continue the current local training. In 2019, Xie et al. [27] proposed a federated optimization asynchronous algorithm FedAsync. When the server received the parameters of each participant, it would immediately update the global model without waiting for other participants to complete this round of training. In 2022, Feng et al. [5] proposed an asynchronous federated learning framework based on blockchain, which uses a proof of work algorithm to encourage more devices to become participants.

2.3 Federated Learning Based on Semi-asynchronous Communication

In federated learning based on semi-asynchronous communication protocol, Chai et al. [2] proposed a framework FedAT that combines synchronous intra-tier training and asynchronous cross-tier training based on the hierarchical strategy. In 2021, Wu et al. [26] proposed a semi-asynchronous federated learning protocol SAFA, which only requires the up-to-date and deprecated clients to be synchronized with the server while the tolerable clients remain asynchronous with the server. At the same time, the enforced synchronization strategy is used to force the stragglers to train with the latest global model. In 2021, Ma et al. [15] proposed a semi-asynchronous federated learning protocol FedSA, which enables the server to aggregate a certain number of local models in the arrival order of each round to minimize the training completion time. Like SAFA, it also uses an enforced synchronization strategy. In 2022, Wang et al. [23] proposed FedCH, which allocates participants into multiple clusters according to different training capacities. Participants in a cluster synchronously forward local updates to the cluster header for aggregation, while all cluster headers asynchronously perform global aggregation. In 2022, Zhou et al. [31] proposed a two-stage weighted K-asynchronous federated learning WKAFL with an adaptive learning rate. In 2022, Liang et al. [13] proposed a semi-asynchronous federated learning protocol Semi-SynFed for IoV systems, designed a client selection scheme to evaluate the state of vehicle nodes to select appropriate clients to participate in the global update, and designed a dynamic server waiting time scheme to adjust the aggregation frequency.

3   Preliminaries

In this section, we provide a brief overview of the federated learning process based on the semi-asynchronous communication protocol. Next, we introduce the process of graph contrastive learning.

3.1   Semi-asynchronous Communication Protocol in Federated Learning

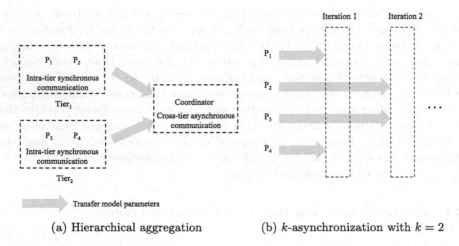

(a) Hierarchical aggregation   (b) k-asynchronization with $k = 2$

Fig. 1. Two typical mechanisms of semi-asynchronous communication protocol for federated learning

The federated learning algorithms based on the semi-asynchronous communication protocol discussed in Subsect. 2.3 can be classified into two main types: hierarchical aggregation [2,23] and k-asynchronization [7,15,24,26,31]. As illustrated in Fig. 1(a), the hierarchical aggregation mechanism divides participants into different tiers (such as $Tier_1$, $Tier_2$) and updates models through intra-tier synchronous and cross-tier asynchronous communication. According to the k-asynchronization mechanism depicted in Fig. 1(b), after receiving k local model parameters(for example, $Iteration$ 1 selects P_1 and P_4 for updating, whereas $Iteration$ 2 selects P_2 and P_3.), the coordinator performs the global aggregation by weighted aggregation and sends the latest global model parameters to the corresponding participants. The remaining participants can continue the current training.

In either case, the local model parameters received by the coordinator may be trained on a stale global model. We refer to the corresponding participant with such a model as a straggler. We represent the staleness of participant n in the ith round as τ_n^i, calculated as the difference between the current round and the previously received global model version.

3.2   Graph Contrastive Learning

Graph contrastive learning [29] uses contrastive learning to maximize the consistency between two different views of a graph to learn a graph representation. In this paper, we take GraphCL [29] as an example to illustrate.

Partition a graph dataset into different subgraphs, assuming that one of the subgraphs is denoted as $G = (V, E)$, each node $v \in V$ is represented by a vector $h_v \in \mathbb{R}^P$ in a graph. Adjacency matrix $A \in \mathbb{R}^{N \times N}$ represents the topological structure of the graph, where $N = |V|$ denotes the number of nodes in the graph. In federated graph contrastive learning, two different views $\hat{G}_i$, $\hat{G}_j$ will be generated by data augmentation for the input graph. Then, the corresponding graph-level representation vectors h_i, h_j are generated by applying an encoder $f(\cdot)$ based on graph neural networks. After that, z_i, z_j which can be used for downstream tasks obtained by Multi-Layer Perceptron(MLP).

$$f(\mathcal{G}) = \text{READOUT}\left(\left\{h_n^{(k)} : v_n \in \mathcal{V}, k \in K\right\}\right) \tag{1}$$

where $h_n^{(k)}$ is the representation vector of the node v_n at the $k - th$ layer. The loss function in the training process of graph contrastive learning can be defined as follows:

$$\ell = -\frac{1}{M}\sum_{m=1}^{M} \log \frac{\exp\left(\text{sim}\left(z_{m,i}, z_{m,j}\right)/\beta\right)}{\sum_{m'=1, m'\neq m}^{M} \exp\left(\text{sim}\left(z_{m,i}, z_{m',j}\right)/\beta\right)} \tag{2}$$

where β is the temperature parameter, which controls the smoothness of the softmax function output.

4   The Proposed Protocol

4.1   Framework

The framework of SWESALT is shown in Fig. 2. A complete round of the training and communication process consists of the following three steps.

Step 1: Adaptive local update. In this step, stragglers will perform fewer local iterations during local training.

Step 2: Global aggregation. The coordinator performs weighted aggregation of the received local model parameters before sending the updated global model parameters to the corresponding participants.

Step 3: Weighted enforced synchronization. If a participant is a straggler, its local model will be updated by weighted aggregation with the latest global model.

The above process is repeated until the target accuracy is reached or a predetermined number of global iterations is completed. The specifics will be described in the following subsection.

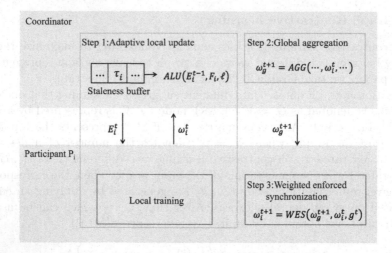

Fig. 2. Framework of SWESALT. The mathematical symbols are explained in subsequent subsections.

4.2 Adaptive Local Update

First, the coordinator calculates the number of local iterations in the subsequent round based on the staleness of each participant in the staleness buffer. When the staleness of participant i exceeds the threshold, fewer local iterations should be assigned to make it participate in the global aggregation as much as possible to reduce the version differences between participants. The formula for calculating the number of local iterations for participant i is as follows:

$$E_i^t = ALU\left(E_i^{t-1}, F_i, \ell\right) = \max\left(1, E_i^{t-1} - \text{round}\left(\alpha * l + (1-\alpha) * F_i\right)\right) \quad (3)$$

where E_i^t is the number of local iterations that participant i needs to execute in the next global round t, E_i^{t-1} represents the number of local iterations for participant i in the $(t-1)$th round of the federated learning process. round($\cdot$) is the rounding function, α is a hyperparameter ranging from $[0,1]$, l represents the maximum lag tolerance for a participant, and F_i represents the computing performance of participant i. Second, participant i will perform E_i^t local iterations and upload its local model to the coordinator after completing training.

4.3 Global Aggregation

After receiving the first k local models, the coordinator performs aggregation and updates the global model using the computation method described in Eq. (4).

$$w_g^{t+1} = AGG\left(\cdots, w_i^t, \cdots\right) = \left(1 - \sum_{n_i \in n_k} \frac{D_i}{D}\right) w_g^t + \sum_{n_i \in n_k} \frac{D_i}{D} w_i^t \quad (4)$$

where n_k is the participants participating in this round of aggregation, D is the total amount of data of all participants, D_i is the amount of data held by participant n_i, and w_i^t is the local model received from participant n_i in round t. After that, the coordinator sends the updated global model parameters to these k participants.

4.4   Weighted Enforced Synchronization

We design a weighted enforced synchronization strategy to alleviate the degradation of accuracy and convergence speed caused by models trained based on stale parameters that the coordinator may receive during semi-asynchronous FedGNN. In this strategy, we consider both model relevance and the percentage of stragglers. Wang et al. [14] have proved that the sign consistency of the local model and the global model can ensure the consistency of the gradient direction. The higher the relevance is, the gradient direction of the local model is more inclined to the global model, facilitating model convergence. Model relevance is measured specifically as follows:

$$r\left(w^t, w_g^{t+1}\right) = \frac{1}{N} \sum_{j=1}^{N} I\left(\text{sgn}\left(w_j\right) = \text{sgn}\left(w_{g,j}\right)\right) \tag{5}$$

where $w^t = \langle w_1, w_2, \ldots, w_N \rangle$ represents the local model with N model parameters, w_g^{t+1} represents the global model. $I(\cdot)$ is 1 if the signs of w_j and $w_{g,j}$ are the same, 0 otherwise, therefore $r\left(w^t, w_g^{t+1}\right) \in [0, 1]$. Furthermore, to prevent stale local models from deviating the global model from the current update direction, especially when there are a significant number of stragglers, we incorporate the proportion of stragglers in the current iteration, denoted as g^t into our strategy. The local model of stragglers with weighted enforced synchronization is updated as:

$$\begin{aligned} w^{t+1} &= WES\left(w_g^{t+1}, w^t, g^t\right) \\ &= \left(r\left(w^t, w_g^{t+1}\right) - g^t\right) * w^t + \left(1 - r\left(w^t, w_g^{t+1}\right) + g^t\right) * w_g^{t+1} \end{aligned} \tag{6}$$

5   Experiments

In this section, we conduct experiments to verify the performance of the proposed protocol SWESALT in terms of runtime and prediction accuracy. The proposed protocol is compared with existing synchronous, asynchronous, and semi-asynchronous protocols on different networks. We implement unsupervised FedGNN, named FedGraphCL, by combining federated learning with GraphCL introduced in Subsect. 3.2.

5.1   Datasets

In the experiments, we used 5 real-world networks [8, 16, 20–22], which are described in detail as Table 1:

Table 1. Real-world networks

Networks	Nodes	Edges	Attributes	Classes
PubMed	19717	88651	500	3
Citeseer	3327	9228	3703	6
Flickr	7575	239738	12047	9
LastFM Asia	7624	27806	7842	18
Blogcatalog	5196	343486	8189	6

5.2   FedGraphCL

In the experiments, we use FedGraphCL for training. Each participant uses data augmentation to generate original and augmented graphs for their subgraphs and then uses GNN for local training. The objective is to minimize Eq. (2). The local models are then uploaded to the coordinator for aggregation, and the participants perform the next round of local training using the latest global model. The node embeddings generated during training can be used for downstream tasks.

5.3   Baseline Protocols

In our experiments, we compare the synchronous communication protocol, Fed-Prox [12], the asynchronous communication protocol, FedAsync [27], and the semi-asynchronous communication protocol, SAFA [26], as well as WKAFL [31].

5.4   Experimental Settings

In the experiments, we train the model on different networks. The total number of participants is set to 50, the number of global iterations is set to 50, the number of local iterations is set to 10 by default, and the learning rate is set to 0.001. We compare SWESALT with baseline protocols in terms of model accuracy and runtime. We assume that the performance of all participants follows a normal distribution, with mu and $sigma$ set to 1 and 0.3, respectively. In addition, to simulate the situation where participants are unable to upload their models due to network failures or other factors, we have assigned a specific crash rate c to each participant. After obtaining the subgraph embeddings of the participants, we cluster them using the K-means algorithm and compare the experimental results of the downstream task, namely community detection. We plan to complete the runtime and accuracy experiments.

In the runtime experiment, the number of participants participating in the global aggregation in each round for synchronous and semi-asynchronous communication protocols is 5, or the pick rate is 0.1. Due to the characteristics of the asynchronous communication protocol, each round of global aggregation is limited to a single participant. Our protocol is compared to baseline protocols with the crash rates c of 0.1, 0.4, and 0.7, respectively. A higher c indicates that a participant is more likely to fail to upload local model parameters.

In the accuracy experiment, we compare the accuracy of SWESALT and baseline protocols measured by NMI. To observe the experiments' results, we select 25, 10, and 5 participants among the 50 to participate in each round of global aggregation. According to the proof of Zhou et al. [31], we can set the average staleness of participants by setting the total number N of participants and the number K of participants in each aggregation:

$$s = \frac{N}{K} \qquad (7)$$

Therefore, in our experiments, the semi-asynchronous protocols SWESALT, SAFA, and WKAFL have three degrees of participant staleness: $50/25 = 2, 50/10 = 5, 50/5 = 10$. However, since only one participant participates in the aggregation during each round of the asynchronous protocol FedAsync, the average staleness of all participants is 50. Since FedProx communicates based on a synchronous protocol, the average staleness of all participants is 0.

5.5   Evaluation Metrics

To compare the model accuracy, we measure it using Normalized Mutual Information (NMI) [17]. In the comparison of runtime, the main goal is to reduce the time spent in the federated learning process, which is calculated as follows:

$$T = \min \left\{ T_b , T_s + \max_k \{ T_k^d + T_k^u + T_k^t \} \right\} \qquad (8)$$

where T_b is the upper bound of the federated learning process time, T_k^d, T_k^u, and T_k^t are the time of downloading the global model, uploading the local model, and training the local model of the kth participant, respectively. In this experiment, referring to the bandwidth setting of SAFA, we set the local bandwidth to 100 MB/s and the coordination bandwidth to 125 MB/s. Therefore, for the coordinator, the time taken to transmit the model is given by:

$$T_s = \frac{m \cdot C}{b_1} \qquad (9)$$

where m represents the number of models to be transmitted, determined by the number of participants that need to obtain the global model, C is the model size, and b_1 is the bandwidth of the coordinator. The time for participant k to download the model depends on model size and local bandwidth:

$$T_k^d = \frac{C}{b_2} \qquad (10)$$

The model upload time of participant k is calculated in the same way as the download time. For participant k, its local training time is as follows:

$$T_k^t = \frac{B_k \cdot E_k}{F_k} \qquad (11)$$

where B_k is the number of batches of participant k, E_k is the number of local iterations of participant k, and F_k is the performance of participant k.

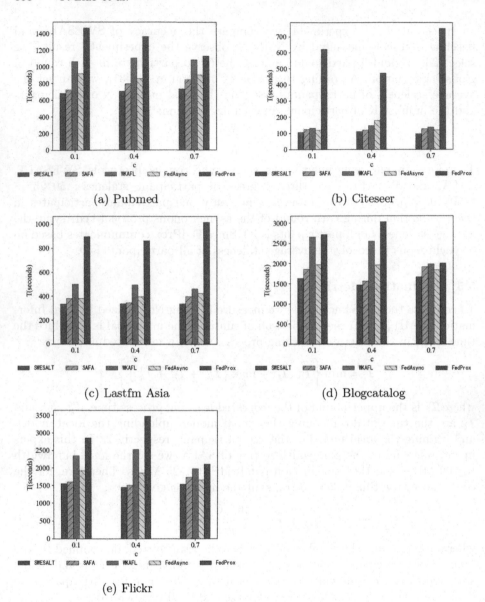

(a) Pubmed

(b) Citeseer

(c) Lastfm Asia

(d) Blogcatalog

(e) Flickr

Fig. 3. The results of runtime experiment

5.6   Runtime Experiment

Figure 3 demonstrates that our protocol requires the least time for 50 global iterations under different networks and crash rates, followed by SAFA, FedAsync, WKAFL, and FedProx. This is due to the fact that our protocol employs the ALU strategy, which reduces the possibility of straggler occurrences. In addition, reducing the number of stragglers decreases the time required for the coordinator to transmit the latest global model to the stragglers. For stragglers that have already appeared, the WES strategy ensures that the stale models will not hinder the convergence of the global model.

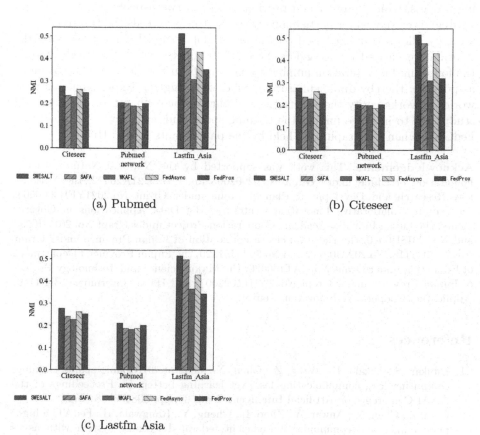

(a) Pubmed

(b) Citeseer

(c) Lastfm Asia

Fig. 4. The results of accuracy experiment

5.7   Accuracy Experiment

As shown in Fig. 4, the NMI values of our protocol are the highest for all experimental settings. The NMI values of FedProx, FedAsync, SAFA, and WKAFL are greatly affected by the crash rate and the staleness. This is due to the fact that the WES strategy in our protocol retains the information carried by stragglers and trains it based on the latest global model. ALU strategy reduces the possibility of stragglers' appearance. The combination of these two strategies prevents the stale models from causing the global model to deviate from the optimal updating direction, which would result in a decline in precision.

6   Conclusions

In this paper, we propose a semi-asynchronous communication protocol (SWE-SALT) for FedGNN to boost the communication efficiency in the federated learning process, which improves on previous works in two aspects. First, the WES strategy is employed for participants whose staleness exceeds the threshold. This strategy allows training based on the latest global model while preserving the information carried by stragglers. Second, stragglers would adaptively update the following local iteration number to participate in the global update as much as possible, thereby diminishing the number of stragglers. Experiments on real-world networks verify the effectiveness of our protocol. In future work, we will study how to improve further the training speed and accuracy of unsupervised FedGNN when the graph data held by the participants is Non-IID.

Acknowledgements. This work was supported by the National Natural Science Foundation of China under Grant No.62002063 and No. U21A20472, the National Key Research and Development Plan of China under Grant No.2021YFB3600503, the Fujian Collaborative Innovation Center for Big Data Applications in Governments, the Fujian Industry-Academy Cooperation Project under Grant No. 2017H6008 and No. 2018H6010, the Natural Science Foundation of Fujian Province under Grant No.2022J01118, No.2020J05112 and No.2020J01420, the Fujian Provincial Department of Education under Grant No. JAT190026, the Major Science and Technology Project of Fujian Province under Grant No.2021HZ022007, and Haixi Government Big Data Application Cooperative Innovation Center.

References

1. Bibikar, S., Vikalo, H., Wang, Z., Chen, X.: Federated dynamic sparse training: computing less, communicating less, yet learning better. In: Proceedings of the AAAI Conference on Artificial Intelligence. vol. 36, pp. 6080–6088 (2022)
2. Chai, Z., Chen, Y., Anwar, A., Zhao, L., Cheng, Y., Rangwala, H.: FedAT: a high-performance and communication-efficient federated learning system with asynchronous tiers. In: Proceedings of the International Conference for High Performance Computing, Networking, Storage and Analysis, pp. 1–16 (2021)
3. Dai, R., Shen, L., He, F., Tian, X., Tao, D.: DisPFL: towards communication-efficient personalized federated learning via decentralized sparse training. arXiv preprint arXiv:2206.00187 (2022)
4. Du, B., Wu, C.: Federated graph learning with periodic neighbour sampling. In: 2022 IEEE/ACM 30th International Symposium on Quality of Service (IWQoS), pp. 1–10. IEEE (2022)
5. Feng, L., Zhao, Y., Guo, S., Qiu, X., Li, W., Yu, P.: BAFL: a blockchain-based asynchronous federated learning framework. IEEE Trans. Comput. **71**(5), 1092–1103 (2021)
6. Fu, X., Zhang, B., Dong, Y., Chen, C., Li, J.: Federated graph machine learning: a survey of concepts, techniques, and applications. ACM SIGKDD Explor. Newsl. **24**(2), 32–47 (2022)

7. Gao, Z., Duan, Y., Yang, Y., Rui, L., Zhao, C.: FedSeC: a robust differential private federated learning framework in heterogeneous networks. In: 2022 IEEE Wireless Communications and Networking Conference (WCNC), pp. 1868–1873. IEEE (2022)

8. Giles, C.L., Bollacker, K.D., Lawrence, S.: Citeseer: an automatic citation indexing system. In: Proceedings of the Third ACM Conference on Digital Libraries, pp. 89–98 (1998)

9. He, D., Du, R., Zhu, S., Zhang, M., Liang, K., Chan, S.: Secure logistic regression for vertical federated learning. IEEE Internet Comput. **26**(2), 61–68 (2021)

10. Hönig, R., Zhao, Y., Mullins, R.: DAdaQuant: doubly-adaptive quantization for communication-efficient federated learning. In: International Conference on Machine Learning, pp. 8852–8866. PMLR (2022)

11. Hu, W., et al.: Open graph benchmark: datasets for machine learning on graphs. Adv. Neural. Inf. Process. Syst. **33**, 22118–22133 (2020)

12. Li, T., Sahu, A.K., Zaheer, M., Sanjabi, M., Talwalkar, A., Smith, V.: Federated optimization in heterogeneous networks. Proc. Mach. Learn. Syst. **2**, 429–450 (2020)

13. Liang, F., Yang, Q., Liu, R., Wang, J., Sato, K., Guo, J.: Semi-synchronous federated learning protocol with dynamic aggregation in internet of vehicles. IEEE Trans. Veh. Technol. **71**(5), 4677–4691 (2022)

14. Luping, W., Wei, W., Bo, L.: CMFL: mitigating communication overhead for federated learning. In: 2019 IEEE 39th International Conference on Distributed Computing Systems (ICDCS), pp. 954–964. IEEE (2019)

15. Ma, Q., Xu, Y., Xu, H., Jiang, Z., Huang, L., Huang, H.: FedSA: a semi-asynchronous federated learning mechanism in heterogeneous edge computing. IEEE J. Sel. Areas Commun. **39**(12), 3654–3672 (2021)

16. McAuley, J., Leskovec, J.: Image labeling on a network: using social-network metadata for image classification. In: Fitzgibbon, A., Lazebnik, S., Perona, P., Sato, Y., Schmid, C. (eds.) ECCV 2012. LNCS, vol. 7575, pp. 828–841. Springer, Heidelberg (2012). https://doi.org/10.1007/978-3-642-33765-9_59

17. McDaid, A.F., Greene, D., Hurley, N.: Normalized mutual information to evaluate overlapping community finding algorithms. arXiv preprint arXiv:1110.2515 (2011)

18. McMahan, B., Moore, E., Ramage, D., Hampson, S., Arcas, B.A.: Communication-efficient learning of deep networks from decentralized data. In: Artificial Intelligence and Statistics, pp. 1273–1282. PMLR (2017)

19. Pan, Q., Zhu, Y.: FedWalk: communication efficient federated unsupervised node embedding with differential privacy. In: Proceedings of the 28th ACM SIGKDD Conference on Knowledge Discovery and Data Mining, pp. 1317–1326 (2022)

20. Rozemberczki, B., Sarkar, R.: Characteristic functions on graphs: birds of a feather, from statistical descriptors to parametric models. In: Proceedings of the 29th ACM International Conference on Information & Knowledge Management, pp. 1325–1334 (2020)

21. Sen, P., Namata, G., Bilgic, M., Getoor, L., Galligher, B., Eliassi-Rad, T.: Collective classification in network data. AI Mag. **29**(3), 93 (2008)

22. Tang, L., Liu, H.: Relational learning via latent social dimensions. In: Proceedings of the 15th ACM SIGKDD International Conference on Knowledge Discovery and Data Mining, pp. 817–826 (2009)

23. Wang, Z., Xu, H., Liu, J., Xu, Y., Huang, H., Zhao, Y.: Accelerating federated learning with cluster construction and hierarchical aggregation. IEEE Trans. Mob. Comput. **22**, 3805–3822 (2022)

24. Wang, Z., et al.: Asynchronous federated learning over wireless communication networks. IEEE Trans. Wireless Commun. **21**(9), 6961–6978 (2022)
25. Wu, C., Wu, F., Lyu, L., Huang, Y., Xie, X.: Communication-efficient federated learning via knowledge distillation. Nat. Commun. **13**(1), 2032 (2022)
26. Wu, W., He, L., Lin, W., Mao, R., Maple, C., Jarvis, S.: SAFA: a semi-asynchronous protocol for fast federated learning with low overhead. IEEE Trans. Comput. **70**(5), 655–668 (2020)
27. Xie, C., Koyejo, S., Gupta, I.: Asynchronous federated optimization. arXiv preprint arXiv:1903.03934 (2019)
28. Yi, L., Gang, W., Xiaoguang, L.: QSFL: a two-level uplink communication optimization framework for federated learning. In: International Conference on Machine Learning, pp. 25501–25513. PMLR (2022)
29. You, Y., Chen, T., Sui, Y., Chen, T., Wang, Z., Shen, Y.: Graph contrastive learning with augmentations. In: Advances Neural Information Processing System, vol. 33, pp. 5812–5823 (2020)
30. Zhou, J., et al.: Graph neural networks: a review of methods and applications. AI Open **1**, 57–81 (2020)
31. Zhou, Z., Li, Y., Ren, X., Yang, S.: Towards efficient and stable K-asynchronous federated learning with unbounded stale gradients on non-IID data. IEEE Trans. Parallel Distrib. Syst. **33**(12), 3291–3305 (2022)

Vietnam Dynasty and Sandpile Modeling

Peng Lu[1,2,3,4] ⓘ, Mengdi Li[1,2,3] ⓘ, and Zhuo Zhang[1,2,3](✉) ⓘ

[1] Department of Sociology, Central South University, Chang Sha 410000, China
sociophysics@hotmail.com
[2] Department of Artificial Intelligence, Central South University, Chang Sha 410000, China
[3] PKU-Wuhan Institute for Artificial Intelligence, Wuhan 430072, China
[4] Research Center for Intelligent Society and Governance, Zhejiang Lab, Hangzhou 311121, China

Abstract. The questions about the emergence, functioning, and decline of empires in human history continue to attract scholarly attention. Conventional research has identified economics, population, climate change, and international relations as important factors that determine the constant rising and falling of empires. Based on them, we proposed a more scientific and advanced method, agent-based modeling, to investigate the life cycle dynamics. The sandpile model is applied to build multi-agent systems. According to the sandpile model, the dissipative structure and chaos theory coincides with the life cycle dynamics, which is evolving periodically. Agent-based sandpile model is applied here to investigate, simulate, and back-calculate Vietnam empires. According to this, we can find the optimal solutions, under which repeated simulations (N = 1000) can perfectly match empires in history. Macroscopically, the number of simulated empires is normally distributed. The average number of simulated empires is 9.634 (≈10), which strictly matches 10 empires in real history. Combining agent-based modeling and simulations, this work unveils the homogeneity or similarity between natural systems (sandpile) and human societies (empires).

Keywords: Sandpile Model · Empire Dynamics · Rise and Fall Mechanism · Agent-based Modeling (ABM)

1 Introduction

In human history, the rise and fall cycles of empires exist all over the world. Empire's cycles have been one of the most mysterious topics for both natural and social scientists. Among the various kinds of political communities, units, and entities that have existed in history, the life cycle dynamics have been the key features of empires, which are ubiquitous and in many ways the precursors of modern national states [1]. The life cycle trajectories of empires are resembling a flat-topped parabola. The rise, development, and decline process of empires are shaped by political changes, economic adjustments, climate change, international relations, and other factors [2]. Many hypotheses or theories are proposed to explain the life circle dynamics, but due to the lack of precision and reproducibility, they don't reveal the core mechanism. Based on the unification of natural

Y. Sun et al. (Eds.): ChineseCSCW 2023, CCIS 2012, pp. 393–405, 2024.
https://doi.org/10.1007/978-981-99-9637-7_29

systems and human society, we propose the hypothesis about self-organized criticality and evolutionary similarity, to reveal the nature of empire cycles. Self-organization refers to biological adaptability to the environment within isolated and closed systems [3]. Self-organized criticality means that the system reaches the threshold automatically and spontaneously, without external interference. When the threshold is reached, the current systemic structure will collapse and start a new evolution again [4]. From the evolutionary similarity, natural and social systems share the same underlying principles in the evolution or development process [5]. Both Vietnam (more than 1000 years) and China (more than 2000 years) have a stable and long process of sequential empires in history. In the wave of studying imperial cycles, the history of Vietnamese empires is an essential part because it is about how human society organized and governed during many centuries of empires [6]. Considering the historical trend of repeated rising and falling empires, it is critical to understand the internal mechanism of Vietnamese empires. Based on the self-organization and evolutionary similarity, we use an agent-based model to explore and back-calculate the internal mechanism and evolutionary dynamics of the Vietnam empires. We obtain the optimal solution of simulations to achieve the highest matching to empires in history.

2 Proposed Mechanism of Dynasties Cycles

2.1 The Chaos Theory

In system science, chaos theory is applied to explore natural phenomena, which emphasizes both observed orders and inner structures [7]. As the pioneer, Edward (1963) deems it as qualitative studies of unstable and aperiodic behaviors in deterministic nonlinear, dynamic, and complex systems [8]. The chaotic system widely exists in both the natural (physical) world and social domains [9], such as social systems applications in economics, political, and management sciences [10]. Empire Life cycles often contain unpredictable activity peaks and longer periods of unstable behaviors. Thus, it provides valuable insights into empire dynamics: **(a) The relationship between stability and instability.** In dynamic systems, chaos is the state between order and disorder, and it is away from the balance of systems. Dynastic cycles are also periodic alternation of regimes, it switches between despotism (rulers tax farmers and hunt bandits) and anarchy (there are no rulers or social cooperation) [11]. This change between despotism and anarchy can also be conceived of as orderly movement in a bigger grouping of moving systems, viewed as components of chaos; **(b) Non-linear development.** Chaos theory is the study of nonlinear dynamic systems [12]. Chaos is a deterministic system, in which there are seemingly random irregular movements, whose behaviors are uncertain, unrepeatable, and unpredictable [13]. Similarly, empires also tend to be characterized by nonlinear relationships and complex interactions that evolve dynamically over time [14, 15]. Each empire rises to a political, cultural, and economic peak and then, begins to decline and fluctuate until it finally collapses and is replaced by a new empire [16]. The transition from an old order to a new one is precisely a non-linear system, **and (c) Butterfly effect.** The Chaos theory assumes that concentration on individual units can yield significant results [17]. This means a small input to the system will produce huge and unanticipated outcomes or changes. In the evolutions of system behaviors, even the micro-level, seemingly insignificant, and easily overlooked initial conditions (inputs) may diverge to unpredictable macro-level system outcomes, which is the Butterfly Effect [18]. In the same way, Empires are complex systems made up of a large number of asymmetrical, interacting components. This termite hill-like construction leaves empires systems in apparent equilibrium to some extent, but a very small trigger can set off a "phase transition" from a benign equilibrium to a crisis [19]. For example, as the first big and unified dynasty founded by ethnic minorities in China, the Yuan Dynasty was overthrown by the peasant uprising, due to political disorder, an underdeveloped economy, corrupt officials, and rejecting Chinese (Han) culture. Known for the military power, the Mongols people established the strongest Yuan Dynasty worldwide, which nevertheless collapsed and returned to its original state quickly [20]. Therefore, the Chaos theory provides new perspectives to our dynastic cycle research.

2.2 The Sandpile Model

The sandpile model is a classic tool to investigate the critical phenomena of dynamic systems, the Abelian sandpile is most commonly used [21, 22]. The sandpile system is a horizontal (flat) platform, with a certain number of sand particles. The platform is stable, then we continue to add a grain randomly on the platform. When the slope of the sandpile reaches the critical point T, the avalanche will happen, and the grains will be equally shared by the neighbors. When the neighbors also reached the critical point T, the cascade avalanche will continue to propagate [23]. Researches concentrate on the self-organized criticality (SOC) and the avalanche threshold T for the sandpile models; **(a) Intrinsic properties.** The SOC plays an indispensable role in the growing and collapsing process of sandpiles, and the threshold of avalanches is the key issue. The size and span of avalanches follow the spatial and temporal power-law distribution [24]. In sandpile models, the inverse avalanches can conjecture the cyclic structure of sandpiles, when existing the absence of a certain spanning branch [25]. The known exponents of spanning branches can determine the avalanched wave sizes, which follow the power-law distribution, with exponent $\alpha = 3/4$ and basic exponent $\tau = 5/4$ in the model [26]. In the model of stochastic energy activation, the avalanches are divided into linear and branched types, in which the collapses transfer grains narrowly to one neighbor or broadly to all neighbors, respectively. The exponents of linear avalanches can be determined by preconditions, and branched avalanches are more similar to the stochastic two-state sandpile [27]; **(b) Capture of the law.** The Abelian sandpile and Bak-Tang-Wiesenfeld (BTW) sandpile can be modeled by computer simulation and then capture the law of the model. In the Abelian sandpile, the avalanched probability is determined by the generators of avalanches (GOAs) and avalanche waves, including landing location, pre-set conditions, and avalanche threshold. The attributions of avalanches include the avalanched size, the amount of cascade collapse, and the avalanche boundary, which are computed by the GOAs [28]. Likewise, based on the Bak-Tang-Wiesenfeld (BTW) model, the size and duration of avalanches in a scale-free network are decided by the degree exponent and observed power-law exponent [29]. Potential links between the spatial and temporal indicators of sandpile avalanches could be captured by connecting the previous and later toppling, which breaks the shortest and longest records, compared to the previous one. The separation distances, recurrence intervals, and degree distributions of farthest recurrences can be also detected by the links [30]; and (c) **Analogy.** The sandpile model concretizes dissipative system theory, and it reflects the systemic cycles from order to disorder during the energy exchange. In the analogy between sandpiles and empires, the sand particles refer to endogenous and exogenous factors. The sandpile structure, which consists of many sand particles, is internally similar to the empire (societal) structure, which consists of many social factors, such as population, economy, climate, and international relationships. The collapse of sandpiles can be considered as the collapse of empires, and the sandpile model is in nature suitable for modeling empire dynamics.

2.3 Our Combined Perspective

Previous theories have applications for both natural and social systems, and they greatly facilitate our sandpile modeling. Chaos theory can be used to model the status shift between system conditions. The dissipative system theory can represent the characteristics of empires, such as nonlinear, non-equilibrium, dynamic, or cyclic development. And it is possible to identify structural and evolutionary characteristics of social systems. Based on the combined theoretical framework, we establish the agent-based sandpile model that follows the principles of chaos theory. Within the chaos theory, empires can be modeled as nonlinear, non-equilibrium, dynamical, and evolutionary systems. The empire system also qualifies the self-organized criticality. When endogenous and exogenous variables (popularity, economy, climate, and foreign relationships) reach their thresholds, the systems will undergo phase transitions, namely, the collapse of old empires and the rise of new empires. The CA-based sandpile model was initially proposed to explore the dynamics of self-organized criticality, and its simulations can therefore perfectly match the rise and fall (life cycles) of real empires in history.

3   Designs and Methods of Agent-Based Model

As an emerging (advanced) technology to study real evolutions by simulations and to reproduce (back-calculate) real dynamic processes, agent models have been widely used in ecology, meteorology, economics, biology, agriculture, sociology, and other social sciences [31]. Therefore, we use ABM to explore the rise and fall dynamics of empires. For now, we see no research on the Vietnam empires from AD 938 to AD 1945. The ODD protocol (overview, design concepts, and details) is applied to describe our model's framework. It can clarify descriptions and improve repeatable researches, which is more scientific [32]. Although the ODD versions have changed multiple times [33, 34], the main skeleton framework is stable, consisting of purpose, entities, state variables, scales, process overview, scheduling, basic principles, initialization, etc. [35]. Here, we present our model according to the ODD protocol principles.

3.1 The Overview

It includes: (a) Purpose and patterns. NetLogo is an ideal tool to simulate complex and dynamic systems, such as the rising and falling of empires. Due to the self-organized criticality (sandpile model) and its chaos attribution (similar evolution patterns of empires), we use Agent-Based Modeling to explore potential laws such as life cycles and durations of empires [2]. It is possible to test and verify the evolutional similarity or connections between natural and social systems. There is a reasonable analogy across the structures, processes, and attributions of empires and sandpiles. For real empires, micro-level factors (population, information, resources, climate, and economy) can cause macro-level calamity. Likewise, in the sandpile model, adding one more sand particle may also trigger the cascading avalanches in the sandpile system; (b) Static Settings of Agents. The sandpile model applied here belongs to the Abelian sandpile models. In NetLogo, we use dynamic state changes of patches to present the dynamics process, where microscopic sand particles construct the macroscopic sandpile system. We set the area of sandpile S = 41 × 41 = 1681 patch2. The spatial state of agents (patches) has three variables or indicators: the "grains-per-patch" refers to how many sand particles the patch already has; the "threshold-value" is the threshold beyond which the sandpile (patches) will collapse; the "drop-location" is which patch (where) the sand particles are added or dropped on. The temporal variable refers to the running ticks, presented by the t; and (c) Process overview and scheduling. At each time t, one sand particle will be added randomly to one patch, and when the sandpile (patch) reaches the critical threshold, the collapse happens until no patches are beyond the threshold. When a patch collapse, it releases or transfers four sand particles to its four neighbors. Each neighbor obtains one particle from the collapsed sandpile and accumulates its own sand particles. If the critical point of neighbors also is overwhelmed, the cascading avalanches will happen. After each time the collapse, the accumulation of sand piles will return to the original value (one).

3.2 Design of Concepts and Mechanisms

It includes: (a) Basic objectives and principles. The key objective of our work is to simulate real empires in history. Using an agent-based sandpile model, the highest standard is to perfectly simulate and match the life cycles (durations) of real empires, from the beginning to rise, peak, and ending. Based on combined perspectives of the dissipative system and chaos theory, both empires and sandpiles have the same systemic structure such as the life cycle dynamics. Based on the self-organized criticality, the system of human society (empires) is inclined to reach the threshold of collapsing or vanishing, which coincides with the sandpile. Hence, the sandpile model becomes the optimal method to simulate the rise and fall cycles of empires in Vietnam; (b) Interactions and Mechanism of Agents. The behavioral rules of individual behaviors and interactions are set as follows. The area of the squared grid is deemed as the territory of empires, where we have all agents (patches). For this empire system, each patch has the attribution of total grain value G, which refers to how many sand particles this patch has. The initial value of G is set for all patches. As the simulation begins, each patch i at the time t has the grain G_{it}. The dynamics of the sandpile system are determined by the grain mechanism in Eq. (1). At each time t, one sand particle will be added to one patch randomly in the system. At the next time $t+1$, the grains of agent i are denoted as $G_{i,t+1}$, which has three possibilities. For the first case, it remains the same, i.e. $G_{i,t+1} = G_{it}$, because no sand particles are added to this patch and no transfers of sand particles either. For the second case, it increases by one, which means that $G_{i,t+1} = G_{it} + 1$, because one drop of sand particle has been added into this patch, or it receives one sand particle from its neighbor whose threshold has been satisfied. When the threshold of this patch i (center) has been reached, the sand particle will collapse on this patch. This (center) patch will lose 4 sand particles ($G_{i,t+1} = G_{it} - 4$), which are transferred to surround four neighbors. Each one of the four neighbors will receive sand particles. This is the normal case within the territory of the system. In four marginal patches that have less than 4 neighbors, the sand particles transferred to non-existing neighbors will disappear from this system.

$$G_{i,t+1} = \begin{cases} G_{it} - 4 & \text{if center} \\ G_{it} + 1 & \text{if neighbor} \\ G_{it} & \text{if outside} \end{cases} \tag{1}$$

3.3 Details of Model Settings

The model initialization includes the initial grains of patches, collapse threshold, and simulation durations: (a) Initialized the variables. In the beginning, the total grain value G is set to all patches. The threshold value for all patches is the critical condition where the patch, as well as the whole sandpile system, collapses. At each time t, we record relative sizes (percentage) of avalanches out of the whole sandpile system. Therefore, in Eq. (2), the relative size is a percentage value that satisfies $Y_t \in [0, 1]$. . It refers to the percentage of collapsed patches out of total patches ($n = 1681$), and therefore the probability of social instability for empires; (b) Empire dynamics. The set S is a time-serial value list, which is consist of all the dynamic values of s_t at each time or iteration. For each simulation, the value set $S = \{t, y_t\}$ records the whole process of the system, from the start ($t = 0$) to the end ($t = t_{max} = T$) of the simulation. The whole process data $S = \{t, y_t\}$ refers to the life cycle trend of several empires, which contains both stable and unstable periods. In reality, the life cycle dynamics are shaped by economic, demographic, military, and other factors. They jointly determine the weak, chaotic, or strong (health) of empires; (c) Divide separate empires. The data $S = \{t, y_t\}$ can be divided into serval empires, according to specific rising and falling of empires. In our modeling, we set the critical crisis threshold to divide empires or dynasties. This critical crisis threshold does not change for the whole process. If the dynamic value s_t exceeds the critical crisis threshold, the degree of chaos and turbulence is too high, which leads to the death of old empires, and the birth of new empires. For a typical empire, the life cycle curve can be captured as $S_d = \{t, y_t\}$ from the start ($t = t_{d0}$) to death ($t = t_{d1}$) of the dth empire; (b) Durations of empires. According to the study of the Vietnam empires [36], the ancient Vietnamese empire becomes an independent country that has discretionary power since AD 907, but the last Vietnam empire collapsed inevitably in AD 1945. In 1945, the Republic of Vietnam formally was established and presented as an end symbol of feudal Vietnamese society. There are roughly ten empires in history with more than 1000 years, from AD 907 to AD 1945. To match these real empires in history, the simulation results $S = \{t, Y_t\}$ should contain 10 empires (Fig. 1).

$$s_t = \frac{\# \; Callapsed \; Patches}{\# \; Total \; Patches} * 100\% \tag{2}$$

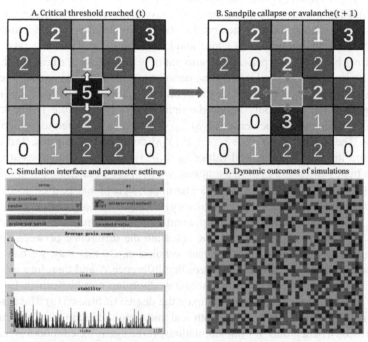

Fig. 1. The rule of lattice dynamics and the interface of the sandpile model. Subfigures A and B show the change rule of dynamic, which consists of many lattices. Subfigure C shows the parameter-setting interface of the sandpile model, and subfigure D indicates the dynamic process.

3.4 Optimal Solution of Real Empires

The results of our agent-based modeling should match empires in Vietnam's history. Before AD 907, there were no empires in Vietnam, because it had been ruled by the China empire for more than 1000 years, from BC 112 to AD 907. In China, a famous general Zhu Wen overtook the weak Tang empire in AD 907, which started the chaotic period of the Five Dynasties and Ten Kingdoms [37]. As China's dominance over Vietnam faded away, Vietnam entered an era of independent and autonomous development. In table one, there were 10 empires in history. The first empire (Ngô Quyền Dynasty) is not stable. The regime was ruled by Khúc Thừa Dynasty, then by the Ngô Quyền Dynasty. It was inherited through several leadership changes during AD 907 and AD 968, and the imperial history of self-governed Vietnam was formed then. Hence, we define the first empire ranges from AD 907 to AD 968 [6]. The simulated results can be displayed in Table one. During the empirical period, we have a series of ten empires or dynasties, namely, the Ngô Quyền dynasty (AD 907 to AD 968), the Đinhs dynasty (AD 968 to AD 980), the Early Lês dynasty (AD 980 to AD 1009), Lýs dynasty (AD 1009 to AD 1225), Trầns dynasty (AD 1225 to AD 1400), Hồs dynasty (AD 1400 to AD 1407), Later Trầns dynasty (AD 1407 to AD 1428), Later Lês dynasty (AD 1428 to AD 1784), Tây Sons dynasty (AD 1784 to AD 1802), and Nguyễns dynasty (AD 1802 to AD 1945). Actually, although most historians have a consensus on the exact duration of these empires, there are still some controversial disputes on the start and end dates of some empires. For instance, the Fourth domination of China and Later Trầns is still controversial, because these regimes belong to one period, but with multiple coexisting or ruling local regimes. Since multiple regimes existed in the same period, we regard them as one regime. We use commonly-believed consensus to take the durations, and some tiny errors are inevitable and acceptable. The commonly-believed empires are listed in Table 1. The history of real empires in history can be denoted by $f_{real}(\cdot)$, which contains ten identified empires in Eq. (2). The set $\{Y_1, Y_2, Y_3, \ldots Y_k, \ldots Y_9, Y_{10}\}$ contains ten empires, and each one refers to specific time-serial paired values $S_d = \{t, y_t\}$. As the simulations are ought to match the trends and features of real empires, we use $f_{sim}(\cdot)$ to denote our ten simulated empires $\{\widehat{Y_1}, \widehat{Y_2}, \widehat{Y_3}, \ldots \widehat{Y_k}, \ldots \widehat{Y_9}, \widehat{Y}_{10}\}$. The upper sign of hat is used to distinguish simulated empires from real empires in history. We have one outcome for $f_{real}(\cdot)$, which has been fixed in history, but has multiple and paralleled simulation outcomes $f_{sim}(\cdot)$. Taking $f_{real}(\cdot)$ as the target function, we calculate the difference between simulation and reality, $\Delta = f_{sim}(\cdot) - f_{real}(\cdot)$, for each simulation. By this way, we can solve the optimal solution $Par^*(\cdot)$, which minimizes the difference Δ and therefore achieves the highest fitness to reality. The optimal solution algorithm can be seen in Eq. (2). We have two standards to calculate and compare the degree of fitness: (a) The macro-level standard is the matching numbers of both real and simulated empires. Real empires in history provide a benchmark for our simulations. If the agent-based model is reasonably designed, the number of simulated empires should equal 10, or close to 10 at least. For multiple simulations, the mean value of the distribution should equal 10 (or close to 10). Under these achievements, the model will be a reliable one; and (b) The micro-level (higher) standard is one-by-one duration matching. Based on the macro-level standard, this is a higher standard. Given the same numbers of empires, we should make sure that the duration of 10 paired empires should be matched, and we can see more $Y_i = \widehat{Y}_i$ cases if we compare simulated and real empires. If the model and simulation satisfy these two standards, we can back-calculate the historical life cycles of the Vietnam empires, based on the optimal solution $Par^*(\cdot)$ in Eq. (3). We traverse related parameters and simulations to find the optimal solution.

$$\begin{cases} f_{real}(\cdot) = \{Y_1, Y_2, Y_3, \ldots Y_i, \ldots Y_9, Y_{10}\} \\ f_{sim}(\cdot) = \{\widehat{Y_1}, \widehat{Y_2}, \widehat{Y_3}, \ldots \widehat{Y_k}, \ldots \widehat{Y_9}, \widehat{Y}_{10}\} \\ Par^*(\cdot) = Argmin[f_{sim}(\cdot) - f_{real}(\cdot)] = Argmin \sum_1^{10} \frac{\left(Y_i - \widehat{Y_i}\right)^2}{n-1} \end{cases} \quad (3)$$

4   Results and Fitness

Within 1000 simulations with different combinations of parameters, we try to find the optimal solution $Par^*(\cdot)$. After repeated simulations and alignments, it indicates that the total grain value G should be 4, and the threshold value be 5. Under the setting of this sandpile model collapse, we can find the optimal solution $Par^*(\cdot)$, a unique combination of parameters. The critical crisis threshold is 0.62, beyond which the old empire dies and the new one rises. The existence of the optimal solution merely supports the validity of our model. Thus, we further investigate the robustness by repeated simulations. Under the optimal solution, we repeat the simulation 1000 times, take the average values, and therefore obtain robust outcomes of simulations (N = 1000). It suggests that the robust outcome of simulations (N = 1000) fits real empires well, according to the following standards or aspects. Therefore, both the validity and robustness of the optimal solution can be supported by our agent-based modeling.

4.1   Distributive Fitness of Simulations

Under the optimal combination of parameters $Par^*(\cdot)$ solved in Eq. (2), we repeat simulations and obtain average values (N = 1000) as the final robust outcome, which can be seen in Fig. 2. According to chaos theory and dissipative system theory, the empire cycle resembles the stochastic and disordered process, which can be shown by our simulation data. For each simulation, a number of empires can be obtained. Besides 10 simulated empires, we also inevitably see other scales of simulated empires, from 6 to 20 empires. The number of simulated empires has 1000 observations, and its distribution is smooth and bell-curved in Fig. 2. Besides, it follows the normal distribution, which is supported by the Q-Q plot because most data points are evenly distributed near the straight $y = x$ line. The mean value is 9.634 (N = 1000), which approximately equals 10 in reality. Hence, we have 10 empires for both simulations and real history. The fitness and robustness of our sandpile model can be guaranteed. Besides, the SD is 2.908272 (N = 1000), which represents that most values are close to the mean of 10, and coefficient variations are low. Meanwhile, we calculated the percentages of common numbers, such as n = 5 (4.30%), n = 6 (7.10%), n = 7 (10.40%), n = 8 (10.70%), n = 9 (13.00%), n = 10 (13.60%), n = 11 (12.00%), n = 12 (9.20%), n = 13 (8.30%), n = 14 (4.00%), and n = 15 (2.20%). Apparently, the density of n = 10 has the highest density. Therefore, our sandpile model can simulate an accurate number of empires and restore the dynamic evolution of real empires in history.

4.2   Durations Matching of 10 Empires

Macroscopically, we have precisely matched the number of 10 empires in Vietnam's history. Microscopically, we have 10 durations of the empires, and the total duration is 1038 years. The optimal solution of our model can match these 10 empires one by one: (a) Ranking 10 real empire durations. The 10 empires and durations are fixed in historical records, which can be seen in Fig. 3. In order to be matched by the simulations, we rank these real empires and their durations in history. In Fig. 3, each color corresponds to one unique simulated and real empire. The first A panel visualizes the original order of

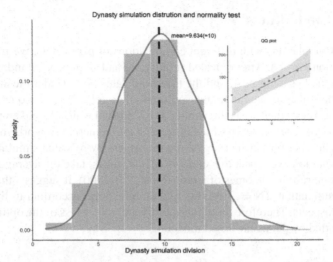

Fig. 2. The distribution of simulations under the optimal parameters (N = 1000). It shows a schematic of the probability density distribution (N = 1000). The mean is 9.634(which can be rounded up to 10) and the SD is 2.91. We verified the normal distribution by the Q-Q plot.

empires in history as well as their durations. The width of each rectangular refers to the duration in years for each empire; (b) Obtaining 136 groups of ranked durations.

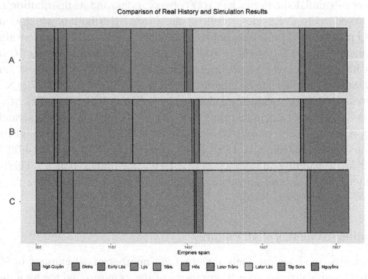

Fig. 3. Panel A shows the durations of 10 empires in history. Panel B indicates the best simulation with 10 empires (durations), out of 136 simulations. Panel C reflects the average (robust) outcome of 136 simulations, which have 10 empires.

From the distribution in Fig. 2, we have 136 cases with n = 10 empires (13.60%) out of 1000 repeated optimal solution simulations. For each one of these 136 simulations, we rank 10 simulated empire durations and obtain 136 groups of 10 ranked durations; (c) The best-ranking matching. For 136 groups of ranked 10 durations, we calculate the 136 differences (Δ) between ranked real and simulated durations. Again, the $ArgMin[\Delta]$ algorithm in Eq. (2) is applied to find the best matching group, which minimizes errors between reality and simulations. Then, we recover or restore the real order of empires in history. The second B panel shows one best simulations, which has well matched real durations in history. For this best simulation, the total duration lasted for 1033 years, which is 5 years shorter than the real total duration (1038 years). Then, we check the one-by-one matching. For each target empire, the durations of real and simulation can be well-matched, with tiny bias mostly less than 8 years. There is only one empire with a duration beyond 300 years, and we also have this one (Later Lê Dynasty) in the B panel; (d) The average duration matching. Besides the best matching group, we use the averaged data of 136 groups as the robust outcome of the 10 ranked empire durations. Then, we restore the order in history to match real empire durations. It indicates that the average duration of 136 simulations (C panel) fit real empires more than the best one (B panel). Most duration gaps between real and simulation pairs are tiny and less than 5 years, and the aggerated duration in the C panel is 1040 years, which is merely two years beyond the 1038 years in history. In reality (Panel A), there are five empires with durations below 50 years, and we also have them (Đinhs Dynasty, Early Lê Dynasty, Hôs Dynasty, Later Trầns Dynasty, & Tây Sơns Dynasty) in panel C. We separately have one case whose duration is between 50 and 100 (Ngô Quyền Dynasty), 100 to 150 (Nguyễns Dynasty), 150 to 200(Trầns Dynasty), and 200 to 250 ranges (Lýs Dynasty). Not only is it exactly the same in terms of interval matching, but every empire time match is also very close to each other. Hence, panel C matches real empires better than panel B.

5   Conclusions and Discussions

The life cycle is a robust rule in both natural and social systems. Life cycles can be short, intermediate, or longer in terms of lifespan. We can use this cyclical rhythm to back-calculate history and predict future trends for several centuries. For the life cycles of Vietnamese empires, historians find the patterns that recurred over time and use them to discover the natural rhythms of social systems. In the previous work, the sandpile model and simulations have been applied to explore the life cycles of China's empires in history. In this work, we also confirm that the Vietnam empire cycles can be investigated by applying the sandpile model. Macroscopically, the rising and falling process of Vietnam empires in history has been changed frequently, and we have 10 empires in total. Under the optimal solution, we repeat simulations 1000 times and calculate the mean value of simulations. It indicates that the mean=9.634($\approx$ 10) and SD = 2.9083, which perfectly matches the number of 10. Thus, we assume that our sandpile model matches real empires at all levels. At the macro-level, the sandpile model matches well the 10 empires of Vietnam, and we can also find ten simulated-real empire pairs. Microscopically, the one-by-one matching of empire durations can be also satisfied.

From AD 907 to AD 1945, the list of 10 empires lasts for 1,038 years in total. In our simulations, the best simulation has merely a gap of 5 years gap, and the multiple simulations also have a gap of 5 years. The simulation is very close to the real history of the Vietnam empires. It can be considered the basic restoration of the history of the Vietnamese empire. The process of history is full of chaos and randomness, so we explore situations other than 10 empires. Therefore, we suppose that the sandpile model perfectly fits real empires in Vietnam. Besides, there are some limitations. First, the division of the Vietnam empires from the different standards or historians is not the same. Therefore, we obtain a consistent division with the mainstream of history by referring to many historical works of literature. Nevertheless, some obscure or different duration remain. Besides, if the simulated results could appropriately match real empires one by one, the simulated model will perfectly restore reality and also predict future development. Since the dynastic cycles of both China and Vietnam empires can be supported by the sandpile model, we further expand the sandpile model to the other empires such as the British and Japanese empires in the world and execute the further examination.

References

1. Suny, R.G.: The empire strikes out: imperial Russia, 'national' identity, and theories of empire. A state of nations: Empire and nation-making in the age of Lenin and Stalin, 23–66 (2001)
2. Taagepera, R.: Patterns of Empire Growth and Decline: Context for Russia. unpublished paper, March (1995)
3. Bondaletov, V., Maslikov, V.: Evolution of sociological knowledge in the field of self-organization of society. In: Economic and Social Development: Book of Proceedings, pp. 1075–1081 (2017)
4. Skokov, V.N., Koverda, V.P., Reshetnikov, A.V.: Self-organization of a critical state and 1/fα-fluctuations at film boiling. Phys. Lett. A 263(4–6), 430–433 (1999)
5. Norgaard, R.B.: Development betrayed: The end of progress and a co-evolutionary revisioning of the future. Routledge (2006)
6. Taylor, K.W.: A History of the Vietnamese. Cambridge University Press (2013)
7. Pryor, R.G., Bright, J.: The chaos theory of careers. Aust. J. Career Dev. 12(3), 12–20 (2003)
8. Lorenz, E.N.: Deterministic nonperiodic flow. J. Atmos. Sci. 20(2), 130–141 (1963)
9. Gregersen, H., Sailer, L.: Chaos theory and its implications for social science research. Hum. Rel. 46(7), 777–802 (1993)
10. Kiel, L.D., Elliott, E.W.: Chaos Theory in the Social Sciences: Foundations and Applications. University of Michigan Press (1996)
11. Usher, D.: The dynastic cycle and the stationary state. Am. Econ. Rev. 1031–1044 (1989)
12. Levy, D.: Chaos theory and strategy: theory, application, and managerial implications. Strateg. Manag. J. 15(S2), 167–178 (1994)
13. Brock, W.A., Hsieh, D.A., LeBaron, B.D., Brock, W.E.: Nonlinear Dynamics, Chaos, and Instability: Statistical Theory and Economic Evidence. MIT Press (1991)
14. Feichtinger, G., Forst, C.V., Piccardi, C.: A nonlinear dynamical model for the dynastic cycle. Chaos, Solitons Fractals 7(2), 257–271 (1996)
15. Piccardi, C.A.R.L.O., Feichtinger, G.: Peak-to-peak dynamics in the dynastic cycle. Chaos Solit. Fract. 13(2), 195–202 (2002)
16. Meskill, J.T.: The Pattern of Chinese History Cycles, Development, or Stagnation? (1965)
17. Murphy, P.: Chaos theory as a model for managing issues and crises. Public Rel. Rev. 22(2), 95–113 (1996)

18. Vandervert, L.R.: Chaos theory and the evolution of consciousness and mind: a thermodynamic-holographic resolution to the mind-body problem. New Ideas Psychol. **13**(2), 107–127 (1995)
19. Ferguson, N.: Complexity and collapse: empires on the edge of chaos. Foreign Aff. **89**, 18 (2010)
20. Liu, Q., Li, G., Kong, D., Huang, B., Wang, Y.: Climate, disasters, wars and the collapse of the Ming Dynasty. Environ. Earth Sci. **77**(2), 44 (2018)
21. Creutz, M.: Abelian sandpiles. Comput. Phys. **5**(2), 198–203 (1991)
22. Levine, L. (2010). What is... a sandpile. In Notices Amer. Math. Soc
23. Nagel, S.R.: Instabilities in a sandpile. Rev. Mod. Phys. **64**(1), 321 (1992)
24. Ivashkevich, E.V., Ktitarev, D.V., Priezzhev, V.B.: Critical exponents for boundary avalanches in two-dimensional Abelian sandpile. J. Phys. A: Math. Gen. **27**(16), L585 (1994)
25. Dhar, D., Manna, S.S.: Inverse avalanches in the abelian sandpile model. Phys. Rev. E **49**(4), 2684 (1994)
26. Priezzhev, V.B., Ktitarev, D.V., Ivashkevich, E.V.: Formation of avalanches and critical exponents in an Abelian sandpile model. Phys. Rev. Lett. **76**(12), 2093 (1996)
27. Manna, S.S., Stella, A.L.: Self-organized random walks and stochastic sandpile: from linear to branched avalanches. Physica A **316**(1–4), 135–143 (2002)
28. Dorso, C.O., Dadamia, D.: Avalanche prediction in Abelian sandpile model. Physica A **308**(1–4), 179–191 (2002)
29. Lee, D.S., Goh, K.I., Kahng, B., Kim, D.: Sandpile avalanche dynamics on scale-free networks. Physica A **338**(1–2), 84–91 (2004)
30. Tarun, A.B., Paguirigan, A.A., Jr., Batac, R.C.: Spatiotemporal recurrences of sandpile avalanches. Physica A **436**, 293–300 (2015)
31. Abar, S., Theodoropoulos, G.K., Lemarinier, P., O'Hare, G.M.: Agent based modelling and simulation tools: a review of the state-of-art software. Comput. Sci. Rev. **24**, 13–33 (2017)
32. Grimm, V., et al.: A standard protocol for describing individual-based and agent-based models. Ecol. Model. **198**(1–2), 115–126 (2006)
33. Grimm, V., Berger, U., DeAngelis, D.L., Polhill, J.G., Giske, J., Railsback, S.F.: The ODD protocol: a review and first update. Ecol. Model. **221**(23), 2760–2768 (2010)
34. Grimm, V., Polhill, G., Touza, J.: Documenting social simulation models: the ODD protocol as a standard. In: Edmonds, B., Meyer, R. (eds.) Simulating social complexity. UCS, pp. 349–365. Springer, Cham (2017). https://doi.org/10.1007/978-3-319-66948-9_15
35. Grimm, V., et al.: The ODD protocol for describing agent-based and other simulation models: A second update to improve clarity, replication, and structural realism. J. Artif. Soc. Soc. Simul. **23**(2) (2020)
36. Lockhart, B.M.: Vietnamese (Dai Viet) Empire. The Encyclopedia of Empire, 1–6 (2016)
37. Juzheng, X.: Old history of the Five Dynasties. Zhonghua Book Company (in Chinese) (1976)

Multi-source Autoregressive Entity Linking Based on Generative Method

Dongju Yang[1,2] and Weishui Lan[1,2(✉)]

[1] Beijing Municipal Key Laboratory on Integration and Analysis of Large-Scale Stream, Beijing 100144, China
[2] Data Research Center for Cloud Computing, North China University of Technology, Beijing 100144, China
yangdongju@ncut.edu.cn, im.lws@mail.ncut.edu.cn

Abstract. The task of entity linking aims to map the entity reference in the text with the unambiguous entity in the knowledge base. However, under the background of the continuous growth of science and technology service platform services, the complexity and diversity of domain semantic information, and the vagueness and ambiguity of natural language, the task of linking industrial chain knowledge graphs and technology service resources faces the following problems: (1) The increase in the types of semantic information in the do-main will lead to the lack of cognition and ambiguity in the entity linking process, which will affect the accuracy of entity linking; (2) the context and interaction of corpus information Dependencies become more complex, making insufficient consideration of the mapping relationship between linked entities. To address the above issues, this paper proposes a generative method and multiple sources of information Autoregressive Entity Linking (GMoAEL), which uses data sets such as unstructured textual descriptions, related reference links, and fine-grained structured types Information and other sources of information are used to build a unified dense representation for entity learning, and an autoregressive model in the form of encoder-decoder is used to adjust the link generation process to handle the complex mapping relationship between in-put and output. This paper uses the AIDA CoNLL-YAGO data set to conduct experiments. Compared with other methods, the Micro-F1 value is 1.6% points ahead, which verifies the feasibility and effectiveness of this method.

Keywords: entity linking · generative · multi-source · autoregressive · mention detection · target sequence

1 Introduction

The technology service platform is an industry hub offering streamlined, full-lifecycle solutions for technology services, elements, and more. By using technologies such as machine learning, it addresses the challenge of standardizing diverse tech services sources. It has also proposed a solution for domain-specific service spaces and matching service resources. The industry knowledge graph, a cornerstone, links various tech service resources and their industry chains.

Y. Sun et al. (Eds.): ChineseCSCW 2023, CCIS 2012, pp. 406–420, 2024.
https://doi.org/10.1007/978-981-99-9637-7_30

However, within the current context, the complexity of domain semantic information within the technology service platform has increased. This complexity presents challenges in linking industry chain knowledge graphs to different technological service resources. These challenges are as follows: (1) The abundance of domain semantic information leads to shallow understanding and introduces ambiguity in recognizing service entities. For instance, underutilizing textual descriptions, service-related references, and detailed structured type information can impact entity linking precision. (2) The intricate context and interdependencies of technological service corpus information must be considered. Neglecting mapping relationships between service entities and not fully leveraging corpus context can result in incomplete entity linkage outcomes. Additionally, natural language itself is inherently vague and ambiguous. Addressing these challenges through natural language processing techniques to enhance the effectiveness of linking industry chain knowledge graphs and technological service resources has become a demanding endeavor.

In response to the aforementioned challenges, this paper introduces a Generative-based Multi-source Autoregressive Entity Linking method (GMoAEL). The paper extensively employs multiple sources: entity textual descriptions from Wikipedia, linked mentions, and fine-grained type information from Freebase. These sources create explicit Entity Representations, integrated into a unified dense representation for entity linking.

During entity linking training, this paper combines an Encoder-Decoder architecture [1] with an autoregressive language model. This approach effectively uses the encoder-decoder structure of entities and their contexts, benefiting from pre-training knowledge. This mechanism adjusts subsequent generation based on prior outputs, enhancing coherence. Ultimately, model training improves the understanding of intricate mapping relationships between inputs and outputs, thus enhancing entity linking effectiveness. The approach primarily connects industry chains, technological services, and the entity linking task through multi-source information embedding.

2 Background

2.1 Entity Linking

Entity Linking [2] is a natural language processing (NLP) task aimed at identifying real-world entities referred to in textual documents and linking them to a knowledge base, thereby establishing associations between textual documents and existing knowledge repositories. This task serves as a fundamental building block for various natural language understanding and knowledge acquisition tasks, such as question answering systems [3], text classification [4], and commercial recommendation systems [5].This task primarily deals with issues of entity mentions and ambiguity, leading to two main subtasks: Mention Detection [6] and Entity Disambiguation [7].

Early entity linking [8] involved two steps: mention detection and entity disambiguation. These used text similarity and entity occurrence probability. Advanced methods employ neural networks, calculating semantic matches between mention and candidate entity context [9]. For instance, Luo et al. [10] introduced a deep semantic matching model using knowledge graphs and descriptive text.

Recently, research into entity linking has progressively introduced techniques such as Long Short-Term Memory (LSTM) and Self-Attention mechanisms. LSTM is used to encode the context on both sides of entity mentions, while Self-Attention employs attention heads to capture essential text around the mention. Martins et al. [11] introduced a model inspired by the Stack-LSTM approach for joint learning of Named Entity Recognition (NER) and entity linking. For entity linking, language modeling approaches provide a new perspective, treating it as a distinct task within language modeling. Taking a BERT-based approach [12], Broscheit et al. [13] redefined entity linking as holistic token classification. Detected entities are categorized as specific tokens in the vocabulary. In contrast, this paper emphasizes generating richer entity representations with enhanced semantic capabilities, capturing entity relationships and contextual consistency. This enhances entity linking accuracy. Unlike early methods, Broscheit et al.'s language model eliminates separate mention detection and entity disambiguation, directly mapping for entity linking.

2.2 Multi-source Semantic Information

In entity linking, knowledge base-provided background semantic information significantly impacts both mention detection and entity disambiguation. For instance, linked mentions and detailed type data from Wikipedia assist mention detection. Likewise, textual entity descriptions facilitate context similarity comparisons.

Recent entity linking research aims to enhance performance via multi-source semantic integration. Navigli et al. [14] used graph-based word sense representations from SemCor for entity disambiguation. Similarly, Zan et al. [15] combined synonym dictionaries, encyclopedic resources, and bag-of-words models for multi-source knowledge-based linking. Additionally, Dredze et al. [16] augmented relevant Wikipedia pages with search engine results to expand candidate entities and enrich background knowledge. In contrast, this study combines Freebase and Wikipedia data using a generative approach, leveraging Freebase's interconnected knowledge points to expand candidates. The study addresses fusion challenges by optimizing encoder loss functions and using an autoregressive model, resulting in multi-source, information-based, autoregressive entity linking.

Multi-source knowledge methods now enhance mention detection and entity disambiguation. By integrating diverse data into existing knowledge bases, they efficiently acquire structured and unstructured information. This approach gains prominence in multi-knowledge base algorithms [17].

2.3 Autoregressive

DE et al. [18] introduced an autoregressive model that replaces vector space linking with sequence-to-sequence denoising pretraining, using BART [19]. Input sequences contain mention pairs, while output sequences correspond to entities for each pair. The model highlights and maps entity mentions using parentheses/brackets to knowledge base concepts. The method employs an encoder-decoder framework, with the encoder translating input mention pairs into vectors for the decoder. This decoder progressively generates the output sequence, providing an entity identifier at each step.

When forming identifiers, the decoder considers prior identifiers and input vectors, maximizing conditional probabilities in training. This entails optimizing the likelihood of generating the correct output sequence given input mention pairs and the desired entity identifier sequence. Furthermore, Sutskever et al. [20] employed constrained decoding to ensure generated names align with a predefined candidate set. This approach effectively governs output, enhancing model accuracy and reliability.

3 Generative-based Multi-source Autoregressive Method

The entity linking task aims to establish accurate mapping relationships between entity mentions present in a text document and target entities within a knowledge base. The proposed approach in this paper, which integrates generative methods and multiple information sources into an autoregressive entity linking framework, is depicted in Fig. 1. The entire process can be broadly divided into five components: multi-source information embedding, mention detection, candidate entity generation, target sequence generation, and discriminative correction. This section will provide an overview of the process by integrating it into two main parts: multi-source information embedding and autoregressive entity linking.

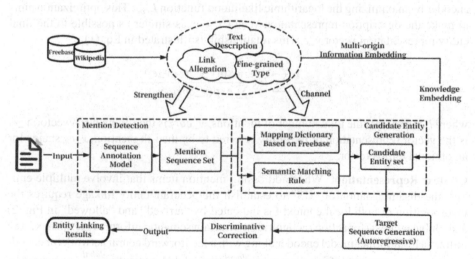

Fig. 1. Flowchart of multi-source regression entity linking

3.1 Multi-source Information Embedding

In the multi-source information embedding step, diverse data like Wikipedia content, entity URLs, and Freebase [21] type information are transformed into high-quality embeddings. This knowledge embedding enhances entity linking by capturing semantic relationships. Figure 2 illustrates the multi-source joint entity information segment of the model.

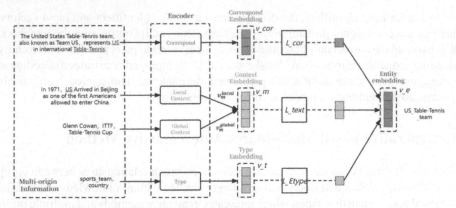

Fig. 2. Multi-source federated entity information

Related Description. In terms of entity-related descriptions, this paper embeds word sequences into a d_w-dimensional vector, thereby creating a sequence of vectors. Subsequently, a convolutional neural network is employed for global average pooling, resulting in v_cor. The paper then jointly optimizes entity representation and related description encoder by maximizing the logarithmic likelihood function L_{cor}. This optimization aims to make the description representation vector v_cor as similar as possible to the final entity representation vector v_e. This relationship is illustrated in Eq. (1).

$$L_{cor} = \frac{1}{N} \sum_{i=1}^{N} log \frac{exp(v\_cor_i \cdot v\_e_i)}{\sum exp(v\_cor_i \cdot v\_c_k)} \tag{1}$$

where N represents the total number of mentions, v_cor_i is the i-th mention vector, v_e_i is the vector representation of the entity referred to by the i-th mention, v_c_k stands for an optional entity vector.

Context Representation. When addressing mention items that involve multiple entities, the disambiguation of "US" to establish the accurate entity linkage requires the incorporation of both local context (as indicated by "arrived" and "allowed" in Fig. 2) and global context (for action recognition). To retain semantic information, this research utilizes a Longformer model encoder along with a feedforward neural network for encoding the representations of local context v_m^{local} and global context v_m^{global}, respectively. Ultimately, these two forms of representation are amalgamated into a unified vector representation denoted as v_m.

Specifically, the local context encoder begins by concatenating the forward h_m^l and backward h_m^r output sequences of a bidirectional LSTM, which capture the contextual information of the mention's surroundings in the text. Subsequently, the representation h_m is passed through a single-layer feedforward neural network to generate the representation v_m^{local}, as depicted in Formula (2).

$$h_m^l = LSTM(u_m, h_{m-1}, s_{m-1}), \quad h_m^r = LSTM(u_m, h_{m+1}, s_{m+1}), \quad h_m = \left[h_m^l; h_m^r \right] \tag{2}$$

where m represents the mention, u_m denotes the low-dimensional word vector of the input mention, h_{m-1} and h_{m+1} correspondingly refer to the preceding and succeeding outputs, and s represents the respective unit state.

Meanwhile, the global context encoder employs a bag-of-words model to extract feature words from all the words in the global context. These feature words are then used to construct a matrix that models the inclusion of word weights, resulting in a feature vector $v_D \in \{0,1\}^{|V_G|}$, where V_G represents the vocabulary in the training dataset. Subsequently, this vector is compressed into a lower-dimensional representation v_m^{global}. Finally, the context encoder concatenates the representations of local and global context, passing them through a single-layer feedforward network to obtain the context embedding vector v_m, as illustrated in Fig. 3.

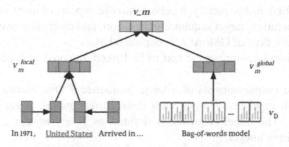

Fig. 3. Local and Global Coding Descriptions

Similarly, this paper employs a joint optimization approach by maximizing the log-likelihood function L_{text}, which is congruent with L_{cor}, to optimize both entity representations and context encoders. This process aims to maximize the resemblance between the context representation vector v_m and the ultimate entity representation vector v_e as much as possible.

Fine-grained Types. In this study, the probability $\sigma(v_t \cdot v_e)$ associated with the entity e and type t is computed using the sigmoid function. The logarithmic likelihood function L_{Etype}, which incorporates information from both entity and type representations, is then maximized to enhance the loss function. This enhancement is represented by Formula (3).

$$L_{Etype} = \frac{1}{|\varepsilon|} \sum_{e \in \varepsilon} log \prod_{t \in T_e} \sigma(v_t \cdot v_e) \prod_{t' \notin T_e} (1 - \sigma(v_{t'} \cdot v_e)) \tag{3}$$

where ε represents the set of fine-grained entities, σ denotes the sigmoid function, t signifies an entity type, and T_e stands for the collection of entity types.

The described encoders convert diverse multi-source data into corresponding vector representations. A fully connected layer then maps these to a fixed-size embedding vector, unifying them. To effectively capture semantic relationships across information types, the argmax function jointly maximizes loss functions. This balances different information source reliability.

Additionally, the strong connections among Freebase knowledge points and their linkage to relevant topics emphasize multi-source semantic relevance. The section leverages embedding vectors from multi-source information, merging them with knowledge embeddings. These are compared to annotated mention sequences in the candidate entity set using similarity measures. This method integrates multi-source information into entity linking.

3.2 Autoregressive Entity Linking

This section provides a comprehensive overview and explanation of the process and design details of the generative self-regressive entity linking. Firstly, it outlines the procedure and algorithm of the multi-source generative self-regressive entity linking method (GMoAEL). Subsequently, it delves into the aspects of mention detection, candidate entity generation, target sequence generation, and discriminative correction. The overall algorithmic flow of GMoAEL is depicted below:

Input: The input comprises the text to be linked, denoted as I, containing entities awaiting linking.

Output: The output consists of a target sequence T that encompasses all entity mentions m from input text I along with their corresponding target entities e in the knowledge base. The target sequence is defined as $T = \{(m_1,e_1),...,(m_j,e_j)\}, j \in N^*$ represents a positive integer.

Step 1: The input text I is preprocessed to generate multiple input sentences $\{i_1,...,i_n\}$. This captures contextual information for the input vectors. Employing a sequence labeling model, it predicts the start and end positions of entity mentions m. Using the labeled positions, it identifies positions corresponding to entity mentions. This creates a set of mention sequences $M = \{m_1,...,m_j\}, j \in N^*$ signifies a positive integer.

Step 2: For each annotated position of an entity mention m, in conjunction with the knowledge base's multi-source embedding vector v_e, the Freebase mapping dictionary, and syntactic rules, a corresponding candidate entity set $C = \{c_1,...,c_k\}, k \in N^*$ is generated.

Step 3: Positions labeled as mentions in input sentences $\{i_1,...,i_n\}$ are replaced with candidate entity sets, forming target sentences $\{t_1,...,t_m\}$. These serve as encoder inputs. Using an autoregressive process, each mention m in target sentences is successively replaced with its top-probability candidate entity c. The most probable candidate entity c becomes the target entity e, combined with the corresponding entity reference m to create the target sequence T.

Step 4: Employing a neural network-based discriminative correction approach, an assessment is made for each candidate entity c and whether it aligns with all the mentions m in the corresponding target sentence t_m. Utilizing the backpropagation algorithm, the parameters of the target sequence generation model are updated to achieve the final discriminative correction outcome.

Step 5: The target sequence T, refined through the discriminative correction process, is presented as the ultimate output for entity linking.

Mention Detection. This study utilizes a mention detection module for annotating mentions in the input text. Initially, the conversion of input sentences into labeled sequences is treated as label-based binary classification. "E" signifies an entity mention or concept label, while "O" represents other labels, this process records potential starting and ending positions for entity mentions.

This study treats the process from labeled sequences to target mentions as a generative problem. Binary cross-entropy loss function is utilized to assess whether each label corresponds to an entity mention. By comparing the predictions with the actual labels, the objective is to minimize the cross-entropy loss L_{bce} and predict the positions of target entities within the input sentences. Ultimately, this process generates a set of mention sequences. Formula (4) in the paper provides a detailed representation of the algorithmic flow.

$$L_{bce} = -\frac{1}{N} \sum_{i=1}^{N} [y_i \cdot \log p(y_i) + (1 - y_i) \cdot \log(1 - p(y_i))] \tag{4}$$

where N represents the number of mentions, y_i is a binary label value of either 0 or 1, and $p(y_i)$ is the probability associated with the label value y_i.

Candidate Entity Generation. The candidate entity generation task combines mention sequences with multi-source embeddings to identify candidate entities for each entity mention. To ensure accuracy and efficiency, this study utilizes a method involving Freebase's mention-entity mapping dictionary (D) and syntactic rules.

Specifically, the mapping dictionary D is created using standard names and aliases of Freebase entities. It consists of a mention domain and an entity domain, stored as < mention; e1,e2,...,en >. Here, mention represents an entity mention stored in the mention domain, and e1,e2,...,en are potential entities stored as Freebase unique identifiers (/m/0600c, for example) in the entity domain.

If an entity mention isn't found in the mapping dictionary D, this paper uses syntax rules to generate candidate entity sets. This involves generating an initial set of candidate entities following syntax rules for categories like personal names and place names. Then, it calculates cosine similarity between the mention and entities in the candidate entity set. If the calculated similarity exceeds a preset threshold β, the top k candidate entities are retained as the final candidate entity set. For a detailed view of the candidate entity generation module, consult Algorithm 1 in Table 1.

Target Sequence Generation. The objective of this section is to replace the entity mentions within the input sentences with their corresponding target entities and generate the corresponding target sequence T. To start, the target sentences are combined with the candidate entity set C and fed into the encoder. Specifically, a autoregressive decoder is employed to generate the target sequence T, wherein each entity mention m is replaced with its most probable candidate entity c.

At each step of target sequence generation, the ongoing sequence T_i influences the subsequent T_{i+1} generation. The decoder computes the conditional probability distribution $P(t_{mi}|ide_{i-1})$ based on prior tokens and input vectors. Here, ide represents the token for the entity mention, replaced by the most probable candidate entity—either as an identifier or in textual form. This facilitates entity linking by comparing tokenized input text with knowledge base entities. An entity identifier is then sampled from this distribution to serve as the current time step's output. This output extends the sequence,

Table 1. Candidate entity generation.

Algorithm 1: candidate entity generation
Input: $M = \{m_1, ..., m_i\}$, mapping dictionary D, threshold β, int k // Here k is topK
Output: candidate entity set $C = \{c_1, ..., c_i\}$
1:     $C \leftarrow init()$ // Initialize C
2:     **for** m in M **do**
3:     | **if** m in D **do**
4:     | | $C \leftarrow D[m]$ // From the dictionary to generate candidate entity sets
5:     | **else**
6:     | | $C \leftarrow$ Grammar rules   // Get candidate entity sets according to grammatical rules
7:     **for** entity in C **do**
8:     | **if** $Sim(entity) < \beta$ **then**   // Filter by cosine similarity
9:     | | remove entity from C // Remove Low Relevance Candidates
10:    **if** $|C| > k$ **then**   // Select the topk candidate entities
11:    | $C \leftarrow$ remainTopkCandidates(C)
12:    **return** C

and the process iterates, using it as input for the next step. This iterative loop persists until the complete output sequence is formed. Algorithm 2 in Table 2 outlines the detailed procedural flow of this approach.

Table 2. Target sequence generation.

Algorithm 2: target sequence generation
Input: $M = \{m_1, ..., m_i\}$, target sentence $\{t_{m1}, ..., t_{mi}\}$, $C = \{c_1, ..., c_k\}$
Output: terget sequence T
1:     $T \leftarrow init()$ // Initialize T
2:     **for** i in target sentence **do**
3:     | $T_i \leftarrow$ autoregressive(i, t_{mi}, m_i, C, ide) // Loop calling autoregressive methods
4:     $T \leftarrow \{T_1, ..., T_i\}$
5:     **return** T
6:     **function** autoregressive(i, t_m, mention, candidate set, ide_{i-1})
7:     | **if** c in C **do**
8:     | | **for** c_k in C **do**
9:     | | | $ide_k \leftarrow P(t_{mi}|ide_{k-1})$ // Forecast the present identifier using the preceding one
10:    | | | $t_{c\_j} \leftarrow t_{m\_i}$ //Gradually replace referent m as its most likely candidate entity c
11:    | | | **return** autoregressive(i, t_{c_j}, m_i, C, ide_k)
12:    | | $(m_i, e_i) \leftarrow (m_i, c_i)$ // Let the most likely candidate entity c act as the target entity e
13:    | | combined with the corresponding entity reference m
14:    | **else**
15:    | | **return** (m_i, e_i)

Discriminative Correction. In this section, a neural network-based correction method is used, representing each candidate entity c as a vector. Simultaneously, all mention vectors in the target sentence are L2 normalized to address computation bias from varying vector lengths. Cosine similarity scores S are then computed between these normalized mention vectors and the candidate entity vector.

Similarity scores S are transformed to the [0,1] range via the sigmoid function, yielding probabilities indicating likelihood of match between a candidate entity and an entity in the target sentence. Backpropagation optimizes target sequence generation model parameters, enhancing prediction accuracy of most probable candidate entity c for each mention m in the sequence. This extends target sequence generation, optimizing model parameters by evaluating candidate-entity matches. This refining process improves target sequence generation further. In training, the model optimizes both target sequence generation and discriminative correction tasks through the mean squared error loss function (Eq. 5).

$$L_{tsg} = (p(t_m|c) - 1)^2 + \sum_{i=1}^{k} \left(p\left(t_{m_i}|c_i\right) - P\left(t_{m_i}|ide_{i-1}\right) \right)^2 \tag{5}$$

where t_m is the target sentence, t_{m_i} is the i-th generated sample, $p(t_{m_i}|c_i)$ is the probability that an entity in the target sequence matches an entity in the candidate sequence, $P(t_{m_i}|ide_{i-1})$ is the i-th generated The conditional probability distribution of the correct identifier in the sample versus the target sentence. The algorithm flow is shown in Algorithm 3 in Table 3.

Table 3. Discriminant correction.

Algorithm 3: discriminant correction
Input: $M = \{m_1,..,m_i\}$, t_m, $C = \{c_1,..,c_i\}$, threshold γ
Output: Bool bool
1:      **for** m in M **do**
2:        **for** c in C **do**
3:          $S \leftarrow c \cdot m/\|c\|\|m\|$ // Cosine similarity calculation
4:          **if** $sig(S) < \gamma$ **then** // Sigmoid function mapping
5:            $P(t_{mi}|ide_{i-1}) \leftarrow L_{tsg}$ //The backpropagation algorithm maximizes probability
6:            autoregressive() $\leftarrow$ tuning $P(t_{mi}|ide_{i-1})$ // Optimal Autoregressive
7:            **return** False
8:          **else**
9:            **return** True

4 Experiments

4.1 Datasets

The AIDA CoNLL-YAGO [22] benchmark dataset is split into standard training, validation, and testing sets following common practice, as detailed in Table 4. AIDA CoNLL-YAGO, derived from CoNLL 2013 entity recognition dataset annotations, is a significant named entity linking dataset released by the Max Planck Institute. It holds a reputation as a extensively annotated benchmark for evaluating entity linking methodologies.

Table 4. AIDA CoNLL-YAGO dataset statistics

Split	Documents	Mentions
Train	942	18540
Dev	216	4791
Test	230	4485

The dataset encompasses multiple text documents, with each document containing one or more named entities. Each named entity is associated with corresponding attributes, including a Wikipedia URL, YAGO2 entity name, and Freebase identifier. Additionally, contextual information for entities is provided, consisting of the words and sentences surrounding the entity within the document.

4.2 Experimental Design

In this study, the baseline model chosen is the "longformer-base-4096," which is based on the RoBERTa architecture and is specifically designed for processing long texts. The model comprises 12 layers, but only the first 8 layers are used in this paper, resulting in 149 million parameters and 12 hidden heads with a size of 768 each. It supports sequences with a maximum length of 4,096.

To enhance model performance, specific training data is employed to fine-tune parameters. Entity, context, and type vectors are restricted to sizes of 200. To mitigate overfitting, a dropout operation with a 0.1 probability is utilized before linear projection during mention identification. Different word-dropout probabilities (0.2 for local context encoder and 0.4 for global context encoder) are also used. Word-dropout replaces randomly chosen mention strings in context with the "unknown" token. Model optimization employs the Adam optimizer with a weight decay of 1e-2 and a learning rate of 1e-4. Training lasts up to 120 epochs using a batch size of 32 across 8 GPUs (RTX 3090 with 24 GB VRAM). Micro-F1 is computed on the validation set. The model's generalization is boosted primarily through techniques like data separation, dropout layers, learning rate adjustments, and regularization weights.

In this paper, entities corresponding to AIDA are treated as real entities. The text linked to these entities' Wikipedia URLs serves as the mention object and input for the encoder. Entity contextual information becomes entity descriptions, and structured data from Freebase identifiers is utilized as entity types. The assessment of mention existence in the knowledge base follows the In-KB setting.

4.3 Validation Set Test Experiment

Testing results on the AIDA dataset are presented in Table 5. Following iterative parameter tuning, our proposed model demonstrates promising performance in the generative autoregressive entity linking task. Compared to the current leading entity linking model on the AIDA dataset, De Cao et al. (2021b), our approach achieves a 1.6% point lead in terms of Micro-F1 score. Unlike De Cao et al., our method leverages multiple entity information sources for joint modeling and knowledge embedding, facilitating entity type-aware representations that capture diverse semantic information, thus enhancing entity linking precision.

Moreover, our method surpasses Kannan Ravi et al. (2021) by 2.2% points. This highlights the efficacy of the generative autoregressive approach in entity linking. Unlike Kannan Ravi et al., our approach places substantial emphasis on context and interdependencies in both mention identification and target sequence generation tasks. The final discriminative correction module further ensures the validity of generated target sequences.

Table 5. Results on the AIDA test set

Method	Micro-F1
Steinmetz and Sack (2013)	42.3
Daiber et al. (2013)	57.8
Piccinno and Ferragina (2014)	73.0
Peters et al. (2019)	73.7
Broscheit (2019)	79.3
van Hulst et al. (2020)	80.5
Kannan Ravi et al. (2021)	83.1
De Cao et al. (2021b)	83.7
GMoAEL(Our model)	**85.3**

4.4 Ablation Studies

This paper conducts ablation experiments from two perspectives to investigate the effect of multi-source joint entity information and the generative approach-based mention identification component on improving entity linking performance.

Firstly, the experiments involve using context information denoted as MS_T, entity-related descriptions denoted as MS_C, and entity type information denoted as MS_E. Secondly, the paper assesses whether the mention identification and target sequence generation tasks within the autoregressive entity linking framework impact the overall entity linking performance. These tasks are respectively referred to as MD and TSG. Detailed results of these experiments can be found in Table 6.

Table 6. Results of ablation studies

MS_T	MS_C	MS_E	MD	TSG	Micro-F1
Ablation of Multi-source Entity Information					
✗	✗	✗			83.7
✓	✗	✗			83.8
✓	✓	✗			83.3
✓	✓	✓			84.2
Ablation of Autoregressive Entity Linking					
✓	✓	✓	✓	✗	84.6
✓	✓	✓	✓	✓	85.3

According to the results shown in Table 6, the paper employs a model with multi-source joint information to analyze the impact of different information sources on entity linking accuracy. From the experimental results, several observations can be made: The model that encodes only contextual information (MS_T) performs similarly to the generative approach, showing that the original model effectively utilizes dataset context. When both contextual information and entity-related descriptions are incorporated (MS_TC), performance slightly declines, likely due to short or incomplete sentences in descriptions, some of which are entity-specific annotations. Introducing fine-grained entity type information considerably enhances performance in the MS_TCE model with an entity type-aware loss. This suggests that explicitly integrating detailed entity type information enhances the context encoder, enabling the acquisition of entity type-aware representations.

5   Conclusions

This paper introduces a groundbreaking approach that combines generative techniques with multiple information sources in an autoregressive entity linking framework. It effectively addresses challenges in traditional entity linking through two key innovations. First, it leverages various dataset sources like unstructured textual descriptions, related mention links, and fine-grained structured type information. This empowers entities to establish a cohesive dense representation, notably enhancing accurate entity linking. Secondly, by integrating mention identification and target sequence generation tasks, the paper devises an autoregressive entity linking method adept at handling intricate context and dependencies within the text corpus. Through training, it learns the intricate mapping relationships among entities. The approach employs open-domain standard datasets, paving the way for future expansion into cross-domain entity linking tasks beyond specific domains. On the AIDA CoNLL-YAGO dataset, the model achieves a remarkable 1.6% point Micro-F1 score lead. Ablation experiments further substantiate the advantages of these innovations.

References

1. Li, J., Sun, A., Ma, Y.: Neural named entity boundary detection. IEEE Trans. Knowl. Data Eng. **33**(4), 1790–1795 (2020). https://doi.org/10.1109/TKDE.2020.2981329
2. Li, T.R., Liu, M.T., Zhang, Y.J., et al.: A Review of Entity Linking Research Based on Deep Learning. Acta Scientiarum Naturalium Universitatis Pekinensis **57**(01), 91–98 (2021). https://doi.org/10.13209/j.0479-8023.2020.077
3. Zhang, T., Jia, Z., Li, T.R., et al.: Open-domain question-answering system based on large-scale knowledge base. CAAI Trans. Intell. Syst. **13**(04), 557–563 (2018). https://doi.org/10.11992/tis.201707039
4. Zhu, M., Celikkaya, B., Bhatia, P., et al.: Latte: latent type modeling for biomedical entity linking. In: Proceedings of the AAAI Conference on Artificial Intelligence. **34**(05), 9757–9764 (2020). https://doi.org/10.1609/aaai.v34i05.6526
5. Ji, S., Pan, S., Cambria, E., et al.: A survey on knowledge graphs: representation, acquisition, and applications. IEEE Trans. Neural Netw. Learn. Syst. **33**(2), 494–514 (2021). https://doi.org/10.1109/TNNLS.2021.3070843
6. Kusum, L., Pardeep, S., Kamlesh, D.: Mention detection in coreference resolution: survey. Appl. Intell.. Intell. **52**(9), 9816–9860 (2022). https://doi.org/10.1007/s10489-021-02878-2
7. Mulang', I O, Singh, K., Prabhu, C., et al.: Evaluating the impact of knowledge graph context on entity disambiguation models. In: Proceedings of the 29th ACM International Conference on Information & Knowledge Management, pp. 2157–2160 (2020). https://doi.org/10.1145/3340531.3412159
8. Daiber, J., Jakob, M., Hokamp, C., et al.: Improving efficiency and accuracy in multilingual entity extraction. In: Proceedings of the 9th International Conference on Semantic Systems, pp.121–124 (2013). https://doi.org/10.1145/2506182.2506198
9. Özge, S., Artem, S., Mikhail, A., Alexander, P., Chris, B.: Neural entity linking: a survey of models based on deep learning. Semantic Web **13**(3), 527–570 (2022). https://doi.org/10.3233/SW-222986
10. Luo, A., Gao, S., Xu, Y.: Deep semantic match model for entity linking using knowledge graph and text. Proc. Comput. Sci. **129**, 110–114 (2018). https://doi.org/10.1016/j.procs.2018.03.057
11. Martins, P.H., Marinho, Z., Martins, A.F.T.: Joint learning of named entity recognition and entity linking. arXiv preprint arXiv:1907.08243, 2019.https://doi.org/10.48550/arXiv.1907.08243
12. Fang, Z., Cao, Y., Li, R., et al.: High quality candidate generation and sequential graph attention network for entity linking. In: Proceedings of the Web Conference, pp. 640–650 (2020). https://doi.org/10.1145/3366423.3380146
13. Broscheit, S.: Investigating entity knowledge in BERT with simple neural end-to-end entity linking[J]. arXiv preprint arXiv:2003.05473. (2020)
14. Navigli, R., Velardi, P.: Structural semantic interconnections: a knowledge-based approach to word sense disambiguation. IEEE Trans. Pattern Anal. Mach. Intell. **27**(7), 1075–1086 (2005). https://doi.org/10.1109/TPAMI.2005.149
15. Zan, H.Y.,Wu, Y.G., Jia, Y.X., et al.: Chinese Micro-blog named entity linking based on multiorigin knowledge. J. Shandong Univ.(Natural Science) **50**(07), 9–16 (2015). https://doi.org/10.6040/j.issn.1671-9352.3.2014.026
16. Dredze, M., Mcnamee, P., Rao, D., et al.: Entity disambiguation for knowledge base population. In: International Conference on Computational Linguistics. Association for Computational Linguistics (2010)
17. Christophides, V., Efthymiou, V., Palpanas, T., et al.: An overview of end-to-end entity resolution for big data. ACM Comput. Surv. (CSUR) **53**(6), 1–42 (2020)

18. Nicola De, C., Gautier, I., Sebastian, R., Fabio, P.: Autoregressive entity retrieval. In: International Conference on Learning Representations (2021b)
19. Lewis, M., Liu, Y., Goyal, N., et al.: Bart: denoising sequence-to-sequence pre-training for natural language generation, translation, and comprehension. arXiv preprint arXiv:1910.13461. (2019)
20. Sutskever, I., Vinyals, O., Le, Q.V.: Sequence to sequence learning with neural networks. In: Advances in Neural Information Processing Systems, 27 (2014). https://doi.org/10.5555/296 9033.2969173
21. Evgeniy, G., Michael, R., Amarnag, S.: "FACC1: freebase annotation of ClueWeb corpora, Version 1 (Release date 2013–06–26, Format version 1, Correction level 0)", June (2013)
22. Hoffart, J., Yosef, M.A., Bordino, I., et al.: Robust disambiguation of named entities in text. In: Proceedings of the 2011 Conference on Empirical Methods in Natural Language Processing, pp. 782–792 (2011)
23. Gupta, N., Singh, S., Roth, D.: Entity linking via joint encoding of types, descriptions, and context[C]//Proceedings of the. Conf. Empirical Methods Natural Lang. Process. **2017**, 2681–2690 (2017). https://doi.org/10.18653/v1/D17-1284
24. Nicola De, C., Wilker, A., Ivan, T.: Highly parallel autoregressive entity linking with discriminative correction. arXiv preprint arXiv:2109.03792 (2021a)
25. Ravi, M.P.K., Singh, K., Mulang, I.O., et al.: CHOLAN: a modular approach for neural entity linking on Wikipedia and Wikidata. arXiv preprint arXiv:2101.09969 (2021)

Improving Voice Style Conversion via Self-attention VAE with Feature Disentanglement

Hui Yuan[1] , Ping Li[1(✉)] , Gansen Zhao[1], and Jun Zhang[2]

[1] School of Computer Science, South China Normal University, Guangzhou, China
{yuanhui2021,gzhao}@m.scnu.edu.cn, liping26@mail2.sysu.edu.cn
[2] College of Education, Shenzhen University, ShenZhen, China
zhangjuniris@szu.edu.cn

Abstract. Voice conversion (VC) is a widely used technique in intelligent speech processing, that aims to modify the speaker's information while preserving the underlying linguistic content. Speech can be divided into five parts: linguistic content, timbre, rhythm, pitch, and accent. Obtaining the disentanglement representation of these components is very useful in many speech analysis and generation applications. Recently, state-of-the-art voice conversion systems have been able to decompose speech into content feature representation and timbre representations. While information such as accent, pitch, and rhythm are still mixed with the content. It is a challenging problem to separate components from speech without explicit annotated information. This paper proposes a voice style conversion model Disentangle-VSC, which can decompose speech into five components without any text labels. We employed an encoder-decoder architecture, utilizing extractors with distinct bottlenecks to extract different features. Then these features are fed as input to the decoder to generate transformed speech. We also apply the self-attention mechanism to capture the relationships between different speech features, thereby further improving the quality of the generated converted speech. The experimental results demonstrate that our model achieves feature disentanglement, and the quality of converted speech is better than that of AutoVC and SpeechSplit. The repository can be found at https://github.com/sanena/Disentangle-VSC.

Keywords: Voice conversion · Feature disentanglement · Style transfer

1 Introduction

Voice conversion (VC) is used to change the non-linguistic information in speech while keeping the linguistic content unchanged. Potential applications of voice conversion include speaker identity conversion [5], and privacy identity protection [17]. Non-linguistic information includes timbre, rhythm, pitch, and accent. Timbre refers to the unique sound characteristics of a speaker, which can make the same phoneme sound distinct when spoken by different individuals. Meanwhile, the speaker's style is primarily manifested in rhythm, pitch, and accent,

Y. Sun et al. (Eds.): ChineseCSCW 2023, CCIS 2012, pp. 421–435, 2024.
https://doi.org/10.1007/978-981-99-9637-7_31

which can vary significantly among speakers. Rhythm describes the speed at which a speaker utters each syllable. Pitch variation conveys the speaker's intonation. Accent refers to the features related to pronunciation and intonation that are associated with specific regions or language backgrounds. Through the variation and combination of these features, speakers are able to express more information, emotions, and linguistic meaning. When it comes to voice conversion, it is important to replicate the prosody of the target speaker, including rhythm, pitch, and accent, when imitating their voice characteristics. Therefore, the implementation of voice conversion requires flexible style transformation capabilities.

Speech feature separation refers to separating different speech features from a speech signal, allowing each feature to be identified or analyzed independently. This has significant applications in the fields of speech signal processing and speech recognition. Traditional methods for speech separation are primarily based on signal processing and mathematical models, such as independent component analysis (ICA) [21], non-negative matrix factorization (NMF) [22], and others. However, these methods often face challenges in accurately separating speech due to the complexity of mixed speech, noise, and interference. In recent years, with the advancement of deep learning techniques, significant progress has been made in speech feature disentanglement using deep neural networks. These methods leverage deep neural network models to learn complex representations and mapping relationships of speech features, achieving separation through training data. Common deep learning models used in this area include variational autoencoder (VAE) [8,9,18,24], generative adversarial network (GAN) [1,2,11], and more. Through speech feature separation, individual speech components can be obtained and further applied to various tasks and application scenarios. For instance, separating speaker features can be used for speaker recognition or multi-speaker conversation processing, while separating speech content can be applied to speech recognition or text-to-speech synthesis. Overall, speech feature separation is a challenging research field that holds great potential for improving the performance of speech-related tasks and enabling a wider range of applications.

Recently, state-of-the-art voice conversion systems have been able to separate speaker-independent information from speaker-related information in speech. The former mainly consists of linguistic content, while the latter pertains to timbre. We summarize some related studies in Table 1. However, aspects such as rhythm, pitch, and accent, which are also associated with the speaker, remain intertwined with the content. Consequently, speech generated by these algorithms only shows differences in timbre compared to the source speech, with the rhythm, pitch, and accent largely unchanged. The successful separation of timbre is attributed to the availability of speaker identity labels, which encompass almost all the timbre-related information. However, annotating features such as rhythm, pitch, and accent poses a significant challenge. This means that disentangling content, rhythm, pitch, and accent without any labels is a difficult task.

Table 1. Summary of recent works. C means Content, U means Timbre, R means Rhythm, P means Pitch, A means Accent, and S means Style.

Researches	text-independent	Components					
		C	U	R	P	A	S
AutoVC [14]	✓	✓	✓	–	–	–	–
SpeechSplit [13]	✓	✓	✓	✓	✓	–	–
IDE-VC [25]	✓	✓	–	–	–	–	✓
VQMIVC [19]	✓	✓	✓	–	✓	–	–
Wang2021 [20]	×	✓	✓	–	–	✓	–
SFEVC [10]	✓	✓	✓	–	–	–	✓

Voice style conversion is a interesting and challenging task. This paper aims to achieve style transformation on timbre, rhythm, pitch, and accent. We propose a model named Disentangle-VSC, which utilizes an encoder-decoder architecture with four encoders and one decoder. Each encoder has a distinct and carefully designed information bottleneck responsible for extracting unique feature representations. The information bottleneck is shaped by the encoder's feature dimensionality constraint and the random resampling operator. The fusion of these features enables the generation of diverse speech styles. In addition, we introduced a self-attention mechanism to capture long-range dependencies. The experimental results on the VCTK dataset indicate that Disentangle-VSC has improved the speech quality of the converted speech and achieved some success in disentangling various speech features. Our major contributions can be summarized as follows:

1. We designed a voice style conversion model called Disentangle-VSC, which can separate speech into five components: content, timbre, rhythm, pitch, and accent.
2. Experimental results indicate that optimizing the encoder's output feature dimensionality can enhance its ability to disentangle speech features.
3. According to experimental results using the dataset named CSTR VCTK Corpus, our model has improved in terms of speaker similarity, speech quality, and the ability to separate different components from speech.

The paper is structured as follows. Section 2 introduces background knowledge. Section 3 describes our proposed methods. The experiments and results are collected in Sect. 4. Finally, we conclude and look forward in Sect. 5.

2 Background

2.1 Variational AutoEncoder

Variational AutoEncoder (VAE) [4] is a random network model consisting of an encoder and a decoder. The encoder and the decoder can be viewed as two functions, one for mapping high-dimensional input x to low-dimensional representation z, and the other for mapping low-dimensional representation z to high-dimensional output $\hat{x}$. Let the prior probability distribution $p(z)$ on the latent variable z be a Gaussian distribution. The encoder tries to infer an approximate posterior probability distribution $q_\phi(z \mid x)$ of a latent variable z given input data x, where ϕ is the parameter weights learned by the encoder. After receiving the input x, the encoder outputs the mean $\mu = (\mu_1, \mu_2, ..., \mu_n)$ and the standard deviation $\sigma = (\sigma_1, \sigma_2, ..., \sigma_n)$. To get the hidden layer code $z = (z_i, z_2, ..., z_n)$, we need to perform the operation of $e^{\sigma_i} \times \epsilon_i$, and then add the result to the mean μ, described as $z_i = e^{\sigma_i} \times \epsilon_i + \mu_i$. In this equation, the auxiliary noise variable $\epsilon = (\epsilon_1, \epsilon_2, ..., \epsilon_n)$ is sampled from the normal distribution, $\epsilon \sim \mathcal{N}(0, \mathbf{I})$. The decoder tries to infer the conditional probability distribution $p_\theta(x \mid z)$ of data x given a latent variable z, where the θ is the parameter weights learned by the decoder. Then use the code z as the input of the decoder to obtain the output $\hat{x}$.

The loss function of VAE contains two terms. The first term $L_{rec}(x, \hat{x})$ is the reconstruction loss between the input data x and the output data $\hat{x}$, calculated by the mean square error ($\mathbb{E}[\cdot]$). And the second term $D_{kl}(q_\phi(z \mid x) \parallel p_\theta(z))$ denotes the Kullback-Leibler divergence [7] between the approximate posterior distribution of latent vectors and the prior distribution. The loss function can be expressed as Eq. (1),

$$L(\theta, \phi; x) = L_{rec}(x, \hat{x}) \; + \; D_{kl}(q_\phi(z \mid x) \parallel p_\theta(z))$$

$$= \mathbb{E}\left[\|x - \hat{x}\|_2^2\right] \; - \; \frac{1}{2}\sum_{j=0}^{k-1}(\sigma_j + \mu_j^2 - 1 - \log\sigma_j). \tag{1}$$

2.2   Attention Mechanism

In sequence tasks, attention allows models to dynamically allocate different weights to different parts of the input sequence or output sequence, enabling more targeted processing of key information. The attention mechanism can be considered as the mapping of a query vector and a set of key-value vector pairs to an output. The multi-head attention mechanism is a mechanism to execute multiple attention functions in parallel, which can simultaneously focus on information from different representation subspaces. The computation process for multi-head attention is as follows Eq. (2):

$$\text{Attention}(Q, K, V) = \text{softmax}\left(\frac{QK^T}{\sqrt{d_k}}\right)V,$$

$$\text{MultiHead}(Q, K, V) = \text{Concat}\left(\text{head}_1, \ldots, \text{head}_h\right)W^O, \tag{2}$$

$$\text{where } \text{head}_i = \text{Attention}\left(QW_i^Q, KW_i^K, VW_i^V\right),$$

where query Q and key K be d_k dimensional, and value V be d_v dimensional. And parameters $W_i^Q, W_i^K \in \mathbb{R}^{d_{\text{model}} \times d_k}, W_i^V \in \mathbb{R}^{d_{\text{model}} \times d_v}, W^O \in \mathbb{R}^{hd_v \times d_{\text{model}}}$

are learnable projection matrices. Self-attention denotes the attention module with $Q = K = V$.

2.3   Information of Speech

In this subsection, we will introduce the speech's features, which are *timbre*, *content*, *rhythm*, *accent*, and *pitch*. In Fig. 1, we list several speech spectrograms and pitch contours to help us understand these components. The content of these voices is 'Please call Stella' with different speakers. The speaker of the left (a) is a slower-speaking woman. The speaker of the middle (b) is a fast-speaking woman. And the speaker of the right (c) is a fast-speaking man.

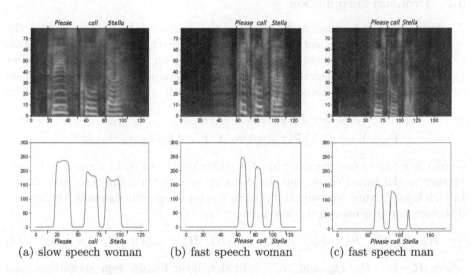

(a) slow speech woman   (b) fast speech woman   (c) fast speech man

Fig. 1. The spectrograms and the pitch contours.

Timbre refers to the speaker's vocal characteristics, which are reflected in the formant frequencies. Formant frequencies are resonant frequency components in the vocal tract. Formants are several horizontal bars parallel to the time axis in the spectrogram.

Content is made up of words in many languages. Each word has a particular formant. By observing Fig. 1, we can know that each segment in the spectrogram corresponds to a word. Multiple words together represent the message that the speech is intended to convey.

Rhythm refers to the patterns and variations in timing and pace within speech. It is related to how long it takes for the speaker to utter each word. The spectrogram is divided into segments, each corresponding to a word, and the length of segments can respond to rhythmic information.

Pitch is related to the fundamental frequency ($F0$) of the voice and responds to vocal pitch information. It can be perceived intuitively by observing the pitch contour.

Accent refers mainly to the differences in the placement of stress on specific words or syllables, which are unique pronunciation patterns and speech characteristics associated with specific geographic or linguistic groups.

3   Architecture

In this section, we will introduce our proposed model, Disentangle-VSC, which can successfully separate the above five components from speech and achieve voice style conversion.

3.1   Problem Formulation

Assuming that it is possible to separate the content information I_C and the speaker's characteristic features from speech S, with the feature information being mutually independent. The timbre I_U, rhythm I_R, pitch I_P, and accent I_A of a speaker are considered speaker-characteristic features. This assumption can be described mathematically as follows Eq. (3):

$$S = \text{Gen}(I_C, I_U, I_R, I_P, I_A),$$
$$P(X, Y) = P(X) P(Y), \text{where } X, Y \in \{I_C, I_U, I_R, I_P, I_A\}. \tag{3}$$

$\text{Gen}(\cdot)$ is a one-to-one mapping function. Our goal is to build a voice style conversion model based on an encoder-decoder architecture, that can extract the hidden layer feature representations from the input speech. Formally, the feature disentangling process can be described as Eq. (4):

$$\boldsymbol{R}_c = h_c(C), \ \boldsymbol{R}_u = h_u(U), \ \boldsymbol{R}_r = h_r(R), \ \boldsymbol{R}_p = h_p(P), \ \boldsymbol{R}_a = h_a(A), \tag{4}$$

where $\boldsymbol{R}_c$, $\boldsymbol{R}_u$, $\boldsymbol{R}_r$, $\boldsymbol{R}_p$, and $\boldsymbol{R}_a$ are hidden layer feature representations, and $h_c(\cdot)$, $h_u(\cdot)$, $h_r(\cdot)$, $h_p(\cdot)$ and $h_a(\cdot)$ are one-to-one mapping functions that transform the input into low-dimensional hidden layer variables.

3.2   Proposed Framework

Disentangle-VSC includes five modules: content encoder, rhythm encoder, pitch encoder, accent encoder, and decoder. Each encoder extracts a specific feature, and then the decoder is used to reconstruct it. Figure 2 illustrates the framework of Disentangle-VSC.

Assuming that there are M speakers in our dataset X, denoted as $X = (X_1, X_2, ..., X_M)^\top$, where each person has N speech items with different utterances, denoted as $X_i = (X_{i1}, X_{i2}, ..., X_{iN})$, then the dataset can be described as a matrix $X_{M \times N}$ with M rows and N columns. During training, a segment $X_{ij} = (X_{ij}^1, X_{ij}^2, ..., X_{ij}^{T_{ij}})$ is randomly selected as the input to the model, where T_{ij} denotes the frame number of the spectrogram, and $i \in [1, M], j \in [1, N]$.

Let $\boldsymbol{x}_{sj} = (x_{sj}^1, x_{sj}^2, ...x_{sj}^{T_{sj}})$ denotes the source speech acoustic feature segment, and $\boldsymbol{x}_{tk} = (x_{tk}^1, x_{tk}^2, ...x_{tk}^{T_{tk}})$ denotes the target speech acoustic feature

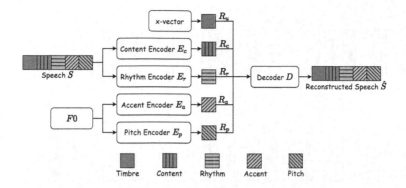

Fig. 2. The framework of Disentangle-VSC.

segment, where $s, t \in [1, M]$, $j, k \in [1, N]$. The process of voice conversion can be described as the following Eq. (5):

$$
\begin{aligned}
\boldsymbol{R}_c &= E_c(\boldsymbol{x}_{sj}), \boldsymbol{x}_{sj} \in X, s \in [1, M], j \in [1, N] \\
\boldsymbol{R}_r &= E_r(\boldsymbol{x}_{tk}), \boldsymbol{x}_{tk} \in X, t \in [1, M], k \in [1, N] \\
\boldsymbol{R}_p &= E_a(\boldsymbol{x}_{tk}), \ \boldsymbol{R}_a = E_p(\boldsymbol{x}_{tk}), \\
\hat{\boldsymbol{x}} &= D(\boldsymbol{R}_c, \boldsymbol{R}_r, \boldsymbol{R}_p, \boldsymbol{R}_a, \boldsymbol{R}_u),
\end{aligned}
\tag{5}
$$

where the content encoder, rhythm encoder, pitch encoder, and accent encoder are $E_c(\cdot)$, $E_r(\cdot)$, $E_p(\cdot)$, $E_a(\cdot)$, respectively. The decoder is represented by $D(\cdot)$. The reconstructed mel-spectrogram, calculated by the decoder, is denoted as $\hat{\boldsymbol{x}}$. The speaker identity $\boldsymbol{R}_u$ is an x-vector embedding extracted from a pre-trained model [16].

The content encoder simulates the posterior distribution $p_\phi(\boldsymbol{R}_c \mid \boldsymbol{x})$ of the latent variable $\boldsymbol{R}_c$ given the input data $\boldsymbol{x}$. While the decoder approximates the conditional distribution $p_\theta(\boldsymbol{x} \mid \boldsymbol{R}_c)$ of the data $\boldsymbol{x}$ given the latent variable $\boldsymbol{R}_c$. The model's loss function is displayed in Eq. (6):

$$
\begin{aligned}
L &= L_{rec}(\boldsymbol{x}, \hat{\boldsymbol{x}}) \ + D_{kl}(p_\phi(\boldsymbol{R}_c \mid \boldsymbol{x}) \ || \ p_\theta(\boldsymbol{R}_c)) \\
&= \mathbb{E}\left[\|\boldsymbol{x} - \hat{\boldsymbol{x}}\|_2^2 \right] - \frac{1}{2} \sum_{j=0}^{k-1} (\sigma_j + \mu_j^2 - 1 - \log \sigma_j).
\end{aligned}
\tag{6}
$$

3.3   Network Architecture

Encoders. As shown in Fig. 3, the network structures of the four encoders are almost the same, but there are still some subtle differences. First, the inputs to the encoders are not exactly the same. The input to the content encoder and the rhythm encoder is an 80-dimensional mel-spectrogram, denoted as S. The mel-spectrogram S is computed with 64ms frame length and 16ms frame hop. The input to the pitch encoder and the accent encoder is 257 bins of one-hot embedding $F0$, which is the pitch contour converted through the logarithm Gaussian

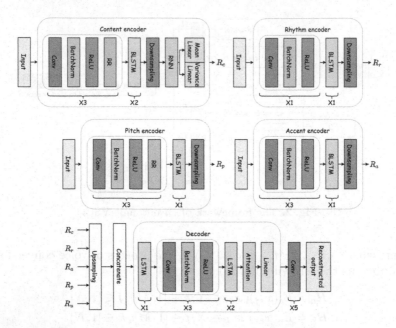

Fig. 3. The details of the encoders and decoder. 'BatchNorm' denotes Batch normalization; 'RR' denotes random resampling module. ×n denotes the module above is repeated n times.

normalized transformation. Second, each encoder has a unique information bottleneck. The dimensions of the content feature code, rhythm feature code, pitch feature code, and accent feature code are 16, 8, 32, and 8, respectively.

Figure 3 shows the detailed structures of the encoders and the decoder. Each encoder consists of a stack of 5×1 convolutional layers and bidirectional LSTM layers. In the content encoder and pitch encoder, each convolutional layer is followed by batch normalization, ReLU activation, and a random resampling module. In the rhythm encoder and accent encoder, each convolutional layer is followed by batch normalization and ReLU activation. The final output of the convolutional layers is fed to the bidirectional LSTM layer to reduce the feature dimension. And then the output of the bidirectional LSTM layer is downsampled to reduce the temporal dimension, producing the hidden layer codes. After these operations, the content encoder also includes an RNN layer, a mean linear layer, and a variance linear layer. To better understand the details of encoders, we list the hyperparameter settings of each encoder in Table 2.

Decoder. First, we upsample the hidden representation to restore the original sampling rate. Second, the speaker identity embedding $\boldsymbol{R}_u$ is repeated along the time dimension to match the time dimension of other latent codes. Then $\boldsymbol{R}_c$, $\boldsymbol{R}_r$, $\boldsymbol{R}_p$, $\boldsymbol{R}_a$ and $\boldsymbol{R}_u$ are concatenated according to the feature dimension as the input of the decoder.

Table 2. Hyperparameter settings of the encoders.

	Content	Rhythm	Pitch	Accent
Conv Layers	3	1	3	3
Conv Dim	512	128	256	128
BLSTM Layers	2	1	1	1
BLSTM Dim	8	4	16	4
Downsample Factor	8	8	8	8
Feature Dim	16	8	64	8

The decoder has three LSTM layers, a three-layer stack of 5×1 convolutional layers, a multi-head self-attention layer, and fully connected layers. Each convolutional layer is followed by batch normalization and ReLU activation. The introduction of self-attention to the VAE framework enhances style transfer, especially for unseen speakers, given the global nature of speaker information. At the last layer, the decoder outputs the reconstructed mel-spectrogram with the same dimension as the input mel-spectrogram. The output channel number of each convolutional layer is 512. Then the output is fed to the two LSTM layers with 1024 hidden width. To better build the details of the spectrogram, we add five 5×1 convolutional layers, and the first four layers use batch normalization and hyperbolic tangent. The channel dimension for the first four layers is 512 and goes to 80 in the last layer.

Finally, we use the WaveNet vocoder [12, 15] pre-trained on the VCTK corpus to generate speech audio files from the mel-spectrogram. The WaveNet vocoder consists of four deconvolution layers. In our implementation, the frame rate of the mel-spectrogram is 62.5 Hz, and the sampling rate of the speech waveform is 16 kHz.

3.4   Why Does It Work?

This section focuses on explaining why Disentangle-VSC can make each encoder extract each intended feature at the training stage.

Firstly, according to the research described in SpeechSplit [13], random resampling can eliminate some rhythm information from the input mel-spectrogram. Therefore, the only encoder that can capture complete rhythm information is the rhythm encoder. Secondly, the content encoder and rhythm encoder have the same input, while the rhythm encoder extracts only rhythm information. The content encoder should capture full content information to recover the entire original speech. Moreover, the pitch contour contains all pitch and accent information. Assuming that the pitch encoder can exclusively extract pitch information while the accent encoder can only extract features related to accent. Each encoder is limited to extracting a single feature from the speech. This proposed approach ensures complete speech information recovery.

Based on the aforementioned assumptions, features I_C, I_U, I_R, I_P, and I_A are mutually independent. When the encoder's information bottleneck is set correctly, the global optimal solution of optimizing the reconstruction loss L_{recon} will generate the decoupled information described in Eq. (4). The reconstruction loss at this time is 0, and the proof can be described as Eq. (7):

$$
\begin{aligned}
\hat{x} &= D(R_c, R_r, R_p, R_a, R_u) \\
&= \text{Gen}(h_c^{-1}(R_c), h_r^{-1}(R_r), h_p^{-1}(R_p), h_a^{-1}(R_a), h_u^{-1}(R_u)) \\
&= \text{Gen}(I_C, I_U, I_R, I_P, I_A) \\
&= x.
\end{aligned}
\tag{7}
$$

4 Experiments

In this section, we will experimentally verify the feature separation ability of Disentangle-VSC, and we will visualize our speech results with mel-spectrogram and pitch contour.

4.1 Configurations

We use the CSTR VCTK corpus [23] as the dataset for our experiments. The CSTR VCTK Corpus includes speech data uttered by 110 English speakers with various accents. For our experiment, the training set contains 50 speakers, each of whom chooses the first 100 speech data, about 10 min. The test set contains all the utterances of six other unseen speakers (3 males and 3 females), and each speaker has a different accent. During training, we employ the Adam optimizer [3] for training with a batch size of 32 for 20k steps. The 80-dimensional mel-spectrogram S and the 257-dimensional normalized pitch contour $F0$ are the acoustic features. The speaker identity representation uses a 512-dimensional x-vector extracted by the pre-trained extractor [16]. The benchmark models are AutoVC [14], and SpeechSplit [13].

4.2 Evaluation Criteria

Objective Evaluation. We use the Mel-Cepstral Distance (MCD) [6] as the objective metric for evaluating the quality of converted speech. MCD is a commonly used objective metric that measures the acoustic feature distance between the target ground truth and the converted utterance. Given two mel-cepstra, $\hat{x} = (\hat{x}_1, \hat{x}_2, ..., \hat{x}_D)^\mathsf{T}$ and $x = (x_1, x_2, ..., x_D)^\mathsf{T}$, MCD can estimate the difference between the two aligned speeches, and the calculation formula in Eq. (8) :

$$
MCD(dB) = \frac{10}{ln10} \sqrt{2 \sum_{d=1}^{D} (\hat{x}_d - x_d)^2},
\tag{8}
$$

where $\hat{x}_d$ and x_d are the dth dimensional coefficients of the converted and the target mel-cepstra, respectively. In terms of spectral distortion, the lower the

MCD, the better the performance of the voice conversion system. To calculate MCD, we chose the first speech samples from the first 10 speakers to construct pairs of test data with consistent content.

Subjective Evaluation. To test the speech quality and the feature separation degree, we also conducted some subjective experiments using the mean opinion score criterion, where 13 different listeners rated 10 converted speech pairs. To ensure fairness, the experimenters wore the same headphones and kept the same volume level throughout the experiment. When evaluating the speech quality, the listeners need to score the quality of the speech heard on a scale from 1 to 5, where 1 point means bad, 2 points mean poor, 3 points mean fair, 4 points mean good, and 5 points mean excellent. When testing the degree of separation of speech features, the listeners need to compare the converted speech and the target speech, thus scoring the similarity of each feature such as rhythm, pitch, timbre, and accent.

4.3   Results

Table 3 presents the results of MCD and the speech quality test for unseen speaker conversion by AutoVC [14], SpeechSplit [13] and our proposed model Disentangle-VSC, when the linguistic content is consistent. The data in Table 3 are derived by averaging the values obtained from calculating all-aspect converted speech. The MCD value obtained by Disentangle-VSC is lower than the MCD value of other models in the baseline. Therefore, in terms of voice conversion performance, our model's performance is slightly better. In male-to-male conversion, the MOS score of Disentangle-VSC is lower than the baseline. But in other conversions, the MOS scores obtained by Disentangle-VSC are higher than those obtained by other baseline models. Therefore, subjectively, our proposed model produces better quality converted speech.

Table 3. Comparison of MCD and MOS for speech quality test with parallel pairs.

Method	MCD	MOS				
		M2M	M2F	F2M	F2F	Avg
AutoVC [14]	8.82	3.11	3.35	2.97	3.29	3.18
SpeechSplit [13]	6.51	3.87	3.21	3.25	3.59	3.48
Disentangle-VSC	5.38	3.64	3.54	3.49	3.59	3.56

Table 4 shows the MOS results of all conversion tests by combining different components with parallel pairs. The data fully demonstrates that our system can separate components from speech successfully. The more components that are converted at the same time, the more obvious the effect will be. And timbre-only conversion performs better, which means the speaker similarity has improved.

Table 4. MOS by combining different components with parallel pairs.

Rhythm Only (R)	Pitch only (P)	Timbre Only (U)	Accent Only (A)
3.50	3.58	3.47	3.32
R + P	R + U	R + A	P + U
3.17	3.26	3.29	3.24
P + A	U + A	R + P + U	R + P + A
3.04	3.43	3.37	3.63
R + U + A	P + U + A	R + P + U + A	–
3.48	2.89	4.56	–

Figure 4 shows the single-aspect conversion results on a speech pair uttering 'Please call Stella'. The source speaker is a slow male speaker with an England accent, and the target speaker is a fast male speaker with an Indian accent. When performing the single-aspect conversion, we only need to modify the input of that specific encoder, while keeping the inputs of other encoders unchanged. For example, when converting only the rhythm, the input to the rhythm encoder should be the target mel-spectrogram, while the inputs to other encoders should still come from the source speech.

As shown in Fig. 4, the rhythm is time-aligned with the target speech when only converted rhythm. In the case of only pitch conversion, the converted speech has the same falling tone on 'call' as the target speech. The converted voice has the same stressed syllables as the target voice on 'Stella' when converting the accent. During timbre conversion, the formant of the converted voice is aligned with those of the target voice.

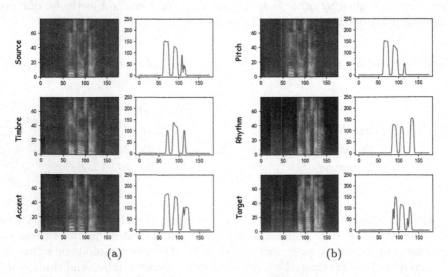

(a)   (b)

Fig. 4. Spectrogram and pitch contours of single-aspect conversion results.

4.4 Discussion

To examine the ability of our model's feature separation, we generated some spectrograms with individual components removed. For example, by setting the input of the content encoder to a tensor with the value 0 and the same size as the source mel-spectrogram, the content can be removed. We change the speaker identity representation to one-hot embedding with all zeros to remove the timbre. Figure 5 illustrates the mel-spectrogram after removing one component.

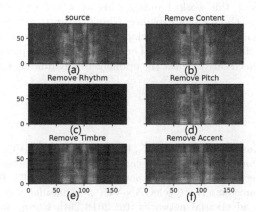

Fig. 5. The spectrogram when one component was removed.

Figure 5 (a) shows the spectrogram of the source speech. In Fig. 5 (b), when the content is removed, the output will be blurred, because certain spectral components in the spectrogram disappear and the energy of the noise decreases. By observing Fig. 5 (c), it is clear that the output is almost empty and no information is visible without the rhythm. The spectrogram is a representation of speech signals in the frequency domain, showing the energy of different frequency components over time. When the rhythm information is removed, the temporal structure of the speech signal disappears, resulting in a spectrogram with a flat energy distribution and no distinct frequency components. Figure 5 (d) illustrates that the output becomes smoother and the harmonic bands are weaker in intensity, after removing the pitch. As shown in Fig. 5 (e), removing the timbre makes the output spectrum's formant position shift. The speaker in this spectrogram may be an average speaker in the dataset. Figure 5 (f) shows that after removing the accent, the output becomes flat, the energy of some regions is reduced or disappears, and the syllable focus of the source speech cannot be seen from the spectrum. These results further validate that our proposed model can decompose speech into different components.

5 Conclusion

This paper presents a voice style conversion model for feature disentanglement. We use the encoder-decoder architecture to modify the number of convolutional layers and feature dimensions of the encoder, allowing us to perform feature disentanglement. Furthermore, we integrate the self-attention layer into the decoder to enhance the voice style conversion task. Our experiments demonstrate that our model improves the speech quality and speaker similarity of converted speech. In future work, we plan to incorporate additional feature extraction algorithms to further reduce the generalization error.

Acknowledgement. We would like to thank all the anonymous reviewers for their insightful comments on this work. Funding This work was supported by the Natural Science Foundation of Guangdong Province, China (Grant No. 2021A1515011607) and the Special Project for Research and Development in Key areas of Guangdong Province, China (Grant No. 2020B0101090003). The opinions in this paper are those of the authors and do not necessarily reflect the opinions of any funding sponsor or the China Government.

References

1. Kameoka, H., Kaneko, T., Tanaka, K., Hojo, N.: StarGAN-VC: non-parallel many-to-many voice conversion using star generative adversarial networks. In: 2018 IEEE Spoken Language Technology Workshop (SLT), pp. 266–273. IEEE (2018)
2. Kaneko, T., Kameoka, H.: CycleGAN-VC: non-parallel voice conversion using cycle-consistent adversarial networks. In: 2018 26th European Signal Processing Conference (EUSIPCO), pp. 2100–2104. IEEE (2018)
3. Kingma, D.P., Ba, J.: Adam: a method for stochastic optimization. In: 3rd International Conference on Learning Representations (2015)
4. Kingma, D.P., Welling, M.: Auto-encoding variational bayes. In: 2nd International Conference on Learning Representations, ICLR (2014)
5. Kinnunen, T., Juvela, L., Alku, P., Yamagishi, J.: Non-parallel voice conversion using i-vector plda: Towards unifying speaker verification and transformation. In: 2017 IEEE International Conference on Acoustics, Speech and Signal Processing (ICASSP), pp. 5535–5539. IEEE (2017)
6. Kubichek, R.: Mel-cepstral distance measure for objective speech quality assessment. In: Proceedings of IEEE Pacific Rim Conference on Communications Computers and Signal Processing, vol. 1, pp. 125–128. IEEE (1993)
7. Kullback, S., Leibler, R.A.: On information and sufficiency. Ann. Math. Stat. **22**(1), 79–86 (1951)
8. Lian, J., Zhang, C., Yu, D.: Robust disentangled variational speech representation learning for zero-shot voice conversion. In: ICASSP 2022–2022 IEEE International Conference on Acoustics, Speech and Signal Processing (ICASSP), pp. 6572–6576. IEEE (2022)
9. Long, Z., Zheng, Y., Yu, M., Xin, J.: Enhancing zero-shot many to many voice conversion via self-attention VAE with structurally regularized layers. In: 2022 5th International Conference on Artificial Intelligence for Industries (AI4I). pp. 59–63. IEEE (2022)
10. Luo, Z., Lin, S., Liu, R., Baba, J., Yoshikawa, Y., Ishiguro, H.: Decoupling speaker-independent emotions for voice conversion via source-filter networks. IEEE/ACM Trans. Audio Speech Lang. Process. **31**, 11–24 (2023)
11. Meftah, A.H., Alashban, A.A., Alotaibi, Y.A., Selouani, S.A.: English emotional voice conversion using StarGAN model. IEEE Access **11**, 67835–67849 (2023)

12. Oord, A.v.d., et al.: WaveNet: a generative model for raw audio. In: The 9th ISCA Speech Synthesis Workshop, p. 125 (2016)
13. Qian, K., Zhang, Y., Chang, S., Hasegawa-Johnson, M., Cox, D.: Unsupervised speech decomposition via triple information bottleneck. In: International Conference on Machine Learning, pp. 7836–7846. PMLR (2020)
14. Qian, K., Zhang, Y., Chang, S., Yang, X., Hasegawa-Johnson, M.: AutoVC: zero-shot voice style transfer with only autoencoder loss. In: International Conference on Machine Learning, pp. 5210–5219. PMLR (2019)
15. Shen, J., et al.: Natural TTS synthesis by conditioning WaveNet on MEL spectrogram predictions. In: 2018 IEEE International Conference on Acoustics, Speech and Signal Processing (ICASSP), pp. 4779–4783. IEEE (2018)
16. Snyder, D., Garcia-Romero, D., Sell, G., Povey, D., Khudanpur, S.: X-vectors: robust DNN embeddings for speaker recognition. In: 2018 IEEE International Conference on Acoustics, Speech and Signal Processing (ICASSP), pp. 5329–5333. IEEE (2018)
17. Srivastava, B.M.L., Vauquier, N., Sahidullah, M., Bellet, A., Tommasi, M., Vincent, E.: Evaluating voice conversion-based privacy protection against informed attackers. In: ICASSP 2020–2020 IEEE International Conference on Acoustics, Speech and Signal Processing (ICASSP), pp. 2802–2806. IEEE (2020)
18. Tobing, P.L., Wu, Y.C., Hayashi, T., Kobayashi, K., Toda, T.: Non-parallel voice conversion with cyclic variational autoencoder. In: Interspeech 2019, 20th Annual Conference of the International Speech Communication Association, pp. 674–678 (2019)
19. Wang, D., Deng, L., Yeung, Y.T., Chen, X., Liu, X., Meng, H.: VQMIVC: vector quantization and mutual information-based unsupervised speech representation disentanglement for one-shot voice conversion. In: Interspeech 2021, 22nd Annual Conference of the International Speech Communication Association, pp. 1344–1348 (2021)
20. Wang, Z., et al.: Accent and speaker disentanglement in many-to-many voice conversion. In: 2021 12th International Symposium on Chinese Spoken Language Processing (ISCSLP), pp. 1–5. IEEE (2021)
21. Wilde, M.M., Martinez, A.B.: Probabilistic principal component analysis applied to voice conversion. In: Conference Record of the Thirty-Eighth Asilomar Conference on Signals, Systems and Computers, 2004, vol. 2, pp. 2255–2259. IEEE (2004)
22. Wu, Z., Virtanen, T., Chng, E.S., Li, H.: Exemplar-based sparse representation with residual compensation for voice conversion. IEEE/ACM Trans. Audio Speech Lang. Process. **22**(10), 1506–1521 (2014)
23. Yamagishi, J., Veaux, C., MacDonald, K., et al.: CSTR VCTK corpus: English multi-speaker corpus for CSTR voice cloning toolkit (version 0.92). University of Edinburgh. The Centre for Speech Technology Research (CSTR) (2019)
24. Yang, J., Zhou, Y., Huang, H.: Mel-S3R: Combining MEL-spectrogram and self-supervised speech representation with VQ-VAE for any-to-any voice conversion. Speech Commun. **151**, 52–63 (2023)
25. Yuan, S., Cheng, P., Zhang, R., Hao, W., Gan, Z., Carin, L.: Improving zero-shot voice style transfer via disentangled representation learning. In: 9th International Conference on Learning Representations, ICLR 2021, Virtual Event, Austria, May 3–7, 2021 (2021)

Deep Reinforcement Learning for Delay and Energy-Aware Task Scheduling in Edge Clouds

Meng Xun[1], Yan Yao[1,2(✉)], Jiguo Yu[2], Huihui Zhang[3], Shanshan Feng[4], and Jian Cao[5]

[1] School of Computer Science, Qufu Normal University, Rizhao, China
[2] Big Data Institute, Qilu University of Technology (Shandong Academy of Sciences), Jinan, China
yaoyanedu@163.com
[3] School of Computer Engineering, Weifang University, Weifang, China
[4] School of Information Science and Engineering, Shandong Normal University, Jinan, China
[5] Department of Computer Science and Engineering, Shanghai Jiao Tong University, Shanghai, China

Abstract. Edge computing is proving to be a promising model, offering low-latency and high-bandwidth services to the end-users. However, due to the dynamic nature of the network and the heterogeneous computing resources, task scheduling in edge clouds remains a challenging problem. In order to solve this problem, we propose a novel task scheduling algorithm for edge clouds based on deep reinforcement learning, which combines a deep Q-learning network with a priority-based action selection strategy. This approach aims to optimize computing resource allocation while minimizing energy consumption in edge nodes. We evaluated the effectiveness of our algorithm using a simulated edge cloud environment and compared it with other advanced task scheduling algorithms. Experimental results indicate that our algorithm outperforms baseline algorithms in terms of delay and energy consumption. In particular, our method improves task completion time and energy efficiency compared to traditional scheduling algorithms.

Keywords: Internet of things · Edge clouds · Task scheduling · Deep reinforcement learning

1 Introduction

The swift evolution of the Internet of Things and 5G technology has given rise to computing-intensive applications, such as augmented reality, autonomous driving, and face recognition. These applications generate substantial volumes of data and impose significant requirements on delay and computational processing power. Nevertheless, end devices are resource-limited, resulting in bottlenecks during the processing of large-scale applications and challenges in providing a persistent power supply. To address these challenges, edge computing has been developed.

© The Author(s), under exclusive license to Springer Nature Singapore Pte Ltd. 2024
Y. Sun et al. (Eds.): ChineseCSCW 2023, CCIS 2012, pp. 436–450, 2024.
https://doi.org/10.1007/978-981-99-9637-7_32

Edge computing involves processing a substantial portion of data on edge devices, which helps save data transmission bandwidth, reduce transmission delays, and minimize energy consumption. Additionally, it protects user data privacy and prevents the leakage of sensitive information [1]. By shifting service requests from centralized cloud computing centers to decentralized edge devices, processing tasks at the edge reduces response time and enhances reliability. Consequently, edge computing is poised to become a crucial computing model in IoT applications. Edge Clouds (ECs) are small clusters of servers deployed near end users, enabling the execution of resource-intensive applications at the network's edge.

Compute offloading is one of the key advantages of edge computing, effectively reducing device energy consumption. In the context of the IoT, task offloading for execution has become increasingly popular, necessitating efficient task scheduling to optimize resource utilization, reduce delay, and conserve energy. Nevertheless, the effective scheduling of tasks in edge clouds is challenging owing to various factors, including the different states, types, and sizes of arriving tasks, the heterogeneity of resources, the dispersion of locations, and the diversity of performance, stability, and cost requirements for different applications.

Existing research on task scheduling in edge clouds commonly employs traditional policies, such as heuristic and stochastic policies. While these policies have been widely adopted, they may not guarantee the required quality of service, particularly in dynamic edge computing environments where task response time is crucial. Some studies have explored the application of machine learning algorithms, but there may be limitations, such as the lack of simultaneous optimization of energy consumption and cost.

In our investigation, we tackle the challenge of estimating the load state of edge nodes in dynamic environments and identifying edge nodes that ensure the required quality of service without overloading or congestion. We formulate the task scheduling problem as a Markov decision process (MDP) and use a DRL technique to determine the optimal policy within the proposed network model. We introduce a Deep Q Network-Action (DQN-A) algorithm that leverages previous operations to achieve optimal scheduling without relying on a mathematical model of the environment.

The remaining sections of the paper are structured as follows: Sect. 2 provides an overview of related work. Section 3 introduces our proposed edge cloud architecture and problem statement. Section 4 presents our proposed solution, namely the DQN-A algorithm. We evaluate the effectiveness of the proposed algorithm and analyze experimental results in Sect. 5. Finally, we summarize the paper.

2   Related Work

Significant progress has been made in the development of task-scheduling algorithms for edge computing. These algorithms can be broadly categorized into three groups: heuristic algorithms, meta-heuristic algorithms, and machine learning algorithms. We will focus on machine learning algorithms here.

Machine learning algorithms, particularly reinforcement learning (RL), have been employed to address task scheduling problems in IoT systems. Robles et al. [2] advocated the use of RL for addressing the edge scheduling problem. They further introduce a novel multi-layer extension of RL (ML-RL) to enable edge agents to seek additional knowledge from higher-level agents. In order to enhance the performance and convergence of RL, Wang et al. [3] introduced an RL task scheduling approach assisted by Digital Twins. Zhao et al. [4] employed several schedulers within a sizable data center. They proposed a multi-agent RL scheduling system that cooperatively learns fine-grained job allocation strategies, ultimately minimizing job execution time. Song et al. [5] introduced an enhanced multi-objective reinforcement learning (MORL) algorithm. This algorithm's objective is to minimize the completion time of the application, the energy consumption of mobile devices, and the usage costs of edge resources. Possebon et al. [6] developed an RL method for automatically balancing network flows. Shahidani et al. [7] introduced an RL fog scheduling algorithm to reduce the latency of requests, especially real-time and delay-sensitive requests.

Current research on task assignments in IoT systems mainly focuses on using reinforcement learning as a potential solution. However, the significant number of edge computing nodes in the system results in a considerable number of candidate task assignment actions for IoT users. This leads to an enormous action space for the task scheduling policy. Reinforcement learning algorithms usually determine the optimal action by comparing the state action values of all candidate actions, which becomes increasingly challenging given the size of the action space.

3   System Model and Problem Statement

3.1   Edge Cloud Architecture

We consider a decentralized edge computing network composed of multiple edge clouds, densely deployed and connected via a fiber-based wired network with sufficient bandwidth. End-users establish connections with edge clouds through wireless links between access points (APs) and users. These edge clouds coexist with APs and deliver services within their coverage area. Figure 1 illustrates the system architecture, where users can submit heterogeneous tasks through their associated APs. Each edge cloud (EC) consists of N edge nodes responsible for handling computational tasks submitted by users. Each edge node comprises a task scheduling module and several Virtual Machines (VMs).

3.2   Communication Model

The task-handling process between the edge node and the user can be divided into three distinct phases: task transmission, task execution, and the delivery of

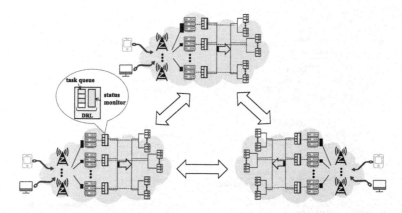

Fig. 1. Edge clouds architecture.

processing outcomes. It's important to note that, as the result of the substantial reduction in data size after task processing, the downlink transmission rate typically outpaces the uplink transmission rate, as stated in [8]. Therefore, this paper excludes considerations related to the delay and energy consumption associated with the processing result return phase and the communication between edge clouds.

During the task transmission phase, we make the assumption that the channel gain between the end device m and the edge node n is H_{mn}. Given that the device's movement during the short duration of task transmission is nearly negligible, we determine the transmission rate of the channel is determined using Shannon's theorem:

$$r_{mn} = B_m log_2(1 + \frac{P_m H_{mn}}{\sigma^2}). \tag{1}$$

Here, B_m represents the channel bandwidth assigned to the task, P_m is the transmission power of the task, and σ^2 is the noise power.

3.3 Task Scheduling Model

As shown in Fig. 2, the task scheduling module is composed of three main components: a task queue, a status monitor, and a task scheduler based on DRL.

The task queue serves as a repository for recording tasks submitted by end-users and enables the execution of various types of tasks.

The status monitor gathers the status information from all tasks and edge nodes, and this information is then used as input for the task scheduler.

The task scheduler is responsible for generating the task allocation plan. It decides which VMs will receive specific tasks for scheduling. It's important to note that the primary focus of this paper is on task scheduling among all VMs within an edge cloud.

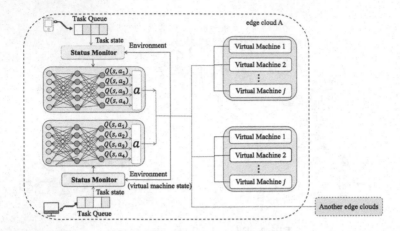

Fig. 2. DRL-based intelligent task scheduling method.

The objective of our model is to reduce the total task cost, which is a composite measure consisting of the weighted sum of delay and energy consumption. To achieve this, we need to calculate the delay of scheduling tasks, which can be divided into three key components: task transmission delay Tr_{mn}, task waiting delay T_{wait}, and task execution delay T_{run}. Thus, the definition of total delay is the sum of these components: $T_{total} = Tr_{mn} + T_{wait} + T_{run}$. In detail, Tr_{mn} denotes the task delay for task i to be transmitted from end device m to edge node n, T_{wait} quantifies the queuing delay experienced prior to the task scheduling, and T_{run} accounts for the delay incurred as the VM processes the task. The expression for Tr_{mn} can be defined as:

$$Tr_{mn} = \frac{Data_i}{r_{mn}}. \tag{2}$$

where $Data_i$ represents the data consumption associated with task i while r_{mn} signifies the transmission rate of the communication channel.

Upon a task's arrival at the edge node, it enters the task queue, at this point, T_{wait} can be defined as:

$$T_{wait} = T_{start} - T_{arrive}. \tag{3}$$

where T_{start} corresponds to the initiation time of task i execution and T_{arrive} denotes the moment when the task reaches the edge node.

In this study, we utilize φ_i as a representation of the task scheduling policy, where φ_i can assume values with the range $1, 2, ..., N$. When $\varphi_i = 1$, it indicates that the computational task is executed in the local edge cloud, and other values indicate that it will be scheduled to execute on the edge cloud corresponding to that value. Thus T_{run} can be defined as:

$$T_{run} = \frac{Cycle_i}{f_{nj}}, \varphi_i = 1. \tag{4}$$

where $Cycle_i$ denotes the CPU cycles consumed by task i, and f_{nj} is the computational resource of the jth VM in the nth edge node, expressed in terms of CPU cycle frequency.

Subsequently, we proceed with the computation of the transmission energy consumption E_{mn} and the execution energy consumption E_{run}. The definitions for E_{mn} and E_{run} are as follows

$$E_{mn} = P_{mn}Tr_{mn}. \tag{5}$$

$$E_{run} = \mu Cycle_i f_{nj}^2, \varphi_i = 1. \tag{6}$$

where P_{mn} is the uplink transmission power of the end device to transfer tasks to the edge node and μ is the energy factor associated with the CPU architecture. The cumulative energy consumption can be denoted as $E_{total} = E_{mn} + E_{run}$. Consequently, the total cost Z_n^{cost} can be defined as:

$$Z_n^{cost} = \lambda T_{total} + (1 - \lambda)E_{total}. \tag{7}$$

where λ is the weight parameter for the delay in edge computing, $\lambda \in [0, 1]$.

3.4 Optimization Problem Formulation

Based on the previous discussions, We define the optimization problem with the aim of minimizing the total cost as follows:

$$P : \min_{\varphi_i, f_{nj}} \sum_{n=1}^{N} Z_n^{cost} \tag{8}$$
$$s.t. : C1 : \quad \varphi_i \in \{1, 2, ..., N\}$$
$$C2 : \quad 0 \le Cycle_i \le f_{nj}$$

where constraint C1 limits each task can be scheduled to one edge node for execution, and C2 defines that the CPU cycles consumed by a task cannot exceed the computational power of the VM processing it.

4 Algorithm Design

Within this segment, we propose the utilization of the DQN network model as a solution to the optimization problem. We aim to decrease the overall cost associated with task scheduling by minimizing both delay and energy consumption.

4.1 Markov Decision Process

Within our specific MDP framework, the agent assumes the role of a task scheduler responsible for selecting the most appropriate VM to execute tasks, considering the present state of the environment. The agent aims to make optimal decisions at every step, minimizing the total cost of the tasks. To avoid local optima, agents need to have a global representation of the features across all edge clouds, rather than solely relying on local features of their respective edge clouds.

State Space. The state space, denoted as $s_t \in S$, is a one-dimensional vector that contains two sets. The first set, s_r, represents the state of the task and includes $Cycle_i$ (the CPU cycles required by the task) and $Data_i$ (the data consumption of the task). The second set, s_x, represents the state of the VMs within each edge cloud and includes R_{n_j} (the remaining CPU cycles of the jth VM in the nth edge cloud) and f_{n_j} (the CPU cycle frequency of the jth VM in the nth edge cloud). Thus, the present state can be represented as follows:

$$s_t = [s_r + s_x] = [Cycle_i, Data_i, ..., R_{nj}, f_{nj}, ...] \quad i = 1, 2, ..., I, j = 1, 2, ..., J. \quad (9)$$

where R_{nj} indicates the memory capacity of the VM.

Action Space. The agent acts by perceiving the current state of the environment. Within our model, the agent's action a_t is defined as selecting a VM for the task, indicating that the computational resources in the chosen VM will be allocated to the present task. The action space can be defined as:

$$a_t = \{a | V_{11}, V_{12}, ..., V_{nj}, ...\} \quad n = 1, 2, ..., N. \quad (10)$$

where V_{nj} denotes the jth VM on the nth edge node.

Reward Function. The environment provides the agent with a reward at time step $t + 1$ in response to the action taken by the agent based on the state observed at time step t. The rewards received are utilized to update the task scheduling strategy, determining on the best action for the next round. In Deep Reinforcement Learning (DRL), the agent aims to achieve maximum rewards. Therefore, we establish the reward function as:

$$r = -\sum_{n=1}^{N} Z_n^{cost} \quad n = 1, 2, ..., N. \quad (11)$$

where Z_n^{cost} stands for the overall cost incurred in scheduling tasks for the nth edge cloud.

4.2   The DQN-A-Based Task Scheduling Algorithm

Utilizing the Deep Q Network-A (DQN-A) algorithm, we address the task scheduling problem. The specific process gets depicted in Fig. 3. The state is first passed to the Main Net, and action is then selected based on the probability distribution. The chosen action is then fed back to the environment, leading to the acquisition of the subsequent state. When a state changes, the agent receives a reward, and this state-action-reward-next state tuple becomes part of the replay experience pool, contributing to the adjustment of the parameters in the Main Net. These parameters are also assigned to Target Net every 50 steps to enhance the stability of the algorithm by reducing the correlation between the evaluated Q values.

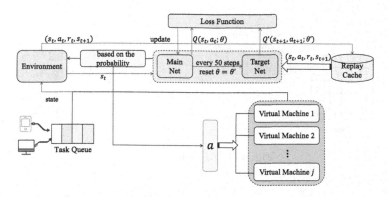

Fig. 3. DQN-A-based task scheduling process.

The DQN algorithm combines a Convolutional Neural Network (CNN) and Q-learning, where the CNN takes raw image data (as states) as input and outputs the value function assessment (Q-value) corresponding to each action [10]. The goal is to find an appropriate action. First, *softmax* regression is employed to convert the Q-values into probability distributions:

$$Q(s_t, a_t) \leftarrow \frac{e^{Q(s_t, a_t)}}{\sum_{v=1}^{V} e^{Q(s_t, a_v)}}. \tag{12}$$

To enhance the accuracy and convergence speed, the Q-values with probabilities less than 10% are removed, and the remaining probabilities are then normalized:

$$Q(s_t, a_t) \leftarrow \frac{Q(s_t, a_t) - Q_{min}}{Q_{max} - Q_{min}}. \tag{13}$$

In a given state, the agent must choose an action, and the sum of the probabilities of all alternative actions should be 1 to ensure a valid decision in each state. Therefore, the sum of the probabilities of all Q-values is converted to 1:

$$Q(s_t, a_t) \leftarrow \frac{Q(s_t, a_t)}{\sum_{p=1}^{P} e^{Q(s_t, a_p)}}. \tag{14}$$

An action is then selected based on the probability distribution, and this action becomes the output of the Main Net. Additionally, we update the Q-value through Bellman's formula for the state-action combination:

$$Q(s_t, a_t) \leftarrow Q(s_t, a_t) + \alpha[r_t + \gamma max_a Q(s_{t+1}, a_t) - Q(s_t, a_t)]. \tag{15}$$

where α represents the learning rate and γ is the discount factor, reflecting the importance of future rewards (ranging from 0 to 1).

As depicted in Fig. 4, the value function Q, in this case, is not a single value but a set of vectors. If we denote the value function as $Q(s_t, a_t; \theta)$, the θ is the weight parameter of the neural network model. Training a neural network

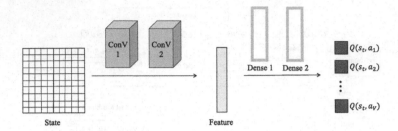

Fig. 4. DQN neural network.

involves optimizing the objective, which is the minimization of the loss function. We define the loss function by comparing the output of the Main Net with that of the Target Net:

$$L(\theta) = E[(r_t + \gamma max_a Q'(s_{t+1}, a; \theta') - Q(s_t, a_t; \theta))^2]. \tag{16}$$

where θ' represents the Target Net parameters and θ is the Main Net parameter. The next step is to update the Main Net parameters by gradient descent:

$$\theta \leftarrow \theta - \alpha \nabla_\theta L(\theta). \tag{17}$$

After a certain number of iterations, the parameter θ of the Main Net is copied to parameter θ' of the Target Net. After adding the target network, the target Q values remain constant over time, which reduces the correlation between the evaluated Q values and enhances the stability of the algorithm.

We outline the proposed intelligent task scheduling algorithm based on DQN-A in Algorithm 1.

5   Experiment

Within this segment, we assess the effectiveness of our introduced task scheduling approach by conducting a comprehensive series of experiments. We provide details of the simulation setup and a thorough analysis of the experimental outcomes.

5.1   Experiment Setup

To examine the performance of our task scheduling algorithm, we carried out a series of experiments using a tower server equipped with 2.8 GHz Intel Core i5 CPU, 16 GB RAM, Python3.9, and CloudSim 4.0, an open-source package widely used [11].

In our experimental setup, we varied the transmission power within the range of 32 mW to 197 mW, while each channel had a bandwidth of 22 MHz. The mini-batch size was configured as 32, the learning rate for the Q-network was set at 0.003, and the discount factor γ was established as 0.7. Task-specific CPU

Algorithm 1. DQN-A Task Scheduling Algorithm.

Input: Number of edge nodes, number of VMs, VMs' computational capabilities, radio bandwidth, parameters for task configuration

Output: VM assignment a_t, the acquired model parameters θ in the Main Net, and the acquired model parameters θ' in the Target Net

Initialize replay cache D to capacity K and the quantity of mini-batches B

Initialize action-value function Q with random model parameters θ, and set up the target action-value function Q' with $\theta' = \theta$

for task num $= 1, I$ **do**

    for step $= 1, T$ **do**

        Obtain the present state s_t in the environment

        if the random number $>$ the probability ε **then**

            Calculate the probability of each action and remove actions with a probability of less than 10%

            Normalize the residual probability

            Calculate the new probability of each action

            Select a_t according to the probability

        else

            For each state, select a random action a_t with probability ε

        end if

        Receive the reward r_t according to the action a_t, then the state transition performs $s_t \rightarrow s_{t+1}$

        Assign $s_{t+1} = s_t$

        Save experiences (s_t, a_t, r_t, s_{t+1}) into the replay cache D

        for b=1, ..., B **do**

            Randomly select a mini-batch of transition (s_t, a_t, r_t, s_{t+1}) within the replay cache D

            Calculate the target Q-values for each example

        end for

        Determine the target Q-values for each example using the function $L(\theta)$

        Update the Main Net parameters θ

        if step $==$ 50 **then**

            Reset $\theta' = \theta$

        end if

    end for

    Return a_t

end for

Return θ and θ'

---

cycle requirements were randomly assigned from a range spanning 5.2×10^8 to 9.8×10^8, and the task arrival rates adhered to a Poisson distribution.

To assess our model's performance, we conducted a comparative analysis with three existing scheduling methods: the DQN algorithm, the dynamic task scheduling optimization algorithm (DTSOA) [12], and the Deep Deterministic Policy Gradient (DDPG) algorithm [13].

The DQN algorithm combines the deep neural network and Q-learning method to approximate the Q-value function, enabling decision-making and learning in unknown environments. The DTSOA algorithm is an improved version based on the dueling DQN algorithm for dynamic task scheduling [12]. The DDPG algorithm combines deep neural networks with the deterministic strategy gradient method, using two networks to estimate action value function more accurately and handle high-dimensional state and continuous action spaces [13].

5.2 Evaluation Results

In the initial phase, we assessed the algorithms with a consistent number of 200 VMs while varying the number of tasks. Our assessment criteria encompassed performance metrics such as delay, energy consumption, and cost. Figure 5 demonstrates the effectiveness of the DQN-A algorithm compared to other approaches in resource allocation and task scheduling.

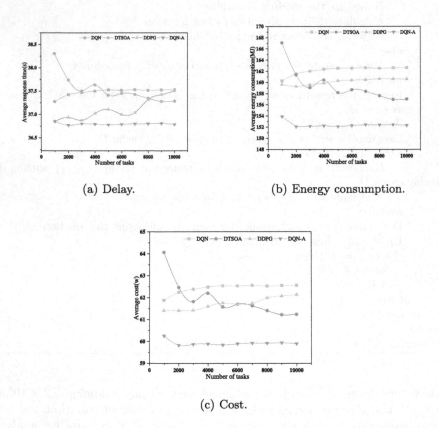

(a) Delay.   (b) Energy consumption.

(c) Cost.

Fig. 5. Delay, energy consumption, and cost versus the number of tasks for different algorithms.

Specifically, Fig. 5(a) shows that the DQN algorithm exhibits a long average response time in the later stages of task scheduling, indicating potential inefficiencies in resource allocation and subsequent inefficient task processing. In contrast, the DQN-A algorithm, which utilizes an intelligent action selection method considering resource availability and workload allocation, notably enhances the efficiency of task processing and reduces the average response time.

Furthermore, in Fig. 5(b), with the task count of 7000, the DQN-A algorithm achieves lower average energy consumption compared to DQN, DTSOA, and DDPG. The energy consumption reduction is at least 3.8%, 6.3%, and 5.1%, respectively. This improvement can be attributed to the real-time feedback mechanism of the DQN-A algorithm, which dynamically adjusts the task allocation strategy based on the system's load and resource utilization. By adapting to actual demand, the algorithm ensures the effective use of energy and prevents energy waste.

Figure 5(c) presents the cost-effectiveness of task scheduling by comparing the delay and energy consumption among different algorithms. The DQN-A algorithm's ability to reduce delay and optimize energy consumption contributes to its improved cost-effectiveness compared to other approaches.

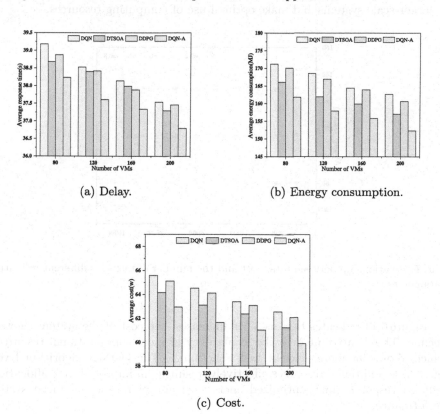

(a) Delay.   (b) Energy consumption.

(c) Cost.

Fig. 6. Delay, energy consumption, and cost versus the number of VMs for different algorithms.

The experimental results in Fig. 6 demonstrate the influence of varying VMs on task scheduling performance, comparing the DQN-A algorithm with other algorithms.

In Fig. 6(a), it is evident that with an increase in VMs, the average response time shows a decline. This decline is attributed to the increased computing capacity of the edge cloud system. With a larger number of VMs, there is an increased capacity for processing tasks, which leads to improved task scheduling and reduced task completion time. The DQN-A algorithm effectively utilizes these additional resources through efficient task allocation, reducing average response time.

Figure 6(b) demonstrates that both the DTSOA and DQN-A algorithms perform better with a smaller scale (fewer VMs). As VMs increases and more resources become available, the DQN-A algorithm demonstrates superior performance. It efficiently allocates tasks, distributes them evenly across the available VMs, reduces energy consumption per task, avoids VM overload, and achieves energy savings. This highlights the capability of the DQN-A algorithm to adapt to larger-scale systems and make optimal use of computing resources.

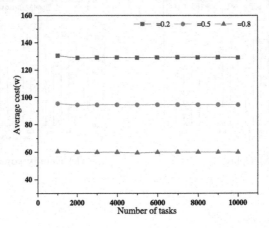

Fig. 7. Relationship between total cost and the number of tasks for different weighting parameters.

Figure 6(c) indicates that as VMs increases, the cost of the system shows a decline. This is attributed to the availability of more computational resources, which allows for more efficient task scheduling. The DQN-A algorithm leverages these additional resources effectively, resulting in improved task allocation, reduced response time, optimized energy consumption, and enhanced system performance.

Figure 7 demonstrates the impact of varying the weighting parameters (λ) on the total system cost, considering the balance of delay and energy consumption. The total system cost is the combination of the delay cost and the energy cost, with appropriate weighting. As shown in Fig. 7, when the proportion of delay cost decreases (i.e., smaller λ values), the total system cost increases. This observation indicates that the energy cost of task processing outweighs the cost of task latency in this scenario. Therefore, reducing energy consumption becomes crucial for minimizing the overall system cost. To effectively manage the system cost, it is important to select the appropriate VM for task scheduling.

6   Conclusion

This paper introduces a novel DQN-A-based intelligent task scheduling algorithm for edge cloud architectures, addressing the critical challenge of load balancing and maintaining application performance in highly variable network environments. Our proposed method dynamically adapts to workload fluctuations, leveraging the powerful sensing and decision-making capabilities of DRL to optimize task assignments. Through a series of experiments, we demonstrated that our DQN-A algorithm significantly outperforms several existing scheduling methods with regard to task delay, energy consumption, and cost. The comprehensive analysis of the experimental results emphasizes the advantages of our approach and establishes its effectiveness in improving task scheduling performance across a range of VM configurations. In our future work, we aim to implement the proposed scheduling framework, utilizing deep reinforcement learning, within a real edge cloud environment. Furthermore, we have plans to integrate the mobility of terminal devices into the scheduling algorithm to achieve an additional boost in system efficiency.

Acknowledgments. This work was supported in part by the National Natural Science Foundation of China (62272256), Shandong Provincial Natural Science Foundation (No. ZR2021MF026), the Piloting Fundamental Research Program of Qilu University of Technology (Shandong Academy of Sciences) (2022XD001, and the Colleges and Universities 20 Terms Foundation of Jinan City China (202228903).

References

1. Zhang, Y., Chen, X., Chen, Y., et al.: Cost efficient scheduling for delay-sensitive tasks in edge computing system. In: 2018 IEEE International Conference on Services Computing (SCC), pp. 73–80 (2018)
2. Robles, A., Skarmeta, A.: A multi-layer guided reinforcement learning-based tasks offloading in edge computing. Computer Networks **220**, 109476 (2022)
3. Wang, X., Ma, L., Li, H., et al.: Digital twin-assisted efficient reinforcement learning for edge task scheduling. In: 2022 IEEE 95th Vehicular Technology Conference: (VTC2022-Spring), pp. 1–5 (2022)
4. Zhao, X., Wu, C.: Large-scale machine learning cluster scheduling via multi-agent graph reinforcement learning. IEEE Trans. Netw. Serv. Manage. **19**(4), 4962–4974 (2022)
5. Song, F., Xing, H., et al.: Offloading dependent tasks in multi-access edge computing: a multi-objective reinforcement learning approach. Futur. Gener. Comput. Syst. **128**, 333–348 (2022)

6. Possebon, I., Silva, B., Da, C., Schaeffer-Filho, A.: Look-ahead reinforcement learning for load balancing network traffic. In: 2022 IEEE Symposium on Computers and Communications (ISCC), pp. 1–6 (2022)
7. Shahidani, R., Fatemeh, A., Ghasemi, A., et al.: Task scheduling in edge-fog-cloud architecture: a multi-objective load balancing approach using reinforcement learning algorithm. Computing **105**, 1337–1359 (2023)
8. Panin, A., Shvechikov, P.: Practical Reinforcement Learning. Coursera and National Research University Higher School of Economics (2017)
9. Arulkumaran, K., Deisenroth, M., Brundage, M., Bharath, A.: Deep reinforcement learning: a brief survey. IEEE Signal Process. Mag. **34**(6), 26–38 (2017)
10. Filhd, M., Oliveira, R., Monteiro, C., et al.: CloudSim plus: a cloud computing simulation framework pursuing software engineering principles for improved modularity, extensibility and correctness. In: Integrated Network & Service Management, pp. 400–406 (2017)
11. Youn, J., Han, Y.: Intelligent task dispatching and scheduling using a deep Q-network in a cluster edge computing system. Sensors (Basel) **22**(11), 4098 (2022)
12. Li, X., Fang, Y., et al.: Resource scheduling for UAV-assisted failure-prone MEC in industrial internet. Drones **7**, 259 (2023)
13. Ran, L., Shi, X., Shang, M.: SLAs-aware online task scheduling based on deep reinforcement learning method in cloud environment. In: 2019 IEEE 21st International Conference on High Performance Computing and Communications, pp. 1518–1525 (2019)

A Comprehensive Review
of the Oversmoothing in Graph Neural
Networks

Xu Zhang[1], Yonghui Xu[2], Wei He[1], Wei Guo[1], and Lizhen Cui[1,2(✉)]

[1] School of Software, Shandong University, Jinan 250101, China
{hewei,guowei}@sdu.edu.cn, clz@sdu.edu.cn
[2] Joint SDU-NTU Centre for Artificial Intelligence Research (C-FAIR),
Shandong University, Jinan 250101, China

Abstract. There are many ways to process graph data in deep learning, among which Graph Neural Network(GNN) is an effective and popular deep learning model. However, GNN also has some problems. For example, after multiple layers of neural networks, the features between nodes will become more and more similar, so that the model identifies two completely different nodes as one type. For example, when two nodes with different structural information output, they are almost the same at the feature level and thus difficult to be distinguished, and this phenomenon is called oversmoothing. For example, in node classification, two completely different types of nodes obtain highly similar node features after model training. How to alleviate and solve the oversmoothing problem has become an emerging hot research topic in graph research. However, there has yet to be an extensive investigation and evaluation of this topic. This paper aims to summarize different approaches to mitigate the oversmoothing phenomenon by providing a detailed research survey. We analyze and summarize proposed research schemes from three aspects currently: topological perturbation, message passing, and adaptive learning, and evaluate the strengths and limitations of existing research by outlining oversmoothing evaluation methods. In addition, we predict and summarize promising and possible research paths in the future. In doing so, this paper contributes to the development of GNN and provides insightful information for practitioners working with GNN and graph data.

Keywords: GNN · Oversmoothing · Topological Perturbation · Adaptive Learning

1 Introduction

In daily life, graph-structured data is everywhere. Graph data has also become a frequently used data set by every researcher. These data sets include person relationship graphs, knowledge graph collections, protein molecular structure collections, etc. However, traditional machine learning methods [25,30,36] usually cannot effectively capture graphs' structural and relational information when processing graph data. The proposal of Graph Convolutional Network (GCN) promoted the development of graph neural network. Its proposed message passing mechanism and domain aggregation function can efficiently obtain the characteristic output of nodes. For example, node classification [1,50], social recommendation [25,41], etc. However, with the development of GCN, some problems have emerged. [21] proposed that during the GCN training process, as the propagation layer deepens, node features become more and more similar, and the distinction between nodes decreases, thus affecting the representation ability and generalization performance of the model. This phenomenon is called oversmoothing of node features.

The presentation of this paper has aroused the extensive attention of researchers on the oversmoothing problem and promoted follow-up research work to solve the oversmoothing problem. [18,43,45] further explain the essence of the problem: graph convolution essentially mixes the representations of adjacent nodes together. Regarding the setting of the number of training layers, if we continue to increase the number of layers, there will be no major difference in the representation output of most nodes in the end. This oversmoothing problem has recently attracted significant attention and research. By designing new model structures [45], aggregation strategies [6,18], topological perturbation [17], and parameterized matrices [55], researchers are committed to improving the representation ability and generalization performance of GNN to cope with the challenges of oversmoothing. Currently, there are no survey papers on the oversmoothing problem. In this article, we classify and summarize the research work done in recent years to alleviate the oversmoothing problem. We propose a classification method according to which current relevant research can be summarized. Classified according to the angle of oversmoothing problem solving. This paper analyzes their solution to help readers understand the impact of this oversmoothing phenomenon on graph neural networks. We summarize and classify related research on mitigating the oversmoothing problem and introduce several oversmoothing measurement methods.

2   Preliminaries

2.1   Definition

First, we have a graph G. The graph G consists of the set V and the set E. Where V is the set of nodes in G, and E is the set of edges in G. Each node $v_i \in V$ in V has an initial representation h_i^0, through message passing and node update rules. In each pass update step t, the representation h_i^t of node v_i can be calculated by the following formula:

$$h_i^t = Update(h_i^{t-1}, Aggregate(h_j^{t-1}, \forall v_j \in \mathcal{N}(v_i))) \tag{1}$$

Among them, Aggregate function means to aggregate the representations of neighbor nodes, such as summing or averaging. And Update function represents the update rule of the node itself, which can be a multi-layer perceptron

(MLP) or other functions. In [21], the oversmoothing problem occurs because as the number of training network layers increases, the feature differences between nodes become smaller and smaller, so that they converge to the point where they are indistinguishable.

This over-convergence problem limits the expressive ability of GNN. In this article, we will define this problem as follows:

Definition 1 (Oversmoothing, OS). *The oversmoothing problem can be expressed using the above pre-defined formula: $h_i^t \approx h_j^t$ As messages are propagated progressively, the embeddings of nodes become more and more similar, so that the node embeddings are indistinguishable and highly similar.*

In [2], Mean Average Distance (MAD) which has often been suggested as a measure of oversmoothing is represented as follows:

$$MAD(G) = \frac{1}{|V|} \sum_{i \in V} \sum_{j \in N(v_i)} 1 - \frac{{h_i^t}^T h_j^t}{||h_i^t|| ||h_j^t||} \tag{2}$$

[54] uses Euclidean distance to represent the feature similarity between node v_i and node v_j:

$$D(h_i, h_j) = \frac{1}{2} \left|\left| \frac{x_i}{||x_i||} - \frac{x_j}{||x_j||} \right|\right| \tag{3}$$

Existing approaches to measure oversmoothing in deep GNN have mainly been based on concept of Dirichlet energy on graphs:

$$\omega(G) = \frac{1}{|V|} \sum_{i \in V} \sum_{j \in N(v_i)} ||h_i^t - h_j^t||_2^2 \tag{4}$$

2.2   Analysis

Topological Perturbation. Topological perturbation can change the connection relationship between nodes, thereby increasing the difference between nodes and reducing the occurrence of oversmoothing phenomenon.

Message Deliver. Message passing is an important mechanism for passing and updating information between nodes. During message passing, a node can only utilize the information of its neighbor nodes, which may lead to local information limitation. Especially in large graphs, nodes may not fully utilize global information.

Adaptive Learning. Adaptive Learning can increase the discrimination of nodes by reducing the connection between nodes or reducing the dimensionality of node features, thereby alleviating the oversmoothing problem. Specifically, Neural sparsification allows the key features of nodes to receive the attention of the model, reduce the dependence on noise and redundant information, and improve the discrimination of nodes.

3   The Proposed Methods of Alleviating Oversmoothing

Table 1. Application of Alleviating OS

Group	Ref.	name	Hard Drop Node	Soft Drop Node	Hard Drop Edge	Soft Drop Edge	Sampling	Regularization	Attention	Residual Connection	Jump Connection	Sparsification	Adaptive Learning	Cora [29]	Citeseer [12]	Pubmed [28]	Reddit [35]	MUTAG [8]	PTC [38]	PROTEINS [9]	NCI1 [40]	PPI [32]	other
Topological Perturbation	[24]	DropGNN	✓					✓										✓	✓	✓			
	[52]	DOTIN	✓					✓												✓	✓		
	[10]	DropNode Regularization	✓					✓						✓	✓	✓		✓		✓	✓		
	[26]	DropEdge			✓			✓						✓	✓	✓	✓						
	[57]	DII-GCN			✓			✓		✓				✓	✓	✓							
	[56]	DropDEdge			✓			✓						✓	✓	✓							
	[13]	SoftEdge				✓		✓										✓	✓		✓		
	[31]	FairDrop			✓			✓						✓	✓								
Delive	[39]	GAT							✓					✓	✓	✓						✓	
	[14]	GraphSAGE					✓								✓		✓						
	[19]	REGNN					✓		✓					✓	✓	✓							
	[45]	JKNet									✓			✓	✓		✓						
	[23]	GraphDrop	✓		✓		✓																①
	[11]	DropMessage						✓	✓					✓	✓	✓							
	[5]	GCNII								✓				✓	✓	✓							
Adaptive Learning	[55]	NeuralSparse										✓		✓	✓		✓						
	[22]	PTDNet						✓				✓	✓	✓	✓		✓						
	[44]	NodeFormer						✓				✓	✓	✓									②
	[49]	SGAT							✓			✓	✓	✓	✓	✓	✓					✓	
	[58]	DGSLN						✓					✓	✓	✓						✓		
	[53]	ADGCN						✓					✓	✓		✓							
	[4]	NAIE						✓					✓	✓	✓	✓							③
	[3]	NSAIR-GCN						✓		✓			✓	✓	✓	✓							
	[2]	ADaEdge						✓		✓			✓	✓	✓	✓							
	[54]	DAGNN						✓		✓			✓	✓	✓	✓	✓						④

① Cornell [7], Wisconsin [33]. ② OGB-Proteins [16]. ③ Wiki [42], BlogCatalog(BC) [37], Flickr [15]. ④ Amazon Computers, Amazon Photo.

We classified related research on alleviating the oversmoothing problem based on the structural characteristics of the neural network model and the representation of the graph structure. This taxonomy can classify graph neural networks into three types, namely topological perturbation, message passing, and adaptive learning.

In Table 1 we show a total of 26 mitigation options. These solutions are divided into three categories based on the raw data and target features of the neural network and the model training process. Table 1 also shows the different data sets used in different scenarios. For example, DAGNN [54] uses trainable vectors to measure the retention scores of different message propagation layers, which can be adaptively adjusted, so it is classified as an adaptive learning type, but we do not classify it as a message propagation type.

3.1   Topological Perturbation Strategies

The topology of a graph involves the connection relationships and structures of nodes and edges, reflecting the relationship between nodes and the information transmission path. Topological perturbation refers to the modification or perturbation of the above topology, such as adding or deleting nodes, adding or disconnecting edges and other operations. In practical application scenarios, graph data may be affected by noise, incomplete information or attacks. Topological perturbations can introduce more variation and uncertainty, breaking the aggregation tendency among nodes, thus helping the model to better understand the adaptability of these perturbations.

Node Perturbation. In node classification tasks, the characteristics of nodes are crucial. Therefore, the perturbation of the nodes greatly affects the accuracy of downstream tasks, and how to perturb the nodes is a direction of current research. DropGNN [24] proposes to randomly drop a part of nodes in GNN calculation. In each forward propagation process, some nodes are randomly selected for discarding according to a certain probability, and they are removed from the graph. Dropping nodes causes the network to perform computations on different subgraphs, thus introducing more variation and diversity. In DOTIN [52], the idea of Graph Attention Network is combined to aggregate multiple low-attention nodes into a virtual node, thus discarding some nodes and alleviating the oversmoothing problem. DropNode Regularization [10] can transfer information more comprehensively and reduce oversmoothing problems by introducing node transition probability and DropNode regularization.

Edge Perturbation. Edge perturbation increases the difference between nodes by adding random edge perturbations in the graph, so that the representation of nodes is no longer over-smooth during the iterative process. In this way, the individual characteristics and local structure information of nodes can be better preserved, and the oversmoothing problem can be alleviated. At the same time, edge perturbation can also strengthen the model from the aspect of data enhancement.

In DropEdge [26], a certain number of edges are randomly discarded in each round of training to achieve an effect similar to data enhancement. Weakening the message passing on the edges can alleviate the occurrence of oversmoothing problems. DII-GCN [57] first obtains multiple different learning sample data through DropEdge, and then uses the feature output of each convolution layer as the initial residual, which has a significant easing effect on the convergence of features. DropDEdge [56] proposes the SNR standard and the feature gain of nodes. By calculating these two evaluation criteria, edges that have a negative impact or have no positive impact on downstream tasks are purposefully removed. SoftEdge [13] proposes data augmentation without deleting edges or nodes, and "soften" the edges by changing the duality of the adjacency matrix so that the values in the adjacency matrix are randomly selected between (0, 1). A new biased edge drop algorithm (FairDrop [31]) to combat homogeneity and enhance fair learning of node features. Flexibility to interpolate between biased edges to fair edges and unbiased edges.

3.2   Deliver Strategies

In graph neural networks, message passing is fundamental for transferring and aggregating information between nodes in a graph structure. It is one of the core mechanisms of GNN to capture the interactions and dependencies between nodes. Message delivery can be analyzed from multiple aspects, such as node information aggregation, iterative delivery, etc.

Attention Strategies. Attention strategy is a technique that enables neighbor nodes to perform adaptive information aggregation. Employing the attention mechanism, the model is capable of dynamically adjusting weights in the aggregation process based on the relevance and similarity between nodes, thereby enabling the identification of crucial information in the graph. This strategy usually introduces attention weights for weighted aggregation of neighbor nodes. These weights are calculated from the relationships and features between nodes, reflecting the degree of mutual influence between nodes.

By introducing adaptive attention weights, GAT [39] can perform accurate information aggregation among neighbor nodes, thereby better retaining individual characteristics and local structural information of nodes, and alleviating the oversmoothing problem. Specifically, the attention weight in GAT is calculated by the similarity between nodes; nodes with higher similarity will get higher weights. This makes neighbor nodes that have a positive impact on downstream tasks more critical, reducing transitive dependencies on other irrelevant nodes. GraphSAGE [14] changes the scope and method of message delivery through sampling and aggregation. Compared with the traditional fully connected message passing, GraphSAGE only considers the information of the local neighborhood reducing the overhead of computation and storage. This change makes the difference between nodes larger, and improves the efficiency and scalability of the model. REGNN [19] combines the ideas in Natural Language Processing, and uses concatenation, element product and absolute element difference to represent the relationship between two nodes. And perform operations such as replacement through the relationship between nodes to aggregate the characteristics of neighboring nodes, resulting in different angles of impact on the own node.

Message Strategies. An excessive number of messaging layers can worsen the issue of oversmoothing. This is due to increased layer count running the risk of balancing out the node characteristics, thereby losing the distinguishing features between nodes. Thus, it is crucial to exercise caution when deciding on the appropriate number of layers for message propagation and feature aggregation techniques across different layers.

By introducing skip connections, JKNet [45] allows information to jump directly between different layers, avoiding the loss and smoothing of information in multi-layer transfer. The independent weight matrix of each skip layer can make the feature representations between different layers maintain the difference, thereby improving the discrimination ability of the model. In addition to skip connections, JKNet also introduces an important mechanism, namely skip weight learning. By learning the weights of different skip layers during training, JKNet can adaptively choose which layer's information is more useful for the current node representation. This can further improve the model's perception of the differences between nodes. GraphDrop [23] From a functional perspective, two dropout functions and a loss function are proposed to calculate the impact of nodes or edges on downstream tasks, and then filter out the negatively impacting nodes and edges. GraphDrop seeks the relational reasoning patterns of subgraphs by maximizing the removal of nodes and edges in subgraphs by penalizing losses, and tries to preserve the logical rules and topological structures of subgraphs through the proposed topology loss. Existing random drop methods usually only consider the random drop of nodes or edges, and do not deal with them uniformly. Since the previous two methods finally act on the message matrix, DropMessage [11] directly performs the drop operation on the message matrix, which can be applied to any message delivery gnn. GCNII [5] is an extension of the normal GCN model, using two simple yet effective techniques: initial residuals and identity mapping. For each GCN layer, a connection is constructed, which is a jump, while the identity mapping constructs an initial identity matrix and fuses it with the weight matrix.

3.3 Adaptive Learning Strategies

Graph data in the actual environment must contain noise. These noises are manifested as edges and nodes that are irrelevant to the final task, which will affect the representation ability of GNN. Some studies have shown that by adaptively selecting key edges or removing task-irrelevant edges and nodes during the learning or training process, the selective learning ability of GNN can be improved while reducing the degree of oversmoothing.

Neural Sparsification Strategies. Neural sparsification can make the model more sensitive to capture differences between nodes by reducing the total number of parameters that need to be learned or tuned. There are usually two ways: sparse node representation and sparse connection weights. Sparse node representation: By limiting the dimensionality of node representations, that is, by sparsifying the representation vectors of nodes, the quantity of parameters can be reduced to avoid oversmoothing. This can be achieved by introducing a sparse regularization term or by using a compression algorithm. Sparse connection weights: In addition to sparse node representations, sparse connection weights are also an effective strategy. By setting the threshold of connection weights and setting some connection weights to zero, the number of parameters of the model can be reduced and the model's ability to perceive the differences between nodes can be enhanced.

NeuralSparse [55] mainly consists of two parts: sparse network and GNN. In sparse networks, edges are selected through some parameterized network methods to ensure that the remaining edges contribute to downstream tasks. GNN is used in the training phase and testing phase to learn from the output graph of the sparse network without sampling from the initial graph. PTDNet [22] is based on the idea of NeuralSparse and believes that there is natural noise in the original graph that affects downstream tasks, and a parameterized network is needed to filter these nodes and edges. On this basis, considering the topological structure properties of the graph, low-rank constraints are implemented on the rank of the matrix, and the implementation method is to add a nuclear norm for regularization. NodeFormer [44] is the first Transformer model to extend all-pair message passing to large node classification graphs. NodeFormer develops a kernelized Gumbel-Softmax operator that is proven to be a well-posed approximation for specific variables, especially the discrete latent structure between data points. SGAN [49] has no corresponding sparse network, but sets a sparse attention coefficient, which is learned under the constraint of l0-norm regularization, and then applies this coefficient to each GNN layer.

Adaptive Strategies. By dynamically adjusting the learning process of the model, the difference of nodes is maintained, and the expression ability and generalization performance of the model are improved. Choosing an appropriate adaptive method requires experimentation and tuning with the characteristics of specific tasks and data sets, which can effectively alleviate oversmoothing.

[2] proposed MADReg and ADaEdge, which are regularizers based on MAD and GNN model through iterative training and edge removal/addition operations according to the prediction results, and adaptively adjust the graph's topology. DAGNN [54] judges how much of the output representation of each propagation layer should be retained by training a retention score. These propagation layers also represent the importance of nodes at different depths. The difference between DGSLN [58] and other models lies in the expansion of the scope of consideration, which links the topology and properties of the initial graph during the propagation process. This idea can be combined into any GNN model,

and is designed for this idea. A complex loss function. ADGCN [53] facilitates the consistent management of interactions among components through end-to-end learning. To achieve the goal that the model can automatically use widely varying graph data, we place learnable parameters. The effect is comparable to manually modifying the parameters' structure precisely. ADGCN consists of three parts, which regulate the information dissemination of the model, control the complexity of the model, and introduce the attention mechanism as a control switch to realize the selective aggregation of information across layers. NAIE [4] adjusts node characteristics in an adaptive manner. First, the topological structure around the smooth node and the properties of the node are integrated through the autoencoder, and then adaptive smoothing parameters are generated for Laplacian smoothing to adjust the influence of neighboring nodes on itself. NSAIR-GCN [3] is an adaptive initial residual depth map convolutional network based on node smoothness.

4   Oversmoothing Evaluation Method

In order to demonstrate the effectiveness of the above scheme in alleviating the oversmoothing problem, we will introduce some evaluation criteria and experimental analysis.

4.1   Theoretical Analysis of Alleviating Oversmoothing

Oversmoothing evaluation indicators can be divided into two methods: process evaluation and result evaluation. The process evaluation focuses on oversmoothing issues within the model and examines node representation similarity, information entropy and node classification performance. The results evaluation focuses on model oversmoothing in different contexts, including different datasets, graph structures, and tasks. Together, these methods are used to deeply evaluate the oversmoothing problem in graph neural networks to help determine model performance and optimization strategies.

4.2   Mitigation Effectiveness Assessment

Evaluating the effectiveness of different solutions in mitigating the oversmoothing problem under different data sets is helpful to analyze their role in a general environment. We list the following indicators for evaluation, through which the mitigation effects of different solutions can be demonstrated.

Classification Accuracy. Generally, there are two types of tasks in classification tasks: node classification and graph classification. In task of node classification, it is necessary to evaluate the node classification accuracy of the model at different levels or iterations. In the graph classification task [48], the graph classification accuracy of the model at different levels or iterations is evaluated. If the classification accuracy of the model does not change significantly in subsequent layers or iterations, there may be an oversmoothing problem.

Nodes Represent Similarity Measures. By computing similarity measures between node representations, such as MAD(Mean Average Distance) [20], Euclidean distance [25,54], Dirichlet energy [27] etc., the degree of oversmoothness of the model in the representation space is evaluated. The values of these similarity measures are negatively correlated with the degree of oversmoothing, with lower values possibly indicating that the node representation is oversmoothed.

Information Entropy and Analysis of Variance. Compute the information entropy and variance of node representations [46] to assess the diversity and difference of representations. Low entropy and variance values may indicate that nodes represent oversmoothing.

Laplacian Score. Laplacian-based eigenvalue analysis method for evaluating smoothness and diversity of node representations. A higher Laplacian Score value [43] indicates better smoothness and diversity of node representations.

Local Structure Preservation. Evaluate the structure-preserving ability of the model on node neighborhoods or subgraphs [51], such as maintaining the neighbor relationship of nodes, the topology of subgraphs, etc. An oversmoothing model may lose detailed information of the local structure.

5 Possible Research Paths

From our summary and analysis, we can see that research on alleviating the oversmoothing problem has become increasingly popular in recent years. For the purpose of a better dealing with the oversmoothing problem in different practical environments, we propose the following promising and possible research paths, which we hope to provide reference for future research.

Theoretical Analysis and Explanation. Further, understand the nature and causes of the oversmoothing problem. Through theoretical analysis and explanation [27], it reveals the connection between the oversmoothing phenomenon and graph structure, data characteristics, and model architecture, and provides theoretical guidance for designing effective mitigation strategies.

Model Design and Optimization. Explore new graph neural network model structures and optimization methods [34] to alleviate the oversmoothing problem. For example, designing an adaptive convolution operation, introducing an attention mechanism or a mechanism to control information dissemination, etc., to strengthen the model's ability to identify and aggregate differences between nodes.

Adaptive Learning and Tuning. Study how to adaptively [47] learn and tune model smoothness during training to balance the smoothness and diversity of node representations. This can be achieved by introducing dynamic hyperparameters, adaptive learning strategies, or feedback-based mechanisms.

Exploration of Practical Application Scenarios The impact of smoothing problems has been studied in practical applications, and corresponding solutions have been developed. For example, prediction of social relationships between characters, accurate recommendation of items [50], and identification of material molecules all involve the degree of oversmoothing of graph neural networks.

Acknowledgements. This paper is partly supported by National Key R&D Program of China No.2021YFF0900800, NSFC No.62202279, Shandong Provincial Key Research and Development Program (Major Scientific and Technological Innovation Project) No.2021CXGC010108, Shandong Provincial Natural Science Foundation No. ZR2022QF018, Shandong Provincial Outstanding Youth Science Foundation No. 2023HWYQ-039, Fundamental Research Funds of Shandong University.

References

1. Bhagat, S., Cormode, G.: Node classification in social networks. In: Proceedings of the 2011 SIAM International Conference on Data Mining, pp. 201–212 (2011)
2. Chen, D., Lin, Y., Li, W., Li, P., Zhou, J., Sun, X.: Measuring and relieving the over-smoothing problem for graph neural networks from the topological view. In: The Thirty-Fourth AAAI Conference on Artificial Intelligence, AAAI 2020, The Thirty-Second Innovative Applications of Artificial Intelligence Conference, IAAI 2020, The Tenth AAAI Symposium on Educational Advances in Artificial Intelligence, EAAI 2020, New York, NY, USA, February 7–12, 2020, pp. 3438–3445. AAAI Press (2020). https://ojs.aaai.org/index.php/AAAI/article/view/5747
3. Chen, H., Li, Y.: Node-smoothness based adaptive initial residual deep graph convolutional network (2022). Available at SSRN 4254779
4. Chen, J., Zhong, M., Li, J., Wang, D., Qian, T., Tu, H.: Effective deep attributed network representation learning with topology adapted smoothing. IEEE Trans. Cybern. **52**(7), 5935–5946 (2022). https://doi.org/10.1109/TCYB.2021.3064092
5. Chen, M., Wei, Z., Huang, Z., Ding, B., Li, Y.: Simple and deep graph convolutional networks. In: Proceedings of the 37th International Conference on Machine Learning, ICML 2020, 13–18 July 2020, Virtual Event. Proceedings of Machine Learning Research, vol. 119, pp. 1725–1735. PMLR (2020). http.//proceedings. mlr.press/v119/chen20v.html
6. Chen, Y., Li, Z., Xiao, X., Zhang, K., Lu, H.: Simple and effective graph convolutional networks with graph attention convolution. In: Proceedings of the AAAI Conference on Artificial Intelligence, pp. 11459–11466 (2020)
7. Danescu-Niculescu-Mizil, C., Lee, L., Pang, B., Kleinberg, J.: Chameleons in imagined conversations: A new approach to understanding coordination of linguistic style in dialogs. In: Proceedings of the 20th ACM SIGKDD International Conference on Knowledge Discovery and Data Mining, pp. 123–132. ACM, New York, NY, USA (2014). https://doi.org/10.1145/2623330.2623623, https://www. cs.cornell.edu/ cristian/Cornell_Movie-Dialogs_Corpus.html

8. Debnath, A.K., Lopez de Compadre, R., Debnath, G.C., Shusterman, A., Hansch, C.: Structure-activity relationship of mutagenic aromatic and heteroaromatic nitro compounds. correlation with molecular orbital energies and hydrophobicity. J. Med. Chem. **34**, 786–797 (1991)

9. Ding, H., Takigawa, I., Mamitsuka, H., Zhu, S.: Similarity-based machine learning methods for predicting drug-target interactions: a brief review. Brief. Bioinform. **15**(5), 734–747 (2014)

10. Do, T.H., Nguyen, D.M., Bekoulis, G., Munteanu, A., Deligiannis, N.: Graph convolutional neural networks with node transition probability-based message passing and DropNode regularization. Expert Syst. Appl. **174**, 114711 (2021). https://doi.org/10.1016/j.eswa.2021.114711

11. Fang, T., Xiao, Z., Wang, C., Xu, J., Yang, X., Yang, Y.: DropMessage: unifying random dropping for graph neural networks. CoRR abs/2204.10037 (2022). https://doi.org/10.48550/arXiv.2204.10037

12. Giles, C.L., Bollacker, K.D., Lawrence, S.: CiteSeer: an automatic citation indexing system. In: Proceedings of the 3rd ACM Conference on Digital Libraries, pp. 89–98. ACM (1998)

13. Guo, H., Sun, S.: SoftEdge: regularizing graph classification with random soft edges. CoRR abs/2204.10390 (2022). https://doi.org/10.48550/arXiv.2204.10390

14. Hamilton, W.L., Ying, R., Leskovec, J.: Inductive representation learning on large graphs. In: Advances in Neural Information Processing Systems, pp. 1024–1034 (2017)

15. Hodosh, M., Young, P., Hockenmaier, J.: Framing image description as a ranking task: data, models and evaluation metrics. J. Artif. Intell. Res. **47**, 853–899 (2013)

16. Hu, W., et al.: Open graph benchmark: datasets for machine learning on graphs. arXiv preprint arXiv:2005.00687 (2021)

17. Jin, W., Barz, B., Li, M.: Graphdiff: differential privacy for graph neural networks via topology change. In: Proceedings of the AAAI Conference on Artificial Intelligence, pp. 11024–11031 (2020)

18. Klicpera, J., Bojchevski, A., Günnemann, S.: Diffusion improves graph learning. In: Proceedings of the 36th International Conference on Machine Learning (ICML), vol. 97, pp. 3651–3661 (2019)

19. Koishekenov, Y.: Reducing over-smoothing in graph neural networks using relational embeddings. CoRR abs/2301.02924 (2023). https://doi.org/10.48550/arXiv.2301.02924

20. Li, H., et al.: DeeperGCN: all you need to train deeper GCNs. In: Proceedings of the 25th ACM SIGKDD International Conference on Knowledge Discovery & Data Mining, pp. 3332–3342. ACM (2020)

21. Li, Q., Han, Z., Wu, X.: Deeper insights into graph convolutional networks for semi-supervised learning. CoRR abs/1801.07606 (2018). http://arxiv.org/abs/1801.07606

22. Luo, D., et al.: Learning to drop: robust graph neural network via topological denoising. In: Lewin-Eytan, L., Carmel, D., Yom-Tov, E., Agichtein, E., Gabrilovich, E. (eds.) WSDM 2021, The Fourteenth ACM International Conference on Web Search and Data Mining, Virtual Event, Israel, March 8–12, 2021, pp. 779–787. ACM (2021). https://doi.org/10.1145/3437963.3441734

23. Mai, S., Zheng, S., Sun, Y., Zeng, Y., Yang, Y., Hu, H.: Dynamic graph dropout for subgraph-based relation prediction. Knowl. Based Syst. **250**, 109172 (2022). https://doi.org/10.1016/j.knosys.2022.109172

24. Papp, P.A., Martinkus, K., Faber, L., Wattenhofer, R.: DropGNN: random dropouts increase the expressiveness of graph neural networks. In: Ranzato, M., Beygelzimer, A., Dauphin, Y.N., Liang, P., Vaughan, J.W. (eds.) Advances in Neural Information Processing Systems: Annual Conference on Neural Information Processing Systems 2021, NeurIPS 2021(December), pp. 6–14, 2021. virtual, vol. 34, pp. 21997–22009 (2021). https://proceedings.neurips.cc/paper/2021/hash/b8b2926bd27d4307569ad119b6025f94-Abstract.html
25. Perozzi, B., Al-Rfou, R., Skiena, S.: DeepWalk: online learning of social representations. In: Proceedings of the 20th ACM SIGKDD International Conference on Knowledge Discovery and Data Mining, pp. 701–710 (2014)
26. Rong, Y., Huang, W., Xu, T., Huang, J.: DropEdge: towards deep graph convolutional networks on node classification. In: 8th International Conference on Learning Representations, ICLR 2020, Addis Ababa, Ethiopia, April 26–30, 2020. OpenReview.net (2020). https://openreview.net/forum?id=Hkx1qkrKPr
27. Rusch, T.K., Bronstein, M.M., Mishra, S.: A survey on oversmoothing in graph neural networks. CoRR abs/2303.10993 (2023). https://doi.org/10.48550/arXiv.2303.10993
28. Sayers, E.W., et al.: PubBed: a resource for curated biomedical literature. Nucleic Acids Res. **39**(Database issue), D1268–D1271 (2011)
29. Sen, P., Namata, G., Bilgic, M., Getoor, L., Galligher, B., Eliassi-Rad, T.: Collective classification in network data. In: AI Magazine, vol. 29, pp. 93–93 (2008)
30. Shervashidze, N., Schweitzer, P., van Leeuwen, E.J., Mehlhorn, K., Borgwardt, K.M.: Weisfeiler-Lehman graph kernels. J. Mach. Learn. Res. **12**(Sep), 2539–2561 (2011)
31. Spinelli, I., Scardapane, S., Hussain, A., Uncini, A.: FairDrop: biased edge dropout for enhancing fairness in graph representation learning. IEEE Trans. Artif. Intell. **3**(3), 344–354 (2022). https://doi.org/10.1109/TAI.2021.3133818
32. Stark, C., Breitkreutz, B.J., Reguly, T., Boucher, L., Breitkreutz, A., Tyers, M.: BioGRID: a general repository for interaction datasets. Nucleic Acids Res. **34**(Database issue), D535–D539 (2006)
33. Street, W.N., Wolberg, W.H., Mangasarian, O.L.: Wisconsin (Original) Breast Cancer Dataset. UCI Machine Learning Repository (1995)
34. Sun, F.: Over-smoothing effect of graph convolutional networks. CoRR abs/2201.12830 (2022). https://arxiv.org/abs/2201.12830
35. Tan, J., Chang, S., Zettlemoyer, L.S.: Linguistically informed character-level language models for unsupervised named entity recognition. arXiv preprint arXiv:1505.05008 (2015)
36. Tang, J., Qu, M., Wang, M., Zhang, M., Yan, J., Mei, Q.: Line: large-scale information network embedding. In: Proceedings of the 24th International Conference on World Wide Web, pp. 1067–1077 (2015)
37. Tang, L., Liu, H.: Relational learning via latent social dimensions. In: Proceedings of the 15th ACM SIGKDD International Conference on Knowledge Discovery and Data Mining, pp. 817–826. ACM (2009)
38. Toivonen, H., Kaski, S., Nikkilä, J., Vähänikkilä, M., Hautaniemi, S.: Statistical evaluation of term occurrences for discovering differentially expressed genes. J. Comput. Biol. **10**(4), 447–464 (2003)
39. Veličković, P., Cucurull, G., Casanova, A., Romero, A., Lio, P., Bengio, Y.: Graph attention networks. In: International Conference on Learning Representations (2018)
40. Wale, N., Karypis, G.: Comparison of descriptor spaces for chemical compound retrieval and classification. Knowl. Inf. Syst. **14**(3), 347–375 (2008)

41. Wang, H., Wang, J., Wang, J., Zhao, M., Zhang, W.: Knowledge-aware graph neural networks with label smoothness regularization for recommender systems. In: Proceedings of the 28th ACM International Conference on Information and Knowledge Management, pp. 1221–1230 (2019)
42. Wikipedia Contributors: Wikipedia (2023)
43. Wu, F., Zhang, T., Souza, A., Fifty, C., Yu, T., Weinberger, K.Q.: Simplifying graph convolutional networks. In: Proceedings of the 36th International Conference on Machine Learning, pp. 6861–6871 (2019)
44. Wu, Q., Zhao, W., Li, Z., Wipf, D., Yan, J.: NodeFormer: a scalable graph structure learning transformer for node classification. CoRR abs/2306.08385 (2023). https://doi.org/10.48550/arXiv.2306.08385
45. Xu, K., Li, C., Tian, Y., Sonobe, T., Kawarabayashi, K.i., Jegelka, S.: Representation learning on graphs with jumping knowledge networks. In: Proceedings of the 35th International Conference on Machine Learning (ICML), vol. 80, pp. 5421–5430 (2018)
46. Xu, K., Li, C., Tian, Y., Sonobe, T., Kawarabayashi, K.i., Jegelka, S.: How powerful are graph neural networks? In: International Conference on Learning Representations (2019)
47. Yan, Y., Hashemi, M., Swersky, K., Yang, Y., Koutra, D.: Two sides of the same coin: heterophily and oversmoothing in graph convolutional neural networks. In: Zhu, X., Ranka, S., Thai, M.T., Washio, T., Wu, X. (eds.) IEEE International Conference on Data Mining, ICDM 2022, Orlando, FL, USA, November 28 - Dec. 1, 2022, pp. 1287–1292. IEEE (2022). https://doi.org/10.1109/ICDM54844.2022.00169
48. Yanardag, P., Vishwanathan, S.: Deep graph kernels. In: Proceedings of the 21th ACM SIGKDD International Conference on Knowledge Discovery and Data Mining (KDD), pp. 1365–1374 (2015)
49. Ye, Y., Ji, S.: Sparse graph attention networks. IEEE Trans. Knowl. Data Eng. **35**(1), 905–916 (2023)
50. Ying, R., He, R., Chen, K., Eksombatchai, P., Hamilton, W.L., Leskovec, J.: Graph convolutional neural networks for web-scale recommender systems. In: Proceedings of the 24th ACM SIGKDD International Conference on Knowledge Discovery & Data Mining (2018)
51. Zeng, S., Yang, J., Liu, W., Liu, Q.: GraphSAINT: graph sampling based inductive learning method. In: International Conference on Learning Representations (ICLR) (2020)
52. Zhang, S., Zhu, F., Yan, J., Zhao, R., Yang, X.: DOTIN: dropping task-irrelevant nodes for GNNs. CoRR abs/2204.13429 (2022). https://doi.org/10.48550/arXiv.2204.13429
53. Zhang, S., Du, L., Li, F., Yu, G., Chen, M.: Propagate deeper and adaptive graph convolutional networks. In: ICLR (2023)
54. Zhang, X., Li, Y., Zhuang, Y., Zhou, Q.: Towards deeper graph neural networks with differentiable group normalization. In: Proceedings of the AAAI Conference on Artificial Intelligence, vol. 33, pp. 4609–4616 (2019)
55. Zheng, C., et al.: Robust graph representation learning via neural sparsification. In: Proceedings of the 37th International Conference on Machine Learning, ICML 2020, 13–18 July 2020, Virtual Event. Proceedings of Machine Learning Research, vol. 119, pp. 11458–11468. PMLR (2020). http://proceedings.mlr.press/v119/zheng20d.html

56. Zhou, X., Wu, O.: Drop "noise" edge: an approximation of the Bayesian GNNs. In: Wallraven, C., Liu, Q., Nagahara, H. (eds.) Pattern Recognition - 6th Asian Conference, ACPR 2021, Jeju Island, South Korea, November 9–12, 2021, Revised Selected Papers, Part II. Lecture Notes in Computer Science, vol. 13189, pp. 59–72. Springer (2021). https://doi.org/10.1007/978-3-031-02444-3_5
57. Zhu, J., Mao, G., Jiang, C.: DII-GCN: dropedge based deep graph convolutional networks. Symmetry **14**(4), 798 (2022). https://doi.org/10.3390/sym14040798
58. Zou, X., Li, K., Chen, C., Yang, X., Wei, W., Li, K.: DGSLN: differentiable graph structure learning neural network for robust graph representations. Inf. Sci. **626**, 94–113 (2023). https://doi.org/10.1016/j.ins.2023.01.059

A Foreground Feature Embedding Network for Object Detection in Remote Sensing Images

Jiahui Wu[1], Yuanzheng Cai[2($\boxtimes$)], Tao Wang[2], Zhiming Luo[3], Senhua Shan[4], and Zuoyong Li[2]

[1] College of Computer and Data Science, Fuzhou University, Fuzhou 350108, China
[2] Fujian Provincial Key Laboratory of Information Processing and Intelligent Control, College of Computer and Control Engineering, Minjiang University, Fuzhou 350108, China
yuanzheng_cai@mju.edu.cn
[3] Department of Artificial Intelligence, Xiamen University, Xiamen 361005, China
[4] Istrong Technology Limited Company, Fuzhou 350108, China

Abstract. Compared with traditional natural images, remote sensing images (RSIs) typically have high resolution. The objects in the images are densely distributed, with heterogeneous orientation and large scale variation, even among objects of the same class. In recent years, object detection algorithms have made great strides in general images, but they are still difficult to meet the challenges that exist in RSIs. Therefore, we propose a foreground feature embedding network (FFE-Net) for object detection in RSIs. To better grasp the object features in RSIs, we design a foreground feature embedding module (FFEM) to learn the foreground features of the object. This is achieved by introducing an additional semantic segmentation branch and embedding the features in the classification and regression branches. Simultaneously, we propose a modified Gaussian function with focal loss (MGFFL) as a way to eliminate the extra background noise from soft labels, making the learned foreground features more robust. Our experimental results on two publicly available remote sensing image datasets, DOTA-v1.0 and HRSC2016, validate the effectiveness of FFE-Net.

Keywords: Oriented object detection (OOD) · Remote sensing images (RSIs) · Multi-task learning

1 Introduction

With the development of remote sensing technology, it has become easier to acquire large-scale optical remote sensing images (RSIs). Consequently, some popular remote sensing datasets [1,2] have been generated as a result. Unlike natural images in general object detection [3], RSIs are typically high resolution and contain much detailed information that can visually reflect the color, shape,

Fig. 1. An example of soft labels. The green rectangular box in the left image is the ground-truth box, and the right image is a mask image using the pixel points inside the ground-truth box. (Color figure online)

texture, and other characteristics of ground objects. Additionally, even objects of the same category in RSIs can exhibit large scale variations and are distributed at different orientations in real-world scenarios. Therefore, oriented object detection (OOD) in RSIs remains a fundamental and challenging task.

In recent years, the widespread use of convolutional neural networks (CNNs) [4] has significantly improved the benchmark performance of object detection tasks. This improved performance can be attributed to the inherent ability of CNNs to efficiently capture complex visual patterns and features, thus enhancing the accuracy and efficiency of object detection algorithms. The proposed residual networks (ResNet) [5] and feature pyramid networks (FPN) [6] with their powerful feature extraction and fusion capabilities have further advanced the field of object detection. Inspired by these advancements, researchers have proposed one-stage (RetinaNet) [7] and two-stage (Faster R-CNN) [8] anchor-based object detection algorithms to enable a comprehensive end-to-end detection process. However, anchor-based algorithms heavily depend on the quality of anchor design for accurate object prediction. Anchor-free algorithm RepPoints [9] avoid the use of anchors by representing the object as a point set and achieves comparable performance to anchor-based algorithms. Shortly afterward, they proposed their respective improved versions, Mask R-CNN [10] and RepPointsv2 [11], to further enhance the performance of both anchor-based and anchor-free algorithms by adding additional segmentation branches in multi-task learning framework.

All of the algorithms mentioned above were originally designed to implement generic object detection, and most of these efforts and algorithms have been rc-implemented in MMRotate [12] for OOD in RSIs. However, due to the complex background information of RSIs, the densely distributed, and cluttered objects, these algorithms yield mediocre detection performance in RSIs.

Therefore, finding solutions for the aforementioned problems has become primary research direction. For instance, R3Det [13] developed a feature refinement module based on RetinaNet [7], which enhances the model representation by reconstructing and aligning features through pixel-wise feature interpolation. To solve the problem of discontinuity of regression angles, Yang *et al.* [14] transformed the angular regression problem into a classification problem, which effectively solves the angular periodicity problem. GWD [15] and KLD [16] transform the arbitrarily rotated rectangular box into a two-dimensional Gaussian distribution, solving the problem that the rotated intersection over union (IoU) is not derivable. Moreover, some methods have demonstrated that additional emantic information improves the classification and localization performance of OOD algorithms.

Mask OBB [17] is based on Mask R-CNN [10]. It utilizes the rotated box obtained by calculating the minimum bounding rectangle for the predicted segmentation map as the detection result. The model performance is improved through the utilization of multi-scale convolution. Furthermore, Both HSP [18] and CDBA-Net [19] have demonstrated that additional semantic segmentation tasks in RSIs can guide feature learning and improve algorithm performance. However, since existing remote sensing datasets [1,2] do not provide precise semantic segmentation labels, most algorithms directly use the pixel points inside the ground-truth box as show in Fig. 1 as soft labels for supervised learning of semantic segmentation branches. This inevitably introduces excessive background noise contained in the rotated boxes, which affects the performance of the algorithm.

Inspired by the work mentioned above, we propose a foreground feature embedding network (FFE-Net) base on RetinaNet [7]. Therefore, FFE-Net is a simple one-stage anchor-based OOD network for RSIs. The main contributions of this paper are summarized as follows:

1) We design a foreground feature embedding module (FFEM) to enrich feature semantic information to improve the classification and regression performance of the model.
2) We propose a modified Gaussian function with focal loss (MGFFL) combined with soft labels for supervised learning of semantic segmentation branch to make the learned features more robust.
3) Our method achieves superior performance on the DOTA-v1.0, HRSC2016 datasets and validates the effectiveness of FFE-Net.

The remainder of this paper is organized as follows: Sect. 2 provides a detailed description of the proposed FFE-Net. The experimental results and analysis are presented in Sects. 3, and 4 is the conclusion.

2   Proposed Method

The introduction of additional semantic segmentation branches for multi-task learning is a way to enhance the classification and localization performance of

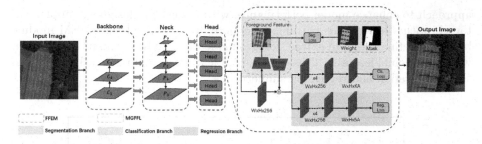

Fig. 2. Pipeline of the proposed FFE-Net. $C_3 - C_5$ indicate the feature maps extracted from the backbone network, and $P_3 - P_7$ denote the feature maps enhanced by the feature pyramid. W and H denote the width and height of the feature maps, and K and A denote the number of categories and the number of anchors.

the object detection algorithm. However, existing remote sensing image datasets lack corresponding instance segmentation labels, and the soft-labeling approach employed by most algorithms is rife with a significant amount of background noise. Therefore, Hence, the primary objective of our research is to optimize the utilization of the supplementary branches features while mitigating the impact of soft labels.

2.1   Overall Framework

Figure 2 depicts the overall network structure of the FFE-Net, primarily comprising the backbone network, feature pyramid, and five heads. Each head consists of three network branches: a semantic segmentation branch, a classification branch, and a regression branch. The backbone network first extracts feature maps at different scales $C_3 - C_5$, followed by utilizing the feature pyramids to fuse these maps and enhance the semantic information. Subsequently, we feed the five obtained feature maps $P_3 - P_7$ into the identical head network structure. For a P_i feature map, we initially pass it through the FFEM to learn object foreground features, then integrate this feature map with the original one. Our proposed MGFFL is able to weight the soft labels in the semantic segmentation branch, thereby enhancing the model's focus on learning crucial objective features. At last stage, we put the refined features into the classification branch and the regression branch to yield the final prediction results. The subsequent subsections provide more detailed introductions to the FFEM and MGFFL, respectively.

2.2   FFEM

Both the anchor-free algorithm RepPointsv2 [11] and the two-stage anchor-based algorithm HSP [18] have demonstrated that incorporating semantic segmentation branches is advantageous for guiding the model to acquire more robust features. We believe that multi-task learning offers a straightforward and effective approach to enhance model performance, with a focus on designing supplementary branches to support learning. Therefore, we developed the FFEM module based on RetinaNet [7] to extract foreground features in RSIs and integrate them with the original features. These augmented features are subsequently input into the classification and regression subnetworks.

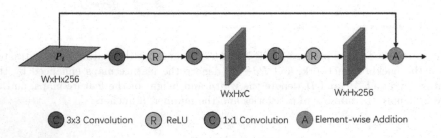

Fig. 3. Structure of the FFEM. The specific meaning of each operation step is described in the second line.

The overall structure of FFEM is illustrated in Fig. 3. Firstly, for each feature map $Pi \in R^{W \times H \times 256}$ from the FPN, we apply a 3×3 convolutional block, followed by passing it through a 1×1 convolutional block beneath the ReLU activation layer. The foreground feature map $Pfg \in R^{W \times H \times C}$ is derived by reducing the channel dimension of the feature map to C using a 1×1 convolutional block, where C denotes the number of categories. This serves as the prediction output for the semantic segmentation branch, utilized for computing the semantic segmentation loss, which is used to calculate the semantic segmentation loss. The channel dimensions are then restored using a 1×1 convolution block and a ReLU activation layer. Ultimately, we add P_i with the restored feature maps to obtain the final feature maps P, which are fed into the classification and regression branches. The entire process can be represented by the following equation:

$$P_{fg} = C_{1 \times 1}(R(C_{3 \times 3}(P_i))) \tag{1}$$

$$P = R(C_{1 \times 1}(P_{fg})) + P_i \tag{2}$$

With the FFEM, we accomplish semantic segmentation branch predictions, while utilizing the learned foreground feature maps to embed the preceding feature maps from the FPN, thereby enhancing the model's classification and localization performance

2.3   MGFFL

Focal loss [7] is a commonly used semantic segmentation loss, and supervised learning in standard object detection datasets [3] usually involves accurate semantic segmentation labels. However, in remote sensing image datasets, the soft-labeling method employed by most algorithms, as depicted in Fig. 1, leads to the introduction of additional background noise. From the figure, we can observe that the points closer to the center of the rotating box are more likely to indicate the target, and the points closer to the edge of the rotating box are more likely to signify the background. Consequently, we calculate the distance from the center point in the middle of the rotation box and employ it as a weight by modifying the Gaussian function to enhance the traditional focal loss. The specific formula for the semantic segmentation loss is as follows:

$$loss_{seg} = \sum_{c=1}^{C} \begin{cases} \dfrac{-1}{Nw} w_{ij}^c \cdot \alpha \cdot (1 - p_{ij}^c)^\gamma \cdot \log(p_{ij}^c) & \text{if } y_{ij}^c = 1 \\ \dfrac{-1}{N}(1 - \alpha) \cdot (p_{ij}^c)^\gamma \cdot \log(1 - p_{ij}^c) & \text{otherwise} \end{cases} \tag{3}$$

where p_{ij}^c is the score of the c-th category in the prediction featmap at position (i, j), y_{ij}^c is the value on the ground-truth mask map, N_w is the sum of w_{ij}^c, and w_{ij}^c is the modified Gaussian function used to calculate the weight of each point in the ground truth box. The specific definitions are as follows:

$$w_{ij}^c = \begin{cases} e^{-\frac{\left|(p_{ij}^c - p_c) \cdot \text{Rot}(\theta)\right|^2}{2 \cdot rat^2}} & \text{if } y_{ij}^c = 1 \\ 0 & \text{otherwise} \end{cases} \tag{4}$$

where p_{ij}^c and p_c the coordinates of the point inside the rotation box and the center, respectively. $Rot\,(\theta)$ is the rotation matrix and $\theta \in [-90°, 90°)$, It is defined as follows:

$$Rot\,(\theta) = \begin{pmatrix} \cos\theta & -\sin\theta \\ \sin\theta & \cos\theta \end{pmatrix} \tag{5}$$

Furthermore, rat is a scaling factor that adjusts the size of the range affected by the Gaussian weighting function by calculating the ratio of the width to the height of the ground-truth box, which is defined as follows:

$$rat = \frac{w}{2} * \left(\frac{w}{h}\right) \tag{6}$$

where w and h are the width and height of the rotating box, respectively. The Gaussian function is modified by introducing the rotation matrix $Rot\,(\theta)$ and the aspect ratio rat of the rotating box, and the obtained Gaussian weights can reflect the orientation and scale information of the object. As shown in Fig. 4, MGFFL can assign more weight to the center of the object than traditional focal loss, while reducing the effect of additional background noise.

2.4   Total Loss

FFN-Net mainly consists of segmentation branch, classification branch and regression branch, the total loss function of the whole algorithm can be expressed as follows:

$$loss = \lambda_1 loss_{cls} + \lambda_2 loss_{reg} + \lambda_3 loss_{seg} \tag{7}$$

Here, we did not experiment meticulously with the change in the weights of the loss function, but simply set λ_1, λ_2, λ_3 all to 1. In this, we use Focal Loss [7] as the classification loss, which is defined as follows:

$$loss_{cls} = -\frac{1}{N} \sum_{c=1}^{C} \begin{cases} \alpha(1 - p_{ij}^c)^\gamma \log(p_{ij}^c) & \text{if } y_{ij}^c = 1 \\ (1 - \alpha)(p_{ij}^c)^\gamma \log(1 - p_{ij}^c) & \text{otherwise} \end{cases} \tag{8}$$

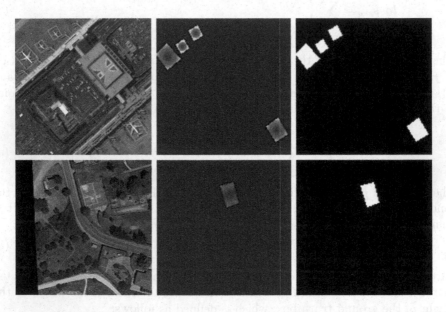

Fig. 4. The weights of modified Gaussian function. The images from left to right are the ground-truth box, the heatmap of the weight, and the soft label.

where N is the number of positive samples, C is denoted as $K \times A$, K is the number of categories and A is the number of anchors. We define p_{ij}^c as the predicted score on the predicted heat map at position (i, j) on channel c, and y_{ij}^c as the ground-truth label at the corresponding position. Finally, we set the hyperparameters α, γ to 0.25, 2.0 respectively.

And for the regression branch, we use L1 Loss as the loss function, which is defined as follow:

$$loss_{reg} = \frac{1}{N} \sum_{j=1}^{N} L1Loss(o_{j,k}, \widehat{o}_{j,k}) \tag{9}$$

where N is the number of positive samples, $o_{j,k}$ is the ground-truth offset, and $\widehat{o}_{j,k}$ is the prediction offset. The semantic segmentation loss has already been introduced in MGFFL, and as shown in Eq. (7), the total loss can ultimately be defined simply as the sum of $loss_{cls}$, $loss_{reg}$ and $loss_{seg}$.

3   Experiments and Result Analysis

3.1   Datasets and Evaluation Metrics

DOTA-v1.0 dataset [1]: DOTA-v1.0 is a large-scale remote sensing image benchmark dataset. With resolutions ranging from 800×800 to 4000×4000, it contains a total of 2806 remote sensing images in various scenes. There are 15 categories and 188,282 instances in these images, including plane (PL), baseball diamond (BD), bridge (BR), ground track field (GTF), small vehicle (SV), large vehicle (LV), ship (SH), tennis court (TC), basketball court (BC), storage tank (ST), soccer-ball field (SBF), roundabout (RA), harbor (HA), swimming pool (SP), and helicopter (HC). All original images are cropped to a uniform resolution of 1024×1024 and overlapped by 200 as the input image.

HRSC2016 dataset [2]: HRSC2016 is a challenging ship detection dataset which contains 1061 satellite images with resolutions ranging from 300×300 to 1500×900. Its training and validation sets and test set contain 436, 181, and 444 images, respectively. All raw images with a maximum scale of no more than 800×512 are used as input images.

Evaluation metrics: The evaluation metric uses the standard VOC2007 format of mean average precision (mAP) with a fixed IoU size of 0.5.

3.2   Implementation Details

MMRotate [12] is used to build FFE-Net and other comparative models. All detectors were fixed with the same random seed for retraining on a single Nvidia RTX A4000 GPU. The backbone networks of all models are ResNet50 [5] pretrained on ImageNet [20] and FPN [6] as neck network for image feature extraction and enhancement. We trained on the DOTA [1] and HRSC2016 [2] datasets for 12 and 72 epochs, respectively. All models use an stochastic gradient descent (SGD) optimizer with a weight decay of 0.0001, an initial learning rate of 0.0025, and a momentum of 0.9. As for the data augmentation operations, we used only random flips on the DOTA-v1.0 dataset and random flips and random rotations on the HRSC2016 dataset.

3.3   Ablation Experiments

Table 1. Ablation experiments of different modules

Settings	PL	BD	BR	GTF	SV	LV	SH	TC	BC	ST	SBF	RA	HA	SP	HC	mAP
Baseline	89.21	77.64	40.36	65.85	77.94	63.50	77.73	**90.90**	82.83	**82.43**	58.95	**62.27**	55.70	65.81	41.77	68.86
+FFEM+ [7]	**89.70**	80.01	41.07	68.45	78.10	65.39	**78.05**	90.88	83.88	81.28	60.04	62.10	54.57	**69.10**	45.07	69.85
+FFEM+MGFFL	89.34	**81.92**	**41.71**	**72.60**	**78.78**	**65.76**	77.99	90.89	**85.84**	82.30	**60.28**	62.25	**58.54**	68.52	**45.14**	**70.79**

To validate the contribution of each module, we conducted ablation experiments on the DOTA-v1.0 dataset using the RetinaNet [7] within the MMRotate framework [12]. As depicted in Table 1, the mAP of the algorithm is improved by 0.99% after incorporating the FFEM into the baseline and using the traditional focal loss [7] as the semantic segmentation loss. Additionally, to mitigate the impact stemming from soft labels, we replaced the traditional focal loss with MGFFL. This replacement further increased mAP by 0.94%, resulting in a total improvement of 1.93% compared with the baseline algorithm.

For each of these categories, we observe that the average precision (AP) of 14 of them exhibits improvement after the incorporation of the designed modules. Among them, BD, GTF and HC improved by 4.28%, 6.75% and 3.37% respectively. The superior performance in most categories is evidence that FFE-Net achieves a degree of performance improvement compared with RetinaNet [7] through FFFM with MGFFL.

3.4   Contrast Experiments

Table 2. Comparisons with different methods on the DOTA-v1.0 test set. The results in bold denote the best results in each column.

Methods	PL	BD	BR	GTF	SV	LV	SH	TC	BC	ST	SBF	RA	HA	SP	HC	mAP
RepPoints [9]	86.78	59.60	35.60	44.14	70.25	51.73	71.27	90.18	69.11	82.75	50.92	57.56	49.05	56.12	12.83	59.19
SASM [21]	86.17	63.67	**47.05**	69.13	72.58	72.94	79.03	90.85	75.58	84.15	48.98	60.72	63.81	58.91	32.32	67.06
RetinaNet [7]	89.21	77.64	40.36	65.85	77.94	63.50	77.73	90.90	82.83	82.43	58.95	62.27	55.70	65.81	41.77	68.86
CSL [14]	**89.62**	80.74	39.61	68.37	76.81	62.26	77.66	90.87	82.31	82.70	58.27	62.57	56.14	63.65	41.55	68.87
KLD [16]	89.60	79.37	38.96	69.94	77.98	65.35	**82.15**	90.89	81.44	81.95	59.48	**63.55**	58.42	68.20	43.18	70.03
R3Det [13]	89.18	75.95	46.03	70.13	76.15	**73.54**	79.29	90.90	77.69	**84.35**	58.44	63.38	**64.47**	62.97	38.90	70.09
GWD [15]	89.42	79.32	41.47	71.60	78.20	65.21	81.96	**90.90**	83.10	82.07	55.16	62.99	59.12	65.48	**45.89**	70.12
FFE-Net (Ours)	89.34	**81.92**	41.71	**72.60**	**78.78**	65.76	77.99	90.89	**85.84**	82.30	**60.28**	62.25	58.54	**68.52**	45.14	**70.79**

Results on DOTA-v1.0 [1]: The results of FFE-Net and other comparison algorithms are shown in Table 2. Compared to some of the current popular detectors, including RepPoints [9], SASM [21], RetinaNet [7], CSL [14], KLD [16], R3Det [13], and GWD [15], it can be observed that FFE-Net achieves a mAP of 70.79%, with improvements of 11.60%, 3.73%, 1.93%, 1.92%, 0.76%, 0.70%, and 0.67%, achieving a better performance. At the same time, we can notice that the FFE-Net algorithm achieves the best detection performance on six classes of targets, namely BD, GTF, SV, BC, SBF, and SP, in comparison with other algorithms. These six classes of targets share certain characteristics, such as having aspect ratios that are generally not very large, and the targets occupying almost the entire area within the ground-truth box. We attribute this phenomenon to the FFEM's capacity to extract these foreground features and employ them for enhancement, thereby effectively boosting the detection performance of these target classes.

Table 3. Detection performance on the HRSC2016 dataset

Method	RepPoints [9]	CSL [14]	RetinaNet [7]
AP50	69.90	83.30	83.80
Method	GWD [15]	FFE-Net (Ours)	KLD [16]
AP50	84.40	85.10	85.40

Fig. 5. Detection results of the proposed FFE-Net on the DOTA-v1.0 data set.

Results on HRSC2016 [2]: As shown in Table 3, the FFE-Net demonstrated competitive performance compared to other algorithms, achieving 85.10% on the VOC2007 AP50 metric while improving 1.30% on the baseline algorithm RetinaNet [7]. Compared to advanced algorithms such as RepPoints [9], CSL [14], GWD [15] and KLD [16], the difference is 15.20%, 1.80%, 0.70% and -0.30% respectively. Since the target objects in the HRSC2016 [2] dataset are all ships, their aspect ratios are usually large, and the larger aspect ratios lead to a wider distribution of the Gaussian weighting function, which results in a smaller weighting of the target edges. However, in reality, only a very small part of the region encompassed by the ground-truth box of the ship's target is background noise, and the vast majority of the region is foreground target. In this case, the MGFFL resulted in some parts that would have been foreground target regions also being assigned smaller weights. Therefore, we believe that this may be the reason for the mediocre results of the FFE-Net algorithm on the HRSC2016 [2] dataset.

From the experimental results on the DOTA-v1.0 and HRSC2016 datasets, it can be concluded that the improvement of FFE-Net is simple and effective, achieving better results on the seven categories in the DOTA-v1.0 dataset. Figure 5 shows the visual detection results of FFE-Net on the DOTA-v1.0 dataset, where we use different coloured borders to indicate the different categories and provide the corresponding category labels in the centre of the borders. It can be seen that FFE-Net can effectively detect different classes or the same class of objects at different scales.

4   Conclusion

In this paper, our proposed FFE-Net is used to improve the remote sensing object detection by introducing semantic segmentation branches. We add semantic segmentation branches to each head network to learn the objective foreground features, and embed the foreground features in the classification and regression branches while learning the objective foreground features through the FFEM. To avoid the additional background noise introduced by soft labels, we also improve the traditional focal loss by MGFFL to make the foreground features learned by the semantic segmentation branch more robust. To verify the effectiveness of FFE-Net, we conducted a series of experiments on the DOTA-v1.0 and HRSC2016 datasets, which proved that the improvement of FFE-Net is simple and effective. In future work, we will continue to explore foreground and background features for oriented object detection in RSIs as a way to obtain superior detection results.

Acknowledgements. This work is partially supported by National Science Foundation of China (61972187), Natural Science Foundation of Fujian Province (2020J01828, 2020J02024, 2022J011112, 2020J01826), Fuzhou Science and Technology Major Project (2022FZZD0112), Fuzhou Technology Planning Program (2021-ZD-284), and the Open Program of The Key Laboratory of Cognitive Computing and Intelligent Information Processing of Fujian Education Institutions, Wuyi University (KLCCIIP2020202).

References

1. Xia, G.S., et al.: DOTA: a large-scale dataset for object detection in aerial images. In: Proceedings of the IEEE Conference on Computer Vision and Pattern Recognition, pp. 3974–3983 (2018)

2. Liu, Z., Yuan, L., Weng, L., Yang, Y.: A high resolution optical satellite image dataset for ship recognition and some new baselines. In: ICPRAM, pp. 324–331 (2017)
3. Lin, T.-Y., et al.: Microsoft COCO: common objects in context. In: Fleet, D., Pajdla, T., Schiele, B., Tuytelaars, T. (eds.) ECCV 2014. LNCS, vol. 8693, pp. 740–755. Springer, Cham (2014). https://doi.org/10.1007/978-3-319-10602-1_48
4. Krizhevsky, A., Sutskever, I., Hinton, G.E.: ImageNet classification with deep convolutional neural networks. Commun. ACM **60**(6), 84–90 (2017)
5. He, K., Zhang, X., Ren, S., Sun, J.: Deep residual learning for image recognition. In: Proceedings of the IEEE Conference on Computer Vision and Pattern Recognition, pp. 770–778 (2016)
6. Lin, T.Y., Dollár, P., Girshick, R., He, K., Hariharan, B., Belongie, S.: Feature pyramid networks for object detection. In: Proceedings of the IEEE Conference on Computer Vision and Pattern Recognition, pp. 2117–2125 (2017)
7. Lin, T.Y., Goyal, P., Girshick, R., He, K., Dollár, P.: Focal loss for dense object detection. In: Proceedings of the IEEE International Conference on Computer Vision, pp. 2980–2988 (2017)
8. Girshick, R.: Fast R-CNN. In: Proceedings of the IEEE International Conference on Computer Vision, pp. 1440–1448 (2015)
9. Yang, Z., Liu, S., Hu, H., Wang, L., Lin, S.: RepPoints: point set representation for object detection. In: Proceedings of the IEEE/CVF International Conference on Computer Vision, pp. 9657–9666 (2019)
10. He, K., Gkioxari, G., Dollár, P., Girshick, R.: Mask R-CNN. In: Proceedings of the IEEE International Conference on Computer Vision, pp. 2961–2969 (2017)
11. Chen, Y., Zhang, Z., Cao, Y., Wang, L., Lin, S., Hu, H.: RepPoints v2: verification meets regression for object detection. Adv. Neural. Inf. Process. Syst. **33**, 5621–5631 (2020)
12. Zhou, Y., et al.: MMRotate: a rotated object detection benchmark using PyTorch. In: Proceedings of the 30th ACM International Conference on Multimedia, pp. 7331–7334 (2022)
13. Yang, X., Yan, J., Feng, Z., He, T.: R3Det: refined single-stage detector with feature refinement for rotating object. In: Proceedings of the AAAI Conference on Artificial Intelligence, vol. 35, pp. 3163–3171 (2021)
14. Yang, X., Yan, J.: Arbitrary-oriented object detection with circular smooth label. In: Vedaldi, A., Bischof, H., Brox, T., Frahm, J.-M. (eds.) ECCV 2020. LNCS, vol. 12353, pp. 677–694. Springer, Cham (2020). https://doi.org/10.1007/978-3-030-58598-3_40
15. Yang, X., Yan, J., Ming, Q., Wang, W., Zhang, X., Tian, Q.: Rethinking rotated object detection with Gaussian Wasserstein distance loss. In: International Conference on Machine Learning, pp. 11830–11841. PMLR (2021)
16. Yang, X., et al.: Learning high-precision bounding box for rotated object detection via Kullback-Leibler divergence. Adv. Neural. Inf. Process. Syst. **34**, 18381–18394 (2021)
17. Wang, J., Ding, J., Guo, H., Cheng, W., Pan, T., Yang, W.: Mask OBB: a semantic attention-based mask oriented bounding box representation for multi-category object detection in aerial images. Remote Sens. **11**(24), 2930 (2019)
18. Xu, C., Li, C., Cui, Z., Zhang, T., Yang, J.: Hierarchical semantic propagation for object detection in remote sensing imagery. IEEE Trans. Geosci. Remote Sens. **58**(6), 4353–4364 (2020)

19. Liu, S., Zhang, L., Lu, H., He, Y.: Center-boundary dual attention for oriented object detection in remote sensing images. IEEE Trans. Geosci. Remote Sens. **60**, 1–14 (2021)
20. Deng, J., Dong, W., Socher, R., Li, L.J., Li, K., Fei-Fei, L.: ImageNet: a large-scale hierarchical image database. In: 2009 IEEE Conference on Computer Vision and Pattern Recognition, pp. 248–255 (2009)
21. Hou, L., Lu, K., Xue, J., Li, Y.: Shape-adaptive selection and measurement for oriented object detection. In: Proceedings of the AAAI Conference on Artificial Intelligence, vol. 36, pp. 923–932 (2022)

Visitors Vis: Interactive Mining of Suspected Medical Insurance Fraud Groups

Rixin Dong[1,2,3,4,5,6,7], Hanlin Liu[1], Xu Guo[1,2,3,4,5,6,7], and Jiantao Zhou[1,2,3,4,5,6,7](✉)

[1] College of Computer Science, Inner Mongolia University, Hohhot, China
cszjtao@imu.edu.cn
[2] National and Local Joint Engineering Research Center of Intelligent Information Processing Technology for Mongolia, Hohhot, China
[3] Engineering Research Center of Ecological Big Data, Ministry of Education, Hohhot, China
[4] Inner Mongolia Engineering Laboratory for Cloud Computing and Service Software, Hohhot, China
[5] Inner Mongolia Key Laboratory of Social Computing and Data Processing, Hohhot, China
[6] Inner Mongolia Key Laboratory of Discipline Inspection and Supervision Big Data, Hohhot, China
[7] Inner Mongolia Engineering Laboratory for Big Data Analysis Technology, Hohhot, China

Abstract. As medical insurance continues to grow in size, the losses caused by medical insurance fraud cannot be underestimated. Current data mining and predictive techniques have been applied to analyze and explore the health insurance fraud population. However, previous studies only provide summary results and do not show the details of comparative analysis during the visit, resulting in the inability of auditors to quickly identify anomalous behavior. In this paper, we propose a visual analytics system for interactive medical insurance fraud detection to support the exploration and interpretation of different access processes. We propose a weighted MinDL to improve the accuracy of visit pattern classification in the time-series modeling process, and design a data analysis model and visual analysis view based on medical insurance fraud characteristics to reveal and explore the characteristics of medical insurance fraud groups. We collaborate with related organizations to design and implement an interactive visualization for medical insurance fraud group detection using real Medicare data and expert interviews The system is effective and practical in detecting and analyzing medical insurance fraud syndicates.

Keywords: Visual Analytics · Health Insurance Fraud · Anomaly detection · Multidimensional data

1 Introduction

Medical insurance fraud is the fraudulent insurance compensation through insurance or fictitious and exaggerated insurance injuries.

Over the past decade, as the scale of medical insurance has grown, the problem of medical insurance fraud has become more serious. According to an estimate, approximately 17 billion to 57 billion funds were misutilized via healthcare frauds under the

Y. Sun et al. (Eds.): ChineseCSCW 2023, CCIS 2012, pp. 479–490, 2024.
https://doi.org/10.1007/978-981-99-9637-7_35

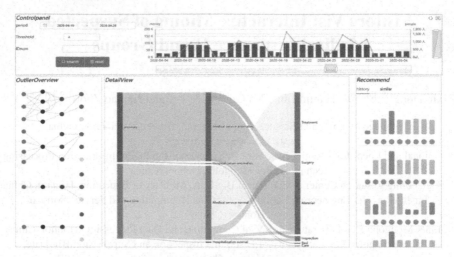

Fig. 1. Visitors Vis system diagram

healthcare-supported scheme discussed by [1]. Therefore, effective mining of fraud cases and tapping into fraudulent groups is essential for reducing economic losses and social harmony. Therefore, Effective mining of fraud cases and tapping into fraudulent groups is important for reducing economic losses and social harmony Fig. 1.

Medical insurance data is characterized by high data latitude, high data volume, and complex correlations, particularly when exploring medical insurance fraud groups, which are complicated by the reliance on interlinking the discovery of medical insurance fraud groups with the attribute analysis of medical insurance data and the process of access. Existing mining methods include processing rules [2] and data comparison [3]. These methods have achieved concrete results, but are limited in many ways due to the single existing fraud model, including the inability to detect common characteristics of offenders and inefficiency. In addition, some scholars have proposed the use of data mining and machine learning methods, but the small proportion of medical insurance data that is fraudulent and is part of an unbalanced sample distribution leads to problems with machine learning methods such as high false positive rates and poor interpretability. Thirdly, there is a lack of visual interaction. Medical insurance auditors can only process and manually analyze data through simple statistical functions provided by existing systems, which can be time-consuming and slow to retrieve.

To address the first challenge, we used a temporal modeling approach to reduce the complexity of exploring medical insurance fraud syndicates by modeling the complete visit process of the attendee as temporal data, we propose a weighted MinDL algorithm to classify different visit patterns using the principle of minimum description length, which is experimentally proven to be more accurate than existing clustering algorithms. To address the remaining challenges, we use multiple logic models to detect and explore Medicare fraud groups and visual analytics to visualize the types of anomalies in attendee and visit processes to improve the interpretability of anomaly detection. The interactive visual analytics system enables medical insurance auditors to understand and manipulate medical insurance data based on their own experience and domain knowledge, allowing them to determine the presence of medical insurance fraud directly in the system and to identify more similar groups of medical fraud for a single medical insurance fraudster. The efficiency of medical insurance auditors has been greatly improved.

2 Related Work

In this section, we summarise the techniques most relevant to our work, including insurance fraud detection methods and health insurance fraud visualization techniques.

2.1 Insurance Fraud Detection Methods

In previous anomaly detection studies for datasets that already have labels, researchers have tended to favor machine learning methods to train anomaly detection models. Francis et al. Proposed an improved support vector machine (svm) approach to detect health insurance fraud using a new standardized approach for health insurance billing records [4]. Wilson et al. Proposed the use of logistic regression as a statistical tool to help identify fraudulent claims [8]. Garta proposed a novel data intelligence technique based on multiple consensus models to maximize the effectiveness of the model in detecting fraudulent transactions [17]. Liu proposed a new lstm-based approach and applied it to fraud detection in telecommunication datasets [18].

Yet most of the data on health insurance fraud is in a situation where labels are missing. So there are some researchers who use data mining methods to detect anomalies. Kumar et al. [5] used data mining techniques for predicting and Johnson et al. [6] proposed a multi-stage approach to detecting fraud between providers and patients, ultimately comparing risk values with risk thresholds to determine the presence of fraud. Applied this method to tax fraud detection. They used Badrank to assign information about known entities in the network and predict the probability that the entity is a fraudster. This probability will be used as an attribute in the clustering to participate in the clustering process. Batal et al. [9] proposed a temporal pattern mining framework for detecting anomalous events in complex multivariate time series. Shin et al. [11] et al. proposed a scoring model which is based on extracting from insurance claims Phua et al.[12] used a combination of back-propagation, plain Bayesian, and C4.5 algorithms to select the best combination of classifiers for data with unbalanced data distribution using a single meta-classifier. Liu et al. [13] proposed a temporal skeletonization approach to reduce the representation of sequences to discover important hidden temporal structures. Yangchang et al. [15] proposed a fraud detection method using the SSIsomap activity clustering method. Jurgovsky et al. [16] utilized the concept of sequence classification to detect credit card fraud.

Some scholars have studied the network topology between doctors and patients, and evidence of possible medical insurance fraud can be obtained from the process of doctor-patient interaction. Jamshid et al. [7] proposed a data enrichment scheme that focuses on the use of social network analysis to help detect systems that provide information hidden in the relationships between entities and is used to broaden the application scenario of classical anomaly detection methods. Liu [10] et al. proposed the concept of time graphs to capture medical event relationships in each time series, with significant improvement for anomalous event prediction. Lin [19] et al. proposed mining and exploring tax evasion populations using visual analytics for performing profit and topological data analysis using visual analytics.

2.2 Medical Insurance Fraud Visualization Techniques

However, The sheer volume of data to be processed for health care data analysis and the complexity of his relationships require highly specialized data processing techniques and visual analytics. Klimov et al. [20] propose the VISITORS system, which enables users to visualize raw data and abstract concepts from multiple patient records at multiple levels of temporal granularity, and to explore these concepts.

Toyoda et al. [21] proposed the use of multiple perspectives to understand overall cost expenditure, which allows interactive visualization of huge amounts of data from raw claims data to understand the analysis of overall healthcare expenditure and local healthcare expenditure with different focuses. Zhou et al. [22] proposed medicare vis, which supports the Spatio-temporal multi-perspective filtering of healthcare data and the analysis of fraud through different categories, different subjects of correlation analysis between frauds. Lv proposed [26] PEVis to identify seasonal variations in anomalies by aggregating different anomaly detection algorithms.

3 Background

As introduced in Sect. 1, our goal is to identify groups of people committing medical insurance fraud. Some core concepts about medical insurance fraud are presented below to help understand the context. Medical insurance fraud falls into the following broad categories.

Service upgrade: The service upgrade is coded as a more expensive reimbursement for the service than the actual process completed. For example, A 30-min service is coded as a 60-min service.

Duplicate claims: Instead of submitting the same bill, a small part, such as the date, is changed to charge the same service twice for the insurance. For example: Instead of submitting an exact copy of the original claim a second time, certain parts, such as the date, are changed in order to receive twice the benefit of the original claim.

4 Requirement Analysis

We conducted a series of structured face-to-face interviews and teleconferences with experts in the field. We focused on three aspects of medical insurance fraud detection: 1) What are the standard practices and their processes for detecting and analyzing medical insurance fraud? 2) What are the main challenges and limitations of current methods for finding and investigating medical insurance fraud groups? 3) What design requirements and tasks are they trying to achieve?

We summarised the expert opinions, further designed a list of requirements, and finally proposed the design of Visitors Vis.

R1 Enable interactive systems to detect suspected fraudulent groups. Different users can quickly find suspected fraud situations of interest based on domain knowledge and experience and configure different parameters to adjust the scope of the suspected group.

R2 Using the computing power of machines to provide data to support users' decisions. Due to a large number of insured persons, it is vital to help users quickly locate suspicious groups. The system should give data support that is difficult for the user to detect directly as they use it.

R3 Support the interactive exploration of people and their attributes who attend medical appointments in similar cases of suspected fraud. In the mining process, we often find a suspected fraudster, and we can perform similarity coding to reflect the suspected fraudster's similar medical population to improve the efficiency of detecting similar fraudulent people.

5 System Design

We propose an interactive medical insurance fraud detection system, Visitors Vis, to help disciplinary officers explore and identify suspected fraudsters. As shown in Fig. 2, the system is divided into three main modules: the data pre-processing module, the data analysis module, and the visual analysis module.

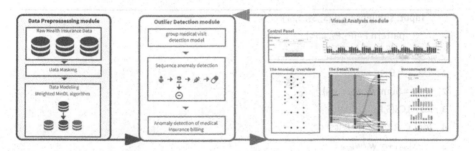

Fig. 2. Visitors Vis Architecture Overview Diagram

The data pre-processing module performs data masking and data modeling. The purpose of data modeling is to stitch together the insured's visit status and billing information into a time series of data to facilitate the understanding and analysis of their data by the relevant personnel. We propose a weighted MinDL algorithm to classify different visit patterns for the same condition and demonstrate its superiority over common clustering algorithms through experiments.

The data analysis module summarizes real fraud cases and investigates fraud groups using data mining techniques to filter out information on attenders with anomalies based on user-set parameters, combined with the user's domain knowledge and experience, to support the user's decision making.

The Visual Analysis module displays individuals of suspected fraud groups and the corresponding contextual detailed evidence through intuitive visualizations. He helps to facilitate the exploration and in-depth investigation of suspected fraudsters through these views.

5.1 Data Preprocessing Module

This module the raw data from collaborators as participant access process data.

Data modeling. Since the medical insurance data is modeled temporally, there are differences in length and sequence for each medical condition thus making anomaly detection more difficult. We propose to treat each visit as the smallest unit of anomaly detection. However, the method has certain drawbacks in the process of practical application. Since the treatment of certain diseases needs to be divided into multiple stages or multiple treatment strategies, which leads to different kinds of treatment modalities for the same disease, if the classification criteria of events are only based on the condition of disease, there will be detection errors brought about by different treatment strategies for the same disease. We introduced the MinDL algorithm [23], which uses the principle of shortest description length to describe each sequence in a two-part representation, i.e., the extracted pattern and the corrections needed to recover the original sequence. To solve the above problem, we correct the expenditure proportion of each visit sequence to the weight of the visit event. Finally, we can classify the different stages of the visit under the same condition name.

Algorithm 1 : Edits

    Input: sequence $S = \{S_1, S_2, ..., S_n\}$
          pattern $P = \{P_1, P_2, ..., P_k\}$
    Output: $\triangle L_{edit}$

1   $\triangle L_{edit} = 0$

2   $w_{total} = Sum(w_1, w_2, ..., w_n)$

3   $lcs = LCS(S, P)$

4   **for** $i \leftarrow 1$ to $len(S+P-lcs)$ **do**

5      $\triangle L_{edit} += w_i/w_{total}$

6   **return** $\triangle L_{edit}$

The weighted MinDL algorithm uses the MDL principle to extract patterns in event sequences. We therefore propose to introduce a new metric (Algorithm 1) to introduce the consumption of visit events to calculate the description cost to meet the analysis requirements.

To demonstrate that the weighted MinDL (WMDL) algorithm proposed in the paper can provide better classification results in the classification of actual visit patterns, we designed comparison experiments to compare WMDL, MinDL and the popular unsupervised classification algorithms nowadays for comparison (Table 1).

In the clustering algorithm, K-Means, GMM, DBSCAN, MinDL, and WMDL algorithms are tried and compared, and the best algorithm is selected for clustering the data.

In order to verify the accuracy of the clustering algorithm in real health insurance data more precisely, we processed a part of the disease data for manual classification

Table 1. Comparison table for evaluation of clustering algorithms

Algorithm	Purity	NMI
K-Means	0.7054	0.7129
GMM	0.8812	0.7938
DBSCAN	0.7918	0.7693
MinDL	0.8371	0.8022
WMDL	**0.8963**	**0.8312**

and conducted experimental evaluation of the above clustering algorithm using external evaluation indexes.

From the experimental results, we can clearly see that the Purity metric and NMI metric using WMDL outperform the mainstream clustering methods in the visit sequence clustering problem. So we choose the WMDL algorithm to classify the visit behavior of different treatment strategies for the same disease.

5.2   Data Analysis Module

Based on case communication and exchange of domain knowledge with relevant staff. The paper summarizes actual fraud cases and designs multi-angle anomaly detection methods for the drawbacks of existing anomaly detection methods.

Apriori-Based Group Medical Visit Detection Model

To detect group visits in medical insurance fraud, we need to find the visit patterns of multiple enrollees. If the visit sequences of a group of size C over a period of time all match the pattern $M = \{(t_a, h_a),...,(t_b, h_b)\}$, then these enrollees are suspected of group visit fraud. Specifically, in the time period $[t_a, t_b]$, if the group G contains C participants and each participant's visit sequence S contains the pattern M, then these participants are a visit group, where C is also called the support degree of the pattern.

Among them, in the frequent item set mining stage, relying on manual computation is very costly in case resources. In order to make the frequent items be mined faster, the paper introduces Apriori algorithm to mine frequent visits and describes the principle of Apriori algorithm and its specific implementation.

Sequence Anomaly Detection.

To our knowledge, many of the methods used to detect health insurance fraud look for suspected fraudsters in terms of the amount of health insurance reimbursement, but few researchers have looked at whether a particular service should exist. After mining, the consultation service can be divided into two categories: frequent sequences and rare sequences.

In this paper, we use the Prefixspan [24] algorithm to mine rare patterns in selected medical procedures. If the probability of occurrence of a rare pattern is below a set threshold, the pattern is deemed to be a suspected fraud.

Anomaly Detection of Medical Insurance Billing

As described in Sect. 3, most Medicare fraud problems manifest as service escalation, i.e., higher-than-average population expenditures.

In this paper, we use COPOD [25] for anomaly detection, which uses a nonparametric approach to obtain empirical covariance from the empirical cumulative distribution, after which the tail probability of the joint distribution of dimensions can be estimated from the empirical covariance.

5.3   The Visual Analysis

As shown in Fig. 1, the Visitors Vis interface consists of four main UI components: A) The Control Panel B) The Outlier Overview shows the suspected fraudsters that match the control panel parameters and explains the reasons for their anomalies C) The Detail View shows the complete visit of the selected suspected fraudster D) The Recommend View shows the topology of all insured persons in relation to the doctor.

Control Panel

Fig. 3. Control Panel

The control panel version (Fig. 3) consists of a parameter selector and a mixture of bar and line graphs. Fraudsters are explored by interactively setting analysis periods or relevant parameters. The bar and line graphs represent the temporal time distribution of the number of enrollees seeking medical treatment and the amount of insurance reimbursement in the original data respectively, a search space that the user can control with their domain knowledge and experience.

Outlier Overview

The exception overview view shows the visits that fit the scope of the control panel. Therefore, the thesis proposes to use a visualization method combining parallel coordinates + arcs to summarize the anomalous cases found by the platform, so that each sub-view represents a visit case as shown in Fig. 4:

In the application of medical insurance fraud exploration, for group visits, the module provides a clear picture of when suspected fraud groups appear together, where they visit,

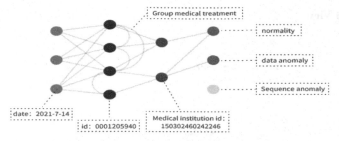

Fig. 4. Exception overview diagram module

and whether their visit data is abnormal. While observing a case, the user can highlight other attributes related to it by selecting the visit attribute of interest with the mouse, making it easier to highlight the characteristics of the selected attribute in the case.

Detail View

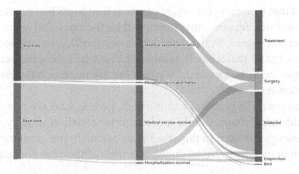

Fig. 5. Exception detail view module

In For the detailed display of anomalous visit behavior, the paper proposes to use the Sankey diagram to visualize the process of treatment as well as consumption details in the visit behavior of the attendee. As shown in Fig. 5, we divide the view into two categories for the purpose of interpretability for abnormal sequences and abnormal consumption, one is the process of abnormal attendee's visit behavior and the other is an "ideal" normal attendee's visit process simulated by retrieving the same attendee with the same strategy for the same disease using Gaussian mixture model. The process of consultation.

In addition, the view uses color coding to highlight the parts that appear abnormal. For example, green represents normal behavior, yellow represents abnormal behavior in an abnormal sequence, and red represents behavior with abnormal consumption values.

Rcommend View

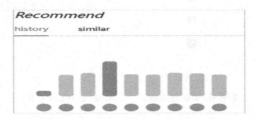

Fig. 6. Recommendation module

Considering the usefulness of the platform, it provides a view of similar abnormal group recommendations. As shown in Fig. 6, the module visualizes the visit events using parallel rectangles and circles.

In the process of using this feature, it is found that historical data retrieval has improved the detection of anomaly detection. In the detection of group medical anomalies, it was found that a certain percentage of group fraudsters had not had such diseases in their history, and this feature could improve the efficiency and accuracy of anomaly detection to a certain extent. In the detection of abnormal consumption and abnormal sequences, it was found that a small number of cases had the exact same visit occurring multiple times in the historical data, which greatly improved the credibility of such abnormal detection results.

In the second part, the platform recommends people who are similar or related to the selected fraudsters through a multi-angle recommendation strategy. The paper uses the concept of energy distance in this module to calculate the similarity to the current visit of the anomalous patient based on the specifics of the visit consumption and visit sequence.

Acknowledgments. This work is supported by the National Natural Science Foundation of China under Grant No.62162046, the Inner Mongolia Science and Technology Project under Grant No.2021GG0155, the Natural Science Foundation of Major Research Plan of Inner Mongolia under Grant No.2019ZD15, and the Inner Mongolia Natural Science Foundation under Grant No. 2019GG372.

References

1. Aldrich, N., Crowder, J., Benson, B.: How much does medicare lose due to fraud and improper payments each year?, Sentinel (2014)
2. Sithic, H.L.; Balasubramanian, T. Survey of insurance fraud detection using data mining techniques. arXiv2013, arXiv:1309.0806
3. V erma, A.; Taneja, A.; Arora, A.: Fraud detection and frequent pattern matching in insurance claims using data mining techniques. In: Proceedings of the 2017 Tenth International Conference on Contemporary Computing (IC3), Noida, India, 10–12 August 2017; pp. 1–7 (2017)

4. Francis, C.; Pepper, N.; Strong, H. Using support vector machines to detect medical fraud and abuse. In: Proceedings of the International Conference of the IEEE Engineering in Medicine & Biology Society , Boston, MA, USA, 30 August–3 September (2011)

5. Kumar, M., Ghani, R., Mei, Z.S.: Data mining to predict and prevent errors in health insurance claims processing. In: Proceedings of the 16th ACM International Conference on Knowledge Discovery and Data Mining. New York: ACM Press, 2010: 65–74 (2010)

6. Johnson, M.E., Nagarur, N.: Multi-stage methodology to detect health insurance claim fraud. Health Care Manag. Sci. **19**(3), 249–260 (2016)

7. Botelho, J., Antunes, C.: Combining social network analysis with semi-supervised clustering: a case study on fraud detection. In: Proceedings of Mining Data Semantics (MDS'2011)in Conjunction with SIGKDD (2011)

8. Jamshidi, S., Hashemi, M.R.: An efficient data enrichment scheme for fraud detection using social network analysis. In: Sixth International Symposium on Telecommunications (IST), (pp. 1082–1087). IEEE (2012)

9. Wilson, J.H.: An analytical approach to detecting insurance fraud using logistic regression. J. Finance Account. **1**, 1 (2009)

10. Batal, I., Fradkin, D., Harrison, J., Moerchen, F., Hauskrecht, M.: Miningrecent temporal patterns for event detection in multivariate time series data. In: Proceedings of the 18th ACM SIGKDD International Conference Knowledge Discovery DataMining (KDD), 2012, pp. 280–288 (2012)

11. Liu, C., Wang, F., Hu, J., Xiong, H.: "Temporal phenotyping from longitudinal electronic health records: A graph based framework. In: Proceedings of the 21th ACM SIGKDD Inernational Conference Knowledge Discovery Data Mining, pp. 705–714 (2015)

12. Shin, H., Park, H., Lee, J., et al.: A scoring model to detect abusive billing patterns in health insurance claims. Expert Syst. Appl. **39**(8), 7441–7450 (2012)

13. Phua, C., Alahakoon, D., Lee, V.: Minority report in fraud detection: classification of skewed data. ACM SIGKDD Explorations Newsl **6**(1), 50–59 (2004)

14. Liu, C., Zhang, K., Xiong, H., Jiang, G., Yang, Q.: 'Temporal skeletonization on sequential data: Patterns, categorization, and visualization.' IEEE Trans. Knowl. Data Eng. **28**(1), 211–223 (2016)

15. Yang, J., Liu, C., Teng, M., Xiong, H., Liao, M., Zhu, V.: Exploiting temporal and social factors for B2B marketing campaign recommendations. In: Proc. IEEE International Conference Data Mining, Nov. 2015, pp. 499–508 (2015)

16. Jurgovsky, J., et al.: Sequence classification for credit-card fraud detection','. Expert Syst. Appl. **100**, 234–245 (2018)

17. Carta, S., Fenu, G., Recupero, D.R., Saia, R.: Fraud detectionfor E-commerce transactions by employing a prudential multiple consensus model, J. Inf. Secur . Appl., vol. 46, pp. 13–22, Jun (2019)

18. Liu, G., Guo, J., Zuo, Y., Wu, J., Guo, R.-Y.: Fraud detection via behavioral sequence embedding. Knowl. Inf. Syst. **62**, 2685–2708 (2020)

19. Lin, Y., Wong, K., Wang, Y., et al.: Taxthemis: Interactive mining and exploration of suspicious tax evasion groups. IEEE Trans. Visual Comput. Graphics **27**(2), 849–859 (2020)

20. Klimov, D., Shahar, Y., Taieb-Maimon, M.: Intelligent visualization and exploration of time-oriented data of multiple patients. Artif. Intell. Med. **49**(1), 11–31 (2010)

21. Toyoda, S., Niki, N.: Visualization-based medical expenditure analysis support system. In: 2015 37th Annual International Conference of the IEEE Engineering in Medicine and Biology Society (EMBC). IEEE, 2015: 1600–1603 (2015)

22. Zhou,J., et al.: MedicareVis: a joint visual analysis method for health insurance anti-fraud. J. Comput.-Aided Design Graph. **33**(09), 1311–1317 (2021)

23. Chen, Y., Xu, P., Ren, L.: Sequence synopsis: Optimize visual summary of temporal event data. IEEE Trans. Visual Comput. Graphics **24**(1), 45–55 (2017)

24. Jian, P., Han, J., Mortazavi-Asl, B., et al.: PrefixSpan: mining sequential patterns efficiently by prefix-projected pattern growth. In: International Conference on Data Engineering. IEEE Computer Society (2001)
25. Li, Z., Zhao, Y., Botta, N., et al.: COPOD: copula-based outlier detection. In: 2020 IEEE International Conference on Data Mining (ICDM). IEEE, 2020: 1118–1123 (2020)
26. Lv, C., Ren, K., Zhang, H., et al.: PEVis: visual analytics of potential anomaly pattern evolution for temporal multivariate data. J. Visual. 1–17 (2021)

CERender: Real-Time Cloud Rendering Based on Cloud-Edge Collaboration

Ziqi He, Yuanyuan Yang, Zhanrong Li, Ningjiang Chen[✉], Anran Zhang, and Yanting Su

School of Computer and Electronic Information, Guangxi University, Nanning 530004, China
chnj@gxu.edu.cn

Abstract. With the maturity of cloud computing and the rise of edge computing, real-time cloud rendering technology has received widespread attention for its ability to solve the problem of low-power mobile devices. Cloud rendering still faces challenges in providing users with stable, high-quality and real-time interactive experiences due to the limitations of the network environment and the cost of computing resources. A cloud-edge collaborative rendering model is proposed in this paper, in order to reduce the computing resource burden on the edge side by using cloud-side computing power and reusing rendering computation results. At the same time, a set of dynamic update strategies is designed to address the high downstream bandwidth burden brought by the model. Finally, experiments show that the introduction of edge computing can significantly reduce network latency and interaction latency compared to cloud-centric solutions. At the same time, by introducing the NetGI component of cloud-edge co-rendering, the frame rate is increased by more than 20% in the scene of large multi-dynamic lighting sources compared with the pure edge-end rendering solution.

Keywords: Cloud Rendering · Edge Computing · Cloud-Edge Collaboration · Computing Resource Cost

1 Introduction

In recent years, users have become increasingly reliant on mobile devices. However, there is a conflict between the portable design of mobile devices and the quality and performance required for rendering [1]. Real-time cloud rendering aims to provide users with a more stable, higher quality, and better real-time interactive experience. Most real-time cloud rendering applications adopt a centralized model. However, centralized cloud computing is subject to network complexity, and it is challenging to guarantee the downstream bandwidth and interaction latency requirements of real-time cloud rendering with access by large-scale concurrent users [2]. Therefore, solving the problem of computing resource costs while enhancing user experience has become a new research direction. By relying on edge servers sinking to the user side and distributed network under the edge computing paradigm, it can effctly avoid the two biggest problems of real-time cloud rendering: latency and bandwidth. At the same time, edge computing

Y. Sun et al. (Eds.): ChineseCSCW 2023, CCIS 2012, pp. 491–501, 2024.
https://doi.org/10.1007/978-981-99-9637-7_36

also has better real-time and privacy. However, the hardware resources of edge nodes are extremely limited, and the cost of improving the hardware performance of edge nodes is too expensive due to the number of edge nodes. As a result, the hardware capability of edge servers has become a new bottleneck.

From the perspective of the rendering process, a real-time cloud rendering model for video streaming based on cloud-edge collaboration is proposed. By leveraging edge computing and reusing computing resources for common information, the latency of real-time cloud rendering systems and the cost of computing resources for edge servers are reduced. At the same time, the use of cloud GPU computing power reduces the burden on the edge side.

2 Related Work

Real-time cloud rendering of video streams has become a mainstream choice in the industry because it can maximize the liberation of clients and give full play to the advantages of cloud computing. In order to tackle problems related to user experience and computing resource expenses, many studies have considered methods such as adaptive bitrate [3, 4], video compression [5, 6]. Instance sharing technology [7, 8] has been widely applied in research aimed at solving computing resource cost problems due to its sharing and reuse properties. However, in previous research, multiple perspective rendering technology was used for GPU sharing. In real-time cloud rendering, users have vastly different viewing angles, and there are usually no reusable parts between multiple views.

ECACG [9] improves the multiplayer cloud gaming experience and operational costs by offloading game rendering tasks to nearby edge servers. Multi-Tier CloudVR [10] utilizes multi-access edge computing to improve the latency brought by remote rendering, enabling the interactive virtual reality experience based on cloud rendering. In addition, there are some studies to reduce the cost of computing resources through scheduling algorithms. Yao et al. [11] combine serverless computing with edge computing and propose a distributed function offloading method ES-DRL based on experience-sharing deep reinforcement learning. This approach can reduce the average latency by about 17%. Although these studies have improved the user experience of real-time cloud rendering systems to some extent, they have not provided better solutions to the cost problem of large-scale deployment of edge servers. Therefore, this paper will focus on solving the problem of computing resource costs. Cloud-edge collaboration and user instance sharing technologies are used to reduce the GPU computing power requirements for real-time cloud rendering by splitting the rendering process, thereby reducing the computing resource cost of edge server deployment.

3 The Framework

The real-time cloud rendering model CERender (Cloud-Edge Render) based on cloud-edge collaboration mainly consists of a cloud center server, multiple edge servers, and multiple clients connected to the edge servers. As shown in Fig. 1, CERender runs in a group of edge servers near the client end that are scheduled uniformly by the cloud central server.

The cloud center server is responsible for providing services and resource scheduling, rendering scene logical calculation, and maintain public rendering information. All relevant information of edge servers is stored in the server database, while user basic information, container images, and other related information are stored in the user information database. The edge server is mainly responsible for running cloud rendering instances and conducting peer-to-peer streaming transmission with users based on the WebRTC protocol. The decoding of audio and video streams and capture of the user's command input are the responsibility of the client. The scene instance serves the cloud rendering instance of all users in the scene, handles its state logic calculation and updates the rendering information according to the changes in the scene. In the communication model with the cloud, this article focuses on communication to obtain cloud indirect lighting rendering information. The update and distribution of rendering information are finished completely by the cloud, and the edge only needs to establish a network connection to the cloud to update the rendering information.

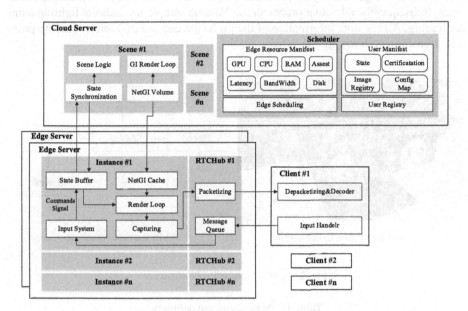

Fig. 1. The Framwork of CERender

4 Cloud-Edge Collaborative Rendering Process

This article splits incident lighting into direct and indirect lighting. As users are almost imperceptible to short-term delay in indirect lighting update, the indirect lighting with complicated calculation is offloaded to the cloud for computation. The direct lighting is completed by the edge server itself.

4.1 Rendering Process of Cloud Center Server

The cloud center server is mainly responsible for indirect lighting rendering calculations of the scene. Based on the DDGI [12], the NetGI indirect lighting component suitable for cloud-edge collaborative rendering is developed. The light probe is used to collect the light irradiance in the scene, and the depth information can be used to better solve the problem of light leakage of the probe. Additionally, the real effect can be approximated gradually through the inter-frame reuse of ray tracing information. Firstly, multiple NetGI Volumes with different priorities that cover the entire scenario are deployed in the initial scene by the cloud center server. Each Volume is a cubic region and containing light probes distributed in groups, as shown in Fig. 2(a). Each probe stores spherical irradiance information and depth information. Each Volume maintains a state matrix of a set of probes, which is used to store the logical index, world-space position, and active state of all probes. The cloud center sets different priorities for Volumes based on the user's activity range, and higher priorities assigned to Volumes around multiple online users. Subsequently, all active probes in the Volume sample the indirect lighting using ray tracing. All the state information of the probe are defined in Table 1, and the probe state transition is shown in Fig. 2(b).

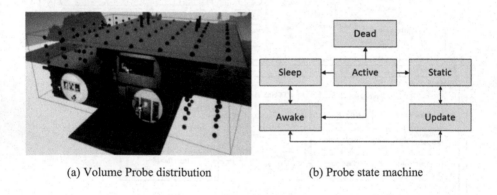

(a) Volume Probe distribution   (b) Probe state machine

Fig. 2. NetGI Volume Probe structure

Table 1. Probe status and definition

State name	Definition
Active	Creat probe
Dead	The probe is located inside the static object
Awake	There are movable dynamic meshes around the probe
Static	Only the static mesh volume is present around the probe
Sleep	The probe is in an open area, and there are no surrounding grids that can be cast by rays
Update	The cloud will update the probe texture to the edge end

4.2 Edge Server Rendering Process

The rendering instance runs in the edge server, which communicates at the same level as the user. Each rendering instance maintains a complete virtual world scene around the user and multiple Volume caches, while also maintaining communication with the cloud center for probe texture updates. When the instance is rendered, direct lighting is computed and combined with the cached indirect lighting texture in the volume for shading. The rendering model used in this paper is:

$$L_0(p, \vec{w}_0) = \int_\Omega K_d \frac{c}{\pi} L_i(p, \vec{w}_i)(\vec{w}_i \cdot \vec{n}_p)d\vec{w}_i + \int_\Omega K_S \frac{DFG}{4(\vec{w}_0 \cdot \vec{n})(\vec{w}_i \cdot \vec{n})} L_i(p, \vec{w}_i)(\vec{w}_i \cdot \vec{n}_p)d\vec{w}_i \quad (1)$$

where $\vec{w}_0$ represents the viewing direction, $\vec{w}_i$ represents the incident direction, $\vec{n}_p$ represents the surface point of p, $L_0(p, \vec{w}_0)$ represents the radiance reflected from point p to the viewing direction $\vec{w}_0$, k_d represents the diffuse component of the BRDF(Bidirectional Reflectance Distribution Function), k_s represents the specular component of the BRDF, and according to energy conservation: $k_d + k_s = 1$. $L_i(p, \vec{w}_i)$ is the radiance of the light received by point p in the incident direction. DFG represents the microfacet distribution function. This article splits incident lighting $L_i(p, \vec{w}_i)$ into direct lighting $L_{dir}(p, \vec{w}_i)$ and indirect lighting $L_{ind}(p, \vec{w}_i)$. Regarding the shading calculation results of the complex indirect lighting $L_r(p, \vec{w}_0)$:

$$L_r(p, \vec{w}_0) = (k_d \frac{c}{\pi}) \int_\Omega L_{ind}(p, \vec{w}_i)(\vec{w}_i \cdot \vec{n})d\vec{w}_i = k_d \frac{c}{\pi} E(\vec{n}_p) \quad (2)$$

For a point p surrounded by Volume, eight probes can always be found around it, and the approximate irradiance $E(\vec{n}_p)$ of point p can be obtained by interpolation based on the irradiance of the eight probes. The final rendering result is shown in Fig. 3.

(a) Direct lighting   (b) Direct lighting+ indirect lighting   (c) Final material effect

Fig. 3. Cloud-edge collaborative rendering results

4.3 Rendering Information Update Strategy

Although edge computing eliminates the bandwidth pressure on cloud center, the collaborative rendering model introduces additional bandwidth consumption. Accordingly, considering the magnitude of changes in different probes, this paper proposes an update strategy that can selectively update lighting probes at an appropriate frequency without affecting the lighting effect:

(1) The subscribed Volumes for the user will save the last probe texture sent to the edge for each non-Dead probe, and the initial value of the texture is set to all zeros.

(2) After the probe texture update described in Sect. 4.1, all non-Dead probes of the subscribed Volumes will perform an difference operation with the last probe texture sent to the edge that they have cached. When the difference value is higher than a certain threshold, the probe will be changed to an Update state. And the probe will no longer participate in the texture updates of ray tracing until the texture synchronization with the edge is completed.

(3) The probe in the Update state will put the updated information into the update queue of all subscribers. Then update the probe texture cache in (1), and exit the Update state.

(4) The cloud server maintains a Volume subscription system for each user, which includes multiple Volume indexes around the user and an update queue. It is defined in the scheduling database of the cloud server and the queue length depends on the network state of the edge server. The cloud server distributes the updated information to each edge server based on the update queue.

5 Experiments and Evaluation

5.1 Experimental Design

This paper uses Unreal Engine 4.27. The client and edge servers are located in two different NAT networks, with a network latency of around 1–2 ms and a bandwidth of 100 mbps. The cloud center server sends scene indirect lighting update information to the edge server from time to time. Maintain a network delay of about 30-50ms with the edge server through delay injection, with a bandwidth of 100Mbps. The edge server synchronizes user state frames with the cloud server based on state synchronization technology. The ICE (Interactive Connectivity Establishment) server is mainly used for NAT traversal between the client and edge servers. The Web Server provides HTTP web page services to clients, and clients access web resources through a browser to access the Web Server. The specific parameters of all servers are shown in Table 2.

To fully test the cloud-edge collaborative rendering model, five scene instances are constructed, including two indoor scenes and three outdoor scenes,. The basic information of all scenes is shown in Table 3. The classroom scene represents a more complex indoor scene with high-precision models and high-resolution textures. The room scene, on the other hand, represents a typical indoor scene with similar Volume and and probe deployments as the classroom scene. In the outdoor scenes, the building scene aims to test the rendering performance under multiple Volumes, while the relic scene explores the impact of multiple dynamic light sources on the system performance.. And the town scene tests system performance in a complex outdoor scene with ultra-high-precision models. Finally, the performance of the system is tested in complex outdoor environments with ultra-high-precision models, such as urban scenes.

Two sets of comparative tests are designed to evaluate the performance of the proposed real-time cloud rendering system. The first set of tests compared the cloud-edge collaborative rendering model with the Unreal official pixel streaming real-time cloud rendering solution deployed in the cloud center. The second set of tests compared the

Table 2. Server configuration

Node	CPU	GPU	RAM	System
Cloud Server	AMD Ryzen 3700X 8-Core Processor 3.6GHZ	NVIDIA GeForce RTX 3070	48 GB	Windows 10
Edge Server	AMD Ryzen 3700X 8-Core Processor 3.6GHZ	NVIDIA GeForce RTX 2070	32 GB	Windows 10
ICE Server	Intel Xeon Cascade Lake 2-Core vcpu 2.5GHZ	/	4 GB	Ubuntu Server 18.04.1 LTS
Web Server	Intel Xeon CPU E5620 8-Core vcpu 2.4GHz	/	16 GB	CentOS 7

NetGI solution of cloud-edge collaboration with the DDGI solution of pure edge rendering. All two sets of experiments were conducted under equivalent hardware conditions. And tests the optimization capabilities of the real-time cloud rendering system in terms of latency, FPS, and bandwidth.

Table 3. Scenario information

Scene	Average number of facets	Average draw call	Number of dynamic light	Volume number	Number of probes/Volume	Number of rays/probe	Total asset size
Classroom	449316	743	2	1	16 * 16 * 8	576	1.97 GB
Room	169025	387	2	1	8 * 8 * 8	288	248 MB
Building	553286	2560	2	9	16 * 16 * 8	720	354 MB
Relic	342705	510	10	2	8 * 16 * 8	576	542 MB
Town	80410040	2973	3	3	16 * 16 * 8	288	11 GB

5.2 Interpretation of Results

Figure 4(a) shows the total interaction latency data within one minute for both the CERender system deployed on the edge server and the Pixel Streaming system deployed in the cloud center. The client records the latency data with the server every second and calculates a weighted average over 10-s intervals. Figure 4(b) shows the latency distribution map within one minute. It is evident that the real-time cloud rendering system based on edge deployment reduces the interaction latency by about 50% compared to the rendering solution based on cloud center deployment. This proves that introducing edge computing can successfully reduce the interaction latency to below 100ms, thereby achieving the real-time interaction requirements of real-time cloud rendering. Furthermore, the distribution statistics chart indicates that the main cause of latency in the traditional center-based deployment scheme is network latency, which can be reduced to several milliseconds by edge computing. However, the client's processing latency a new bottleneck of latency.

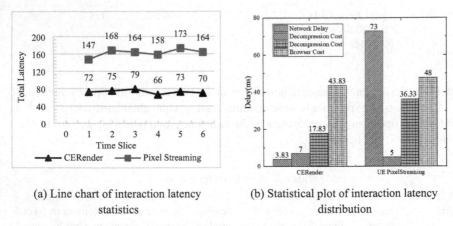

(a) Line chart of interaction latency
statistics

(b) Statistical plot of interaction latency
distribution

Fig. 4. Comparison of latency

Figure 5 shows the FPS data comparison between the CERender instance based on NetGI and the pixel streaming instance based on DDGI launched on the edge server in the five scenes. It can be observed that the FPS improvement is most significant in scenes with multiple Volumes and multiple light sources, such as the building and relic scenes, with a framerate increase of about 25%. The building scene has multiple non-overlapping Volumes covering all areas, and the relic scene has a directional light, a skylight, four spotlights, and four point lights set within the viewing range, which may be the reason for the significant FPS improvement. Indicating that the cloud-edge collaborative rendering model proposed in this paper is more suitable for larger-scale multiplayer online virtual scenes with multiple light sources.

In the complex outdoor scene, i.e., the town scene, although there is an FPS improvement, the degree of improvement is relatively small compared to the above two outdoor scenes. This is likely due to high-precision face rendering and soft shadow calculations becoming the new computational bottleneck. In the indoor scenes, the relatively simple room scene has a certain FPS improvement, while the FPS of the classroom scene almost does not improve, which may be attributed to the overly complex soft shadow calculations and reflection probes in the classroom scene.

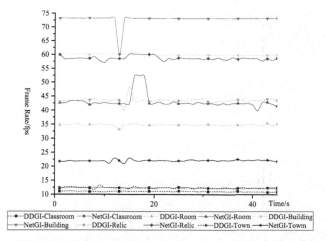

Fig. 5. Statistical plot of frame rate for single client access

Figure 6 and Fig. 7 show the FPS data comparison between multiple CERender instances based on NetGI and multiple pixel streaming instances based on DDGI launched on the edge server in the five scenes. It can be found that the FPS improvement is more significant in the building and relic scenes compared to Fig. 5. This further proves that the cloud-edge collaborative rendering model proposed in this paper can effectively reduce rendering computation consumption in large scenes and multiple light source environments. At the same time, in the room and town scenes, the FPS has also been improved to some extent. This demonstrates that when rendering computations other than indirect lighting calculations become the rendering bottleneck, the cloud-edge collaborative rendering approach can still reduce rendering computation consumption to some extent.

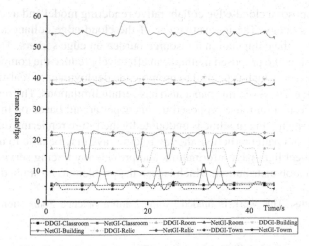

Fig. 6. Statistical plot of frame rate of dual client access

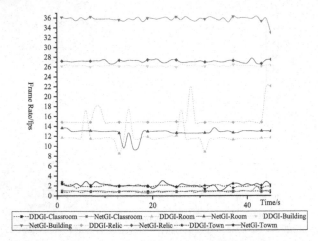

Fig. 7. Statistical plot of frame rate accessed by three clients

In brief, the above series of experiments fully validate the effectiveness of the cloud-edge collaborative real-time cloud rendering model proposed in this paper. By introducing edge computing, it reduces a lot of network latency and interaction latency compared to the cloud center solution. Compared to a pure edge-based rendering approach, introducing the NetGI component led to a frame rate improvement of over 20% in large, dynamic, multi-light source scenes, which also means that the GPU computational power consumption is reduced by over 20% at the same frame rate. The fluctuation depends on the specific scene and number of user accesses.

6   Conclusion

This article proposes a cloud-edge collaborative rendering model and a rendering information update strategy. The innovative use of the cloud-edge collaborative rendering approach reduces the computational resource burden on edge servers. Through experimental verification, the proposed method can effectively reduce the computing resource cost of edge servers, which is helpful to promote the deployment of real-time cloud rendering at the edge. However, this paper also has certain limitations. The rendering model and lighting information reuse proposed in this paper are all based on the rasterization pipeline, while ray tracing pipeline is undoubtedly the future rendering direction. Based on path tracing and path prediction, the ray tracing rays may be able to use the probe's approach to collect light path information, and provide ray tracing services to the edge through information distribution, which is also the problem to be studied in the future.

Acknowledgments. This work is funded by the Natural Science Foundation of China (No. 62162003).

References

1. Dong, Y., Peng C.: Multi-GPU multi-display rendering of extremely large 3D environments. Vis. Comput., 1–17 (2022)
2. Sadeeq, M., Abdulkareem, N., Zeebaree, S., et al.: IoT and cloud computing issues, challenges and opportunities: a review. Qubahan Acad. J. 1(2), 1–7 (2021)
3. Huang, T., Sun, L.: Deepmpc: a mixture abr approach via deep learning and Mpc. In: 2020 IEEE International Conference on Image Processing, pp. 1231–1235 (2020)
4. Chen, H., Lu, M., Ma, Z., et al.: Learned resolution scaling powered gaming-as-a-service at scale. IEEE Trans. Multimedia 23, 584–596 (2020)
5. Mossad, O., Diab, K., Amer, I., et al. DeepGame: efficient video encoding for cloud gaming. In: Proceedings of the 29th ACM International Conference on Multimedia, Chengdu, China, pp. 1387–1395 (2021)
6. Illahi, G., Gemert, T., Siekkinen, M., et al.: Cloud gaming with foveated video encoding. ACM Trans. Multimed. Comput. Commun. Appl. 16(1), 1–24 (2020)
7. Bhojan, A., Ng, S., Ng, J., et al.: CloudyGame: enabling cloud gaming on the edge with dynamic asset streaming and shared game instances. Multimedia Tools Appli. 79(43), 32503–32523 (2020)
8. Li, L., Yang, B., Bao, C., et al.: DroidCloud: scalable high density AndroidTM cloud rendering In: Proceedings of the 28th ACM International Conference on Multimedia, pp. 3348–3356 (2020)
9. Gao, Y., Zhang, C., Xie, Z., et al.: Cost-efficient and quality-of-experience-aware player request scheduling and rendering server allocation for edge-computing-assisted multiplayer cloud gaming. IEEE Internet Things J. 9(14), 12029–12040 (2021)
10. Mehrabi, A., Siekkinen, M., Kämäräinen, T., et al.: Multitier cloudvr: leveraging edge computing in remote rendered virtual reality. ACM Trans. Multimed. Comput. Commun. Appl. 17(2), 1–24 (2021)
11. Yao, X., Chen, N., Yuan, X., et al.: Performance optimization of serverless edge computing function offloading based on deep reinforcement learning. Fut. Generation Comput. Syst. 139, 74–86 (2023)
12. Majercik, Z., Guertin, J., Nowrouzezahrai, D., et al.: Dynamic diffuse global illumination with ray-traced irradiance fields. J. Comput. Graph. Tech. 8(2), 1–30 (2019)

Auxiliary Diagnosis of Pneumonia Based on Convolutional Attention and Parameter Migration

Jianfei Zhang[✉] and Bo Zhang

College of Computer and Control Engineering, Qiqihar University, Qiqihar, China
13079602468@163.com

Abstract. Traditional deep learning models have limited ability to extract features from pneumonia images. This study combines convolutional attention modules with transfer learning to improve the model's feature extraction ability and simplify training.This article has discovered an improved CBAM-Xception neural network pneumonia model. This network uses Xception as the main network, and combines with the convolutional attention CBAM module to enhance the expression of lesion information and suppress irrelevant information interference; At the same time, transfer learning is introduced to prevent over fitting when the sample data amount is small. In order to evaluate the effectiveness of the optimization model, experimental simulation tests were conducted on the Mendeley Data public pneumonia dataset. The improved model achieves 94.2% accuracy in classifying four images of COVID-19, bacterial pneumonia, viral pneumonia and normal chest on the test set, and the optimization effect is significant. In order to further verify the performance of this method, the experiment divided the small sample data set to train the model, and divided the large sample data to test the generalization performance of the model. The results show that the model in this paper has good generalization ability. This model can provide an important basis for the auxiliary diagnosis and treatment of pneumonia.

Keywords: pneumonia · CBAM · transfer learning · Xception

1 Introduction

Since the COVID-19 pandemic, the word pneumonia has gradually become active in public view.Pneumonia is prone to infection in children and the elderly with weak resistance, and the mortality rate is increasing. As of May 16, 2023, there were approximately 676.1 million COVID-19 [1] cases worldwide and approximately 6 million 880 thousand million deaths from COVID-19.

With the development of computer hardware performance, artificial diagnosis is no longer the only solution. Hospitals have brought computer-assisted diagnosis (CAD) [2] into clinical practice to facilitate doctors' reference and diagnosis. There are many different solutions for computer-aided diagnosis of pneumonia at home and abroad.Yuan Maozhou [3] used the LBP(Local Binary Pattern) algorithm and gray level co-occurrence matrix to extract the lung region features of the image, and the obtained features were recognized using a support vector machine classifier for the lung image. However, the new algorithm requires manual threshold setting, and the extracted lung features are similar. Yue Lu et al. [4] applied the decision tree algorithm to the data of 200 children with pneumonia, and finally achieved an accuracy rate of 80%. Jun et al. [5] used support vector machines [6] to classify two types of interstitial pneumonia, and compared with the recognition results of artificial pneumonia, the results showed a difference of only 5% to 6%. In the implementation scheme of pneumonia recognition, traditional algorithms have excellent performance, but with the gradual increase of data sets, the performance of traditional algorithms, both in terms of robustness and recognition efficiency, is unsatisfactory.

With the development of artificial intelligence and big data, artificial intelligence has been active in the field of disease image recognition as a new solution in recent years. Deep learning [7], as a popular solution in artificial intelligence, includes branch methods such as convolutional neural networks [8], and is gradually being applied to disease recognition. Zhou Qihao et al. [9] combined deep dense aggregation structure with DenseNet-201 and proposed a deep learning based classification network DLDA-A-DenseNet, which aggregates feature information from different stages and classifies the dataset provided by the China Chest CT Image Survey and Research Association. The recognition accuracy improved by 2.24% compared to the original DenseNet-201. Guo Yi et al. [10] used GhostNet lightweight network to simplify DenseNet network parameters, and classified the open COVID-19 dataset. Under the condition of ensuring the recognition accuracy of 83%, the medical computer took 236 ms. Khanun Roisatul Ummah et al. [11] evaluated Watershed segmentation, smoothing image method of Median and Gaussian filters, and other image preprocessing methods for automatic detection of new coronal pneumonia based on CT images. In order to further improve the classification accuracy of the model, scholars often increase the number of layers of the network. Although networks with more layers have improved classification accuracy, their parameters are far more than shallow networks, increasing the difficulty of model training and posing a serious challenge to computer performance. Therefore, this paper proposes a CBAM-Xception neural network that combines the convolutional attention CBAM [12] module with transfer learning [13]. Convolutional attention enhances the feature extraction ability of the model. Transfer learning is performed on the parameters trained in ImageNet [14] data, allowing the model to quickly fit the parameters, thereby reducing the burden of computer performance.

2 Model Selection and Improvement

2.1 Transfer Learning

During the actual data collection process, it is difficult to collect medical images of pneumonia due to patient privacy issues, as well as complex features of pneumonia lesions, varying sizes of lesions, and different manifestations of different lesions at different time points, making it difficult for pneumonia data to form a standard training database. However, using a small amount of data sets to train in the Xception network can result in model overfitting. Therefore, this article uses migration learning to pre train the model on the ImageNet dataset, and then migrate parameters with stronger general feature extraction capabilities to the Xception network. On this basis, the model is trained to improve the accuracy of model recognition and reduce the difficulty of computer training.

2.2 CBAM Module

Various types of pneumonia lesions vary in size at different stages and tend to concentrate in a single area. Allowing the model to assign more parameter weights to the lesion area will improve the recognition accuracy of the model. Therefore, this article introduces a CBAM module that integrates spatial attention and channel attention to improve the feature extraction ability of the model, extracting diverse lesion features in both spatial and channel aspects, and allocating more weight of model parameters to focus areas. The CBAM module structure is shown in Fig. 1. After combining the CBAM module with the Xception main network, the CBAM module extracts the focus features output from the Xception main network through both spatial and channel aspects, making the model focus on the focus area. The feature map output from the Xception main network is multiplied by the feature map output from the attention module to enhance the expression ability of features in the spatial channel dimension.

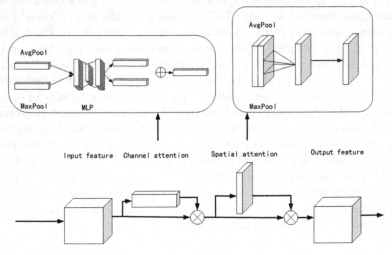

Fig. 1. CBAM module structure

2.3 CBAM Xception Transfer Learning Pneumonia Detection Model

This article proposes a convolutional attention neural network CBAM-Xception for pneumonia lesion recognition by introducing the CBAM module, and simplify the model training process through transfer learning. The CBAM-Xception model consists of an

Xception module, a CBAM module, and a fully connected layer module. The Xception module and CBAM module extract the features of the input pneumonia image and submit the extracted features to the classification module for classification. The model structure is shown in Fig. 2. The Xception feature extraction block contains deep separable convolutions. Deep separable convolution has a lower number of parameters than conventional convolution but shares the same feature extraction capability. The CBAM module includes channel attention modules and spatial attention modules. Better results can be achieved than an attentional mechanism that focuses only on the channel. The fully connected classification module and Softmax function classify the extracted features and output the confidence levels of four types of pneumonia labels.

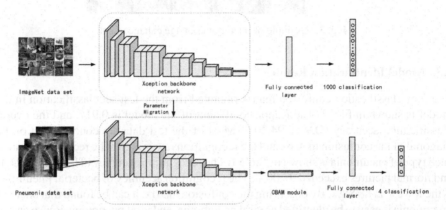

Fig. 2. CBAM Xception transfer learning pneumonia detection model structure

3 Experiment and Analysis

3.1 Data Set

The data used in this paper is the pneumonia dataset from Mendeley Data, and the images of bacterial pneumonia, viral pneumonia, COVID-19 and other pneumonia are taken as research objects. To prevent network overfitting, four data enhancement operations are performed on the original dataset, including random rotation angle, random horizontal flip, shear change angle, and horizontal offset. The image enhancement effect is shown in Fig. 3.

3.2 Experimental Setup

Divide the pneumonia image dataset into training, validation, and testing sets in a ratio of 8:1:1. The experiment was conducted under the Windows 10 operating system, with Python version 3 6. The version of Tensorflow is 2.2.0. The model is constructed using the TensorFlow deep learning framework. The parameter optimizer is a gradient descent function, and the average cross entropy is a loss function. Train 100 samples per training session.

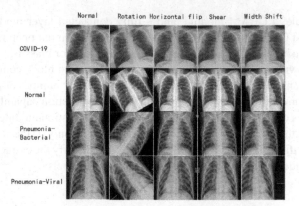

Fig. 3. Example of pneumonia image enhancement

3.3 Model Identification Results

The four classification confusion matrix obtained from the test set classification in this model is shown in Fig. 4. The Kappa coefficient of the model is 0.917, and the overall classification accuracy (OA) is 94.20%. Most of the test data are concentrated on the diagonal of the confusion matrix, and the recognition rate is high. The recognition rate of each type of pneumonia is shown in Table 1. The recognition accuracy of both COVID-19 and normal pictures exceeded 97.00%; The recognition accuracy of bacterial pneumonia is the lowest, at 88.88%. By observing the confusion matrix, it can be found that bacterial pneumonia is easy to be identified as viral pneumonia, and viral pneumonia is also easy to be mistakenly classified as bacterial pneumonia by the model. Based on the comparison of the dataset, it can be seen that there is a small difference between bacterial pneumonia and viral pneumonia, making it prone to classification errors.

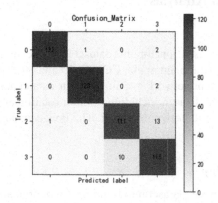

Fig. 4. Identification result confusion matrix

Table 1. The recognition rate of different schemes in each type of pneumonia image

Types of pneumonia	Xception training from zero		CBAM-Xception training from zero		CBAM-Xception transfer learning	
	Accuracy	Recall	Accuracy	Recall	Accuracy	Recall
COVID-19	0.960	0.902	0.952	0.983	0.976	0.992
Normal	0.952	0.856	1.000	0.850	0.984	0.992
Pneumonia-Bacterial	0.800	0.645	0.816	0.729	0.888	0.917
Pneumonia-Viral	0.400	0.685	0.536	0.728	0.920	0.871

3.4   Model Performance Evaluation.

Ablation Experiment.   The ablation experiment was used to verify the effect of CBAM module and transfer learning, and compare the effects of Xception from zero training, CBAM-Xception from zero training, and CBAM-Xception transfer learning. The results of the ablation experiment are shown in Table 2. The three methods used the same experimental environment and dataset, only changed the experimental comparison section. By comparing the accuracy, loss value, and recall of the three methods, the performance of the methods is determined. The training process of different methods on the pneumonia dataset is shown in Figs. 5.

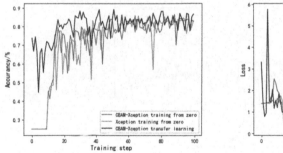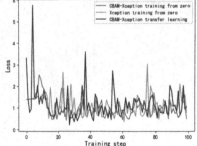

Fig. 5. Comparison between different schemes

In Fig. 5, it can be seen that the recognition accuracy of our method is superior to other methods. After adding transfer learning, the model achieves higher accuracy and lower loss value, and the model can converge quickly. After adding the CBAM attention module to the network, the classification accuracy improved by 4.8% (Table 2). Therefore, transfer learning and CBAM module effectively enhance the ability of the model to extract pneumonia features. The above experiments show that CBAM-Xception transfer learning method can improve the accuracy of pneumonia classification for pneumonia dataset.

Generalization Performance Verification.   On data with the same probability distribution, partitioning a small number of datasets to train the model and testing a large

Table 2. Comparison of experimental results

Model	Transfer learning	CBAM model	Accuracy/%
Xception training from zero			77.8
CBAM-Xception training from zero		✔	82.6
CBAM-Xception transfer learning	✔	✔	94.2

amount of data on the model can evaluate the generalization performance of the model. In this experiment, the training set and test set are exchanged, and the ratio between the training, validation set, and test set is 1:1:8. The transfer learning CBAM-Xception network model is trained with a training set with a small amount of data, and then the model is evaluated with a verification set and a test set with a large amount of data. The training process of model loss value and accuracy is shown in Fig. 6.

In Fig. 6, overfitting is normal because the number of training sets is too small. The accuracy rate has gradually converged, and the classification accuracy rate has reached about 70%. In the iteration interval from 0 to 20, the loss value also increases gradually due to overfitting of the model. The classification results of this model on the test set are shown in Table 3.

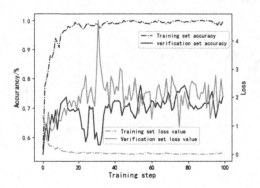

Fig. 6. Model generalization validation results

Table 3. Validation of pneumonia image classification results through generalization ability

Types of pneumonia	COVID-19	Normal	Pneumonia-Bacterial	Pneumonia-Viral	All pneumonia
Accuracy/%	96.7	81.8	39.2	81.5	74.8

In Table 3, it is found that the model has a strong generalization ability in COVID-19, reaching an accuracy rate of 96.7%, and surpasses the Xception model in the classification and recognition of bacterial pneumonia and viral pneumonia. The accuracy of the test set is 3% less than that of the Xception model, which indicates that the model in this paper has excellent generalization.

4 Conclusion

This paper proposes a scheme combining convolutional attention CBAM module and transfer learning. The accuracy of 94.2% was achieved on the Mendeley Data public pneumonia dataset, and the improved model has higher recognition rate and excellent generalization compared to the original Xception model, providing a certain reference for the auxiliary diagnosis and treatment of pneumonia. In future work, the number of training images for bacterial pneumonia and viral pneumonia should be increased to further improve the classification performance of the model. In summary, this article has clinical significance and practical value, providing a good research method and approach for the auxiliary diagnosis of pneumonia.

References

1. Johns Hopkins university. COVID-19 Dashboard by the Center for Systems Science and Engineering at Johns Hopkins University. (16 May 2022).https://coronavirus.jhu.edu/map.html
2. Shiraishi, J., Li, Q., Appelbaum, D., et al.: Computer-aided diagnosis and artificial intelligence in clinical omaging. Seminars Nuclear Med. **41**(6) (2011)
3. Maozhou, Y.: Research on feature extraction and classification of X-ray lung images. Dalian University of Technology (2019). DOI:https://doi.org/10.26991/d.cnki.gdllu.2019.003229
4. Yue, L., Ma, L., Wei, B.: Research on children Pneumonia Clinical Syndrome Classification model based on decision tree algorithm. Electronic Test **05**, 243–244 (2013)
5. Jun, S., Park, B., Seo, J.B., Lee, S., Kim, N.: Development of a computer-aided differential diagnosis system to distinguish between usual interstitial pneumonia and non-specific interstitial pneumonia using texture- and shape-based hierarchical classifiers on HRCT images. J. Digital Imaging, **31**(2) (2018)
6. Hearst, M.A., Dumais, S.T.: Support vector machines. IEEE Intell. Syst. Appli. **13**(4) (1998)
7. Sun, Z., Xue, L., Xu, Y., et al.: Overview of deep learning. Appli. Res. Comput. **29**(08), 2806–2810 (2012)
8. Zhou, F., Jin, L., Dong, J.: A review of convolutional neural networks. Chin. J. Comput. **40**(06), 1229–1251 (2017)
9. Zhou, Q., Zhang, J., Pu, Z., et al.: COVID-19 CT image classification method combined with deep layer dense aggregation. Appli. Res. Comput., 1–8 (2023).https://doi.org/10.19734/j.issn.1001-3695.2022.08.0502
10. Guo, K., Du, Q.C., Wu, A., et al.: COVID-19 recognition technology based on lightweight neural network. Chin. J. Med. Phys. **39**(10), 1263–1269 (2022)
11. Ummah, K.R., et al.: Effect of image pre-processing method on convolutional neural network classification of COVID-19 CT scan images. Inter. J. Innov. Comput. Inform. Control **18**(6), 1895–1912 (2022) https://doi.org/10.24507/ijicic.18.06.1895
12. Zhang, N., Wu, H., Han, X., et al.: Tomato disease recognition method based on multi-scale and attention mechanism. J. Zhejiang Agricul. **33**(07), 1329–1338 (2021)
13. Lin, C., Zhang, G., Yang, J., et al.: Ttransfer learning based recognition for forestry business images. J. Nanjing Forestry Univ. (Nat. Sci.), **44**(04), 215–221 (2020)
14. Li, F.-F., Jia, D., Kai, L.: ImageNet: Constructing a large-scale image database. J. Vis. **9**(8) (2010)

End-to-end Relation-Enhanced Learnable Graph Self-attention Network for Knowledge Graphs Embedding

Shengchen Jiang[1], Hongbin Wang[1(✉)], and Xiang Hou[2]

[1] Faculty of Information Engineering and Automation, Kunming University of Science and Technology, Kunming 650500, China
whbin2007@126.com
[2] College of Automation, Chongqing University, Chongqing 400044, China

Abstract. The knowledge graphs embedding performance of the classic graph convolutional network has been limited due to the large-scale knowledge information. The complex knowledge information requires the model for better learnability rather than linearly weighted qualitative constraints. By studying the structural characteristics of the knowledge graph and investigation the imbalance of knowledge information, the end-to-end relation-enhanced learnable graph self-attention network for knowledge graphs embedding is proposed in this work. A relation-enhanced adjacency matrix is constructed to take into account the incompleteness of the knowledge graph. The convolutional knowledge sub-graph is introduced by using a graph self-attention network to obtain the entity node information's global encoding and relevance ranking. The training effect of the Convolutional Knowledge Base (convKB) model is improved by changing the construction of negative samples, and a better reliability score in the decoder can be obtained. The experimental results on the data set FB15k-237 and WN18RR show that the proposed method achieves better scores than the compared methods in terms of Hits@10 and MRR.

Keywords: Knowledge Graphs Embedding · Relation-enhanced · Convolutional Knowledge sub-graph · Negative Samples Construction

1 Introduction

The knowledge graph plays an essential role in the semantic network and benefits various downstream applications, such as personalized recommendation [1] and question answering [2], and enhanced word embedding [3]. The knowledge information is represented by a network structure consisting of triples, where the nodes and the connection edges refer to the entity information and the multi-relation information among entities, respectively [4,5], as shown in Fig. 1.

However, symbolic knowledge of network structure can not be analyzed by machine learning, which leads to insufficient analysis and utilization of knowledge

Y. Sun et al. (Eds.): ChineseCSCW 2023, CCIS 2012, pp. 510–524, 2024.
https://doi.org/10.1007/978-981-99-9637-7_38

base information. The knowledge graph embedding aims to convert the graph structural information to a low-dimensional dense vector representation [6]. With the development of neural networks, Nguyen et al. [7] proposed the convKB model, which uses a convolutional neural network to capture feature interactions among triples, and better Knowledge Graphs Embedding performance was achieved. Most neural networks use the connection information to construct a graph adjacency matrix [8,9]. Velikovi et al. [10] proposed a graph network with the self-attention mechanism added to the graph convolutional network. It calculates the weights of different relations on entities to obtain superior results. However, current methods do not consider the interconnection and interaction of the triples in the knowledge graph. In order to solve these problems, based on the existing researches, this paper proposes an end-to-end relation-enhanced learnable graph self-attention network for knowledge graphs embedding.

2   Related Work

The existing knowledge graphs embedding method is mainly based on the transformation between entities. Bordes et al. [11] proposed the TransE model based on the idea that the head-entity could get the tail-entity through relationship translation. Subsequent studies, such as TransH [12], TransR [13], TransD [14], KG2E [15] and TranSparse [16], are carried out by extending the embedding space of entities and relationships. Ebisu et al. [17] changed the embedded space into sphere to obtain a more comprehensive entity and relation embedding in spherical space. Sun et al. [18] defined the relationship as the rotation from head-entity to tail-entity to obtain the knowledge graphs embedding in complex space.

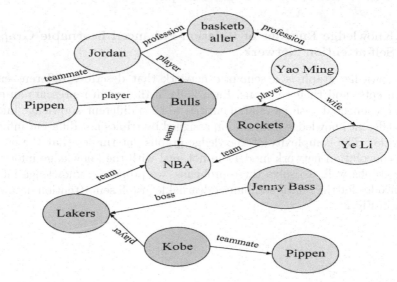

Fig. 1. Local knowledge graph.

To capture more feature interactions between the embeddings, the ConvE [19], ConvKB [7] and InteractE [20] models are proposed. Those models trained the knowledge embedding matrix through the credibility score function and improved the expressiveness. Trouillon et al. [21] managed various binary relations through complex embedding. Cai et al. [22] used the generative adversarial network to enhance the quality of negative samples. Recently, graph convolutional networks have been widely used [8,23]. Shang et al. [24] extended the ConvE model by using a graph convolution network, maintaining the transformation characteristics between entities and relationships. Current methods are devoted to preserving the symmetry and antisymmetry relation properties to improve the expressiveness [25–28]. Chen et al. [29] and Zhang et al. [30] combined the bidirectional influence between entities and relationships by considering the relationship edge information. Hamilton et al. [31] integrated the logical query information into the knowledge graphs embedding by performing the logical operation in the low-dimensional embedded space.

However, the classic graph convolutional network might not be able to well process the information owing to its imbalance. Moreover, the knowledge complexity determines that the models would need better learnability rather than linearly weighted qualitative constraints.

3   Methodology

This work proposes the end-to-end relation-enhanced learnable graph self-attention network for knowledge graphs embedding. The method consists of two modules: the knowledge encoder for the self-attention network and the knowledge decoder for reconstructing the negative sample.

3.1   Knowledge Encoder of Relation-Enhanced Learnable Graph Self-attention Network

The knowledge graph is a semantic network that describes different entities (or concepts) and their relations. Each node in the graph represents an entity, which is connected with its related entities to form different knowledge information. Different knowledge information assigned by triples has different influences on entities. The complexity of knowledge graphs determines that the ordinary graph convolution network model can not deal with the knowledge information in the graphs well. To solve these problems, we propose a knowledge information encoder for the relation-enhanced learnable graph self-attention network, as shown in Fig. 2.

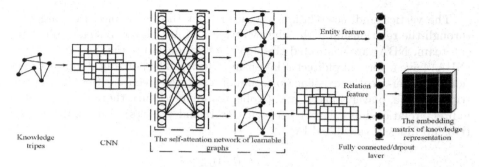

Fig. 2. Knowledge encoder based on relation-enhanced learnable graph self-attention network.

Relation-enhanced learnable graph self-attention network is an extension of the classical Graph Convolution Network (GCN) model. We construct the relation-enhanced adjacency matrix for the incompleteness of the knowledge graph. The entity node representation from the previous layer is used as the input in the current layer network for each node in the graph. The entity representation matrix of the output is obtained through the relation-enhanced self-attention network by:

$$H_m^L = GKConv(AH^L W_{conv}) \tag{1}$$

where $GKConv$ is the knowledge graph convolution sub-layer, A is the relation-enhanced adjacency matrix, $H^L \in R^{n \times F^L}$ is the entity representation matrix of L layer learnable graph self-attention network, F^L is the entity representation dimension and W_{conv} is the trainable parameter matrix.

In order to diminish the effect of the knowledge graph incompleteness on knowledge representation, indirect relationship attributes between entities are added into the adjacency matrix. The indirect relationship attributes including vertical and horizontal indirect relationships, as shown in Fig. 3.

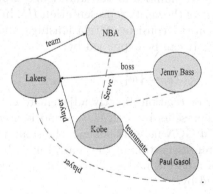

Fig. 3. Indirect relationships of the knowledge graph.

The vertical indirect relationship means that the two triples are connected through the relationship path. The two triples (Kobe, player, Lakers) and (Lakers, team, NBA) are connected through the relationship paths. So, (Kobe) and (NBA) have a vertical indirect relationship (Serve). The horizontal indirect relationship refers to the existence of common entity between entities. In the two triples (Kobe, player, Lakers) and (Kobe, teammate, Paul), there is a horizontal indirect relationship (player) between (Paul) and (Lakers). The indirect relationship index is calculated by:

$$r_{ij} = (\frac{1}{2})^{(k-1)}(\frac{1}{2})^p \tag{2}$$

where $\frac{1}{2}$ is the relationship attenuation coefficient, k is the relationship path length, and p is the horizontal indirect path length between entities. If $k = 1$, it is a direct relationship, and the correlation is 1. Set the attenuation index to $k - 1$. The shortest path is taken when there are multiple paths between two entities. We assume that in this work, there can only be one relationship between entity pairs. The indirect relationship attributes between directly adjacent entities are not calculated. In this way, the relation-enhanced adjacency matrix $\mathbf{A}$ is constructed by:

$$\mathbf{A} = \begin{cases} 1 & direct\ relationship \\ r_{ij} & indirect\ relationship \\ 0 & no\ relationship \end{cases} \tag{3}$$

where r_{ij} is the indirect relationship path length. For the relation-enhanced learnable graph self-attention network, the high-level feature representation of entities in the knowledge graph is extracted through the convolutional neural network by:

$$H^1 = conv(e_1, e_2, \cdots, e_n) \tag{4}$$

where $conv$ is the convolutional operation, e_i is the input characteristic of $i - th$ entity and n is the entity number in the knowledge graph. The CNN model obtains the input matrix of the entity representation H^1. In this work, the feature representation of an entity (consists of relationships and entities) is directly connected to the entity. It can be expressed by:

$$e_i = \{w_1^i, w_2^i, \cdots, w_m^i\} \tag{5}$$

where w_m^i is the entity or relation directly adjacent to entity e_i. m is set to 50. The empty entity is represents by $< EMP >$ and is used to make up for the deficiency. The classical GCN network assigns the same weight to the adjacent nodes. It obtains the representation of the central node by aggregating the feature representations of adjacent nodes. The attention weights between different entities can be obtained by:

$$e_{ij} = \sigma(h_i^L, h_j^L) \tag{6}$$

where $h_i^L \in R^{(F^L)}$ and $h_j^L \in R^{(F^L)}$ are the feature representation of entities e_i and e_j at the layer L of the relation-enhanced learnable graphs self-attention network, respectively. σ is the feedforward neural network of single layers with *LeakyReLU* as the activation function (negative input slope $\alpha = 0.2$). Attention weights between entity nodes are obtained through the normalization of scores calculated by single-layer feedforward neural network:

$$a_{ij} = \frac{exp(LeakyReLU(W_a^T[h_i^L \parallel h_j^L]))}{\sum_{g \in N_i} exp(LeakyReLU(W_a^T[h_i^L \parallel h_g^L]))} \tag{7}$$

where $W_a^T \in R^{2F^L}$ is the weight matrix of the feedforward neural network and $\parallel$ is the connection operation of vectors. A relevance matrix $P \in R^{n \times n}$, $P_{ij} = a_{ij}$ is formed. Through an aggregation of the neighboring entities, the entity node representation of the fusion graph structure information can be obtained by:

$$h_i^{'} = \sigma(\sum_{g \in N_i} a_{ij} h_j^L) \tag{8}$$

where N_i is the adjacency nodes set of entity e_i. In this work, we constructed the relation-enhanced adjacency matrix $\mathbf{A}$ of the knowledge graph, which reduces the negative effects of an incomplete knowledge graph on knowledge representation. Meanwhile, considering that there are a large number of entity nodes in the graph, we make references to the work in [32] with the multi-head self-attention mechanism to acquire a better and more stable representation of the entity. The final encoding representation of entity nodes is obtained by weighted summation of correlation weights between connected nodes:

$$h_i = concate(\parallel_{k=1}^{S} \sigma(\sum_{g \in N_i} a_{ij}^k h_j^L)) \tag{9}$$

where *concate* is the connection operation of vectors and S is the number of self-attention mechanism.

In the knowledge graph, the connection of each entity can reflect the semantic information of the entity. Due to the different connection conditions of each entity, it is impossible to convolve the entity information in the knowledge graph directly by using convolutional neural networks. Therefore, we construct a convolutional knowledge sub-graph to perform the convolutional operation on the aggregated entity representation, as shown in Fig. 4.

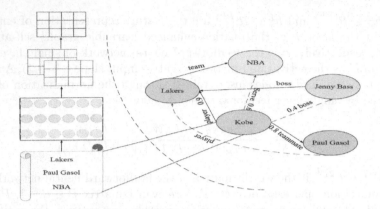

Fig. 4. Convolutional knowledge sub-graph.

The convolutional knowledge sub-graph of the entity (Kobe) is (Laker, Paul, NBA). The characteristic representation is obtained by performing the convolution operation on the convolutional knowledge sub-graph.

We extract the T entities with the most relevance for each entity through the correlation matrix $\mathbf{P}$ and construct the convolutional knowledge sub-graph by:

$$H_c = g(H, W, T) \tag{10}$$

$$W = A \cdot P \tag{11}$$

$$P = \frac{\sum_{i \in S} P_i}{S} \tag{12}$$

where g is the construction function of convolutional knowledge sub-graph, $\mathbf{P}$ refers to the correlation obtained by the multi-head self-attention mechanism, $\mathbf{P}$ is the average value of each self-attention mechanism, S is the number of self-attention mechanisms and T refers to the number of neighboring nodes with the greatest correlation. If the neighboring node is less than T, then empty entity $< EMP >$ is adopted for supplement. $\mathbf{A}$ refers to the relation-enhanced adjacent matrix of the knowledge graph. The final relevance matrix $\mathbf{W}$ of adjacent nodes is obtained through matrix point multiplication. The entity representation is calculated through the convolutional neural network by:

$$H^{L+1} = conv(W_1 H_c + b_1) \tag{13}$$

where W_1 and b_1 are convolution layer parameters and $H_c \in R^{n \times T \times m}$ is the knowledge sub-graph of entity. The convolution operation is performed on the convolutional knowledge sub-graph to obtain an entity representation matrix $H^{L+1} \in R^{n \times F^{L+1}}$ as the output. We construct a convolutional knowledge sub-graph, realizing the convolution operation in the graph convolution network and reducing the model parameters. At the same time, the multi-layer convolution network can be integrated into the entity node information aggregation according to the graph structure. It improves the representation ability of the classic graph convolution network.

The relational embedding matrix is built on the assumption that entity information can explain and reflect the relation information. The embedding matrix $\mathbf{H}$ of entities is used to search the entity pairs corresponding to each relation category. 20 entities are selected as the information representation text according to each relationship category and its representation is obtained by:

$$R_i = conv(W_r X_i + b_r) \tag{14}$$

where X_i is the information feature representation of $i - th$ relation category, composed of representations of entity pairs directly connected with relation categories. W_r and b_r are the parameters of CNN. R_i is the feature representation of the $i - th$ relation category. The relational embedding matrix $\mathbf{R}$ is obtained according to Equation (14). Then the entity embedding matrix $\mathbf{H}$ is combined with the relation embedding matrix $\mathbf{R}$ to obtain the embedding matrix $\mathbf{U}$ of knowledge representation with the final encoding.

3.2   Knowledge Decoder of Improved Negative Samples Construction

The knowledge graph is a network structure composed of triples, and the decoder aims to define a reliability score function f that makes the positive triples score higher than that of negative triples. The embedding representation $U_i = [v_i^h, v_i^r, v_i^t] \in R^{3 \times d}$ of knowledge information is obtained based on the relation-enhanced learnable graphs self-attention network, where v_h, v_r, v_t are the representations of head-entity, relation and tail-entity of knowledge triples, respectively. d is the dimension. The convolution operation is conducted for each dimension of the vector representation of knowledge triples:

$$v_i = conv(WU_{i,:} + b) \tag{15}$$

where $U_{i,:} \in R^{3 \times 1}$ is i^{th} dimensional representation of triple. The convolutional kernel is $W \in R^{(3 \times 1)}$. The convolution of triples is performed repeatedly in each dimension. In order to maintain the conversion properties of the triplet, the connection operation is chosen by:

$$v = [v_1, v_2, \cdots, v_d] \tag{16}$$

where $v \in R^{1 \times d}$ is the feature representation of triples after convolution. Such a connection operation extracts the global feature information of triples and maintains the triples transformation characteristics. To acquire abundant feature information, different convolution kernels are set to achieve the multi-channel convolution operation:

$$v_i^\tau = conv(W^\tau U_{i,:} + b^\tau) \tag{17}$$

where W^τ and b^τ are the convolution layer parameters of τth convolutional channel. The triple feature representation of each channel is connection to obtain the triple representation $V_i = [v^1, v^2, \cdots, v^t] \in R^{(1 \times td)}$, where t is the number of convolution channels. The reliability score of triple is calculated by:

$$f(U_i) = \sigma(W_z V_i + b_z) \tag{18}$$

where W_z and b_z are the full connection layer parameters. We improved the training effect of negative samples on the convKB model by changing the construction of negative samples to obtain a better reliability score in the decoder. The negative samples are updated according to the reliability score after each iteration by:

$$f(U_i') = \sigma(W_z V_i' + b_z) \tag{19}$$

where U_i' is a negative sample for U_i:

$$U_i' = (h', r, t') \in \left\{ (h', r, t') \mid h' \in \varepsilon, h' \neq h \right\} \cup \left\{ (h, r, t') \mid t' \in \varepsilon, t' \neq t) \right\} \tag{20}$$

During the negative samples construction, the random replacement method is used to prevent the occurrence of simultaneous replacement of the head-entity and tail-entity that are still positive samples. The same weight matrix W_z and b_z are used for calculating the negative sample score without considering model loss or parameters updating. The triple with the highest reliability score is selected as the negative samples:

$$U_i' = max(f(U_1'), f(U_2'), \cdots, f(U_q')) \tag{21}$$

where q is the number of constructed negative samples. The chosen negative sample participates in the next iteration for model training and are updated according to its score. To improve the calculation efficiency, 100 negative samples are randomly selected for each positive sample. Then, the triple with the highest reliability score is used as the final negative sample. The model parameters are trained through the loss function:

$$\iota = \sum_{U \in \xi \cup \xi'} log(1 + exp(g(U)f(U))) + \frac{\lambda}{2} ||W||_2^2 \tag{22}$$

$$\mathbf{A} = \begin{cases} -1 & U \in \xi \\ 1 & U' \in \xi' \end{cases} \tag{23}$$

where ξ and ξ' represent the set of positive and negative samples, respectively. The parametric matrix W of the model is regularized by $L2$. Based on the optimization of the loss function, the reliability score of positive triples is higher than that of negative triples. A higher-quality knowledge embedding can be obtained by optimizing the embedding matrix of knowledge representation for the relation-enhanced learnable graphs self-attention network.

4   Experiment

4.1   Experimental Settings

In this work, the output vector of the convolution layer is set to 64 dimensions. The number of the convolution kernels is set to 500 with a dropout of 0.6. The number of negative samples constructed by each positive sample is 100, and the one with the highest reliability score is selected as the negative sample. The Adam optimizer is used with a learning rate of 0.0001 for the end-to-end model training. The parametric regularization ratio is 0.001, the batch size is 128 and the epoch number is 800.

The performance of the proposed approach is verified on two benchmark data sets: WN18RR [19] and FB15k-237 [20], which are the subsets of WN18 [11] and FB15k [11], respectively. WN18RR consists of 40943 entities and 11 types of relation categories. The training, validation and test data sets contain 86835, 3034 and 3134 triples, respectively. FB15k-237 contains 14541 entities and 237 relation categories. There are 272115, 17535 and 20466 triples in the training, validation and test data sets, respectively. In WN18RR and FB15k-237, the reversible relationship is removed, making the task of knowledge representation and knowledge base completion more authentic.

4.2   Evaluation Criteria

The reliability score function f on the triples of the test data sets [11] are used to evaluate the performance. A group of negative triples is built for each triple tested by randomly replacing its head and tail entities. Three benchmark evaluation indicators MR, MRR and $Hits@10$ are employed. MR indicates the average value of the correct label ranking in the probability distribution vector. The smaller the value, the better the performance. MRR represents the average value of the reciprocal of the correct label ranking in the probability distribution vector. Larger values indicate better performances. $Hits@10$ represents the probability of the correct label rank in top ten, where larger values indicate better performances.

4.3   Results and Discussion

Experiment 1. To verify the effects of the size T of convolutional knowledge sub-graphs on the results of entity linking prediction, tests have been performed with T equals to 10, 20, 30, 40 and 50. The results are listed in Table 1.

Table 1. Performance of different knowledge sub-graphs size T

T	MR	MRR	$Hits@10$
10	346	0.341	52.5
20	323	0.353	54.9
30	304	0.367	55.6
40	**272**	**0.376**	**56.1**
50	311	0.370	56.3

The optimal performance is achieved when $T = 40$. It could be that the size of the knowledge sub-graph increases and more adjacent entity node information can be used. Thus, the convolution obtains a richer feature representation. Since the proposed knowledge sub-graphs are structured by relevance sort, when the knowledge sub-graph reaches a certain level, less relevant entity node information is likely to generate redundant information to the central entity.

Experiment 2. Different numbers of the self-attention mechanisms h are tested to verify the effect of self-attention mechanisms on the entity linking prediction performance. The results are listed in Table 2.

The results show that, as the number h of attention mechanisms increases, each indicator has been improved accordingly. Particularly, the optimal performance is achieved when h=10. It is because when h increases, a more stable features representation can be obtained.

Experiment 3. FB15k-237 data set is used to verify the contribution of knowledge encoder. Three models are tested: the convKB model [7], GCN + convKB model (GConKB) and the proposed relation-enhanced learnable graph self-attention network + convKB model (R-GATKB-N). The results are listed in Table 3.

The addition of the GCN-based knowledge encoder exerts a minor influence on the knowledge representation quality. Only the Hits@10 indicator shows an

Table 2. Performance of different numbers h for self-attention mechanisms

h	MR	MRR	$Hits@10$
1	359	0.347	53.1
2	329	0.349	53.7
4	321	0.358	54.6
6	305	0.366	55.3
8	307	0.370	55.8
10	**272**	**0.376**	**56.1**
12	291	0.373	55.9
14	310	0.368	55.4

improvement. It gives an increasing number of high-quality knowledge representations, but MRR indicator implies that some triples are poorly presented. Compared with the classical GCN model, Hits@10 increases by 4.4 relative value 51.7%.

Table 3. Performance of different models

Model	MR	MRR	$Hits@10$
convKB	**257**	**0.396**	51.7
GConKB	376	0.337	53.4
R-GATKB-N	272	0.376	**56.1**

Experiment 4. FB15k-237 data set is used to compare the proposed method with other eight state-of-the-art works. The results are listed in Table 4.

Table 4. Comparison between baseline and proposed model

Model	MR	MRR	$Hits@10$
TransE [11]	347	0.294	46.5
DISTMULT [33]	254	0.241	41.9
COMPLEX [21]	339	0.247	42.8
KBGAN [22]	–	0.278	45.8
ConvE [19]	246	0.316	49.1
ConvKB [7]	257	**0.396**	51.7
RotatE [18]	**177**	0.338	53.3
SACN [24]	–	0.350	54.0
R-GAT	324	0.357	54.4
R-GATKB	298	0.373	55.6
R-GATKB-N	272	0.376	**56.1**

The absent data noted '–' in Table 4 indicates that there is no reported score in the original work. R-GAT is the experimental result of adding the relation-enhanced adjacency matrix. R-GATKB is with the cobination of relation-enhanced adjacency matrix and convolution knowledge sub-graph. R-GATKB-N is R-GATKB with improved negative samples. The results reveal that the self-attention network considers more comprehensive information from knowledge graphs and improves the learnability of the model. Based on the graph structure and relation-enhanced adjacency matrix, the learnability of the model can be improved by considering the imbalance of knowledge information and convolutional knowledge sub-graphs.

Experiment 5. WN18RR data set is used to test the applicability of the proposed method. The testing results are shown in Table 5.

The results indicate that the proposed method can improve the performance in terms of $Hits@10$ and MRR on WN18RR data set by comparing with the latest research results of SACN [24].

Table 5. Comparison of different models on WN18RR

Model	MR	MRR	$Hits@10$
TransE [10]	3384	0.226	50.1
DISTMULT [33]	5110	0.430	49.0
COMPLEX [21]	5261	0.440	51.0
KBGAN [22]	–	0.213	48.1
ConvE [19]	5277	0.460	48.0
ConvKB [7]	**2554**	0.248	52.5
RotatE [18]	3340	0.476	**57.1**
SACN [24]	–	0.470	54.0
R-GATKB-N	3169	**0.488**	55.4

5   Conclusions

To deal with the complexity and large-scale knowledge information, a relationship enhanced self attention knowledge graph embedding network of learnable graph is proposed in this paper. The proposed approach increases the flexibility and learnability of the network through the graph self attention mechanism with convolutable knowledge sub-graph. According to the experimental results analysis, the relationship information in the knowledge graphs presented an important impact on knowledge representation, and the complexity of knowledge information is an important constraint affecting the effect of knowledge representation. The experimental results on the data set FB15k-237 and WN18RR show that the proposed method achieves better performance in terms of Hits@10 and MRR.

Acknowledgements. This work is partly supported by National Key R&D Program of China (Grant No. 2018YFB1402900), National Natural Science Foundation of China (Grant No. 61966020) and Chongqing Social Science Foundation (Grant No. 2020YBTQ130).

References

1. Wang, H., Zhang, F., Xie, X., Guo, M.: DKN: deep knowledge-aware network for news recommendation. In: Proceedings of WWW, pp. 1835–1844 (2018)
2. Huang, X., Zhang, J., Li, D., Li, P.: Knowledge graph embedding based question answering. In: Proceedings of WSDM, pp. 105–113 (2019)
3. Mancini, M., Camacho-Collados, J., Iacobacci, I., Navigli, R.: Embedding words and senses together via joint knowledgeenhanced training. CoRR abs/1612.02703 (2016)
4. García-Durán, A., Bordes, A., Usunier, N., Grandvalet, Y.: Combining two and three-way embedding models for link prediction in knowledge bases. J. Artif. Intell. Res. **55**, 715–742 (2016)
5. Nickel, M., Murphy, K., Tresp, V., Gabrilovich, E.: A review of relational machine learning for knowledge graphs. Proc. IEEE **104**(1), 11–33 (2015)

6. Rossi, A., Firmani, D., Matinata, A., Merialdo, P., Barbosa, D.: Knowledge graph embedding for link prediction: a comparative analysis. ACM Trans. Knowl. Discovery Data **15**(2), 1–49 (2021)
7. Nguyen, D.Q., Nguyen, T.D., Nguyen, D.Q., Phung, D.: A novel embedding model for knowledge base completion based on convolutional neural network. arXiv preprint arXiv:1712.02121 (2017)
8. Schlichtkrull, M., Kipf, T.N., Bloem, P., van den Berg, R., Titov, I., Welling, M.: Modeling relational data with graph convolutional networks. In: Gangemi, A., et al. (eds.) ESWC 2018. LNCS, vol. 10843, pp. 593–607. Springer, Cham (2018). https://doi.org/10.1007/978-3-319-93417-4_38
9. Kalchbrenner, N., Grefenstette, E., Blunsom, P.: A convolutional neural network for modelling sentences. In: Proceedings of the 52nd Annual Meeting of the Association for Computational Linguistics, vol. 1, pp. 655–665 (2014)
10. Velickovic, P., Cucurull, G., Casanova, A., Romero, A., Liò, P., Bengio, Y.: Graph attention networks. arXiv preprint arXiv:1710.10903 (2017)
11. Bordes, A., Usunier, N., Garcia-Duran, A., Weston, J., Yakhnenko, O.: Translating embeddings for modeling multi-relational data. In: Advances in Neural Information Processing Systems, pp. 2787–2795 (2013)
12. Wang, Z., Zhang, J., Feng, J., Chen, Z.: Knowledge graph embedding by translating on hyperplanes. In: Twenty-Eighth AAAI Conference on Artificial Intelligence, pp. 1532–1543 (2014)
13. Lin, Y., Liu, Z., Sun, M., Liu, Y., Zhu, X.: Learning entity and relation embeddings for knowledge graph completion. In: Twenty-ninth AAAI Conference on Artificial Intelligence, pp. 1–7 (2015)
14. Ji, G., He, S., Xu, L., Liu, K., Zhao, J.: Knowledge graph embedding via dynamic mapping matrix. In: 53rd Annual Meeting of the Association for Computational Linguistics and the 7th International Joint Conference on Natural Language Processing, pp. 687–696 (2015)
15. He, S., Liu, K., Ji, G., Zhao, J.: Learning to represent knowledge graphs with gaussian embedding. In: Proceedings of the 24th ACM International on Conference on Information and Knowledge Management, pp. 623–632. ACM (2015)
16. Ji, G., Liu, K., He, S., Zhao, J.: Knowledge graph completion with adaptive sparse transfer matrix. In: Thirtieth AAAI Conference on Artificial Intelligence, pp. 985–991 (2016)
17. Ebisu, T., Ichise, R.: TorusE: knowledge graph embedding on a lie group. In: Thirty-Second AAAI Conference on Artificial Intelligence, pp. 1–8 (2018)
18. Zhiqing, S., Zhi-Hong, D., Jian-Yun, N., Jian, T.: RotatE: knowledge graph embedding by relational rotation in complex space. arXiv preprint arXiv:1902.10197 (2019)
19. Dettmers, T., Minervini, P., Stenetorp, P., Riedel, S.: Convolutional 2D knowledge graphembeddings. In: Thirty-Second AAAI Conference on Artificial Intelligence, pp. 1–9 (2018)
20. Vashishth, S., Sanyal, S., Nitin, V., Agrawal, N., Talukdar, P.: Interacte: improving convolution-based knowledge graph embeddings by increasing feature interactions. arXiv preprint arXiv:1911.00219 (2019)
21. Trouillon, T., Welbl, J., Riedel, S., Gaussier, é., Bouchard, G.: Complex embeddings for simple link prediction. In: International Conference on Machine Learning, pp. 2071–2080 (2016)
22. Cai, L., Wang, W.Y.: KBGAN: adversarial learning for knowledge graph embeddings. In: Proceedings of the 2018 Conference of the North American Chapter

of the Association for Computational Linguistics: Human Language Technologies, vol. 1, pp. 1–11 (2018)

23. Defferrard, M., Bresson, X., Vandergheynst, P.: Convolutional neural networks on graphs with fast localized spectral filtering. In: Proceedings of NIPS, pp. 3837–3845 (2016)

24. Shang, C., Tang, Y., Huang, J., Bi, J., He, X., Zhou, B.: End-to-end structure-aware convolutional networks for knowledge base completion. arXiv preprint arXiv:1811.04441 (2018)

25. Nathani, D., Chauhan, J., Sharma, C., Kaul, M.: Learning attention-based embeddings for relation prediction in knowledge graphs. In: Proceedings of the 57th Annual Meeting of the Association for Computational Linguistics, pp. 4710–4723 (2019)

26. Ding, B., Wang, Q., Wang, B., Guo, L.: Improving knowledge graph embedding using simple constraints. In Proceedings of ACL, pp. 110–121 (2018)

27. Kazemi, S.M., Poole, D.: Simple embedding for link prediction in knowledge graphs. In: Proceedings of NIPS, pp. 4289–4300 (2018)

28. Xu, C., Li, R.: Relation embedding with dihedral group in knowledge graph. In: Proceedings of ACL, pp. 263–272 (2019)

29. Chen, H., Sun, X., Tian, Y., Perozzi, B., Chen, M., Skiena, S.: Enhanced network embeddings via exploiting edge labels. In: Proceedings of the 27th ACM International Conference on Information and Knowledge Management, pp. 1579–1582 (2018)

30. Zhang, W., Paudel, B., Zhang, W., Bernstein, A., Chen, H.: Interaction embeddings for prediction and explanation in knowledge graphs. In: Proceedings of the Twelfth ACM International Conference on Web Search and Data Mining, pp. 96–104 (2019)

31. Hamilton William L., Payal, B., Marinka, Z., Dan, J., Jure, L.: Embedding logical queries on knowledge graphs. In: Advances in Neural Information Processing Systems, pp. 2026–2037 (2018)

32. Vaswani, A., et al.: Attention is all you need. In: Advances in neural information processing systems, pp. 5998–6008 (2017)

33. Yang, B., Yih, W.-T., He, X., Gao, J., Deng, L.: Embedding entities and relations for learning and inference in knowledge bases. arXiv preprint arXiv:1412.6575 (2014)

Research on Signal Detection and System Recognition Techniques in Private Internet of Things

Jiayu Jiang(✉), Bin Wang, Pengfei Sun, and Bang Li

Harbin Institute of Technology, Harbin 150001, China
Jjy963537621@163.com

Abstract. P-IoT is an IoT transmission system proposed for users in the private network industry, which has the advantages of high reliability, high security and strong coverage capability compared with the existing IoT system, it has great application potential. However, there is a amount of unused spectrum in sub-1 GHz private network band now. How P-IoT can exploit the spectrum holes has become a hot research issue. In order to improve the utilization rate of spectrum resources, P-IoT can obtain the information about whether the spectrum is be used, and about network system which is using the frequency band through signal detection and system recognition. This can provide supports for P-IoT to formulate the utilization strategy of idle spectrum. In this paper, signal detection and system recognition technology of P-IoT are studied. This paper selects energy detection to detect narrowband private network signals and recognize the broad/narrowband private network signals. Taking the modulation modes of TETRA, PDT and dPMR as the classification objects, this paper also implements system recognition algorithms including binary trees and neural network classifiers, and further compares and analyzes the proposed algorithms. The simulation results show that the proposed recognition methods for P-IoT can effectively recognize the three private network signals. The results of this paper provide reference and support for the subsequent works that utilize unused spectrum, such as spectrum allocation and spectrum collaboration.

Keywords: Private IoT · Signal detection · Modulation recognition

1 Introduction

With the vigorous development of Internet of Things technology, users in private network industries such as police and government have increasingly urgent needs for Internet of Things. The Internet of Things technology can provide the sensing, transmission and application of information required by private network users such as fingerprints, environmental monitoring, and biochips. It can also create intelligent police, medical, governmental systems and other industry systems with the IoT system as the main body, and provide efficient smart solutions for private network users. For example, in the smart medical private network system, IoT medical devices can be used to collect a

Y. Sun et al. (Eds.): ChineseCSCW 2023, CCIS 2012, pp. 525–535, 2024.
https://doi.org/10.1007/978-981-99-9637-7_39

large amount of medical data, and remote cloud servers can be used to analyze the data to help advance medical activities [1]. However, in some authorized frequency bands of private network communications, there is no corresponding IoT access technology to meet the needs of private network users. The Private-IoT (P-IoT) technology that fits with the characteristics of private network comes from this.

Although the introduction of P-IoT has expanded the functions of private network, it has also brought pressure on spectrum resources. At present, 70% of the private network frequency bands below 1 GHz (sub-1 GHz) are unused, which prevent the maximum utilization of the spectrum and the rapid development of P-IoT. Therefore, it is necessary to utilize idle spectrum to improve the spectrum utilization rate of P-IoT.

In order to make more flexible use of spectrum holes, the key technology adopted by P-IoT is signal detection and system recognition. The former first judges whether the current frequency spectrum is being used, and the latter identifies the private network system adopted by the authorized private network users of the current frequency band. On this basis, the cooperation within the P-IoT network or the cooperation between P-IoT and the narrowband private network can help formulating appropriate resource allocation and transmission strategies, and then to combine with follow-up technologies to complete the use of spectrum holes. In addition, the theory of cognitive radio (CR) can also be applied to the P-IoT system to form a cognitive P-IoT solution, which uses wireless communication technology to integrate local perception information and environmental information, apply to the field of automatic driving [2, 3].

At present, the overall Internet of Things construction in my country's private network industry is still immature, and P-IoT is also in the process of technical research and standardization. Paper [4] proposed the necessity of building IoT for private network users, but adopted traditional technologies such as LPWAN as its access network. Paper [5, 6] clearly proposed P-IoT technology, and pointed out the possibility of using the spectrum hole in the private network frequency band, but did not analyze the recognition technology for P-IoT. In addition, the research on system recognition has relatively mature theories, the algorithms can be divided into two categories: the likelihood-based (LB) recognition algorithm [7] and the feature-based (FB) algorithm [8, 9]. But there is a lack of application in the private network background.

Considering the background of high demand for spectrum resources under the private network system, this paper studies the signal detection and system recognition methods under the P-IoT system. This paper compares and analyzes the performance and applicability of different detection and recognition methods in the context of P-IoT, which provides reference and support for subsequent technologies to use private network spectrum holes, such as spectrum analysis, spectrum decision-making, spectrum switching and spectrum allocation technologies.

2   The Scheme Design of Signal Detection and System Recognition in P-IoT

Firstly, it is necessary to clarify the objects and characteristics of detection and identification in this paper. This paper mainly studies the sub-1 GHz narrowband P-IoT system. This frequency band has strong interference avoidance ability. Common narrowband digital private networks in this band include TETRA, dPMR and PDT. The modulation method of TETRA is π/4-DQPSK [10] and the modulation method of dPMR and PDT is 4FSK [11, 12]. The process of P-IoT signal detection and system recognition is shown in Fig. 1.

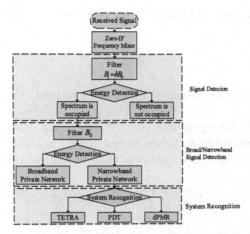

Fig. 1. Process of signal detection and private network system recognition

The overall process can be divided into three parts: 1) Signal detection: determining whether the frequency band is occupied; 2) Broad/Narrowband signal detection: changing the bandwidth for the second filter to distinguish broad/narrowband signals; 3) System recognition: artificial or machine learning methods are used to extract signal features and recognize the modulation modes of the signals of three systems.

2.1 Energy Detection and Broad/Narrowband System Signals Recognition

At present, the receiver of the narrowband digital private network generally adopts the zero-IF receiving technology. Based on zero-IF technology, P-IoT can complete the energy detection of baseband signals, and can complete the detection of broad/narrowband signals by adjusting the filter bandwidth and comparing the energy of received signals.

Narrowband private network signals have almost zero spectral energy beyond the 30 kHz, while broadband signal bandwidth can reach several MHz to tens of MHz. If the narrowband signal spectrum is taken as the benchmark, when the bandwidth is expanded by k times for filtering, the energy of the received narrowband signal will remain approximately unchanged, while it of the broadband signal will be expanded by k times. Therefore, broad/narrowband signals can be distinguished by observing the change of the filtered signal energy.

The specific process of P-IoT signal detection and broad/narrowband signal distinction is as follows:

This initial signal is filtered with bandwidth of $B1 = kB0$ to obtain signal $y0(t)$. Carry out N-point sampling on $y0(t)$, the sampling period is Ts, the signal $y1(t)$ is obtained, and then the energy detection is performed, the detection statistic $Y1$:

$$Y_1 = \frac{1}{N} \sum_{k=1}^{N} |y_1(k)|^2 - \sigma_1^2 \tag{1}$$

where σ_1^2 is the noise power of Gaussian noise after zero-IF reception and filtering:

$$\sigma_1^2 = \frac{1}{N} \sum_{k=1}^{N} |n(k)|^2 \tag{2}$$

By comparing the detection statistic $Y1$ with the threshold $\lambda 1$, a judgment conclusion can be drawn.

If the result of the first signal detection is that the signal exists, the signal is sent to a digital filter with bandwidth B_0 for the second filtering to obtain the signal $y2(t)$, and the energy detection is performed again, and the detection statistic is

$$Y_2 = \frac{1}{N} \sum_{k=1}^{N} |y_2(k)|^2 - \sigma_1^2/k \tag{3}$$

The decision statistic is

$$Y = |Y_1/Y_2| \tag{4}$$

The decision statistic Y is compared with the threshold to get the decision result of broad/narrowband signal. If Y is approximately 1, the decision result is narrowband signal, and if Y is approximately k the decision result is broadband signal.

2.2 System Recognition Algorithm Based on Modulation Method

This paper adopts the recognition method based on feature extraction, the recognition process can be divided into two steps: feature extraction and classifier recognition. The signal features used for feature extraction are high-order cumulants and instantaneous features. According to different classifiers, the recognition algorithm can be divided into algorithm based on decision tree, BP and Convolutional neural network.

The high-order cumulant as a classification feature has a certain resistance to Gaussian noise in the channel, so the high-order cumulant is often used in signal recognition [13]. The modulation methods to be recognized in this paper are divided into two types. Two modulation modes, 4FSK and $\pi/4$-DQPSK, can be distinguished by the eighth-order cumulant (Table 1.).

PS in the table is the symbol power of the complex signal. Therefore, the absolute value of X is used as one of the recognition features, the threshold $\lambda_1 = Ps^4/2$:

$$T_1 = |C_{80}| \tag{5}$$

The high-order cumulants of PDT and dPMR are equal, so they cannot be distinguished based on it. However, PDT and dPMR signals can be recognized by calculating the frequency offset of the signal through phase difference.

Table 1. Higher order cumulant of 4FSK and π/4-DQPSK

	C_{20}	C_{21}	C_{42}	C_{60}	C_{63}	C_{80}
4FSK (dPMR、PDT)	0	P_s	$-P_s^2$	0	$4P_s^3$	0
π/4-DQPSK (TETRA)	0	P_s	$-P_s^2$	0	$4P_s^3$	P_s^4

The frequency offset of the k-th symbol is:

$$T_k = \frac{1}{N-1} \sum_{i=1}^{N-1} \frac{\Phi_k(i+1) - \Phi_k(i)}{2\pi \Delta t} \tag{6}$$

where $\Phi_k(i)$ is the phase of the sampled signal at i-th sampling interval, N is the number of sampling points and Δt is the sampling interval.

The decision statistics are defined as follows to detect M symbols:

$$T_2 = \frac{1}{M-1} \sum_{k=1}^{M} \left(T_k - \frac{1}{M} \sum_{k=1}^{M} T_k \right)^2 \tag{7}$$

This formula describes the sample variance of the frequency offset. According to the theoretical frequency offset of PDT, the variance is about 2099520, and the variance of the frequency offset of the dPMR signal is about 612500, the middle value is set as the threshold λ2. If $T2 > λ2$, the signal is recognized as dPMR. If $T2 < λ2$, the signal is recognized as PDT. The flow chart of the system recognition algorithm based on the decision tree is shown in Fig. 2.

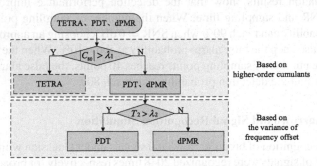

Fig. 2. Narrowband private network system recognition process based on eighth-order cumulant and variance of frequency offset

In addition, this paper also uses BP neural network and convolutional neural network for feature extraction and recognition. The BP neural network still needs to manually extract signal features, while the convolutional neural network eliminates the manual feature extraction step, the neural network automatically extracts features for training and for subsequent judgments [14].

3   Simulation Results and Analysis

3.1   Energy Detection Simulation

Figure 3(a) is the Receiver Operating Characteristic (ROC) curves of the signal detection of the energy detection algorithm at different SNR, where Pf is the false alarm probability and Pd is the detection probability. The SNR corresponding to the curves from top to bottom are 0dB, −3 dB and −6 dB, respectively. Figure 3(b) shows the relationship between the ROC curve and the number of sampling points. The sampling points corresponding to the curves from top to bottom are 40, 20, and 5 respectively. The simulation uses the LTE signal with a bandwidth of 2 MHz as the broadband signal. The number of detections is 1024 times.

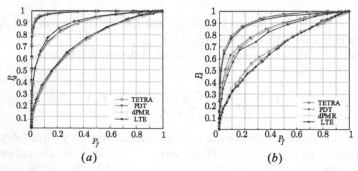

Fig. 3. ROC curves of signal detection: (a) under different SNR ($N = 30$; (b) under different sampling points ($SNR = -3$dB

The simulation results show that the detection performance improves with the increase of SNR and sampling time. When the number of sampling points is 30, the detection probability can reach 90% when SNR = 0 dB, choosing an appropriate threshold value can also keep the false alarm probability at about 10%. When the channel SNR is -3dB and the number of sampling points reaches 40 points, the false alarm probability can reach 20% and the detection probability can reach 80%.

3.2   Broad/Narrowband Signal Recognition Simulation

Simulate the recognition of broad/narrowband signals under Gaussian white noise channel. Four types of signals were recognized 2048 times respectively for broad/narrowband recognition. The SNR was −2 dB, the number of sampling points was 1024, and the relationship curve between its recognition performance and threshold value is shown in Fig. 4.

According to the simulation results, when the threshold value is 1.3, the broad/narrowband signal discrimination rates of the broadband signal and the three narrowband signals are close to 100%.

After determining that the threshold value is 1.3, different sampling point numbers N were selected to analyze the broad/narrowband recognition simulation results of four

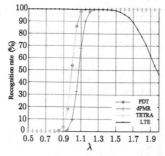

Fig. 4. Recognition performance of broad/narrowband signals under different threshold values ($SNR = -2$dB)

types of signals under different signal-to-noise ratios. The recognition was performed 500 times, and their performance is shown in Fig. 5(a) and (b), respectively.

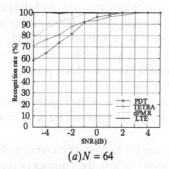
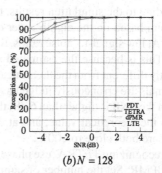

Fig. 5. Recognition performance of broad/narrowband signals under different signal-to-noise ratios

According to the above simulation results, the recognition performance of the four signals improves with the increase of the number of sampling points. The simulation results show that when the number of sampling points is 128, the recognition rate of each type of signal is more than 90% when the SNR is -3 dB.

The energy spectrum distribution characteristics of narrowband signals will be affected by noise, and the probability of being misjudged as broadband signals increases under low SNR. The detection statistic is the value obtained by subtracting the filtered noise power from the energy detection result, which reduces the error rate of broad/narrowband signal recognition under low SNR.

3.3 Narrowband Private Network System Recognition Simulation

Recognition Based on Higher-Order Cumulants and Frequency Offset Variance.
Set the number of sampling points to 15000, and the threshold to $Ps^4/2$, where Ps is the symbol power of the complex signal, which is set to 2W. Under this condition, the

Gaussian white noise channel is recognized 1000 times, and the recognition performance is shown in Fig. 6.

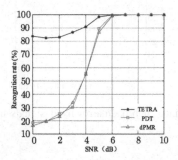

Fig. 6. Recognition performance of π/4-DQPSK and 4FSK based on eighth-order cumulant

According to the simulation results, the recognition performance of the private network system based on the eighth-order cumulant improves as the signal-to-noise ratio increases. At low signal-to-noise ratios, the recognition performances of PDT and dPMR are poor. This is because the estimated value of the eighth-order cumulant of noise is significantly different from the theoretical value of 0. When the SNR is low, the PDT and dPMR signals are erroneously judged as TETRA signals with high eighth-order cumulant. When the SNR is higher than 6 dB, the estimated value of the eighth-order cumulant is close to the theoretical value, and at this time, the recognition rates of π/4-DQPSK and 4FSK are both close to 100%.

After recognizing TETRA, use phase difference in the AWGN channel to distinguish PDT and dPMR. Set the number of sampling points to 750, the number of recognitions to 1000, and the threshold value to 1356010. The relationship between the recognition performance of PDT and dPMR based on the sample variance of the frequency offset and the SNR is shown in Fig. 7.

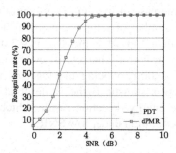

Fig. 7. Recognition performance of PDT and dPMR based on the sample variance of the frequency offset

Simulation result shows that when the SNR is low, the recognition rate of PDT is close to 100% while that of dPMR is close to 0. This is due to the large noise power, which leads to large fluctuations in the frequency offset measured by phase difference, which makes the variance statistic value too large. Based on the simulation results of the above methods, the algorithm of artificially extracted features has better recognition performance only when the SNR is higher than 5dB.

System Recognition Based on BP Neural Network. The BP neural network input consists of 10,000 training data sets for each of the three signals. Each data set includes two features, the eighth-order cumulant and the sample variance of the frequency offset, extracted manually from the signal, and their corresponding labels. The neural network has two hidden layers, each with eight neurons. The structure of the BP neural network is shown in Fig. 8, where w represents weight and b represents bias.

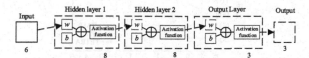

Fig. 8. Structure of the BP neural network

The transfer function of the neurons in the hidden layer is the tansig function, and the transfer function of the neurons in the output layer is the logsig function. The training was conducted for 543 times with a target error of 10^{-10}. The ratio of training set to test set was 80%:20%. The recognition performance obtained is shown in Fig. 9.

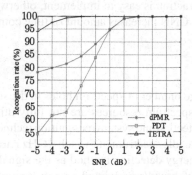

Fig. 9. System recognition performance based on BP neural network

Simulation results show that at lower SNR, the method based on BP neural network has better performance compared to the method of manual feature extraction. When the SNR is 0dB, the success rate of PDT and dPMR signal recognition can reach 95%, and that of TETRA signal recognition can approach 100%.

System Recognition Based on Convolutional Neural Network. The convolutional neural network used in this paper consists of an input layer, six convolutional layers, a fully connected layer and an output layer. After each convolutional layer, there is a batch normalization layer, a rectified linear unit (RELU) layer and a max pooling layer.

In the last convolutional layer, the max pooling layer is replaced by an average pooling layer. The input of the convolutional neural network is 10,000 sets of data for each of the three signals. Each set of data includes the signal itself and the corresponding label. The number of trainings is 1000 times. The ratio of training set, verification set, and test set is 80%: 10%: 10%. The recognition performance is shown in Fig. 10.

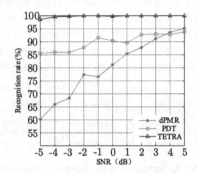

Fig. 10. System recognition performance based on convolutional neural network

Based on the simulation results of the above three recognition methods, the method of manually extracting features has poor recognition performance under low SNR, while the recognition method based on neural network has better recognition performance under low SNR. For the two neural network methods, the BP neural network can be used when the feature extraction is easy to implement, otherwise CNN can be used for recognition. However, the CNN increases amount of time complexity.

4 Conclusions

At present, there are a large number of spectrum holes in the sub-1GHz private network frequency band, and the spectrum resources are not fully utilized. This paper mainly studies the P-IoT signal detection and system recognition technology to provide technical support for P-IoT to use the idle spectrum of the sub-1GHz narrowband private network.

This paper uses the energy detection method as the signal detection algorithm and realizes the recognition of broad/narrowband signals according to the difference in energy ratio before and after the two filters. In terms of the modulation recognition, the algorithm of artificially extracted features has higher requirements on SNR, while the method based on neural network has better performance than binary tree classification method under low SNR.

The narrowband private network system and its standards are still evolving, such as new versions like PDT 2.0, and future research needs to design corresponding idle spectrum utilization schemes as the system changes. In addition, it is necessary to combine the P-IoT Ad hoc network technology to study the cooperative sensing scheme suitable for P-IoT, and explore the performance of various technologies in the complex private network communication environment.

References

1. Guo, Y., Xie, X., Qin, C., Wang, Y.: Fog computing federated learning system framework for smart healthcare. In: CSCW 2021. CCIS, vol 1491. Springer, Singapore (2022). https://doi.org/10.1007/978-981-19-4546-5_11
2. Wang, R., Zhao, L.: Application of anti-collision early warning system for 5g internet of vehicles. In: Hung, J.C., Chang, J.-W., Pei, Y., Wei-Chen, Wu. (eds.) Innovative Computing. LNEE, vol. 791, pp. 677–684. Springer, Singapore (2022). https://doi.org/10.1007/978-981-16-4258-6_84
3. Thandavarayan, G., Sepulcre, M., Gozalvez, J.: Cooperative perception for connected and automated vehicles: evaluation and impact of congestion control. IEEE Access **8**, 197665–197683 (2020)
4. Miao, Y., Shao, B., Xie, W.: Exploration of the application of private Internet of Things in broadband converged networks. Police Technol., 12–15 (2017)
5. Sun, P., Song, Z., Yu, Y.: Research on private-internet of things technology. Mobile Commun. **42**(07), 92–96 (2018)
6. Sun, P., Yu, Y., Wang, Y.: Innovative application of private-internet of things in emergency field. Mobile Commun. **43**(03), 12–17 (2019)
7. Wen, W., Mendel, J.M.: Maximum-likelihood classification for digital amplitude-phase modulations. IEEE Trans. Commun. **48**(2), 189–193 (2000)
8. Donoho, D.L., Huo, X.: Large-Sample modulation classification using hellinger representation. In: 1997 First IEEE Signal Processing Workshop on Signal Processing Advances in Wireless Communications (1997)
9. Zhu, X., Lin, Y., Dou, Z.: Automatic recognition of communication signal modulation based on neural network. In: 2016 IEEE International Conference on Electronic Information and Communication Technology (ICEICT) (2017)
10. GB/T 15539–1995. Technical specifications for trunked mobile radio systems (1995)
11. GA/T 1056–2013. Technical specifications for Police Digital Trunking (PDT) communication system (2013)
12. ETSI TS 102 658 V2.5.1. Digital Private Mobile Radio (dPMR) using FDMA with a channel spacing of 6,25 kHz (2015)
13. O'Shea, T.J., Johnathan Corgan, T., Clancy, C.: Convolutional radio modulation recognition networks. In: Jayne, C., Iliadis, L. (eds.) EANN 2016. CCIS, vol. 629, pp. 213–226. Springer, Cham (2016). https://doi.org/10.1007/978-3-319-44188-7_16
14. Zhao, X., Guo, C., Li, J.: Mixed recognition algorithm for signal modulation schemes by high-older cumulants and cyclic spectrum. J. Electron. Inf. Technol. **38**(3), 674–680 (2016)

Research on Traffic Flow Prediction and Traffic Light Timing Recommendation Technology Based on Vehicle Data Analysis

Tong Wang, Shuyu Xue, Guangxin Yang$^{(\boxtimes)}$, Shan Gao, Min Ouyang, and Liwei Chen

Harbin Engineering University, Harbin 150000, China
{wangtong,1803669455}@hrbeu.edu.cn

Abstract. In view of the fact that traditional traffic signal systems cannot provide dynamic and flexible timing schemes for modern high-volume urban road traffic, this paper predicts road traffic flow from a global perspective and provides reasonable strategies for traffic signal timing based on this. By analyzing data to predict future road traffic flow and providing reasonable strategies for corresponding traffic signals, this paper proposes a time series prediction method based on recurrent neural network(TSPR). To reduce prediction errors, multiple segmented predictions were performed, and the selection of relevant parameters was determined through simulation analysis. The accuracy of the TSPR algorithm was demonstrated by comparing its prediction results with those of SVR [1], CART, and BPNN [2], and the rationality of multiple segmented predictions was demonstrated by comparing them with one-time multi-segment predictions. Based on the TSPR prediction results, in order to rationally set up traffic lightsGreen time ratio to improve the overall income, this paper combines the prediction results with the DQN [3] algorithm and applies it to the field of traffic light control, proposing a traffic light timing recommendation model based on prediction. Compared with the traditional DQN algorithm, the overall return of the DQN algorithm can be improved after the traffic light timing is recommended by TSPR prediction, thereby achieving an increase in benefits.

Keywords: Vehicle data analysis · Traffic flow prediction · Traffic light timing recommendation

1 Related Work

In intelligent signal light control, the rise of artificial intelligence provides new solutions for traffic light control, such as the introduction of fuzzy control by Ikidid A et al. [4]; the use of model-free reinforcement learning represented by

Supported by organization Springer Nature.

Q-learning, Fei LUO et al. [5] proposed an online control algorithm based on improved reinforcement learning, which is aimed at the problem of slow convergence speed of Q-learning The algorithm was improved to speed up the iterative process of Q-learning. Evolutionary algorithms are also widely used to solve traffic signal scheduling problems. Ng S C et al. [6] used a genetic algorithm to optimize the timing of traffic light cycles at an intersection located in Hong Kong, resulting in a significant improvement in the overall performance of the network.

Considering the influencing factors of road traffic conditions from a single time or space perspective cannot extract all the characteristics that affect traffic flow changes. Traffic flow spatiotemporal prediction research is a comprehensive consideration of spatiotemporal factors, using historical observation data from adjacent road sections to predict the future traffic flow of a certain road section [7–11].

In view of this, this paper focuses on the road traffic flow prediction and traffic light control problems, and conducts research from two aspects: traffic flow pre-diction and traffic light timing recommendation based on prediction. The contributions of this paper are as follows: (1) In terms of traffic flow prediction, a time series prediction method based on RNN (TSPR) is proposed, and the selection of relevant parameters is determined through simulation analysis. The accuracy of the TSPR algorithm was demonstrated by comparing its prediction results with those of SVR, CART, and BPNN, and the rationality of multiple segmented predictions was demonstrated by comparing them with one-time multi-segment predictions. (2) The DQN traffic signal control algorithm with added traffic flow prediction was tested. Compared with directly applying the DQN algorithm, the performance of the traffic light timing recommendation algorithm based on traffic flow prediction improved by about 27.3%.

2 Theoretical Model and Implementation

2.1 Recurrent Neural Networks

Recurrent Neural Network (RNN) is a type of neural network that models and processes sequence data [12]. Unlike traditional Feedforward Neural Networks, RNNs have recurrent connections and can model the temporal relationships within a sequence.

The main idea of RNN is to introduce recurrent connections between the hidden layers of the network, allowing the network to retain previously processed information [13,14] and apply it to the current input. Due to the strong mobility and randomness of daily travel vehicles [15], some commonly used algorithms (such as support vector machines and decision trees) have difficulty learning the intrinsic connections between traffic flow data, thereby reducing the accuracy of prediction. In response to this problem, this paper combines the idea of Recurrent Neural Networks (RNN) for use in the field of traffic flow prediction. The method can effectively capture the potential relationships between data and make more accurate predictions. On this basis, a time series prediction method based on

RNN (TSPR) is further proposed to perform future multi-segment prediction of urban traffic flow, thereby achieving long-term planning.

2.2   Recurrent Neural Networks

First, the traffic flow prediction framework is given, which is divided into two parts: offline and online, as shown in Fig. 1. This paper uses Beijing cab real-time data for prediction and validation.

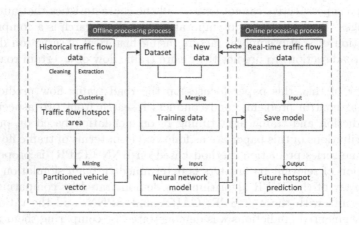

Fig. 1. Future traffic flow hotspot prediction framework

The framework process is implemented through the following steps: (1) Clean the original data of the vehicle's historical trajectory, delete invalid information, duplicate information, and non-Beijing data. (2) According to the GPS longitude and latitude information of the vehicle in the trajectory, it is projected onto ArcGIS Map to obtain the vehicle hotspot area. (3) According to the timestamp information in the trajectory, the number of vehicles in each area at each time period is counted to obtain the regional vehicle vector. (4) Determine the vehicle number prediction model, and the regional vehicle data is used as the training set to form a prediction model. (5) Obtain the latest vehicle information in the current area and input it into the trained prediction model. The output of the model is the predicted number of vehicles. At the same time, cache the newly acquired data. When it reaches a certain amount, merge it with the training set and return to step (5).

2.3   RNN-Based Traffic Hotspot Segmentation Prediction Method

In urban traffic flow prediction, it is difficult for classical BP neural networks to learn the intrinsic connections of time series data due to the temporal nature of drivers' travel intentions. To address this issue, this paper combines the ideas of Recurrent Neural Networks (RNN) for predicting future traffic flow in a region.

For predicting the number of vehicles in a region, this paper adopts a Recurrent Neural Network (RNN) as the prediction model. The input to the model is the number of vehicles in the previous d segments, and the output is the number of vehicles in the $d + 1$ segment, i.e., the input layer of the RNN is a d-dimensional vector and the output layer is a 1-dimensional vector. However, to optimize the traffic flow system in the long term, it is not enough to obtain predictions for only the nearest future time period. Therefore, this paper further proposes a Time Series Prediction Based on RNN (TSPR) method to predict the number of vehicles in multiple future segments for the entire city, thus achieving long-term planning. First, perform data processing and obtain dataset D, where $k = 0, 1, 2, \cdots$ corresponds to different datasets D_k. Then, 70% of dataset D_k is used as training data for input into the RNN, and the remaining 30% is used as test data. After parameter tuning and other related optimizations, a KRNN model related to K is trained and saved.

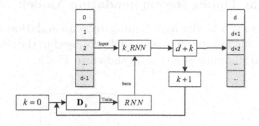

Fig. 2. RNN-based segmentation prediction model

In application, the latest d segments of vehicle information generated by each region are obtained, and then the number of vehicles in the current future period is predicted in segments. During prediction, the corresponding k_RNN model is loaded according to the target segment, and the d segments of vehicle data are input into the prediction model. The output of the model is the predicted value for the corresponding time period. Finally, all predicted values are combined into a vector as the basis for recommendation. The structure of TSPR is shown in Fig. 2.

According to different values of k, TSPR can effectively learn the intrinsic connection between the input and output time segments during each training session. Through multiple segmented predictions, the number of vehicles in each future time period in the hotspot region can be accurately predicted. The predicted number of vehicles in each future time period is combined into a predicted vehicle number vector for recommendation. At the same time, it is necessary to continuously update the training set. Each region will generate actual vehicle information, which is cached. When the cached data reaches a certain volume, it is merged into the training set and retrained. As the training data accumulates, the resulting traffic flow prediction model will have stronger fitting capabilities, thus ensuring the validity of the dataset and the accuracy of the prediction results. The specific steps are shown in Table 1.

Table 1. TSPR solution process

Step.

1. Initialization
    Obtain the vector v of the number of vehicles in the latest d time periods under each vehicle hotspot region;
    Set the time interval k between the target time period to be predicted and the time period of vector v to 0;
2. Construct dataset
    Construct the regional vehicle information vector into dataset D_k;
    Build a Recurrent Neural Network model, use D_k as the training set to train the Recurrent Neural Network, and obtain k_RNN;
    Input the vehicle number vector v into k_RNN to predict the number of vehicles in the target time period;
3. Strategy improvement
    Let $k = k + 1$, predict the number of vehicles in the next time period, and return to step (2)

2.4 Traffic Light Timing Recommendation Model

This section describes a traffic light timing recommendation system that combines the TSPR traffic flow prediction model proposed in the previous subsection. First, the system framework is given, as shown in Fig. 3.

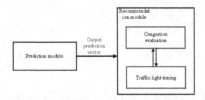

Fig. 3. RNN-based segmentation prediction model

To better utilize the predicted data, it is necessary to introduce reinforcement learning based on the predicted data to construct a more reasonable traffic light timing scheme. The process of updating the DQN algorithm net-work is as follows.

Technique introduced by DQN is the experience replay strategy, which stores data obtained from interactions with the environment during training in the form of a quadruplet $< s_t, a_t, r_t, s_{t+1} >$ in the experience replay pool and trains the neural net-work through uniform sampling of samples. Since continuous experience samples in reinforcement learning are temporally correlated, learning is performed through small batch sampling to improve training efficiency. The neural network also requires a large amount of data for training to reach convergence. The experience replay mechanism can reuse experience samples to accelerate the convergence speed of the algorithm. Our traffic light prediction vector is also added at this step, by converting the prediction of future traffic flow at a certain intersection into a quadruplet. The data used for network update is independently and identically distributed, breaking the correlation between samples,

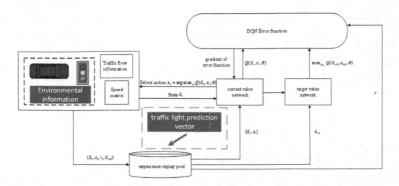

Fig. 4. DQN intersection traffic signal control system with added prediction vector

which helps to accelerate the convergence speed of the algorithm and ensure its correctness and stability (Fig. 4).

3 Experimental Section

3.1 Prediction Results and Performance Comparison

In our traffic flow prediction model, we use a neural network to train and make predictions based on historical vehicle data. The dataset is obtained using the vehicle information extraction method described in Sect. 2.3

$$D_k = \{(x_1, y_1), (x_2, y_2), \cdots, (x_m, y_m)\} \tag{1}$$

Of the dataset, 70% (21 d) is used for training the neural network, while the remaining 30% (9 d) is used as a test set. The time step for each segment is set to $Ts = 15$ minutes, with a historical length of $d = 1$ used for prediction. Let $k = 0$, meaning there is no time interval between input and output data in the RNN. Support Vector Machines and Decision Trees are used as comparison algorithms for prediction. The average results of the test set prediction are shown in Figs. 5 and 6.

Figures 5 and 6 shows the results of using the same dataset to train and make predictions with SVR, CART, BP neural network, and TSPR models. It can be seen that the TSPR model has overall excellent predictive performance, accurately reproducing the trend of vehicle count changes for each time period when compared to historical data. The comparison of prediction errors for SVR, CART, BP neural network, and TSPR is shown in Fig. 6. RMSE and MRE are root mean square error and mean relative error.

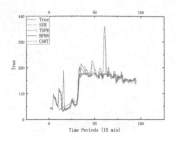

Fig. 5. Comparison of prediction algorithms

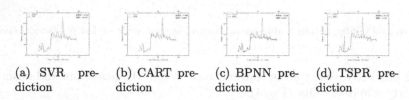

(a) SVR pre-
diction

(b) CART pre-
diction

(c) BPNN pre-
diction

(d) TSPR pre-
diction

Fig. 6. Algorithm error comparison

3.2   Segmented Prediction

In the segmented prediction method based on RNN introduced in Sect. 3.3, the number of neurons in the output layer of the RNN is 1, and each prediction only yields the number of vehicles for a future time period. TSPR obtains prediction data for each future segment through multiple predictions and then combines the data from each segment to obtain a multi-segment prediction result. However, when per-forming regression prediction on data, the neural network itself can achieve one-time multi-segment prediction for the future by increasing the number of neurons in the output layer [16]. For example, to predict the passenger count for a region in the next 6 time periods, simply set the number of neurons in the RNN output layer to 6 to complete a one-time prediction. This section compares the results of one-time multi-segment prediction to explain why this paper adopts multiple segmented predictions instead of one-time multi-segment prediction.

Based on the TSPR introduced in Sect. 2.2 and the regional information mining in Sect. 2.3, 70% of the dataset D_k is used as a training set and the remaining 30% as a test set. Let $k = 1, 2, \cdots, d = 1$, meaning that the number of vehicles for a historical time period in a given region is used to predict the number of vehicles for the next three time periods. The RNN has one neuron in both the input and output layers, and k_RNN models related to k are trained separately. The average prediction results and corresponding errors for the 9-day test set data are shown in Fig. 7.

As can be seen from Fig. 8, as the distance between the input and output segments of the RNN increases, the prediction error of the TSPR model increases. This indicates that the relationship between segments decreases with increasing

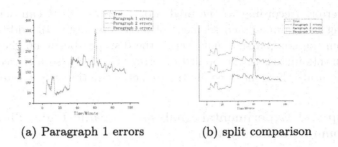

(a) Paragraph 1 errors   (b) split comparison

Fig. 7. Algorithm error comparison

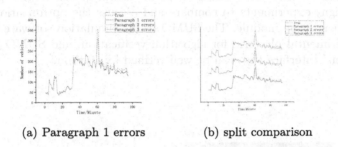

(a) Paragraph 1 errors   (b) split comparison

Fig. 8. Error of multi-segment prediction results

distance, which is related to the weakening of the relationship between vehicle counts as the time interval increases in reality. As a comparison algorithm, the dataset for one-time multi-segment prediction can be represented as:

$$D_k = \{(x_1, y_1), (x_2, y_2), \cdots, (x_m, y_m)\} \tag{2}$$

wherein:

$$
\begin{aligned}
&x_1 = (x_0, x_1, \cdots, x_{d-1}), y_1 = (x_d, x_{d+1}, \cdots, x_{d+k}) \\
&x_2 = (x_1, x_2, \cdots, x_d), y_2 = (x_{d+1}, x_{d+2}, \cdots, x_{d+1+k}) \\
&\qquad \vdots \\
&x_m = (x_m, x_{m+1}, \cdots, x_{m+d-1}), y_m = (x_{m+d}, x_{m+d+1}, \cdots, x_{m+d+k})
\end{aligned}
\tag{3}
$$

Let the historical length $d = 1$ and $k = 2$, meaning that the number of segments predicted at once is 3. Still taking 70% of D_k as the training set, the average prediction results for each segment obtained through multi-segment prediction in the remaining 30% test set are shown in Fig. 8.

Comparing the prediction results in Figs. 7 and 8, it is not difficult to see that multi-segment prediction can obtain prediction results for multiple future segments at once, and the prediction errors for the three segments are very close. However, since the model training has to take into account the accuracy of multi-segment prediction at the same time, it cannot fully learn the relationship between each segment's output and input, resulting in a generally larger prediction error. According to the prediction results, TSPR can achieve maximum fitting by training each segment of data separately. In addition, it can be seen from the comparison that even if the distance be-tween the input and output segments increases, the prediction error of TSPR also increases, but it is still more accurate than one-time multi-segment prediction at the same distance.

3.3   Setup and Experimental Analysis of Traffic Light Timing Recommendation System

To verify the effectiveness and evaluate the performance of the traffic light timing recommendation system based on prediction proposed in this paper, this section designs experiments to compare and discuss the optimization effect of the recommendation module. The SUMO traffic simulation software is selected as the experimental platform for algorithm verification, and SUMO provides a Traci external interface that can be well verified by Python.

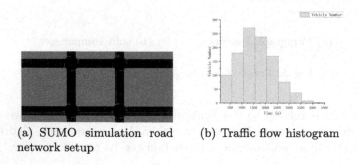

(a) SUMO simulation road network setup   (b) Traffic flow histogram

Fig. 9. Simulation environment settings

Figure 9(a) shows the setup of the simulated experimental environment. The road simulation experiment parameters are set based on the characteristics of dense inter-section distribution, small spacing, strong correlation, and large traffic flow on the main roads of the urban road network. A two-way six-lane road is set up, with the inner lane for left turns and straight ahead, the middle lane for straight ahead, and the rightmost lane for right turns. The sequence is set as first south-north straight ahead and right turn, south-north left turn, then east-west straight ahead, right turn and left turn, with a yellow light time of 3 s.

Figure 9(b) shows the relationship between time and the total number of vehicles in the four intersections. It can be seen that there are peak and normal moments in the vehicle count setting, with 75% allocated for straight ahead at each moment and the rest for right or left turns. As can be known from actual traffic experience, frequent adjustment of phase differences will reduce the effective use time of phases. Com-pared to phase differences, signal timing adjustments can be more frequent to adapt to real-time traffic changes.

To more objectively evaluate the performance of the algorithm, the average waiting delay is used as an evaluation indicator. The model is trained until convergence, and the algorithm in this section is compared with the Fixed Time algorithm and the DQN algorithm without prediction in the above simulation environment. The Fixed Time algorithm uses the default values of SUMO as the fixed timing strategy parameters, setting the green-red phase duration at intersections to 35 s and the yellow phase duration to 3 s (Fig. 10).

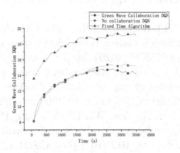

Fig. 10. Traffic flow histogram.

4   Conclusion

In this paper, we have addressed the problem of traffic flow prediction and traffic light timing recommendation based on vehicle data analysis. We have proposed a time series prediction method based on recurrent neural network (TSPR) to predict future road traffic flow and provide reasonable strategies for corresponding traffic signals. We have also combined the TSPR prediction results with the DQN algorithm and applied it to the field of traffic light control, proposing a traffic light timing recommendation model based on prediction.

Our results show that the TSPR algorithm has high accuracy and rationality in predicting traffic flow, and that it can improve the performance of the DQN algorithm in traffic light control by about 27.3%. We have demonstrated the advantages of our methods over existing approaches such as SVR, CART, BPNN, and traditional DQN algorithm by conducting experiments on real-world vehicle data and using SUMO traffic simulation software.

References

1. da Silva Santos, C.E., Sampaio, R.C., dos Santos Coelho, L., Bestard, G.A., Llanos, C.H.: Multi-objective adaptive differential evolution for SVM/SVR hyperparameters selection. Pattern Recogn. **110**, 107649 (2021). https://doi.org/10.1016/j.patcog.2020.107649
2. Geng, G., Lu, S., Duan, C., Jiang, H., Xiang, H.: Design of autonomous vehicle trajectory tracking controller based on Neural Network Predictive Control. Proc. Inst. Mech. Eng. D: J. Automobile Eng. 09544070221150023 (2023). https://doi.org/10.1177/09544070221150023

3. Zafar, H., Utkovski, Z., Kasparick, M., Stanczak, S.: Transfer learning in multi-agent reinforcement learning with double q-networks for distributed resource sharing in v2x communication. In: WSA 2021; 25th International ITG Workshop on Smart Antennas, pp. 1–6. VDE (2021). https://doi.org/10.48550/arXiv.2107.06195

4. Ikidid, A., Abdelaziz, E.F., Sadgal, M.: Multi-agent and fuzzy inference-based framework for traffic light optimization. Int. J. Interact. Multimedia Artif. Intell. (2023). https://doi.org/10.9781/ijimai.2021.12.002

5. Luo, F., Bai, M.: Decision optimization of traffic scenario problem based on reinforcement learning. J. Comput. Appl. **42**(8), 2361 (2022). https://doi.org/10.1016/j.engappai.2016.01.001

6. Ng, S.C., Kwok, C.P.: An intelligent traffic light system using object detection and evolutionary algorithm for alleviating traffic congestion in Hong Kong. Int. J. Comput. Intell. Syst. **13**(1), 802–809 (2020). https://doi.org/10.2991/ijcis.d.200522.001

7. Yang, H., Zhang, X., Li, Z., Cui, J.: Region-level traffic prediction based on temporal multi-spatial dependence graph convolutional network from GPS data. Remote Sens. **14**(2), 303 (2022). https://doi.org/10.3390/rs14020303

8. Wang, J., Wang, W., Liu, X., Yu, W., Li, X., Sun, P.: Traffic prediction based on auto spatiotemporal multi-graph adversarial neural network. Physica A **590**, 126736 (2022). https://doi.org/10.1016/j.physa.2021.126736

9. Zhou, X., Zhang, Y., Li, Z., Wang, X., Zhao, J., Zhang, Z.: Large-scale cellular traffic prediction based on graph convolutional networks with transfer learning. Neural Comput. Appl. **34**, 5549–5559 (2022). https://doi.org/10.1007/s00521-021-06708-x

10. Zhang, Y., Li, Y., Zhou, X., Luo, J., Zhang, Z.L.: Urban traffic dynamics prediction–a continuous spatial-temporal meta-learning approach. ACM Trans. Intell. Syst. Technol. **13**(2), 1–19 (2022). https://doi.org/10.1145/3474837

11. Tang, J., Zeng, J.: Spatiotemporal gated graph attention network for urban traffic flow prediction based on license plate recognition data. Comput. Aided Civil Infrastruct. Eng. **37**(1), 3–23 (2022). https://doi.org/10.1111/mice.12688

12. Ran, X., Shan, Z., Fang, Y., Lin, C.: Travel time prediction by providing constraints on a convolutional neural network. IEEE Access **6**, 59336–59349 (2018). https://doi.org/10.3390/s19092063

13. Ran, X., Shan, Z., Fang, Y., Lin, C.: A convolution component-based method with attention mechanism for travel-time prediction. Sensors **19**(9), 2063 (2019). https://doi.org/10.3390/s19092063

14. Sen, J., Liu, M., Gu, X., Han, Y.: Predicting traffic travel time with a dual-parameter convolutional theory model. Comput. Eng. Appl. **56**(20), 258–263 (2020)

15. Benchang, Z.: Prediction of supply and demand for online drivers and passengers based on time series. Huazhong University of Science and Technology (2019)

16. van Lint, H., Hoogendoorn, S.P., van Zuylen, H.J.: State space neural networks for freeway travel time prediction. In: Dorronsoro, J.R. (eds.) Artificial Neural Networks – ICANN 2002. ICANN 2002. Lecture Notes in Computer Science, vol. 2415. Springer, Berlin, Heidelberg (2002). https://doi.org/10.1007/3-540-46084-5_169

Towards Distributed Graph Representation Learning

Hanlin Zhang[1], Yue Zhang[2], Wei He[1], Yonghui Xu[3(✉)], and Lizhen Cui[1,3]

[1] School of Software, Shandong University, Jinan 250101, China
`zhanghanlin@mail.sdu.edu.cn`, {`hewei,clz`}`@sdu.edu.cn`
[2] School of Physics and Electronic Information Engineering,
Qinghai Normal University, Xining 810016, China
[3] Joint SDU-NTU Centre for Artificial Intelligence Research (C-FAIR),
Shandong University, Jinan 250101, China
`xu.yonghui@hotmail.com`

Abstract. Distributed graph representation learning refers to the process of learning graph data representation in a distributed computing environment. In the process of distributed graph representation learning, nodes need to exchange data frequently, making data transmission crucial in this context. The content of data transmission, including plaintext data, ciphertext data, and model parameters, affects the performance, computational and communication costs, and privacy protection of distributed graph representation learning. However, there is currently a lack of comprehensive investigations into distributed graph representation learning. This paper fills this gap by conducting a detailed study on distributed graph representation learning and summarizing various methods for transmitting different types of content. We review the applications and evaluation methods of distributed graph representation learning and, through an analysis of the strengths and limitations of existing research, provide insights into the future development directions of distributed graph representation learning.

Keywords: Distributed · Graph Representation Learning

1 Introduction

As the scale and complexity of real-world graph data increase, traditional graph representation learning methods face significant challenges. These methods typically rely on a single computing node and cannot efficiently handle large-scale graph data. Furthermore, the distribution of data storage and computing resources in a distributed environment presents new challenges for graph representation learning [12]. Therefore, an innovative approach is needed to address the learning and representation of large-scale graph data.

Distributed graph representation learning is an approach that distributes graph data across multiple nodes for learning [17]. In this approach, the graph

Y. Sun et al. (Eds.): ChineseCSCW 2023, CCIS 2012, pp. 547–557, 2024.
https://doi.org/10.1007/978-981-99-9637-7_41

data is partitioned into subgraphs and distributed across multiple computing nodes. Each node independently processes local graph data and learns global graph representation through information exchange and model fusion. Distributed graph representation learning offers several advantages [37]. Firstly, it can handle large-scale graph data by leveraging parallel computing and distributed storage for efficient processing capabilities. Secondly, distributed graph representation learning can utilize multi-source data for joint learning, thereby enhancing the quality and generalization ability of graph representation.

In this survey, we categorize and study distributed graph representation learning methods based on the content of data transmission. This categorization is based on the critical role of data transmission in distributed graph representation learning [29]. Different types of content transmission have distinct advantages and limitations for achieving efficient distributed graph representation learning. Categorizing methods based on content transmission helps us analyze and compare each method in depth, revealing their underlying principles and characteristics. Additionally, we gain a better understanding of the impact of different content transmissions on the performance and effectiveness of distributed graph representation learning.

This survey contributes in several aspects. Firstly, we provide a comprehensive investigation summarizing the latest research progress in distributed graph representation learning. Secondly, we delve into the concepts, advantages, and challenges of distributed graph representation learning. Thirdly, we propose a classification method based on the content of data transmission, enabling a systematic categorization and study of distributed graph representation learning. Finally, we identify key challenges and future research directions for distributed graph representation learning.

2 Preliminaries

Before delving into the investigation, it is necessary to define distributed graph representation learning. This approach faces various challenges, particularly in the transmission of different types of content in a distributed environment. Therefore, we will analyze the meanings and characteristics of transmitting plaintext data, ciphertext data, and model parameters.

2.1 Definition

Definition 1 (Distributed Graph Representation Learning, DGRL).
A process for learning representation of graph data within a distributed computing environment. It involves partitioning the original graph data into subgraphs, which are distributed across computing nodes. Each node independently processes its subgraph to learn its specific representation. Techniques like information exchange and model fusion facilitate sharing and integration of learned representation, leading to a global representation of the entire graph.

2.2   Analysis

Transmission of Plaintext Data. In DGRL, one common approach is to transmit the subgraph data between computing nodes without encryption or obfuscation. This method offers the advantage of lower computational overhead, leading to improved overall system performance and efficiency [41]. As a result, our focus is on enhancing computational efficiency and minimizing communication time and resource costs.

Transmission of Ciphertext Data. To address the privacy and security concerns associated with transmitting plaintext data, another approach is to use encryption techniques to transmit graph data in a distributed environment. Encrypted data transmission ensures the confidentiality of the transmitted data and protects it from unauthorized access. However, the encryption process introduces additional computational overhead, including encryption and decryption, which can potentially impact overall performance.

Transmission of Model Parameters. Federated learning [14] has gained significant attention in the field of DGRL in recent years. It enables collaborative model training without the need to directly share raw data. Instead, nodes exchange model parameters to collectively learn the global graph representation. This approach ensures data privacy and minimizes the risk of exposing sensitive information during transmission.

3   The Proposed DGRL Taxonomy

Based on the definition of DGRL and the classification based on transmission content in Sect. 2, we propose a content-based classification method for DGRL. This classification method categorizes DGRL into three types. We analyzed 24 different methods for DGRL, as shown in Table 1. These methods are classified into three types based on the content of transmission. Table 1 summarizes the methods and datasets used in the experiments.

3.1   Transmission of Plaintext Data

In DGRL, there are two main approaches: full-batch training and mini-batch training. Here, we focus on how to improve computational efficiency and reduce communication time and resource overhead, without considering privacy protection and data security issues.

Full-Batch Training. Full-batch training refers to the scenario where the entire graph data, including all nodes and edges, is involved in the computations and updates in each training iteration. The goal of full-batch training is to process the entire graph data simultaneously to capture global information. However,

Table 1. Application of Distributed Graph Representation Learning

	Ref.	name	Full-batch training	Mini-batch training	Symmetric encryption	Asymmetric encryption	Differential privacy	Homomorphic encryption	Secure multiparty computation	Horizontal federated learning	Vertical federated learning	Federated transfer learning	Cora [28]	Citeseer [28]	PubMed [21]	Reddit [9]	DGBN [9]	MovieLens [8]	PPI [7]	Proteins [27]	IMDB [5]	Amazon [18]	other
Transmission of Plaintext Data	[16]	NeuGraph	✓													✓	✓					✓	①
	[10]	Roc	✓													✓	✓		✓			✓	
	[19]	DistGNN	✓														✓	✓		✓			②
	[30]	FlexGraph	✓														✓				✓		③
	[39]	AGL		✓									✓					✓	✓				④
	[11]	SALIENT		✓													✓						
Transmission of Ciphertext Data	[32]	SecGNN						✓					✓	✓	✓								
	[13]	Privacy-Preserving DistributedGraph Filtering						✓															
	[35]	FedPerGNN					✓													✓			⑤
	[34]	FedGNN					✓													✓			⑥
	[42]	PGPregel					✓													✓			
	[20]	P²CG							✓				✓	✓	✓								
	[4]	FedSGC							✓				✓	✓	✓								
	[25]	A Hybrid Secure ComputationFramework								✓			✓										
Transmission of model parameters	[40]	FedSage+								✓			✓	✓	✓								⑦
	[23]	FedNI								✓													⑧
	[38]	FedGCN								✓			✓	✓				✓					
	[2]	FedGraph								✓			✓	✓	✓	✓	✓						
	[22]	FedVGCN									✓		✓	✓	✓	✓							
	[3]	Graph-Fraudster									✓		✓	✓	✓	✓							
	[1]	VFGNN									✓		✓	✓	✓	✓			✓				
	[24]	Relation Leaksin Vertical Federated Learning									✓		✓	✓	✓								
	[15]	FTL-NGCF										✓											⑨
	[31]	FedGraph-KD										✓									✓	✓	⑩

①BlogCatalog social network. ②AM. ③FB91. ④UUG. ⑤⑥Flixster, Douban, YahooMusic. ⑦MSAcademic. ⑧ABIDE, ADNI. ⑨Gowalla, Yelp2018, Amazon-Book. ⑩NCI1.

due to the involvement of the entire graph data, the computational and memory requirements per training iteration are usually high. To address the computational and memory overhead in full-batch training, distributed full-batch training adopts several workload balancing methods. For example, NeuGraph [16] evenly partitions each vertex's features into multiple segments to achieve finer-grained workload partitioning, which are then assigned to different GPU threads for computation. Roc [10] introduces a cost model to predict the computation time of each GNN layer on inputs and generates balanced workload partitions in each iteration to adjust workload distribution. FlexGraph [30] uses edge-cutting techniques to divide the graph into different partitions and learns a cost function to estimate the training cost of a given GNN model. DistGNN [19] introduces the Delayed Remote Partial Aggregation (DRPA) algorithm to overlap computations and communications, enabling overlap between inter-epoch computations and communications. This approach improves computational efficiency and reduces communication time and resource overhead.

Mini-batch Training. Another approach is mini-batch training, where the training data is divided into multiple mini-batches for training. In distributed mini-batch training, each compute node processes its assigned mini-batch data in parallel. For example, AGL [39] precomputes the k-hop neighbors of each vertex and utilizes distributed pipelines and MapReduce infrastructure to accelerate the generation process. Dynamic mini-batch allocation refers to dynamically assigning mini-batches to worker nodes to ensure timely access to mini-batches for each compute node and alleviate workload imbalance. SALIENT [11] employs a lock-free input queue for dynamic mini-batch allocation. In this approach, there is no static correspondence between the CPU responsible for sampling and the GPU responsible for model computation. When a CPU generates a mini-batch, it is assigned to the target worker node based on the stored number in the queue at the generation time.

3.2   Transmission of Ciphertext Data

With the widespread use of large-scale graph data, protecting the privacy of node features, labels, and structural information has become a research focus. In this regard, the use of encryption techniques is a common method for privacy protection. We will discuss encryption techniques and their applications in protecting the privacy of graph data.

Symmetric Encryption. Symmetric encryption uses the same key for encrypting and decrypting data. It has the advantage of high encryption efficiency and low computational overhead, making it suitable for large-scale distributed graph data transmission. SecGNN [32] uses random vectors as keys to encrypt and decrypt the node's features, labels, and structural information. In [13], the encryption function uses multiplication noise as the encryption vector, generating encrypted data for nodes by multiplying private data with the encryption vector.

Asymmetric Encryption. Asymmetric encryption uses a public key and a private key for encryption and decryption operations. When transmitting graph data, the sender encrypts the data using the receiver's public key, and the receiver decrypts the ciphertext using their private key. However, asymmetric encryption algorithms are relatively time-consuming, with significant computational overhead for encryption and decryption, which may pose performance bottlenecks in large-scale distributed graph data transmission. FedPerGNN [35] and FedGNN [34] use symmetric encryption as a means of privacy protection. In these papers, the server generates and sends a public key to the clients for encrypting local project IDs. The clients encrypt the project IDs using the public key, generate ciphertext, and upload it to a third-party server to match the same projects.

Differential Privacy. Differential privacy is a privacy protection concept that seeks a balance between individual data privacy and data analysis. In DGRL, multiple data holders can merge their data for collaborative learning while protecting sensitive information such as node attributes and connectivity through the application of differential privacy techniques. The PGPregel [42] system adopts the ϵ-edge-DP model, aiming to hide the existence of individual edges in the graph to prevent the inference of edge existence through inter-datacenter communication in subgraphs. P^2CG [20] introduces a differential privacy-based algorithm to protect the structural information of the graph. Differential privacy protection can be achieved by adding Laplace noise to the adjacency matrix.

Homomorphic Encryption. Homomorphic encryption enables computations on ciphertext without decryption. During graph data transmission, sender encrypts using homomorphic encryption, receiver performs computation on ciphertext and decrypts results. However, it has computational overhead, low performance, and limited support for graph representation learning algorithms. FedSGC [4] assumes there are only two clients without a central server. The topology structure and node features are owned by the two clients. The client with node labels is the active party for creating an encryption key pair. The client encrypts sensitive information using additive homomorphic encryption (AHE) and sends it to the other party for GNN model parameter update.

Secure Multi-party Computation. Secure multi-party computation allows multiple participants to perform computations without revealing their private inputs and obtain the computation results. However, MPC may involve a significant amount of communication overhead, especially when multiple participants and large-scale data are involved, which can increase communication costs. In [25], a framework combining secure multi-party computation and hardware security extension (SGX) introduces a hybrid secure computation framework that combines the advantages of MPC and SGX, reducing communication overhead and improving security guarantees.

3.3   Transmission of Model Parameters

In DGRL, participants can share model parameters through federated learning to compute local graph representation models and transmit the updated model parameters to other participants. Through federated learning, participants can share their learned knowledge and model parameters to improve the overall performance of graph representation learning.

Horizontal Federated Learning. Participants share model parameters while having different graph data. Each participant computes the graph representation model locally and then transfers the local model parameters to other participants for collaborative training and updating of the model. FedSage+ [40] trains a node generator on the client-side that can predict the number of missing neighboring nodes and reconstruct node features. FedNI [23] improves the quality of generated node features by adding a discriminator to the node generator. FedGCN [38] proposes a strategy where, at the start of training, clients collect average neighbor node features from other clients to address the issue of information scarcity.

FedGraph [2] designs a server sampling strategy based on reinforcement learning to reduce the computational cost of GNN model training.

Vertical Federated Learning. Participants have the same graph data but may have different features. Participants share model parameters to compute local graph representation models and transmit and update the local model parameters. FedVGCN [22] is a vertical federated learning framework for preserving data privacy in Graph Convolutional Networks (GCN). The framework is applicable to scenarios where graph data is vertically partitioned and can be extended to existing GCN models. Graph-Fraudster [3] generates adversarial perturbations by exploiting privacy leakage and node gradient information in Graph Neural Networks-based Vertical Federated Learning (GVFL), to deceive the server model. VFGNN [1] is a graph neural network learning paradigm for vertical federated learning, specifically designed for node classification tasks with privacy protection in data vertically partitioned environments. In [24], the research focused on relation inference attacks within VFL, revealing the risks of leaking sample relationships.

Federated Transfer Learning. Participants have different graph data and model parameters. Some participants transfer a portion of their model parameters to other participants, enabling knowledge transfer and model sharing to enhance the overall graph representation learning performance. FTL-NGCF [15] is a personalized recommendation framework based on federated transfer learning and Neural Graph Collaborative Filtering (NGCF). It aims to balance the accuracy of personalized recommendations with privacy protection. FedGraph-KD [31] approach utilizes the idea of transfer learning to address the model heterogeneity issue. Clients can inherit some learned knowledge from the pre-trained D-GNN model and apply it to their own datasets to improve the performance of the local model.

4   DGRL Evaluation Methods

In order to assess the effectiveness of DGRL, we proceeded with theoretical analysis and experimental evaluations of the evaluation methods for DGRL.

4.1   Theoretical Analysis of DGRL

The evaluation methods for DGRL can also be categorized into three types: plaintext transmission, encrypted transmission, and model parameter transmission. For plaintext transmission, we focus on the data transmission speed and bandwidth consumption. For encrypted transmission, we emphasize privacy protection and data security. For model parameter transmission, we can draw insights from traditional federated learning evaluation methods. By comprehensively employing these evaluation methods, we can assess the performance and effectiveness of DGRL in practical applications.

4.2   Experimental Evaluation Metrics

Transmission Speed and Bandwidth Consumption. This evaluation emphasizes the speed of data transmission and the required bandwidth in the process of DGRL. Fast and efficient data transmission can enhance the overall system performance, reducing training time and communication overhead.

Privacy Protection. Privacy protection is a crucial consideration in DGRL [33]. The evaluation method should assess the degree of privacy protection during data transmission and processing. This includes the application of encryption or privacy protection techniques to sensitive data, ensuring that participants' privacy is not compromised or misused.

Computational Consumption. Evaluating the computational resources involved in DGRL is important. This evaluation should consider the computational complexity and memory usage of model training, as well as the computational capabilities and resources required by participants for local computation and communication.

5   Promising Future Research Directions

Our survey clearly indicates that research in DGRL is receiving increasing attention. However, numerous challenges remain to be addressed in order to make this technology capable of meeting the challenges in practical applications. To better tackle the issues in future DGRL, we identify the following research directions.

Trade-Off Between Privacy Protection and Model Performance. The process of transmitting graph data and model parameters introduces computational and communication overheads due to privacy protection measures. Therefore, it is essential to strike a balance between protecting privacy and maintaining model performance [26]. Researchers need to explore the effectiveness and costs of privacy protection methods to ensure robust graph representation learning performance while safeguarding privacy.

Privacy Attacks and Vulnerabilities. Despite the application of privacy protection techniques, potential privacy attacks and vulnerabilities still exist [35]. Attackers may leverage encrypted data analysis or exploit other side-channel information to infer sensitive information. Consequently, comprehensive privacy risk assessments are required, along with the design of defense mechanisms to mitigate various types of privacy attacks.

Communication and Computational Overheads. Participants need to frequently exchange graph data and model parameters, performing computations and updates. This process incurs significant communication and computational overheads, especially when dealing with a large number of participants and massive graph data [6]. Thus, research is needed to investigate efficient communication and computational strategies that reduce overheads and enhance the scalability and efficiency of the system.

Data Imbalance and Non-uniform Distribution. In distributed environments, different participants may possess graph data that is imbalanced or non-uniformly distributed [36]. This can result in some participants contributing fewer data to the model training process, thereby impacting the overall model performance. Addressing the challenges of data imbalance and non-uniform distribution is crucial to ensure that all participants can contribute and benefit fully.

Acknowledgments. This work was supported by the National Key R&D Program of China No.2021YFF0900800, the NSFC No.62202279, the Shandong Provincial Key Research and Development Program (Major Scientific and Technological Innovation Project) No.2021CXGC010108, the Shandong Provincial Natural Science Foundation No.ZR2022QF018, the Shandong Provincial Outstanding Youth Science Foundation No.2023HWYQ-039, the Fundamental Research Funds of Shandong University.

References

1. Chen, C., et al.: Vertically federated graph neural network for privacy-preserving node classification. In: IJCAI, pp. 1959–1965. ijcai.org (2022)
2. Chen, F., Li, P., Miyazaki, T., Wu, C.: Fedgraph: federated graph learning with intelligent sampling. IEEE Trans. Parallel Distributed Syst. **33**(8), 1775–1786 (2022)
3. Chen, J., Huang, G., Zheng, H., Yu, S., Jiang, W., Cui, C.: Graph-fraudster: adversarial attacks on graph neural network-based vertical federated learning. IEEE Trans. Comput. Soc. Syst. **10**(2), 492–506 (2023)
4. Cheung, T.H., Dai, W., Li, S.: Fedsgc: federated simple graph convolution for node classification. In: IJCAI Workshops (2021)
5. Fu, X., Zhang, J., Meng, Z., King, I.: MAGNN: metapath aggregated graph neural network for heterogeneous graph embedding. In: WWW, pp. 2331–2341. ACM / IW3C2 (2020)
6. Guo, Y., Zhao, R., Lai, S., Fan, L., Lei, X., Karagiannidis, G.K.: Distributed machine learning for multiuser mobile edge computing systems. IEEE J. Sel. Top. Signal Process. **16**(3), 460–473 (2022)
7. Hamilton, W.L., Ying, Z., Leskovec, J.: Inductive representation learning on large graphs. In: NIPS, pp. 1024–1034 (2017)
8. Harper, F.M., Konstan, J.A.: The movielens datasets: history and context. ACM Trans. Interact. Intell. Syst. **5**(4), 19:1–19:19 (2016)
9. Hu, W., et al.: Open graph benchmark: datasets for machine learning on graphs. In: NeurIPS (2020)

10. Jia, Z., Lin, S., Gao, M., Zaharia, M., Aiken, A.: Improving the accuracy, scalability, and performance of graph neural networks with roc. In: MLSys. mlsys.org (2020)
11. Kaler, T., et al.: Accelerating training and inference of graph neural networks with fast sampling and pipelining. In: MLSys. mlsys.org (2022)
12. Klauck, H., Nanongkai, D., Pandurangan, G., Robinson, P.: Distributed computation of large-scale graph problems. In: SODA, pp. 391–410. SIAM (2015)
13. Li, Q., Coutino, M., Leus, G., Christensen, M.G.: Privacy-preserving distributed graph filtering. In: EUSIPCO, pp. 2155–2159. IEEE (2020)
14. Li, T., Sahu, A.K., Talwalkar, A., Smith, V.: Federated learning: challenges, methods, and future directions. IEEE Signal Process. Mag. **37**(3), 50–60 (2020)
15. Liu, Y., Fang, S., Wang, L., Huan, C., Wang, R.: Neural graph collaborative filtering for privacy preservation basedon federated transfer learning. Electron. Libr. **40**(6), 729–742 (2022)
16. Ma, L., et al.: Neugraph: Parallel deep neural network computation on large graphs. In: USENIX Annual Technical Conference, pp. 443–458. USENIX Association (2019)
17. Malewicz, G., et al.: Pregel: a system for large-scale graph processing. In: SIGMOD Conference, pp. 135–146. ACM (2010)
18. McAuley, J.J., Targett, C., Shi, Q., van den Hengel, A.: Image-based recommendations on styles and substitutes. In: SIGIR, pp. 43–52. ACM (2015)
19. Md, V., et al.: Distgnn: scalable distributed training for large-scale graph neural networks. In: SC, p. 76. ACM (2021)
20. Miao, X., et al.: P^2cg: a privacy preserving collaborative graph neural network training framework. VLDB J. **32**(4), 717–736 (2023)
21. Namata, G., London, B., Getoor, L., Huang, B., Edu, U.: query-driven active surveying for collective classification. In: 10th International Workshop on Mining And Learning with Graphs. vol. 8, p. 1 (2012)
22. Ni, X., Xu, X., Lyu, L., Meng, C., Wang, W.: A vertical federated learning framework for graph convolutional network. CoRR abs/2106.11593 (2021)
23. Peng, L., Wang, N., Dvornek, N., Zhu, X., Li, X.: Fedni: Federated graph learning with network inpainting for population-based disease prediction. IEEE Transactions on Medical Imaging (2022)
24. Qiu, P., et al.: Your labels are selling you out: Relation leaks in vertical federated learning. IEEE Transactions on Dependable and Secure Computing (2022)
25. Ren, Y., Jie, Y., Wang, Q., Zhang, B., Zhang, C., Wei, L.: A hybrid secure computation framework for graph neural networks. In: PST, pp. 1–6. IEEE (2021)
26. Rodríguez, E., Otero, B., Canal, R.: A survey of machine and deep learning methods for privacy protection in the internet of things. Sensors **23**(3), 1252 (2023)
27. Rossi, R.A., Ahmed, N.K.: The network data repository with interactive graph analytics and visualization. In: AAAI, pp. 4292–4293. AAAI Press (2015)
28. Sen, P., Namata, G., Bilgic, M., Getoor, L., Gallagher, B., Eliassi-Rad, T.: Collective classification in network data. AI Mag. **29**(3), 93–106 (2008)
29. Shao, Y., et al.: Distributed graph neural network training: a survey. CoRR abs/2211.00216 (2022)
30. Wang, L., et al.: Flexgraph: a flexible and efficient distributed framework for GNN training. In: EuroSys, pp. 67–82. ACM (2021)
31. Wang, S., Xie, J., Lu, M., Xiong, N.N.: Fedgraph-kd: an effective federated graph learning scheme based on knowledge distillation. In: BigDataSecurity/HPSC/IDS, pp. 130–134. IEEE (2023)

32. Wang, S., Zheng, Y., Jia, X.: Secgnn: privacy-preserving graph neural network training and inference as a cloud service. IEEE Transactions on Services Computing (2023)
33. Wu, B., et al.: A survey of trustworthy graph learning: Reliability, explainability, and privacy protection. arXiv preprint arXiv:2205.10014 (2022)
34. Wu, C., Wu, F., Cao, Y., Huang, Y., Xie, X.: Fedgnn: federated graph neural network for privacy-preserving recommendation. CoRR abs/2102.04925 (2021)
35. Wu, C., Wu, F., Lyu, L., Qi, T., Huang, Y., Xie, X.: A federated graph neural network framework for privacy-preserving personalization. Nat. Commun. **13**(1), 3091 (2022)
36. Wu, N., Yu, L., Yang, X., Cheng, K.T., Yan, Z.: Federated learning with imbalanced and agglomerated data distribution for medical image classification. arXiv preprint arXiv:2206.13803 (2022)
37. Yang, S., Chen, W., Zhang, X., Liang, C., Wang, H., Cui, W.: A graph-based model for transmission network vulnerability analysis. IEEE Syst. J. **14**(1), 1447–1456 (2020)
38. Yao, Y., Jin, W., Ravi, S., Joe-Wong, C.: Fedgcn: convergence and communication tradeoffs in federated training of graph convolutional networks. arXiv preprint arXiv:2201.12433 (2022)
39. Zhang, D., et al.: AGL: a scalable system for industrial-purpose graph machine learning. Proc. VLDB Endow. **13**(12), 3125–3137 (2020)
40. Zhang, K., Yang, C., Li, X., Sun, L., Yiu, S.: Subgraph federated learning with missing neighbor generation. In: NeurIPS, pp. 6671–6682 (2021)
41. Zheng, C., et al.: Bytegnn: efficient graph neural network training at large scale. Proc. VLDB Endow. **15**(6), 1228–1242 (2022)
42. Zhou, A.C., Qiu, R., Lambert, T., Allard, T., Ibrahim, S., Abbadi, A.E.: Pgpregel: an end-to-end system for privacy-preserving graph processing in geo-distributed data centers. In: SoCC, pp. 386–402. ACM (2022)

Author Index

Printed in the United States
by Baker & Taylor Publisher Services